Lecture Notes in Computer Science

Lecture Notes in Artificial Intelligence   **14158**

Founding Editor

Jörg Siekmann

Series Editors

Randy Goebel, *University of Alberta, Edmonton, Canada*
Wolfgang Wahlster, *DFKI, Berlin, Germany*
Zhi-Hua Zhou, *Nanjing University, Nanjing, China*

The series Lecture Notes in Artificial Intelligence (LNAI) was established in 1988 as a topical subseries of LNCS devoted to artificial intelligence.

The series publishes state-of-the-art research results at a high level. As with the LNCS mother series, the mission of the series is to serve the international R & D community by providing an invaluable service, mainly focused on the publication of conference and workshop proceedings and postproceedings.

Fabian Meder · Alexander Hunt ·
Laura Margheri · Anna Mura · Barbara Mazzolai
Editors

Biomimetic and Biohybrid Systems

12th International Conference, Living Machines 2023
Genoa, Italy, July 10–13, 2023
Proceedings, Part II

 Springer

Editors
Fabian Meder ⓘ
Italian Institute of Technology
Genoa, Italy

Alexander Hunt ⓘ
Portland State University
Portland, OR, USA

Laura Margheri ⓘ
Italian Institute of Technology
Genoa, Italy

Anna Mura ⓘ
Radboud University
Nijmegen, The Netherlands

Barbara Mazzolai ⓘ
Italian Institute of Technology
Genoa, Italy

ISSN 0302-9743   ISSN 1611-3349 (electronic)
Lecture Notes in Artificial Intelligence
ISBN 978-3-031-39503-1   ISBN 978-3-031-39504-8 (eBook)
https://doi.org/10.1007/978-3-031-39504-8

LNCS Sublibrary: SL7 – Artificial Intelligence

This Springer imprint is published by the registered company Springer Nature Switzerland AG
The registered company address is: Gewerbestrasse 11, 6330 Cham, Switzerland

Preface

These proceedings contain the papers presented at the 12th International Conference on Biomimetic and Biohybrid Systems (Living Machines 2023) in Genoa, Italy, July 10–13, 2023. The international conferences in the Living Machines series focus on the intersection of research on novel life-like technologies inspired by the scientific investigation of biological systems, biomimetics, and research that seeks to interface biological and artificial systems to create biohybrid systems. The conference aims to highlight the most exciting research in both fields united by the theme of "Living Machines."

Gaining a deep understanding of the essence of life is an essential prerequisite for advancing artificial technology. There are two fundamental principles to consider. Firstly, technology should serve life and living beings. Its development should aim to improve the well-being and quality of life of all living organisms. Secondly, as researchers, our primary objective should be the development of sustainable technologies that harmoniously integrate with Earth's ecosystems and the inherent life within them. The escalating environmental pollution and resulting climate changes pose significant challenges that must be addressed. This situation presents humanity with an unprecedented and monumental challenge, arguably the greatest we have ever encountered. As researchers, it is imperative for us to look deeper into how living systems solve issues and explore ways to translate these solutions into technology.

By studying and emulating the strategies and mechanisms found in living systems, we can strive to develop innovative technologies that are not only efficient and functional but also environmentally friendly and sustainable. This approach requires a multidisciplinary effort, combining knowledge from biology, ecology, engineering, and other relevant fields. The Living Machines conference embodies and promotes this vision by bringing together researchers from various disciplines such as engineering, biology, computational science, and materials science. These researchers propose technical solutions that draw inspiration from a wide range of biological mechanisms found in nature. These mechanisms span from the nervous system to motion, sensing, and materials in plants and animals. The conference also encompasses biohybrid systems, where artificial technology directly interacts with biological systems.

The Living Machines conference series was first organized by the Convergent Science Network (CSN) of biomimetic and biohybrid systems to provide a mechanism for ensuring this communication. It is a focal point for gathering world-leading researchers and the presentation and discussion of cutting-edge research at the boundary of biology and engineering. This year's Living Machines conference upheld this esteemed legacy by showcasing biologists and engineers who have dedicated their careers to advancing biomimetic and biohybrid systems. Furthermore, the event provides an opportunity to introduce and support numerous young researchers in this rapidly expanding field. This emphasis on nurturing emerging talent ensures continued growth and innovation within the realm of biomimetics and biohybrid systems.

The papers in these proceedings encompass the research submissions to the conference, and from these submissions, a careful selection was made for oral and poster presentations. The articles underwent rigorous evaluation, with an average of 2.7 reviewers per paper, conducted in a single-blind review process. A total of 66 papers were received, and the acceptance rate for publication in the proceedings was 87%. This indicates that a significant portion of the submitted research met the standards set by the conference organizers and reviewers. Moreover, the 180 reviewers who contributed to the evaluation provided authors with detailed comments, typically offering comprehensive suggestions rather than brief, superficial responses. To illustrate the depth of the review process, one article received over 100 comments from a reviewer. This level of engagement demonstrates the commitment of the reviewers to support the authors by offering valuable suggestions for improving their work. Following revisions, most papers underwent a second round of review. The meticulous evaluation and revision process ensures that the papers included in these proceedings represent a high standard of research in the field of biomimetic and biohybrid systems.

The main conference was a three-day in-person meeting with single-track oral presentations and six plenary talks taking place in Genoa, Italy, preceded by a one-day event with four workshops and four tutorials. The conference venue, the Aquarium of Genoa, was selected to further underline the importance of life for the conference where the participants were surrounded by over 800 animal and vegetal species and over 15000 living specimens in one of Europe's biggest aquariums. This setting added an immersive and enriching dimension to the conference, aligning with its focus on biomimetic and biohybrid systems. The plenary speakers were Peter Fratzl (Max Planck Institute of Colloids and Interfaces, Germany), Eleni Stavrinidou (Linköping University, Sweden), Marco Dorigo (Université Libre de Bruxelles, Belgium), Oussama Khatib (Stanford University, USA), Kyu-Jin Cho (Seoul National University, South Korea), and Olga Speck (University of Freiburg, Germany). Session themes included: Bioinspired materials, actuators, sensors I+II; Human-robot interaction, rehabilitation and learning; Joints and muscles; Biohybrid systems and interactions; Invertebrate locomotion and perception mechanisms; Computational tools and modelling; Bioinspiration under water; and Biomimetics analyzed. Additionally, a Science Café was organized on "Living Machines: the Origin and the Future" that was open to the public and moderated by Nicola Nosengo, Chief Editor, Nature Italy.

We wish to thank the many people that were involved in making Living Machines 2023 possible. The conference would not have been possible without the dedication, efforts, and support of numerous individuals. Additional guidance and support were provided by the Living Machines International Advisory Board. We would also like to thank the authors and speakers who contributed their valuable work to the conference. A significant acknowledgment goes to the reviewers who dedicated their time and expertise. Lastly, we would like to express our gratitude to the volunteers, sponsors, and all other individuals who contributed their time, resources, and support to ensure the smooth running of Living Machines 2023.

June 2023
Fabian Meder
Alexander Hunt
Laura Margheri
Anna Mura
Barbara Mazzolai

Organization

General Chair

Barbara Mazzolai   Istituto Italiano di Tecnologia, Italy

Program Chairs

Fabian Meder   Istituto Italiano di Tecnologia, Italy
Alexander Hunt   Portland State University, USA

Local Organization

Laura Margheri   Istituto Italiano di Tecnologia, Italy

Communication Chairs

Giuliano Greco   Istituto Italiano di Tecnologia, Italy
Anna Mura   Radboud University, The Netherlands
Valeria Delle Cave   Istituto Italiano di Tecnologia, Italy

Workshop and Tutorial Chairs

Wenqi Hu   Max-Planck-Institute for Intelligent Systems,
     Germany
Li Wen   Beihang University, China

International Steering Committee

Minoru Asada   Osaka University, Japan
Joseph Ayers   Northeastern University, USA
Hillel Chiel   Case Western Reserve University, USA
Mark Cutkosky   Stanford University, USA
Marc Desmulliez   Heriot-Watt University, UK

José Halloy	Université Paris Cité, France
Koh Hosoda	Osaka University, Japan
Alexander Hunt	Portland State University, USA
Holger G. Krapp	Imperial College London, UK
Cecilia Laschi	National University of Singapore, Singapore
Nathan Lepora	University of Bristol, UK
Uriel Martinez-Hernandez	University of Bath, UK
Barbara Mazzolai	Istituto Italiano di Tecnologia, Italy
Fabian Meder	Istituto Italiano di Tecnologia, Italy
Anna Mura	Radboud University, The Netherlands
Tony Prescott	University of Sheffield, UK
Roger Quinn	Case Western Reserve University, USA
Masahiro Shimizu	Osaka University, Japan
Thomas Speck	Albert-Ludwigs-Universität Freiburg, Germany
Nicholas Szczecinski	West Virginia University, USA
Falk Tauber	Albert-Ludwigs-Universität Freiburg, Germany
Paul F. M. J. Verschure	Radboud University, The Netherlands
Vasiliki Vouloutsi	Technology Innovation Institute, United Arab Emirates
Victoria Webster-Wood	Carnegie Mellon University, USA

Reviewers

Andrew Adamatzky	University of the West of England, UK
Ian Adams	Case Western Reserve University, USA
Adepapo Alabi	University of Cincinnati, USA
Emanuel Andrada	University of Jena, Germany
Yasmin Ansari	Scuola Superiore Sant'Anna, Italy
Paolo Arena	University of Catania, Italy
Serena Armiento	Istituto Italiano di Tecnologia, Italy
Daniel Aukes	Arizona State University, USA
Jessica Ausborn	Drexel University, USA
Robert Baines	Yale University, USA
Simeon Bamford	Istituto Italiano di Tecnologia, Italy
Giacinto Barresi	Istituto Italiano di Tecnologia, Italy
Anil Bastola	University of Nottingham, UK
Lucia Beccai	Istituto Italiano di Tecnologia, Italy
Sofia Belardinelli	University of Naples Federico II, Italy
Paolo Bollella	University of Bari, Italy
Brandon Caasenbrood	Eindhoven University of Technology, The Netherlands

Genci Capi	Hosei University, Japan
Ragesh Chellattoan	Istituto Italiano di Tecnologia, Italy
Ziyu Chen	Technical University of Munich, Germany
Tiffany Cheng	University of Stuttgart, Germany
Francesca Ciardo	Istituto Italiano di Tecnologia, Italy
Kliton Cikalleshi	Istituto Italiano di Tecnologia, Italy
David Correa	University of Waterloo, Canada
Marco Crepaldi	Istituto Italiano di Tecnologia, Italy
Mark Cutkosky	Stanford University, USA
Giulia D'Angelo	Istituto Italiano di Tecnologia, Italy
Simon Danner	Drexel University, USA
Doris Danninger	Johannes Kepler University Linz, Austria
Riddhi Das	Istituto Italiano di Tecnologia, Italy
Edoardo Datteri	University of Milan, Italy
Cem Balda Dayan	Max Planck Institute for Intelligent Systems, Germany
Emanuela Del Dottore	Istituto Italiano di Tecnologia, Italy
Osman Yirmibeşoğlu	Yale University, USA
Volker Dürr	Bielefeld University, Germany
Matt Ellis	University of Sheffield, UK
Muhammad Farhan	Helmholtz-Zentrum Hereon, Germany
Isabella Fiorello	Istituto Italiano di Tecnologia, Italy
Daniel Flippo	Kansas State University, USA
Fabrizio Gabbiani	Baylor College of Medicine, USA
Luigi Garaffa	University of Padua, Italy
Marcello Garcia	University of the Basque Country, Spain
Benoît Girard	Pierre and Marie Curie University, CNRS, France
Evripidis Gkanias	University of Edinburgh, UK
Axel Gorostiza	University of Cologne, Germany
Benjamin Gorrisen	KU Leuven, Belgium
Lorenzo Guiducci	Max Planck Institute for Colloids, Germany
Wesley Guo	Stanford University, USA
Tamar Gutnick	Okinawa Institute of Science and Technology, Japan
Joe Hays	United States Naval Research Laboratory, USA
Shinishi Hirai	Ritzumeikan University, Japan
Alexander Hunt	Portland State University, USA
Bohyun Hwang	Korea Aerospace University, South Korea
Jacqueline Hynes	Brown University, USA
Auke Ijspeert	EPFL, Switzerland
Hiroyuki Ishii	Waseda University, Japan
Ludger Jansen	University of Rostock, Germany

Alejandro Jimenez-Rodriguez   University of Sheffield, UK
Seonggung Joe   Istituto Italiano di Tecnologia, Italy
Julie Jung   University of Utah, USA
Behnam Kamare   Istituto Italiano di Tecnologia, Italy
Lorenzo Kinnicutt   Boston University College of Engineering, USA
Holger Krapp   Imperial College London, UK
Sebastian Kruppert   University of Freiburg, Germany
Maarja Kruusmaa   Tallinn University of Technology, Estonia
Cecilia Laschi   National University of Singapore, Singapore
Florent Le Moël   University of Edinburgh, UK
Binggwong Leung   Vidyasirimedhi Institute of Science and
                               Technology, Thailand
Junnan Li   Technical University of Munich, Germany
Vittorio Lippi   University of Freiburg, Germany
Matteo Lo Preti   Istituto Italiano di Tecnologia, Italy
Kees Lokhorst   Wageningen University, The Netherlands
Huub Maas   University of Amsterdam, The Netherlands
Michael Mangan   University of Sheffield, Opteran, UK
Stefano Mariani   Istituto Italiano di Tecnologia, Italy
Andrea Marinelli   Istituto Italiano di Tecnologia, Italy
Marcos Maroto   Charles III University of Madrid, Spain
Edgar A. Martinez Garcia   Universidad Autónoma de Ciudad Juárez, Mexico
Uriel Martinez-Hernandez   University of Bath, UK
Arianna Mazzotta   Istituto Italiano di Tecnologia, Italy
Stu McNeal   Portland State University, USA
Edoardo Milana   University of Freiburg, Germany
Stefano Mintchev   ETH Zurich, Switzerland
Charanraj Mohan   Istituto Italiano di Tecnologia, Italy
Sumit Mohanty   AMOLF, The Netherlands
Alessio Mondini   Istituto Italiano di Tecnologia, Italy
Sara Mongile   Istituto Italiano di Tecnologia, Italy
Kenneth Moses   Case Western Reserve University, USA
Anna Mura   Radboud University, The Netherlands
Indrek Must   University of Tartu, Estonia
Giovanna Naselli   Istituto Italiano di Tecnologia, Italy
Noel Naughton   University of Illinois, USA
Nir Nesher   Hebrew University of Jerusalem, Israel
Huu Nhan Nguyen   JAIST, Japan
Jasmine Nirody   University of Chicago, USA
William Nourse   Case Western Reserve University, USA
Luca Padovani   University of Rome, Italy
Luca Patanè   University of Messina, Italy

Linda Paterno	Scuola Superiore Sant'Anna, Italy
Andrew Philippides	University of Sussex, UK
Telmo Pievani	University of Padua, Italy
Maria Pozzi	University of Siena, Italy
Saravana Prashanth Murali Babu	SDU Biorobotics, Denmark
Thorsten Pretsch	Fraunhofer IAP, Germany
Boris Prilutsky	Georgia Tech, USA
Qiukai Qi	University of Bristol, UK
Roger Quinn	Case Western Reserve University, USA
Nicholas Rabb	Tufts University, USA
Giulio Reina	Politecnico di Bari, Italy
Leonardo Ricotti	Scuola Superiore Sant'Anna, Italy
Shane Riddle	Case Western Reserve University, USA
Donato Romano	Scuola Superiore Sant'Anna, Italy
Taher Saif	University of Illinois Urbana-Champaign, USA
Vanessa Sanchez	Stanford University, USA
Francisco Santos	Radboud University, The Netherlands
Rob Scharff	Hong Kong University of Science and Technology, China
Milli Schlafly	Northwestern University, USA
Andrew Schulz	Georgia Tech, USA
Marianna Semprini	Istituto Italiano di Tecnologia, Italy
Kim Seungwon	KIST, South Korea
Ebrahim Shahabishalghouni	Istituto Italiano di Tecnologia, Italy
Edoardo Sinibaldi	Istituto Italiano di Tecnologia, Italy
Thomas Speck	University of Freiburg, Germany
Osca Sten	Istituto Italiano di Tecnologia, Italy
Germán Sumbre	ENS Paris, France
Xuelong Sun	University of Lincoln, UK
Gregory Sutton	University of Lincoln, USA
Nicholas Szczecinski	West Virginia University, USA
Falk Tauber	University of Freiburg, Germany
Yonas Teodros Tefera	Istituto Italiano di Tecnologia, Italy
Thomas George Thuruthel	University College London, UK
Kadri-Ann Valdur	University of Tartu, Estonia, Imperial College London, UK
Lorenzo Vannozzi	Scuola Superiore Sant'Anna, Italy
Julian Vincent	Heriot-Watt University, UK
Francesco Visentin	University of Verona, Italy
Francesco Wanderlingh	University of Genoa, Italy
Barbara Webb	University of Edinburgh, UK
Victoria Webster-Wood	Carnegie Mellon University, USA

Contents – Part II

Biohybrid Systems and Interactions

Contents – Part I

Bioinspiration Under Water

Invertebrate Locomotion and Perception Mechanisms and Thereof Inspired Systems

Joints and Muscles

Model Reveals Joint Properties for Which Co-contracting Antagonist Muscles Increases Joint Stiffness

Isabella Kudyba and Nicholas S. Szczecinski[✉] [ID]

West Virginia University, Morgantown, WV 26506, USA
nicholas.szczecinski@mail.wvu.edu

Abstract. A challenge in robotics is to control interactions with the environment by modulating the stiffness of a manipulator's joints. Smart servos are controlled with proportional feedback gain that is analogous to torsional stiffness of an animal's joint. In animals, antagonistic muscle groups can be temporarily coactivated to stiffen the joint to provide greater opposition to external forces. However, the joint properties for which coactivation increases the stiffness of the joint remain unknown. In this study, we explore possible mechanisms by building a mathematical model of the stick insect tibia actuated by two muscles, the extensor and flexor tibiae. Muscle geometry, passive properties, and active properties are extracted from the literature. Joint stiffness is calculated by tonically activating the antagonists, perturbing the joint from its equilibrium angle, and calculating the restoring moment generated by the muscles. No reflexes are modeled. We estimate how joint stiffness depends on parallel elastic element stiffness, the shape of the muscle activation curve, and properties of the force-length curve. We find that co-contracting antagonist muscles only stiffens the joint when the peak of the force-length curve occurs at a muscle length longer than that when the joint is at equilibrium and the muscle force versus activation curve is concave-up. We discuss how this information could be applied to the control of a smart servo actuator in a robot leg.

Keywords: Hill muscle · musculoskeletal modeling · insect · leg · joint · servo

1 Introduction

In biologically-inspired robotics, a limitation to function and mobility is the materials and devices available to construct and control robots. A common and readily-available actuator for robot limbs is the servo motor. The speed and position of a servo motor are easily controllable via feedback control, but the output torque must also be controlled if the robot is to interact with the environment and people properly (e.g., as in impedance control (Hogan 1985)). In nature, animals have evolved over millions of years to interact with their environment (e.g., walking, running, climbing) without damaging themselves or their environment and serve as a model for how robots may more readily control the forces they exert on the world. If the force control of animals can be mimicked by robots, then their motion may become less "robotic" and they may become more capable of walking and accomplishing other tasks.

F. Meder et al. (Eds.): Living Machines 2023, LNAI 14158, pp. 3–19, 2023.
https://doi.org/10.1007/978-3-031-39504-8_1

Animals may control the forces they exert on the environment by controlling the stiffness of their joints (Houk 1979). Animals have groups of antagonistic muscles that apply moments about the joints to move the body, e.g., the biceps and triceps muscles in the human arm that flex and extend the elbow joint. When simultaneously activated (i.e., "co-contracted") by the nervous system, the muscles increase the stiffness of the joint (i.e., the moment exerted in response to a change in angle) and can do so at many different angles (Zajac 1989; Blickhan et al. 2007). In this way, animals can resist external forces while producing the same motion (Matheson and Dürr 2003; Zakotnik et al. 2006). However, the properties a joint must possess to have the ability to increase joint stiffness by co-contracting antagonist muscles remain unknown. To investigate this question, we modeled a pair of antagonistic muscles that actuate an insect leg joint.

To ensure our model is physiologically plausible, we based our work on extensive characterization and modeling of the stick insect extensor tibiae muscle and the dynamics of the femur-tibia joint (Guschlbauer et al. 2007; Blümel et al. 2012a, b; von Twickel et al. 2019). The tibia is actuated by an antagonistic pair of muscles, the extensor and flexor tibiae. These are pinnate muscles with relatively simple geometry, e.g., their lengths are approximately sinusoidal functions of the femur-tibia angle (Guschlbauer et al. 2007; von Twickel et al. 2019). As in these previous studies, we modeled each muscle as a Hill-type muscle with an elastic element in parallel with the contractile element. The contractile element's force is a function of the muscle's activation and is limited by a force-length curve. Experiments show that the shape of the force-length curve depends on the activation of the muscle (Guschlbauer et al. 2007; Blümel et al. 2012a). All these features are present in our model. However, because we are primarily interested in understanding the stiffness of the joint (not its entire impedance), we omit the force-velocity curve from our model. In addition, because the activation dynamics of the flexor tibiae have not been characterized, the antagonist muscles in our model are both tuned like the extensor tibiae. Such a model prevents us from obscuring underlying principles of joint stiffness due to asymmetrical muscle parameters.

In this study, we investigate how muscle co-contraction may increase joint stiffness by constructing a mathematical model of an antagonistic pair of muscles that actuate an insect leg joint. Our overall approach is to set the activation of each muscle, calculate the joint's equilibrium angle, displace the joint from equilibrium, calculate the restoring moment generated by the muscle forces, and use this information to calculate the joint's stiffness. We calculated the dependence of this stiffness on four parameters:

1. the presence of the parallel elastic element,
2. the shape of the function that maps muscle activation to contractile element force (i.e., sigmoidal or linear),
3. the shape of the force-length curve (i.e., sine function as in Blümel et al. 2012a or polynomial as in Shadmehr and Arbib 1992), and

4. whether or not the peak of the force-length curve depended on muscle activation (Blümel et al. 2012a).

We find that for the parameters of the extensor tibiae muscle, co-contracting the muscles only stiffens the joint if:

- the peak of the force-length curve occurs at a muscle length *longer* than the muscle at joint equilibrium length **OR**
- if the function that maps muscle activation to contractile element force is concave-up.

In the discussion, we summarize our findings, discuss their relevance to the neural control of animal behavior, and propose how these findings could be applied to the control of walking robots.

2 Methods

2.1 Joint Model

The stiffness of a muscle joint, k $\left(\frac{mN \cdot mm}{rad}\right)$, can be calculated following Eq. 1, where τ is the joint torque (mN $\cdot$ mm) and θ is the joint angle (rad). The joint stiffness can be represented as the derivative of the torque with respect to the angle,

$$k = \frac{d\tau}{d\theta}. \tag{1}$$

The force in each muscle can be calculated, and then the moment arm lengths of each muscle are crossed with the corresponding forces to calculate the torque applied to the joint, as shown in Fig. 1 and Eq. 2. In Eq. 2, F_{extn} and F_{flex} are the extensor and flexor forces, and r_{extn}, r_{flex} are the respective maximum moment arm lengths,

$$\tau = F_{extn}r_{extn}\sin\theta - F_{flex}r_{flex}\sin\theta. \tag{2}$$

In this model, the length of the moment arms changes as the angle changes. This model neglects any pinnation angle of muscles, because this angle is so small in comparison with the orientation of the muscles and femur themselves (Blümel et al. 2012a). In addition to this simplification, we have assumed that the muscle resting lengths, resting moment arm lengths, and optimal force outputs are equal in the extensor and flexor. In future work these values can be changed based on parameters measured from the flexor tibiae or other muscles that actuate other joints.

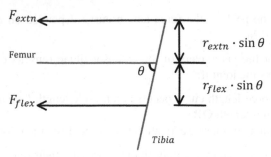

Fig. 1. Muscle forces produce a torque with moment arm lengths, r, that change with respect to the joint angle, θ.

2.2 Calculating Muscle Force

From the Hill-type muscle model, the force of a muscle is produced by a contractile element (CE), which is controlled by active dynamics from the nervous system, a parallel element (PE) that mimics the elastic and viscous forces of the inactivated muscle, and a series elastic element (SEE) that mimics the muscle's spring-like properties when activated (Zajac 1989). Because of their arrangement, the forces of the CE and PE add, and this sum is equal to the tension in the SEE, as well as the total force of the muscle. This relationship is shown in Eq. 3 and Fig. 2A,

$$F_{muscle} = F_{CE} + F_{PE} = F_{SEE}. \tag{3}$$

Note that previous studies by Blümel et al. (2012a) calculate muscle force as a function of the muscle fiber length, not muscle length (differentiated in Fig. 2B). However, we express our model in terms of muscle length, by replacing the fiber length with change of the muscle length, as a function of the joint angle and maximum moment arm lengths. As the joint angle increases, the length of the extensor decreases and the length of the flexor increases. The difference in these parameters does not impact the accuracy of this study but is noted for clarity.

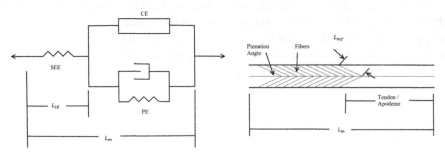

Fig. 2. A) The series elastic element (SEE), contractile element (CE), and parallel element (PE) produce the muscle force according to Eq. 4. B) The length of the muscle fibers compared to the length of the muscle.

The series elastic element produces a force shown in Eq. 4 where k_{SE} is the spring constant of the series elastic element and L_{SE} is the length of the series elastic element (Guschlbauer et al. 2007),

$$F_{SEE} = k_{SE} \cdot L_{SE}^2. \tag{4}$$

In steady state, the length of the muscle and force of the muscle do not change with time, so damping forces are omitted from the model. The elastic property of the parallel element follow Eq. 5, where k_1 and k_2 are spring constants and L_{mf} is the length of the muscle fibers (Blümel et al. 2012b). Figure 3 shows the relationship between F_{PE} and change in muscle length from the joint equilibrium length.

$$F_{PE} = k_1 e^{k_2 \cdot L_{mf}}. \tag{5}$$

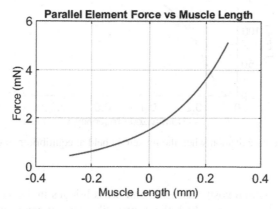

Fig. 3. Parallel element force against muscle length deviation from rest.

The contractile element (CE) produces force F_{CE} through activation dynamics, where excitation of the nervous system results in a force in the sarcomeres of the muscle tissue. F_{CE} depends on the maximum force that the muscle can produce, the activation of the muscle (A_{act}), the length of the muscle, and the speed at which the muscle is contracting (Zajac 1989). Because we are focusing on joint stiffness during tonic muscle activation, we are neglecting the speed at which the muscle is contracting. As a result, the contractile element force is the product of the maximum force the muscle can exert (F_{max}), the activation of the muscle, and a function of the muscle length (F_L) shown in Eq. 6 (Zajac 1989),

$$F_{CE} = F_{max} \cdot A_{act} \cdot F_L. \tag{6}$$

To account for the muscle activation component of the CE force, the normalized frequency of the motor neurons, f, is a fraction of maximum motor neuron excitation, normalized to 200 Hz, the maximum frequency observed in the extensor muscle during walking (Guschlbauer et al. 2007). In doing so this value can be thought of as a percentage of maximum excitation. Previous work shows that the motor neuron frequency does not correlate linearly with the contractile element force, but instead is a sigmoid curve shown in Fig. 4 (Blümel et al. 2012a). When holding the extensor at the length which the joint is at equilibrium and exciting the extensor motor neuron, Blümel et al. measured the force output vs. motor neuron excitation. Note that in Blümel et al. 2012a, they refer to the normalized motor neuron frequency as act. They fit this curve, using Eqs. 7 and 8, where A_{act} represents the muscle activation. A_{act} is then used as a multiplier in Eq. 9 to calculate F_{CE} (Blümel et al. 2012a). Figure 4 shows the muscle force plotted against normalized motor neuron frequency, the rate at which the CE force increases with respect to this neuron excitation is larger at lower frequencies.

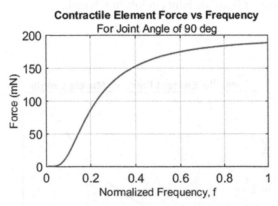

Fig. 4. Muscle force vs activation when the muscle is held at equilibrium angle. Accounted for in Eqs. 7 and 8.

Because of the actin/myosin filaments and cross bridges in the sarcomere, there is an optimized muscle length in which the contractile element can produce the greatest amount of force, and this happens when the muscle is stretched or is longer that at muscle length at joint equilibrium (Zajac 1989). Guschlbauer et al. found that at lower activation states, this peak occurs at a longer muscle length than at higher activations (Guschlbauer et al. 2007). Blümel et al. fit this phenomenon by describing the force-length relationship as a sine curve, which allowed for a shifting peak as muscle activation increased. This required the addition of a "frequency", ω (with units mm^{-1}), that is dependent on the motor neuron frequency. The calculation for ω is shown in Eq. 7, where $curv_\omega$ is an animal-dependent constant. Putting this all together, F_{CE} is shown in Eq. 9 and Fig. 5A (Blümel et al. 2012a),

$$\omega = 2.5 + \frac{1}{[curv_\omega \cdot (f + 0.05)]^2},$$ (7)

$$A_{act} = 15e^{-1.06\omega},$$ (8)

$$F_{CE} = F_{max} \cdot A_{act} \cdot F_L = F_{max} \cdot A_{act} \cdot \frac{1 + sin\left(\omega L_{mf} - \left(\frac{\pi}{2} + 2.7\omega\right)\right)}{2}.$$ (9)

Note that at very low activations, the equation produces a curve that does not follow the pattern at higher activations. This error is discussed further in the discussion.

To study the effects that each of these aspects has on the stiffness of the joint and create an estimate that can be better used in robotic applications, we analyze the CE force equation derived from Blümel et al. and create our own CE force equations that can be manipulated more easily in our model. Instead of a sine curve for the force-length curve, we use a parabola in vertex form, similar to the approach taken in other models (Cofer et al. 2010; Shadmehr and Arbib 1992). This allows us to shift the curve's peak easily, while maintaining similar force magnitudes from the constructed sine curve. To incorporate the non-linearity of the force and activation relationship, we can alter the muscles' activation, but we also test a linear relationship between the force and activation, when $A_{act} = f$. If a linear relationship produces a similar stiffness result to the non-linear relationship, the linear relationship may be used in servo-motor control to simplify and accelerate calculations. Equation 10 details the CE force we manipulate to compare with stiffness. In this equation, a changes the width of the curve, h shifts the peak with respect to the length of the muscle, and F_{max} is the maximum force of the curve,

$$F_{CE} = A_{act} \cdot \left[a(\Delta L_m - h)^2 + F_{max} \right]. \tag{10}$$

The shift in the force-length curve's peak can be altered with the activation state by using Eq. 11, where ϵ is machine epsilon. This was added so when the activation is 0, the result will not be undefined, but has a negligible effect on the shifting of the parabola. h_1 and h_2 are determined from the maximum and minimum peak shifts in the curve. These maximum and minimum shifts will resemble the look of the sine curve that was measured in the stick insect and can be shown in Fig. 5B. Note that $Shift_{max}$ was computed when normalized frequency is 10%. This adds little error to the equation at low frequencies:

$$h(f) = \frac{h_1}{f + \epsilon} + h_2, \tag{11}$$

$$h_2 = \frac{Shift_{max} - 1}{1 - \frac{1}{Shift_{min}}}, \tag{12}$$

$$h_1 = Shift_{min} - h_2. \tag{13}$$

Figure 5 below compares the sine curve measured from the actual stick insect with the parabola function of Eq. 10 where the non-linear muscle activation is used, and the muscle length at which the peak of the parabola occurs decreases as activation increases. Figure 5C shows the parabola function where the length at which the peak occurs is constant and linear muscle activation relationship. Figure 5D shows the peak of the curve at a constant value, but with sigmodal activation. These different ways of calculating muscle force are labeled and detailed in Table 1 for further comparison.

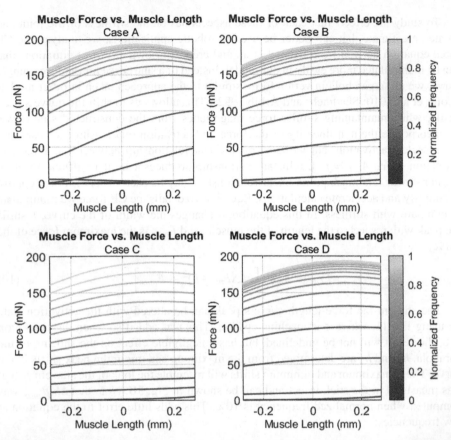

Fig. 5. A) Muscle force plotted against muscle length with increasing motor neuron frequency according to Blümel et al. (2012a). The equation for force is Case A detailed in Table 1. The force-length relationship is the sine curve measured from the actual stick insect. Note that at lower motor neuron frequencies, the equation produces maximum force at a very short length, which is addressed in the discussion. B) Muscle force using the parabolic force-length curve in vertex form, where h-shift in the peak of the graph is dependent on motor neuron frequency and muscle activation is non-linear. The force produced in this graph is Case B in Table 1. C) Muscle force using parabolic force-length curve, where h-shift in the peak of the graph is constant and muscle activation is linear. D) Muscle force using parabolic force-length curve, where h-shift is constant and muscle activation is nonlinear according to Eq. 8.

In Case C, the force-length relationship is modeled as a concave-down parabola. In this case, the parabola's shift along the length axis is not dependent on activation state, unlike in real muscles. Figure 6 compares the force-length curve for multiple levels of normalized frequency and values of h.

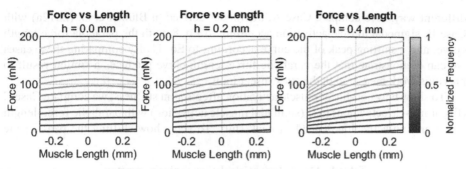

Fig. 6. Muscle force plotted against muscle length deviation from rest with increasing activation in Case C. Relationship plotted is the concave down parabola, where h represents a shift in the peak of the graph (i.e., the muscle length which produces the greatest active force).

2.3 Calculating the Stiffness

Using MATLAB R2022a, we calculate the force of each muscle by adding the contractile and passive forces for every angle and every activation state. The net torque is calculated and plotted for every activation combination of the extensor and flexor muscles. Figure 7 shows an example of torque vs. joint angle for equal coactivation. The stiffness was calculated using the centered difference approximation for the closest values of torque equal to zero, shown in Eq. 14. In this calculation, $\Delta\theta = 1° = 0.017$ radian:

$$k = \frac{d\tau}{d\theta} \approx \frac{\tau(\theta + \Delta\theta) - \tau(\theta - \Delta\theta)}{2\Delta\theta}. \tag{14}$$

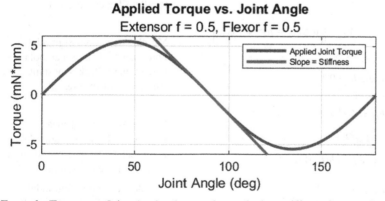

Fig. 7. Example Torque vs. Joint Angle plot used to calculate stiffness for set of activation combinations. Stiffness is calculated when torque is at the closest values to zero.

2.4 Testing Muscle Force Components

To analyze how different muscle parameters affect joint stiffness, we test different details that make up force, noted in Table 1. In the various cases, muscle force is calculated in different ways. We compare Case A, the model derived in Blümel et al. (2012a) with Case B, sigmodal muscle activation according to Eq. 8, with the parabola force length curve, and a shifting peak of the curve according to Eq. 11. By comparing these cases we can demonstrate that the parabolic force-length curve produces a similar result to previous work measured in the stick insect joint.

To show how non-linear muscle activation affects joint stiffness, we compare Case C (linear muscle activation) to D (sigmodal muscle activation) with parabolic force-length curve and no activation-dependent peak shift. To show how shifting the peak of the

Table 1. Muscle Force Calculation Testing parameters

Case	Muscle Force Equation	Properties
A	$F_m = F_{max} \cdot A_{act} \cdot$ $\dfrac{1 + sin(\omega L_{mf} - (\frac{\pi}{2} + 2.7\omega))}{2} + k_1 e^{k_2 \cdot L_{mf}}$	Muscle Activation: Sigmodal Force Length Curve: Blümel Sine Curve Force Length Peak: Dependent on f Parallel Element: Present
B	$F_m = A_{act} \cdot \left[a(\Delta L_m - h)^2 + F_{max} \right]$, $+ k_1 e^{k_2 \cdot L_{mf}}$ where $h = h(f)$ (Eq. 11)	Muscle Activation: Sigmodal Force Length Curve: Parabola Force Length Peak: Dependent on f Parallel Element: Present
C	$F_m = f \cdot [a(\Delta L_m - h)^2 + F_{max}]$, $+ k_1 e^{k_2 \cdot L_{mf}}$ where $h = \{0, 0.1, 0.2, 0.3, 0.4\}$	Muscle Activation: Linear Force Length Curve: Parabola Force Length Peak: Constant Parallel Element: Present
D	$F_m = A_{act} \cdot \left[a(\Delta L_m - h)^2 + F_{max} \right]$, $+ k_1 e^{k_2 \cdot L_{mf}}$ where $h = 0.1$	Muscle Activation: Sigmodal Force Length Curve: Parabola Force Length Peak: Constant Parallel Element: Present
E	$F_m = f \cdot \left[a(\Delta L_m - h)^2 + F_{max} \right]$, $+ k_1 e^{k_2 \cdot L_{mf}}$ where $h = h(f)$ (Eq. 11)	Muscle Activation: Linear Force Length Curve: Parabola Force Length Peak: Dependent on f Parallel Element: Present
F	$F_m = F_{max} \cdot A_{act}$ $\cdot \dfrac{1 + sin(\omega L_{mf} - (\frac{\pi}{2} + 2.7\omega))}{2}$	Muscle Activation: Sigmodal Force Length Curve: Blümel Sine Curve Force Length Peak: Dependent on f Parallel Element: Absent
G	$F_m = A_{act} \cdot \left[a(\Delta L_m - h)^2 + F_{max} \right]$, where $h = h(f)$ Eq. 11)	Muscle Activation: Sigmodal Force Length Curve: Parabola Force Length Peak: Dependent on f Parallel Element: Absent

force-length curve affects joint stiffness, Case C includes multiple force-length curves with static but differing peaks between 0 mm and 0.4 mm.

Comparing Case C to E and Case D to B shows how the force-length curve's peak shifting dependence on motor frequency alters the stiffness, for a linear activation and the sigmodal activation, respectively. This analysis compares a constant peak shift to the peak shift dependent on motor neuron frequency according to Eq. 11.

Lastly, to analyze what affect the parallel element has on stiffness, in cases A and F we compare the Blümel et al. (2012a) model with and without the parallel element. Additionally, we compare the parabolic force-length curve with non-linear muscle activation and shifting peak with motor neuron frequency as observed in the animal, with and without the parallel element in Cases B and G.

The parameters used to calculate values of forces and their origin are listed in Table 2. Note that parameter values for the extensor muscle are used for both the extensor and flexor (see note in introduction). When choosing animal dependent parameters, animal E in Table 1 of Blümel et al. 2012b was used.

Table 2. Extensor parameter values used in model.

Parameter	Value	Source
r_{extn}	0.28 mm	Fig. 5 Guschlbauer et al. 2007
L_{mf}	1.41 mm	Fig. 3B Guschlbauer et al. 2007
F_{max}	189 mN	Table 1 Blümel et al. 2012b
$curv_\omega$	4.51 mm$^{0.5}$	Table 1 Blümel et al. 2012b
k_1	$3.13 \cdot 10^{-3}$ mN	Table 1 Blümel et al. 2012b
k_2	4.38 mm^{-1}	Table 1 Blümel et al. 2012b
a	$-200 \frac{mN}{mm^2}$	Not measured in animal
$Shift_{min}$	0.1 mm	Fig. 6a Blümel et al. 2012a
$Shift_{max}$	0.4 mm	Fig. 6a Blümel et al. 2012a

3 Results

Because the muscles in this model are equal and opposite, the equilibrium angle is 90 degrees when the muscles are activated the same amount. All stiffness graphs detailed below are plotted for a joint angle of 90 degrees. Figure 8 plots the joint stiffness against the motor neuron frequency for all cases listed in Table 1. Figure 8A shows Cases A through E and Fig. 8B shows Cases A, B, F, and G. Case A contains the most biological detail, including a sinusoidal force-length curve whose peak shifts to shorter lengths as muscle activation increases. Although the model contains some simplifications (see Methods), this model is likely closest to the animal's physiology. Co-activating the antagonist muscles increases the stiffness by a factor of 20 relative to the relaxed joint.

However, the joint stiffness decreases with muscle activation greater than approximation 20%. Furthermore, the stiffness of the joint is negative for some low motor neuron frequencies. This is due to the way the model from Blümel et al. (Eq. 9, Fig. 5A) maps from motor neuron frequency to muscle force. This is addressed in the Discussion.

Altering the form of the functions within the model shows the effect that each has on joint stiffness. When the sinusoidal force-length curve is replaced with a parabolic curve whose peak shifts with muscle activation (Case B), the peak stiffness is only about 8 times the baseline joint stiffness. Despite this difference, the maximum joint stiffness occurs at the same normalized frequency as in Case A, about 20%. This is where the inflection point of the activation curve occurs, suggesting that co-contracting antagonist muscles can stiffen the joint if the activation curve is concave-up. However, if the peak of the force-length curve does not shift with muscle activation (Case D), the joint stiffness always increases with increasing activation. This suggests that the location of the force-length curve's peak also affects joint stiffness. If the muscle activation is made a linear function of motor neuron frequency and the force-length parabola's peak is constant, the joint stiffness increases linearly with increasing motor neuron frequency (Case C). With linear activation and force-length curve peak shifting (Case E), stiffness increases linearly with motor neuron frequency and has a greater stiffness at lower frequencies.

Figure 8B enables the comparison of how the parallel element affects the stiffness of the joint. Because this element is in parallel with the contractile element, it simply raises the stiffness of the joint at all muscle activations.

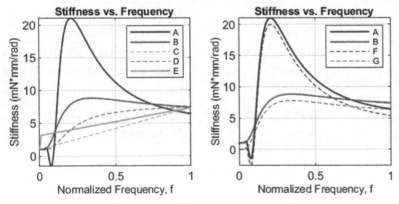

Fig. 8. A) Stiffness vs. Normalized motor neuron frequency for Cases A through E of Table 1. B) Stiffness vs. Normalized motor neuron frequency for Cases A, B, F, and G. Cases F and G are equivalent to Cases A and B respectively, minus the parallel element force.

Figure 9 shows the joint stiffness as a function of muscle activation for Case C in which the constant force-length curve peak shift is varied from 0 to 0.4 mm. As the peak of the force length curve is shifted a greater amount, the stiffness that the joint can achieve through co-contraction increases. When the peak shift is 0 mm, co-contracting the muscles does not stiffen the joint. This suggests that the force-length curve, a property of the active muscle, plays an important role in the stiffening of the joint during antagonist co-contraction.

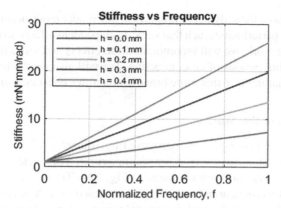

Fig. 9. Joint stiffness vs. muscle activation for Case C. Greater peak shifts (shown in Fig. 6) create greater maximum stiffness.

4 Discussion

To better understand how co-contracting antagonist muscles stiffens an animal's joint (Houk 1979; Blickhan et al. 2007), we developed a mathematical model of the muscular actuation of an insect joint based on experimental measurements and previous models (Guschlbauer et al. 2007, Blümel et al. 2012a, b; von Twickel et al. 2019). Each muscle in our model is a Hill muscle with a sigmoidal muscle activation curve, a parallel elastic element, a force-length curve, and an angle-dependent moment arm about the joint. Because we are interested in stiffness, we omitted the inertia of the distal limb segment and velocity-dependent terms in the muscle model, e.g., the force-velocity curve. By systematically altering the model, we found that co-activating the muscles increases joint stiffness if the peak of the force-length curve occurs at a muscle length longer than that at joint equilibrium or if the function that maps muscle activation to contractile element force is concave-up.

4.1 Limitations and Future Work

Although this study provided some insight into the joint properties by which co-contracting antagonist muscles may stiffen a joint, it has limitations as a model of the animal's joint. In the stick insect, the flexor muscle has a longer moment arm than the extensor, higher PE forces and maximum contractile forces, and unknown CE force-length dependence (Guschlbauer et al. 2007). Future studies may more accurately model the animal's joint by approximating the flexor's unique parameter values. To the authors' knowledge, no study measures the stiffness of the femoral/tibial joint in the stick insect and how it depends on muscle activation. Such data would be valuable for creating a more biologically accurate model.

Another limitation of this study is the omission of dynamic muscle properties, such as the force-velocity curve and the series elastic element. These properties are known to affect the force a muscle develops when the joint is disturbed from equilibrium (Zajac 1989; von Twickel et al. 2019). As a result, our model only approximates the full behavior of a leg joint. Without these dynamic properties, our model most closely models a joint undergoing a slow perturbation, such that velocity-dependent effects do not dominate the response. In future work, we will incorporate these effects and test whether they affect joint stiffness during periods of co-contraction. We will also need a broader definition of stiffness than that in Eq. 1 that more broadly quantifies resistance to perturbations.

4.2 Implications of this Work

For the sine wave force-length curve proposed by Blümel et al. (Case A), the model deviates from the qualitative pattern at low motor neuron frequencies, with peak muscle force occurring at very short muscle lengths (Fig. 5A). This error occurs at 15% and less of normalized motor neuron frequency and is caused by a shifting in the sine curve. When data was taken from the stick insect, only muscle forces for some motor neuron frequencies were measured. When constructing the sine curve, Blümel et al. may not have accounted for motor neuron frequencies less than 30 Hz. Because of this, forces and stiffnesses measured with normalized frequencies less than 15% should be neglected when analyzing the sine curve data.

As an alternative to the sine force-length curve in Case A, we created the parabolic force-length curve in Case B (Fig. 5A and 5B). There are some differences in the magnitude of muscle force related to motor neuron frequency. At 10% of max normalized frequency, the largest percent difference between the two calculations for F_M for every joint angle was 106%, such a high value can be attributed to the error in the sine curve for frequencies less than 15% of maximum. However, at higher frequencies, the parabolic equation better matches the Blümel et al. sine curve. At 80% maximum normalized frequency, the largest percent difference between these two curves was 26%. At maximum motor neuron frequency, the largest percent difference was 6%. In future work, better approximations for the biological sine curve will allow for closer approximations for muscle force. When comparing the stiffness curves in Fig. 8A, Case A creates a noticeably greater joint stiffness than Case B, although the general shape of the curves is the same. Both curves produce a peak stiffness around 20% of maximum motor neuron frequency, and then decrease to a stiffness of about 7 $\frac{\text{mN·mm}}{\text{rad}}$ at full motor neuron excitation. The difference in maximum stiffness is probably due to the non-linearity of the peak shifting noted in Eq. 11. We derived this equation as an approximation of the shifting of the peak in the sine curve, but its accuracy could be improved e.g., by replacing it with a second-order Taylor approximation of the sinusoidal relationship from Blümel et al. 2012a. However, because the shape of the stiffness curves in Fig. 8A is similar, we infer that the parabolic force-length curve does not fundamentally alter the behavior of the joint.

In Case C, when the peak of the force-length curve, h, is constant, shifting h to be longer increased the maximum stiffness the joint could produce, shown in Fig. 9. When the shift of the peak of the force length curve is zero, as in the F_{CE} is largest when the muscle is at joint equilibrium length, then the joint stiffness does not increase with increasing motor neuron frequency. For this reason, the maximum force that the muscle can provide must occur when the muscle is stretched past its length at joint equilibrium for stiffness to increase with motor neuron activation. The greater this shift, the greater stiffness the joint can produce. Comparing Case C (linear muscle activation and constant peak shift) with Case D (sigmodal muscle activation and constant peak shift), we found that the non-linear muscle activation creates a non-linear relationship between motor neuron frequency and joint stiffness. The non-linear relationship between motor neuron frequency and muscle force also creates a maximum stiffness around 20% of maximum excitation.

When this peak shift is dependent on activation in Case E, $h = h(f)$, the dependency on motor neuron frequency in Case E increases the stiffness for lower frequencies, however the stiffness still increases with increasing frequency. This means that when the peak shift is a function of frequency, the maximum joint stiffness is not changed from the linear case when $h = 0.1$ mm, as shown in Case C in Fig. 8A.

Looking at Cases B and D allows us to compare how the stiffness changes with a peak dependent on motor neuron frequency when the muscle activation is nonlinear. Looking at Fig. 8A we observe that when the peak shift is dependent on motor neuron frequency (Case B) the maximum stiffness is much higher than in the constant peak case (Case D). Therefore, by comparing Cases C to E and Cases B to D we find that when the peak of the force length curve decreases with respect to motor neuron frequency, the stiffness that the joint can produce increases for lower motor neuron frequencies.

Lastly, we compare how removing the parallel element affects the stiffness in Cases A to F and B to G. When the parallel element was removed from the systems the magnitude of the stiffness decreases by a small amount and does not alter the relationship to motor neuron frequency, as shown in Fig. 8B. This phenomenon is observed both in the sine curve based (Case A) function and in the parabola function (Case B). Although including the parallel element in the model only increases the stiffness by little, the PE also sets the minimum stiffness the joint can have. If the PE were to be removed from the muscles, they would be allowed to have zero stiffness when activation is zero. To conclude, including the parallel element would be necessary for controlling a servo motor for setting minimum stiffness, but does not have much of an effect on stiffness at higher motor neuron firing frequencies.

4.3 Application to Robotics

Variable stiffness actuators (or more generally, variable impedance actuators) have been of interest in the field of robotics for several decades (for a review, see Wolf et al. 2016). Such actuators are of particular interest in the field of "collaborative robotics" (i.e., cobots), which must operate safely around humans (for a review, see Et Zaatari et al. 2019). Recently, some work has been done on modeling the joint stiffness of animals for use in robotics. Takuma et al. 2011 created a humanoid robot, *Kojiro*, with tendon-driven actuators that can resist applied forces from the environment by increasing the stiffness of joints. Zhang et al. 2022 analyzed the variable stiffness in human joints and neurological signals and matched them with a variable stiffness actuator to perform a lifting experiment. In both studies the actuators can change stiffness to adapt to the environment. However, the actuators in both cases were not just servo motors acting as a joint. For example, Kojiro's tendon-drive actuators are elastic bands that act as tendon and muscle, contracted by servo motors (Takuma et al. 2011). Zhang et al. 2022 implemented an extra stiffening motor with belt and circular springs surrounding the drive motor to stiffen the joint. These solutions are clever and effective, but add to the size, weight, and mechanical complexity of the robot. In the future, we seek to apply the lessons learned from our current study to develop a software solution to be used with compact, commercially available smart-servo actuators. Nonetheless, more research is required to apply principles from animal muscle activation to develop more effective control strategies for the stiffness of a walking robot's leg joints in real time.

Acknowledgements. This work was funded by NSF DBI NeuroNex 2015317 to NSS. This work was also funded by NSF IIS 2113028 to NSS.

References

Blickhan, R., Seyfarth, A., Geyer, H., Grimmer, S., Wagner, H., Günther, M.: Intelligence by mechanics. Philos. Trans. R. Soc. A: Math. Phys. Eng. Sci. **365**(1850), 199–220 (2007). https://doi.org/10.1098/rsta.2006.1911

Blümel, M., Hooper, S.L., Guschlbauer, C., White, E.W., Büschges, A.: Determining all parameters necessary to build Hill-type muscle models from experiments on single muscles. Biol. Cybern. **106**(10), 543–558 (2012a). https://doi.org/10.1007/s00422-012-0530-5

Blümel, M., Guschlbauer, C., Daun-Gruhn, S., Hooper, S.L., Büschges, A.: Hill-type muscle model parameters determined from experiments on single muscles show large animal-to-animal variation. Biol. Cybern. **106**(10), 559–571 (2012b). https://doi.org/10.1007/s00422-012-0530-6

Cofer, D.W., Cymbalyuk, G., Reid, J., Zhu, Y., Heitler, W.J., Edwards, D.H.: AnimatLab: a 3D graphics environment for neuromechanical simulations. J. Neurosci. Methods **187**(2), 280–288 (2010). https://doi.org/10.1016/j.jneumeth.2010.01.005

El Zaatari, S., Marei, M., Li, W., Usman, Z.: Cobot programming for collaborative industrial tasks: an overview. Robot. Auton. Syst. **116**, 162–180 (2019). https://doi.org/10.1016/j.robot.2019.03.003

Guschlbauer, C., Scharstein, H., Buschges, A.: The extensor tibiae muscle of the stick insect: biomechanical properties of an insect walking leg muscle. J. Exp. Biol. **210**(6), 1092–1108 (2007). https://doi.org/10.1242/jeb.0272

Hogan, N.: Impedance control: an approach to manipulation: part I—theory. J. Dyn. Syst. Meas. Contr. **107**(1), 1–7 (1985). https://doi.org/10.1115/1.3140702

Houk, J.C.: Regulation of stiffness by skeletomotor reflexes. Annu. Rev. Physiol. **41**(1), 99–114 (1979). https://doi.org/10.1146/annurev.ph.41.030179.000531

Matheson, T., Dürr, V.: Load compensation in targeted limb movements of an insect. J. Exp. Biol. **206**(18), 3175–3186 (2003). https://doi.org/10.1242/jeb.00534

Shadmehr, R., Arbib, M.A.: A mathematical analysis of the force-stiffness characteristics of muscles in control of a single joint system. Biol. Cybern. **66**(6), 463–477 (1992). https://doi.org/10.1007/BF00204111

Takuma, S., Urata, J., Nakanishi, Y., Okada, K., Inaba, M.: Whole body adapting behavior with muscle level stiffness control of tendon-driven multijoint robot. In: IEEE International Conference on Robotics and Biomimetics (2011). https://doi.org/10.1109/robio.2011.6181623

Von Twickel, A., Guschlbauer, C., Hooper, S.L., Büschges, A.: Swing velocity profiles of small limbs can arise from transient passive torques of the antagonist muscle alone. Curr. Biol. **29**(1), 1-12.e7 (2019). https://doi.org/10.1016/j.cub.2018.11.016

Wolf, S., et al.: Variable stiffness actuators: review on design and components. IEEE/ASME Trans. Mechatron. **21**(5), 2418–2430 (2016). https://doi.org/10.1109/TMECH.2015.2501019

Zajac, F.E.: Muscle and tendon: properties, models, scaling, and application to biomechanics and motor control. Crit. Rev. Biomed. Eng. **17**(4), 359–411 (1989). https://doi.org/10.1113/jph ysiol.1965.sp007626

Zakotnik, J., Matheson, T., Dürr, V.: Co-contraction and passive forces facilitate load compensation of aimed limb movements. J. Neurosci. **26**(19), 4995–5007 (2006). https://doi.org/10.1523/JNE UROSCI.0161-06.2006

Zhang, X., Huang, L., Niu, H.: Structural design and stiffness matching control of bionic variable stiffness joint for human-robot collaboration. Biomimetic Intell. Robot. **3**, 100084 (2022). https://doi.org/10.1016/j.birob.2022.100084

Biarticular Muscles Improve the Stability of a Neuromechanical Model of the Rat Hindlimb

Kaiyu Deng[1](✉), Alexander J. Hunt[2], Hillel J. Chiel[1], and Roger D. Quinn[1]

[1] Case Western Reserve University, Cleveland, OH, USA
kxd194@case.edu
[2] Portland State University, Portland, OR, USA

Abstract. This study introduces a novel neuromechanical model of rat hindlimbs with biarticular muscles producing walking movements without ground contact. The design of the control network is informed by the findings from our previous investigations into two-layer central pattern generators (CPGs). Specifically, we examined one plausible synthetic nervous system (SNS) designed to actuate 3 biarticular muscles, including the Biceps femoris posterior (BFP) and Rectus femoris (RF), both of which provide torque about the hip and knee joints. We conducted multiple perturbation tests on the simulation model to investigate the contribution of these two biarticular muscles in stabilizing perturbed hindlimb walking movements. We tested the BFP and RF muscles under three conditions: active, only passive tension, and fully disabled. Our results show that when these two biarticular muscles were active, they not only reduced the impact of external torques, but also facilitated rapid coordination of motion phases. As a result, the hindlimb model with biarticular muscles demonstrated faster recovery compared to our previous monoarticular muscle model.

Keywords: Rat · Biarticular Muscles · Synthetic Nervous System · Stabilization Analysis

1 Introduction

Recent technological advancements have led to the development of legged robots that exhibit greater agility and stability, even when encountering unexpected perturbations during various locomotor tasks [1–4]. Despite these impressive developments, there is a growing interest in the remarkable ability of animals to effectively solve low-level joint/gait coordination problems while adapting to changes in their environment. This highlights the importance of studying natural mechanisms and suggests that researchers can gain valuable insights into the development of more advanced bio-inspired robots and prosthetic devices.

Despite the existence of promising bio-inspired robots [5–10] and artificial neural controllers [11–15], our current understanding of the mechanisms behind dynamic and robust walking is still insufficient for the development of robots that mimic mammalian

© The Author(s), under exclusive license to Springer Nature Switzerland AG 2023
F. Meder et al. (Eds.): Living Machines 2023, LNAI 14158, pp. 20–37, 2023.
https://doi.org/10.1007/978-3-031-39504-8_2

locomotion. Although the strategies and neural systems responsible for mammalian locomotion patterns are not yet fully understood, cat locomotion studies using split-belt treadmills suggest that the spinal cord and its associated peripheral nervous system are pivotal in generating and adapting these patterns [16–18]. This is consistent with T.G. Brown's finding that the cat spinal cord can generate a locomotor rhythm in the absence of input from higher centers and afferent feedback [19].

Subsequent investigations confirmed Brown's findings and led to the development of the widely accepted concept of central pattern generators (CPGs). These are neural circuits located within the central nervous systems of invertebrates and vertebrates that can generate rhythmic, coordinated movements such as swimming [20], walking [21–23], heartbeat [24], breathing and gasping [25]. The "half-center" model [21] is a widely used model of the spinal CPG that produces rhythmic alternating activity of flexor and extensor motoneurons during locomotion.

However, the presence of "non-resetting deletions" [26], observed in the movement of decerebrate cats cannot be explained by a simple "half-center" structure. These "non-resetting deletions" refer to instances where motoneuron activities are absent for a few cycles, but then reappear without a phase shift. To address this issue, Rybak's group proposed a computational model of the two-layer CPG [27], which allows for separate control of walking rhythm timing and motoneuron activity pattern during locomotion.

Our previous work incorporated a two-layer CPG into a neuromechanical model of rat hindlimbs [15], which successfully reproduced repetitive forward walking and "non-resetting deletions". However, this neuromechanical model was limited by its simplistic musculoskeletal configuration with pairs of antagonist muscles at each joint. As a result, the stability investigations from this model were potentially incomplete. To address this issue, we have expanded the musculoskeletal configuration to include biarticular muscles in a simplified model [28] and a full-muscle model [29]. Our current goal is to investigate how biarticular muscles could contribute to the stabilization of the simulation model during walking. Specifically, we explore how biarticular muscles linking hip and knee joint are actuated with a plausible neural configuration that utilizes the preferred CPG parameters reported in a previous work by our group [30].

2   Methods

To simulate the rat hindlimb walking with biarticular muscles, we used Animatlab [31], a simulation software that allows for the creation of synthetic nervous systems (SNSs) and actuation of biomechanical bodies with proprioceptive feedback. The simulations were conducted in the Vortex physics engine (CM Labs, Montreal, Quebec), which is integrated into Animatlab and provides realistic physical simulations.

2.1   Biomechanical Modeling

The biomechanical model of the rat hindlimb (shown in Fig. 1A) and muscle parameter values are consistent with our previous model [28]. As in the previous model, the hindlimb is constrained to move in the sagittal plane and is actuated by the eight most prominent muscles used in forward locomotion. The hindlimb model consists of five monoarticular muscles, including Iliopsoas (IP) and Biceps femoris anterior (BFA), which actuate the hip joint; grouped Vastii (VA), which actuates the knee joint; and Soleus (SO) and Tibialis anterior (TA), which actuate the ankle joint. The model also includes three biarticular muscles shown in red font, including Biceps femoris posterior (BFP) and Rectus femoris (RF), which link the hip and knee joint and are the primary focus of investigation in this study; while Gastrocnemii (GA) spans the knee and ankle joint.

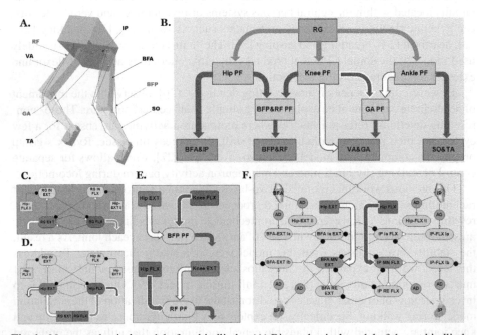

Fig. 1. Neuromechanical model of rat hindlimbs. (A) Biomechanical model of the rat hindlimbs from our previous work [28], muscle labeled in red font are biarticular muscles. (B) Schematic of the general neural control network for a single rat hindlimb. (C) General rhythm generator configuration. (D) Pattern formation network for the hip joint. (E) Intermediate integration layer for the BFP and RF muscles. GA PF similarly combines Ankle EXT and Knee FLX signals. (F) Sensory-motor network for the hip monoarticular muscle pair (BFA & IP). Identical network designs are used for BFP and RF, VA and GA, and SO and TA. IP: Iliopsoas; BFA: Biceps femoris anterior; BFP: Biceps femoris posterior; SO: Soleus; RF: Rectus femoris; VA: Vastii; GA: Gastrocnemii; TA: Tibialis anterior. RG: Rhythm generator; PF: Pattern formation; MN: motoneuron; IN: Interneuron; EXT: Extensor; FLX: Flexor; RE: Renshaw cell; AD: Adaptor. Color codes are used to distinguish between neurons and connections. Extensor oscillators are colored blue, while flexor oscillators are colored red. Motoneurons are colored brown, interneurons are colored yellow, and pink indicates intermediate pattern formation interneurons for biarticular muscles. Flexor signals are indicated by arrows with solid fill and white outline, while extensor signals are represented by arrows with a white fill and solid outline. Arrows with both solid fill and outline indicate that all signals are conducted to the next region.

AnimatLab uses a basic linear Hill muscle model from Shadmehr's work [32, 33] to generate force and it is illustrated in Fig. 2 below.

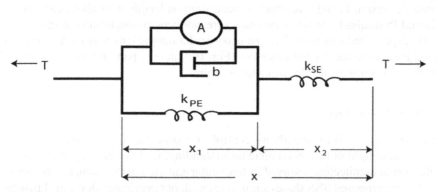

Fig. 2. AnimatLab Muscle Model. Adapted from Shadmehr's work [32, 33].

The muscle model is a spring-damper system with user pre-defined length-tension and stimulus-tension relationships. Tension, T, developed in the muscle is determined by the following equation:

$$\frac{dT}{dt} = \frac{k_{se}}{b}\left(k_{pe}\Delta x + b\dot{x} - \left(1 + \frac{k_{pe}}{k_{se}}\right) \cdot T + A\right)$$

where Δx is the muscle length minus the resting length (if negative, $\Delta x = 0$), $\dot{x}$ is the muscle contraction velocity, k_{se} is the series elastic stiffness and k_{pe} is the parallel elastic stiffness, b is the linear muscle damping, and A represents the activation level of the muscle described by:

$$A = A_m * A_l$$

where A_m is the stimulus-tension factor:

$$A_m = \frac{F_{max}}{1 + e^{C(V_0-V)} + B}$$

where F_{max} is the maximum muscle force, C describes the slope of the sigmoid, V is the membrane voltage of the motor neuron, and V_0 and B describe the V and F offsets of the sigmoid. A_l is the length-tension factor described as:

$$A_l = 1 - \frac{(l - l_{rest})^2}{l_{width}^2}$$

where l_{rest} describes the length at which the muscle can provide the most force and l_{width} describes the length from l_{rest} at which the muscle can provide no force. Details of the muscle parameter design can be found in Deng et al. [28].

The afferent feedback used in this paper are simplified representations of types Ia, Ib, and II (shown in Fig. 1) in mammalian systems modeled by Animatlab. Ia feedback is sensitive to muscle velocity $\dot{x}$ and total muscle length x, Ib feedback is dependent on the muscle tension T, and II feedback is dependent on length of parallel elastic element x_1. Ia and Ib feedback are synapsed onto correspondent motoneuron pools as shown in Fig. 1F. Type II feedback from the hip monoarticular muscles (namely BFA and IP) were applied directly to the rhythm generator (Fig. 1C) and the pattern formation networks (Fig. 1D) to coordinate the extensor-flexor timing.

2.2 Neural Modeling

The precise mechanisms underlying control of biarticular muscles are not yet fully understood. In light of this incomplete understanding, we have developed a hypothesis for the neural architecture involved in biarticular muscle control, which is depicted in Fig. 1B. The proposed SNS shares similarities with our previously developed two-layer CPG network, but features an additional intermediate layer between the CPG network and the sensory-motor network. This layer processes pattern signals from related joints and integrates them to produce more precise and accurate patterns for biarticular muscle control.

In Fig. 1, panels B through F, we employed a color scheme to differentiate between neurons and connections. Specifically, the extensor oscillators are denoted by the color blue, while flexor oscillators are represented by the color red. In addition, motoneurons are depicted in brown, interneurons in yellow, and the intermediate pattern formation interneurons for biarticular muscles in pink. To further differentiate between flexor and extensor signals, arrows with a solid fill and white outline are used to indicate flexor signals, while arrows with a white fill and solid outline depict extensor signals. Arrows that feature both solid fill and outline indicate that all signals are transmitted to the following region.

In this study, each neuron node depicted in Fig. 1 represents the average activity of a population of spiking neurons, and functions as a leaky integrator [34]. All neurons are modeled as conductance-based, non-spiking compartments; action potentials were neglected in the model to increase computational efficiency and reduce runtime [35]. This simplification allows us to focus on how signals are transmitted through synapses and how groups of neurons contribute to network behaviors.

The membrane voltage of a neuron node, V, may be seen as a proxy for the spiking frequency of a spiking neuron. V varies according to the differential equation:

$$C_m \frac{dV}{dt} = G_m(E_{rest} - V) + \sum_{i=1}^{n} G_{s,i} \cdot (E_{s,i} - V)$$
$$+ I_{app} + G_{NaP}(E_{NaP} - V) \cdot m_\infty \cdot h$$

where I_{app} is external stimulus, E_{rest} is the resting potential of the neuron, t is the time variable and E stands for a constant reference voltage (i.e. reversal potential). C_m and G_m are the capacitance and conductance of the cell membrane, respectively. The conductance, $G_{s,i}$ is a threshold linear function of the ith incoming (i.e. presynaptic) neuron's voltage. Synapses communicate via piecewise-linear functions described as:

$$G_{s,i} = g_{s,i} \cdot min\left(max\left(\frac{V_{pre} - E_{lo}}{E_{hi} - E_{lo}}, 0 \right), 1 \right)$$

where $g_{s,i}$, E_{lo}, and E_{hi} are constants representing the ith synapse's maximum conductance, its lower threshold, and its upper threshold, respectively. $G_{NaP}(E_{NaP} - V)$ is a persistent sodium current present in the oscillator neurons with voltage-dependent channel activation and deactivation described by m and h:

$$\frac{dh}{dt} = \frac{h_\infty(V) - h}{\tau_h(V)}, \quad \tau_h(V) = \tau_h \cdot h_\infty(V) \cdot \sqrt{A_h \cdot \exp(-S_h(V - E_h))}$$

For each instance of ion use, m_∞ and h_∞ values were adjusted to match with other CPG models developed in the field [36, 37]. Both m_∞ and h_∞ are sigmoidal function described below:

$$z_\infty = \frac{1}{1 + A_z \cdot \exp(-S_z(V - E_z))}$$

where z represents either m or h, „ and A (factor), S (slope) and E (reversal potential) are constant parameters, specific to m or h.

The oscillators in the PF incorporate the same persistent sodium current as the RG ones, which means that they can produce the same rhythm as RG neurons. In our prior analysis of the two-layer CPG, we primarily investigated the perturbation response of a single joint (the hip joint) [30]. In this paper, we will investigate how the two-layer CPG performs in controlling multiple joints while responding to different disturbances. Our previous investigations [30] showed how different parameters affect coordination between the RG and PF layers and provides the basis for the parameters chosen in this work and reported in the Appendix (Tables 1 and 2). The maximum conductance value (g_c) between the RG and PF, are as follows: 0.1 μS for the hip joint, 0.05 μS for the knee joint, and 0.02 μS for the ankle joint. This allocation of maximum conductance followed the report from our previous investigations of the two-layer CPG, which suggested that more distal segments require greater flexibility in responding to perturbations.

Figure 3 provides a graphical representation of the activation of neurons in a two-layer CPG that controls multiple joints in the hindlimb under unperturbed conditions. The rhythm generator sets the oscillatory frequency of the joint movements, whereas the pattern formation network modulates the amplitude of the oscillations and the phase relationship between the joints.

In particular, each joint's CPG oscillates at a consistent frequency (time for one step cycle is around 0.59 s), which is regulated by the rhythm generator. However, the pattern formation network of each joint exhibits a distinct phase timing (i.e. when compared to RG) that is unique to that joint. The hip joint exhibits a 5.74% phase delay, while the knee advances 6.35% and ankle advances 8.32% in phase. This is consistent with our previous report on g_c: The connection strength results in a trade-off between phase-locking potentials and the amount of phase difference that can exist between the two layers.

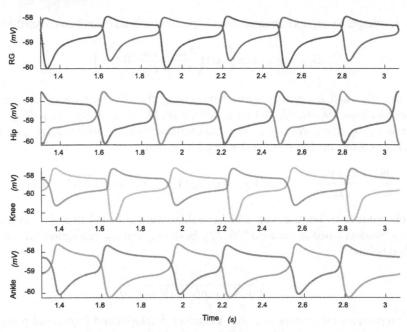

Fig. 3. Neuron activity for the two-layer CPG controlling multiple joints. The rhythm generator controls the overall timing of the network. Each joint pattern formation network exhibit different phase timings, all while maintaining the same oscillation frequency. The hip joint exhibits a 5.74% phase delay, while the knee joint advances 6.35% and the ankle joint advances 8.32% in phase. However, the period for one step for all these joints persists at 0.59 s per cycle. The blue lines represent the membrane voltage for extensor neurons, and the red lines stand for flexor neuron voltages.

3   Results

We started by manually adjusting the connection strengths and feedback weights of the hindlimb model, fine-tuning it until it was capable of sustaining its own weight while achieving repetitive forward walking with biarticular muscles. To further evaluate the performance of the model, we then suspended the pelvis of the model in the air to allow the model to perform repetitive movements without ground contact. We did this because in later experiments, we disabled the biarticular femoral muscles (BFP and RF) which are important for supporting the body's weight during movement.

We first perturbed the simulation model by introducing external currents to different layers of the two-layer CPG and analyzed the model's response. Subsequently, we applied torque to the hindlimb model's right femur under three different circumstances: with the BFP and RF muscles active and functioning normally, with only passive tension in the BFP and RF (by disabling the motoneuron projection), and with the BFP and RF muscles fully disabled, rendering the model monoarticular at the hip joint.

3.1 CPG Perturbation Test

Applying an external stimulus current with a magnitude of 2 nA to the flexor neuron of the rhythm generator from 2 s to 2.1 s (orange area in Fig. 4) resulted in a rapid short step, followed by a 15.44% phase–delayed step cycle after the perturbation, and subsequent step cycles exhibited a 15% phase delay.

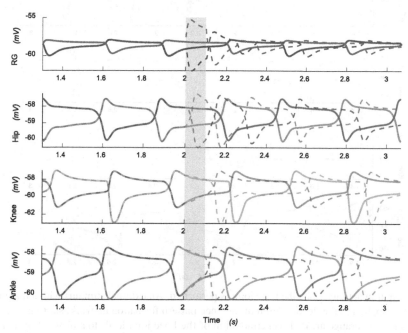

Fig. 4. Neuron activity when the RG layer is perturbed. An external stimulus with a magnitude of 2 nA is applied to the flexor neuron of the rhythm generator, starting at 2 s and ending at 2.1 s (orange area). The external stimulus causes a rapid short step with phase delay of 15.44% for the next step cycle after injection, followed by 15% phase delays for the subsequent step cycles. Strong connections ($g_c = 0.1uS$) ensure that the hip strictly follows the signal patterns from the rhythm generator, while weak connections ($g_c = 0.05uS$ for the knee and $g_c = 0.02uS$ for the ankle) result in a less perturbed phase (with a skipped step) of the knee and ankle joints. However, the knee and ankle still follow the phase timing from the rhythm generator after the perturbation. Blue lines represent the membrane voltage for extensor neurons, and the red lines stand for flexor neuron voltages. The solid lines represent the nominal activation of neurons in the two-layer CPG, while the dashed lines indicate the neuron activations during perturbed motion.

And the resulting patterns depicted in Fig. 4 demonstrate that a strong connection enables the hip joint to closely adhere to the signal patterns from the rhythm generator (5.74% phase delays). In contrast, weak connections result in a less disturbed phase (with a skipped step) of the knee and ankle joints during the disturbance. In either case, after injection, the neuron activity from the knee and ankle remains synchronized with the phase timing from the rhythm generator (i.e. the knee advances 6.35% and ankle advances 8.32% in phase).

Applying a 2 nA external current to the flexor neuron of the knee pattern formation network from 2 s to 2.1 s (orange area in Fig. 5) produces results that contradict previous experiments involving only antagonistic muscle pairs.

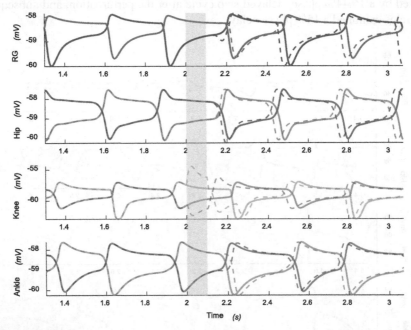

Fig. 5. Neuron activity when the knee joint is perturbed. An external stimulus with a magnitude of 2 nA is applied to the flexor neuron of the knee pattern formation network, starting at 2 s and ending at 2.1 s (orange area). This perturbation of the knee joint leads to a phase shift in all the joints. To clarify, the initial step after injection involves advancing the rhythm generator by 5%, the hip joint by 5.3%, the knee joint by 6.7%, and the ankle joint by 3%. Then, in the subsequent steps, all joints are advanced by 5.2% in response to the phase-advanced rhythm generator signal. The membrane voltage of extensor neurons is indicated by blue lines, while that of flexor neurons is represented by red lines. The solid lines represent the nominal activation of neurons in the two-layer CPG, while the dashed lines indicate the neuron activations during perturbed motion.

In our prior research on the rat hindlimb simulation model with antagonist muscles, we found that perturbing the pattern formation network of a single joint did not affect the neuron activations of the rhythm generator or the motion of other joints. However, in this current study, we observed a phase shift in other joints when an excitatory stimulus is applied to the knee flexor neuron of the pattern formation network. Specifically, after injection, the first step cycle is advanced by 5% for the rhythm generator, 5.3% for the hip joint, 6.7% for the knee joint and 3% for the ankle joint. Subsequently, following the signal from the phase-advanced rhythm generator, all the joints are advanced by 5.2% in the following steps.

3.2 Joint Torque Perturbation Test

Figure 6 presents neural activity in the pattern formation network for all muscles during air-walking. The activation pattern for the monoarticular pairs in the hip joint (BFA and IP, color-coded as blue and red which stand for extension and flexion neuron voltage), respectively, generally follows the signal pattern depicted in Fig. 3. The same applies to the monoarticular pairs in the ankle joint (TA and SO). The same applies to the monoarticular muscles pairs (TA and SO) in the ankle joint. Since these muscles actuate only a single joint, they require a more straightforward signal pattern to execute their respective movements. In contrast, the biarticular muscles BFP (present in cyan line), RF (present in magenta line), and GA (present in pink line) integrate patterned signals from multiple joint networks, necessitating more complex signaling. As a result, these muscles exhibit a more intricate activation pattern than monoarticular muscles, which, in turn, generates a complex motion to control movement across multiple joints.

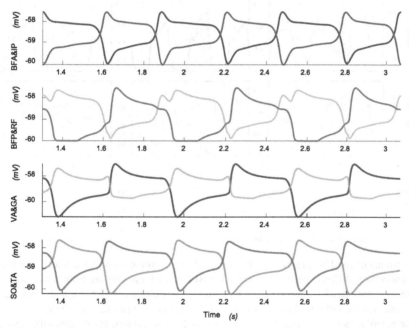

Fig. 6. Neural activity in the pattern formation network for all the muscles during air-walking. The monoarticular hip muscles BFA and IP, ankle muscles TA and SO generally follow the signal activation pattern presented in the Fig. 3, whereas the biarticular muscles BFP, RF, and GA integrate signal patterns from the actuated joints. Blue lines represent the membrane voltage for extensor neurons, and the red lines represent the flexor neuron voltages. The cyan line shows the activation for BFP, magenta presents the membrane voltage for RF, and the pink line depicts the GA.

When an external torque of 0.1 Nm is applied to the right femur in the simulation, the response of the biarticular muscles model under three different conditions during air-walking can be distinguished. As can be seen in Fig. 7, the magnitude of the phase changes due to the external torque is significantly less in the biarticular muscle models, regardless of whether there is active tension on the muscle or not. Thus, we conclude that biarticular muscles can reduce the impact of external perturbations. However, this reduction in perturbation also influences the motion of other joints, such as the knee and ankle.

Comparison of nominal and perturbed motions of the leg reveals that active BFA and RF muscles result in faster restoration when compared to model in which they are disabled. Interestingly, it was found that the biarticular muscle model with only passive tension was unable to return to its original step timing after the perturbation ended.

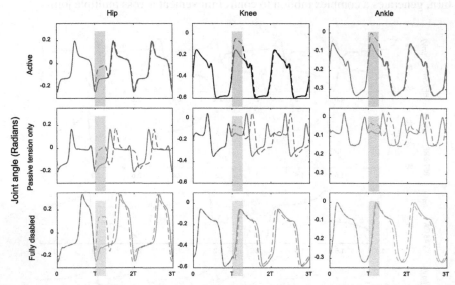

Fig. 7. Nominal (solid lines) and perturbed (dashed lines) joint motion for the biarticular muscles model under three different conditions: when the BFP and RF muscles are fully active (first row); when there is only passive tension on the BFP and RF muscles (second row); and when the BFP and RF muscles are fully disabled (third row). The joint motion profiles are depicted using blue lines for hip joint motion (orange areas shows when the external torques are applied), black lines represent knee motion, and red lines stand for ankle motion. The perturbation is an external torque with magnitude − 0.1 Nm applied to the right femur, starting at the beginning of the second stride and lasting for 30 percent of the stride period. During the perturbed motion, the full activation of the BFA and RF muscles results in better stability when compared to the monoarticular hip joint condition, as it enables faster and better recovery to the original step timing.

4   Discussion

In this work, we present a neuromechanical model of a rat hindlimb with biarticular muscles. We expanded on our previous study of biarticular muscle models [28] by examining the neural control of this model. In other previous work, we conducted an in-depth investigation of the two-layer CPG [30] and gained a better understanding of the design of these neural controllers. In this work, we integrated our prior findings to design a hypothesized SNS that actuates the biarticular muscles BFP and RF muscles connecting the hip and knee joints, and the GA muscle spanning the knee and ankle joint.

Biarticular muscles play an important role in locomotion. Previous research by Markin's group [38] and Shevtsova et al. [39] has proposed how biarticular muscles are controlled. Specifically, they suggest that the BFP and RF muscles have their own individual pattern formation networks. This enables more precise control of these muscles, but complicates the design of the SNS, and may require additional animal data to help tune the parameters in these individual pattern formation networks. Similarly, our hypothesized neural architecture comprises multiple components that collectively govern the timing and coordination of movement between the joints. Specifically, the rhythm generator plays a critical role in regulating the overall timing of steps, adjusting the timing of movement phases in each individual joint. The pattern formation networks for hindlimb joints receive input from the rhythm generator and distribute signals to the corresponding muscles and intermediate layers, which is necessary for coordinating the movements of the biarticular muscles. Notably, a difference in our network is that the muscles are organized into reciprocal synergist pairs and receive signal projections from joint level pattern formation networks.

In the CPG perturbation test, we found that the rhythm generator plays a crucial role in controlling the overall timing of the hindlimbs. Specifically, each pattern formation network of the joints displays distinct phase timings that are sensitive to perturbations applied at the rhythm generator layer. Strong connections between the rhythm generator and the hip joint enable the hip joint to closely adhere to the RG step timing during perturbations, while weaker connections lead to less disturbed phase timings in the knee and ankle joint. Importantly, the results observed in this study differ from those reported in previous works for monoarticular actuation. Specifically, we found that disrupting the knee's pattern formation network resulted in changes in motion at all the joints. Specifically, changes in knee kinematics affected the intermuscular coordination between the hip and knee joint, resulting in a cascade of effects. Changes in knee joint motion affected both the hip joint's motion and the phase of the rhythm generator. As the rhythm generator's phase shifts, the direct connection between the ankle and the rhythm generator causes the ankle phase to become correlated with the RG timing. These findings support our previous analysis of the two-layer CPG and confirm our expectations regarding the perturbation response of the system.

Based on the air-walking perturbation test simulation results, we discovered that biarticular muscles can significantly reduce the impact of external torque. This is evidenced by the smaller phase changes observed in the fully active biarticular muscle models compared to the monoarticular muscle models. However, this reduction in perturbation also influences the motion of other joints due to the multi-joint linkage through biarticular muscles. Additionally, our analysis revealed that activating the BFA and RF muscles resulted in faster restoration after the perturbation compared to the model with the biarticular muscles disabled. Interestingly, the biarticular muscle model with only passive tension on the muscle was unable to revert back to its original step timing after the perturbation ended, likely due to the considerable magnitude of passive tension as reported in our previous work [28]. A possible explanation for this is that the passive tension in the biarticular muscles acts as a large damper in the absence of active tension. This dampening effect reduces the impact of external torques and minimizes internal adjustments.

There are some limitations in our work that must be carefully considered. For instance, the muscle model utilized in AnimatLab does not employ a hyperbolic force-velocity relationship for the contractile element. It is possible that different muscle models may have an effect on the quantitative results, though we anticipate the qualitative results will remain the same. Furthermore, the joint angle ranges differ significantly between the three different situations in the air-walking perturbation test. As the models being compared are not optimally tuned, we can only conclude that the normal active biarticular muscle is less affected by external torque and exhibits faster restoration after perturbation, which provides more stability compared to the fully disabled model. It is still unclear if all these results will remain the same when each model is tuned for ground walking and the perturbations are applied in a more realistic environment. Indeed, previous results from our work indicate that all differences seen in neural perturbation and air-walking tests may functionally result in little to no difference when applied to ground walking [30].

While this work has shed light on the functional role of biarticular muscles in stabilizing perturbed locomotion, there are several limitations stemming from the lack of detailed rat locomotion and EMG data. However, these limitations do not diminish the value of our findings, which offer important insights into this complex phenomenon and provide guidelines for designing a neural controller for a biomechanical model with biarticular muscles. Moving forward, future research should investigate the impact of different SNS designs and noise on the stability of the model, and should also compare the results with neural controllers hypothesized by researchers in parallel studies. Also, a more in-depth analysis investigating perturbations with different amplitude, timing and directions is necessary to support our conclusion on a more general basis. Overall, this work highlights the significance of biarticular muscles in stabilizing the rat hindlimbs during perturbed locomotion, and the broader implications of our findings for understanding animal locomotion.

Acknowledgements. This work was supported by grants from the NSF DBI 2015317 as part of the NSF/CIHR/DFG/FRQ/UKRIMRC Next Generation Networks for the Neuroscience Program.

Appendix

List of Acronyms

CPG Central pattern generator
SNS Synthetic nervous system
BFP Biceps femoris posterior
RF   Rectus femoris
GA   Gastrocnemii
IP   Iliopsoas
BPF Biceps femoris anterior
VA   Vastii
SO   Soleus
TA   Tibialis anterior
RG   Rhythm generator
PF   Pattern formation
MN Motoneuron
IN   Interneuron
RE   Renshaw cell
EXT Extensor
FLX Flexor
AD   Adaptor

Table 1. Neural parameters

Neuron	$C_m(nF)$	$G_m(\mu S)$	E_r (mV)	$G_{Na}(\mu S)$	A_h	S_h	E_h (mV)	τ_h (ms)	A_m	S_m	E_m (mV)	τ_m (ms)
RG	5	1	−60	1.5	0.5	−0.6	−60	350	1	0.2	−40	2
PF	5	1	−60	1.5	0.5	−0.6	−60	350	1	0.2	−40	2
MN	5	1	−100	0	–	–	–	–	–	–	–	–
IN	5	1	−60	0	–	–	–	–	–	–	–	–

Table 2. Synapse parameters.

Synapse	g (μS)	E_s (mV)	E_{lo} (mV)	E_{hi} (mV)
RG to IN	2	−40	−60	−40
IN to RG	2	−70	−60	−40
Between RG	0.01	−40	−60	−40
PF to IN	2	−40	−60	−40
IN to PF	1.61	−70	−60	−40
PF to MN	/→/	−10	−60	−50
RG to Hip	0.1	−40	−60	−40
RG to Knee	0.05	−40	−60	−40
RG to Ankle	0.02	−40	−60	−40
Hip to BFP	0.967	−40	−60	−40
Hip to RF	0.236	−40	−59	−40
Knee to BFP	0.365	−40	−59	−40
Knee to RF	0.872	−40	−60	−40
Knee to GA	1	−40	−60	−40
Ankle to GA	0.3	−40	−59	−40
PF to Ia	0.5	−40	−60	−55
Between Ia	0.5	−70	−60	−40
Ia to MN	2	−100	−60	−40
MN to RE	0.5	−40	−100	−10
Between R	0.5	−70	−60	−40
R to MN	0.5	−100	−60	−40
R to Ia	0.5	−70	−60	−40

PFs to MNs	g (μS)
BFA	2
IP	3
BFP	6.4
RF	5.8
VA	5
GA	4
SO	8
TA	2

References

1. Bouman, A., et al.: Autonomous Spot: Long-Range Autonomous Exploration of Extreme Environments with Legged Locomotion (2020)
2. Feng, S., Whitman, E., Xinjilefu, X., Atkeson, C.G.: Optimization based full body control for the atlas robot. In: Proceedings of the 2014 IEEE-RAS International Conference on Humanoid Robots, pp. 120–127. IEEE, Madrid, Spain, November 2014
3. Hubicki, C., et al.: ATRIAS: design and validation of a tether-free 3D-capable spring-mass bipedal robot. Int. J. Robot. Res. **35**, 1497–1521 (2016). https://doi.org/10.1177/027836491 6648388
4. Hutter, M., et al.: ANYmal - a highly mobile and dynamic quadrupedal robot. In: Proceedings of the 2016 IEEE/RSJ International Conference on Intelligent Robots and Systems (IROS), pp. 38–44, October 2016
5. Geng, T., Porr, B., Worgotter, F.: Self-stabilized biped walking under control of a novel reflexive network. In: Proceedings of the 2005 IEEE/RSJ International Conference on Intelligent Robots and Systems, pp. 3269–3274, August 2005

6. Ijspeert, A.J., Crespi, A., Ryczko, D., Cabelguen, J.-M.: From swimming to walking with a salamander robot driven by a spinal cord model. Science **315**, 1416–1420 (2007). https://doi.org/10.1126/science.1138353

7. Yang, W., Kim, H., You, B.J.: Biologically inspired self-stabilizing control for bipedal robots. Int. J. Adv. Rob. Syst. **10**, 144 (2013). https://doi.org/10.5772/55463

8. Szczecinski, N.S., et al.: Introducing MantisBot: hexapod robot controlled by a high-fidelity, real-time neural simulation. In: Proceedings of the 2015 IEEE/RSJ International Conference on Intelligent Robots and Systems (IROS), pp. 3875–3881. IEEE, Hamburg, Germany, September 2015

9. Kimura, H., Fukuoka, Y., Cohen, A.H.: Adaptive dynamic walking of a quadruped robot on natural ground based on biological concepts. Int. J. Robot. Res. (2016).https://doi.org/10.1177/0278364907078089

10. Hunt, A., Szczecinski, N., Quinn, R.: Development and training of a neural controller for hind leg walking in a dog robot. Front. Neurorobot. **11** (2017). https://doi.org/10.3389/fnbot.2017.00018

11. Kim, J.-Y., Park, I.-W., Oh, J.-H.: Walking control algorithm of biped humanoid robot on uneven and inclined floor. J. Intell. Robot. Syst. **48**, 457–484 (2007). https://doi.org/10.1007/s10846-006-9107-8

12. Schilling, M., et al.: A hexapod walker using a heterarchical architecture for action selection. Front. Comput. Neurosci. **7**, 126 (2013). https://doi.org/10.3389/fncom.2013.00126

13. Szczecinski, N.S., Brown, A.E., Bender, J.A., Quinn, R.D., Ritzmann, R.E.: A neuromechanical simulation of insect walking and transition to turning of the cockroach Blaberus discoidalis. Biol. Cybern. **108**(1), 1–21 (2013). https://doi.org/10.1007/s00422-013-0573-3

14. Hunt, A., Schmidt, M., Fischer, M., Quinn, R.: A biologically based neural system coordinates the joints and legs of a tetrapod. Bioinspiration Biomim. **10**, 055004 (2015). https://doi.org/10.1088/1748-3190/10/5/055004

15. Deng, K., et al.: Neuromechanical model of rat hindlimb walking with two-layer CPGs. Biomimetics **4**, 21 (2019)

16. Forssberg, H., Grillner, S., Halbertsma, J., Rossignol, S.: The locomotion of the low spinal cat II. Interlimb coordination. . Acta Physiol. Scand. **108**, 283–295 (1980). https://doi.org/10.1111/j.1748-1716.1980.tb06534.x

17. Frigon, A., Hurteau, M.-F., Thibaudier, Y., Leblond, H., Telonio, A., D'Angelo, G.: Split-belt walking alters the relationship between locomotor phases and cycle duration across speeds in intact and chronic spinalized adult cats. J. Neurosci. **33**, 8559–8566 (2013). https://doi.org/10.1523/JNEUROSCI.3931-12.2013

18. Frigon, A., Thibaudier, Y., Hurteau, M.-F.: Modulation of forelimb and hindlimb muscle activity during quadrupedal tied-belt and split-belt locomotion in intact cats. Neuroscience **290**, 266–278 (2015). https://doi.org/10.1016/j.neuroscience.2014.12.084

19. Brown, T.: The Intrinsic Factors in the Act of Progression in the Mammal, Royal Society of London (1911)

20. Grillner, S., McCLELLAN, A., Sigvardt, K., Wallén, P., Wilén, M.: Activation of NMDA-receptors elicits fictive locomotion in lamprey spinal cord in vitro. Acta Physiol. Scand. **113**, 549–551 (1981). https://doi.org/10.1111/j.1748-1716.1981.tb06937.x

21. Brown, T.G.: On the nature of the fundamental activity of the nervous centres; together with an analysis of the conditioning of rhythmic activity in progression, and a theory of the evolution of function in the nervous system. J. Physiol. **48**, 18–46 (1914). https://doi.org/10.1113/jphysiol.1914.sp001646

22. Hägglund, M., Dougherty, K.J., Borgius, L., Itohara, S., Iwasato, T., Kiehn, O.: Optogenetic dissection reveals multiple rhythmogenic modules underlying locomotion. PNAS **110**, 11589–11594 (2013). https://doi.org/10.1073/pnas.1304365110

23. Bässler, U., Büschges, A.: Pattern generation for stick insect walking movements—multisensory control of a locomotor program. Brain Res. Rev. **27**, 65–88 (1998). https://doi.org/10.1016/S0165-0173(98)00006-X
24. Arbas, E.A., Calabrese, R.L.: Ionic conductances underlying the activity of interneurons that control heartbeat in the medicinal leech. J. Neurosci. **7**, 3945–3952 (1987). https://doi.org/10.1523/JNEUROSCI.07-12-03945.1987
25. Tryba, A.K., Peña, F., Ramirez, J.-M.: Gasping activity in vitro: a rhythm dependent on 5-HT2A receptors. J. Neurosci. **26**, 2623–2634 (2006). https://doi.org/10.1523/JNEUROSCI.4186-05.2006
26. Grillner, S., Zangger, P.: On the central generation of locomotion in the low spinal cat. Exp. Brain Res. **34**, 241–261 (1979)
27. Rybak, I.A., Shevtsova, N.A., Lafreniere-Roula, M., McCrea, D.A.: Modelling spinal circuitry involved in locomotor pattern generation: insights from deletions during fictive locomotion. J. Physiol. **577**, 617–639 (2006). https://doi.org/10.1113/jphysiol.2006.118703
28. Deng, K., Szczecinski, N.S., Hunt, A.J., Chiel, H.J., Quinn, R.D.: Kinematic and kinetic analysis of a biomechanical model of rat hind limb with biarticular muscles. In: Vouloutsi, V., Mura, A., Tauber, F., Speck, T., Prescott, T.J., Verschure, P.F.M.J. (eds.) Biomimetic and Biohybrid Systems. Living Machines 2020. LNCS, vol. 12413, pp. 55–67. Springer, Cham (2020). https://doi.org/10.1007/978-3-030-64313-3_7
29. Young, F., Rode, C., Hunt, A., Quinn, R.: Analyzing moment arm profiles in a full-muscle rat hindlimb model. Biomimetics **4**, 10 (2019). https://doi.org/10.3390/biomimetics4010010
30. Deng, K., et al.: Biomechanical and sensory feedback regularize the behavior of different locomotor central pattern generators. Biomimetics **7**, 226 (2022). https://doi.org/10.3390/biomimetics7040226
31. Cofer, D., Cymbalyuk, G., Reid, J., Zhu, Y., Heitler, W.J., Edwards, D.H.: AnimatLab: a 3D graphics environment for neuromechanical simulations. J. Neurosci. Methods **187**, 280–288 (2010). https://doi.org/10.1016/j.jneumeth.2010.01.005
32. Shadmehr, R., Arbib, M.A.: A mathematical analysis of the force-stiffness characteristics of muscles in control of a single joint system. Biol. Cybern. **66**, 463–477 (1992). https://doi.org/10.1007/BF00204111
33. Shadmehr, R., Wise, S.: A Mathematical Muscle Model
34. Szczecinski, N.S., Hunt, A.J., Quinn, R.D.: Design process and tools for dynamic neuromechanical models and robot controllers. Biol. Cybern. **111**(1), 105–127 (2017). https://doi.org/10.1007/s00422-017-0711-4
35. Szczecinski, N.S., Quinn, R.D., Hunt, A.J.: Extending the functional subnetwork approach to a generalized linear integrate-and-fire neuron model. Front. Neurorobot. **14** (2020). https://doi.org/10.3389/fnbot.2020.577804
36. Markin, S.N., Klishko, A.N., Shevtsova, N.A., Lemay, M.A., Prilutsky, B.I., Rybak, I.A.: Afferent control of locomotor CPG: insights from a simple neuromechanical model. Ann. N. Y. Acad. Sci. **1198**, 21–34 (2010). https://doi.org/10.1111/j.1749-6632.2010.05435.x
37. Daun-Gruhn, S., Büschges, A.: From neuron to behavior: dynamic equation-based prediction of biological processes in motor control. Biol. Cybern. **105**, 71–88 (2011). https://doi.org/10.1007/s00422-011-0446-6

38. Markin, S., Klishko, A., Shevtsova, N., Lemay, M., Prilutsky, B., Rybak, I.: A neuromechanical model of spinal control of locomotion. In: Prilutsky, B., Edwards, D. (eds.) Neuromechanical Modeling of Posture and Locomotion, pp. 21–65. SSCN. Springer, New York, NY (2016). ISBN 978-1-4939-3267-2. https://doi.org/10.1007/978-1-4939-3267-2_2

39. Shevtsova, N., Hamade, K., Chakrabarty, S., Markin, S., Prilutsky, B., Rybak, I.: Modeling the organization of spinal cord neural circuits controlling two-joint muscles. In: Prilutsky, B., Edwards, D. (eds.) Neuromechanical Modeling of Posture and Locomotion, pp. 121–162. SSCN. Springer, New York, NY (2016). ISBN 978-1-4939-3267-2. https://doi.org/10.1007/978-1-4939-3267-2_5

Multimodal Parameter Inference for a Canonical Motor Microcircuit Controlling Rat Hindlimb Motion

Clayton Jackson[1](✉) , Matthieu Chardon[2] , Y. Curtis Wang[3] ,
Johann Rudi[4] , Matthew Tresch[5] , Charles J. Heckman[6] ,
and Roger D. Quinn[1]

[1] Department of Mechanical and Aerospace Engineering,
Case Western Reserve University, Cleveland, OH 44106-7222, USA
clayton.jackson@case.edu
[2] Interdepartmental Neuroscience, Northwestern University, Chicago, IL, USA
[3] Department of Electrical and Computer Engineering, California State University,
Los Angeles, CA 90032, USA
[4] Department of Mathematics, Virginia Tech, Blacksburg, VA 24060, USA
[5] Department of Biomedical Engineering Northwestern University,
Evanston, IL 60208, USA
[6] Department of Physical Therapy and Human Movement Sciences,
Northwestern University, Evanston, IL 60208, USA

Abstract. This work explored synaptic strengths in a computational neuroscience model of a controller for the hip joint of a rat which consists of Ia interneurons, Renshaw cells, and the associated motor neurons. This circuit has been referred to as the Canonical Motor Microcircuit (CMM). It is thought that the CMM acts to modulate motor neuron activity at the output stage. We first created a biomechanical model of a rat hindlimb consisting of a pelvis, femur, shin, foot, and flexor-extensor muscle pairs modeled with a Hill muscle model. We then modeled the CMM using non-spiking leaky-integrator neural models connected with conductance-based synapses. To tune the parameters in the network, we implemented an automated approach for parameter search using the Markov chain Monte Carlo (MCMC) method to solve a parameter estimation problem in a Bayesian inference framework. As opposed to traditional optimization techniques, the MCMC method identifies probability densities over the multidimensional space of parameters. This allows us to see a range of likely parameters that produce model outcomes consistent with animal data, determine if the distribution of likely parameters is uni- or multi-modal, as well as evaluate the significance and sensitivity of each parameter. This approach will allow for further analysis of the circuit, specifically, the function and significance of Ia feedback and Renshaw cells.

This work was supported by NSF DBI 2015317 as part of the NSF/CIHR/DFG/FRQ/ UKRI-MRC Next Generation Networks for Neuroscience Program.

Keywords: Sensori-motor Control · Markov chain Monte Carlo ·
Neuromechanical Simulation

1 Introduction

Mammilian locomotion continues to be a much researched topic in the world of neuroscience. It is commonly accepted that the rhythmic activity during locomotion arises from descending commands from pattern generator networks in the spinal cord [16,17]. The activity from pattern generators is then modulated by neural circuits and sensory feedback at the output stage before controlling muscle activity. We have designed one of these output stage neural circuits after the works of Hultborn et al. [10] which we refer to as the Canonical Motor Microcircuit (CMM). The CMM modeled in this work does not include gamma motoneurons as in the Hultborn model for simplicity [10]. This network, consisting of Ia interneurons, Renshaw cells, and motor neurons, is included in numerous other neural models of locomotor circuitry. [8,9,12,18,23]. However, these works primarily focus on the pattern generator networks and largely ignore the role of the CMM in modulating these commands. Aside from studies showing that the neurons in this model are active in mammals during locomotion, the role of the CMM and of the specific neurons within the CMM remains unknown [21].

The aim of this work is to enhance our understanding of the CMM through the use of neural and biomechanical modeling. While the ideal approach would involve recording neural activity in the spinal cord *in vivo*, this method can be challenging and resource-intensive. Therefore, we aim to use modeling as a complementary tool to aid in these experiments. By working with neuroscientists, we can use these models to test theories, design future experiments, and provide insights into experimental results.

Modeling neural and biomechanical systems is challenging, tuning these models is often nontrivial. Hand-tuning the networks is one possible method, but is often time consuming and impractical. Another possible method is the Functional Subnetwork Approach (FSA) [28]. This method describes the tuning of small networks to perform addition, subtraction, multiplication, division, integration, and differentiation. These smaller networks can then be joined to create large networks without the need for global optimization [28]. The FSA can be useful in designing neural circuits, though when modeling existing circuits, it may not be clear how to divide the network into subnetworks. In these cases, we can turn to more traditional optimization techniques. Gradient-based optimization is likely not an option as these systems tend to be highly nonlinear. Other methods, such as particle swarm optimization, are reliant on initial values and like gradient-based optimization, are susceptible to getting stuck in local minima [14,15]. While genetic algorithms can use mutation to avoid local minima, they share one large downside with other methods in this application. These optimization methods produce one result and often tell little to nothing about the solution space. This paper examines a tuning method for the CMM using a Markov chain Monte Carlo (MCMC) approach to solve a parameter estimation problem in a Bayesian inference framework. This parameter inference method has been used to tune a single Hodgkin-Huxley style neuron, but has not yet been used to tune a network of neurons [31]. The MCMC method is advantageous for this application because it provides a view of the solution space as a whole, showing the significance and sensitivity of each parameter. In this way, we can use the results to analyze the components of the network.

2   Methods

2.1   Modeling

We first create a biomechanical model of a rat hindlimb to be controlled by the CMM. The physics engine and biomechanical modeling for this work were done in Mujoco [29]. An existing model of the hindlimb with muscles to control the hip, knee, and ankle in three dimensions, modeled in Opensim, was taken and converted to the format needed for Mujoco [7,11,24]. The model was then simplified to only two muscles, a flexor-extensor muscle pair controlling the hip joint in the sagittal plane. In this model, the pelvis is fixed and the leg air steps without ground contact. These simplifications to the model were chosen as a starting point; future models will expand to include the complete array of muscles and control of all joints. The simplified model in Mujoco can be seen in Fig. 1.

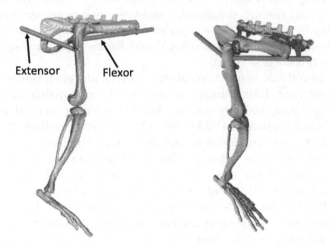

Fig. 1. Biomechanical model of a rat right hindlimb in Mujoco with a flexor/extensor muscle pair (red). (Color figure online)

Mujoco implements a Hill muscle model which is similar to that of Opensim. The key differences are that Mujoco assumes the tendons are inelastic and that the pennation angle is zero [7, 24, 29]. For this work, the default muscle parameters in Mujoco were used. The muscle force, F_M, can be found using the equation [29]:

$$F_M = (F_L(L) \cdot F_{Vel}(Vel) \cdot act(V_{MN}) + F_P(L)) \cdot F_0 \qquad (1)$$

where F_L is the active force as a function of length, L is the length of the muscle, F_{Vel} is the active force as a function of velocity, Vel is the velocity of the muscle, F_P is the passive force, F_0 is the peak active force at zero velocity and is computed in the model compiler, and act is the muscle activation as a function of the corresponding motor neuron potential, V_{MN}. In this model, we use a sigmoid muscle activation function. Examples of the F_L and F_{Vel} curves are shown in Fig. 2.

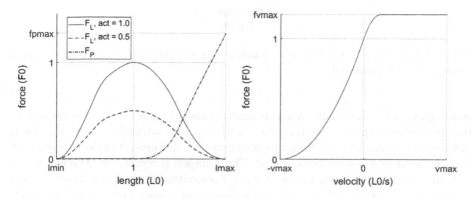

Fig. 2. Mujoco muscle modeling. Left: F_P curve and F_L curve with various activation. The activation function simply scales the F_L curve. The F_L curve is centered around L0, which is the resting length of the muscle as computed in the model compiler. Right: F_{Vel} curve. [29]

We then create the neural model of the CMM, shown in Fig. 3, to control muscle activation of the biomechanical model. The neural modeling and simulation in this work was done in Python using SNS-Toolbox [20]. The neurons were modeled using a non-spiking leaky-integrator model:

$$C\frac{dV}{dt} = I_{app} - I_{leak} + \sum_{i=1}^{n} I_{syn_i} \qquad (2)$$

where C is the membrane capacitance, V is the membrane voltage, I_{app} is an applied current, I_{leak} is the membrane leak current, and I_{syn_i} are the synaptic currents. The benefit of using this neural model is that it allows for a single non-spiking neuron to approximate the average activity of populations of spiking neurons [32]. The synaptic currents are modeled using conductance based synapses:

$$I_{syn_i} = g_{max_i} \cdot \min\left(\max\left(\frac{V_{pre} - E_{lo_i}}{E_{hi_i} - E_{lo_i}}, 0\right), 1\right) \cdot (E_{syn_i} - V(t)) \qquad (3)$$

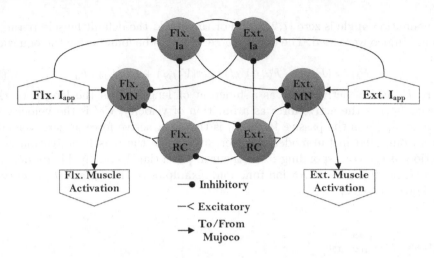

Fig. 3. CMM Neural Model in SNS-Toolbox. Ia: Ia inhibitory neuron. MN: Motor Neuron, RC: Renshaw cell.

where g_{max} is the maximum synaptic conductance, V_{pre} is the membrane potential of the pre-synaptic neuron, E_{hi_i} and E_{lo_i} are saturation and threshold parameters, respectively, which are properties of the pre-synaptic neuron, and E_{syn} is the synaptic reversal potential. The synaptic reversal potential was set to -100 mV for inhibitory synapses and 0 mV for excitatory synapses. The leak current in Eq. 2 estimates the net effect of sodium, potassium, and chloride channels with a net membrane conductance G, and a resting potential E_R:

$$I_{leak} = G \cdot (V(t) - E_R). \tag{4}$$

The neural model incorporates Ia afferent feedback from muscle spindles to the respective Ia inhibitory and motor neurons. We model this as a discharge rate from the muscle spindles. It was found that for the Hill muscle model, the discharge rate, is proportional to the tension of the muscle [25]. We can then model the afferent feedback as an applied current:

$$I_{app} = m \cdot T + b \tag{5}$$

where T is the muscle tension, m is a gain to convert from muscle tension to a current, and b is a y-offset.

Tables 3 and 2 show the parameter values used in this model for the parameters not explored in the MCMC search (Table 1).

In order to run the neural and biomechanical models together, we first initialize the neurons at their resting potentials. The biomechanical model is initialized with the hip in slight flexion. This causes the limb to fall due to gravity at the beginning of the simulation, initially exciting the neurons. Using the forward Euler method, we then repeat the following for a desired number of iterations:

Table 1. Neural Parameters. MN: Motor Neuron. Ia: Ia inhibitory Neuron. RC: Renshaw Cells

	E_R(MV)	E_{hi}(MV)	E_{lo}(MV)
MN	−62	−54.53	−78
Ia	−60	−40	−62
RC	−50.5	−40	−60

Table 2. Muscle Feedback Applied Current Parameters.

	m	b
I_{app} to Ext Ia	0.4565	−0.5617
I_{app} to Flx Ia	3.5385	−0.7185
I_{app} to Ext MN	0.0106	−0.9210
I_{app} to Flx MN	0.5036	0.0411

1. Run one timestep of the neural model in SNS-Toolbox using muscle feedback from Mujoco as inputs.
2. Feed the motor neuron potentials from the previous timestep into the sigmoidal muscle activation function.
3. Take one timestep in the biomechanical model in Mujoco using the calculated muscle activation.
4. Get the muscle tension from Mujoco to input to the next step of the neural model.

In earlier works, both the biomechanical and neural models were run in Animatlab2 [6]. While it was beneficial to have both models in the same software, the simulation time in Animatlab2 was slow, which greatly impacted the computation time for automating the parameter search. By utilizing newly available software tools, SNS-Toolbox and Mujoco, simulation time was decreased from 10.21 to 2.48 s on average when compared to Animatlab2.

2.2   Markov Chain Monte Carlo

Previous iterations of this work aimed to hand-tune similar models to produce oscillatory motion in the hip joint [13]. While this method proved to be successful, the results provided little information about the significance or sensitivity of parameters in the models. To address these shortcomings, we implement an automated parameter search for the maximum synaptic conductance, g_{max}, in the CMM shown in Fig. 3 using a Markov chain Monte Carlo (MCMC) method. This method is centered around Bayes theorem [5]:

$$P(g_{max}|y) = \frac{P(y|g_{max}) \cdot P(g_{max})}{P(y)} \tag{6}$$

where $P(g_{max}|y)$ is the posterior (conditional probability for parameters g_{max}, given the data y), $P(y|g_{max})$ is the likelihood (conditional probability of the data y given the parameters g_{max}), g_{max} is the prior (probability of the parameters), and $P(y)$ is called evidence (probability of the data y). The evidence term is a constant, therefore Bayes theorem is typically used in the form:

$$P(g_{max}|y) \propto P(y|g_{max}) \cdot P(g_{max}). \tag{7}$$

The prior term is designed to take into account known information about the parameters. As there is little known about the CMM, unbiased priors were used. These priors were uniform distributions with lower and upper bounds of 0 and 8 microSiemens, respectively. The likelihood term is based on a loss function which was designed to match the simulated data of the hip angle to data of the hip trajectory of a rat walking on a treadmill as collected by Alessandro et al. [2]. Rather than explicitly trying to match the simulated and animal data, the loss function aims to mimic certain aspects of the motion:

$$loss = l_{freq} + l_{sw/st} + l_{smooth} + l_{oscillate} \tag{8}$$

where l_{freq} is the percent error of the frequency of oscillations between the simulated and animal data, $l_{sw/st}$ is the percent error of the swing to stance ratio. The percent error is calculated as:

$$\%Error = \left| \frac{v_S - v_A}{v_A} \right| \tag{9}$$

where v_S is the simulated value and v_A is the value from the animal data. The smoothness term in the loss function, l_{smooth}, is the mean of the second derivative of the simulated hip angle squared.

$$l_{sw/st} = mean\left(\left(\frac{d^2\theta}{dt^2} \right)^2 \right) \tag{10}$$

The last term in the loss function is designed to promote solutions which oscillate, $l_{oscillate}$ is the inverse of the number of peaks in the simulated hip angle vs. time.

$$l_{oscillate} = \frac{1}{num\_peaks} \tag{11}$$

The likelihood probability density is then defined as:

$$P(y|g_{max}) = e^{-loss} \tag{12}$$

where the loss depends on the data, y, and parameters, g_{max}: $loss = loss(g_{max}, y)$.

To begin the MCMC, we first choose a sampling method. In this work, we have chosen an adaptive Metropolis-Hastings algorithm [26]. The Metropolis-Hastings algorithm is typically a good choice when the conditional probability

$P(y|g_{max})$ cannot be drawn from directly [4]. As previously stated, we aim to determine if the distribution of likely parameters is uni- or multi-modal. To do this we run an adaptive parallel tempering MCMC using the PyPESTO library in python [19,27]. Parallel tempering is a technique used in MCMC to help chains traverse high posterior density regions and overcome local optima. Multiple chains are run in parallel where each chain has a unique starting point and runs its own Metropolis-Hastings random walk. Similar to simulated annealing algorithms, a temperature is computed for each chain and varies according to Vousden et al. [30]. We then assign a term, β where $0 < \beta < 1$ and is inversely related to the temperature of the chain: $\beta = 1/T$. This β term is then applied as an exponent to the posteriors of the given chain, resulting in $P^{\beta}(g_{max}|y)$. This newly scaled posterior is then what is used to calculate the acceptance ratio in the Metropolis-Hastings algorithm. The impact of the β term is that chains at higher temperatures can more easily explore the entire prior distribution for parameters, while chains at lower temperatures can sample from regions of high probability more efficiently [30]. Additionally, chains may perform swaps at certain intervals, swapping their parameters while maintaining their temperature.

3   Results

The parallel tempering MCMC with an adaptive Metropolis-Hastings random walk algorithm was successful in its ability to explore the multidimensional parameter space, finding that the posterior is multi-modal with two distinct regions of parameters with acceptable loss values. We present marginals of the posterior showing the relationships between parameters. Figure 4 shows four of these marginalized densities.

Here, we observe two modes in the posteriors. One mode showing the Renshaw cells inhibits Ia interneurons more strongly than they do motor neurons, while the other indicates that the synapse from the extensor Renshaw cell to the extensor Ia inhibitory neuron has a maximum synaptic conductance close to zero (Fig. 4C). This would suggest that there are no synapses between these neurons. We are able to dismiss these results as it is known that Renshaw cells inhibit Ia inhibitory neurons [21]. The marginal densities in Fig. 4 also show that the two modes in the posterior densities may overlap for certain parameters (Fig. 4B).

To further examine the results, we look at the hip angle for the simulated data and animal data. Figure 5 shows a variety of joint trajectories and their associated cost. The parameter values used in these plots can be found in Table 3. Note that the loss function in Eq. 8 only aims to match certain properties of the trajectory, and therefore, the joint trajectories from the simulation may not match the animal data completely. The results in Fig. 5 show a variety of joint trajectories, all of which indicate that the CMM is capable of producing oscillatory behavior without the input of a pattern generator.

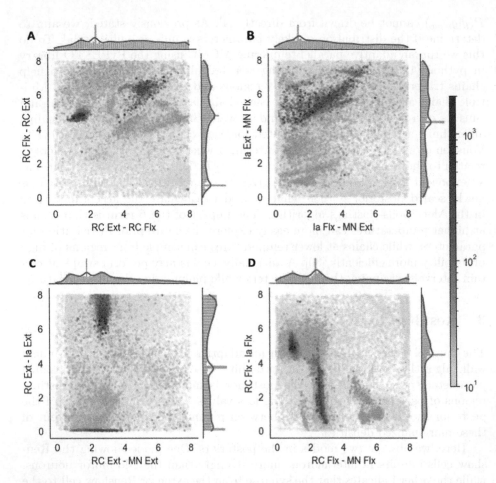

Fig. 4. Partial solution map of the posterior for the 12 parameter search of maximum synaptic conductance of the CMM model. Axes are labeled as: pre-synaptic - post-synaptic neurons. For example: RC Ext - Ia Ext represents the synapse where the RC Ext. is the pre-synaptic neuron and the Ia Ext. is the post-synaptic neuron. 1D marginals are shown above and to the right of each subplot, which tell the search range and the normalized distribution. The other portion of each subplot shows the 2D marginals of pairs of parameters with the x- and y-axes being the range of the respective parameter. Each point in the 2D marginals is a sample found in the MCMC search. The color of the point is associated with the posterior, with the darker colors indicating a large posterior, and therefore a lower loss. The darkness of the point also indicates the density of the area, with more prominent color indicating more points overlapping. This figure shows 4 of the 66 2D marginals, the complete set can be found at: https://github.com/cxj271/Living-Machines-2023

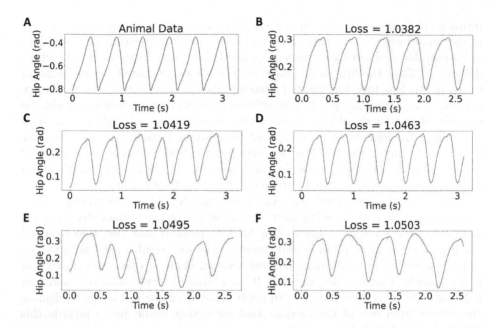

Fig. 5. Hip angle vs. time of a rat walking on a treadmill as it compares to the simulated data. A) Hip angle in the sagittal plane recorded from a rat walking on a treadmill. B-F) Solutions found from the MCMC search and their associated loss.

Table 3. Parameter Values for Simulations in Fig. 5

Fig. 5 Subplot	Loss	RC Flx to RC Ext	RC Ext to RC Flx	Ia Ext to MN Flx	Ia Flx to MN Ext	RC Ext to Ia Ext	RC Ext to MN Ext	RC Flx to Ia Flx	RC Flx to MN Flx
B	1.0382	4.7841	1.4200	6.3990	3.9774	6.9240	2.8318	5.0318	0.9442
C	1.0419	4.7357	1.0733	5.3191	2.3385	6.4873	2.5085	4.8937	0.8550
D	1.0463	4.8273	1.4041	5.0100	1.7797	6.0296	2.7741	4.8000	0.9119
E	1.0495	4.8319	1.4309	5.6222	3.0556	6.7807	2.5516	4.8108	1.0417
F	1.0503	4.1899	1.6269	4.9527	2.2418	6.3311	2.8697	4.9122	1.0798

4   Discussion

The results in Figs. 4 and 5 show that the parallel tempering MCMC method can successfully be used to automate the parameter search of a neural circuit to control a biomechanical model to exhibit a desired behavior. While the simulation results from the MCMC shown in Fig. 5 show difference in joint trajectory from the animal data, they share similarities in frequency of oscillations and swing to stance ratios. This is a result of the design of the loss function in Eq. 8. Many iterations of loss functions were tested to determine an appropriate equation to generate different results. Other loss functions included: mean squared error, mean absolute error, energy distance, Pearson Correlation, and Dynamic time warping [1,3,22]. Additionally, we explored the inclusion other terms to the current loss function such as a root mean square error and errors in the amplitude of oscillation. These attempts produced results with a variety of undesirable characteristics such as sharp changes in velocity or results which did not oscillate the hip joint. Issues such as these prompted the inclusion of terms in the loss function which promoted smooth trajectories and oscillatory motion (l_{smooth} and $l_{oscillate}$). The differences in joint trajectories may also be a result of using a simplified model of the rat hindlimb with only two muscles controlling the joint motion as opposed to applying muscle synergies. Further testing and refining the loss function may provide better results in the sense of hip trajectories. However, designing and selecting a "good" loss function is a difficult process for automated parameter search and optimization.

Unlike traditional optimization methods, the MCMC results provide a posterior density (Fig. 4), allowing us to see the whole picture rather than a single solution of the parameter space. The MCMC method was also able to avoid getting stuck at local minima and found acceptable results with no need for initial guesses and no information about the parameters other than upper and lower bounds. Furthermore, the MCMC was able to locate multiple modes in the posteriors. We were then able to apply what we know in biology to dismiss the results from one of the modes. Another option would be to include this knowledge in the priors.

The final results confirmed some expectations. It was thought that the Renshaw cells more strongly inhibit Ia inhibitory neurons than motor neurons. This was found in previous iterations of the work through hand-tuning and confirmed through the posterior densities in Figs. 4C and 4D [13]. The posterior of the mutual inhibition of the Renshaw cells in Fig. 4A show a tight spread of losses. Therefore, it can also be inferred that these synapses are sensitive to change and play a significant role in muscle control. The sensitivity and significance of the remaining synaptic conductances can be examined in a similar fashion using the posteriors presented in Fig. 4. For example, the Ia-MN synapses (Fig. 4B), are insensitive compared to the RC-RC synapses (Fig. 4A) as the darker region in the posterior is more spread out.

It should be noted that the posteriors shown in Fig. 4 were found using animal data of a rat walking at one frequency and swing stance ratio. While is likely that using animal data with different frequencies and swing stance ratios would cause changes in the posterior of the synaptic conductances, the results presented should not be dismissed. It is important to remember that this circuit receives a rhythmic input which was omitted in these experiments. Future works will further analyze the modes found in the posteriors, exploring how this system responds to the additional rhythmic input. We can then determine if tuning this circuit to oscillate at one frequency is beneficial when driven at other frequencies. It is also possible that small changes in the desired frequency and swing stance ratio would result in small shifts in the posteriors of the synaptic conductances. These small shifts may be due to synaptic plasticity, which may be accounted for by expanding the neural model to include synaptic plasticity.

The MCMC method for tuning neural circuits provides promising results which may help to make neural modeling more readily and widely used in computational neuroscience. In future works, the models will also be expanded to include control of the hip in three-dimensions as well as control of the knee and ankle joints. We will also explore how changes to the scale of the biomechanical model impact changes to the neural model. It is known that as the length scale of the biomechanical model increases, inertial forces become more dominant leading to changes in muscle activity during normal gait [33]. However, changes in the neural control which drives this activity have not yet been explored. The use of the MCMC method for parameter searching will allow us to develop more complex models and begin to answer these larger questions.

References

1. Müller, M.: Dynamic time warping. In: Müller, M. (ed.) Information Retrieval for Music and Motion, pp. 69–84. Springer, Heidelberg (2007). https://doi.org/10.1007/978-3-540-74048-3_4
2. Alessandro, C., Rellinger, B.A., Barroso, F.O., Tresch, M.C.: Adaptation after vastus lateralis denervation in rats demonstrates neural regulation of joint stresses and strains. eLife **7**, e38215 (2018). https://doi.org/10.7554/eLife.38215
3. Benesty, J., Chen, J., Huang, Y., Cohen, I.: Pearson correlation coefficient. In: Cohen, I., Huang, Y., Chen, J., Benesty, J. (eds.) Noise Reduction in Speech Processing. Springer Topics in Signal Processing, pp. 1–4. Springer, Heidelberg (2009). https://doi.org/10.1007/978-3-642-00296-0_5
4. Calvetti, D., Somersalo, E.: Sampling: the real thing. In: Calvetti, D., Somersalo, E. (eds.) Introduction to Bayesian Scientific Computing: Ten Lectures on Subjective Computing. STAMS, pp. 161–182. Springer, New York (2007). https://doi.org/10.1007/978-0-387-73394-4_9
5. Chen, Z.: An overview of Bayesian methods for neural spike train analysis. Comput. Intell. Neurosci. **2013**, 1–17 (2013). https://doi.org/10.1155/2013/251905. http://www.hindawi.com/journals/cin/2013/251905/
6. Cofer, D., Cymbalyuk, G., Reid, J., Zhu, Y., Heitler, W.J., Edwards, D.H.: AnimatLab: a 3D graphics environment for neuromechanical simulations. J. Neurosci. Methods **187**(2), 280–288 (2010). https://doi.org/10.1016/j.jneumeth.2010.01.005. https://linkinghub.elsevier.com/retrieve/pii/S0165027010000087
7. Delp, S.L., et al.: OpenSim: open-source software to create and analyze dynamic simulations of movement. IEEE Trans. Biomed. Eng. **54**(11), 1940–1950 (2007). https://doi.org/10.1109/TBME.2007.901024
8. Deng, K., et al.: Biomechanical and sensory feedback regularize the behavior of different locomotor central pattern generators. Biomimetics **7**(4), 226 (2022). https://doi.org/10.3390/biomimetics7040226. https://www.mdpi.com/2313-7673/7/4/226
9. Deng, K., et al.: Neuromechanical model of rat hindlimb walking with two-layer CPGs. Biomimetics **4**(1), 21 (2019). https://doi.org/10.3390/biomimetics4010021. https://www.mdpi.com/2313-7673/4/1/21
10. Hultborn, H., Lindstrm, S., Wigstrm, H.: On the function of recurrent inhibition in the spinal cord. Exp. Brain Res. **37**(2) (1979). https://doi.org/10.1007/BF00237722
11. Ikkala, A., Hämäläinen, P.: Converting Biomechanical Models from OpenSim to MuJoCo (2020). https://doi.org/10.48550/ARXIV.2006.10618

12. Ivashko, D., Prilutsky, B., Markin, S., Chapin, J., Rybak, I.: Modeling the spinal cord neural circuitry controlling cat hindlimb movement during locomotion. Neurocomputing **52–54**, 621–629 (2003). https://doi.org/10.1016/S0925-2312(02)00832-9. https://linkinghub.elsevier.com/retrieve/pii/S0925231202008329
13. Jackson, C., Nourse, W.R.P., Heckman, C.J., Tresch, M., Quinn, R.D.: Canonical motor microcircuit for control of a rat hindlimb. In: Hunt, A., et al. (eds.) Biomimetic and Biohybrid Systems, vol. 13548, pp. 309–320. Springer, Cham (2022). https://doi.org/10.1007/978-3-031-20470-8_31
14. Kennedy, J., Eberhart, R.: Particle swarm optimization. In: Proceedings of ICNN 1995 - International Conference on Neural Networks, Perth, WA, Australia, vol. 4, pp. 1942–1948. IEEE (1995). https://doi.org/10.1109/ICNN.1995.488968. http://ieeexplore.ieee.org/document/488968/
15. Lee, K.Y., Park, J.: Application of particle swarm optimization to economic dispatch problem: advantages and disadvantages, pp. 188–192 (2006). https://doi.org/10.1109/PSCE.2006.296295
16. Lindén, H., Petersen, P.C., Vestergaard, M., Berg, R.W.: Movement is governed by rotational neural dynamics in spinal motor networks. Nature **610**(7932), 526–531 (2022). https://doi.org/10.1038/s41586-022-05293-w. https://www.nature.com/articles/s41586-022-05293-w
17. MacKay-Lyons, M.: Central pattern generation of locomotion: a review of the evidence. Phys. Ther. **82**(1), 69–83 (2002). https://doi.org/10.1093/ptj/82.1.69. https://academic.oup.com/ptj/article/82/1/69/2837028
18. McCrea, D.A., Rybak, I.A.: Organization of mammalian locomotor rhythm and pattern generation. Brain Res. Rev. **57**(1), 134–146 (2008). https://doi.org/10.1016/j.brainresrev.2007.08.006. https://linkinghub.elsevier.com/retrieve/pii/S0165017307001798
19. Miasojedow, B., Moulines, E., Vihola, M.: An adaptive parallel tempering algorithm. J. Comput. Graph. Stat. **22**(3), 649–664 (2013). https://doi.org/10.1080/10618600.2013.778779. http://www.tandfonline.com/doi/abs/10.1080/10618600.2013.778779
20. Nourse, W.R.P., Szczecinski, N.S., Quinn, R.D.: SNS-toolbox: a tool for efficient simulation of synthetic nervous systems. In: Hunt, A., et al. (eds.) Biomimetic and Biohybrid Systems, vol. 13548, pp. 32–43. Springer, Cham (2022). https://doi.org/10.1007/978-3-031-20470-8_4
21. Pratt, C.A., Jordan, L.M.: IA inhibitory interneurons and Renshaw cells as contributors to the spinal mechanisms of fictive locomotion. J. Neurophysiol. **57**(1), 56–71 (1987). https://doi.org/10.1152/jn.1987.57.1.56. https://www.physiology.org/doi/10.1152/jn.1987.57.1.56
22. Rizzo, M.L., Székely, G.J.: Energy distance. Wiley Interdisc. Rev.: Comput. Stat. **8**(1), 27–38 (2016). https://doi.org/10.1002/wics.1375. https://onlinelibrary.wiley.com/doi/10.1002/wics.1375
23. Rybak, I.A., Stecina, K., Shevtsova, N.A., McCrea, D.A.: Modelling spinal circuitry involved in locomotor pattern generation: insights from the effects of afferent stimulation: modelling afferent control of locomotor pattern generation. J. Physiol. **577**(2), 641–658 (2006). https://doi.org/10.1113/jphysiol.2006.118711. https://onlinelibrary.wiley.com/doi/10.1113/jphysiol.2006.118711
24. Seth, A., et al.: OpenSim: simulating musculoskeletal dynamics and neuromuscular control to study human and animal movement. PLoS Comput. Biol. **14**(7), e1006223 (2018). https://doi.org/10.1371/journal.pcbi.1006223

25. Shadmehr, R., Wise, S.P.: The Computational Neurobiology of Reaching and Pointing: A Foundation for Motor Learning. Computational neuroscience, MIT Press, Cambridge (2005)
26. Spencer, S.E.: Accelerating adaptation in the adaptive Metropolis-Hastings random walk algorithm. Aust. New Zealand J. Stat. **63**(3), 468–484 (2021). https://doi.org/10.1111/anzs.12344. https://onlinelibrary.wiley.com/doi/10.1111/anzs.12344
27. Stapor, P., et al.: PESTO: parameter EStimation TOolbox. Bioinformatics **34**(4), 705–707 (2018). https://doi.org/10.1093/bioinformatics/btx676. https://academic.oup.com/bioinformatics/article/34/4/705/4562504
28. Szczecinski, N.S., Hunt, A.J., Quinn, R.D.: A functional subnetwork approach to designing synthetic nervous systems that control legged robot locomotion. Front. Neurorobot. **11**, 37 (2017). https://doi.org/10.3389/fnbot.2017.00037. http://journal.frontiersin.org/article/10.3389/fnbot.2017.00037/full
29. Todorov, E., Erez, T., Tassa, Y.: MuJoCo: a physics engine for model-based control. In: 2012 IEEE/RSJ International Conference on Intelligent Robots and Systems, pp. 5026–5033 (2012). https://doi.org/10.1109/IROS.2012.6386109. ISSN 2153-0866
30. Vousden, W.D., Farr, W.M., Mandel, I.: Dynamic temperature selection for parallel tempering in Markov chain Monte Carlo simulations. Monthly Notices R. Astron. Soc. **455**(2), 1919–1937 (2016). https://doi.org/10.1093/mnras/stv2422. https://academic.oup.com/mnras/article-lookup/doi/10.1093/mnras/stv2422
31. Wang, Y.C., et al.: Multimodal parameter spaces of a complex multi-channel neuron model. Front. Syst. Neurosci. **16** (2022). https://www.frontiersin.org/articles/10.3389/fnsys.2022.999531
32. Wilson, H.R., Cowan, J.D.: Excitatory and inhibitory interactions in localized populations of model neurons. Biophys. J. **12**(1), 1–24 (1972). https://doi.org/10.1016/S0006-3495(72)86068-5. https://linkinghub.elsevier.com/retrieve/pii/S0006349572860685
33. Young, F.R., Chiel, H.J., Tresch, M.C., Heckman, C.J., Hunt, A.J., Quinn, R.D.: Analyzing modeled torque profiles to understand scale-dependent active muscle responses in the hip joint. Biomimetics **7**(1), 17 (2022). https://doi.org/10.3390/biomimetics7010017. https://www.mdpi.com/2313-7673/7/1/17

Towards a Soft Artificial Larynx: A Biomimetic Design

Jasmine Pozzi[1,2]([⊠]) [iD], Arianna Conte[1,2] [iD], Martina Maselli[1,2] [iD],
Maria Raffaella Marchese[3] [iD], Andrea Nacci[4] [iD], and Matteo Cianchetti[1,2] [iD]

[1] The BioRobotics Institute, Scuola Superiore Sant'Anna, Pisa, Italy
{Jasmine.pozzi,Arianna.conte,Martina.maselli,
Matteo.cianchetti}@santannapisa.it
[2] The Department of Excellence in Robotics and AI, Scuola Superiore Sant'Anna, Pisa, Italy
[3] Unità Operativa Complessa di Otorinolaringoiatria, Dipartimento di Neuroscienze, Organi di
Senso e Torace, Fondazione Policlinico Universitario A. Gemelli IRCSS, Rome, Italy
Mariaraffaella.marchese@policlinicogemelli.it
[4] ENT, Audiology and Phoniatrics Unit, University Hospital of Pisa, Pisa, Italy
A.nacci@med.unipi.it

Abstract. The larynx is one of the smallest but also one of the most complex organs in the human body, with three main functions: breathing, swallowing, and phonation. In case of total laryngectomy, all these functions are missing. Currently, they are replaced with a tracheal stoma and a vocal prosthesis, which give many physical and social problems to the subject.

The long-term aim of this work is to create an implantable artificial larynx, able to reproduce all the larynx functions. Here, we present the first steps toward the creation of the artificial organ. We analyzed the larynx of different animal classes, to find basic structures and movements, shared among all the Tetrapoda. We used these models as a guide for simplifying the human larynx to obtain a functional design. We found that two cartilages (i.e., the cricoid and the arytenoids) and three muscles (i.e., the posterior cricoarytenoid, the lateral cricoarytenoid, and the thyroarytenoid) are common to all the studied species. Based on this, we proposed a larynx design, suggesting also possible materials, whose validity will be tested in the near future.

Keywords: Biomimetics · Artificial Organs · Soft Robotics

1 Introduction

1.1 The Larynx Anatomy

The larynx is one of the smallest but also one of the most complex organs in the human body. It follows the pharynx, is connected to the esophagus, and continues into the trachea. It has a single horseshoe-shaped bone, called the hyoid bone, which supports the entire laryngeal structure, connecting it to the jaw and the base of the tongue. The larynx structure is mainly composed of four cartilages (see *Fig.* 1). From the supraglottic to the subglottic portion [1]:

– The *epiglottis*, connected to the hyoid bone and thyroid cartilage, whose function is to protect the airways from food entry during the swallowing phase, together with the vertical and horizontal movements of the larynx, and the closure of the vocal folds.
– The *thyroid* cartilage, which allows to stretch the vocal folds to modulate the frequency of the voice. It makes contact respectively with the overlying hyoid bone and the underlying cricoid cartilage.
– The *cricoid* cartilage, which is the only cartilage that completely surrounds the airways with its ring shape, keeping them open. Its malformation leads to their narrowing and consequent respiratory obstruction. It is connected inferiorly to the trachea, superior-anteriorly to the thyroid, while posteriorly it supports the two arytenoid cartilages.
– Two *arytenoid* cartilages, which hold the vocal folds. Their movements (i.e., sliding forward and backward, lateral oscillation, and rotation along the vertical axis), guaranteed by the intrinsic muscles of the larynx, allow the opening and closing of the vocal folds and, therefore, in the first instance, the production of speech. They are pyramidal in shape and are connected to the cricoid cartilage.

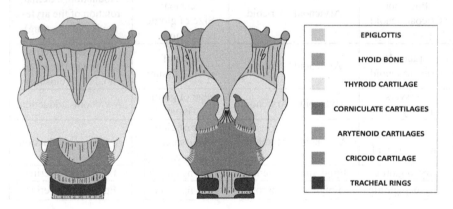

Fig. 1. Schematization of the human larynx.

The vocal folds (VF) are connected to the arytenoid cartilages on one side and the thyroid cartilage on the other side. They are formed by 5 different layers, divided into three groups according to their mechanical properties [2]:

– the mucosa (cover), composed of epithelium and superficial lamina propria
– the ligament, composed of medial and deep lamina propria
– vocal muscle (body)

The complex micro-anatomy of the vocal folds enables phonation through their vibration when closed. On the contrary, when open, they allow the passage of air for breathing [3].

An elastic cone holds the vocal folds above the cricoid cartilage, keeping them in place and connected to the laryngeal structure.

The laryngeal muscles can be divided into intrinsic and extrinsic muscles [1, 3]. The intrinsic muscles originate and remain in the larynx and their function is to control sound during vocal production. They, indeed, regulate the tension, length, shape, and positioning of the vocal folds, working on the movement of the arytenoid cartilages. There are 8 pairs of intrinsic muscles, whose functions are schematized in *Table* 1.

Table 1. Laryngeal intrinsic muscles. Their insertion points on the cartilages and the respective functions are specified.

Muscle	Insertion Points	Regulation	Function
Cricothyroid	Thyroid – Cricoid	Vocal ligament tension	Cricoid withdrawal; Thyroid lowering and protrusion; Vocal folds tension
Thyroarytenoid	Arytenoid – Thyroid	Vocal ligament tension	Thyroid retraction; Vocal folds shortening
Posterior Cricoarytenoid	Arytenoid – Cricoid	Vocal ligament tension; Size of glottic fissure	Abduction, external rotation of the arytenoids (VF opening)
Lateral Cricoarytenoid	Arytenoid – Cricoid	Size of glottic fissure	Adduction, internal rotation of the arytenoids (VF closure)
Transverse Interarytenoid	Arytenoid – Arytenoid	Size of glottic fissure	Arytenoids adduction
Lateral Interarytenoid	Arytenoid – Arytenoid	Size of glottic fissure; Laryngeal inlet	Arytenoids adduction
Aryepiglottic	Epiglottis – Arytenoid	Laryngeal inlet	Epiglottis lowering
Thyroepiglottic	Epiglottis – Thyroid	Laryngeal inlet	Epiglottis lowering

The extrinsic muscles support and position the larynx, move it vertically during breathing and swallowing, allow relative movements of the cartilages and hyoid bone with each other, and, in addition, involuntarily influence the positioning of the vocal folds by dilating and narrowing the glottal fissure. There are more than 10 pairs of extrinsic muscles. In *Table* 2 only a few examples were shown but it is already appreciable their role in narrowing the laryngeal lumen and lowering the entire larynx to protect the airways from food entry.

Despite the important action of the extrinsic muscles in the real larynx, we decided to neglect their movements because their function is secondary in the artificial one. As we will underline later, the key role in lung protection during swallowing is, indeed, attributed to the closure of the vocal folds, to which movements we will refer throughout the paper.

Table 2. Laryngeal extrinsic muscles. Their insertion points and the respective functions are specified. Only a few examples are shown; a detailed list is reported in [3].

Muscle	Insertion Points	Function
Sternohyoid	Hyoid – Sternum	Hyoid lowering
Sternothyroid	Thyroid – Sternum	Hyoid lowering; Thyroid lowering Larynx lowering
Thyrohyoid	Hyoid – Thyroid	Hyoid lowering; Thyroid elevation
Stylohyoid	Hyoid – Jaw	Hyoid elevation; Hyoid withdrawal

The complex anatomy of the larynx and its position in the human body, allows it to perform three vital functions: *swallowing* (sphincteric action), preventing the food bolus from passing through the respiratory tract; *breathing*, guaranteeing the passage of inhaled and exhaled air; the *phonatory*, allowing the emission of sounds with consequent formation of the voice.

1.2 The Laryngectomy and the Current Prostheses

There are about 185.000 new cases of laryngeal carcinoma between men and women every year [4] and the surgical practice remains the only solution for the treatment of the advanced stages. This practice consists of a total laryngectomy, which involves the removal of the entire larynx and all the structures connected to it. Hence, there is a complete disconnection between the upper and lower airways and between airways and the digestive tract, resulting in the loss of all three laryngeal functions. To compensate for this lack, it is necessary to create a stoma in the remaining portion of the trachea, through which the patient can breathe. However, its creation involves many complications for the patient itself: (i) absence of a real larynx implies an alteration of the humidity and temperature of the inspired air; (ii) involves a direct connection between the lungs and the external environment, facilitating the entry of pathogens, the onset of infections and chronic pulmonary diseases. Moreover, a unidirectional voice prosthesis is often inserted. This prosthesis compensates for the loss of voice, allowing laryngectomee patients to create sounds immediately after its implantation. Through the occlusion of the stoma, mostly performed by placing a finger on the stoma itself, the pulmonary air is deflected through the prosthesis, to the pharyngoesophageal segment, where the vibration of the mucosa generates the sound to produce speech, amplified by the buccal cavity which works as a sounding board [3]. However, the voice produced by the prosthesis is aperiodic and disharmonic, poorly fluent and unpleasant, with masculine frequencies even in the case of female patients. The quality of the vocal product, together with the need to close the stoma with a finger makes him/her feel very uncomfortable in public contexts and leads him/her to take refuge from social life. However, voice prostheses are unanimously considered the rehabilitation method of first choice for voice recovery. Among these, the gold standard is represented by the Provox® Vega™ unidirectional voice prosthesis [5].

Alternatively, the phonatory function can be performed through (i) the esophageal speech or (ii) the so-called electrolarynx or laryngophone. In the first case, the air from the stomach, following speech-therapy exercises, is redirected to the esophagus, where the sound is produced by the mucosa tissue vibration. This is a hands-free method, but it has many disadvantages such as the difficulty in learning it, the short duration of the speech, and the quality of the voice. Only a small percentage of patients use this method [6]. In the second case, the subject must press a cylindrical device, composed of an electrically driven vibration plate and powered by a battery, against the neck skin. The vibration generated at the vibration plate is percutaneously guided into the oral cavity, producing the sound. The method is easy to master but uncomfortable because the subject must hold the device and press a button with the finger to control it. Moreover, the voice produced is monotonic, close to a buzzer, and hard to hear. Some studies are focusing on the improvement of this device, trying to control it with the myoelectric signals of the sternohyoid muscle in the neck, avoiding the use of hands [7]. Nevertheless, the device will be composed of several components (i.e., electrodes, a battery, an amplifier, a transducer, a sound actuator, and a control unit signal processor) and the voice quality will be not satisfactory.

In any case, a total artificial larynx, intended as an implantable prosthesis that recreates the real mechanical properties of the natural larynx, is still missing.

One innovative approach to studying new prostheses regards the simulation of parts of the human body with materials similar to human tissue which is one of the emerging applications in the field of soft robotics [8]. This field allows the development of artificial organs increasingly similar to their anatomical counterparts, replicating mechanical characteristics and functionality. Given the anatomical complexity of the larynx, researchers have moved towards the development of artificial larynx as platforms for clinical investigations that can be useful for understanding laryngeal pathologies. Nevertheless, a total artificial implantable larynx, able to replace the current vocal prosthesis, does not exist.

The long-term aim of this work, taking advantage of the technologies related to soft robotics, is to develop an implantable artificial larynx, with functional properties similar to the natural organ and, therefore, able to recreate all three functions of the real larynx. The transplant of the artificial organ will allow the removal of the stoma, reducing recurrent lung diseases, the reunification of the upper airways with the digestive tract, and the improvement of the quality of the vocal product, given by the integration of artificial vocal folds. Thus, the absence of the stoma and a better voice quality will make significant improvements inside the physical and psychological sphere of the laryngectomee patient.

Here, we present the first steps toward the creation of the artificial larynx. The essential anatomical components of the larynx structure were identified to obtain a functional design and possible materials for its manufacture were proposed.

2   The Biomimetic Approach

It is quite clear that reproducing such a complex organ in its entirety, from an engineering point of view, is not possible. A simplification of the natural model is needed. Usually, this simplification relies on a functional synthesis of the essential parts of the model. The elements that are fundamental for reproducing the underlying working principle are identified and their functionality is artificially replicated.

We implemented this simplification as the identification of the cartilaginous and muscular structures that are strictly necessary for the performance of the basic larynx functions, following the conventional approach. However, in this work, we introduce a further possibility. Although this work aims at developing an artificial larynx for humans, we believe that the model to consider should not be necessarily only the human larynx. A further justification for our simplified approach is that the richness of human speech is the result not only of the complexity of the larynx but also of the supraglottic structures (i.e., mouth and tongue).

Hence, to answer our question, we looked at the animal kingdom at large. The larynx in the animal kingdom has several shapes as an adaptation to the environments where animals live. The study of different taxa can be very helpful in finding a larynx structure, which is, certainly, completely different from the human one, but implementing in a simplified way similar characteristics. The idea was to look for simpler models in other Tetrapoda and use them as a further guide to develop an artificial larynx for humans, a sort of cross-bioinspiration. There are different taxonomic categories ranging from the kingdom, which includes, for example, all animals and is therefore very vast, to the species, which is, on the opposite, very specific since two species belonging to the same genus can differ from each other even only for the color of the spots. We chose to analyze the Superclass Tetrapoda because it encompasses all the animal classes which conquered the mainland thanks to their four legs (i.e. amphibians, reptiles, birds, and mammals). Below this category, these classes can no longer be combined. Above this, it should be considered the infraphylum of the gnathostomes, hence, animals with a jaw. This would also include fishes that we did not consider due to their completely different characteristics.

The very first step of this process (which constitutes the main contribution of this work) is to identify the common structures of all the different classes. However, this is not meant to be a review and, therefore, we will be very general in the description of the various anatomical structures of the larynx.

2.1 The Amphibians

Among the class Amphibia, we considered the order Anura, i.e. the amphibians with four limbs and without a tail after the metamorphosis (frogs, toads, and treefrogs).

Generally speaking, the anurans produce distinctive and simple calls, characterized by high intensity and a simple timing pattern [9]. Their larynx is much simpler than the human one and the same basic structures are present in all species (see *Fig.* 2), even in species able to produce ultrasounds (*Odorrana tormota*) [10, 11] or secondary aquatic, specialized in underwater communication (i.e. family Pipidae) [12, 13]. An example is *Hyla arborea*. As in humans, it has a cartilaginous framework formed by two cartilages: a ring-shaped cricoid and a couple of arytenoids attached to the cricoid, on which they can rotate. There is no epiglottis. Also, the hyoid is a hyaline cartilage with just some calcified points. For our work, we did not consider the hyoid, since, in most cases, this structure remains even after the laryngectomy. The vocal folds are called T-folds, since they are the thickening of a membrane that covers the arytenoids, made by elastic tissue, without a multilayer structure [14]. Nevertheless, their vibration, and two lateral vocal sacs for sound amplification, allow the sound, and their removal prevents sound production. *H.*

arborea has just four pairs of muscles: one dilatator larynges muscle, which is the most highly conserved across species, and three constrictor larynges muscles. They are all considered extrinsic muscles of the larynx since frogs lack muscles inside the larynx.

Some species, *Engystomops pustulosus* as an example, are subjected to strong mating competition and, hence, they produce two distinct sounds: an obligatory whine and a facultative chuck. This is due to lateral extensions of connective tissue from the vocal folds, the frenulum labii vocalis, whose swelling creates two laryngeal fibrous masses (FM). These masses vibrate with the vocal folds to produce the chuck. The removal of the fibrous masses prevents the chuck production but has no effect on the vocal folds' vibration and, hence, on the whine production. An additional cartilage called basal cartilage is present as support of the vocal frenulum. The dilatator muscle gains more complexity, and it is divided into two separate bundles of fibers with different orientations [15]. The function of each muscle is specified in *Table* 3.

If the reader is interested in the topic, we suggest reading the review [16].

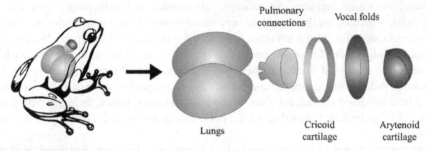

Fig. 2. Schematization of the anuran larynx. *Hyla arborea* is shown as an example. Positioning of the laryngeal apparatus within the anuran body and schematic representation of the its elements. The vocal folds are housed inside the combined arytenoid and cricoid cartilages.

2.2 The Reptiles

The vocalization ability, within the class Reptilia, is lower than that of amphibians. The reptilian sound-producing mechanisms represent a random assemblage, without a central evolutionary tendency. They produce non-vocal sounds, straining the air exhalation without using vocal folds or using tracheal specializations. Among vocal reptiles, we can find some geckos (order Squamata), some turtles (order Testudines or Chelonia), and some alligators (order Crocodilians).

The anatomy of the gecko's larynx will not be introduced in detail, because it is very similar to that of anurans [17].

The terrestrial chelonians (tortoises) present a cricoid cartilaginous ring and two arytenoid cartilages. The hyoid is cartilaginous, just partially calcified and it assumes the role of the thyroid cartilage in mammals, which is missing here [18]. There is no epiglottis, although it is described in *Chelonoidis denticulate*, belonging to the same genus of *Chelonoidis carbonaria*, which, conversely, lacks this cartilage [19]. Chelonians lack true vocal folds, but they have two bands of elastic tissue, directly inserted on the arytenoids and the hyoid, which works precisely as the thyroid. These bands are positioned differently from those of amphibians: the amphibians' fibroelastic bands projected into the lumen of the larynx, stretched between the dorsal and ventral wall of the cricoid, while the chelonians ones are positioned between the arytenoids and the hyoid, which works precisely as the thyroid and are directly inserted on the cartilages. For the first time, these fibroelastic bands are a specialization of the larynx wall and glottal lips rather than being a fold into the laryngeal lumen, and they are completely supported by the cartilages. Some species, such as *Testudo graeca* and *Testudo marginata*, present some finger-shaped, low-frequency resonating chambers, the diverticula, which improve the harmonic structure of emitted sounds. These structures have been found only in the tracheal membrane of the king cobra (*Ophiophagus hannah*), the mangrove ratsnake (*Gonyosoma oxycephalum*), and other related ophidian species, in which these structures are demonstrated to be related to phonation [18]. The chelonians' larynx musculature is very simple with only two pairs of extrinsic muscles that work on the opening and closure of the arytenoids: the dilator larynges muscle and the constrictor larynges muscle (see *Table* 3). The elastic bands can actually also be stretched. Since tortoises lack intrinsic muscles (for example the cricothyroid muscle in mammals) their tension is given by the movement of the hyoid away from the cricoid. This movement could be given by the m. constrictor contraction or by the contraction of the muscles of the tongue. The latter hypothesis is particularly appealing because when vocalizing, tortoises fully extend their neck, open their mouth, and completely lift their tongue. The larynx structure of sea turtles is similar to those of terrestrial chelonians with a pair of arytenoid cartilages, moved by the muscle dilator, and a cricoid ring, compressed against the hyoid by the muscle constrictor [20].

The American alligator (*Alligator mississippiensis*) has a cricoid ring and two arytenoids, with a cartilaginous hyoid. However, it displays a large vocal ability with a complex vocal repertoire, thanks to multilayer vocal folds, very similar to those of mammals. There are only two muscles but with a greater ability to play on the closure and tension of the vocal folds [21, 22] (see *Table* 3).

A more detailed review can be found in [23], while a more evolutionary view of the larynx through the non-avian reptiles, starting from the dinosaurs can be found in [24].

2.3 The Songbirds

Among the Tetrapoda, the songbirds are the most peculiar. They have, indeed, a unique vocal organ called syrinx. The syrinx is located at the caudal end of the trachea before the lungs. Due to its location, it does not protect the airways during swallowing (as the larynx does) but it regulates the airflow from and to the lungs and modulates the airflow during sound production. It has a cylindrical cartilage, the tympanum (working as the thyroid cartilage), with a bifurcation at the caudal end. This bifurcation represents two different sound sources. Each sound source, indeed, has 2 labia (one lateral and one medial labium), which represent the vibrating structures for the vocalization (see *Fig.* 3). The labia are generally composed of an extracellular matrix, rich in elastin, collagen, and hyaluronic, between two layers of epithelium. Their structure could be uniform or multilayer, which guarantees a wider range of frequencies. It is possible to note a strong similarity with the human vocal folds. The two different sound sources allow songbirds to produce two independent tones simultaneously: the left source generates lower frequencies while the right one produces higher frequencies with a certain degree of overlap. The control is given by two extrinsic muscles and four intrinsic muscles [25, 26] (see *Table* 3).

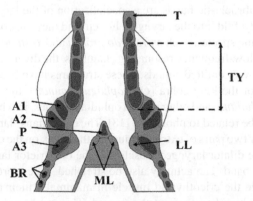

Fig. 3. Schematic cross-section of the syrinx. The cartilaginous components are showed in dark blue; the labia are showed in pink. Abbreviations: T: tracheal ring; Ty: tympanum; A1–A3: trachea-bronchial semi-rings; P: pessulus; BR: bronchial rings; ML: medial labium; LL: lateral labium. (Color figure online)

Echolocating birds has also a syrinx to orient themselves in the night with broadband clicks. Their syrinx has no intrinsic muscles but only two extrinsic muscles. When the stern-tracheal muscle pulls the trachea caudally, it closes the labia and hence the airflow, producing a click; when the trachea-lateral muscle shortens the trachea, stretches the syrinx, and opens the labia, restoring the airflow and producing the second click [27]. Also, ostrich, emu, and cassowary lack intrinsic muscles and can cover a small range of frequencies. This is probably because they are the first birds that evolved the syrinx [28, 29].

A larynx is still present in all songbirds, but it is no longer the vocal organ. It is at the upper end of the trachea and the caudal end of the pharynx and regulates the airflow, working as a filter for sound properties. It is composed of four cartilages: cricoid, procricoid, and two arytenoids. The epiglottis and the thyroid cartilage are not present. There are two types of larynges: kinematic and akinematic. The first is typical of parrots and passerine birds, which can vary the size and the shape of the larynx, thanks to both intrinsic and extrinsic muscles, while the second is typical of chickens, pigeons, and herons, which cannot. This variability does not seem to affect breathing but probably plays a role in the feeding and vocalization mechanisms [29]. The intrinsic muscles of a kinematic larynx are shown in *Table* 3.

2.4 The Mammals

Terrestrial mammals present a larynx structure that is similar to the human larynx. The changes we can find are due to the necessity of reaching higher or lower fundamental frequencies than expected for their body mass for sexual selection, territory defence, or sound propagation [30–34].

In underwater mammals (cetaceans) the vocal folds' position and viscoelastic properties change but the larynx structure is the same of terrestrial mammals [35, 36], thus not repeated here.

Table 3. Principal muscles of each studied animal class: amphibians in green, reptiles in orange; birds in blue. In reptiles, Testudo stands for order Testudines; Alligator stands for order Crocodilians. In songbirds, the syrinx and larynx muscles are described separately. Mammals are not reported. The muscles' insertion points on the cartilages and their functions are specified. Abbreviations: A.: arytenoids; FM: fibrous masses; VF: vocal folds; LL: lateral labia; ML: medial labia

Class		Muscle		Insertion Points	Function
Amphibians		Dilator	Superficial	Arytenoid – Hyoid	A. opening
			Deep	Arytenoid – Cricoid	FM stretching
		Anterior constrictor		Arytenoid – Cricoid	A. closure
		Externus constrictor		Arytenoid – Hyoid	
		Posterior constrictor		Arytenoid – Cricoid	VF closure
Reptiles	Testudo	Dilator		Arytenoid – Cricoid	A. opening
		Constrictor		Hyoid – Cricoid	A. closure VF stretching
	Alligator	Crico-arytenoid	Cranial	Arytenoid – Cricoid	VF opening
			Caudal	Hyoid – Cricoid	VF closure
		Constrictor	Ventral Dorsal	Arytenoid – Hyoid	VF closure; stretching
Birds	Syrinx	Tracheobronchial	Ventral		LL opening
			Dorsal		LL closure
		Syringeal	Ventral		LL tension
			Dorsal		ML closure
	Larynx	Dilator		Arytenoid – Cricoid	A. opening
		Constrictor		Arytenoid – Cricoid Arytenoids Cricoid – Procricoid	A. closure

3   Results and Discussion

3.1   The Larynx Common Structures

The larynx anatomy is too complex to be reproduced in each of its elements, but a perfect reproduction of the larynx may not be necessary to replicate all vital functions if some compromises are accepted. A simplification of the human model is needed. The aim of the present work is to find the basic structures and movements that guarantee the performance of the three larynx functions in the simplest possible way. Different species belonging to the amphibians (order Anura), reptiles (order Squamata, Testudines, Crocodilians), songbirds, and mammals were studied.

A schematization of the various structures present in each class has been provided in *Fig.* 4.

For what concern the cartilages, there are two essential structures: the cricoid cartilage and the arytenoid cartilages, present in every analyzed species.

Specifically, the cricoid is the fixed point of the larynx, since it gives a structure to the organ, keeping the airways open and preventing the larynx from collapsing on itself. Additionally, in basal sauropsids (amphibians and some reptiles such as geckos) it holds vibrating elastic bands, while, in the evolutionarily youngest therapsids, it is the anchor point of the arytenoids.

The arytenoids are fundamental for the opening and closing of the glottis. In amphibians, they are the only protection of the underlying airways. In songbirds, where the phonation role is delegated to the syrinx, the arytenoids are moved by several muscles just to adjust the size and shape of the laryngeal chamber. In some reptiles (i.e., Crocodilians) and in mammals they hold the vocal folds, so that, the movements of these cartilages allow for different positions of the vocal folds, which, in turn, guarantee a wide vocal repertoire.

The thyroid cartilage and the epiglottis are generally missing, except for the mammal's larynx.

Regarding the muscles, the analysis was much more complex. The muscles' name changes depending on the animal class, and even within the same class. In the present study, for simplicity, each muscle in each class was assigned to the corresponding muscle in humans, according to the function it performs (see Table 4 for a visual representation of this comparison).

From this study, it turned out that only three muscles were strictly necessary for life: the muscle that abducts and externally rotates the vocal folds (i.e., the posterior cricoarytenoid muscle), the muscle that adducts the vocal folds and closes the glottis (i.e., lateral cricoarytenoid muscle), and the muscle that stretches the vocal folds (i.e., thyroarytenoid muscle) (*Fig.* 4).

Table 4. Correspondences between the muscles of the human and other animal classes' larynx/syrinx. In reptiles, the muscles of the Testudines' species are in blue; the muscles of the Crocodilians' species are in orange. In Birds, the muscles related to the syrinx are in light pink; the muscles related to the larynx are in violet. The extrinsic muscles are not mentioned.

Humans	Frogs	Reptiles	Songbirds
Posterior Cricoarytenoid	Dilator larynges	Dilator larynges	Ventral trachea-bronchial
		Cranial cricoarytenoid	Dilator larynges
Lateral cricoarytenoid	Constrictor larynges	Constrictor larynges	Dorsal syringeal
		Caudal cricoarytenoid	Cricoarytenoid constrictor
Cricothyroid		Constrictor larynges	Ventral + Dorsal syringeal
Thyroarytenoid	Posterior constrictor	Dorsal and Ventral constrictor	Cricoarytenoid constrictor
Inter-arytenoid			Dorsal trachea-bronchial
			Interarytenoid constrictor
			Intercricoid constrictor

3.2 The Larynx Design

We proposed a first functional design for the development of a human artificial larynx (see *Fig.* 5) considering only the laryngeal structures (cartilages and muscles) common to all animal classes, and, hence, the structures included in the intersection showed in *Fig.* 4.

Starting from the cartilages, the prototype must have a ring-shaped cricoid cartilage to keep the airways open. It is present in all studied species, even in those without a high vocalization complexity. Its dimension referred to the human ones [3]: 10 mm in height, with an external diameter of 35 mm and an internal one of 25 mm; three motionless 20 mm high pillars distribute on the cricoid cartilage were added to connect it, in the future, to the hyoid bone. The cartilage is lower than its natural counterpart, which is 65 mm in height, reaching 30 mm in height which is the minimum height that the larynx can have to be connected to the hyoid bone on the upper side and the trachea on the lower side. As in every considered species, also in our prototype, the epiglottis is missing. The function of the epiglottis could be replaced by the closure of the vocal folds, to protect the lungs from food entry during swallowing, as already happens in humans. The epiglottis has, indeed, just an additional supporting role. Would be of interest, for future works, to understand why the other Tetrapoda do not have this cartilage and, conversely, mammals have evolved it if not strictly necessary. In the view of a simplified model, also the role of the extrinsic muscles during swallowing could be omitted and this function delegated exclusively to the vocal folds. More in general, the role of the extrinsic muscles could be neglected in the creation of the entire prosthesis. It is, indeed, enough that the entire larynx moves up and down, without relative movements of the cartilages, to allow for both swallowing and breathing. The vertical movements of the artificial organ will be

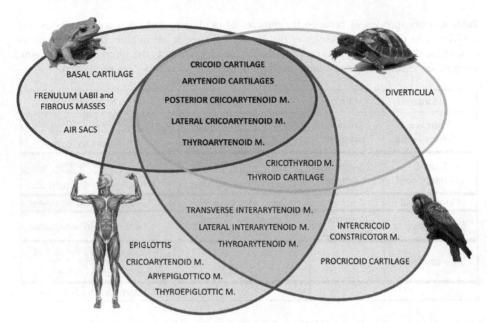

Fig. 4. Visual representation of laryngeal muscles and cartilages in the studied animal class. The common structures are highlighted in bold. In the figure are shown, as examples, the frog *Hyla arborea* (amphibians, green circle); the tortoise *Testudo hermanni* (reptiles, yellow circle); a parrot from genus Ara, subfamily Arinae, family Psittacidae (songbirds, blue circle); the human (mammals, red circle). In birds, components from syrinx and larynx were put together for simplicity. (Color figure online)

guaranteed by the hyoid bone, which is generally maintained during laryngectomy and will represent the anchor point of the prosthesis.

Hence, the movements of the vocal folds turn out to be even more important. They must be open during breathing, to allow the passage of air, and close during phonation to produce sounds through their vibration. Moreover, their closure must be a tight closure, since the epiglottis is not present, and the vocal folds have to protect the airways during swallowing. The movements of opening and closing of the vocal folds are not linear but rotational; moreover, in humans, their maximum opening/closing distance is 15 mm (each vocal fold has to move laterally by 7.5 mm from the glottal line) and the maximum elongation in tension is 30% of the initial length [37]. All these properties are guaranteed by the laryngeal muscles.

According to *Fig. 4*, we can reproduce these movements with three muscles: the posterior cricoarytenoid, which opens the vocal folds; the lateral cricoarytenoid, which closes the vocal folds without stretching them; and the thyroarytenoid, which stretches the vocal folds. The opening and closure of the glottis allow the air to pass through the airways from one side and the vocal folds to vibrate. The tension of the vocal folds guarantees a tight closure of the glottis during swallowing. Different tensions of the vocal folds guarantee different voice tones. Without this modulation, the voice would be a monotonic voice but at the early stage of this work, it may be acceptable.

A preliminary and simplified schematization has been created as a CAD (computer-aided design) model in SOLIDWORKS® software and it is reported in *Fig. 5*. Here, we reproduced also the vocal folds, connected to the arytenoids, to show their movements driven by the three selected muscles.

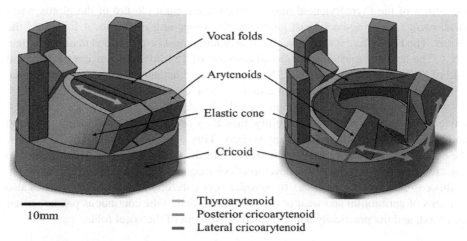

Fig. 5. Proposed design of the human artificial larynx. The arytenoid cartilages are reported as part of the future actuation system. The vocal folds are in the scheme, integrated in the elastic cone. The actions of the three selected muscles are shown with arrows: the posterior cricoarytenoid muscle (in orange), opens the vocal folds; the lateral cricoarytenoid muscle (in blue) closes the vocal folds; the thyroarytenoid muscle stretches the vocal folds. (Color figure online)

4 Future Challenges

Future steps include the selection of materials that meet requirements in terms of mechanical properties for each reproduced component. Vocal folds have been already extensively studied and their production is described in [38]. The elastic cone is a membrane that must be stiff enough to close the glottis, support the vocal folds, and not vibrate with the airflow, but, at the same time, it must be elastic enough not to impair the movements of the vocal folds. Unfortunately, the elastic cone has never been characterized from a mechanical point of view, thus quantitative data are currently missing. In any case, it could be possible to refer to a range of elastic moduli between the tendon, whose modulus is comparable to that of vocal folds, and the cartilage [39]. The same lack of data applies to the cricoid cartilage, but a reasonable approximation may be represented by the tracheal ring (average elastic modulus of 4 MPa) [40–42]. For both the elastic cone, within which the vocal folds need to be integrated, and the larynx cartilages, a thorough evaluation of available elastomers needs to be performed and mechanical testing should consider their deformation and rate in operative conditions.

One of the biggest challenges ahead is the selection and development of the most suitable actuation technology to replicate the most important active capabilities of the larynx: the motion of the vocal folds. However, the motion pattern of the vocal folds involves two different planes. At rest, the vocal folds must be open (also for safety reasons, in case of failure). A first movement is the closure of the vocal folds, mimicking the action of the lateral cricoarytenoid muscle, so that the subject can speak through their vibrations. A second movement should result in the tension of the vocal folds, mimicking the action of the thyroarytenoid muscle, to ensure a tight closure of the glottis when swallowing. A spring-back must guarantee the reopening of the vocal folds and the glottis. The two different and sequential movements must be performed in no more than 0.5 s. The actuator must allow a glottal opening of 15 mm and a tension of the vocal fold of 30% of their initial length [37]. Moreover, the actuator must have enough force to move not only the vocal folds but also the elastic cone they are attached to.

A final yet important open point regards the durability of the device. Currently, voice prostheses have limited durability, thus they are designed to be easily extracted and replaced periodically, without any surgery. This is a valid a safe approach, but how the entire artificial organ can be removed without the need for surgery remains an open question. Another possibility is to develop a device conceived for long-term implantation. In this case, it would be necessary to consider very carefully the material properties also in terms of antibiofilm and wear of the prosthesis, due to the continuous passage of air and food, and the practically uninterrupted movement of the vocal folds.

5   Conclusions

The larynx is one of the smallest but also one of the most complex organs of the entire human body. In order to create an artificial larynx, simplification is necessary.

To do that, we looked at the animal kingdom to find the basic laryngeal structures and movements, common to different species among Tetrapoda, from sauropsids to therapsids to mammals. We used these simpler models as a guide for proper simplification of the human larynx.

Hence, based on these cross-species study, we proposed a new design for a human artificial larynx. Our model includes a motionless ring-shape cricoid cartilage, which gives the structure to the larynx and allows the connection to the trachea. The arytenoid cartilages are essential in all analyzed species, and they will be included in the actuation system. We considered the movements given by only three muscles: the opening of the vocal folds by the posterior cricoarytenoid muscle, their closure by the lateral cricoarytenoid muscle, and their tension by the thyroarytenoid muscle.

We obtained a design that aims to be the basic architectural skeleton of a total artificial larynx, able to perform all the three functions of the natural larynx (breathing, protection, and phonation).

Moreover, we suggested some suitable materials for the creation of the various components of the prosthesis, as well as, the ongoing challenges in its implementation were presented. Finally, the functionality and validity of this new design will be tested in the near future.

Acknowledgments. This work has been partially supported by Consorzio Interuniversitario Istituto Nazionale di Ricerche in Foniatria "Guido Bartalena" (INRF) and Fondazione Terzo Pilastro – Internazionale through the Larynx project.

References

1. Piazza, C., Ribeiro, J.C., Bernal-Sprekelsen, M., Paiva, A., Peretti, G.: Anatomy and physiology of the larynx and hypopharynx. In: Anniko, M., Bernal-Sprekelsen, M., Bonkowsky, V., Bradley, P.J., Iurato, S. (eds.) Otorhinolaryngology, Head and Neck Surgery, pp. 461–471. Springer, Heidelberg (2010). https://doi.org/10.1007/978-3-540-68940-9_49
2. Hirano, M., Kakita, Y.: Cover-body theory vocal fold vibration. In: Daniloff, R (ed.) Speech Science, pp. 1–46 (1985)
3. Simpson, B., Rosen, C.: Operative Techniques in Laryngology. Springer, Heidelberg (2008). https://doi.org/10.1007/978-3-540-68107-6
4. Cancer Today [Internet] (2023). https://gco.iarc.fr/today/home. Accessed 24 May 2023
5. Provox® Vega™ - Atos Medical [Internet] (2023). https://www.atosmedical.it/product/provox-vega. Accessed 24 May 2023
6. Tyburek, K., Mikołajewski, D., Rojek, I.: Analysis of phonetic segments of oesophageal speech in people following total laryngectomy. Appl. Sci. **13**(8), 4995 (2023)
7. Oe, K.: An electrolarynx control method using myoelectric signals from the neck. J. Robot. Mechatron. **33**(4), 804–813 (2021)
8. Laschi, C., Mazzolai, B., Cianchetti, M.: Soft robotics: technologies and systems pushing the boundaries of robot abilities. Sci. Robot. **1**(1), eaah3690 (2016)
9. Wilczynski, W., McClelland, B.E., Rand, A.S.: Acoustic, auditory, and morphological divergence in three species of neotropical frog. J. Comp. Physiol. A **172**(4), 425–438 (1993). https://doi.org/10.1007/BF00213524
10. Shen, J.X.: Ultrasonic vocalization in amphibians and the structure of their vocal apparatus. In: Handbook of Behavioral Neuroscience [Internet], pp. 481–491. Elsevier (2018). https://linkinghub.elsevier.com/retrieve/pii/B9780128096000000457. Accessed 23 May 2023
11. Suthers, R.A., et al.: Voices of the dead: complex nonlinear vocal signals from the larynx of an ultrasonic frog. J. Exp. Biol. **209**(24), 4984–4993 (2006)
12. Yager, D.D.: A unique sound production mechanism in the pipid anuran *Xenopus borealis*. Zool. J. Linn. Soc. **104**(4), 351–375 (1992)
13. Araújo, O.G.S., Pugener, L.A., Haddad, C.F.B., Da Silva, H.R.: Morphology and development of the hyolaryngeal apparatus of *Pipa arrabali* (Anura: Pipidae). Zool. Anz. **269**, 78–88 (2017)
14. Hermida, G.N., Farías, A.: Morphology and histology of the larynx of the common toad *Rhinella arenarum* (Hensel, 1867) (Anura, Bufonidae). Acta Zool. **90**(4), 326–338 (2009)
15. Lagorio, A.D., Grewal, K., Djuhari, S., Le, K., Mulhim, R., Gridi-Papp, M.: The Arylabialis Muscle of the Túngara Frog (*Engystomops pustulosus*). Anat. Rec. **303**(7), 1966–1976 (2020)
16. Narins, P.M., Fay, R.R., Feng, A.S., Popper, A.N.: Hearing and Sound Communication in Amphibians. Springer, New York (2006). https://doi.org/10.1007/978-0-387-47796-1
17. Brumm, H., Zollinger, S.A.: Vocal plasticity in a reptile. Proc. Roy. Soc. B Biol. Sci. **284**(1855), 20170451 (2017)
18. Sacchi, R., Galeotti, P., Fasola, M., Gerzeli, G.: Larynx morphology and sound production in three species of Testudinidae. J. Morphol. **261**(2), 175–183 (2004)
19. Polanco, J.B.A., Mamprim, M.J., Silva, J.P., Inamassu, L.R., Schimming, B.C.: Computed tomographic and radiologic anatomy of the lower respiratory tract in the red-foot tortoise (*Chelonoidis carbonaria*). Pesquisa Veterinária Bras. **40**(8), 637–646 (2020)
20. Fraher, J., et al.: Opening and closing mechanisms of the leatherback sea turtle larynx: a crucial role for the tongue. J. Exp. Biol. **213**(24), 4137–4145 (2010)
21. Riede, T., Li, Z., Tokuda, I.T., Farmer, C.G.: Functional morphology of the *Alligator mississippiensis* larynx with implications for vocal production. J. Exp. Biol. **218**(7), 991–998 (2015)

22. Riede, T., Tokuda, I.T., Farmer, C.G.: Subglottal pressure and fundamental frequency control in contact calls of juvenile *Alligator mississippiensis*. J. Exp. Biol. **214**(18), 3082–3095 (2011)
23. Russell, A.P., Bauer, A.M.: Vocalization by extant nonavian reptiles: a synthetic overview of phonation and the vocal apparatus. Anat. Rec. **304**(7), 1478–1528 (2021)
24. Yoshida, J., Kobayashi, Y., Norell, M.A.: An ankylosaur larynx provides insights for bird-like vocalization in non-avian dinosaurs. Commun. Biol. **6**(1), 152 (2023)
25. Riede, T., Goller, F.: Peripheral mechanisms for vocal production in birds – differences and similarities to human speech and singing. Brain Lang. **115**(1), 69–80 (2010)
26. Schmidt, M.F., Wild, J.M.: The respiratory-vocal system of songbirds. In: Progress in Brain Research [Internet], pp. 297–335. Elsevier (2014). https://linkinghub.elsevier.com/retrieve/pii/B978044463488700015X. Accessed 23 May2023
27. Suthers, R.A.: Vocal mechanisms in birds and bats: a comparative view. Anais Acad. Bras. Ciênc. **76**(2), 247–252 (2004)
28. Elemans, C.P.H., et al.: Universal mechanisms of sound production and control in birds and mammals. Nat. Commun. **6**(1), 8978 (2015)
29. Homberger, D.G.: The avian lingual and laryngeal apparatus within the context of the head and jaw apparatus, with comparisons to the mammalian condition: functional morphology and biomechanics of evaporative cooling, feeding, drinking, and vocalization. In: Maina, J.N. (ed.) The Biology of the Avian Respiratory System, pp. 27–97. Springer, Cham (2017). https://doi.org/10.1007/978-3-319-44153-5_2
30. Riede, T., Titze, I.R.: Vocal fold elasticity of the Rocky Mountain elk (*Cervus elaphus nelsoni*) – producing high fundamental frequency vocalization with a very long vocal fold. J. Exp. Biol. **211**(13), 2144–2154 (2008)
31. Frey, R., Volodin, I., Volodina, E., Soldatova, N.V., Juldaschev, E.T.: Descended and mobile larynx, vocal tract elongation and rutting roars in male goitred gazelles (*Gazella subgutturosa*Güldenstaedt, 1780): goitred gazelle vocal anatomy and rutting calls. J. Anat. **218**(5), 566–585 (2011)
32. Klemuk, S.A., Riede, T., Walsh, E.J., Titze, I.R.: Adapted to roar: functional morphology of tiger and lion vocal folds. PLoS ONE **6**(11), e27029 (2011)
33. Frey, R., Gebler, A.: Mechanisms and evolution of roaring-like vocalization in mammals. In: Handbook of Behavioral Neuroscience [Internet], pp. 439–450. Elsevier (2010). https://linkinghub.elsevier.com/retrieve/pii/S1569733910700540. Accessed 23 May 2023
34. Frey, R., Volodin, I., Volodina, E.: A nose that roars: anatomical specializations and behavioural features of rutting male saiga. J. Anat. **211**(6), 717–736 (2007)
35. Reidenberg, J.S., Laitman, J.T.: Discovery of a low frequency sound source in Mysticeti (baleen whales): anatomical establishment of a vocal fold homolog. Anat. Rec. Adv. Integr. Anat. Evol. Biol. **290**(6), 745–759 (2007)
36. Reidenberg, J.S., Laitman, J.T.: Generation of sound in marine mammals. In: Handbook of Behavioral Neuroscience [Internet], pp. 451–465. Elsevier (2010). https://linkinghub.elsevier.com/retrieve/pii/S1569733910700552. Accessed 23 May2023
37. Deguchi, S., Kawahara, Y., Takahashi, S.: Cooperative regulation of vocal fold morphology and stress by the cricothyroid and thyroarytenoid muscles. J. Voice **25**(6), e255–e263 (2011)
38. Conte, A., et al.: A biorobotic simulator of vocal folds for the reproduction and analysis of electroglottographic signals. In: 2021 IEEE 4th International Conference on Soft Robotics (RoboSoft) [Internet], New Haven, CT, USA, pp. 90–96. IEEE (2021).https://ieeexplore.ieee.org/document/9479296/. Accessed 23 May 2023
39. Liu, J., Zheng, H., Poh, P., Machens, H.G., Schilling, A.: Hydrogels for engineering of perfusable vascular networks. Int. J. Mol. Sci. **16**(7), 15997–16016 (2015)
40. Trabelsi, O., Del Palomar, A.P., López-villalobos, J.L., Ginel, A., Doblaré, M.: Experimental characterization and constitutive modeling of the mechanical behavior of the human trachea. Med. Eng. Phys. **32**(1), 76–82 (2010)

41. Pauken, C.M., Heyes, R., Lott, D.G.: Mechanical, cellular, and proteomic properties of laryngotracheal cartilage. Cartilage **10**(3), 321–328 (2019)
42. Demott, C.J., et al.: Ultra-high modulus hydrogels mimicking cartilage of the human body. Macromol. Biosci. **22**(11), 2200283 (2022)

A Multibody Approach for the Finger Force Estimation of a Robotic Hand

Andrea Grazioso[1,2]($\boxtimes$), Chiara Danese[1,2], Giovanni Antonio Zappatore[2], and Giulio Reina[1]

[1] Department of Mechanics, Mathematics and Management, Politecnico di Bari, via Orabona 4, 70126 Bari, Italy
{andrea.grazioso,chiara.danese,giulio.reina}@poliba.it
[2] BionIT Labs Company, Via Cracovia 1, 73010 Soleto, Italy
g.zappatore@bionitlabs.com
https://bionitlabs.com/it/

Abstract. This article focuses on the finger force estimation in Adam's Hand, a polyarticulated myoelectric prosthesis for transradial and upper level amputations. The main features of the prosthesis are briefly discussed and a multibody model of the device is presented. A test is carried out to measure the maximum forces exerted by the distal phalanges when the fingers are in a fully opened configuration and the results are compared with the simulation for a preliminary validation of the model. Goals, instrumentation and methods of the testing campaign are described in detail.

Keywords: Myoelectric-Hand · Prosthetics · Multibody modeling · Finger force estimation · Upper-limb prosthesis · Robotics · Underactuation

1 Introduction

The human hand is a work of art: 21 degrees of freedom for the hand itself, 6 for the wrist, together with the well-known thumb opposition capability, make for an outstanding and powerful tool that can perform highly sophisticated movements, from power to precision tasks, sense the world around as well as operate on it. Unfortunately, the upper limb amputation, intended as the removal of any part of the forearm or arm, severely reduces the user's autonomy and the capability of performing daily living, working and social activities. A serious handicap that afflicts three million people in the world, and this number is constantly increasing: only in Italy and United Kingdom by approximately 9000 every year, 80% of which concerns the hand [1]. As reported in [2], it is estimated that in the United States 185,000 persons lose an upper or lower limb every year.

This research was funded by Regione Puglia in the frame of the RIPARTI project (POC PUGLIA FESR-FSE 2014/2020) entitled "VINCI (GiVIng a haNd To mediCal robotIcs)".

To date, the prosthetic market of the upper limb is worth $ 285 million and by 2027 is estimated that its value will double. Despite the development of new technologies, in the world only 50 % of the amputees wear a prosthesis, while 37 % of them, even if not using any device, say they would reconsider the use of a prosthesis if only technology could be less expensive.

Four types of prosthetic hands are currently used to restore most abilities and human dexterous tasks. Cosmetics are the first of these, they restore the cosmetic appearance, but do not have any actively moving part. Working/recreational prosthesis are customized for a specific function or recreational activity while body-powered prosthesis use body movements to operate flexing of the elbow (transhumeral and higher amputation levels only) and opening and closing of a terminal device (hook or hand). The other type is myoelectric/external powered prosthesis that are powered by a battery system and are usually controlled by EMG signals generated during muscle contractions. There is also a hybrid of the latter two that combine the use of body power and external power [3]. Moreover, prostheses can also be classified on the basis of the level of amputation: transcarpal, wrist disarticulation, transradial, elbow disarticulation, transhumeral, shoulder and forequarter disarticulation.

Among all, myoelectric powered prosthesis represent the most promising method of replicating human hand functionality because of their potential to provide all of the Degrees of Freedom (DoFs) of a human hand in an intuitive manner without any power input from the user [4]. Currently there are many high-performance myoelectric prosthetic hands. Some of these are Bebionic [5], Hero Arm [6], I-Limb Ultra Revolution [7], LUKE Arm (radial configuration) [8], Michelangelo Hand [9], TASKA Hand [10] and VINCENT Evolution 3 [11]. The relevant characteristics that qualify and distinguish the devices are the overall DoFs, number of actuators, available sizes, weight, maximum grasp and carry load, number of grip patterns. These properties were chosen over time from a point of view of usability, which can be the most important factor for the end user [12].

EMG signals can be used to control myoelectric prostheses. They are easier to use in transradial prostheses, as they are compact and easier to place in a prosthetic socket. Most of the sensors are produced by the same companies that develop prosthetic solutions and they are organized according to manufacturer and their configuration, dimensions, weight, gain adjustment, type of terminals and type of signal processing [13]. Usually two or three EMG electrodes are located in the socket in correspondence to specific muscles capable of emitting electrical signals to open and close the prosthetic hand. The number of movements can be increased employing specific (e.g., sequential) control strategies which are usually still far from being natural, thus contributing to the scarce capabilities and acceptance of myoelectric prostheses [14].

One of the main features of a prosthesis is certainly its weight. Although the human hand has an average weight of 400 g, prosthetic hands with the same weight have been reported by users as being too heavy. However, this can depend on many variables, such as the age and gender of the user. Taking this into account, it is important that the users can choose between different options of models that better matches her/his body characteristics. From a general point-of-view, most of the manufacturers have prosthetic hands available in different sizes.

The capacity of performing tasks with higher strength is another user requirement identified in [1]. A study showed the average amount of grasp force required for daily living to be about 68 N [15], a good indicator of the amount of force the prosthesis should exercise. The most common actuator used in prosthetics to achieve the desired performance is a direct current (DC) motor. Small and lightweight motors are used as they can be packaged in the hand or forearm. In order to reduce the speed and increase the limited torque from these devices, gearing, lead screws, and even harmonic drives may be used. Many prosthesis, including Adam's Hand, incorporate non-backdriveable mechanisms for the system to present a higher autonomy and to improve the durability of the actuators; this is due to the fact that, even in the presence of external applied forces, no power is required to hold the fingers in place. Some works found in the literature also recommend the implementation of automated object grasping and slip prevention to reduce the attention of the user, allowing the performing of other parallel tasks [16]. The thumb accounts for up to 40% of the entire functionality of the human hand [17] and its design in any anthropomorphic prosthetic hand is extremely important. In most of the prosthetic hands the thumb is actuated in flexion/extension (simple closing or opening) and features a passive abduction/adduction rotation directly controlled by the user.

2   Adam's Hand

Adam's Hand is a highly innovative robotic hand proposed by BionIT Labs, an emerging developer of prosthetic technology (see Fig. 1). It stands out as one of the most promising polyarticulated myoelectric hand prostheses suitable for upper limb amputations. The name ADAM'S Hand is an acronym for "A Dialogic Adaptive Modular Sensitive" Hand. The device aims to mimic as much as possible the human hand dexterity while reducing the overall complexity of the system through the principle of underactuation [18], i.e., roughly speaking, the driving of a large number of degrees of freedom by means of a limited number of actuators. In other words, the ultimate goal is to power the opening and closing motions of all the fingers collectively with the aid of a single actuator. This is achieved by resorting to differential systems, that is mechanisms "for which the degree of freedom is two and which may accept two inputs to produce one output or, may resolve a single input into two outputs" [19]. The bevel gear differential transmission mechanism patented by the manufacturer of Adam's Hand [20] manages to automatically distribute the power delivered by one actuator, a DC motor, to provide for the flexion/extension of all the proximal and distal phalanges of the index, middle, ring and little fingers; in doing so, it also ensures passive adaptivity: when the motion of one or more fingers is prevented, the remaining finger(s) should continue to move. Moreover, while grabbing an object, the force tends to equally distribute among the fingers, making it possible to apply large grasping forces and a stable grasp [21]. Moreover, as an added benefit of the increased compliance, the hand is particularly robust to external disturbances that tend to open and/or close the fingers, since these compensate each other; this aspect is of utter importance to patients that do not have limb proprioception. Nevertheless, there are many other underactuated prostheses, one of the most important is the Pisa/IIT SoftHand [22], that uses a continuous tendon transmission to achieve a differential effect. The second DC motor equipped by Adam's Hand drives the flexion/extension motion of the thumb, whose abduction is instead passively controlled by the user.

Fig. 1. Adam's Hand by BionIT Labs.

As shown in Fig. 1, the terminal device is secured to the user's stump by means of a prosthetic socket custom-made by the orthopedic technician; the connection between these two components is guaranteed by a quick-disconnect wrist unit which represents the industry standard and allows passive pronosupination of the prosthetic hand. Alternately, a demonstration unit can be used to test Adam's Hand without the prosthetic socket. Moreover, Adam's Hand is meant to be used in combination with a cosmetic glove that improves aesthetics and makes the prosthesis waterproof and dustproof.

3   Multibody Modeling of Adam's Hand

The ultimate purpose of the present work is to develop a multibody model of the prosthesis Adam's Hand. Such goal, given the complexity of the system being modeled, has to be tackled by relying on specifically dedicated software, in order to leverage on the increasing availability of computational resources [23,24].

The software chosen for the task in question is MSC Adams (acronym for Automated Dynamic Analysis of Mechanical Systems), used both in academic research and engineering; in particular, the graphical user interface of the multi-purpose View suite is used to place and connect together all the required elements. As suggested by Fig. 2, a divide-and-conquer strategy is adopted in pursuing the objective, as the overall structure of the hand prosthesis is split into six major submodels: one for each of the four fingers (index, middle, ring and pinkie), the differential drive mechanism and the frame. These submodels are first modeled and tested independently from one another, then copied and joined together to form the final complete assembly. As evident from Fig. 2, particular care is devoted in importing into MSC Adams the Parasolid files of the real CAD geometries and assigning them to the corresponding rigid parts of the different subsystems: this not only as an assist to the visualization, but also as a way to compute the inertial properties of various parts and compare them to those of the real counterparts.

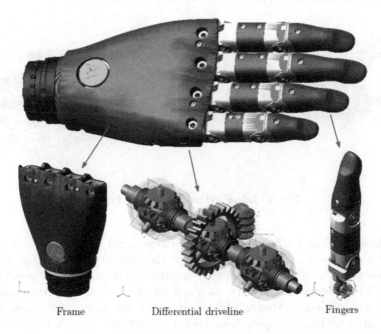

Frame   Differential driveline   Fingers

Fig. 2. Multibody model of Adam's Hand.

The frame submodel is simply constituted of one rigid part to which the other elements, namely the differential line and the fingers, are constrained. The single finger comprises two phalanges: the proximal phalanx is hinged to the frame of the hand at one end and to the distal phalanx at the other end. Both the joints, named metacarpal phalanx (MCP) and distal interphalanx (DIP) respectively, are modeled as revolute joints that allow the rotation about axes perpendicular to the plane in which the flexion/extension motion of the finger takes place. Consequently each finger has two degrees of freedom with respect to the palm of the hand, while one single torque input is provided from the differential drive for actuation. The power delivered by the motor through the differential stages actuates the gear train for the finger to open and close as requested by the user.

Since the mechanism is underactuated, the trajectory followed by the finger is not known a priori as it depends on the shape and position of the object being grasped.

The submodel of the differential driveline represents the core of the digital twin of Adam's Hand, since it is the foundation of the passive grasping capability exhibited by the prosthesis in question. In Fig. 3, a schematic representation of the differential driveline of Adam's Hand is reported. As already mentioned, Adam's Hand is driven by only two motors, the first enables the movement of index, middle, ring and pinkie, the second allows the thumb flexion/extension. Adam's hand has an underactuated, intuitive and easy-to-use mechanism that adapts to the shape and size of the object thanks to the differential mechanism shown in Fig. 3. The main DC motor is coupled with a 26:1 gear reducer, so that the generated electromechanical torque undergoes a first increase. The resulting torque, indicated as T_{gm} in Fig. 3, is applied to the worm screw of a worm gearset and represents the only input to the differential line. The torque applied to the

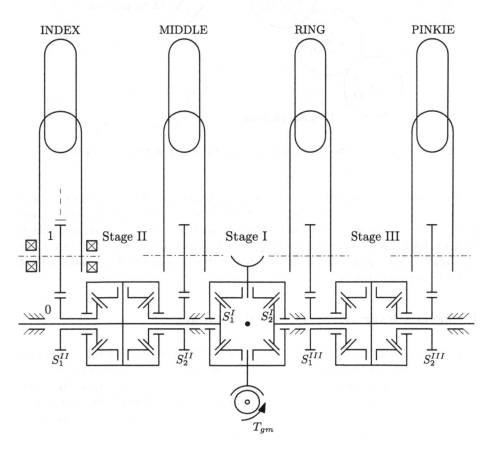

Fig. 3. Differential driveline scheme of Adam's Hand.

drive gear of the index finger, indicated with the number 1 in Fig. 3, is calculated from T_{gm} according to the following equation

$$T_1 = T_{gm} \cdot \eta \cdot \tau \tag{1}$$

where τ and η are the reduction ratio and the efficiency of the transmission line from the worm gear to gear 1 that is assumed approximately equal to 30%. A kinematic scheme of the gear train for a typical two-phalanx finger is shown in Fig. 4.

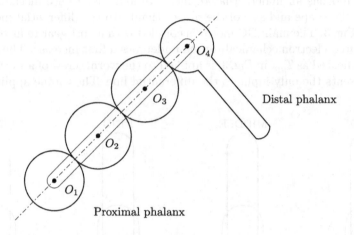

Fig. 4. Kinematic scheme of the gear train for a typical two-phalanx finger.

The result of the meticulous modeling of the described mechanism is shown at the bottom center of Fig. 2. The model comprises 54 moving parts, constrained to each other by means of 54 revolute joints and 61 gear force instances. Each phalanx joint features a rotational spring. It takes about 5 min to run a 5-s simulation of the opening and closing cycle of the fingers, obtained using a Intel i-7 CPU working at 2.7 GHz.

4   Forces Exerted by Distal Phalanges

As directly linked with the intended use of the prosthesis, the forces expressed by the fingers are of primary importance. Therefore, an experimental setup is proposed to measure such forces in a clear and simple way, having at the same time the necessity to use as few tools and resources as possible. The performed test is shortly described and the obtained values are assumed as a basis for a preliminary validation of the multibody model.

4.1   Experimental Test

The purpose of the performed test is to assess the forces that the whole mechanism of Adam's Hand is capable of expressing at the finger tips. The test is carried out using a bench vice, a Demo Unit and ThunderCell Battery for the power supply and a digital gauge by SAMA Tools for measuring the force. The test facility is illustrated in Fig. 5: the Demo Unit with Adam's Hand is clamped in the vice to firmly secure it in place during testing. Given that the output power of the prosthesis depends on many factors, the battery state of charge being one of the prominent, care is taken to ensure that the ThunderCell Battery is fully charged to perform all the repetitions under the same conditions.

The prosthesis is positioned with the back facing the work table on which the force gauge is fixed; this choice is dictated by the express intention of executing the tests by letting the fingers, each one at a time, pull rather than press: in this way the tractive interaction between the tested finger and the measurement device is much more stable than the compressive one that would result if the test were to be performed by pushing against the probe. Therefore, a cable (a fishing wire featuring a maximum allowed traction load of 350 N) is used to tie the distal phalanx to the hooked probe of the force gauge.

The force gauge is anchored to the plate of a fixture system (see Fig. 5). Since the prosthesis is held in place and not moved during the tests, each one of the fingers is at a different height with respect to the workbench, so that a versatile way to reposition the measuring instrument is needed. Four screws inserted into the threaded holes at the corners of the fixture plate are used to this end: by fastening these screws the gauge can be lowered or raised at will, thus preventing the traction cable to be angled. The single test is executed by powering the prosthesis through the Demo Unit. All the fingers close with the exception of the tested one that starts to pull the wire while the gauge samples the traction force with a frequency of 10 Hz. An on/off drive mode is selected to power the prosthesis through the Demo Unit, i.e. the maximum allowed current is supplied to the motor according to the limit set on firmware for the normal mode. In this way, it is possible to evaluate the maximum gripping force that can be exerted by each finger. At the beginning of each test, special care is given that the finger under test does not hit the hard stop of the distal joint, as this would introduce an additional factor in the analysis.

Fig. 5. Test facility.

4.2   Multibody Simulation: Results and Comparison

A simulation of the multibody model represented in Fig. 2 is arranged to numerically replicate the force test described in the preceding section. The goal is to perform a preliminary validation of the multibody model by comparing the numerical results with the outcome of the experimental test. As shown in Fig. 6 the cable used during the test to hook the distal phalanx to the probe of the force gauge is modeled as a spring force. The action and reaction points of such force belong to the distal phalanx part and to the ground part respectively (points A and B in Fig. 6(b)).

Both these markers are placed to exactly match the position at which the cable is tied during the experimental test. The stiffness of the spring is specified by importing into the software a spline that defines the relationship of force F to deformation s according to the following equation

$$F(s) = Ks \left(\frac{\arctan \alpha s}{\pi} + \frac{1}{2} \right) \tag{2}$$

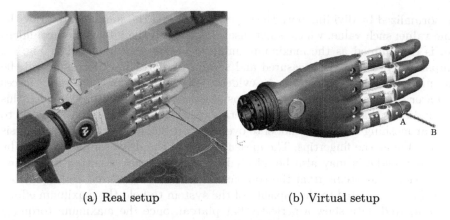

(a) Real setup   (b) Virtual setup

Fig. 6. Experimental setup in (a) real and (b) virtual environment.

where $K = 5 \cdot 10^3 \, \text{N/mm}$ is the traction stiffness of the linkage between the tested finger and the measurement device, and α is a dimensionless factor. By assigning a value of 800 to α, Eq. (2) ensures that the stiffness sharply yet continuously transitions from almost zero when $s < 0$ up to the desired value K for $s > 0$, thus resembling the behaviour of a pulling cable.

The simulations are performed by applying a torque to the screw of the worm gearset that constitutes the input to the differential drivetrain shown in Fig. 3. The magnitude of such torque has to be carefully chosen in accordance with that provided by the gearmotor equipped by the prosthesis. Considered that the torque constant of the electric motor is equal to 4.44 Nmm/A and the supplied current reaches a maximum value of 3 A in normal operation mode, a driving torque of 277 Nmm is to be expected if an efficiency equal to 0.83 is assumed for the 26:1 speed reducer. The torque is applied through a step command that approximates the Heaviside step function with a cubic polynomial as follows

$$T = \begin{cases} T_0 & \text{if } t \leq t_0 \\ T_0 - a\Delta^2 \left(3 - 2\Delta\right) & \text{if } t_0 < t < t_1 \\ T_1 & \text{if } t \geq t_1 \end{cases} \tag{3}$$

where $a = T_1 - T_0$ is the difference between the torque T_1 at the final time t_1 and the torque T_0 at the initial time t_0, and $\Delta = (t - t_0) / (t_1 - t_0)$. By suitably imposing the initial conditions, the simulations are performed starting from a configuration in which all fingers are fully closed except for the tested one which is instead open and hooked to the pulling cable. The function (3) is then set to smoothly ramp up the torque from zero up to the desired final value in 1.7 s, in order to mimic the gradually increasing torque provided by the motor. In all cases the actuation starts at the time $t_0 = 1 \, \text{s}$.

During the simulations, as the fingers other than the tested one fully close, the force due to the elongation of the cable spring increases and finally reaches the steady value representing the maximum finger force. The results shown below are normalized by dividing both the experimental and the simulated data by the same value: such value, which is not disclosed to keep the information confidential, is determined as the maximum simulated force. In Fig. 7 and in Fig. 8 a comparison between the measured and simulated normalized forces for all the four modeled fingers is shown. As evident, all the measured maximum forces are lower than those computed by means of the proposed multibody model: this may indicate that the lack of losses terms other than the friction assigned to the gear meshing causes the model to overestimate the forces that the prosthesis can develop at the fingertips. The measurement of the drive torque provided by the real prosthesis may also be affected by uncertainties. Another interesting observation that stems from the comparison between measured and simulated force curves is related to the capacity of the system to hold the maximum effort: the computed data show a perfectly flat plateau once the maximum torque is reached; thanks to the presence of a self-locking worm-gear drive, the force firmly holds its value even when the driving torque is removed. Differently, the real measurements highlight in all cases a slight force decrease once the motor ceases to provide torque to the worm gear. This may be due to the relaxation of the stresses of all the components placed between the driving couple and the fingertips, which are obviously not infinitely rigid as those that populate the model. Therefore, such phenomenon cannot be captured by the model, unless special flexible bodies are introduced as compliance terms. Finally, the rising of torque depends on the dynamics of the pulling cable, as it affects how much the force oscillates in the first rising region and how rapidly it increases in the second rising region. The discrepancies between real and simulated rising edges that can be seen in Fig. 8, can be also explained by considering the approximation introduced in the simulation when modelling the cable as a single spring element rather than a series of discrete elements.

In Table 1 the maximum values of the measured and simulated normalized forces are reported: As highlighted in the last column, despite the limitations previously suggested by the analysis of the curves, the percentage differences are satisfactory, thus proving the effectiveness of a relatively simpler model in mimicking much of the behaviour of the analyzed mechanical system. The forces reported in Table 1 are computed taking into account the transmission efficiency.

Table 1. Normalized force exerted by the fingers: comparison between measured and simulated maximum values.

Finger	Measured Force [−]	Simulated Force [−]	Difference [%]
Index	0.77	0.79	+2.0
Middle	0.62	0.64	+2.3
Ring	0.85	0.88	+2.9
Little	0.97	1.00	+2.9

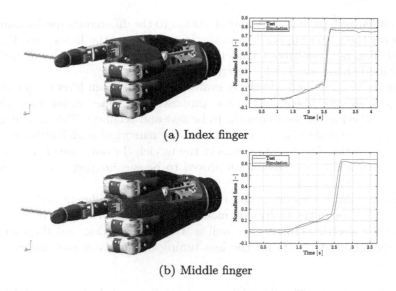

Fig. 7. Comparison between real and simulated normalized force for (a) index and (b) middle finger.

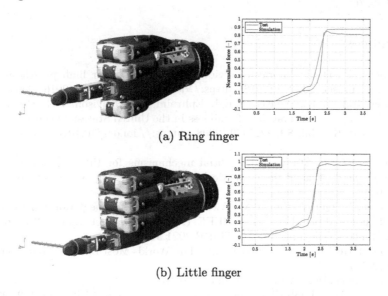

Fig. 8. Comparison between real and simulated normalized force for (a) ring and (b) little finger.

5   Conclusions and Future Developments

In this paper, we introduced Adam's Hand, a myoelectric hand prosthesis suitable for transradial and upper level amputations. The main features of the device were summarized, paying particular attention to the differential mechanism that distributes the power supplied by a single actuator to the index, middle, ring and little fingers. A multibody model specially developed to create a digital twin of the robotic hand was briefly described.

In order to easily and effectively evaluate the maximum forces expressed by the fingers, an experimental setup was proposed that relies on few tools readily available, allowing the measurement to be fast and accurate. The measured values were used to perform a first validation of the numerical model: although there is room for further future refinements of the model, the outcome of the comparison between reality and simulation proved to be encouraging, with percentage differences lower than 3%.

Hopefully, future research efforts will be focused on different activities, such as the integration of the multibody model with subsystems of the thumb assembly and the electric actuators, as well as the identification and the execution of specific laboratory tests for the fine tuning of numerous parameters of the model.

Acknowledgements. The financial support of the project Agricultural inTeroperabiLity and Analysis System (ATLAS), H2020 (Grant No. 857125) is gratefully acknowledged.

References

1. Cordella, F., et al.: Literature review on needs of upper limb prosthesis users. Front. Neurosci. **10**, 209 (2016). https://doi.org/10.3389/fnins.2016.00209
2. Ziegler-Graham, K., MacKensie, E.J., Ephraim, P.L., Travison, T.G., Brookmeyer, R.: Estimating the prevalence of limb loss in the United States: 2005 to 2050. Arch. Phys. Med. Rehabil. **89**, 422–429 (2008). https://doi.org/10.1016/j.apmr.2007.11.005
3. Zappatore G.A., Study of differential mechanisms for the underactuation of a robotic hand, Master thesis in Mechanical Engeneering, University of Salento (2016)
4. Damerla, R., Qiu, Y., Sun, T.M., Awtar, S.: A review of the performance of extrinsically powered prosthetic hands. IEEE Trans. Med. Robot. Bionics **3**(3), 640–660 (2021). https://doi.org/10.1109/TMRB.2021.3100612
5. Ottobock Healthcare GmbH. BeBionic: The Worlds Most Lifelike Bionic Hand, pp. 1–3 (2017)
6. Open Bionics. Hero Arm User Manual (2019)
7. Touch Bionics. I-Limb Ultra Revolution Brochure, no. 694 5462, pp. 1–2 (2013)
8. Mobius Bionics. Luke Arm System Datasheet (2017)
9. Otto bock Healthcare GmbH. Fascinated with Michelangelo (2017)
10. Taska Prosthetics, "Taska Hand," 2018. [Online]. Available: http://www.taskaprosthetics.com. [Accessed: 19-Feb-2019]
11. Vincent Systems. VINCENTevolution3: design and function in perfection (2019)
12. Belter, J.T., Segil, J.L., Dollar, A.M., Weir, R.F.: Mechanical design and performance specifications of anthropomorphic prosthetic hands: a review. J. Rehabil. Res. Dev. **50**(5), 599–618 (2013). https://doi.org/10.1682/JRRD.2011.10.0188

13. Calado, A., Soares, F., Matos, D.: A review on commercially available anthropo-morphic myoelectric prosthetic hands, pattern-recognition-based microcontrollers and sEMG sensors used for prosthetic control. In: 2019 IEEE International Conference on Autonomous Robot Systems and Competitions (ICARSC), Porto, Portugal, pp. 1–6 (2019). https://doi.org/10.1109/ICARSC.2019.8733629
14. Atzori, M., Müller, H.: Control capabilities of myoelectric robotic prostheses by hand amputees: a scientific research and market overview. Front. Syst. Neurosci. **9**, 162 (2015). https://doi.org/10.3389/fnsys.2015.00162. PMID: 26648850; PMCID: PMC4663252
15. Belter, J.T., Dollar, A.M.: Performance characteristics of anthropomorphic prosthetic hands. In: IEEE International Conference on Rehabilitation Robotics (2011)
16. Hermens, H., et al.: Myoelectric forearm prostheses: state of the art from a user-centered perspective. J. Rehabil. Res. Dev. **48**(6), 719 (2011)
17. Ouellette, E.A., McAuliffe, J.A., Caneiro, R.: Partial-hand amputations: surgical principles. Atlas of Limb Prothetics: Surgical, Prosthetic, and Rehabilitation Principles, Chapter 7A (1992)
18. Birglen, L., Laliberté, T., Gosselin, C.: Springer Tracts in Advanced Robotics, Underactuated Robotic Hands. Springer, Heidelberg (2008). https://doi.org/10.1007/978-3-540-77459-4
19. IFToMM: terminology for the theory of machines and mechanisms. Mech. Mach. Theor. **26**(5), 435–539 (1991)
20. Zappatore G.A., Dimastrogiovanni M., Longo A., Tinella D., Accogli A.: Mano robotica Sottoattuata. Registration number 102022000012392, Ministry of Economic Development, Italian Patent and Trademark Office (2022)
21. Zappatore, G.A., Reina, G., Messina, A.: Analysis of a highly underactuated robotic hand. Int. J. Mech. Control **18**(2), 17–24 (2018)
22. Catalano, M.G., Grioli, G., Farnioli, E., Serio, A., Piazza, C., Bicchi, A.: Adaptive synergies for the design and control of the Pisa/IIT SoftHand. Int. J. Robot. Res. **33**(5), 768–782 (2014). https://doi.org/10.1177/0278364913518998
23. Grazioso, A., Galati, R., Mantriota, G., Reina, G.: Multibody simulation of a novel tracked robot with innovative passive suspension. In: Niola, V., Gasparetto, A., Quaglia, G., Carbone, G. (eds.) IFToMM Italy 2022. Mechanisms and Machine Science, vol. 122, pp. 139–146. Springer, Cham (2022). https://doi.org/10.1007/978-3-031-10776-4_17
24. Grazioso, A., Ugenti, A., Galati, R., Mantriota, G., Reina, G.: Introducing Polibot: a high mobility tracked robot with innovative passive suspensions. In: 11th Asia-Pacific Regional Conference of the ISTVS (2022)

A Pneumatic Bending Actuator System Inspired by the Avian Tendon Locking Mechanism

Peter Kappel[1,2](✉) (iD), Lukas Kürner[1,2] (iD), Thomas Speck[1,2,3] (iD), and Falk Tauber[1,2] (iD)

[1] Plant Biomechanics Group (PBG) Freiburg, Botanic Garden of the University of Freiburg, University of Freiburg, Freiburg im Breisgau, Germany
peter.kappel@biologie.uni-freiburg.de

[2] Cluster of Excellence livMatS @ FIT – Freiburg Center for Interactive Materials and Bioinspired Technologies, University of Freiburg, Freiburg im Breisgau, Germany

[3] Freiburg Center for Interactive Materials and Bioinspired Technologies (FIT), University of Freiburg, Freiburg im Breisgau, Germany

Abstract. The tendon locking mechanism (TLM) in the avian foot allows birds to perch on a tree or grasp prey for long periods of time with low energy input. In this study, we present a soft robotic pneumatic bending actuator system inspired by the TLM, consisting of three flexible main components. The first component is an index finger-sized soft robotic pneumatic bending actuator (SPA) with a 90° pre-curved shape that stretches in the opposite direction to classical designs when pressurized. The other two components are a tendon that interconnects the SPA's air chambers and a soft pneumatic tendon sheath (SPTS) that can lock the movement of the tendon. The SPTS requires 160 kPa of pressurized air to release the tendon and locks it through an elastic ligament-based design when actuation stops. The bending actuator can thus be fully stretched with as little as 60 kPa, while generating up to 4.61 ± 0.38 N of block force. This design allows the construction of grippers that can be operated at low air pressure and do not require actuation while gripping and holding objects.

Keywords: Soft robotics · Soft machines · Biomimetics · Additive manufacturing · FDM printing

1 Introduction

Soft machines are a promising alternative to classical rigid robots. That is because they are particularly suitable for applications in which their soft, compliant properties are advantageous, such as in interaction with sensitive objects and living creatures like humans [1]. Due to these properties, soft machines are also ideal for abstracting and transferring principles of soft and elastic movements from animate nature. To recreate such animate movements, soft machines depend on actuators that can use various mechanism to generate motions such as flexion, extension, elongation, contraction, twisting or a combination thereof [2]. Commonly, actuation principles that can be integrated into the flexible material are used, like soft fluid actuators with pneumatic networks (Pneu-Nets) [3]. PneuNets are widely used, as they are easy to manufacture and are actuated

© The Author(s), under exclusive license to Springer Nature Switzerland AG 2023
F. Meder et al. (Eds.): Living Machines 2023, LNAI 14158, pp. 84–100, 2023.
https://doi.org/10.1007/978-3-031-39504-8_6

by compressed air, which is a well-established energy source in industrial and research facilities. PneuNet actuators are hollow structures made from elastic material. The hollow cavity is subdivided into interconnected chambers, the so-called pneumatic network, whose walls expand when pressurized. By "strategically" arranging air chambers and selectively thinning the sidewalls of the chambers facing each other, it is possible to create membranes that expand in a predetermined direction and interact with each other, resulting in bending deformations of the actuator [4].

Pneumatic bending actuators are ideal fingers in soft robotic grippers because they can generate the required deformation themselves [5]. However, a disadvantage of PneuNet actuators is that they require continuous actuation for as long as they are intended to bend, and the force generated is in proportion to the air pressure applied. Moreover, sustaining deformation during actuation can make the actuators susceptible to leakage and wear [6].

To overcome the need for continuous actuation, researchers have developed bi-stable actuators [7, 8], actuators with changes in stiffness [9–11], and pre-stretched constructions [12]. These innovations can improve the reliability and longevity of pneumatic bending actuators, making them more practical for use in soft robotics. Pre-stretching is a particular interesting solution since it can negate the need for a permanent pressurization for closure. Pal et al. (2019) for example used air pressure in the opposite way for stretching instead of bending [12]. Pre-stretching the expandable silicone layer with the pneumatic cavities and gluing it to an expansion-limiting layer resulted in bending with sufficient force for gripping and holding due to the relaxation of the material when unpressurized. Nevertheless, even with such a pre-stretched construction, the absolute air pressure needed for actuation increases in proportion with the force the actuator can generate.

As noted above, due to their inherent compliance, soft robots are ideal for application in human-machine interaction or at places with unpredictable conditions. Such applications could be autonomous service robots or active parts of prosthetics. In such scenarios, constant access to pneumatic infrastructure is often not reliably available, meaning their energy supply has to be autonomous too. Solutions for providing an autonomous pressure supply could be compressed air cartridges that have a limited reservoir or autonomous pumps that provide compressed air onboard from another energy source [13, 14]. An example for a state-of-the-art onboard pressure generator is a credit card sized pneumatic pump that generates 2.34 kPa air pressure at an applied voltage of 8 kV [14].

Accordingly, reducing the air pressure required by actuator systems bring pneumatic soft robotics closer to autonomous applications. The air pressure for pneumatic bending actuators can be reduced if the elements that stabilize the actuator in the flexed state do not work against an intended straightening, as shown for the pre-stretched actuator. One solution is to change the stiffness of the actuator depending on the desired state. This can be achieved, for example, by implementing a backbone made of a second stiffer material whose stiffness can be thermally changed, such as a shape memory material [11].

This study aims to create a pneumatic bending actuator system that requires reduced air pressure. As such this paper presents a pneumatic bending actuator system based on the avian tendon locking mechanism (TLM, Fig. 1A), which would allow the bending actuator to be actuated with low air pressure while maintaining a high blocking force. The TLM is a mechanism in the foot of birds, such as the American crow (*Corvus brachyrhynchos*), that allows the flexor tendon to run freely through the tendon sheath until flexion of the digit occurs. Flexion causes the tendon sheath and the dorsal side of the tendon to come into contact with their structures, which results in the locking of the movement of the tendon. This allows the flexion of the digit to be maintained with little energy expenditure when grasping prey or tree branches [15]. Figure 1B schematically shows how the actuator system could be constructed from a pre-curved pneumatic network actuator, with a soft pneumatic tendon sheath (SPTS) and a flexible tendon. Since 3D printing allows the fabrication of designs with more complex geometries and pneumatic networks, all parts could be printed by Fused Deposition Modeling (FDM). The high tensile strength of the flexible filaments [6] also enables the realization of new and more complex designs.

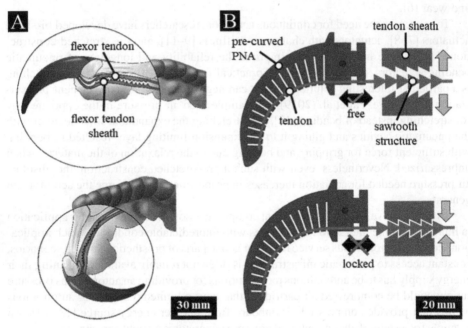

Fig. 1. Avian tendon locking mechanism (TLM) and a schematic for the construction of a TLM inspired bending actuator system with pneumatic network and tendon. **A:** A longitudinal section of digit II of the foot of the American Crow (*Corvus brachyrhynchos*) illustrates the TLM. During extension of the digit (upper schema), the flexor tendon (red) can move freely, while flexion of the digit (lower schema) leads to contact and engagement between the distal part of the tendon and the flexor tendon sheath (blue). Schematic by Lucia Brunhold, based on Quinn & Baumel (1990) [15] **B:** Schematic for a soft robotic TLM inspired pneumatic network actuator (PNA) with an integrated tendon (red). The pre-curved PNA (gray) straightens when pressurized and bends back when depressurized. The tendon is not meant to hinder the actuator during intended extension (upper schema), but to fixate and support it during bending. The soft pneumatic tendon sheath (SPTS) locks the tendon when not actuated (lower schema). (Color figure online)

2   Materials and Methods

The actuator system was 3D printed from flexible filament using FDM. In order to position the three flexible components in space and optimally arrange them in relation to each other, a modular and adjustable fixture was also 3D printed from rigid material. Characterization was performed by measuring the opening distance of the tendon sheath and the actuator's bending angle and block force against applied air pressure.

2.1   3D Printing and Materials

The soft components (pneumatic bending actuator (PNA), pneumatic tendon sheath (SPTS) and tendon) were designed in CAD and fabricated by FDM printing from transparent Filaflex Ultra-Soft 70A (Recreus Industries, S. L., Spain) filament with a diameter of 1.75 mm. Table 1 shows an overview of the print parameters. The manufacturing platforms used were three Prusa i3 MK3S+ (Prusa Research, Czech Republic) upgraded with Hemera direct drive extruder print heads (E3D-Online Ltd., United Kingdom) and customized software and post-processing scripts [16]. The print head nozzles had a diameter of 0.4 mm. The slicing of the 3D models and the adjustment of the printing parameters were carried out in Prusa Slicer (Prusa Research a.s., version 2.4.2 + win64, Prague: Prusa Research a.s., 2022). Therein the extrusion width was set to 0.3 mm. The nozzle temperature was set to 220 °C and the print bed temperature to 60 °C. Layer height was set to 0.1 mm, with the exception of the first layer, which was set to 0.2 mm. The regular print speed was 10 mm/s, while overhangs were printed at a higher speed of 20 mm/s to reduce sagging of the extruded filament. Parts were printed with 10 solid top and bottom layers and a minimum of 5 perimeters. Infill density was set to 95% with an infill angle of 0°. Extrusion factors were set in the custom G-code to 1.25, 1.15, and 1.15 for perimeters, infill, and overhangs, respectively. 3DLAC Adhesive Spray (3DLAC, Spain) was used to improve adhesion of the fabricated part to the print bed during fabrication. Isopropanol was applied to the edges of the printed objects to facilitate removal of the finished prints from the print bed.

Table 1. Print parameters for the manufacture of the flexible parts (PNA, SPTS and tendon) of the TLM actuator system. The extrusion factors are multiplier for the preset values (depending on the slicer software used) for standard filaments such as PLA. The used material was transparent Filaflex Ultra-Soft 70A.

Parameter	Value	Unit
Filament diameter (Filaflex 70A)	1.75	mm
Nozzle diameter	0.4	mm
Extrusion width	0.3	mm

(continued)

Table 1. (*continued*)

Parameter	Value	Unit
Print temperature	220	°C
Bed temperature	60	°C
Layer height – first layer	0.2	mm
Layer height – every other layer	0.1	mm
Print speed – regular	10	mm/s
Print speed – overhangs	20	mm/s
Solid top and bottom layers	10	
Perimeters	5	
Infill density	95	%
Infill angle	0	°
Extrusion factor – perimeters	1.25	
Extrusion factor – infill	1.05	
Extrusion factor – overhangs	1.05	

2.2 Construction of the Tendon Locking Mechanism Inspired Pneumatic Bending Actuator System

The tendon locking mechanism inspired soft pneumatic actuator system (TLM-SPA) was realized by combining a pre-curved soft pneumatic network actuator (SPA) with a tendon and a soft pneumatic tendon sheath (SPTS). All three components were FDM printed as single parts from flexible TPU with a shore hardness of 70A.

In the avian foot, the main function of the flexor tendon is to transmit the force of the flexor muscles to the joint of the digit and to flex it. The TLM within the foot blocks the tendon in the flexed state of the digit, thus keeping it in flexion and reducing the required muscle contraction. This blocking of the tendon sheath at a low actuation level served as inspiration for our design. As such a soft pneumatic tendon sheath (Fig. 2A–D) was developed. To allow the SPTS to block the tendon in the unactuated state, it needed to consist of two similar halves connected by four planar ligaments. The cross-sectional area of the two outer ligaments is 10 mm^2, and 5 mm^2 of the two inner ones, and the height in the direction of elongation is 9.4 mm and 9 mm, respectively. Each half contains two interconnected air chambers, each with a membrane (dimensions: 17.3 mm × 18 mm × 0.7 mm) facing the corresponding membrane of the other half with a distance of 0.8 mm. The aim was to keep the dimensions of the SPTS as small as possible. The dimensions finally chosen were derived from the limitations of the printing process and the functionality of the SPTS. When compressed air is applied to the SPTS, the membranes expand and push the halves away from each other (Fig. 2D). The flexible ligaments counteract this separation and exert a force that causes the channel halves to return to each other once the actuation stops. In the center of the SPTS, the halves form a channel with a saw-tooth structured roof and bottom for the tendon (Fig. 2C). In the depressurized state, the saw-teeth of both halves have a distance of 0.8 mm from each other, which is less than

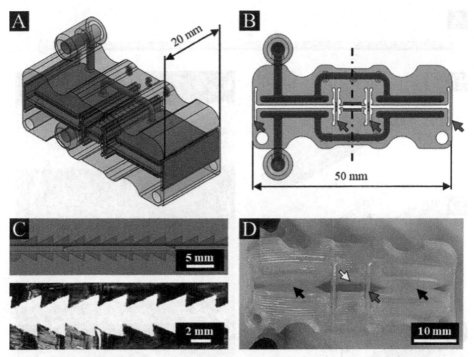

Fig. 2. Soft pneumatic tendon sheath (SPTS). **A:** Isometric view of the SPTS CAD design. The solid parts are illustrated as transparent to provide visibility of the pneumatic network cavity (green), the four laminar ligaments (purple) and the saw-tooth structures of the central tendon channel (yellow). **B:** Frontal view of the SPTS with similar coloring as in **A**, with the ligaments are marked by purple arrows. **C:** Longitudinal section view of the saw-tooth structure of the SPTS central tendon channel in the CAD design (top) and in the cut FDM print (bottom). The dashed line in **B** indicates the section plane. **D:** FDM printed pneumatic tendon sheath actuated with 180 kPa. Expansion of the membranes (black arrows) stretches the four ligaments (one marked with a purple arrow) and increases the distance of the two parts of the central tendon channel (white arrow). (Color figure online)

the thickness of the flat part of the tendon (1 mm). When the SPTS is pressurized, the distance between both halves increases and the structured segment of the tendon can pass otherwise it is blocked.

The tendon (Fig. 3) has a rectangular plane design (1 mm × 4 mm), which aids the FDM printing process, and a total length of 216 mm. In order to be blocked by the SPTS, the tendon was designed to have a structured area with saw-teeth where every second tooth was omitted (Fig. 3F). This teeth structure lead to blocking that was stronger than the force the actuator could generate during actuation and worked better than designs more close to the tissue structure of the biological role model, for example, with bulbs (Fig. 3B+C) or an uninterrupted tooth pattern (Fig. 3D+E). The teeth were aligned opposite to that of the tendon sheath and had a base area of 1.45 × 4 mm and a height of 0.75 mm, of which every second tooth was recessed. This teeth set-up proved to be effective in blocking the tendon. A tendon with this structure could not be released from its blockage by actuation of the

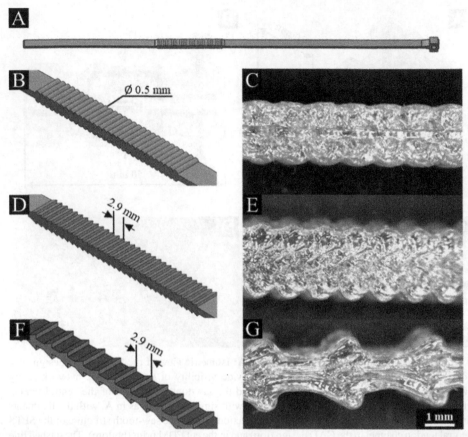

Fig. 3. Artificial tendon for the TLM bending actuator system and development steps of the tendon's structure. **A:** General view of the CAD design of the entire artificial tendon with structured part and head for fixation in the actuators tip. **B:** First approach with a structure design close to the biological role model, which should interlock with the SPTS teeth and block the movement of the tendon, but also pass with minimal friction trough the actuated SPTS. The bulbs diameter of 0.5 mm matched the height of the SPTS teeth. **C:** Side view of the FDM printed structure from **B** revealed unwanted fusion of the bulbs. The locking effect in combination with SPTS was not sufficient to prevent slipping of the tendon. **D:** First approach of a saw-tooth-like tendon structure to enhance the interlocking. **E:** Side view of the FDM printed structure from **D** also revealed fusion of the teeth. **F:** Finally used saw-tooth tendon structure. Removal of every second tooth from design **D** enhanced interlocking with SPTS and blocking of the tendon's movement more than sufficient. **G:** Side view of the FDM printed structure from **F**. (Color figure online)

SPA. The maximum thickness of the tendon in the structural area was designed as 2.5 mm (CAD design). A measurement of the actual thickness of the printed tendons showed an average thickness of 2.30 ± 0.08 mm (MW $\pm$ SD, n = 8). At the apical end, the tendon had a 4 mm x 4 mm head for fixation in the tip of the SPA.

Instead of a conventional bending actuator, a pneumatic network actuator has been developed that works alternative to conventional bending actuators (Fig. 4). Meaning when air is compressed, the actuator straights rather than bends. The actuator is designed

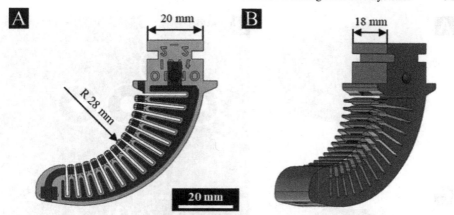

Fig. 4. Pre-curved pneumatic network bending actuator. **A:** Side view of the pre-curved actuator CAD design. The solid parts are illustrated as transparent to provide visibility of the pneumatic network cavity (green) and the tendon channel (brown). **B:** View from diagonal front on the pre-curved actuator CAD design. (Color figure online)

with a 90° curvature between its base and tip. After actuation, the actuator is bent back into its pre-curved state by the material relaxing. The base area of the actuator is 18 mm × 20 mm and the inner radius is 28 mm in side view. In the finished assembly, a weight is attached to the basal end of the tendon whose intended function is to reset and tighten the flexible tendon, but not to bend the actuator. Since there is no actuation in bending direction, the backbone of the actuator (outer radius) gradually converges toward the tip. In this way, the backbone supports the pre-curved posture of the actuator. There are 16 chambers with 30 membranes that decrease in width uniformly from a basal membrane area of the first chamber (basal end) with a size of 12.74 mm × 12.74 mm. To hold and guide the tendon, the chambers have material extensions on their inner radius that form a channel. The tendon is threaded into this channel through the opening in the tip of the actuator, and its head is form-fitted. The entire system – consisting of all three flexible components – was mounted in a modular fixture for the experiments, which also allowed the components to be properly positioned relative to each other.

2.3 TLM Actuator System Fixture

The tendon locking mechanism inspired soft pneumatic actuator system (TLM-SPA) consists of three main flexible parts, a pre-curved soft pneumatic network actuator (SPA), a soft pneumatic tendon sheath (SPTS) and a tendon. To fixate and spatially arrange the three flexible parts of the TLM-SPA, a custom-made, modular fixture (Fig. 5) was designed and fabricated by FDM printing from polylactic acid filament (PLA+, Filamentworld, Germany). The flexibility of the tendon caused it to not retract properly through the channel and jam when the actuator bent back after extension. Therefore, in order to keep the tendon taut and achieve proper retraction, the structure included a component with ball bearing guide rollers that deflected the basal end of the tendon in the direction of gravity with low friction. This allowed a reset weight (23.8 g) to be attached to the basal end of the tendon. Using a weight rather than a spring provided a uniform tensile force on the tendon.

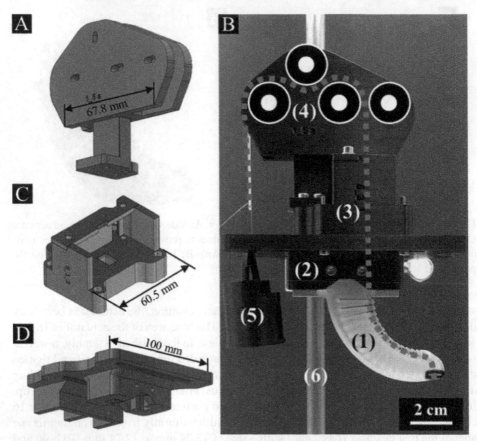

Fig. 5. Rigid TLM actuator system fixture from PLA+. The fixture consists of four FDM printed parts, ball bearings (hidden, indicated as black circles) and screws. **A:** CAD design of the ball bearing mount. **B:** Complete flexible TLM actuator system mounted on its modular PLA+ fixture. The actuator (1) is mounted at its base to the base plate (2) which is hold by a laboratory stand (3). The tendon sheath is inlaid into a rigid frame for adjustable positioning (4). The tendon (orange dashed line) is inserted into the actuator and guided through the tendon sheath and a module with ball bearing guide rollers (5). At its basal end, the tendon is connected to a weight container (6) for proper retraction. **C:** CAD design of the SPTS mount. **D:** CAD design of the base plate with actuator mounting. The two gaps are for positioning of the SPTS mounting from **C**. (Color figure online)

2.4 Actuator Characterization

To determine the operating pressure of the tendon sheath used in the block force measurements the opening width of its tendon channel was tested with regard to applied air pressure. The combined TLM actuator system was characterized by the bending angle and block force.

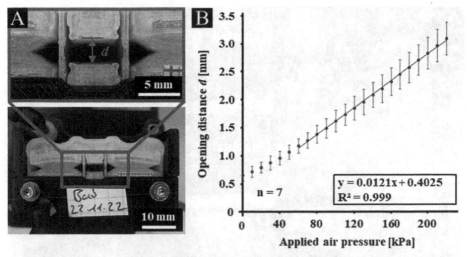

Fig. 6. Characterization of the opening width of the soft pneumatic tendon sheath (SPTS). **A:** SPTS in its rigid frame (black, FDM printed, PLA+) during testing with 220 kPa applied air pressure. The opening distance (d) was defined as the distance between the innermost edges of the upper and lower teeth of the central channel. **B:** Opening distance (d) plotted against applied air pressure in 10 kPa increments. Data points and error bars represent mean and standard deviation, respectively ($n = 7$). For the data points from 60 kPa on, a linear equation was fitted to the graph ($R^2 = 0.999$). (Color figure online)

The opening width of the tendon channel was determined as a function of the applied air pressure in order to obtain the minimum operating pressure required to open the SPTS wide enough for the tendon to slide through frictionless (Fig. 6). To characterize displacement, digital images were taken from a perspective that was orthogonal to the plane of motion at air pressures between 0 and 220 kPa in increments of 10 kPa, and the width was measured with Fiji (version 2.9.0, Schindelin et al., 2012; ImageJ version 1.53t). All data were normally distributed (Shapiro test, $p > 0.05$) and showed homoscedasticity (Levene test, $p > 0.05$). Therefore, the data in Fig. 6B are presented as means with standard deviation SD. From 60 kPa on, a linear equation ($R^2 = 0.999$) was fitted to the graph to describe this range more precisely. Here, the opening width increases at a rate of 0.012 mm per kPa. Based on the results two opening distances were used for the block force measurements: 220 kPa (C2, no contact of the tendon sheath to the tendon teeth, based on the design dimensions) and 160 kPa (C3, no contact between tendon sheath and tendon, based on observations due to deviations dimensions between design and printed model).

For the bending angle measurements, the actuator had a line-shaped marking at the side of its tip included in its design. The line marking was horizontally aligned when the relaxed, pre-curved actuator was mounted on a fixture in downward orientation. When the actuator was pressurized, it straightened and the marking approached a vertical orientation. The bending angle was defined as the angle between the horizontal baseline of the actuator and a reference line placed through the line marking at its tip (Fig. 7A). The applied air pressure for the bending angle measurement was increased in 5 kPa

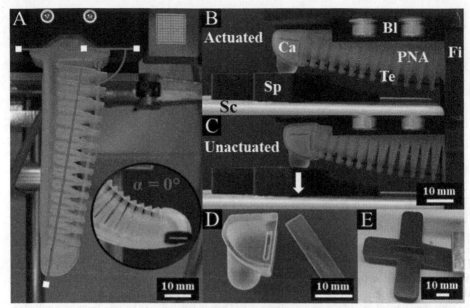

Fig. 7. Measurement of bending angle α and block force of the pre-curved pneumatic network actuator (PNA). **A:** The bending angle was defined as the angle between the baseline of the actuator and a reference line placed parallel to a linear marking at the side of the tip of the actuator. The line marking was included into the design with an orientation horizontal (α = 0°) to the mounting of the pre-curved actuator when not actuated (round picture). Since the form of the tip does not change due to actuation, full straightening of the PNA backbone corresponds to α ≥ 100°. **B:** Setup for the block force measurement with a laboratory scale. To prepare the measurement, the pre-curved pneumatic network actuator (PNA) was at its base mounted to a solid fixture (Fi) made from PLA. The tendon (Te) is for better illustration made from black TPU. To straighten the actuator, it was actuated until its backbone was over the entire length in contact with the horizontal blocking plate (Bl). The actuation was hold until a scale (Sc) was with a lifting platform lifted as close as possible to the actuator without touching. To control the contact point and minimize the influence of friction forces, a solid cap (Ca) on the tip of the PNA and a cross-shaped Spacer (Sp) were used. **C:** Unactuated PNA during block force measurement. The arrow indicates the direction of force that was measured. **D:** A solid cap (Ca) ensured that the block force was transferred to the scale at a specific point of the actuators tip. **E:** Since the PNA narrows from its base to its tip, a spacer, mounted on the scale, prevented parts of the actuator other than the tip from touching the scale's surface. The cross-shape of the spacer ensured a uniform distribution of force on the scale and the groove minimized contact area. Both components (**D+E**) in combination also reduced the influence of frictional forces on the measurement. (Color figure online)

increments starting from 0 kPa and stopped when the back of the bending actuator was fully straightened. In contrast to the main body of the actuator, the solid tip does not deform when the actuator is pressurized, which means full straightening of the PNA backbone corresponds to α ≈ 100°. Since the actuation was done in increments, full straightening was reached at the pressure with α ≥ 100°. The bending angle was also determined from digital photographs using Fiji.

For block force measurements, the actuator was mounted on a fixture so that it straightens horizontally when pressurized and bends downward when depressurized (Fig. 7B). A laboratory scale (Denver Instrument DL-2, Denver Instrument GmbH, Germany) was used to measure the maximum block force at the tip of the actuator. The scale was placed on a laboratory lift that allowed accurate height adjustment and positioning without contact to the actuator but could get close enough under the actuator tip to block its bending movement directly when depressurized. A PLA+ plate above it blocked any upward movement of the actuator. To measure the block force at a specific and comparable point on the actuator tip, a 3D-printed cap (VeroClear™, Stratasys Inc.) with a half sphere facing the scale was plug on the tip (Fig. 7D). To ensure that only the half sphere of the cap touched the scale, a PLA+ spacer was placed on its surface (Fig. 7E). Since the design of the actuator caused it to lengthen and shorten during pressurization and depressurization, the spacer was designed with a groove. The groove was lubricated with Vaseline and acted as a rail for the half sphere of the cap to minimize the influence of shear forces perpendicular to the block force vector. The weight indicated by the scale was recorded 60 s after depressurization and converted into Newton. For each configuration, four measurements were taken 15 s apart and the highest force value was taken as the maximum force for that specimen.

The TLM actuator system was tested in four configurations. To test the basic behavior of the actuator, the first configuration contained only the pre-curved actuator, while configurations 3–4 tested the system with all its components under different conditions. In configurations 2 and 3, the SPTS was pressurized to 220 kPa and 160 kPa, respectively, to determine the operating pressure required to open the SPTS wide enough to minimize friction with the tendon.

In addition, the configurations were designed for helping to evaluate the effect of any friction between the tendon and other parts of the system, as well as of the weight attached to the end of the tendon. In the fourth configuration, the system was tested depressurized and relaxed, meaning that the actuator was in its pre-curved relaxed state and the tendon was taut and retracted when blocked by the relaxed SPTS. Since no actuation and therefore no intended change in bending occurs in this final configuration, only block force measurements were performed here. Nevertheless, to prepare the block force measurements, the actuator needed to be pressurized against the resistance of

Table 2. Overview of the experimental procedure of a tested actuator. C1: Pre-curved soft pneumatic actuator (SPA) tested without a tendon or tendon sheath (SPTS). C2–C4: Whole TLM SPA system tested, either without tendon locking at 220 kPa (C2) or 160 kPa (C3) air pressure on the SPTS or with depressurized SPTS and locked tendon (C4). Bending angle: The applied air pressure was increased by 5 kPa per actuation. Block force: The actuation was performed in preparation for the measurement, until the SPA was fully straightened, and between the four measurements to remove the load from the actuator.

Testing order	→						
Experiment	Bending angle			Block force			
Configuration	C1	C2	C3	C1	C2	C3	C4
Actuation per configuration	10	12		4			
Sum of actuations: SPA	50						

the blocked tendon until its full extension (straight actuator back). Seven SPA specimen were used for the tests. The samples were dependent samples because each of the seven actuator systems was tested in both experiments (bending angle and block force) and in all of the corresponding configurations (Table 2).

2.5 Statistical Analysis

GNU R (version 2022.12.0+353, RStudio Inc.) and MS Excel (Microsoft Corporation, United States) were used for statistical analysis and data presentation. The Shapiro-Wilk test (shapiro.test) was used to test a normal distribution of a dataset. For multiple sets of normally distributed data, the Levene test (leveneTest) was used to assess whether they were homoscedastic. If the data sets were, both normally distributed and homoscedastic, they were considered parametric. If either one or both criteria were not met, they were considered nonparametric. To test for statistically significant differences between multiple paired and nonparametric data sets, the Friedman test (friedman_test) followed by Wilcoxon post hoc tests (wilcox_test, paired = TRUE) were used. For bending angle data, we determined areas of linear tendency to fit a linear equation to the graphs. We used the coefficient of determination R^2 to estimate the lower threshold (air pressure) of the approximately linear range. The lower threshold of the linear range was estimated by taking out the bending angles for lower air pressure levels starting from 0 kPa until R^2 reached 0.999.

3 Results

The bending behavior of the pre-curved actuator during actuation was investigated by measuring its bending angles (Fig. 8) under three different configurations (C1-C3). C1 tested just the pre-curved actuator alone and in C2 and C3 the whole system (actuator, tendon sheath (SPTS) and tendon) was tested only differing in the amount of air pressure applied on the tendon sheath to open it (C2: 220 kPa, C3: 160 kPa). The bending angle was measured from the pre-curved, relaxed position of the actuator until it fully straightened which was defined as $\alpha = 100°$. Therefore, the measurement series ran for C1 from 0 kPa to 50 kPa and for C2 and C3 up to 60 kPa applied air pressure, each with increments of 5 kPa per measurement. Because not all data were normally distributed (Shapiro test, $p \leq 0.05$), bending angles are presented as median and IQR. Since C1 showed a linear tendency for the whole pressure range, a linear equation was fitted to its full data set. The bending behavior of C2 and C3 started increasing slowly at low air pressures and converged into a range with a linear tendency at higher air pressures. Accordingly, a linear equation was fitted for the linear range of the data of C2 and C3 starting at 30 kPa and 40 kPa, respectively. The lower thresholds of the fits were estimated by taking out the bending angles for lower air pressure steps (starting from 0 kPa) until R^2 reached 0.999.

At 0 kPa, the pre-curved actuator without the tendon (C1) was 9.15° (IQR: 0.87°) above its designed pre-curvature at the starting bending angle, which was defined as 0°. In opposite when the tendon was inserted (C2, C3) the starting angle distributed around the defined curvature of 0° (C2: −0.91°, IQR: 2.59° and C3: 0.50°, IQR: 2.3°). In configuration 1, the actuator reached 105.51° (IQR: 2.44°) at 50 kPa applied air pressure, while for configuration 2 and 3 it reached comparable bending angles of 102.59°

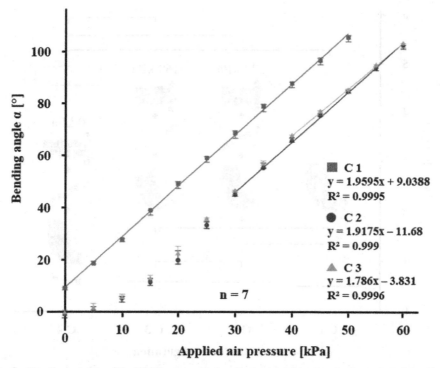

Fig. 8. Bending angles of the TLM pneumatic bending actuator system in the test configurations C1–3. Under C1, the pre-curved actuator was tested alone and under C2 and C3, the whole system (actuator, tendon sheath and tendon) was tested with the tendon sheath opened at 220 kPa and 160 kPa, respectively. The data are plotted against the applied air pressure, which was increased in 5 kPa steps until the actuator reached full extension ($\geq 100°$). Full extension was reached for C1 at latest at 50 kPa and for C2 and C3 at 60 kPa. The data points and error bars represent median and IQR (n = 7). Linear equations were fitted to the linear range of the data, with lower thresholds estimated by R^2. (Color figure online)

(IQR: 1.55°) and 103.24° (IQR: 1.6°) at 60 kPa. The theoretically needed air pressure to reach the exact angle of 100° was calculated by the fitted linear equations as 46.4 kPa for C1, 58.2 kPa for C2 and 58.1 kPa for C3.

To determine the maximal generated force at the tip of the bending actuator, the block force was measured (Fig. 9). In addition to the previously introduced configurations for the bending angle tests, a fourth configuration C4 was added for the block force measurements. In C4, the SPTS was not pressurized and thus blocked the tendon. To bring the pre-curved actuator in the straightened position, which is necessary for the block force measurement, it had to be shortly actuated. The air pressure the bending actuators needed during the preparation for full straightening was 63.6 ± 2.3 kPa (mean ± SD) for configuration C1 and 68.6 ± 3.5 kPa for C2 and C3. To fully straighten the actuator, measurements under configuration 4 required around 3.5 times more air pressure (240 ± 0 kPa) than under the configurations without the locked tendon (C1–3).

The pre-curved actuator alone (C1) generated a block force of 0.49 ± 0.03 N. With integrated tendon and an opened SPTS, the bending actuator already reached significantly higher (Wilcoxon tests, p ≤ 0.05) block forces than in C1 (C2: 0.56 ±

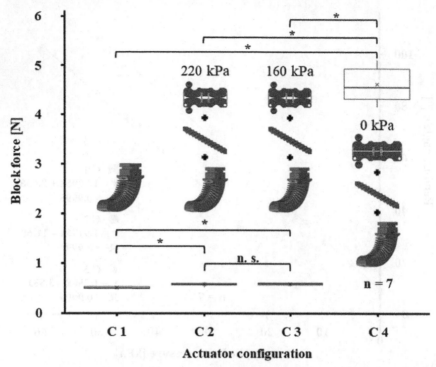

Fig. 9. Block force of the TLM pneumatic bending actuator system for the test configurations C1–4. Under C1, the pre-curved actuator was tested alone and under C2 and C3, the whole system (actuator, tendon sheath and tendon) was tested with the tendon sheath opened at 220 kPa and 160 kPa, respectively. In C4, the actuator and SPTS were depressurized during testing and the tendon locked. The small pictures illustrate the various configurations. Data are represented as Tukey box and whisker plots (n = 7). Boxes show the IQR, with the lower and upper border being equal to the first and third quartiles. Whiskers stretch to the minimum and maximum value within 1.5 times the IQR. Medians are shown as centerlines and means as crosses (×). Brackets show the statistical difference, which was tested with a Friedman test followed by post hoc pairwise Wilcoxon tests for repeated measurements (paired = TRUE). Adjustment of the p-values was done according to the FDR method. Stars indicate the value of significance (n. s. = not significant, * $p \leq 0.01$). (Color figure online)

0.034 N, C3: 0.57 ± 0.03 N). No statistically significant difference was found between the two configurations with different levels of SPTS actuation (C2 and C3, Wilcoxon test, p > 0.05). Configuration 4 clearly had the highest value concerning the block force with 4.61 ± 0.38 N, which was significantly different from all other configurations (Wilcoxon tests, p ≤ 0.05).

4   Conclusion and Outlook

The presented actuator system successfully realizes a bio-inspired approach that combines a pre-curved pneumatic network bending actuator with a soft robotic tendon locking mechanism. As a result, a bending actuator system was created that bends in the unactuated state due to material relaxation, thus reducing the duration of compressed air required for operation. The ability to lock and release of the tendon increases the stiffness (block force up to 4.6 N) passively without trading off its flexibility and low pressure needed for fully straightened (60 kPa and 160 kPa for SPTS). The mechanism concerning the blocking direction is the same for both. The bird's tendon as well as the artificial tendon is strongly blocked in the direction of extension and can just slip into the direction of flexion if a strong enough pulling force would occur. Since the tendon's purpose was to stiffen passively the actuator, it was not moved (pulled) by an actuator in the direction of flexion. Additional modification could also add active actuation for bending to flex the actuator above its initial pre-curvature. Nevertheless, the displayed TLM actuator system gets along without rigid actuators such as electro-motors, which are commonly used for cable-driven systems. Another advantage of the system is the fast response when the actuator bends or the tendon sheath depressurizes, since both motions are initiated by the relaxation of the flexible material, which is during actuation pre-stretched. For comparison, Zhang et al. (2019) developed a stiffness-tunable soft actuator that they described as "fast-responding". It used a shape memory polymer layer that could change between soft and stiff by temperature change but it needed 32 s per cycle [11]. Other solutions comparable to our system – that increased the possible loading of an otherwise low energy consuming bending actuator – are based on rigid bodies and therefore do not represent soft robotics [17, 18] or are combinations of rigid and flexible materials [9]. Other designs have to overcome a high energy barrier, e.g. for bi-stable approaches [7, 8]. For instance, Crowley et al. (2022) [9] presented an actuator comparable to the one presented, but used a multi-material approach. Crowley's actuator used a component with positive layer jamming instead of a tendon, which could generate quite high gripping forces, but had the disadvantage of requiring an actuation pressure of 310 kPa to drive the layer jamming during bending.

In future studies, the reaction speed of the system will be investigated in more detail. Furthermore, due to the construction with no fixed connection between the actuators' air chambers and the tendon, the bending actuator has good flexibility and therefore the prerequisite for adapting to a variety of shapes. To assess the form fitting potential and the influence of such flexibility on the structure of the actuator, suitable tests such as stiffness measurements will be carried out.

In addition, the actuator system presented has a high potential for grippers that need to grasp and hold particularly fragile objects. The actuator alone generates a low block force (0.47 N), while the mechanism leads to a shape adaptation to the object by blocking the tendon. Thus, in the application, the system should only apply a counterforce to the gripped object that is equal to the forces acting through the object (e.g., gravitational force). A gripper with the TLM bending actuators presented here should therefore only grip with as much force as is necessary to hold an object without the use of sensors. The system will be further investigated and developed in its use as a low energy consumption multi finger gripper system.

Funding. Funded by the Deutsche Forschungsgemeinschaft (DFG, German Research Foundation) under Germany's Excellence Strategy – EXC-2193/1 – 390951807.

References

1. Rus, D., Tolley, M.T.: Design, fabrication and control of soft robots. Nature **521**(7553), 467–475 (2015). https://doi.org/10.1038/nature14543
2. Schaffner, M., et al.: 3D printing of robotic soft actuators with programmable bioinspired architectures. Nat. Commun. **9**(1), 878 (2018). https://doi.org/10.1038/s41467-018-03216-w
3. Ilievski, F., et al.: Soft robotics for chemists. Angew. Chem. **123**(8), 1930–1935 (2011). https://doi.org/10.1002/ange.201006464
4. Mosadegh, B., et al.: Pneumatic networks for soft robotics that actuate rapidly. Adv. Funct. Mater. **24**(15), 2163–2170 (2014). https://doi.org/10.1002/adfm.201303288
5. Wang, Z., Chathuranga, D.S., Hirai, S.: 3D printed soft gripper for automatic lunch box packing. In: 2016 IEEE International Conference on Robotics and Biomimetics (ROBIO), pp. 503–508. IEEE (2016). https://doi.org/10.1109/ROBIO.2016.7866372
6. Kappel, P., Kramp, C., Speck, T., Tauber, F.J.: Application-oriented comparison of two 3D printing processes for the manufacture of pneumatic bending actuators for bioinspired macroscopic soft gripper systems. In: Hunt, A., Vouloutsi, V., Moses, K., Quinn, R., Mura, A., Prescott, T., Verschure, P.F.M.J. (eds.) Biomimetic and Biohybrid Systems, pp. 54–67. Springer International Publishing, Cham (2022). https://doi.org/10.1007/978-3-031-204 70-8_6
7. Tang, Y., et al.: Leveraging elastic instabilities for amplified performance: spine-inspired high-speed and high-force soft robots. Sci. Adv. **6**(19), eaaz6912 (2020). https://doi.org/10.1126/sciadv.aaz6912
8. Wang, X., Khara, A., Chen, C.: A soft pneumatic bistable reinforced actuator bioinspired by Venus Flytrap with enhanced grasping capability. Bioinspir. Biomim. **15**(5), 056017 (2020). https://doi.org/10.1088/1748-3190/aba091
9. Crowley, G.B., Zeng, X., Su, H.-J.: A 3D printed soft robotic gripper with a variable stiffness enabled by a novel positive pressure layer jamming technology. In IEEE Robot. Autom. Lett. **7**(2), 5477–5482 (2022). https://doi.org/10.1109/LRA.2022.3157448
10. Wei, Y., et al.: A novel, variable stiffness robotic gripper based on integrated soft actuating and particle jamming. So. Ro., **3**(3), 134–143 (2016). https://doi.org/10.1089/soro.2016.0027
11. Zhang, Y.-F., et al.: Fast-response, stiffness-tunable soft actuator by hybrid multimaterial 3D printing. Adv. Funct. Mater. **29**(15), 1806698 (2019). https://doi.org/10.1002/adfm.201 806698
12. Pal, A., Goswami, D., Martinez, R.V.: Elastic ernergy storage enables rapid and programmable actuation in soft machines. Adv. Funct. Mater. **30**(1), 1906603 (2020). https://doi.org/10.1002/adfm.201906603
13. Wehner, M., et al.: Pneumatic energy sources for autonomous and wearable soft robotics. So. Ro. **1**(4), 263–274 (2014). https://doi.org/10.1089/soro.2014.0018
14. Diteesawat, R.S., Helps, T., Taghavi, M., Rossiter, J.: Electro-pneumatic pumps for soft robotics. Sci. Robot. **6**(51), abc3721 (2021). https://doi.org/10.1126/scirobotics.abc3721
15. Quinn, T.H., Baumel, J.J.: The digital tendon locking mechanism of the avian foot (Aves). Zoomorphology **109**, 281–293 (1990). https://doi.org/10.1007/BF00312195
16. Conrad, S., Speck, T., Tauber. F.J.: Tool changing 3D printer for rapid prototyping of advanced soft robotic elements. Bioinspir. Biomim. **16**(5), (2021). https://doi.org/10.1088/1748-3190/ac095a
17. Nacy, S., Abbood, W., Dermitzakis, K.: Tendon type robotic gripper with frictional self-locking mechanism. IJAER **13**(9), 14393–14401 (2018)
18. Hsu, J., Yoshida, E., Harada, K., Kheddar, A.: Self-locking underactuated mechanism for robotic gripper. In: 2017 IEEE International Conference on Advanced Intelligent Mechatronics (AIM), pp. 620–627. IEEE (2017). https://doi.org/10.1109/AIM.2017.8014086

Study and Preliminary Modeling of Microstructure and Morphology of the Elephant Trunk Skin

Behnam Kamare[1,2]([✉]) [iD], Matteo Lo Preti[1,2] [iD], Irene Bernardeschi[2] [iD],
Simone Lantean[2] [iD], Paule Dagenais[3,4] [iD], Michel Milinkovitch[3,4] [iD],
and Lucia Beccai[2] [iD]

[1] The BioRobotics Institute, Scuola Superiore Sant'Anna, 56025 Pontedera, PI, Italy
Behnam.Kamare@iit.it
[2] Soft BioRobotics Perception Lab, Istituto Italiano di Tecnologia, 16163 Genova, GE, Italy
[3] Laboratory of Artificial and Natural Evolution (LANE), Department of Genetics and
Evolution, University of Geneva, 30, Quai Ernest-Ansermet, 1211 Geneva, Switzerland
[4] SIB Swiss Institute of Bioinformatics, 30, Quai Ernest-Ansermet, 1211 Geneva, Switzerland

Abstract. The mechanical properties and microstructural characteristics of elephant skin have been investigated in this study to gain insights into its exceptional robustness, deformability, and touch sensitivity. Specifically, skin samples from the elephant trunk were thoroughly analyzed to understand their morphology and inner structure. The mechanical behavior of different skin layers was assessed through uniaxial tensile and indentation tests, enabling the retrieval of their mechanical parameters. To better comprehend the microstructure of the skin, two simplified numerical models were developed. The first model elucidated the role of the discrete island-shaped structure of the epidermis, which allows the skin to elongate while maintaining its robustness. The second model focused on the epidermal ridges, demonstrating their influence in increasing local strain under indentation stimuli. These investigations into the natural properties of elephant skin have significant implications for the design of a new generation of artificial skins that exhibit remarkable sensitivity, toughness, and deformability. The findings presented in this study contribute to the advancement of biomimetic materials and inspire innovative approaches in various fields, ranging from robotics to prosthetics and beyond.

Keywords: Elephant · Trunk skin · Skin Morphology · Skin biomechanics

1 Introduction

The elephant proboscis, an organ that allows this animal to explore and navigate the world through smell and touch, possesses a remarkable natural design exemplified by its wrinkled skin. This unique skin is robust, so elephants can undertake demanding tasks such as uprooting trees in challenging environments characterized by high temperatures and dust, and highly deformable and sensitive, enabling delicate manipulation

F. Meder et al. (Eds.): Living Machines 2023, LNAI 14158, pp. 101–114, 2023.
https://doi.org/10.1007/978-3-031-39504-8_7

of various objects, including leaves. The trunk skin exhibits a distinctive combination of mechanical traits, offering protection from external collisions and abrasions while maintaining sensitivity and facilitating flexibility and deformation in multiple directions during organ elongation, bending, and torsion. These exceptional characteristics can inspire the development of new artificial skins, where the biomechanical principles derived from this natural model can guide design [1].

Previous studies [2, 3] have explored biological armors in armadillos, alligators, leatherback turtles, and other species, inspiring the development of tough, flexible, and lightweight body armors. However, investigations into elephant skin have been limited due to the challenges associated with sample collection and data gathering. Early studies by Smith [4] in the late 19th century described the skin's micro-anatomy of Elephas maximus (Asian elephant) skin, focusing on various regions and noting differences in epidermal morphology, including the presence or absence of sweat and sebaceous glands and hair follicles. In the 70 s, Luck et al. [5] conducted a more detailed histological examination of the skin of Hippopotamus amphibious and Loxodonta Africana (African elephant), comparing the epidermal anatomy of these species. Notably, the thickness of the elephants' epidermis and the regularity of their papillary ridges were found to differ from those of the hippopotamus. Subsequent studies by Spearman et al. [6] focused on the histology of the flank epidermis in adult female Loxodonta, investigating the localization of key chemical components for keratinization of the stratum corneum.

Elephant skin has recently gained increased attention within the scientific community due to its distinctive characteristics. Martins et al. [7] shed light on how the island-like structure of elephant skin origins from the local bending mechanical stress and fractures of the stratum corneum, while Schulz et al. [8] examined the role of folds and wrinkles in the elongation of the elephant trunk from a kinematic perspective. Additionally, Paule et al. [9] conducted a comprehensive analysis of the skin morphology of African and Asian elephants using 3D mesh reconstruction techniques, exploring mechanical performance, kinematic strategies, and functional morphology of the elephant trunk. Despite these diverse investigations, the role of microstructure and morphology in the deformability and sensitivity of trunk skin remains incompletely characterized.

The mechanical complexity of the skin arises from its structure, which comprises multiple layers and components. As illustrated in Fig. 1, the skin consists of three primary layers: epidermis, dermis, and hypodermis. The epidermis, the outermost layer, of the skin, is composed of the stratum corneum (SC) and the viable epidermis (VE) [10–12]. The SC, characterized by a discrete island shape structure known as SC islands, is the skin's outermost barrier. The dermis, a dense fibrous tissue between the epidermis and subcutaneous tissue, contains collagen, elastin, and other extracellular components. It is divided into the papillary dermis (PD) and the reticular dermis (RD). Dermal papillae (DP), small finger-like projections, extend from dome-like structures called epidermal ridges and play a crucial role in skin structure and function. The PD is a thin layer interpenetrated with the viable epidermis, consisting of loose connective tissue, while the reticular dermis is a deeper and thicker layer of dense connective tissue constituting the bulk of the dermis [13]. The hypodermis, or subcutaneous tissue, lies beneath the dermis. It comprises adipose and connective tissue, providing insulation, and padding for the body. It contains blood vessels, nerves, and lymphatic vessels supplying skin and underlying tissues. Collectively, the dermis and hypodermis layers are referred to as the "cutis" or "corium" [4, 14, 15], with the dermis constituting the upper layer, and the hypodermis the lower layer.

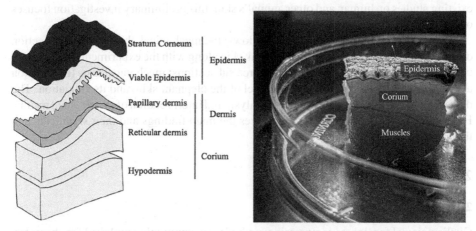

Fig. 1. Elephant skin structure. (Left) Schematic illustration of the distinct layers of elephant skin, comprising the epidermis, dermis, and hypodermis. (Right) Photograph capturing a sample of elephant trunk skin (*Elephas maximus*), vividly presenting the texture and visual characteristics of the skin in its original form, effectively highlighting the different skin layers.

Pham et al. [16], investigated the 3D microstructures of human skin, focusing on the strain energy density concentration in mechanoreceptors' location, highlighting the focalizing and localizing effect that enhance the sensitivity of specific mechanoreceptors. Similar strategies can be applied to studying the tactile capabilities of the mammalian elephant skin, necessitating extensive research by biologists to describe mechanoreceptor types and their distribution across the skin [4].

This study examines the morphology and microstructure of small portions of Asian elephant trunk skin, providing preliminary insights into the role of specific features in strain concentration enhancement. The ultimate objective is to extract fundamental principles for designing robust, deformable, and sensitive artificial skins. Consequently, this investigation focuses on exploring the unique characteristics of elephant skin, with particular emphasis on the role of the discrete island-like structure in deformability. Furthermore, the impact of external loads on the mechanical deformation of skin microstructures, such as epidermal ridges, is analyzed. For both mechanical tests and modeling, the skin is considered a bi-layered structure composed of epidermis and corium. Since the epidermis is stiffer than the corium [6, 14, 15], it can severely limit the deformability of the skin as a whole. Two scenarios are simulated: the first examines the separation of SC islands under tension, whereas the second investigates the mechanical behavior of the sample under indentation forces.

Previous studies on human skin have shown the value of histological images in observing intricate layers and microstructures, and techniques such as second harmonic generation (SHG) [17] microscopy have been widely employed to examine collagen fibers arrangement. Characterization of skin mechanical properties has utilized various methods, including micro/nano indentation [18], and atomic force microscopy (AFM) [19]. Finite element methods (FEM) have been frequently employed [16] to analyze stress and strain distribution in the skin under different load conditions. Building upon existing studies on human and other animal's skin, this preliminary investigation focuses on various aspects of elephant skin.

The organization of the paper is as follows: the mechanical characterization section describes the characteristics of natural trunk skin along with the experimental procedures used. The results section is divided into three subsections: mechanical tests (indentation and tensile testing), a biomechanical model of the elephant skin, and its validation. The discussion section provides an in-depth analysis and interpretation of the obtained results. Finally, the conclusions section summarizes the main findings and their significance in the field.

2   Materials and Methods

2.1   Mechanical Characterization

Cyclic uniaxial tension or compression methods are commonly employed for characterizing biological tissues. However, additional mechanical tests are necessary to comprehensively understand their mechanical behavior under complex loading scenarios, like indentation [20, 21].

Sample Preparation. Elephant skin samples were obtained from the trunk of a deceased Asian elephant that had resided in Zürich Zoo, Switzerland. A high-resolution 3D scan of the entire trunk surface was performed at Tierspital (Zurich, Switzerland), providing detailed morphology information of the trunk's skin (Fig. 2A left [8]). For uniaxial tests, three samples (1, 2, and 3 in Fig. 2A) with approximate dimensions of 6x1x1 cm were carefully cut from the proximal part of the elephant trunk skin along the longitudinal direction, as depicted in Fig. 2. Accurate consideration of the actual dimensions of each sample was ensured for precise stress/strain calculations. This involved measuring the cross-sectional dimensions at multiple points along each sample and deriving the average value to be used in stress and strain calculation. For indentation tests, three smaller cube-shaped samples, approximately 10 mm in length, were cut from sample 4 (Fig. 2A). Frozen skin samples were dissected from the underlying muscles using a scalpel, which was also employed to separate the epidermis and the corium layer for indentation tests. Subsequently, the two layers were slowly defrosted at room temperature. The samples were rehydrated in a 10M phosphate buffer saline (PBS) solution for 30 min. In this experiment, only the corium layer of the skin was exposed to PBS, while the epidermis layer remained unaffected.

The current state-of-the-art procedures for skin layer separation [14, 15, 19, 20] do not facilitate uniform detachment of the epidermis and corium layers for long samples required in uniaxial tensile tests. Therefore, the skin layers were not separated, and the skin was tested for stress-strain characterization. However, in the case of indentation tests, smaller samples were necessary, and the epidermis was separated from the corium. Given that the corium of the elephant skin is significantly softer than the epidermis, this

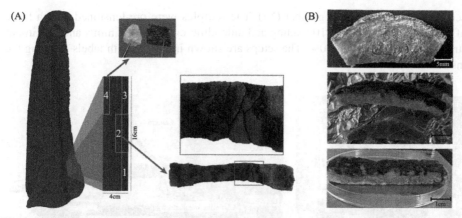

Fig. 2. Anatomical site and preparation process of elephant skin samples. (A) 3D high-resolution scan of the Asian elephant trunk surface. Three larger samples were taken from the proximal region (approx. 1.3 m from the tip) and used for uniaxial tests (the surface of sample 2 is shown with highlighted wrinkles in the inset). Three smaller samples were obtained from sample 4 (one sample is shown) and used for indentation tests. (B) Illustration of the sample preparation process, including freezing (top), muscle separation (middle), and rehydration through immersion in PBS solution (bottom).

characterization can effectively reflect the prominent mechanical differences present throughout the skin.

Experimental Setups and Testing Protocol. A custom indentation setup (Fig. 3) was used to perform the indentation tests, which integrated one orthogonal manual micrometric translation stage (M-105.10, Physik Instrumente, Karlsruhe, Germany), and a micrometric servo-controlled translation stage (M-111.1DG, Physik Instrumente, Karlsruhe, Germany) mechanically interfaced with a triaxial load cell (ATI Nano 17, ATI Industrial Automation, Inc., Apex, NC, USA). The sample was probed using a conical tip with a circular top surface (diameter: 3 mm) that was connected to the load cell. Given that samples' properties tend to degrade, three spatially close samples were tested for 9 indentation cycles each at a speed of 0.1 mm/s.

Concerning tensile tests, a different setup was built to obtain the stress-strain behavior of skin samples. The samples were positioned in the setup with an aluminum clamping mechanism. A common problem with uniaxial tests on biological tissues is the slippage of the samples [21]. To address the slippage issue, screw clamps were deployed in our experimental setup to effectively ensure a secure and tight grip on the samples during the testing process, minimizing any potential movement or slippage. Additionally, to further enhance the stability of the samples, sandpapers were used between the clamps and the sample surfaces at the contact points. This additional measure helped to prevent any unintended movement or displacement during the testing procedures. A tensile force was applied by a micrometric servo-controlled translation stage (M-414.1DG, Physik Instrumente, Karlsruhe, Germany), and measured through a uniaxial load cell (Burster 8431with USB Interface 9206, Burster gmbh & co kg, Gernsbach, Germany). Force data were synchronized with the frame of a recorded video from a Teledyne Dalsa camera, acquired through a frame grabber (NI). The samples were pre-tensioned with a force of 0.3 N and subjected to 10 loading and unloading cycles at 0.2 mm/s and maximum strain of 10%, 20%, and 30%. The setups are shown in Fig. 3, with labels showing the instrumentation.

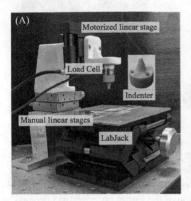
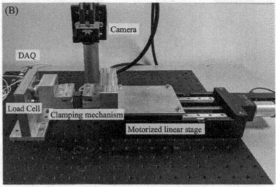

Fig. 3. Custom setups for mechanical characterization of elephant skin. (A) Three-degree-of-freedom (3DoF) setup used for indentation testing. (B) The experimental setup for uniaxial tensile testing features a high-resolution camera and a custom fixture for skin sample clamping.

2.2 Biomechanical Modeling

Optical microscopy images of samples obtained from the proximal part of the elephant trunk were used to investigate the role of SC islands in skin deformation (Fig. 4). The layers' profile was traced and extruded to replicate the geometry, resulting in a Finite Element (FE) model of the sample. In the simulation, one end of the FE model was fixed, while an increasing displacement was applied to the free end (Fig. 6B). The maximum applied strain was set to 30%, consistently with experiments conducted on real samples.

The deformation occurring during contact of the trunk skin with an external object exerting pressure was then studied by fixing the bottom layer of the sample and prescribing a displacement to the top layer. It is worth noting that incompressibility was considered for both layers. This scenario aimed to determine the distribution of stress and strain throughout the sample and identify the maximum strain and stress areas. The hypothesis suggests that certain skin features, such as epidermal ridges, contribute to the localization effect, thereby stimulating mechanoreceptors sensitive to deformation which could be located near such features in the skin [16]. Thus, enhancing the overall tactile sensitivity of the skin. This idea is investigated by evaluating and comparing the equivalent strain between skin layers under normal compressive force. For modeling, the X-axis represents the trunk direction, the Z-axis is normal to the skin surface, and the Y-axis is normal to the XZ plane. The equivalent strain (2) describes the strain states over the body and is calculated from the components of the strain matrix (1) as follows [16]:

$$\varepsilon = \begin{bmatrix} \varepsilon_{xx} & \varepsilon_{xy} & \varepsilon_{xz} \\ \varepsilon_{yx} & \varepsilon_{yy} & \varepsilon_{yz} \\ \varepsilon_{zx} & \varepsilon_{zy} & \varepsilon_{zz} \end{bmatrix} \tag{1}$$

$$\varepsilon_{eqv} = \left(\frac{1}{1+\upsilon}\right)\sqrt{\frac{\left(\varepsilon_{xx}-\varepsilon_{yy}\right)^2 + \left(\varepsilon_{yy}-\varepsilon_{zz}\right)^2 + \left(\varepsilon_{zz}-\varepsilon_{xx}\right)^2 + 6\left(\varepsilon_{xy}^2 + \varepsilon_{yz}^2 + \varepsilon_{zx}^2\right)}{2}}$$

(2)

where ε represents the strain and υ is the Poisson's ratio.

A mock-up with the same geometry as the natural skin was fabricated to validate the FE model. Two molds were 3D printed using an SLA 3D printer (Form 2, Formlabs), one for the stiff top layer and another for the soft bottom layer, based on the virtual image of the bi-layer structure of the natural skin. A transparent top layer was necessary to observe the skin's inner structure and its deformation upon stretching and compression. The inner part had to be visible to be compared to the FE model. In this preliminary study, silicone-based materials were used to simulate the mechanical behavior of skin layers (Fig. 5A). Polydimethylsiloxane (PDMS, with a ratio of 10:1 polymer: curing agent) was used for the epidermis, and Ecoflex 0030 for the corium layer.

The PDMS was chosen due to its shore hardness of A40 [22], which is significantly larger than the Ecoflex series (Shore hardness 00 to 50). The shore hardness measures the indentation resistance of a material using a durometer. The Shore 00 Hardness Scale measures very soft rubbers and gels, while the Shore A Hardness Scale covers flexible mold rubbers that range from very soft to hard, with semi-rigid plastics measured at the high end of the scale [23]. PDMS is considered a medium-soft material, while Ecoflex is classified as the softest silicone. Additionally, PDMS has a transparent structure that enables observing changes in the internal structure, particularly in reproduced dermal ridges, upon indentation and stretching. This transparency is crucial for validating the finite element model with the digital image correlation (DIC) method, as defined below. This difference in stiffness between the two materials allows the simulation of the different layers of natural skin while retaining the ability to analyze the deformation of the internal structure.

For the corium layer, Ecoflex 0030 was chosen for two main reasons. Its non-linear behavior closely resembles the corium layer, as demonstrated in the results (Fig. 5A). Secondly, it provides a strong bond with PDMS, which is not always true for other Ecoflex silicones. A pink color (Electric Pink PMS 812c) was added to the Ecoflex 0030 to distinguish the intermediate layer, facilitating the identification during the analysis.

Digital Image Correlation (DIC) is a non-contact optical measurement technique that enables full-field deformation measurements of a sample's surface, which can be compared to the predictions made by FE simulations [24]. DIC is widely employed to validate FE models in various engineering and scientific fields. The method involves tracking changes in pixel intensity patterns between images of the sample surface taken before, during, and after deformation. By using an appropriate image correlation algorithm, DIC can estimate the full field 2D or 3D displacement. A video of the mock-up undergoing uniaxial deformation was recorded while measuring the reaction force using the load cell by the uniaxial test setup (Fig. 3A). The trajectories of 14 specific points on the mock-up were tracked using Tracker software (Version 6.1.2 from Open-Source Physics) and compared to the results of two FE models (as shown in Fig. 7). The first FE model was based on the mechanical properties obtained through characterization of

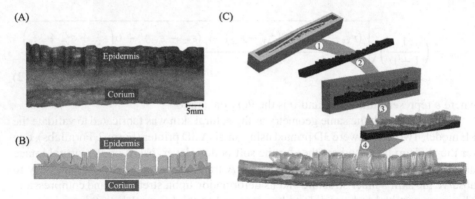

Fig. 4. a) Optical microscopy image used to develop the FE model, b) Corresponding FE model used to investigate skin deformations upon traction and indentation. c) Fabrication process of elephant skin mockup 1. 3D printed mold for Corium layer, filled with Ecoflex 0030; 2. Demolded Corium layer; 3. 3D printed mold for attaching Epidermis and Corium, with Corium layer inserted and PDMS poured; 4. Demolded bi-layer skin mockup.

natural skin. In contrast, the second model incorporates the mechanical properties of artificial materials.

3 Results

3.1 Mechanical Tests

The epidermis was separated from the corium layer of the samples to perform indentation tests. The mechanical behavior of the layers under indentation is reported in Fig. 5A. The epidermis layer shows a linear behavior, with displacement proportional to the applied force, whereas the corium layer shows a nonlinear behavior. Indeed, the corium layer shows an almost linear response to indentation depths up to 1 mm, with a minimal increase in applied force (from 0 to 0.3N). This suggests that the corium layer offers little resistance to deformations in the early stages. However, it then enters a nonlinear phase (toe region), where the required applied force starts increasing. When the strain increases to 2 mm, the applied force goes from 0.3N to 3.2N. This nonlinear behavior and the difference in reaction force in the different stages of displacement could be attributed to the orientation of collagen fibers within the skin [10, 20, 21].

The three skin samples used for uniaxial tensile tests were taken from the same anatomical region of the trunk and tested as a whole since separating the corium and epidermis layer was impossible for longer samples. The classic J-shaped force-displacement behavior, which is commonly observed in soft tissues, is also observed in the uniaxial tests (Fig. 5B). However, it is interesting to note the high variability in the mechanical behavior of these three samples, despite their proximity.

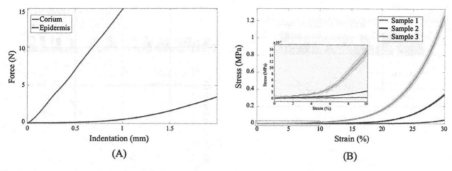

Fig. 5. Mechanical characterization of elephant skin. (a) Force-displacement curves from indentation testing of the epidermis and the corium layers. (b) Stress-strain curves obtained from uniaxial testing of whole skin samples taken from the longitudinal ventral slice of the elephant trunk.

3.2 Biomechanical FE Model of the Elephant Trunk Skin

Mechanical tests on elephant skin layers show that the elephant skin has two main parts with different behaviors. This aspect was exploited for simplifying the complex multi-layered structure of the natural skin into a bi-layer structure for modeling purposes. This simplification made the model computationally inexpensive while still representing the mechanical features of the elephant skin to test.

Strain State in Skin Layers under Indentation Force. When compressive forces are exerted on the skin, the maximum equivalent strain occurs around the epidermal ridges and the intermediate layer between the epidermis and corium. Figure 6A shows the equivalent strain for the corium and the epidermis while varying the displacement in the two layers.

Separation of Epidermis Islands upon Uniaxial Force. Figure 6B shows that the epidermis layer, despite having a larger volume and being stiffer than the corium layer, requires less energy to deform. In this bi-layer model, the volume of the epidermis is 1853.56 mm^3 and the volume of the corium is 2108.40 mm^3. This indicates the impact of the discrete structure of epidermis islands on its mechanical behavior. Indeed, the epidermis does not undergo high stresses upon stretching and it does not limit deformation while it still acts as a protective layer. This emphasizes the importance of the presence of the epidermis islands for maintaining the deformability of the epidermis layer and is further illustrated by the comparison of elastic strain energy in Fig. 6b for the two skin layers.

Validation of Model. Figure 7B shows the force-displacement curves obtained for the FE model of skin with mechanical properties of natural skin (orange), the FE model of skin with mechanical properties of artificial material (yellow), and the mock-up (blue).

The results of tracking 14 points identified both in the FE model of the artificial skin and in the mock-up show a similar trend, while the FE model with natural skin properties is quite different. This divergence is ascribed to the different mechanical behavior of the silicone-based elastomers and the natural layer of the skin.

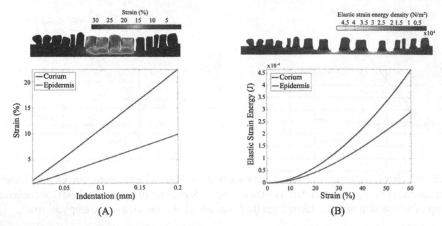

Fig. 6. Mechanical analysis of elephant skin model. (A) Strain distribution in the model under indentation force. The color legend indicates that the maximum equivalent strain occurs in the corium layer and epidermal ridges. (B) Top: Elastic strain energy density J for skin layers upon stretching. Bottom: J for skin layers. Despite being stiffer than the corium, the epidermis requires less energy to deform, highlighting the influence of morphology on mechanical behavior.

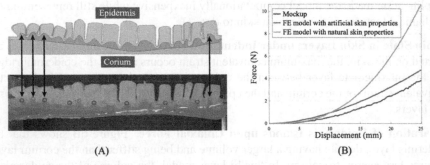

Fig. 7. Comparison of point tracking and force-displacement for tensile stretching between mock-up and FE model. (a) Points used for tracking in the mock-up and FE model. (b) Comparison of force-displacement curves between the mock-up and FE model.

4 Discussion

Elephant skin comprises several layers with a complex and highly convoluted geometry in certain regions, making it challenging to separate them, especially when longer samples are required (Fig. 1). In a previous study by Boyle et al. [19], whole-skin samples were used for uniaxial tests, while the AFM method involved separating all skin layers. In this study, uniaxial tests were conducted on the entire skin sample. Indeed, the small thickness of the single skin layers (hundreds of μm), their highly convoluted architecture in some regions like the tip, and the low availability of elephant skin samples, make it extremely hard to characterize every layer separately. Therefore, for the sake of simplification, only the epidermis (stratum corneum and viable epidermis) and corium (dermis and hypodermis) layers were mechanically separated for characterization through indentation. This simplification was based on a notable difference in thickness and toughness between the epidermis and the rest of the elephant skin. The indentation tests revealed a linear behavior for the epidermis. In contrast, the corium showed a nonlinear behavior with a minimal increase of the reaction force for indentation depths up to 10% strain, followed by a rapid increase. The indentation force applied to the epidermis was approximately one order of magnitude higher than the one applied for the corium at a strain of 20% (15 N and 0.5 N, respectively), confirming that the epidermis is stiffer than the corium. This significant contrast in their mechanical behavior justifies using a bi-layer model, despite data being obtained from defrosted rather than fresh tissue samples.

Uniaxial tensile tests were performed on three longitudinal samples (whole skin) taken from the same anatomical region of the elephant trunk, expecting to observe similar mechanical behavior. However, the results indicated in Fig. 5B demonstrated high variability in the mechanical response of these samples. Biological tissues typically exhibit plastic deformation after the first uniaxial loading cycle, resulting in an increase in sample length [21]. Subsequent cycles do not experience tension until a certain strain threshold is reached, known as the preconditioning effect [10].

This effect introduces significant hysteresis between loading-unloading cycles. To obtain consistent and repeatable experimental results, preconditioning was performed, and in these experiments, it was found that elephant skin reached a steady state after 5 cycles. In the uniaxial experiments, each sample underwent ten tensile cycles. The first five cycles were considered preconditioning effects and the second five were considered stable responses for data analysis. The average of these 5 cycles with corresponding standard deviation is shown in Fig. 5B. Since more wrinkles were observed on the softer samples (samples with higher plastic deformation) this theory was formulated that wrinkles might play a role. Sample 1, exhibiting the lowest resistance against uniaxial tensile testing, shows a high number of wrinkles perpendicular to the loading axis (90°). In contrast, sample 3, which had the highest resistance, only had one wrinkle oriented at approximately 45°. Sample 2 (median sample) has more wrinkles than Sample 1, but they are oriented along the loading axis between 0 and 45°. However, the presence of wrinkles on the skin could be a secondary result of another factor, i.e., the irreversible orientation and elongation of collagen fibers under loading. Tissue softening and plastic deformation in uniaxial tests can be related to the deformation of fibers [17]. Further studies are needed to investigate the mechanisms of wrinkle formation on the skin and its relationship with the underlying skin structures, like collagen fibers. Moreover, the results were obtained from defrosted samples, and it would be valuable to compare the current data with that retrieved from fresh samples or in vivo tests.

A bi-layer FE model was developed to explore the mechanisms that enable the elephant skin to be simultaneously tough and deformable. The first simulation showed how SC islands separate upon stretching, and the elastic strain energy was compared for the epidermis and corium layers. The stiffer and larger volume of the epidermis was expected to require higher energy to deform compared to the corium layer. However, the results showed the opposite trend. This suggests that the presence of channels in the elephant skin, in addition to their role in absorbing and maintaining moisture [6], leads to the formation of an island-like structure in SC that influences the mechanical behavior of the skin. The simulation suggests that if the epidermis did not have the separated island shape structure, this stiff and tough layer would have significantly limited the local deformability.

This study investigates the microstructure of elephant skin to identify distinctive skin characteristics contributing to its thickness and resilience. The long-term goal is to develop a comprehensive model that can investigate the distribution of strain energy density throughout different areas of the skin when subjected to external stimuli (e.g., compressive forces, traction in different directions), like previous studies in human skin. For instance, Pham et al. [16] examined microstructures' impact on human skin's sensitivity by using FEM to model various skin regions, focusing on mechanoreceptor locations.

To deeply investigate the relationship between the biomechanical features of elephant skin and tactile sensitivity, information about the different types and distribution of mechanoreceptors in elephant skin would be required (also referred to as 'morphological computation' related to sensory organs [1, 25]). The second model in this study addressed the role of epidermal ridges under normal compressive force, confirming that these structures experience the highest equivalent strain. Utilizing this localized effect could inspire the development of artificial skins with thickness, resilience, and sensitivity. Furthermore, future studies should explore the effects of other microstructures, such as dermal papillae, on focalizing strain energy density and enhancing deformation.

To validate the accuracy of the FE model, a mock-up of elephant skin was created using artificial materials. PDMS 10:1 was chosen for the epidermis layer and Ecoflex 0030 for the corium layer. The transparency of PDMS allowed for observation of the inner skin's structure, and its relative hardness compared to Ecoflex 0030 closely resembled the difference in the mechanical behavior of elephant skin layers. However, while aiming to choose materials with similar mechanical behavior to natural elephant skin, the materials did not fully meet this objective. Specifically, although Ecoflex 0030 exhibits nonlinear behavior similar to natural corium, it behaves differently under high strains. It was observed that the force-displacement curves for natural corium exhibit a J-shaped curve with three loading phases [10, 20, 21, 26]: first, stretching of easily stretched elastic fibers, second, reorientation of collagen fibers along the load axis, and third stretching of collagen fibers. However, the artificial materials behaved differently in the second and third phases, which may be attributed mainly to the absence of any fiber-like arrangement (in addition to other characteristics of natural skin, such as interstitial fluid and pores) which implementation was not addressed at this stage of the research. Further investigations are required to develop artificial skin that matches the mechanical behavior of natural skin.

5   Conclusions

This study provides insights into the investigation and preliminary modeling of elephant trunk skin, aiming to understand the impact of its unique structure on stress distribution and deformation. Elephant skin exhibits a complex structure composed of different layers, with the epidermis as the stiffest and most superficial layer acting as a protective barrier for the softer underlying layers. The epidermis also possesses a discrete island-like structure that promotes overall skin deformation. The numerical model used in the investigation is a simplified bi-layer structure, and the model parameters were obtained through the mechanical characterization of skin samples. Simulations were conducted in simplified scenarios which demonstrated that the islands in the superficial layer do not experience high stresses and do not limit deformation during uniaxial tensile tests. Another scenario involved applying a compressive force to the epidermis, revealing that the maximum strain occurs around epidermal ridges. Future work will investigate more complex stimulation scenarios representing realistic situations of skin interaction with the environment and explore the role of smaller microstructures like dermal papillae in order to optimize the FE model. Additionally, improved mock-ups with biomimetic 3D morphology will be developed using new materials to validate the numerical model.

Acknowledgments. The authors would like to thank the following people from the Istituto Italiano di Tecnologia: Seonggun Joe for the support in developing the experimental set up; Simone Lantean, Rosalia Bertorelli, and Maria Summa, for their support in samples' preparation. The authors also would like to thank the Zoo Zurich (Switzerland) for providing the trunk of an Asian elephant and Henning Richter, Maya Kummrow and Jean-Michel Hatt at the Tierspital (Zurich, Switzerland) for CT scans of the Asian elephant trunk. This work received funding from the European Union's Horizon 2020 research and innovation program under grant agreement No. 863212 (PROBOSCIS project).

References

1. Astreinidi Blandin, A., Bernardeschi, I., Beccai, L.: Biomechanics in soft mechanical sensing: from natural case studies to the artificial world. Biomimetics **3**(4), 32 (2018)
2. Yang, W., Chen, I.H., Gludovatz, B., Zimmermann, E.A., Ritchie, R.O., Meyers, M.A.: Natural flexible dermal armor. Adv. Mater. **25**(1), 31–48 (2013)
3. Ghazlan, A., Ngo, T., Tan, P., Xie, Y.M., Tran, P., Donough, M.: Inspiration from Nature's body armours–A review of biological and bioinspired composites. Compos. Part B Eng. **205**, 108513 (2021)
4. Smith, F.: Histology of the skin of the elephant. J. Anat. Physiol. **24**(Pt 4), 493 (1890)
5. Luck, C., Wright, P.: Aspects of the anatomy and physiology of the skin of the hippopotamus (H. amphibius). Q. J. Exp. Physiol. Cogn. Med. Sci. Transl. Integr. **49**(1), 1–14 (1964)
6. Spearman, R.: The epidermis and its keratinisation in the African elephant (Loxodonta africana). Afr. Zool. **5**(2) (1970)
7. Martins, A.F., et al.: Locally-curved geometry generates bending cracks in the African elephant skin. Nat. Commun. **9**(1), 1–8 (2018)
8. Schulz, A.K., et al.: Skin wrinkles and folds enable asymmetric stretch in the elephant trunk. Proc. Natl. Acad. Sci. **119**(31), e2122563119 (2022)
9. Dagenais, P., Hensman, S., Haechler, V., Milinkovitch, M.C.: Elephants evolved strategies reducing the biomechanical complexity of their trunk. Curr. Biol. **31**(21), 4727–4737 (2021)
10. Joodaki, H., Panzer, M.B.: Skin mechanical properties and modeling: A review. Proc. Inst. Mech. Eng. Part H: J. Eng. Med. **232**(4), 323–343 (2018)
11. Kolarsick, P.A., Kolarsick, M.A., Goodwin, C.: Anatomy and physiology of the skin. J. Dermatol. Nurses Assoc. **3**(4), 203–213 (2011)
12. Gilaberte, Y., Prieto-Torres, L., Pastushenko, I., Juarranz, Á.: Anatomy and Function of the Skin. In: Nanoscience in Dermatology, Elsevier, pp. 1–14 (2016)
13. Chu, D.H.: Development and structure of skin. In: Klaus Wolf et al (ed), Fitzpatrick" s Dermatology in General Medicine seven edition (2008)

14. Van Scott, E.: Mechanical separation of the epidermis from the corium. J. Invest. Dermatol. **18**(5), 377–379 (1952)
15. Felsher, Z.: Studies on the adherence of the epidermis to the corium. Proc. Soc. Exp. Biol. Med. **62**(2), 213–215 (1946)
16. Pham, T.Q., Hoshi, T., Tanaka, Y., Sano, A.: Effect of 3D microstructure of dermal papillae on SED concentration at a mechanoreceptor location. PLoS ONE **12**(12), e0189293 (2017)
17. Witte, M., Rübhausen, M., Jaspers, S., Wenck, H., Fischer, F.: A method to analyze the influence of mechanical strain on dermal collagen morphologies. Sci. Rep. **11**(1), 7565 (2021)
18. Navindaran, K., Kang, J.S., Moon, K.: Techniques for characterizing mechanical properties of soft tissues. J. Mech. Behav. Biomed. Mater., 105575 (2022).
19. Boyle, C.J., et al.: Morphology and composition play distinct and complementary roles in the tolerance of plantar skin to mechanical load. Sci. Adv. **5**(10), eaay0244 (2019)
20. Geerligs, M.: Skin layer mechanics. Eindh: TU Eindhoven (2010)
21. Remache, D., Caliez, M., Gratton, M., Dos Santos, S.: The effects of cyclic tensile and stress-relaxation tests on porcine skin. J. Mech. Behav. Biomed. Mater. **77**, 242–249 (2018)
22. Sales, F.C., Ariati, R.M., Noronha, V.T., Ribeiro, J.E.: Mechanical characterization of PDMS with different mixing ratios. Procedia Struct. Integr. **37**, 383–388 (2022)
23. Meththananda, I.M., Parker, S., Patel, M.P., Braden, M.: The relationship between Shore hardness of elastomeric dental materials and young's modulus. Dent. Mater. **25**(8), 956–959 (2009)
24. Moerman, K.M., Holt, C.A., Evans, S.L., Simms, C.K.: Digital image correlation and finite element modelling as a method to determine mechanical properties of human soft tissue in vivo. J. Biomech. **42**(8), 1150–1153 (2009)
25. Preti, M.L., Thuruthel, T.G., Gilday, K., Beccai, L., Iida, F.: Mechanical sensing in embodied agents. In: IOP Conference Series: Materials Science and Engineering, p. 012013. IOP Publishing (2022)
26. Brown, I.A.: A scanning electron microscope study of the effects of uniaxial tension on human skin. Br. J. Dermatol. **89**(4), 383–393 (1973)

Development of a Robotic Rat Hindlimb Model

Evan Aronhalt[1]([✉])[iD], Eabha Abramson[1][iD], Clarus Goldsmith[2][iD],
Emanuel Andrada[3][iD], William Nourse[4][iD], Gregory Sutton[5][iD],
Nicholas Szczecinski[2][iD], and Roger Quinn[1][iD]

[1] Department of Mechanical and Aerospace Engineering, Case Western Reserve
University, Cleveland, OH 44106, USA
`era32@case.edu`
[2] Department of Mechanical and Aerospace Engineering, West Virginia University,
Morgantown, WV 26505, USA
[3] Institute of Zoology and Evolutionary Research, Friedrich-Schiller University, Jena,
Germany
[4] Department of Electrical, Computer, and Systems Engineering, Case Western
Reserve University, Cleveland, OH 44106, USA
[5] School of Life Sciences, University of Lincoln (UK),
Brayford Pool, Lincoln LN6 7TS, UK

Abstract. This paper discusses the design decisions, process, and
results for a set of robotic rat hindlimbs scaled up to 2.5 times the size
of the rat. The design is inspired by a previous model from within our
lab, but includes a variety of improvements to further the utility and biological accuracy of the model. The robot is comprised of two legs with
four motors each to actuate sagittal rotations of the hip, knee, and ankle
joints as well as an internal hip rotation. The motor's torque, inertial,
viscous, and stiffness properties are characterized for dynamic scaling
to be properly implemented in the future control scheme. With direct
position commands, the robot's joint movements are able to reflect those
of the rat, proving its validity as a test bed for the implementation of
future neural control schemes.

Keywords: Rat hindlimb · Robot · Dynamic scaling

1 Introduction

Robot locomotion capabilities are continuously advancing. Robots today are better able to traverse complex environments through advanced mechanical design

This work was supported by NSF RI 1704436 and also DFG FI 410/16-1 and NSF DBI
2015317 as part of the NSF/CIHR/DFG/FRQ/UKRI-MRC Next Generation Networks
for Neuroscience Program.

and control schemes. One source of inspiration for robot design is the animal kingdom. Animals have evolved over many years to navigate through a variety of environments with relative ease, a capability that is still being developed and perfected in robots. Several robots that have taken inspiration from biology are Drosophibot, Puppy, and MIT Cheetah 3, based on the fruit fly, whippet, and cheetah, respectively [2,8,10].

Outside of the lab's previous hindlimb model and a model produced by Shi et al. [7,15], rat robots have yet to be explored in great depth. A rat is a prime candidate for a biologically inspired robot for a variety of reasons. A robot with the locomotion ability of a rat could have many practical uses. Furthermore, rat data is both readily available and easily acquired if needed due to the commonality of testing on rats. In addition, there are few legged robots with a similar dynamic scale to rats, which makes it interesting from a scientific perspective. This paper discusses the design decisions for and philosophies behind the design of a set of robotic rat hindlimbs.

2   Design

2.1   Previous Iteration

A previous robotic rat hindlimb model was developed by Emmett Donnelley-Power, from which inspiration was taken and a variety of design decisions were kept, shown in Fig. 1 [7].

This robot has two legs each with three degrees of freedom consisting of sagittal plane rotation at the hip, knee, and ankle. The limbs are approximated by rods, and they are actuated by Dynamixel MX-64 and AX-12A servo motors (Robotis, Seoul, South Korea). The two legs are connected by a connector piece located where the pelvis would exist. This connector piece is then free to translate vertically but not horizontally or rotationally through the rod in the center of the assembly and the two drawer slides in the back. The mount allows for self-supported walking movements without the system actually moving forward, removing the need for a treadmill or wheels. The basic principles of this robot, i.e. using motors to control each joint, approximate robot size, serial control, and general mount design, were carried over to the new design.

2.2   Limb and Joint Design

The new robot described in this paper consists of two legs with three limb segments each: the femur, tibia, and foot, a pelvis, and an electronics mount on top. Each leg has 4 degrees of freedom: sagittal rotation at the hip, knee, and ankle, and femoral long axis rotation at the hip. The decision to use these 4 degrees of freedom was informed by experimentally gathered data of joint angles during rat trot as well as data from Dienes et al.'s paper on 3 dimensional rat hindlimb walking analysis [6].

In our experiments, which were approved by the Committee for Animal Research of the State of Thuringia, Germany (registry number: 02-060/16),

Fig. 1. Robot rat hindlimb model created by Emmett Donnelley-Power. One should note the center fixture where the pelvis should be, as this is one of the larger changes in the updated model. The fixture on this model tended to lean backwards, as the slider joints connected to each motor would easily become loose. Also, the fixture was much wider than the pelvis would have been, leading to inaccuracy in the limb placement. In addition, one can see that all of the limb segments are in plane with each other. In the animal, the limb segments share parallel planes, but are slightly out of plane with each other.

rats moved across a 2.3 m walking track, at their preferred speeds. Body and limb kinematics were collected by using a bi-planar high-speed x-ray fluoroscope (Neurostar, Siemens, Erlangen, Germany) and two synchronized standard light high-speed cameras (SpeedCam Visario g2, Weinberger, Erlangen, Germany) at 500 Hz. X-ray raw video data was first undistorted (batchUndistort routine, www.xromm.org). Manual digitization of the landmarks was performed in SimiMotion (SimiMotion Systems, Unterschleißheim, Germany). Knee, ankle and metatarsophalangeal joint angles were computed as three-point angles. To estimate the three-dimensional rotations occurring at the hip, we computed the relative Cardian angles (x-y-z) between the pelvis and a plane formed by the hip joint, the knee joint and the ankle joint (Fig. 2), for further information see [1].

The three sagittal plane rotations were chosen as they all have a range of motion greater than 60° (Fig. 3). Thus, they were all deemed essential for three dimensional walking. The hip is the logical next place to add degrees of freedom to allow locomotion out of the sagittal plane. Changes in the hip joint position

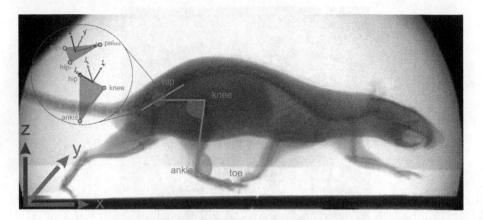

Fig. 2. X-ray image of a rat during trot. Superimposed are the analyzed body segments and joint angles. Knee, ankle and metatarsophalangeal joint angles were computed as three-point angles. Hip three-dimensional rotations were estimated by computing the Cardian angles between the pelvis (composed by both hip joints and the pelvis cranial marker) and a plane formed by the hip joint, the knee joint, and the ankle joint.

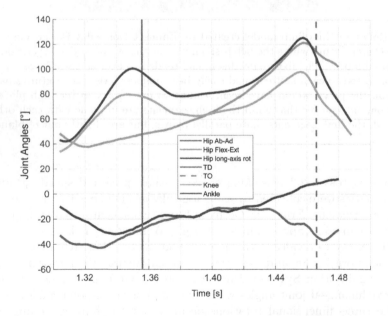

Fig. 3. Joint angle data for the rat hindlimb over one step. Assuming that the knee, and ankle mainly work as revolute joints, the motion of the plane formed by the hip, knee and ankle relative to the pelvis display three-dimensional hip kinematics. Ab-Ad: abduction/adduction. Flex-Ext: flexion/extension. TD: touch-down, TO: toe-off. Positive Hip Flex-Ext values indicate hip extension. Positive values in long axis rotation indicate femoral internal rotation while the foot is moved towards lateral. Positive Ab-Ad values indicate adduction.

have the greatest effect on limb placement during gait due to the joint's placement at the beginning of the leg chain. As such, changes in hip position move the entire leg and can have a great effect on foot movement. In addition, the second degree of freedom found in the knee joint of a rat is barely noticeable, and the other degrees of freedom in the ankle joint are used primarily for foot stability [12].

Only one other joint was included due to space limitations on the robot, increased robot mass, and diminishing returns in accuracy for increased design complexity. The hip internal and external rotation was chosen over hip abduction and adduction due to it having an overall greater range of motion. The data from Dienes et al. shows hip internal rotation having a range of motion of approximately 30° compared to the hip adduction range of motion of 10° [6]. However, abduction/adduction may be important to the hindlimb locomotion, and the effects of these rotations will be explored in future work.

The limbs were created from 3 dimensional models by Hunt et al. [11] and adapted into Solidworks 3D model files (Solidworks Corp., Waltham, MA). The choice to create the limbs in the shape of rat bones instead of an arbitrary shape was guided by several factors. The primary reason was that all attachment points between limb segments could be easily placed where they are found in the animal. In addition, force transfer within the limb segments would be slightly more accurate to the animal since the position of the joints is accurate. This only applies to the joint reaction force, and only partially, as the lack of musculature greatly changes the force distribution of the system.

The foot design had to be changed due to a lack of structural integrity in the bony foot model. The current foot is longer and thicker than an actual rat foot would be, with a slight convex curvature to help with sliding along the ground (Fig. 4). This behavior is normally accounted for by the metatarsophalangeal joints which were omitted from the design for the sake of reducing complexity [18].

Fig. 4. Comparison between new (left) and old (right) foot design.

The robot is 2.5 times larger than a female Sprague-Dawley rat. Limb segment length data were obtained from Johnson et al. [12]. This length scale was chosen for practical purposes. It is easier to work with components at this scale and the high efficiency motor/transmissions were available for this robot size.

For the sagittal plane attachment points, the driving motor is mounted on the proximal limb segment using a circular mounting face. For example, the motor driving the tibia is mounted at the bottom of the femur. The limb segment being driven is attached to the driving motor via the motor's shaft by a hole in the limb segment with a flat to match that of the motor shaft. This connection is then secured by placing a bolt through a hole on the flat of the motor shaft and limb segment hole, minimizing slip between the shaft and limb segment.

The hip internal rotation motors were mounted onto the pelvis. A connector piece and a bracket were then used to mount this motor and the hip sagittal rotation motor. The hip internal rotation motors were raised vertically so that the final position of the hip sagittal rotation axis matched that in the animal. In addition, careful attention was given to making sure the axes of rotation of these two joints intersected to create a partial ball-and-socket joint instead of two separate rotational joints, meaning that the two rotational axes intersected throughout the entire gait cycle. Finally, the ball of the femur and the socket of the hip were used to position the limb at the correct location. Both attachments are shown in Fig. 5.

All structural components were printed using the Markforged Mark Two 3D printer (Markforged, Watertown, MA). They were primarily made with the

Fig. 5. Left: Attachment between the femur (green) and tibia (red) at the knee joint. The motor driving the tibia is attached to the previous limb segment (the femur) securely by the circular pattern of three screws shown in the picture. The motor shaft is secured to the tibia both by the flat seen on the shaft and the hole as well as the screw and nut seen travelling through the tibia and motor shaft; utilizing both of these methods minimizes slippage of the shaft when driving the tibia. **Right:** Hip assembly for the left leg. The sagittal hip rotation motor, driving the femur (green), is attached to the L bracket (yellow), which is then attached to the connector piece (pink) that is driven by the motor responsible for the internal and external rotation of the hip. That motor is attached to the pelvis (blue). (Color figure online)

company's proprietary filament, Onyx, with the addition of varying amounts of carbon fiber supports. All limb segments were carbon fiber reinforced since they will be transferring the forces of walking. The bracket, connector piece, and bottom of the pelvis were also fully reinforced to hold the weight of an entire leg assembly. Carbon fiber was omitted from the top of the pelvis and in the electronics mount, since these areas will be lightly loaded.

The electronics mount is attached to the top of the pelvis and houses the eight electronic speed controllers used by the motors, the power board, and the Controller Area Network (CAN) board, where all eight motors' CAN cables are connected. CAN will be discussed in the Sect. 2.3. All motors are powered by one off-board 24 V power supply and communicate with an Arduino Teensy 4.0 Microcontroller (PJRC, Sherwood, USA) located slightly off-board the robot.

The mount was designed similarly to the one used in Donnelly-Power's robot; it allows for self-supported walking movements while keeping the robot in place by restraining the pelvis with a rod and spring to provide support and allow vertical motion through clamping the base. However, only one rod was used instead of a rod with drawer rails to reduce friction. In addition, a bearing was put inside of the pelvis during printing to further reduce friction during walking. The full Solidworks assembly is shown in Fig. 6.

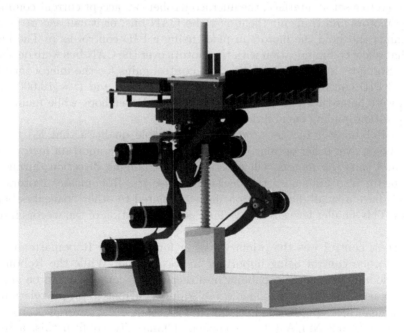

Fig. 6. Full rat hindlimbs and pelvis model in Solidworks with electronics. The bars on the mount are for the stability of the robot, particularly during the limb pushing against the ground. The electronics at the top include the CAN and power boards near the back of the robot and the eight speed controllers housed near the front.

2.3   Motor Testing and Characterization

Despite rats using 38 muscles in their hind legs [19], electric motors were chosen as the actuators for the robot for practical purposes. Artificial muscles such as McKibbens have many advantages in terms of more closely modeling the animal [10]. However, they also have many disadvantages, such as requiring an air compressor and valves. Thus, it is easier to develop an autonomous robot to run outside of the lab using motors, which is the end goal of this project.

The previous model also uses motors, but instead uses Dynamixel MX-64 and AX-12A motors (Robotis, Seoul, South Korea). We decided against using Dynamixels for this project because we desired greater torque, greater backdrivability and better feedback.

We chose Robomaster M2006 (DJI, Shenzhen, China) motors with C610 speed controllers for all joints in the robot. These motors use the Controller Area Network (CAN) bus protocol to communicate with each other and the Teensy microcontroller (PJRC, Sherwood, USA). CAN bus is a form of serial communication where the motors are connected to each other instead of needing to all be individually connected to the microcontroller [3].

The main low level control software, written in C++, runs on the microcontroller and continually sends commands to the motors over the CAN bus. While connected to a serial interface, the microcontroller can accept current commands for the motors and transmit them over the CAN bus, or it can accept position commands and hold the motors in place using a PID control loop. The header files that allow communication with the motors over the CAN bus were developed by the Stanford Robotics Club [13]. The control gains for the microcontroller's onboard PID control loop are P = 100,000, I = 5,000, and D = 10,000. These values were hand-tuned to minimize rise time and overshoot while maintaining good position-holding capabilities.

The Robomaster motors have several desirable qualities that led to them being chosen over other options. Backdrivability was an important factor, as the limbs and thus the motors will constantly be changing direction during gait. Form factor also influenced the decision to use the Robomaster motors. The M2006's have a small diameter front face compared to other "pancake-shaped" motors. This smaller face size allows for easier integration of the motors into the robot.

Current control was the primary reason for using the Robomaster motors, due to torque control being important in locomotion. While the Robomaster motors do not possess the capability of direct torque control, it can be approximated by using current control and establishing a current-to-torque relationship. The manufacturer specifications claim that the motor has a torque constant of approximately 0.2 Nm/A (DJI, Shenzhen, China). To confirm this, a testing procedure was developed to measure the torque the motor produces when commanded a specific current value. A rod was attached to the motor output shaft about its end. Then, a current command was sent so that the motor would begin to rotate. The rod would then collide with a scale, from which the scale reading would be converted to a force, and then that force converted to a torque based on the rod length. This process was repeated for different currents, starting at 0 A and increasing by 0.1 A until reaching 3.5 A. The motor's rated maximum continuous current is 3 A. The final torque constant obtained through experimentation was 0.2657 Nm/A, with Fig. 7 showing all of the tests. This is a 32.85% increase from the manufacturer specified torque constant.

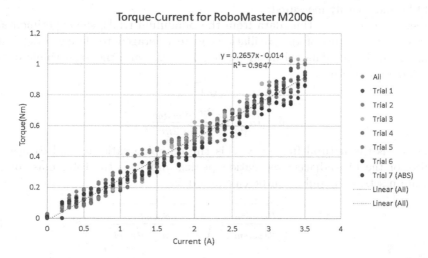

Fig. 7. Experimental torque vs. current relationship for the RoboMaster M2006 motor.

In this paper, the robot is controlled by animal joint angles being given as position commands to the motors. This is done to test the design and strength of the robot.

The manufacturer specifications of the motor claim the motors can produce 1 Nm of maximum continuous torque. We discovered that the maximum torque the motor could produce was just over 1 Nm at stall. If the limb is fully extended, the gravitational torque on the hip sagittal motor will be 0.58 Nm, which is slightly greater than half of the stall torque. This extreme scenario would not occur during normal walking; the gravitational torque seen would be less, thus we believe the motors will have sufficient torque.

In addition to the current-to-torque relationship, other quantities need to be measured to facilitate correct dynamic scaling: the motor's internal moment of inertia from the rotor (J_{motor}), damping coefficient from electromagnetic field effects in the coils (c_{motor}), and stiffness from the proportional gain of the PID loop (k_{motor}). The testing procedure utilized for this characterization is similar to that used for Drosophibot [8]. For J_{motor} and c_{motor}, this process involves attaching a weighted pendulum to the motor and recording the motor's position during freely rotating pendulum oscillations. These oscillation tests were conducted both while the motor was non-powered and while the motor was powered with no commanded position set. Both the damping and stiffness require power to the motor to be present, so removing power isolates the effects of J_{motor} in the setup. Powering the motor without a commanded position then adds damping into the system without adding stiffness, as the PID loop is not utilized. The exact mass placed at the end of the pendulum varied depending on the test conducted. For inertia testing, a mass of 500 g was used to minimize inertia of the pendulum and make the motor's inertia easier to measure. For damping tests, a mass of 1000 g was used to increase the number of oscillations so that c_{motor} could be more easily measured.

Using the angle vs. time data from the pendulum trials, the experimentally observable properties of the oscillations were leveraged to derive J_{motor} and c_{motor}. Namely, the damped natural frequency (ω_d) and the logarithmic decrement (δ) were utilized:

$$\omega_d = \omega_n \sqrt{1 - \zeta^2} \tag{1}$$

$$\delta = ln\frac{\theta_1}{\theta_2} = \frac{2\pi \cdot c_{motor}}{\omega_d \cdot 2m} \tag{2}$$

where ω_n is the natural frequency, ζ is the damping ratio, θ_1 and θ_2 are the heights of the two adjacent oscillation peaks, and m is the total mass of the pendulum setup. ω_n and ζ can be calculated as:

$$\omega_n = \sqrt{\frac{k_{system}}{J_{system}}} = \sqrt{\frac{k_{pend}}{J_{motor} + J_{pend}}} \tag{3}$$

$$\zeta = \frac{\delta}{(2\pi)^2 + \delta^2} \tag{4}$$

where k_{pend} is the stiffness of the pendulum due to gravity:

$$k_{pend} = g \cdot m \cdot L_{pend} \tag{5}$$

And J_{pend} is the pendulum's moment of inertia:

$$J_{pend} = m \cdot L_{pend}^2 \tag{6}$$

L_{pend} is the length of the pendulum. Equations 3–6 can be substituted into Eqs. 1 and 2, and the equations reordered to produce equations to solve for J_{motor} and c_{motor} from easily calculated or observed quantities:

$$J_{motor} = \frac{k_{pend}}{\omega_d^2}(1 - \frac{\delta}{\sqrt{(2\pi)^2 + \delta^2}}) - J_{pend} \tag{7}$$

50 inertia trials and 50 damping trials were recorded, then MATLAB (The MathWorks, Natick, Massachusetts) scripts were used to compile and evaluate the data. A moment of inertia of $J_{motor} = 0.00392 \pm 0.00188\,\mathrm{kgm}^2$ (47.9% error), a damping ratio of $\zeta = 0.119 \pm 0.0109$ (9.20% error), and a damping coefficient of $1.617 \pm 0.146\,\mathrm{Ns/m}$ (9.03% error) were calculated.

This testing procedure was developed for Dynamixel servos, which can monitor their sensory components without powering the motor. Robomaster M2006 motors do not have a manner with which to do this while the motor is powered off, resulting in damping being present during the inertia tests. This issue contributes to the error in the calculated inertia, and will be addressed in future tests by using point tracking in video recordings instead of relying on the motor's sensory components.

Stiffness testing is based on the angular application of Hooke's law to the pendulum:

$$\tau = k_{motor} \Delta\theta \tag{8}$$

where $\Delta\theta$ is the difference between the commanded angle of the motor (θ_{com}) and actual angle (θ_{act}), and τ is the torque produced by the motor. The pendulum was positioned to press down on a scale such that a $\Delta\theta$ was produced. The scale reading was then converted to a torque value based on the pendulum length. This process was repeated for several commanded positions (and thus different $\Delta\theta$ values) to create a τ vs $\Delta\theta$ curve. k_{motor} was then calculated as the linear slope of this curve. After 5 trials, the stiffness of the motor under the present PID controller was found to be 8.40 Nm/rad.

2.4   Dynamic Scaling

The goal is for the robot to move dynamically similar to the rat. Animals of different length and dynamics require different forces to drive their locomotion. For example, insect locomotion is dominated by viscous moments during the swing phase of the limb and elastic forces to hold the limb in place during stance phase, similar to how a spring behaves [9]. Large mammal locomotion is dominated by the inertial forces of the limb following the muscle activation at the start of swing phase.

To be scaled accurately, first the forces active during rat swing phase and stance phase must be characterized; the same distribution of torques must then be present in the robotic model. Young et al. discusses the distribution of rat hindlimb torques at the hip joint below, at, and above rat scale [20]. At rat scale, the ground reaction force, or load, is dominating the muscle torque response. At horse scale, inertia is dominating the muscle torque. In their work, Young et al. use the correlation coefficient to determine the relative contribution of forces to the hip joint torques. Gravitational forces play slightly more of a role in smaller scale animals than larger animals, but are mostly overpowered by other forces at both scales. As such, the correlation coefficient may overstate the importance of gravitational forces, but remains a valuable resource to convey the impact of scale on torque contributions from viscoelastic vs. inertial forces.

At the rat scale, inertial forces have a relative contribution of 0.7 to the hip joint torques, whereas the viscoelastic forces have a relative torque contribution of -0.6, where a correlation of positive 1 means it completely dominates the motion, and a correlation of negative 1 means it does not affect the motion at all. Looking at the robot scale of 2.5 times the size of the rat, the linear correlation coefficient for inertial forces increases to 0.9, and the viscoelastic and gravitational forces decrease to about -0.8. As the size of the rat increases, the system becomes more inertially dominated. However, the desired locomotion behavior of the robot is that of a rat at true scale, not at 2.5 times scale, meaning the inertial forces of the robot model must be decreased to more accurately reflect the original size rat.

Presently, the motor's motion is stiffness dominated, as the motor's stiffness greatly outweighs its damping and inertia. This is not accurate to the rat's load dominated movement, but can be altered by changing parameters in the PID controller. The PID controller gains are currently set high to achieve a quick response, which means the motor stiffness is similarly high. The motor stiffness was further tested, this time decreasing the P gain from 100,000 to 50,000, which in turn resulted in a stiffness of 5.40 N/m compared to the previous 8.40 N/m. Further testing is required to obtain a stiffness value low enough that will result in locomotion that is more accurate to that of the rat and to see how low the stiffness can be without affecting robot performance. If a low enough stiffness is not practical, increasing the walking speed will shift the system towards being more inertially dominated [9]. Matching these dynamic properties will lead to the correct driving forces of locomotion, and subsequently the correct overall kinematics.

3   Results

Using position feedback, the commanded and actual positions were compared in the left leg, shown in Fig. 8. At this scale, there is no perceptible deviation from the commanded positions, which are the rat locomotion data on a 2.5 times time scale. This is to be expected, as these positions are being directly commanded

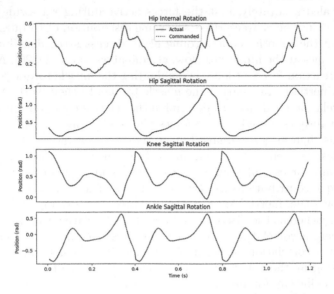

Fig. 8. Commanded and actual joint angles. Commanded joint angles are the animal joint angles at a 2.5 times time scale.

to the motor with high gains in a PID controller. This helps validate the model as being structurally sound and ready to use with future controllers by showing it is capable of reaching the rat hindlimb's range of motion. Further testing is required to ensure that the robot joint angles match those of the animal defined in the coordinate system in Fig. 3.

A video of the robot walking with commanded joint angles can be seen here: https://youtube.com/shorts/l7PZNlQlln8?feature=share, with a picture of the robot in Fig. 9.

Fig. 9. Present model of the robotic rat hindlimbs.

4   Discussion and Conclusions

In this work, a robot model of rat hindlimbs was created. The model was designed based on animal data scaled up in length by a factor of 2.5. The leg segments were 3D printed using continuous strands of carbon fiber for strength. They are models of the rat bones. The robot limb segment connections are designed to provide direct transmission of the motor output and maintain structural integrity. The hindlimbs are capable of the rat's range of motion during normal walking, with sagittal plane rotations at the hip, knee, and ankle, and a hip internal rotation, for a total of four joints in each leg. Robomaster M2006 motor's are used to actuate all of the joints. The motor's internal moment of inertia, damping, and stiffness were experimentally characterized under the present control scheme to provide data that will be used for future dynamic scaling. Using a PID controller, the leg joints can move as commanded.

Despite the simplifications of reducing the overall degrees of freedom in the hip, ankle, and metatarsophalangeal joints, the robot was able to produce a gait that matched the joint angles of the animal. This proves the robot to be a sufficient testbed for future control schemes.

There are several other improvements and iterations to be made to the model in the future. The first and most important addition will be the implementation of a synthetic nervous system (SNS) to control the hindlimbs. SNS apply models of animal nervous systems to robotic control [17].

An SNS will be used for the robotic rat hind legs that is based on the two-layer central pattern generator (CPG) model proposed by Rybak et al. and further tested and developed by Deng et al. [4,5,14]. The two layer model allows for independent control of the CPG's oscillation frequency and the motorneuron patterning. The Deng et al. SNS will be tested on this robot. A model proposed by Song et al. which uses groups of slow, intermediate, and fast V2a interneurons to change the speed of locomotion and may be more accurate to vertebrate spinal control will be explored in future work [16].

While achieving SNS control for the robot is the next primary goal, there are other small improvements that could be made to improve the model. A compliant foot could help offset the errors in toe position that arise from treating the foot as a completely rigid body and removing the metatarsophalangeal joints. A possible design inspiration could come from Drosophibot, which uses a rigid tendon moving through the foot segments connected to a spring to create a compliant foot mechanism [8]. This design mimics the feet seen in insects and not mammals, but basic principles could still be adapted to a different design for a rat. The test stand is sufficient to test early stages of the hindlimb walking, but more in depth testing will require the robot to actually use its walking to provide forward locomotion. This will require a tether to above a treadmill.

Acknowledgements. We would like to thank Emmett Donnelly-Power for his help in understanding the design philosophy behind his previous rat hindlimb robot. We would also like to thank Fletcher Young for providing data used for the scaling analysis.

References

1. Andrada, E., et al.: Limb, joint and pelvic kinematic control in the quail coping with steps upwards and downwards. Sci. Rep. **12**(1), 15901 (2022). https://doi.org/10.1038/s41598-022-20247-y
2. Bledt, G., Powell, M.J., Katz, B., Di Carlo, J., Wensing, P.M., Kim, S.: MIT cheetah 3: design and control of a robust, dynamic quadruped robot. Other repository, January 2019. Accessed 17 Aug 2020. ISBN: 9781538680940. Publisher: Institute of Electrical and Electronics Engineers (IEEE)
3. Corrigan, S.: Introduction to the Controller Area Network (CAN), May 2016. https://www.ti.com/lit/pdf/sloa101

4. Deng, K., et al.: Biomechanical and sensory feedback regularize the behavior of different locomotor central pattern generators. Biomimetics **7**(4), 226 (2022). https://doi.org/10.3390/biomimetics7040226

5. Deng, K., et al.: Neuromechanical model of rat hindlimb walking with two-layer CPGs. Biomimetics **4**(1), 21 (2019). https://doi.org/10.3390/biomimetics4010021

6. Dienes, J., Hicks, B., Slater, C., Janson, K.D., Christ, G.J., Russell, S.D.: Comprehensive dynamic and kinematic analysis of the rodent hindlimb during over ground walking. Sci. Rep. **12**(1), 19725 (2022). https://doi.org/10.1038/s41598-022-20288-3

7. Donnelley-Power, E.: Design of a rat hindlimb robot and neuromechanical controller. Master's thesis, Case Western Reserve University, Cleveland, Ohio, January 2022

8. Goldsmith, C., Szczecinski, N., Quinn, R.: Drosophibot: a fruit fly inspired biorobot. In: Martinez-Hernandez, U., et al. (eds.) Living Machines 2019. LNCS (LNAI), vol. 11556, pp. 146–157. Springer, Cham (2019). https://doi.org/10.1007/978-3-030-24741-6_13

9. Hooper, S.L., et al.: Neural control of unloaded leg posture and of leg swing in stick insect, cockroach, and mouse differs from that in larger animals. J. Neurosci. **29**(13), 4109–4119 (2009). https://doi.org/10.1523/JNEUROSCI.5510-08.2009

10. Hunt, A., Szczecinski, N., Quinn, R.: Development and training of a neural controller for hind leg walking in a dog robot. Front. Neurorobot. **11**, 18 (2017). https://doi.org/10.3389/fnbot.2017.00018

11. Hunt, A.J., Szczecinski, N.S., Andrada, E., Fischer, M., Quinn, R.D.: Using animal data and neural dynamics to reverse engineer a neuromechanical rat model. In: Wilson, S.P., Verschure, P.F.M.J., Mura, A., Prescott, T.J. (eds.) LIVINGMACHINES 2015. LNCS (LNAI), vol. 9222, pp. 211–222. Springer, Cham (2015). https://doi.org/10.1007/978-3-319-22979-9_21

12. Johnson, W.L., Jindrich, D.L., Roy, R.R., Reggie Edgerton, V.: A three-dimensional model of the rat hindlimb: musculoskeletal geometry and muscle moment arms. J. Biomech. **41**(3), 610–619 (2008). https://doi.org/10.1016/j.jbiomech.2007.10.004

13. Kau, N.: DJI C610 + M2006 interface library, November 2022. Original-date: 20 September 2020

14. Rybak, I.A., Shevtsova, N.A., Lafreniere-Roula, M., McCrea, D.A.: Modelling spinal circuitry involved in locomotor pattern generation: insights from deletions during fictive locomotion: modelling spinal circuitry involved in locomotor pattern generation. J. Physiol. **577**(2), 617–639 (2006). https://doi.org/10.1113/jphysiol.2006.118703

15. Shi, Q., et al.: Development of a small-sized quadruped robotic rat capable of multimodal motions. IEEE Trans. Robot. **38**(5), 3027–3043 (2022). https://doi.org/10.1109/TRO.2022.3159188. conference Name: IEEE Transactions on Robotics

16. Song, J., et al.: Multiple rhythm-generating circuits act in tandem with pacemaker properties to control the start and speed of locomotion. Neuron **105**(6), 1048–1061 (2020). https://doi.org/10.1016/j.neuron.2019.12.030

17. Szczecinski, N.S., Hunt, A.J., Quinn, R.D.: A functional subnetwork approach to designing synthetic nervous systems that control legged robot locomotion. Front. Neurorobot. **11**, 37 (2017). https://doi.org/10.3389/fnbot.2017.00037

18. Varejão, A.S.P., et al.: Motion of the foot and ankle during the stance phase in rats: rat ankle angle during stance. Muscle Nerve **26**(5), 630–635 (2002). https://doi.org/10.1002/mus.10242

19. Young, F., Rode, C., Hunt, A., Quinn, R.: Analyzing moment arm profiles in a full-muscle rat hindlimb model. Biomimetics **4**(1), 10 (2019). https://doi.org/10.3390/biomimetics4010010
20. Young, F.R., Chiel, H.J., Tresch, M.C., Heckman, C.J., Hunt, A.J., Quinn, R.D.: Analyzing modeled torque profiles to understand scale-dependent active muscle responses in the hip joint. Biomimetics **7**(1), 17 (2022). https://doi.org/10.3390/biomimetics7010017

Toward a More Realistic 3D Biomimetic Soft Robotic Tongue to Investigate Oral Processing of Semi-solid Foods

Alejandro Avila-Sierra$^{(\boxtimes)}$ (ID), Yurixy Bugarin-Castillo (ID), Juluan Voisin, Vincent Mathieu, and Marco Ramaioli (ID)

Université Paris-Saclay, INRAE, AgroParisTech, UMR SayFood, 91120 Palaiseau, France
alejandro.avila-sierra@inrae.fr

Abstract. The current *in vitro* experiments reproducing food oral processing are not fully representative of the oral anatomy and of the biomechanics of the human tongue. Creating an *in vitro* device imitating the intricate interfacial and mechanical features, as well as the combination of motions of the human tongue, is critical to gain a quantitative understanding of how fluids and foods interact with oral surfaces. We present here a unique pneumatic three-dimensional multi-degree-of-freedom soft robotic actuator – the Biomimetic Soft Robotic Tongue (BSRT) – that embodies the mechanical performance and wettability of the human tongue, with realistic movements, and the surface roughness of the human tongue papillae. The present study presents a promising technology that can be used to realistically simulate the bolus dynamics in a variety of individual conditions, paving the way to design personalized food products meeting individual needs.

Keywords: Biomimetic tongue · soft robotics · oral processing · oral propulsion · semi-solid foods

1 Introduction

In humans, eating and swallowing are complex neuromuscular activities, involving more than 20 muscles. The physiology of normal ingestion and swallowing of liquids is described by the Four-stage Model [1] which consists of the oral preparatory and oral transit phases, as well as the pharyngeal and esophageal stages of swallowing. The oral preparation stage begins with the introduction of the food product in the mouth and ends when the food bolus is ready for swallowing. Once placed into the mouth, liquids and semi-solid foods are mainly subjected to heating, shearing, squeezing, dilution, and chemical breakdown by salivary enzymes [2–4]. For liquids, the bolus is held in the anterior part of the tongue against the hard palate and surrounded by the upper dental arch. To prevent liquid from entering the oropharynx before the swallow is triggered, the oral cavity is sealed posteriorly by the contact between the soft palate and tongue. Although liquids tend to be consumed quite rapidly – bolus texture is mostly maintained from ingestion to the swallow onset [1] – semi-solid foods may take a little longer, because their oral preparation is heavily influenced by tongue movements that both exert shear

F. Meder et al. (Eds.): Living Machines 2023, LNAI 14158, pp. 131–140, 2023.
https://doi.org/10.1007/978-3-031-39504-8_9

forces and facilitate saliva mixing to modulate the rheological properties of the ingested foods [4, 5]. The oral transit stage, on the other hand, is a voluntary phase that begins with the posterior propulsion of the bolus by the tongue towards the back part of the oral cavity, i.e., pharynx, and ends with initiation of the pharyngeal phase of swallowing. In either phase, oral preparatory or oral transit, the tongue moves, squeezes, and twists the food bolus, resulting in a complex combination of motions that are extremely difficult to emulate.

Current *in vitro* experiments attempting to reproduce oral food processing lack complete accuracy in capturing the intricacies of the oral anatomy and physiological biomechanics of the human tongue. While the importance of rheology and tribology in measuring food texture is widely recognized [6–9], there is no system yet capable of realistically simulating the dynamic changes that occur in the human oral cavity when semi-solid foods are ingested. The tongue, being a soft tissue comprising micro-asperities known as papillae (such as fungiform and filiform papillae), contributes to precise oral friction and lubrication, aided by tongue wettability. These factors play a crucial role in controlling biophysical functions like sensory perception and food transport [10], ultimately affecting the amount of residue remaining in the mouth after swallowing. Therefore, it is crucial to develop a system that accurately mimics the intricate architectural, chemical, and mechanical features, as well as the complex motions of the human tongue. Such a system is essential for gaining a comprehensive and quantitative understanding of how fluids and foods interact with the surfaces of the oral cavity.

Several *in vitro* devices imitating different aspects of human swallowing were proposed in the literature, as discussed in [11]. In this paper, we present a unique pneumatic multi-degree-of-freedom soft robotic actuator that, emulating the heterogeneity of papillae, mechanical performance, and wettability of the human tongue, can move realistically at a three-dimensional geometry. With the ability to adjust the actuation pattern according to the individual's features and needs (e.g., a healthy tongue pattern can be tuned to simulate altered tongue strength and poor tongue coordination), the artificial tongue can mimic clinically relevant bolus dynamics depending on the characteristics of the food ingested, while operating within a realistic environment (i.e., salivary lubrication and chemical action, temperature, and representative oral stresses and forces).

2   Materials and Methods

The pneumatic soft robotic actuator, designed to resemble the human tongue, possesses external dimensions that align with the 320-row area detector computed tomography scans of a healthy adult oral cavity, generously provided by [12]. To create the soft actuator, a platinum-catalysed silicone rubber (Ecoflex® 00-30, Smooth-on Inc., Pennsylvania, U.S.A) is employed, which possesses a hardness comparable to that of the human pharynx [13]. The silicone rubber is prepared following the guidelines provided by the supplier. Utilising a MakerBot Replicator 2® 3D printer, the tongue moulds are manufactured using PLA material. The manufacturing process of the tongue mould can be visualised in Fig. 1.

For the assessment of surface wettability, contact angle measurements of a water droplet (10 µL) at an equilibrium state are conducted using the sessile drop technique.

In order to modify the wettability of Ecoflex 00-30, a surfactant (Span 80, 0.5 wt %) is introduced, as elaborated in [14]. A high-speed camera (model ac A2040-120 um, Basler, Ahrensburg, Germany) captures the temporal evolution of the contact angle, while the data processing is carried out using ImageJ® software. According to previous studies, the addition of Span 80 at this concentration does not significantly impact the tensile response of Ecoflex 00-30, which remains at 77 ± 9 and 75 ± 4 kPa, respectively [14].

Table 1. Topographical features (average size and papillae density) data of human tongue surface in a middle section of the tongue [10]

Type of papillae	Density (per 10^{-4} m^2)	Diameter (μm)	Height (μm)
Fungiform	13.5 ± 1.5	878.0 ± 97.0	390.0 ± 72.0
Filiform	160.0 ± 30.0	355.0 ± 40.0	195.0 ± 6.5

The biomimetic texturing of the surface of the soft actuator is based on the topographical *in vivo* data (average size and papillae density) of the human tongue reported by [10], listed in Table 1. The realistic tongue-like surface was designed using Fusion 360® (Autodesk, Inc., France), generating a model surface pattern (10×10 mm) with a random spatial distribution of filiform and fungiform papillae, avoiding overlapping. The surface texturing mould was 3D printed in resin using an ElegooMars 2P® printer. This biomimetic surface was employed to mould-cast the upper surface of the soft actuator as depicted in Fig. 1A.

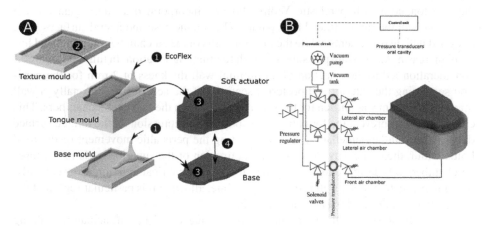

Fig. 1. Manufacturing process (A) and schematics of the pneumatic system (B) used to fabricate and control the soft robotic tongue actuator. Manufacturing process stages: (1) pouring of the Ecoflex mixture into the moulds, (2) adding the surface texturing mould (if used), (3) de-moulding of the cured soft actuator and its base, and (4) final glueing of both parts.

The control algorithm responsible for orchestrating the inflation and deflation of the air chambers was implemented in Arduino IDE v1.8.16 (Arduino AG, Chiasso,

Switzerland), utilising an Arduino Uno board (Arduino AG, Chiasso, Switzerland) for precise control over the pumping sequence. Through a pneumatic system, the soft tongue deformation is regulated by finely adjusted solenoid valves and a rotary vane vacuum pump. To monitor and maintain optimal air pressure within the lines, pressure transducers are employed, with the maximum inflation pressures being adjusted as required using a pair of needle valves. Capturing the actuation pattern at a rapid rate of 100 frames per second was made possible by employing a high-speed camera (model ac A2040-120 um, Basler, Ahrensburg, Germany).

3 Design of the Biomimetic Soft Robotic Tongue (BSRT)

In this section, we delve into the intricate internal design of the soft actuator, drawing inspiration from the structure of the human tongue. Furthermore, we explore the actuation patterns employed, aimed at replicating the dynamic movements of food boli that hold clinical significance within the oral cavity.

3.1 Soft Actuator to Investigate the Oral Preparatory Stage of Semi-solid Foods

Figure 2A presents a comprehensive 3D computer-aided design (CAD) representation of the soft actuator designed to replicate the oral preparation phase of food. This includes detailed posterior and longitudinal cross-section views, complete with precise dimensions derived from the oral cavity anatomy of a healthy adult [12]. The design of the air chambers within the soft actuator took into account the findings presented by [14], where finite element method (FEM) simulations were conducted. These simulations modeled the soft tongue as a hyperelastic Yeoh solid and incorporated a Lagrangian contact condition with the rigid artificial hard palate. The tongue base and lateral surfaces were assigned null displacements, while the interior walls of the air chambers experienced linearly increasing/decreasing pressure to simulate inflation/deflation. In this study, careful consideration led to the selection of an optimal wall thickness of 2 mm for the partition separating the anterior and posterior sections of the actuator. Additionally, a wall thickness of 1 mm was chosen for the separation between the two lateral chambers. This choice aimed to prevent the formation of a spoon-like depression on the tongue surface during lateral inflation/deflation, thus facilitating the peristaltic movement of the food bolus within the oral cavity. Notably, the inclination of the superior walls in the three air chambers was designed to induce pronounced asymmetrical inflation. Consequently, the thinnest section of the wall is the first to inflate, allowing this particular region of the tongue to reach the hard palate at a faster rate.

Figure 2B showcases the inflation/deflation sequence of the soft actuator, enabling the execution of several crucial lingual functions: (1) the compression of food against the hard palate to disrupt its initial structure and form a cohesive bolus, (2) the anterior-posterior transport of food, and (3) and (4) the lateral displacement of the food bolus to facilitate thorough mixing with saliva. Furthermore, Fig. 2C illustrates the recorded pressure profiles during the oral processing of a representative semi-solid food, specifically apple puree.

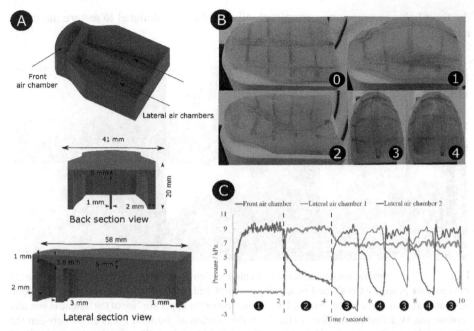

Fig. 2. Soft robotic tongue actuator designed to replicate the oral preparation phase of semi-solid foods. (A) CAD representation of the soft actuator, including posterior and longitudinal cross-section views, and dimensions. (B) inflation/deflation sequence of the soft actuator, simulating: (1) food compression against the hard palate, (2) food anterior-posterior transport, and (3) and (4) the lateral displacement of the food bolus to facilitate thorough mixing with saliva. (C) pressure profiles recorded during the oral processing of apple puree (5 mL).

To initiate the actuation sequence, food is manually loaded into the artificial oral cavity where the soft actuator is situated through the upper opening (Fig. 3, stage i). At this stage, both lateral air chambers remain deflated, creating suction through the assistance of a rotary vane vacuum pump. The actuation sequence commences with the simultaneous inflation of the two lateral air chambers (stage 1), generating a substantial compression force (<50 kPa; maximum pressure from the air inlet) to exert on the food bolus against the artificial hard palate, thereby modifying its structure. Extensive clinical studies involving a significant number of healthy individuals have indicated a range of maximum tongue pressures spanning from 10 to 80 kPa, with an average value of 35 ± 10 kPa [15]. Following the initial inflation, the anterior air chamber is subsequently inflated along with a simultaneous deflation of both lateral air chambers to apply gentle pressure on the food bolus against the hard palate, effectively shifting it to the middle region of the tongue surface (stage 2). The anterior chamber is then deflated, followed by a combined inflation and deflation of the lateral air chambers in an alternating manner (stages 3–4). This synchronized inflation and deflation enable the peristaltic guidance and lateral movement of the food bolus within the oral cavity, facilitating effective mixing with saliva. This actuation sequence can be repeated and adjusted as needed until a consistent bolus is achieved, primed for the subsequent propulsion stage. Once the food bolus preparation is completed, all chambers are deflated to restore the initial undeformed configuration (Fig. 2B, Image 0).

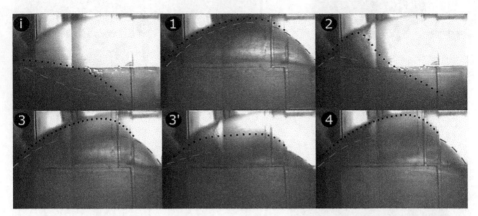

Fig. 3. The soft robotic tongue actuator is located within an artificial oral cavity for simulating the intricate process of oral food processing, exemplified by the manipulation of a model food substance such as apple puree (5 mL). The delineation of the upper surface of the tongue is visually represented by a dashed red line, while the major portion of the food bolus exists between the upper surface of the tongue and a discernible pointed black line. The simulated stages of food oral processing encompass essential actions, including (1) compressing the food against the hard palate, (2) food anterior-posterior transport, and (3) and (4) lateral displacement of the food bolus to enable comprehensive mixing. Image (i) depicts the beginning of the actuation sequence, where the food is manually inserted into the artificial oral cavity. At this stage, the lateral air chambers are not inflated and generate suction. Image (3') shows the moment when the lateral chambers come together during the alternating inflation and deflation pattern.

3.2   Soft Actuator to Investigate the Oral Propulsion Stage of Food Boli

Figure 4A presents a CAD representation of the soft actuator designed to replicate the oral propulsion phase of semi-solid foods based on a previous model [14, 16], including a longitudinal cross-section view and dimensions. A 2 mm wall thickness was selected for the wall separating the anterior and posterior sections of the actuator, and 1 mm for the back wall of the tongue to facilitate the peristaltic motion of the food bolus across the oral cavity, especially when the posterior chamber gets deflated under vacuum. The inflation/deflation sequence of the soft actuator allows to perform the two key lingual functions (i) food bolus containment prior to swallowing, and (ii) transportation of the ready-to-swallow food bolus towards the pharynx for initiating swallowing. Furthermore, Fig. 4B illustrates the recorded pressure profiles during the oral propulsion stage of a representative semi-solid foods.

Representative images of the actuation sequence for the oral propulsion of semi-solid foods are shown in Fig. 2C and 2D, both empty and containing a semi-solid food bolus (5 mL of apple puree), including for the latter the phases of (a) bolus feeding, (b) propulsion, (c) swallowing and (d) residues left in the oral cavity after the swallow.

The actuation sequence starts by inflating the posterior air chamber to ensure bolus containment (1). The ready-to-swallow food bolus is introduced manually and placed in the front part of the soft actuator surface. After bolus loading, suction generated by a rotary vane vacuum pump induces a rapid deflation of the posterior air chamber (2), which is followed by the inflation of the anterior one (3) to squeeze the bolus against the hard palate, guiding peristaltically the bolus towards the pharynx. Here, the contact pressure between the soft actuator and the palate will depend on the food bolus characteristics [14, 17]. Finally, a rapid re-inflation of the posterior air chamber (4), with the anterior still fully inflated, enables to clear the bolus tail from the oral cavity. Then, both chambers are deflated, (5) and (6), to return to the initial undeformed configuration.

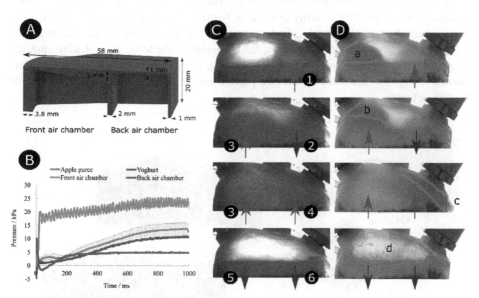

Fig. 4. Soft robotic tongue actuator designed to replicate the oral propulsion phase of semi-solid foods. (A) longitudinal cross-section view, including dimensions, (B) pressure profiles recorded during the oral processing of both apple puree and yoghurt (5 mL each), and (C and D) representative images of the soft robotic tongue actuator for the oral propulsion stage of semi-solid foods. Column (C) shows the inflation (red) and deflection (blue) sequence of the actuator air chambers to simulate the peristaltic movement of the human tongue in an artificial oral cavity. Column (D) shows, along with the inflation/deflection sequence, the *in vitro* swallowing process of a food bolus (apple puree): (a) bolus feeding, (b) propulsion, (c) swallowing and (d) residues left in the oral cavity after the swallow.

3.3   Upper Surface Texturing of the Soft Actuator

Biomimetic surfaces offer valuable insights into the intricate interactions between the tongue and food, as highlighted in previous studies [10, 18]. However, relying solely on surface roughness (S_a) falls short of achieving the desired level of tongue biomimicry. The mechanics of food perception and transport are significantly influenced by the interplay of oral friction, particularly influenced by the densely populated micropapillae [19], and the wettability [14] of the human tongue surface. Recognizing the critical role these factors play, our study capitalizes on the flat 3D biomimetic tongue surface developed by [10], taking it a step further by fabricating the pioneering 3D biomimetic soft robotic tongue. This remarkable innovation enables the realistic simulation of food oral transport within the oral cavity.

To recreate the tongue surface faithfully, we used precise *in vivo* data containing comprehensive information about the geometry and density of filiform and fungiform papillae per unit area (refer to Table 1). These data served as a foundation for meticulously imitating the tongue surface, as described in Sect. 2, adopting a random and non-overlapping distribution of papillae. While fungiform papillae exhibit dome-shaped structures surrounded by an array of filiform papillae, the filiform papillae themselves manifest as clusters of slender cylinders, approximately half the width and height of individual fungiform papillae [10]. The CAD model of the tongue mimicking surface, measuring 10 x 10 mm, and used for 3D printing, is visually depicted in Fig. 5A. Furthermore, Fig. 5B illustrates the surface pattern model applied to the upper surface of the soft actuator.

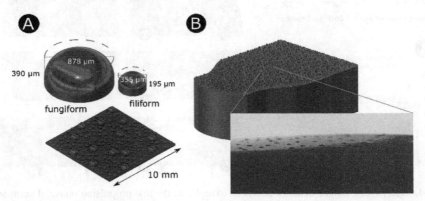

Fig. 5. 3D Biomimetic Soft Robotic Tongue (BSRT). Image (A) showcases the intricate 3D computer-aided design (CAD) model of the artificial papillae, meticulously crafted based on average in vivo data [10]. This model includes a surface area of 10 x 10 mm, incorporating a randomized distribution of both fungiform and filiform papillae. Moreover, (B) features a captivating snapshot of the model surface pattern expertly applied to the upper surface of the soft actuator. This image was captured using a digital camera, showcasing the soft robotic tongue surface at a magnification of 50x.

The introduction of surface texturing to the soft robotic tongue may introduce intriguing modifications to its wetting properties. Detailed findings regarding the equilibrium contact angle are presented in Table 2, encompassing various surface conditions of interest, namely smooth Ecoflex 00-30, Ecoflex 00-30 infused with a surfactant (Span 80), and the latter supplemented with topographical features. In its smooth state, Ecoflex 00-30 exhibits a contact angle of approximately 85°, signifying its inherently hydrophobic nature. However, the addition of a surfactant to the Ecoflex mixture remarkably enhances its wettability, resulting in contact angles of approximately 34°. Conversely, the incorporation of surface structure reduces wettability by a factor of two, yielding an average contact angle of approximately 68°. Notably, this range aligns with reported values found in literature for oral tissues. For instance, studies on pig tongues have indicated contact angles of approximately 77° [10], while in vivo human gingival surfaces have demonstrated contact angles ranging from 72° to 79° [20].

Table 2. Equilibrium contact angle (ECA) of water (10 μL) on various compositions of the tongue surface. Average data of at least four repeats, along with the standard deviation.

Tongue composition	ECA (°)
Ecoflex	85.2 ± 4.8
Ecoflex + surfactant	34.4 ± 3.8
Ecoflex + surfactant + surface texture	68.1 ± 3.8

Therefore, the emergence of this novel biomimetic device, presenting a 3D human tongue-like actuator with a soft hydrophilic silicone surface adorned with randomly distributed papillae-like asperities (including both fungiform and filiform), holds great promise. This innovative tool enables the investigation of oral processing and the transport of liquid and semi-solid foods with an unprecedented level of realism, closely emulating the contact and compression pressures applied by humans during the intricate stages of food oral processing and transport.

4 Conclusions

The design of a unique pneumatic multi-degree-of-freedom soft robotic actuator – called the Biomimetic Soft Robotic Tongue (BSRT) – is reported here to investigate the oral preparatory stage and the transport of liquid and semi-solid food within the oral cavity. The BSRT imitates the surface roughness heterogeneity of the human papillae and the compliance and wettability of the tongue, moving realistically at a three-dimensional geometry. This technology can be used to realistically simulate the bolus dynamics in a variety of individual conditions, paving the way to design personalized food products meeting individual needs.

Acknowledgement. This work was funded by HORIZON MSCA PF2021, SENSINGTech project.

References

1. Matsuo, K., Fujishima, I.: Textural changes by mastication and proper food texture for patients with oropharyngeal dysphagia. Nutrients **12**(6), 1613 (2020)
2. Engelen, L., et al.: A comparison of the effects of added saliva, alpha-amylase and water on texture perception in semisolids. Physiol. Behav. **78**, 805–811 (2003)

3. De Wijk, R.A., et al.: Explaining perceived oral texture of starch-based custard desserts from standard and novel instrumental tests. Food Hydrocolloids **20**, 24–34 (2006)
4. Prinz, J.F., et al.: In vitro simulation of the oral processing of semi-solid foods. Food Hydrocolloids **21**, 397–401 (2007)
5. Aguayo-Mendoza, M.G., et al.: Oral processing behavior of drinkable, spoonable and chewable foods is primarily determined by rheological and mechanical food properties. Food Qual. Prefer. **71**, 87–95 (2019)
6. Sethupathy, P., et al.: Food oral processing and tribology: instrumental approaches and emerging applications. Food Rev. Intl. **37**(5), 538–571 (2020)
7. Panda, S., et al.: Development of model mouth for food oral processing studies: present challenges and scopes. Innov. Food Sci. Emerg. Technol. **66**, 102524 (2020)
8. He, Y., et al.: Current perspectives on food oral processing. Annu. Rev. Food Sci. Technol. **13**, 167–192 (2022)
9. Marconati, M., et al.: The role of extensional rheology in the oral phase of swallowing: an in vitro study. Food Funct. **11**, 4363–4375 (2020)
10. Andablo-Reyes, E., et al.: 3D biomimetic tongue-emulating surfaces for tribological applications. ACS Appl. Mater. Interfaces **12**, 49371–49385 (2020)
11. Marconati, M., et al.: A review of the approaches to predict the ease of swallowing and post-swallow residues. Trends Food Sci. Technol. **86**, 281–297 (2019)
12. Kobayashi, Y., et al.: Velopharyngeal closure analysis using four dimensional computed tomography: a pilot study of healthy volunteers and adult patients with cleft palate. BMC Med. Imaging **19**, 54 (2019)
13. Fujiso, Y., et al.: Swall-E: a robotic in-vitro simulation of pharyngeal swallowing. J. Biomech. **18**, 06 (2018)
14. Marconati, M.: In vitro models for the formulation of easy-to-swallow products. PhD thesis, University of Surrey, U.K. (2019)
15. Alsanei, W.A.: Tongue pressure - a key limiting aspect in bolus swallowing. PhD thesis, University of Leeds, U.K. (2015)
16. Marconati, M., et al.: A soft robotic tongue to develop solutions to manage swallowing disorders. arXiv:2003.01194v1 [physics.med-ph] (2020)
17. Lavoisier, A., et al.: A novel soft robotic pediatric in vitro swallowing device to gain insights into the swallowability of mini-tablets. Int. J. Pharm. **629**, 122369 (2022)
18. Ranc, H., et al.: Friction coefficient and wettability of oral mucosal tissue: changes induced by a salivary layer. Colloids Surf. A **276**, 155–161 (2006)
19. Lauga, E., et al.: Sensing in the mouth: a model for filiform papillae as strain amplifiers. Front. Phys. **4**, 35 (2016)
20. Van der Meia, H.C., et al.: On the wettability of soft tissues in the human oral cavity. Arch. Oral Biol. **49**, 671–673 (2004)

Optimization of Kirigami-Inspired Fingers Grasping Posture in Virtual Environments

Anderson B. Nardin[1,2](✉) ⓘ, Seonggun Joe[1] ⓘ, and Lucia Beccai[1] ⓘ

[1] Soft BioRobotics Perception, Istituto Italiano di Tecnologia, 16163 Genova, GE, Italy
anderson.nardin@iit.it
[2] The BioRobotics Institute, Scuola Superiore Sant'Anna, 56025 Pontedera, PI, Italy

Abstract. Robotic grasping has been conceived as pivotal in achieving a broad spectrum of mechanical functionalities, including motion planning and perceptions via proprio- or exteroceptive sensory feedback control. In the last decade, these efforts have led to the development of artificial grippers that can provide multiple grasping modalities while handling various objects. Nonetheless, most of today's grippers require a particular posture for a given set of functions and tasks with fixed scenarios, which results in concreating grasping pipelines for known and unknown objects. In this work, a double-fingered gripper is presented using a kirigami pattern. To optimize the posture of two kirigami-inspired fingers, SOFA (Simulation Open Framework Architecture) is employed, and we focus on how the posture of two fingers influences to forming of a set of contact points concerning the target object. Overall, the optimal posture of the kirigami-inspired two-fingered gripper is demonstrated.

Keywords: Kirigami · SOFA · Grasping posture

1 Introduction

Robotic grasping capable of a broad spectrum of mechanical functions is a pivotal task that has been pursued in a multi-disciplinary approach that spans from the mechatronic design of the gripper to higher-level domains, e.g., incorporating sensory feedback [1, 2]. This effort enabled robotic grippers that can provide multiple grasping modalities with respect to a wide variety of objects while allowing for interaction with the environment [3, 4]. However, it is worth noting that such particular grasping mechanisms are valid for given tasks with particular scenarios and generally require a sequence of movements to perform the grasping for known and unknown objects in order to negotiate different objects in sudden contingencies (e.g., at different physical states, sizes, configuration, friction force, stiffness, etc.) [5, 6]. Two approaches can be undertaken to address these open challenges: exploring novel design principles to resolve cluttered scenes [3], while the other involves implementing higher-level control through perceptive feedback [7]. In general, gripper developments have hugely relied on symmetric postures/configurations of the fingers when this is possibly not the optimal solution [8–10].

F. Meder et al. (Eds.): Living Machines 2023, LNAI 14158, pp. 141–154, 2023.
https://doi.org/10.1007/978-3-031-39504-8_10

Different types of robotic grippers that do not require prior knowledge of the objects have been presented. More importantly, soft grippers using high deformability or flexibility of inherent soft materials have shown promising potential, allowing them to engage objects having different shapes, stiffness, dimensions, etc. [6]. Moreover, pioneered studies on bioinspired designs demonstrated the ability to safely interact with the environment [11, 12]. Indeed, the observation of natural grippers reveals a tendency towards the asymmetry of fingers. From crabs and lobster pincers, Fig. 1, to complex primate hands, nature wisely devised, exploited and evolved asymmetries to generate excellent grippers.

Fig. 1. Natural grippers present important asymmetries on the fingers positions. Crab (left) and lobster (right) are just a few natural examples that apply grippers endowed with asymmetric fingers [13].

Among the possible design strategies, soft grippers composed of programmed actuators through flexible metamaterials are capable of complex tasks using less input energy compared with their conventional counterparts [14]. These extraordinary performances are mainly due to the tunable mechanical properties of the metamaterial. More specifically, metamaterials can accommodate ultrahigh stiffness and strength-to-weight ratio, or unusual properties, such as a negative Poisson's ratio, which is rarely found in nature, and a negative coefficient of thermal expansion [15–17]. Herein, unlike other types of metamaterials, kirigami enables programmed mechanical characteristics (i.e., force, stiffness, deformation ratio, etc.) through a topological transformation. More importantly, given that such topological transformations allow for the optimized material distribution within a given design space, a lightweight design can be achieved by reducing structural density. In particular, this design strategy is remarkable in accomplishing the strength and flexibility of the mechanisms because any unnecessary regimes that might interfere with the desired gripper movements are removed.

More recently, due to the rapid development of artificial intelligence and 3D printing technologies, it is possible to fabricate sophisticated prototypes that integrate sensors together with computational resources [18, 19]. Indeed, these lead many researchers and developers to create innovative and intelligent rigid robots. However, the soft robotics domain requires seamless integration of the sensor and actuator in order to avoid hindering desired kinematic trajectories while ensuring high precision and accuracy of the sensor [20]. Additionally, non-linearity and hysteresis issues during closed-loop control must also be addressed [21]. These remain open challenging topics and are still being actively explored.

With these in mind, this work focuses on the analysis of a kirigami-based two-fingered soft gripper and its interaction with objects by using SOFA (Simulation Open Framework Architecture). In literature, kirigami represents metamaterials, which are generally composed of hierarchical unit cuts on a 2D layer [22, 23]. Depending on the arrangement of unit cuts (also corresponding unit cells), programmable deformations are achieved. Indeed, in our preliminary study [16], we presented a new design strategy in 3D, allowing for programmable soft actuators by tuning the aspect ratio and wall thickness ratio of the kirigami unit cell made of soft material (Thermo-PolyUrethane, TPU). As a key feature of this approach, it is noted that the axial stiffness of the overall structure is strongly influenced by the wall thickness ratio and that the aspect ratio enables its finer tuning. Thus, the design principle of two kirigami-inspired fingers is based on distributing kirigami unit cells having different aspect ratios, resulting in bending when the tendon is upon contraction. Finally, with two kirigami-inspired fingers, the primary objective of this work is to optimize their postures and understand how the posture of two fingers influences to forming of a set of contact areas with respect to different shapes of the objects.

2 Methodology

2.1 Design of Kirigami-Inspired Finger

Concept design. Figure 2 shows the concept design of the kirigami-inspired finger. The asymmetry geometry is employed, and the kirigami unit cells having different aspect ratios are applied at the ventral and dorsal sides of the finger, respectively (see Fig. 2(b) and (c)). Such distribution of kirigami unit cells having different aspect ratios induces asymmetrically distributed structural stiffness, resulting in bending when subjected to external force and/or deformation. More in detail, an inward bending toward the ventral side of the finger occurs mainly due to relatively weak stiffness rather than the dorsal side. Once the tendon contracts, the ventral side undergoes shortening, while the dorsal side exhibits elongation.

Quasi-Static Characteristics. To understand better the mechanical behavior of the kirigami-inspired finger, a quasi-static analysis is performed by means of ANSYS 19.2 (ANSYS Inc., Canonsburg, PA, USA), as depicted in Fig. 3(a). The tendon is fixed to the ventral side of the finger, which has a 3.7 mm eccentric distance (e) from the mass center, as depicted in Fig. 3(a). The simulation setup was built by creating a node where the tendon is fixed and imposing deformation in the z-direction. We employ the hyperplastic

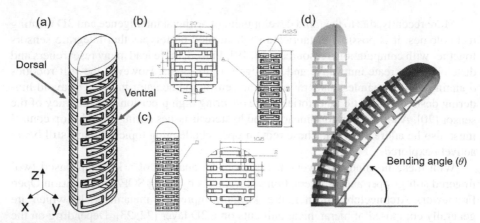

Fig. 2. Concept design of the kirigami inspired finger. (a) isometric view. (b) ventral part of the finger consisting of two kirigami unit cells with aspect ratios of 5 and 2.5, respectively. (c) dorsal part of the finger consisting of kirigami unit cell with aspect ratio of 5, (d) the bending angle measurement.

3D printing material (Flexible Resin 80A, Formlabs, Somerville, MA, USA) as a base material. In our simulations, the kirigami-inspired finger exhibits the bending movement upon compressive strain, which is mainly due to the flexibility of the topologically transformed structure rather than the hyperelasticity of the material. Moreover, to reduce the computational cost that could occur at the hyperelastic modeling, a linear mechanical analysis is performed by employing the following mechanical characteristics of the material (as summarized in Table 1).

Table 1. Material properties.

Properties	Dimensions
Tensile strength [MPa]	8.9
Stress at 100% strain [MPa]	6.3
Bulk modulus [MPa]	2.25
Elongation at break [%]	120
Poisson's ratio	0.4

Figure 3(b) shows the inward bending of the kirigami-inspired finger when the tendon contracts. The ventral side undergoes structure instability (i.e., buckling) mainly due to the compressive strain, while the dorsal side is upon the tensile strain. The maximum stresses at the ventral and dorsal sides are less than the tensile strength of the material used; thereby, it is worth noting that mechanical and/or material failures are unlikely to occur. Moreover, as plotted in Fig. 3(d), a large bending up to 84.3 deg can be accomplished due to the kirigami tessellations.

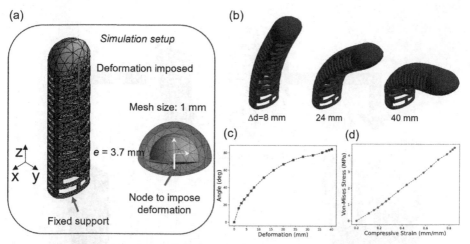

Fig. 3. Finite Element Analysis results. (a) Simulation setups. (b) Stress responses with respect to the deformation imposed, showing bending movements when subjected to 8mm, 24mm, and 40 mm, respectively. (c) The relationship of bending angle versus deformation imposed. (d) The relationship of Von-Mises Stress versus Compressive Strain.

2.2 Simulation Framework

Simulation Open Framework Architecture (SOFA). SOFA is an open-source C ++ library with a modular construction to handle programming interactive physical simulations of rigid and deformable objects considering several aspects such as geometric modeling, computational mechanics, numerical analysis, collision detection, and haptic feedback, among others [24].

Simulated objects are composed of three models: a deformation model with the independent degrees of freedom (DOFs), the mass, and constitutive laws; a collision model that describes the geometry of contacts; a visual model with rendering parameters. The different models are synchronized using a procedure called mapping to propagate forces and displacements of mesh nodes.

The simulations performed are composed of a scene or environment where three objects are present (a fourth object, a supporting plane for the target, is temporarily kept at the beginning of the simulations until the moment when a finger touches the surface of the target). The different models of the objects on the environment, kirigami fingers and target, can be seen in Fig. 4, where the deformation model represents the deformable mechanics using Finite Element Method (FEM); that is why the target is not represented since it is a rigid (i.e., incompressible) body, the collision model is responsible for detecting the contact, while the visual model handles the rendering processes.

A dynamic system of particles, simulation nodes, is employed to construct the deformable solids where the nodes' coordinates are their independent DOFs and accelerations $\mathbf{a}$ are guided by Eq. 1. Position and velocity are described by $\mathbf{x}$ and $\mathbf{v}$ vectors, respectively. Force functions are represented by $\mathbf{f}$, while $\mathbf{M}$ and $\mathbf{P}$ are mass and projection matrices, respectively. The projection matrix imposes boundary conditions on

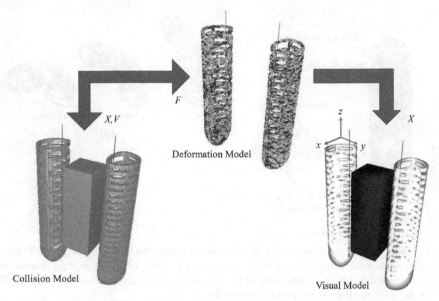

Fig. 4. Three representations of the scene. The deformation, collision and visual models deal with the mechanical behavior, contact policies, and objects visualization respectively. Mappings are used to propagate forces (F), velocities (V) and positions (X) between the models.

movements.

$$\mathbf{a} = \mathbf{PM}^{-1} \sum_{i=initial}^{final} \mathbf{f}_i(\mathbf{x}, \mathbf{v}) \tag{1}$$

SOFA applies Lagrange multipliers to address complex constraints [25], e.g., contacts between moving objects depending on their relative position. Given the linearization performed in each step of the simulation by a Taylor series expansion to the first order, Eq. 2, where i represents the initial value of the variable, the constraint problem is expressed by Eq. 3 (the partial derivatives are stiffness and damping matrices respectively), where p_f is the final value of external forces. Alternatively, we can express the simplified Eq. 4 where $\mathbf{H}$ contains the holonomic and nonholonomic constraints and λ represents the Lagrange multipliers.

$$\mathbf{f}(\mathbf{x}_i + d\mathbf{x}, \mathbf{v}_i + d\mathbf{v}) = f_i + \frac{\partial \mathbf{f}}{\partial \mathbf{x}} d\mathbf{x} + \frac{\partial \mathbf{f}}{\partial \mathbf{v}} d\mathbf{v} \tag{2}$$

$$\left(\mathbf{M} + dt \frac{\partial \mathbf{f}}{\partial \mathbf{v}} + dt^2 \frac{\partial \mathbf{f}}{\partial \mathbf{x}}\right) d\mathbf{v} = -dt \left(f_i - p_f + dt \frac{\partial \mathbf{f}}{\partial \mathbf{x}} \mathbf{v}_i - \mathbf{H}^T \lambda\right) \tag{3}$$

$$\mathbf{A} d\mathbf{v} = \mathbf{b} + dt \mathbf{H}^T \lambda \tag{4}$$

Equations 5 represent, respectively, bilateral interactions, such as attachments and sliding joints, and unilateral interactions, such as contact and friction.

$$\Phi(x_1, x_2...) = 0$$
$$\Psi(x_1, x_2...) \geq 0$$

(5)

The matrix **H** can be understood as the Jacobian between physics and constraint spaces. For two objects, we have Eqs. 6.

$$\mathbf{H}_1 = \left[\frac{\partial \Phi}{\partial x_1}; \frac{\partial \Psi}{\partial x_1}\right]$$

$$\mathbf{H}_2 = \left[\frac{\partial \Phi}{\partial x_2}; \frac{\partial \Psi}{\partial x_2}\right]$$

(6)

The system to be solved is given by Eqs. 7 for two different bodies.

$$\mathbf{A}_1 d\mathbf{v}_1 = \mathbf{b}_1 + dt\mathbf{H}_1^T \lambda$$
$$\mathbf{A}_2 d\mathbf{v}_2 = \mathbf{b}_2 + dt\mathbf{H}_2^T \lambda$$

(7)

In the first step, with $\lambda = 0$, we obtain a free motion $d\mathbf{v}^f$. After integration, we obtain $\mathbf{x}^f$. In the second step, with $\mathbf{b} = 0$, λ is calculated using the Gauss-Seidel algorithm [26]. Then, the motion is computed following Eqs. 8.

$$\mathbf{x}_1 = \mathbf{x}_1^f + dt \cdot d\mathbf{v}_1^c$$
$$\mathbf{x}_2 = \mathbf{x}_2^f + dt \cdot d\mathbf{v}_2^c$$
$$d\mathbf{v}_1^c = dt\mathbf{A}_1^{-1}\mathbf{H}_1^T \lambda$$
$$d\mathbf{v}_2^c = dt\mathbf{A}_2^{-1}\mathbf{H}_2^T \lambda$$

(8)

Target Description. We use the inertia tensor to characterize the mass distribution of a rigid body relative to a reference frame. The reference frame {A} is attached to the rigid body, which has its inertia tensor expressed in Eq. 9. In the main diagonal, it presents the mass moments of inertia, and the others are mass products of inertia.

$$^A I = \begin{bmatrix} I_{xx} & -I_{xy} & -I_{xz} \\ -I_{xy} & I_{yy} & -I_{yz} \\ -I_{xz} & -I_{yz} & I_{zz} \end{bmatrix}$$

(9)

where the elements are given by Eqs. 10 because the body is composed of differential volume elements, dv, and material of density ρ.

$$I_{xx} = \iiint_V (y^2 + z^2)\rho dv$$
$$I_{yy} = \iiint_V (x^2 + z^2)\rho dv$$
$$I_{zz} = \iiint_V (x^2 + y^2)\rho dv$$
$$I_{xy} = \iiint_V xy\rho dv \tag{10}$$
$$I_{xz} = \iiint_V xz\rho dv$$
$$I_{yz} = \iiint_V yz\rho dv$$

Considering a body of uniform density, mass m, rectangular shape, and center of mass on its centroid, represented in Fig. 5, we can obtain the inertia tensor described at the body's center of mass, Eq. 11, designed in the programmed simulation. The target has the dimensions $w = 20$ mm, $h = 20$ mm, $l = 60$ mm, and mass $m = 15$ g.

$$^C I = \begin{bmatrix} \frac{m}{12}(h^2 + l^2) & 0 & 0 \\ 0 & \frac{m}{12}(w^2 + h^2) & 0 \\ 0 & 0 & \frac{m}{12}(l^2 + w^2) \end{bmatrix} \tag{11}$$

This well-known yet important result represents the selected target, but also evidences the versatility and potentiality of the simulation environment to deal with different objects by considering the fundamental body's characteristics.

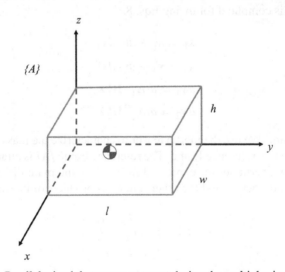

Fig. 5. Parallelepiped that serves as target during the multiple simulations.

2.3 Simulation Protocol

The design of robotic systems is conducted to obtain desired specifications. Such specifications can be qualitative, quantitative, driven by an application, constrained by the integration with other parts, by the fabrication process, etc. The design process difficulty is directly related to the number of specifications. In our approach, the interaction between bodies is essential. Then, initially, the fingers that compose our gripper is defined by the relative displacement between fingers; this metric ranges from -50 mm to 50 mm with steps of 10 mm for each simulation. Considering this domain, an optimal performance index can be sought.

The bodies are subject to gravity ($g = 9.81$ m/s^2), and the tendon-driven kirigami fingers have their curvature/bending and structural deformation defined by the imposed pulling wire. The latter varies linearly from 0 to 8 time-dependent steps. The meshes' nodes are considered for contact detection, and they are treated as contact points in our analysis since they can provide measurable and precise discretization of the surfaces. At the beginning of the simulations, a supporting plane prevents the target object from free-falling. Such a plane disappears once the contact between the fingers and the target is detected.

The fingers have the same mass of 10 g. While finger #2 (right side) has its initial position on space varying the posture or configuration of the gripper, finger #1 (left side) has its base position (where it is placed in its coordinate frame) fixed with respect to an inertial frame on space at coordinates (0 mm, 0 mm, 0 mm). The target position, defined by its center of mass, is placed at coordinates (-40 mm, 22 mm, 0 mm).

Model-based design processes can be iterative through numerical optimization methods, e.g., gradient-descent algorithms or via evolutionary algorithms evaluating candidates which evolve over generations. In our case, the choice of extensively testing the possibilities arises as the most straightforward.

3 Result and Discussion

Figure 6 presents a comparison of relative displacements' (-20 mm, 0 mm, 20 mm) number of contact points along the time, illustrating different postures of the fingers during the simulations on key moments of runtime.

At the beginning of the simulations, finger #2 is placed at a certain distance from finger #1, considering the direction in which the gravity is applied. The illustrations at 0 s show the relative distance between fingers. The blue, orange, and green frames represent the displacements of -20 mm. 0 mm, and 20 mm, respectively. The number of contact points at this phase is due to the presence of a supporting plane which is kept until the detection of contact between any finger and the target surface.

Once the finger contact is detected on the target surface, the supporting plane that sustained the target and avoided its free falling is removed from the virtual environment allowing the pure interaction of fingers and target to govern the state, progress and success of the grasping task. At this phase, it is common to observe the target sliding between the fingers while these struggle to keep the target in position. These variations in the number of contact points can be understood as in-hand movements. The blue framed and the orange framed illustrations at 1 s present an exemplified frame of this phase for the -20 mm and 0 mm displacement, respectively, while the green framed illustration at 0.6 s represents the configuration with the displacement of 20 mm at the same phase.

As evidenced by the last illustrations of the fingers for each relative displacement, for this set of simulations, only when finger #2 is positioned at -20 mm with respect to finger #1, the grasping is successful, i.e., the object is enveloped and holds by the fingers (blue framed illustration at 1.5 s). Displacements of 0mm (orange framed illustration at 1.5 s, possibly the most intuitive configuration/posture) and 20 mm (green framed illustration at 1 s) fail to perform the desired grasping task.

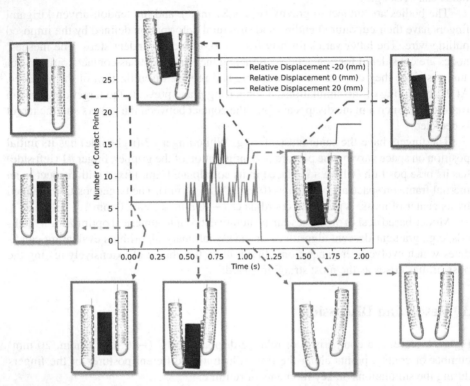

Fig. 6. Comparative evolution of the fingers on different relative displacement between fingers. The colors blue, orange, and green represent the relative displacement configuration of -20 mm, 0 mm, and 20 mm, respectively.

Simulations on the virtual environment generate data to compare consistency and success in performing the grasping task considering the different relative displacements of finger #2 with respect to finger #1. In total, eleven different simulations, each representing a different gripper, have been performed with displacements of −50 mm, −40 mm, −30 mm, −20 mm, −10 mm, 0 mm, 10 mm, 20 mm, 30 mm, 40 mm, and 50 mm. Figure 7 presents a graph with the number of contact points, i.e., points where the fingers touch the target, at the end of the simulation time. This graph evidence that, among the set of different displacements, only simulations where the fingers have been separated by -40 mm, −30 mm, −20 mm, and −10 mm successfully hold the target since the fingers were still in contact with the target at the end of the simulation, i.e., the number of contact points have been different from zero. The other displacements failed to fulfill the grasping task. It is worth mentioning that the configuration with −20 mm displacement presented the highest number of contact points; this indicates a good enveloping of the target comparatively to the other gripper postures, e.g., the symmetric alternative does not bear the target until the end of the simulation.

A remarkable result is presented at the −30 mm displacement; the variation on the slope sign that produces a local minimum can sound irrational. Nevertheless, its behavior is perfectly justifiable by considering the geometries of the involved objects once the fingers themselves present a characteristic curvature due to the force applied on the tendons and their inherent flexibility, and the gravity applied to the target that moves it and misaligns its center of mass and contact points. All these aspects together exemplify the challenge and the beauty of multi-body interaction.

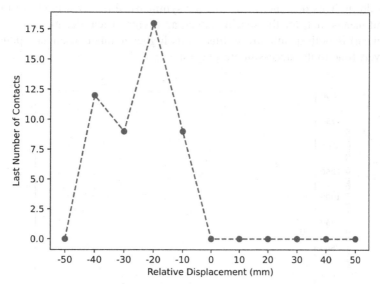

Fig. 7. Number of contact points where the fingers touch the target surface at the end of the simulation. Only relative displacement of −40 mm, −30 mm, −20 mm, and −10 mm managed to grasp and hold the target until the end of the simulation time.

Notwithstanding that the last number of contacts indicates success in grasping, it is necessary a more comprehensive analysis of the dynamic behavior of the grippers (one can understand the different positioning of fingers as possibilities of distinct grippers) when interacting with the target. From the moment when a finger touches the target, tc, to the end of the simulation, tf, the number of contact points, n_c, is integrated to generate I_c, in general terms represented by Eq. 12. This procedure provides a quality index related to each gripper in performing the grasping along the time.

$$I_c = \int_{tc}^{tf} n_c dt \tag{12}$$

Figure 8 presents the integral of the number of contacts obtained by time-discrete definite integration for each considered relative displacement. This graph represents the dynamic characteristic of the grippers defined by their proper fingers' relative displacement. Then, each gripper has its own enveloping signature represented by the number of contact points during the procedure of grasping, i.e., the number of contacts along the time. It is important to highlight the performance obtained by the gripper with −20 mm relative displacement between fingers. That configuration shows the best performance, i.e., the highest index comparatively to the other options tested. These results represent a particularity of the grippers for the selected target object.

About the result for the symmetrical case (0 mm displacement), it is evident its performance falls far from optimal for the selected target object. Indeed, a careful analysis of the simulation frames reveals that the gripper struggles to hold the object while it slides and falls down. This does not mean that the symmetrical design would fail for every target, but means that, for the specific target, an asymmetrical design (with −20 mm displacement) is both quantitatively (due to its higher number of contact points) and qualitatively (due to its successful grasping) superior.

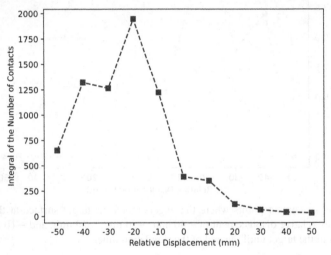

Fig. 8. Graph representing the dynamic characteristic of each gripper defined by the specific relative displacement.

4 Conclusion

The outcomes obtained through simulations showed that, against common intuition, an asymmetric design can be beneficial and surpass the performance of grippers with symmetric fingers (at least for the selected target object). For this reason, this research is useful for the optimal practical design of robotic grippers. This approach can assist the design by justifying the dimensions and posture/configuration of the fingers on a gripper. Moreover, this concept's reasoning and roots originate from observations of natural manifestations.

For future implementation, taking into account the enhancement of realism, feasibility, and applicability, considerations like hyperelastic models of the materials, different initial positions of all the fingers (including finger #1) with respect to the target center of mass, targets with different shapes and irregular distribution of masses (e.g., convex, non-convex, flat, deformable, fragile, etc.), different displacement range/step, and the number of fingers could be investigated. The asymmetric design can be decisive when applying different grasping approaches exploiting the fingers' actuation, stiffness, adhesion, suction, etc.

References

1. Carbone, G.: Grasping in Robotics. Springer London, London (2013). https://doi.org/10.1007/978-1-4471-4664-3
2. George, J.A., et al.: Biomimetic sensory feedback through peripheral nerve stimulation improves dexterous use of a bionic hand. Sci. Robot. **4**, eaax2352 (2019). https://doi.org/10.1126/scirobotics.aax2352
3. Babin, V., Gosselin, C.: Mechanisms for robotic grasping and manipulation. Annu. Rev. Control Robot. Auton. Syst. **4**, 573–593 (2021). https://doi.org/10.1146/annurev-control-061520-010405
4. Homberg, B.S., Katzschmann, R.K., Dogar, M.R., Rus, D.: Robust proprioceptive grasping with a soft robot hand. Auton. Robot. **43**(3), 681–696 (2018). https://doi.org/10.1007/s10514-018-9754-1
5. Zaidi, S., Maselli, M., Laschi, C., Cianchetti, M.: Actuation technologies for soft robot grippers and manipulators: a review. Curr. Rob. Rep. **2**(3), 355–369 (2021). https://doi.org/10.1007/s43154-021-00054-5
6. Shintake, J., Cacucciolo, V., Floreano, D., Shea, H.: Soft robotic grippers. Adv. Mater. **30**, 1707035 (2018). https://doi.org/10.1002/adma.201707035
7. Low, J.H., et al.: Hybrid tele-manipulation system using a sensorized 3-D-printed soft robotic gripper and a soft fabric-based haptic glove. IEEE Robot. Autom. Lett. **2**, 880–887 (2017). https://doi.org/10.1109/LRA.2017.2655559
8. Yuan, J., Guan, R., Du, L., Ma, S.: A robotic gripper design and integrated solution towards tunnel boring construction equipment. In: 2020 IEEE/RSJ International Conference on Intelligent Robots and Systems (IROS), Las Vegas, NV, USA, pp. 2650–2655. IEEE (2020). https://doi.org/10.1109/IROS45743.2020.9341200
9. Elangovan, N., Gerez, L., Gao, G., Liarokapis, M.: Improving robotic manipulation without sacrificing grasping efficiency: a multi-modal, adaptive gripper with reconfigurable finger bases. IEEE Access **9**, 83298–83308 (2021). https://doi.org/10.1109/ACCESS.2021.3086802
10. Kang, B., Cheong, J.: Development of two-way self-adaptive gripper using differential gear. Actuators. **12**, 14 (2022). https://doi.org/10.3390/act12010014
11. Zhou, L., Ren, L., Chen, Y., Niu, S., Han, Z., Ren, L.: Bio-inspired soft grippers based on impactive gripping. Adv. Sci. **8**, 2002017 (2021). https://doi.org/10.1002/advs.202002017
12. Manti, M., Hassan, T., Passetti, G., D'Elia, N., Laschi, C., Cianchetti, M.: A bioinspired soft robotic gripper for adaptable and effective grasping. Soft Robot. **2**, 107–116 (2015). https://doi.org/10.1089/soro.2015.0009
13. Unsplash: Beautiful Free Images & Pictures | Unsplash. https://unsplash.com/. Accessed 30 Mar 2023
14. Rafsanjani, A., Bertoldi, K., Studart, A.R.: Programming soft robots with flexible mechanical metamaterials. Sci. Robot. **4**, eaav7874 (2019). https://doi.org/10.1126/scirobotics.aav7874

15. Joe, S., Bernabei, F., Beccai, L.: A review on vacuum-powered fluidic actuators in soft robotics. In: Olaru, A. (ed.) Rehabilitation of the Human Bone-Muscle System. IntechOpen (2022). https://doi.org/10.5772/intechopen.104373

16. Joe, S., Totaro, M., Beccai, L.: Analysis of soft Kirigami unit cells for TUNABLE stiffness architectures. In: 2021 IEEE 4th International Conference on Soft Robotics (RoboSoft), New Haven, CT, USA, pp. 343–350. IEEE (2021). https://doi.org/10.1109/RoboSoft51838.2021. 9479210

17. Hou, X., Silberschmidt, V.V.: Metamaterials with negative Poisson's ratio: a review of mechanical properties and deformation mechanisms. In: Silberschmidt, V.V., Matveenko, V.P. (eds.) Mechanics of Advanced Materials. EM, pp. 155–179. Springer, Cham (2015). https://doi.org/ 10.1007/978-3-319-17118-0_7

18. Verma, D., Dong, Y., Sharma, M., Chaudhary, A.K.: Advanced processing of 3D printed biocomposite materials using artificial intelligence. Mater. Manuf. Process. **37**, 518–538 (2022). https://doi.org/10.1080/10426914.2021.1945090

19. Zheng, P., et al.: Smart manufacturing systems for Industry 4.0: conceptual framework, scenarios, and future perspectives. Front. Mech. Eng. **13**(2), 137–150 (2018). https://doi.org/10. 1007/s11465-018-0499-5

20. Tiziani, L.O., Hammond, F.L.: Optical sensor-embedded pneumatic artificial muscle for position and force estimation. Soft. Robot. **7**, 462–477 (2020). https://doi.org/10.1089/soro.2019. 0019

21. Joe, S., Wang, H., Totaro, M., Beccai, L.: Sensing deformation in vacuum driven foam-based actuator via inductive method. Front. Robot. AI. **8**, 742885 (2021)

22. Sareh, S., Rossiter, J.: Kirigami artificial muscles with complex biologically inspired morphologies. Smart Mater. Struct. **22**, 014004 (2013). https://doi.org/10.1088/0964-1726/22/1/ 014004

23. Jin, L., Forte, A.E., Deng, B., Rafsanjani, A., Bertoldi, K.: Kirigami-inspired inflatables with programmable shapes. Adv. Mater. **32**, 2001863 (2020). https://doi.org/10.1002/adma.202 001863

24. Faure, F., et al.: SOFA: a multi-model framework for interactive physical simulation. In: Payan, Y. (eds.) Soft Tissue Biomechanical Modeling for Computer Assisted Surgery. Studies in Mechanobiology, Tissue Engineering and Biomaterials, vol. 11, pp. 283–321. Springer Berlin (2012). https://doi.org/10.1007/8415_2012_125

25. Duriez, C., Dubois, F., Kheddar, A., Andriot, C.: Realistic haptic rendering of interacting deformable objects in virtual environments. IEEE Trans. Vis. Comput. Graph. **12**, 36–47 (2006). https://doi.org/10.1109/TVCG.2006.13

26. Duriez, C., Guébert, C., Marchal, M., Cotin, S., Grisoni, L.: Interactive simulation of flexible needle insertions based on constraint models. In: Yang, G.-Z., Hawkes, D., Rueckert, D., Noble, A., Taylor, C. (eds.) MICCAI 2009. LNCS, vol. 5762, pp. 291–299. Springer, Heidelberg (2009). https://doi.org/10.1007/978-3-642-04271-3_36

Computational Tools and Modelling

BrainX3: A Neuroinformatic Tool for Interactive Exploration of Multimodal Brain Datasets

Vivek Sharma[✉], Raimon Bullich Vilarrubias, and Paul F. M. J. Verschure[✉]

Donders Institute for Brain, Cognition and Behaviour, Radboud University, Nijmegen, The Netherlands

{vivek.sharma,paul.verschure}@donders.ru.nl

Abstract. BrainX3 is a neuroinformatic tool for the exploration, analysis, modelling and simulation of brain data using interactive visualisations that facilitate the exploration and discovery of new insights by scientists and clinicians. We describe the design principles and architecture of the platform and the general features of the software. We present BrainX3 Radiology, an application built on top of the platform that targets the localisation of brain lesions and the analysis of their impact on brain function for rapid and efficient access to high-quality integrated multi-modal brain data together with tools for analysis and semantic interpretation. We also argue that tools such as BrainX3 provide platforms for the creation of synthetic and hybrid biological-synthetic brain-like systems which can provide the key control structures for future Living Machines.

Keywords: BrainX3 · semantome · NeuroImaging · brain modelling · synthetic brains · anatomy · physiology · semantome

1 Vision and Approach

The behaviour of biological and synthetic living machines is controlled by their brain. This implies that to study and create such systems, we need dedicated tools that can assist us in linking the anatomy and physiology of brains to their function. Hence, we anticipate a convergence of the tools used to analyze biological and synthesize artificial brains. Here we present an example of this convergence an interactive neuroinformatics platform called BrainX3 featuring 3D visualization, analysis, and simulation of human neuroimaging, electrophysiological data and brain models [1, 2]. The tool supports neuroscientists and clinicians to advance research and clinical use cases on personalized medicine diagnostics, and prognostics and supports intervention decisions. One of the key features of the BrainX3 platform is the possibility to explore and interact with brain datasets directly and in an intuitive and semantically enhanced way. The user can load different data types in the graphical user interface such as Magnetic Resonance Imaging (MRI), Diffusion Tensor Imaging (DTI), Electroencephalography (EEG), Stereoelectroencephalography (SEEG), and their derived data (such as structural and functional connectome) and semantic corpora from available text databases and knowledge graphs

[3]. All this data can be explored in an interactive way using advanced 3D visualizations and interaction techniques that are more effective than other desktop tools [4]. In addition, the empirical data set can be augmented with synthetic data generated by simulations.

BrainX3 software is designed with these principles in mind:

- Human-in-the-loop, emphasizing exploration and interaction with heterogenous and complex data.
- Ingestion of multi-modal data.
- Simulation of neural models including empirical data and parameters.
- Immersive, to work on desktops and large screens, immersive rooms, and virtual reality Head Mounted Displays (HMD).
- Cognitive interfaces using wearables and sensors support interaction.
- Use of standards for personal data use, sharing and organization, adopting existing solutions for modelling and simulation and using available brain atlas.
- Accuracy in the visualization and analysis methods, using validated libraries and algorithms.
- Research and clinical use, targeting a more general solution for research use and specific use cases to be used in clinical practice.

1.1 State of the Art

Several commercial solutions for visualization and analysis exist. The majority are developed for specific acquisition systems and are directly designed by the manufacturers of the device. Source code and file formats are often proprietary and not accessible to the overall research community. In the past decades, many different projects have been developed offering free alternatives to commercial solutions, which have now reached a high level of maturity. Some of these tools such as Slicer, Freesurfer, SPM, EEGLab, Fieldtrip, Brainstorm, MNE, NEST, BRAIN, Nengo, IQR, and TVB tools have been largely adopted by the research community becoming a standard [5–16].

Slicer. 3D Slicer is an open-source software platform for medical image informatics, image processing, and three-dimensional visualization.

Brainstorm. A collaborative open-source application is written in Matlab dedicated to MEG and EEG data visualization and processing, with an emphasis on cortical source estimation techniques and their integration with anatomical magnetic resonance imaging using a graphical user interface.

FieldTrip is a MATLAB toolbox that contains a set of separate (high-level) functions; it does not have a graphical user interface. The toolbox functions can be combined into an analysis pipeline, i.e., a MATLAB script containing all steps of your analysis.

SPM software package has been designed for the analysis of brain imaging data sequences.

Freesurfer Analysis and visualization of structural and functional neuroimaging data from cross-sectional or longitudinal studies.

EEGLab is an interactive Matlab toolbox for processing continuous and event-related EEG, MEG and other electrophysiological data. EEGLAB offers a structured programming environment with a GUI for storing, accessing, measuring, manipulating and visualizing event-related EEG data.

MNEtools is a software package that provides comprehensive analysis tools and workflows including preprocessing, source estimation, time-frequency analysis, statistical analysis, and several methods to estimate functional connectivity between distributed brain regions.

NEST is a simulator for spiking neural networks that puts a special emphasis on network dynamics, structure, and size. NEST includes models from information processing, to network activity dynamics and learning plasticity, which can be simulated either by using the Python package PyNEST or by using their standalone application.

BRAIN Free and open source, Brian is a simulator for spiking neural networks. It enables scientists to quickly and effectively simulate models of spiking neural networks. These models might include novel dynamical equations, interactions with the surrounding environment, and experimental procedures.

NENGO Nengo is a Python library for creating and modeling extensive neural networks. Nengo can build complex spiking and non-spiking neural simulations. Nengo is extremely flexible and expandable. You can specify your own neuron types and learning rules, receive input directly from hardware, design and operate deep neural networks, control robots, and even mimic your model on a different neural simulator or neuromorphic hardware.

IQR is a multi-level neuronal simulation environment. Neuronal models can be created graphically and be further analysed and visualized in-line. IQR can be used to simulate very detailed brain structures in more robot-based models.

TVB The Virtual Brain (TVB) is a full brain activity simulator, mainly operating at a large scale. It can compute simulated signals from the source level (centres of the brain regions) to EEG, sEEG, and MEG. It supports personalization of the operations through large-scale connectivity (extracted from a patient DWI, T1 scans) as well as from annotations on pathologies coming out of literature (TVBase, TVB-O).

1.2 Previous Work

BrainX3 started as a neuroinformatic tool to explore complex data of the brain. The first version (v1.0) of the software was created using the Unity video game engine (Unity Technologies). This environment has helped to create a different approach for visualization and interaction with multiple brain data modalities such as connectome, MRI, electrophysiology, simulation, and semantic information (see Fig. 1). This version also was designed to work on multiple platforms: desktop, VR and immersive rooms. Several studies describe the features and use cases implemented with this version on connectome analysis [17] network dynamics [18] localization of lesions in epileptic patients for neurosurgical interventions [19] analysis of language areas [20] and validation of theoretical models of episodic memory [21]. Also, several studies have been conducted to evaluate immersive visualization and interactions [4, 22, 23], interfaces that use the conscious and unconscious reaction of the user to regulate information [24] and sound interfaces [25]. While the first version of BrainX3 offers great features to develop and explore visualization and interaction approaches, the unity environment has not been designed to work with neuroinformatic datasets.

Fig. 1. BrainX3 1.0 in the XIM immersive room. A visualization of the connectome, MRI and the cortical brain surface (on the left screen) and semantic information of selected brain areas.

2   BrainX3 2.0

2.1   Architecture and Development Methodology

BrainX3 is designed as a layered architecture with four different levels: Graphical User Interface (GUI), Application Core, Native, and Specific Plugins. The GUI layer implements the user interfaces and interactions for the specific platforms (Desktop, VR, Immersive Rooms, and Web). The core layer implements the different classes that handle the internal application logic, interfacing with the GUI layer and the plugin modules. Finally, we have native plugins that handle data and visualization and specific plugins that provide functionalities in the neuroinformatic domain (Fig. 2).

The idea is to decouple the user interface from the internal application logic and, at the same time, the internal logic from the data types and components. The first decoupling is possible by mapping the native events of each GUI component to an internal representation of these events and a mapping between an internal representation of the multimodal data and their relationship to a native user interface representation. The second decoupling is achieved by implementing plugins using the Model-View-Controller pattern. Thus, Plugins have an internal representation of their data, implement their logic and handle their description of how to represent the data graphically, but not the actual graphical representation.

BrainX3 2.0 is implemented using the Python programming language and uses external libraries: Qt [26] for the GUI, VTK [27] for the 3D visualization, and several open-source libraries to manage neuroimaging and electrophysiological data. The GUI offers

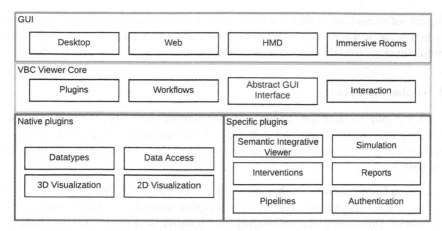

Fig. 2. BrainX3 architecture.

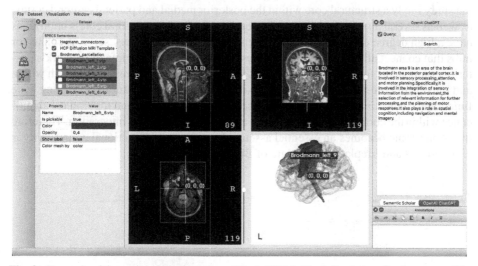

Fig. 3. Example of the main window display of BrainX3 2.0. The left window displays accessible datasets including atlases and imaging data. The middle window is for the visualisation of imaging data and 3D representation of the brain. The right window is the Semantome of BrainX3 which uses API-based search engines to fetch recent research articles and uses OpenAI chat GPT to answer queries.

a multimodal exploration framework, where the user can access a logical organization of the dataset, a semantic corpora query, a 3D scene, and temporal signals plots. At the same time, the VTK's 3D scene presents the anatomical data along with the results of image post-processing and results from analysis and simulations (see Fig. 3). All the raw data and its derivatives are stored using the Brain Imaging Data Structure (BIDS). The BIDS data format allows the universal compatibility of Neuroimaging datasets across different softwares [28]. BrainX3 follows an iterative development, integration, and prototyping strategy, where the various components are advanced and combined in phases to implement the overall solution under the continuous guidance of user feedback.

2.2 Global Features

BrainX3 is built to integrate the bits and pieces of existing tools in the field of Neuroimaging into one platform. The software includes unique features that are integrated and are under constant development. In this section, we list and explain the main features of BrainX3.

Hangmann Connectome. The human cerebral cortex is divided into physically distinct and functionally specialized sections by a complex network of cortico-cortical axonal connections. Diffusion spectrum imaging, non-invasive, was used to identify these networks throughout and across cortical hemispheres in individual human volunteers [29]. According to the researchers, the large-scale structural brain networks generated from the study imply a structural core within the posterior medial and parietal cerebral cortex, as well as several discrete temporal and frontal modules. The structural core's brain areas have a high degree of strength and betweenness centrality, and they serve as connector hubs that connect all key structural modules (Fig. 4). The human default network's posterior components form the structural core, which is made up of brain areas. Both within and outside of core areas, a substantial association between structural and resting-state functional connectivity is reported. Because of the core's spatial and topological significance within the cortex, it is thought to play a key role in functional integration. Therefore the connectome becomes an essential asset to the software as functional connectivity is an important and irreplaceable feature of BrainX3.

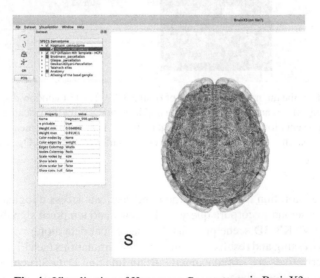

Fig. 4. Visualisation of Hangmann Connectome in BrainX3.

Data. BrainX3 provides a comprehensive interface for loading and visualizing various types of neuroimaging data. The software is capable of handling MRI, iEEG, tractography, and functional connectivity data, making it an invaluable resource for researchers and clinicians alike.

MRI data can be loaded and visualized in various formats, including T1, T2, and diffusion-weighted imaging. This allows for a thorough analysis of structural brain features, such as grey matter, white matter, and cerebrospinal fluid. iEEG data can also be displayed in both raw and processed formats, and the software enables the visualization of individual channels, as well as averaged data. This feature provides a detailed understanding of electrical brain activity and its patterns.

BrainX3 also facilitates the visualization of tractography data in 3D, allowing for a clear view of the neural connections between different regions of the brain.

Furthermore, the software provides the capability to analyze and display functional connectivity data. This feature allows for the exploration of functional brain networks, such as resting-state networks or task-specific networks.

Atlases. BrainX3 offers multiple atlases to serve different research purposes, as each atlas may have different levels of detail, resolution, and labelling schemes. For example, some atlases may focus on brain regions that are important for a specific function, while others may provide a comprehensive mapping of the entire brain. Moreover, different atlases may use different imaging techniques or datasets, leading to variations in the boundaries and labelling of brain regions. Researchers may choose a specific atlas based on their research question and the level of detail required for their study. Therefore, having multiple brain atlases available can provide researchers with a variety of resources to study the brain's structure and function.

Brodmann and Glasser Atlas. Brodmann [30] and Glasser [31] are popular brain atlases used in neuroscience research. Based on histological variations in cellular architecture, the Brodmann atlas, which bears the name of the German neurologist Korbinian Brodmann, divides the cerebral cortex into 52 areas. Each area, or Brodmann area, has a number given to it and is linked to a particular set of abilities, including language, motor control, and sensory processing. To explore brain shape and function, the Brodmann atlas is frequently utilized as a reference book. On the other hand, the Glasser atlas is a more contemporary brain atlas that employs functional connectivity patterns to delineate 180 cortical areas in each hemisphere of the human brain. The Glasser atlas, which is based on information from resting-state fMRI, attempts to offer a more precise and thorough representation of the functional organization of the brain. The Glasser atlas has gained popularity as a tool for investigating brain connections and determining the functional networks in the brain.

The fact that they offer a standard framework for investigating the brain and comparing data from various investigations makes the Glasser and Brodmann atlases crucial tools in neuroscience research. These atlases help researchers gain a deeper understanding of the relationship between the anatomy and operation of the brain and behaviour and cognition. We utilized the Python VTK library to generate 3D structures of atlas labels (Fig. 5). By leveraging VTK's polygonal meshing and visualization capabilities, we were able to create high-quality and interactive 3D representations of anatomical structures, which allowed for a better understanding and analysis of the underlying data.

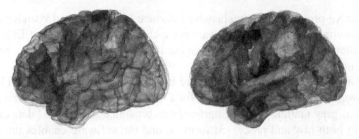

Fig. 5. Visualization of 3D structures of Brodmann (right) and Glasser (left) atlases.

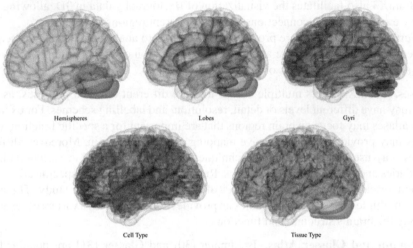

Hemispheres   Lobes   Gyri

Cell Type   Tissue Type

Fig. 6. Visualization of 3D structures of Talairach Atlas at its hierarchical level.

Talairach Atlas. The BrainX3 renders a 3-D Talairach Atlas [32] which is a detailed brain atlas that contains high-resolution colour tracings from MRI scans of a 60-year-old female. It consists of 27 axial sections, ranging from + 65 mm to –40 mm in the z-axis, with a section spacing of 2–5 mm. The images were digitized with a resolution of 0.43 mm, and each structure was segmented using colour discrimination and thresholding. A contiguous 1-mm 3D Talairach atlas volume was created from the reference images using resampling and nearest neighbour interpolation. The anatomical structure-naming scheme used for organizing the numerous 3D anatomical regions is based on volume occupancy and is organized into five hierarchical levels: Hemisphere, Lobe, Gyrus, Tissue type, and Cell type. Each volume of interest (VOI) is defined using 3D coordinates and a unique code for anatomical labelling. The labelling scheme provides explicit boundaries for labelled brain structures, and the entire brain volume is fully labelled at each hierarchical level.

Anatomy. BrainX3 gives a thorough 3D anatomical atlas of the human brain (Fig. 7). Users can examine the many anatomical structures in detail, allowing for a deep exploration of the brain's anatomy and organization. The anatomical atlas provides a complete picture of the different lobes, nuclei, and pathways that make up the brain, enabling users

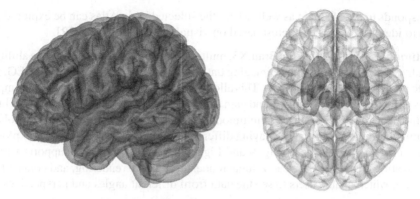

Fig. 7. Visualization of 3D structures of Anatomy (left) and Atlas of Basal Ganglia (right).

to navigate through the brain with ease and precision thanks to the 3D brain visualization feature.

Atlasing of Basal Ganglia. BrainX3 also offers a detailed subcortical probabilistic atlas based on 7T MRI's ultra-high resolution in-vivo anatomical imaging [33] (Fig. 7). Six subcortical nuclei can be found in that atlas: the striatum, the globus pallidus internal and external segment, the subthalamic nucleus, the substantia nigra, and the red nucleus. The atlas can capture the anatomical heterogeneity within healthy populations for each of the included subcortical nuclei.

Region of Interest. The BrainX3 window displays the uploaded MRI brain scan in three alternative orientations (axial, coronal, and sagittal), enabling users to adjust the image's contrast and brightness for the best possible visualization and the potential discovery of structural anomalies. In addition, the Point of Interest (POI) functionality in BrainX3 enables users to navigate and explore MRI scans (Fig. 8). The user can either manually input the coordinates or use a slider to move across all the planes of the MRI which

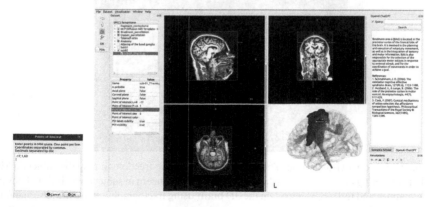

Fig. 8. The POIs tab in BrainX3 can be used to define the coordinates of the interest and can be overlapped with the subject's MRI and 3D representation of the Brain to extract information like the name of the brain area from the choice of atlas and fetch information on it from the Semantome.

corresponds to the 3D brain as well, where the selected brain Atlas can be explored and used to identify regions of interest based on visual inspection of the MRI.

Multimodal Visualisation. In BrainX3, multimodal visualisation refers to the ability to visualize different types of neuroimaging data, such as MRI, fMRI, PET, and EEG, in a single interface (Fig. 9 and Fig. 10). This allows neuroscientists and clinicians to compare and contrast the different datasets and gain a more comprehensive understanding of brain function and structure. BrainX3's multimodal visualization framework includes tools for aligning, co-registering, and overlaying different datasets, as well as tools for exploring the data in 2D and 3D space (Fig. 9 and Fig. 10). The platform also supports various visualization techniques, such as volume rendering, surface rendering, and connectivity mapping, which enable users to see the data from different angles and perspectives.

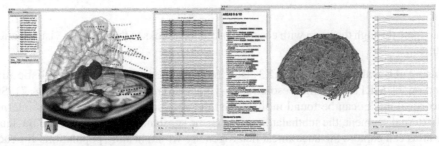

Fig. 9. The BrainX3 desktop application. On the left, visualization of anatomical structures and imaging with intracranial recordings localization and signals. On the right, visualization of a connectome displaying Knowledge information of a selected Brodmann area and node activity.

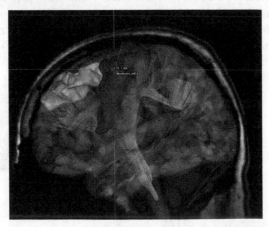

Fig. 10. MultiModal visualisation: The brainX3 provides the freedom to map the subject's MRI onto a 3D rendering of a brain, where the identified area of concern in subject-specific analysis can also be mapped and further examined on the 3D brain using tractography, atlases, and semantome feature of BrainX3.

In addition, BrainX3's multimodal visualization framework is integrated with other analysis tools, such as signal processing and machine learning algorithms, to enable users to explore the data more comprehensively and interactively. Overall, multimodal visualization in BrainX3 provides a powerful tool for understanding complex brain datasets, enabling neuroscientists and clinicians to make more informed decisions in research and clinical practice.

Connection Exploration. We have introduced a feature to study the anatomical connectivity between brain areas provided by the atlases contained in BrainX3 (see Atlas section) (Fig. 9 and Fig. 11). The BrainX3 uses HCP Diffusion MRI Template - HCP1065 for the representation of anatomical connectivity [34–37], which allows users to visually examine the connections between different brain regions. The afferent and efferent white matter pathways associated with a particular (clicked) region of the 3D brain will be visible if the connection mode is activated. This makes it possible to visualize the anatomical connections between various brain regions.

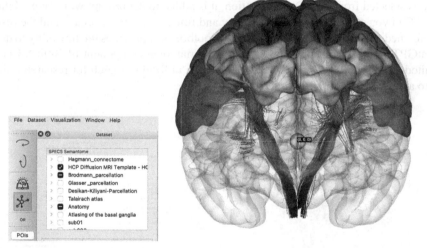

Fig. 11. BrainX3 in connection exploration mode. **3a**: Screenshot of the top left side of the BrainX3 desktop application. The exploration mode can be activated by clicking on the icon highlighted in red (highlighted here in this figure for clarity). **3b**: After activating exploration mode and selecting the Brodmann areas of interest, by clicking on each area the white matter tracts will appear, showing the anatomical connectivity of the selected area and other areas of the brain.

It is possible to limit the visualization of tractography data to specific brain regions of interest instead of displaying all tracts originating from the brain. This can be achieved through the utilization of the AND and OR options in BrainX3.

Currently, only the Brodmann Atlas has this functionality implemented; however, future work will also add white matter tractography for the other Atlases in BrainX3.

The Semantome. One design principle of BrainX3 is that the user has immediate access to the semantic information of structural and functional data [3] To achieve this we have interfaced BrainX3 with several search engines and databases. BrainX3 features the semantic scholar, which serves as a comprehensive toolbox for staying up-to-date with the latest developments and briefly summarizing the functionality of various brain regions. This system leverages Semantic Scholar [38], an AI-powered academic search engine designed to provide relevant and thorough search results for scientific research. The search engine's advanced technology enables it to understand the meaning behind the text of scientific publications, including their abstracts, citations, and other metadata and uses machine learning algorithms to analyze and classify publications based on their content, relevance, and impact (Fig. 12). The semantome is an API-based search engine integrated into BrainX3, enabling users to search or look up specific brain regions. The results retrieved from the API are then presented in a tabular format in the semantome window. Additionally, BrainX3's semantic scholar window displays the title and abstract of research articles, providing users with a high-level overview and helping them determine relevance. Users can further investigate an article by clicking on it to open the full text in their browser. To incorporate the latest advancements and leverage the full potential of AI, BrainX3 now includes OpenAI's chatGPT [39]. When a brain area is selected from the 3D visualization, it is added to the prompt with the predefined text "Can you explain briefly the anatomy and functions of brain area:", and the results are fetched and displayed in a text box. The toolbox also provides the flexibility to query ChatGPT in the search box (Fig. 12). The semantome component of BrainX3 is not limited to searching brain regions; it can also be utilized to search for research articles or to ask ChatGPT questions related to the brain.

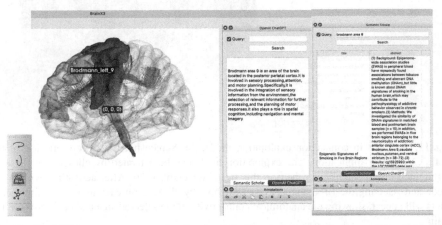

Fig. 12. BrainX3's semantome mode. On the left, the semantome mode can be activated by clicking on the icon highlighted in red (highlighted here in this figure for clarity). On the right, by clicking on a brain area, the information about such a brain area is displayed in two windows. One is the Semantic Scholar, which displays the scientific literature on the selected brain area. On the other window, the OpenAI chatGPT can be used to fetch anatomical and functional information.

The main drawback of ChatGPT is its tendency to provide inaccurate information, which poses a particular problem in academic publishing. The data utilized by ChatGPT is sourced from 2021 and earlier, limiting its relevance. While ChatGPT can be a valuable resource for researchers seeking to validate answers or detect issues in their work, it is crucial to acknowledge that it lacks adequate training to fact-check technical subjects [40].

Annotations. The annotation window in BrainX3 is a convenient feature that enables users to take notes and write while exploring and analyzing the brain. This window is designed to provide a dedicated space for users to record their observations, insights, and ideas as they navigate through the different brain regions and structures. Users can annotate the 3D visualization or any other relevant material in the software and refer to it later for analysis or reference. This feature is particularly useful for researchers, students, and professionals who need to keep track of their thoughts and insights as they study the brain. With the annotation window, users can maintain a detailed and organized record of their analysis and findings.

Reports. The report feature in BrainX3 is a powerful tool that enables users to generate a comprehensive report of their analysis and observations made during their exploration of the brain. This feature is particularly useful for researchers, clinicians, and other professionals who need to document their findings. With the report feature, users can create a customized report that may include information; for example; about the identification of lesion areas and observations made from functional connectivity of the brain using EEG data. The report can be generated in PDF format and can be easily shared with other members of the team. This functionality assists users in keeping a structured and comprehensive record of their analysis, facilitating efficient collaboration and knowledge-sharing.

Cloud. The vision of the platform is to provide data storage and analysis services in the cloud connected to intervention services. The vision is the deployment of a clinical workflow that covers multimodal data collection, brain model personalization for diagnostics and prevention and the use of clinical decision support on interventions, integrating services for visualization, interaction, machine learning, analysis pipelines, modelling, simulation and expert knowledge databases for improving patient-specific diagnosis and treatment. The platforms will provide services to manage and monitor patient data generated by the intervention systems (such as behavioural or physiological data) and it will be integrated with other infrastructures services such as the one provided by the EBRAINS platform to create more complex personalized medicine services for diagnostics and prognostics accessing clinical datasets and services for modelling and simulation. The platform is designed to integrate and scale-up data, resources, and services of multiple platforms with appropriate data security and privacy protection (see Fig. 13).

3   Case Study

3.1   BrainX3 Radiology Use-Case

BrainX3 Radiology is a solution for clinical decision support on the identification of brain lesions and the network of associated brain regions and functions that can be affected.

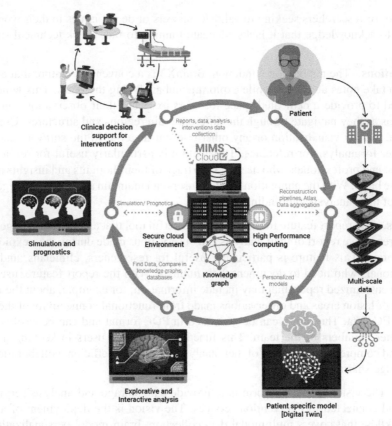

Fig. 13. Multi-scale patient data is collected and stored at the hospitals. The patient's data is integrated through advanced fusion and is used to build a patient-specific Whole Brain Model for interactive exploration and analysis by clinicians to detect lesions and their impact on the brain's networks. The platform provides simulation tools to show possible evolutions of the lesion and how brain functionality is globally affected. The data and associated information are used to support decisions and plan interventions under the guidance of clinicians. The Neurorehabilitation interventions manage the process and collect behavioural and performance data that is used to monitor and evaluate the impact of the interventions.

The development of CT and MRI technology in radiology has improved the visualisation of the structural changes in the brain after an injury which has had a great impact on the acute treatment of patients with brain injuries for instance in accurate thrombectomy post-stroke. In parallel, functional imaging techniques (PET, fMRI) have accelerated the development of the field of cognitive neuroscience. However, thus far functional/cognitive neuroscience has yet not been integrated to its full potential in the treatment of patients with brain injuries. The frustration shared among health care providers is that there is a vast amount of information in the technologies used by the health care system. Still, its accessibility is very limited due to system organization,

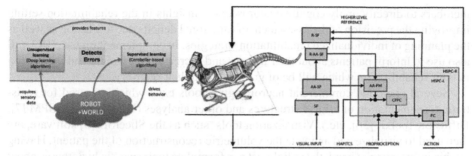

Fig. 14. The HELCA control architecture: Left: The two-phase Neuromorphic control architecture of BHyQ comprises an unsupervised and supervised loop, which are connected in a closed loop through behavioural feedback [45]. The unsupervised learning component extracts sensory features according to the underlying structure of the extero- and interoceptive sensory signals. The supervised learning modules receive those features, together with pre-defined haptic and kinematic error signals to refine and drive action. Finally, the modified behaviour changes the sensory experiences, and thus their underlying structure, requiring a refinement of the extracted features. Right: HELCA applied to BHyQ for the acquisition of visually-guided predictive collision avoidance through the anticipatory activation of the stepping reflex. A standard feedback controller (FC) is steered by predicted kinematic error signals through a counterfactual predictive controller (CFPC) [48]. The action-aware forward model (AA-FM) acquires associations between collision error signals (detected with haptic sensing) to issue anticipated impact signals that through the CFPC module anticipate avoidance action. The modules extracting action-aware sensory features (AA-SF) and recurrent action-aware sensory features (R-AA-SF) are higher-level unsupervised deep learning networks that process unimodal (e.g. vision) or multimodal (high-level visual features and proprioception) to identify latent states, which enable AA-FMs to learn predicting collisions with looming obstacles.

as well as the diversity of specialisations among the potential users. Indeed, it is commonly believed that the adoption of Artificial Intelligence methods in radiology will revolutionize the field creating the area of radiomics [41]. The standard radiology workflow includes the acquisition of data, the preprocessing of images after the acquisition, image-based clinical tasks such as feature extraction and diagnosis, and subsequent discussion in the clinical team to decide on a course of action. Current neuroinformatics and artificial intelligence techniques also advanced in HBP/EBRAINS, show great promise in optimizing this pipeline. However, in addition to the advanced processing of data by algorithms, the results of this process need to be transformed into actionable medical insights for human users in the medical team and also patients. It is exactly at this step where BX3 provides added value. BX3 will use a combination of visualization, data processing techniques, simulation, and semantic interpretation to bridge the gap between radiology and the clinical setting which is expected to have a direct impact on rehabilitation. The clinical team will interact through a common tool where radiological findings will not merely be of importance in the acute management of brain injury but will be integrated into a tool that allows a clinical team to directly analyse structure-function relationships by linking advanced visualization and analysis to semantic access via structure databases such as the EBRAINS knowledge graph, or the semantome [3]. Through this unique combination of features, BX3 will empower physicians and team members to directly apply cognitive neuroscience insights in the rehabilitation setting improving the precision of the assessment of functional deficits due to a lesion as well as the planning of individualized rehabilitation strategies. In complementary use, BX3 will also use to inform patients about their injuries and increase their insight and motivation in their rehabilitation which will be of great value in their recovery.

Several open and commercial neuroimaging tools exist which are used for registration, segmentation of critical structures and other analyses (Freesurfer [6], SPM [7], Diffusion Toolkit [36], etc.). Visualization tools, such as the Slicer3D [5] software, are then used to visualize and annotate the volumetric reconstruction of the patient. Having all this information at hand, the radiologist can formulate their specific hypotheses about the location of the lesion. So far, this process requires the analysis and the comparison in parallel of different sources of data from multiple modalities (e.g., clinical history of the patient from the hospital database, volumetric data, and similar cases registered in the clinical and scientific literature). Individual repositories must be accessed and dedicated software is required to operate on each dataset.

The above-mentioned workflow implies the adoption of different technologies running on several workstations and the sharing of information across different groups of clinicians which can slow down the overall process and may be prone to errors. Moreover, the necessity to learn different applications for different functions introduces additional costs in terms of human resources and time. The clinical practice described above may thus benefit from the approach proposed in BX3, where all the necessary processing, analytical and interpretative pipelines are integrated into a common framework, whereas the underlying computations are made transparent to the user.

4 Future Steps

Our current work focuses on training a UNet architecture for automatic lesion detection using the Stroke Imaging and Lesion Segmentation Challenge (SILSC) dataset which is a large, curated, open-source dataset of neuroimaging data from stroke patients, to train a UNet architecture [42] for automatic lesion detection. The dataset includes T1-weighted MRI images, diffusion-weighted MRI images, and corresponding lesion segmentations for over 1,000 stroke patients. The UNet architecture has been shown to be effective for segmentation tasks in medical imaging, particularly for brain lesions, due to its ability to capture spatial information and preserve fine details. Several studies have demonstrated the successful use of UNet for automated lesion segmentation in stroke patients (e.g., [1, 2]). Once trained, our model has the potential to accurately and efficiently detect stroke lesions, which could assist clinicians in diagnosis and treatment planning. The implementation of such a model in clinical settings could lead to improved patient outcomes and more efficient use of healthcare resources.

Integrate Neuroimaging Modalities: BrainX3 can be expanded to integrate different neuroimaging modalities such as EEG, MEG, fMRI, PET, and CT scans. This will allow researchers to combine different types of data to gain a better understanding of brain activity and its relationship with behaviour.

Develop Signal Processing GUI: BrainX3 can incorporate a signal processing GUI that enables users to preprocess EEG, MEG, and fMRI data in a simple and user-friendly manner. The GUI could include options for filtering, artifact removal, and other preprocessing steps that are commonly used in neuroimaging.

Implement Biophysical Models: BrainX3 can incorporate biophysical models that simulate brain activity, such as neural mass models or neural field models. These models could be used to predict the effects of different brain disorders or injuries and their potential treatments.

Analyze Brain Activity In A 3D Environment: BrainX3 can create a 3D environment where researchers can visualize and analyze brain activity. This could include the ability to explore brain networks and connectivity, visualize functional and structural brain data, and perform statistical analyses on brain data.

Develop Visualization Tools For Different Neuroimaging Modalities: BrainX3 can develop visualization tools specific to different neuroimaging modalities. For example, EEG data can be visualized as scalp maps, time-frequency representations, and source reconstructions. MEG data can be visualized as magnetic fields or source reconstructions, and fMRI data can be visualized as activation maps or connectivity matrices.

Enable Data Sharing and Collaboration: BrainX3 can enable data sharing and collaboration between researchers, allowing them to work together on large-scale projects and share data and analysis tools. This could be achieved through cloud-based solutions or shared databases.

Develop Machine Learning Tools: BrainX3 can host machine learning tools that enable researchers to analyze large and complex datasets. These tools could be used to classify brain activity patterns, predict treatment outcomes, or identify biomarkers of different brain disorders.

Future Use Case: BrainX3 Building a Hybrid Robot Control Architecture
We follow a synthetic methodology to test our models of the brain [43]. By leveraging recent developments in computational neuroscience, machine learning, mechanical engineering, and material science, Counterfactual Assessment and Valuation for Awareness Architecture—CAVAA (European Commission, EIC 101071178) project advances a neuromorphic control architecture for a high-mobility, high-dexterity, and compliant biomorphic robot (BHyQ) that operates robustly and safely in unstructured environments [44, 45]. Due to the many degrees of freedom of soft robots and the complexity of their environments, CAVAA adopts a biologically based approach to address the fundamental robotics challenge of offering robust control in the face of an a priori unknown and huge state-space. Based on the cerebellum's neuromorphic control principles, the CAVAA architecture will learn to regulate BHyQ [46].

BrainX3 acts as a starting point; where for instance the spiking neural network of the cerebellum could be modeled and simulated. The simulated data can be visualized and fed to the biomorphic robotic systems.

These are just a few possible future steps for BrainX3. As technology and research continue to advance, there will likely be many more exciting developments in the field of neuroimaging and brain modeling.

5 Conclusions

BrainX3 is a neuroinformatics platform that supports research and clinical use cases on both personalized medicine diagnostics and prognostics and intervention decisions and the construction of synthetic brains. The platform features 3D visualization, analysis, and simulation of human neuroimaging, electrophysiological data, and brain models. BrainX3 is designed with the principles of human-in-the-loop, immersive, cognitive interfaces, standards for personal data use, sharing, and organization, accuracy in visualization and analysis methods, and targeting research and clinical use.

Several commercial solutions for visualization and analysis exist but the majority are developed for specific acquisition systems and have proprietary source code and file formats that are not accessible to the overall research community. The free alternatives to commercial solutions such as Freesurfer, SPM, EEGLab, Fieldtrip, Brainstorm, and MNE [5–11] tools have been largely adopted by the research community and have now reached a high level of maturity.

BrainX3 2.0 is designed with a layered architecture with four different levels: Graphical User Interface (GUI), Application Core, Native, and Specific Plugins. The architecture is decoupled, allowing the user interface to be mapped to an internal representation of the multimodal data and its relationship to a native user interface representation, and plugins to implement their logic and handle their description of how to represent the data graphically. BrainX3 2.0 is implemented using the Python programming language and uses external libraries: Qt for the GUI, VTK for the 3D visualization, and several open-source libraries to manage neuroimaging and electrophysiological data.

In conclusion, BrainX3 is a powerful tool that offers researchers and clinicians the ability to explore and interact with different brain datasets directly and intuitively. BrainX3 2.0 offers improvements over the first version with a decoupled architecture that allows for easier development and management of the platform. While there are several commercial and free alternatives available, BrainX3 offers unique features that are not present on other platforms. First, BrainX3 has the potential to further advance research and clinical applications in neuroinformatics, personalized medicine diagnostics, and prognostics. Moreover, BrainX3 is not merely restricted to neuroinformatics but also offers the possibility to integrate and interact with recent developments in neuroscience and models of neuromorphic architectures. BrainX3 acts as a bridge between empirical data and the artificial brain allowing it to make neuromorphic robotic systems more biologically plausible. BrainX3 has the potential to offer sufficient flexibility to incorporate new models or tune the ones that are already in place and contribute to the advancement of artificial brain models' biological realism. As we have shown, BrainX3 provides tools to visualize, analyze, model, and simulate multi-modal data. It bridges the gap between various modalities of neuroimaging, brain models, and any prospective applications and uses, such as clinical, education, and research, as an integrative neuroinformatic tool. BrainX3 can be a convergent point to create and view particular brain-like data that will subsequently be applied to such brain-inspired systems in the context of expanding the use of artificial systems that are inspired by the brain in various domains. As a result, BrainX3 not only offers tools to improve research and clinical applications but also serves as a point of convergence for tools in neuroinformatics and links biological data with artificial brains1.

Acknowledgements. We thank Pedro Omedas and Toni Gurgui for their invaluable contribution to Python codes and technical help.

This research work is funded by the European Commission's Counterfactual Assessment and Valuation for Awareness Architecture—CAVAA (European Commission, EIC 101071178), AI in Stroke Neurorehabilitation — AISN (European Commission, EIC 101057655), Personalised Health cognitive assistance for RehAbilitation SystEm — PHRASE (European Commission, EIC 101058240).

References

1. Arsiwalla, X.D., Betella, A., Bueno, E.G., Omedas, P., Zucca, R., Verschure, P.F.M.J.: The dynamic connectome: a tool for large-scale 3D reconstruction of brain activity in real-time. In: 27th Conference on Modelling and Simulation (2013). https://doi.org/10.7148/2013-0865
2. Zucca, R., et al.:."BrainX: A Virtual Reality Tool for Neurosurgical Intervention in Epilepsy" (2017)
3. Arsiwalla, X.D., et al.: Connectomics to semantomics: addressing the brain's big data challenge. Procedia Comput. Sci. **53**, 48–55 (2015)
4. Betella, A., et al.: Understanding large network datasets through embodied interaction in virtual reality. In: Virtual Reality International Conference (2014). https://doi.org/10.1145/2617841.2620711
5. Fedorov, A., et al.: 3D Slicer as an image computing platform for the quantitative imaging network. Magn. Reson. Imaging **30**(9), 1323–1341 (2012). https://doi.org/10.1016/j.mri.2012.05.001
6. Fischl, B.: FreeSurfer. Neuroimage **62**(2), 774–781 (2012)
7. Ashburner, J.: Computational anatomy with the SPM software. Magn. Reson. Imaging **27**(8), 1163–1174 (2009)
8. Delorme, A., Makeig, S.: EEGLAB: an open-source toolbox for analysis of single-trial EEG dynamics including independent component analysis. J. Neurosci. Methods **134**(1), 9–21 (2004). https://doi.org/10.1016/j.jneumeth.2003.10.009
9. Oostenveld, R., Fries, P., Maris, E., Schoffelen, J.: FieldTrip: open source software for advanced analysis of MEG, EEG, and invasive electrophysiological data. Comput. Intell. Neurosci. **2011**, 1–9 (2011). https://doi.org/10.1155/2011/156869
10. Tadel, F., Baillet, S., Mosher, J.C., Pantazis, D., Leahy, R.M.: Brainstorm: a user-friendly application for MEG/EEG analysis. Comput. Intell. Neurosci. **2011**, 1–13 (2011). https://doi.org/10.1155/2011/879716
11. Gramfort, A., et al.: MEG and EEG data analysis with MNE-Python. Front. Neurosci. **7**(267), 1–13 (2013). https://doi.org/10.3389/fnins.2013.00267
12. Peyser, A., et al.: NEST 2.14. 0 (No. FZJ-2017–07289). Jülich Supercomputing Center (2017)
13. Stimberg, M., Brette, R., Goodman, D.F.: Brian 2, an intuitive and efficient neural simulator. Elife **8**, e47314 (2019)
14. Bekolay, T., et al.: Nengo: a python tool for building large-scale functional brain models. Front. Neuroinform. **7**, 48 (2014)

15. Bernardet, U., Verschure, P.F.: iqr: a tool for the construction of multi-level simulations of brain and behaviour. Neuroinformatics **8**, 113–134 (2010)
16. Sanz Leon, P., et al.: The virtual brain: a simulator of primate brain network dynamics. Front. Neuroinform. **7**, 10 (2013)
17. Arsiwalla, X.D., et al.: Network dynamics with BrainX3: a large-scale simulation of the human brain network with real-time interaction. Front. Neuroinform. **9**, 118694 (2015). https://doi.org/10.3389/fninf.2015.00002
18. Arsiwalla, X.D., et al.: Connectomics to semantomics: addressing the brain's big data challenge1. Procedia Comput. Sci. **53**, 48–55 (2015). https://doi.org/10.1016/j.procs.2015.07.278
19. Daniel, P., et al.: BrainX3.: a virtual reality tool for neurosurgical intervention in epilepsy (2017)
20. Zegarek, G., Arsiwalla, X.D., Dalmazzo, D., Verschure, P.F.M.J.: Mapping the language connectome in healthy subjects and brain tumor patients. In: Villa, A.E.P., Masulli, P., Pons Rivero, A.J. (eds.) ICANN 2016. LNCS, vol. 9886, pp. 83–90. Springer, Cham (2016). https://doi.org/10.1007/978-3-319-44778-0_10
21. Estefan, D.P., et al.: Coordinated representational reinstatement in the human hippocampus and lateral temporal cortex during episodic memory retrieval. Nat. Commun. **10**(1), 2255 (2019). https://doi.org/10.1038/s41467-019-09569-0
22. Betella, A., et al.:.BrainX 3. In: Virtual Reality International Conference (2014). https://doi.org/10.1145/2617841.2620726
23. Betella, A., et al Advanced interfaces to stem the data deluge in mixed reality. Zenodo (CERN European Organization for Nuclear Research) (2013). https://doi.org/10.1145/2503385.2503460
24. Cetnarski, R., et al.: Symbiotic adaptive interfaces: a case study using BrainX3. In: Blankertz, B., Jacucci, G., Gamberini, L., Spagnolli, A., Freeman, J. (eds.) Symbiotic 2015. LNCS, vol. 9359, pp. 33–44. Springer, Cham (2015). https://doi.org/10.1007/978-3-319-24917-9_4
25. Papachristodoulou, P., Betella, A., Manzolli, J.: Augmenting the navigation of complex data sets using sonification: a case study with BrainX3. In: 2015 IEEE 2nd VR Workshop on Sonic Interactions for Virtual Environments (SIVE) (2015). https://doi.org/10.1109/sive.2015.7361284
26. Riverbank Computing | Introduction. (n.d.). https://www.riverbankcomputing.com/software/pyqt/. Accessed 27 Mar 2023
27. VTK - KitwarePublic. (n.d.). https://vtk.org/Wiki/VTK
28. Gorgolewski, K.J., et al.: The brain imaging data structure, a format for organizing and describing outputs of neuroimaging experiments. Sci. data **3**(1), 1–9 (2016)
29. Hagmann, P.: From diffusion MRI to brain connectomics (No. THESIS). EPFL (2005)
30. Brodmann, K.: Vergleichende Lokalisationslehre der Grosshirnrinde in ihren Prinzipien dargestellt auf Grund des Zellenbaues von Dr. K. Brodmann (1909)
31. Glasser, M.F., et al.: A multi-modal parcellation of human cerebral cortex. Nature **536**(7615), 171–178 (2016). https://doi.org/10.1038/nature18933
32. Talairach, J.: Co-planar stereotaxic atlas of the human brain. 3-D proportional system: an approach to cerebral imaging (1988)
33. Keuken, M.C., et al.: Quantifying inter-individual anatomical variability in the subcortex using 7 T structural MRI. Neuroimage **94**, 40–46 (2014)
34. Yeh, F.C., et al.: Population-averaged atlas of the macroscale human structural connectome and its network topology. Neuroimage **178**, 57–68 (2018). https://doi.org/10.1016/j.neuroimage.2018.05.027
35. Yeh, F.C., Tseng, W.Y.I.: NTU-90: a high angular resolution brain atlas constructed by q-space diffeomorphic reconstruction. Neuroimage **58**(1), 91–99 (2011)

36. Yeh, F.C., Wedeen, V.J., Tseng, W.Y.I.: Generalized q-sampling imaging. IEEE Trans. Med. Imaging **29**(9), 1626–1635 (2010)

37. Wang, R., Benner, T., Sorensen, A.G., Wedeen, V.J.: Diffusion toolkit: a software package for diffusion imaging data processing and tractography. In: Proc Intl Soc Mag Reson Med, vol. 15, no. 3720 (2007)

38. Lo, K., Wang, L.L., Neumann, M., Kinney, R.M., Weld, D.S.: S2ORC: The Semantic Scholar Open Research Corpus. In: Annual Meeting of the Association for Computational Linguistics (2020)

39. OpenAI. GPT-3 Language Models (2021). https://platform.openai.com/docs/models/gpt-3-5

40. Wen, J., Wang, W.: The future of ChatGPT in academic research and publishing: A commentary for clinical and translational medicine. Clinical and Translational Medicine, **13**(3) (2023). https://doi.org/10.1002/ctm2.1207

41. Hosny, A., Parmar, C., Quackenbush, J., Schwartz, L.B., Aerts, H.J.: Artificial intelligence in radiology. Nat. Rev. Cancer **18**(8), 500–510 (2018). https://doi.org/10.1038/s41568-018-0016-5

42. Zhou, Z., Rahman Siddiquee, M. M., Tajbakhsh, N., Liang, J.: UNet++: a nested U-Net architecture for medical image segmentation. In: Stoyanov, D., et al. (eds.) DLMIA/ML-CDS -2018. LNCS, vol. 11045, pp. 3–11. Springer, Cham (2018). https://doi.org/10.1007/978-3-030-00889-5_1

43. Verschure, P.F.M.J., Prescott, T.J.: A living machines approach to the sciences of mind and brain. The handbook of living machines: research in biomimetic and biohybrid systems, 15–25 (2018)

44. Verschure, P.F., Voegtlin, T., Douglas, R.J.: Environmentally mediated synergy between perception and behaviour in mobile robots. Nature **425**(6958), 620–624 (2003)

45. Dario, P., et al.: Robot companions for citizens. Procedia Comput. Sci. **7**, 47–51 (2011). https://doi.org/10.1016/j.procs.2011.12.017

46. Falotico, E., et al.: Connecting artificial brains to robots in a comprehensive simulation framework: the neurorobotics platform. Front. Neurorobot. **11**, 2 (2017). https://doi.org/10.3389/fnbot.2017.00002

47. Herreros, I., Arsiwalla, X.D., Verschure, P.F.M.J.: A forward model at Purkinje cell synapses facilitates cerebellar anticipatory control. In: Neural Information Processing Systems, vol. 29, pp. 3828–3836 (2016)

Sporify: An Automated Tool to Quantify Spores in Z-Stacked 3D Samples

Oscar Sten[1,2](✉) iD, Emanuela Del Dottore[1](✉) iD, Giulia Raffaele[1,3,4] iD,
Marilena Ronzan[1] iD, Nicola M. Pugno[2,5](✉) iD, and Barbara Mazzolai[1](✉) iD

[1] Bioinspired Soft Robotics Laboratory, Istituto Italiano di Tecnologia,
Via Morego 30, 16163 Genova, Italy
{oscar.sten,emanuela.deldottore,barbara.mazzolai}@iit.it
[2] Laboratory for Bioinspired, Bionic, Nano, Meta Materials and Mechanics, Department of
Civil, Environmental and Mechanical Engineering, University of Trento, Via Mesiano 77,
38122 Trento, Italy
nicola.pugno@unitn.it
[3] Department of Science and Technology for Human and Environment, Università Campus
Bio-Medico di Roma, Via Álvaro del Portillo 21, 00128 Roma, Italy
[4] Department of Biology, Università degli Studi di Napoli Federico II, Via Vicinale Cupa Cintia
21, 80126 Napoli, Italy
[5] School of Engineering and Materials Science, Queen Mary University of London, Mile End
Road, London E1 4NS, UK

Abstract. In recent years, fungi have attracted avid interest from the research
community. This interest stems from several motives, including their network
creation capabilities and fundamental role in the ecosystem. Controlled laboratory
experiments of fungal behaviors are crucial to further understanding their role and
functionalities.

In this paper, we propose a method for automating the quantification and
observation of fungal spores. Our approach consists of four steps: 1) a Z-stack
image acquisition of the sample is performed, 2) a detection algorithm is applied to
all Z-planes, 3) clustering of spores detected in different Z-planes, 4) determination
of the optimal Z-plane for each cluster through an ad-hoc focus measure. We
compared the spore count obtained through the automated tool to a manual count
and the count obtained by applying the detection algorithm to a single plane. The
result is a highly automated, non-invasive tool to determine spore count, estimate
each spore depth, and retrieve an all-in-focus image to analyze further.

Keywords: Fungi · Image processing · Automated analysis

1 Introduction

In nature, some species of terrestrial plants establish symbiotic relationships with fungi,
known as mycorrhiza, to gain nutrients and exchange carbon, the metabolic resource
essential for fungi growth [1]. The mycorrhizae create underground connections between
plants creating a network called Common Mycorrhizal Network (CMN). Since CMNs

© The Author(s) 2023
F. Meder et al. (Eds.): Living Machines 2023, LNAI 14158, pp. 178–192, 2023.
https://doi.org/10.1007/978-3-031-39504-8_12

often extend through forests forming large networks with a structure that recalls the World Wide Web, CMNs have also been named the Wood Wide Web [2, 3].

Due to their role in carbon recycling, the symbiotic relationship between plants and fungi has increasingly attracted researchers' interest [4, 5]. Controlled experiments conducted in a laboratory setting are critical for better understanding the role and functional mechanisms behind the plant-fungus symbiotic relationship. Laboratory experiments can guarantee controlling specific parameters to help identify and characterize their effects on the organisms' growth. Prior to this is the analysis of the spores in the medium.

In order to automate the quantification of fungal spores, several computational approaches have been proposed, specifically involving digital image analysis. In 1993, Paul et al. proposed an image analysis method to automate the assessment of spore viability and germination characteristics in the mold fungus *P. chrysogenum*. In their work, images of spores were acquired with a monochrome microscope. The images were binarized through manual thresholding, and diverse morphological filtering operations were applied to remove undesired objects and to separate spore and germination parts [6]. Computational tools to count the spores in a petri dish sample through image analysis have been proposed in [7–11]. Melo et al. (2019) proposed a two-step approach. First, circular objects are detected with the Circular Hough Transform (CHT), a commonly used algorithm for detecting circular image features [7]. Then, an artificial neural network removes false positives based on their RGB colors [7]. Vidal et al. (2019) proposed a semi-automated approach with an interface allowing users to apply different operations. In particular, the user sets two thresholds to perform double thresholding. Then, diverse morphological filters can be applied, removing objects that are too big, too small, or too elongated [8]. Xu et al. (2009) proposed a series of filtering operations for segmenting and counting isolated pathogenic spores in an image [9]. Tahir et al. (2017) collected pathogenic airborne spores onto glass slides using an air sampling unit and then used a support vector machine model trained with hand-crafted features and histogram-oriented gradient features to detect the spores [11].

Additionally, several studies have proposed techniques for the automated identification of airborne pathogenic spores. Wang et al. proposed a machine learning-based approach for classifying captured spore species using diffraction features [12]. Tahir et al. (2018) utilized a dataset of 40,800 labeled images of five species of pathogenic fungi sampled with an air sampling unit on an adhesive, transparent tape, to train and cross-validate a deep learning-based classifier [13, 14]. Using model-based object recognition, Perner et al. (2004) classified airborne pathogenic spore species photographed on a microscopic slide [15]. Zhao et al. (2019) collected a dataset of 40,000 anthrax bacterial spores that were cultivated, filtered, and photographed on a glass slide. A deep learning-based classifier was trained and validated using these labeled images to segment the spores [16]. However, all the mentioned studies on automated spore quantification work on 2D images.

Despite their reduced dimensions ([30–140] μm of diameter) [17], spores are 3D objects that can lose important features if acquired in a single focal plane. In microscopy, this is done by acquiring the sample at multiple focal depths in a Z-stack, multiple planes over the depth axis, and combining them into an extended depth-of-field (EDF) image

[18]. The various techniques for creating EDF images assess the value of a certain criterion, called focus measure (FM), to determine the plane in which the sample is more focused [18]. The most used techniques are Gradient-based FMs that emphasize prominence of the edges in the image [19], Laplacian-based FM that emphasize the quantity of edges in the image [19], and Wavelet-based FM that utilizes wavelet transforms to analyze and enhance all the frequency components of an image [15]. Both Gradient based and Laplacian based FMs may constitute good options to estimate the depth of spores, however, they may include edges that are not of our interest (hyphae, morphological artifacts). In this study, we aimed at defining an FM adapted to spores, by considering the prominence of the border of the spore, which becomes more defined when the spore is in focus.

In this work, we leverage spore information by employing Z-stacked microscope images. Specifically, we propose a method for automatic 1) detection and quantification of spores of *Rhizophagus irregularis*, a widely studied mycorrhizal fungus, in a live sample, 2) estimation of each spore's relative centroidal Z-position, and 3) acquisition of in-focus image patches of all the spores in the sample. The paper is structured as follows. We present sample preparation, acquisition, and the image analysis process developed (Sect. 2). We show the results of the spore detection and count, compare the proposed Z-stack-leveraged method to the results obtained by applying the detection algorithm to a single Z-plane, and show a qualitative comparison between our FM and some well-known general-purpose FMs (Sect. 3). Finally, we discuss some aspects regarding the validity of our tool for observing and quantifying fungal spores, discuss some future perspectives for spore vitality assessment (Sect. 4), and conclude with final remarks (Sect. 5).

2 Methodology

2.1 Sample Preparation

Spores of *Rhizophagus irregularis* (MUCL 41833), formerly *Glomus intraradices,* were purchased from GINCO (http://www.mbla.ucl.ac.be/ginco-bel).

Spores were cultured in Petri dishes (12×12 cm^2) containing minimal medium (M), with pH 5.5, and gelling agent (gellan gum 3000 mg/l). The M medium is a culture medium with minimal nutrient content explicitly developed for spores germination by Bécard and Fortin (1988) [20]. The medium was sterilized by autoclaving at 121 °C for 15 min and then poured into Petri dishes in an aseptic environment under the laminar-flow hood. After the medium was solidified, 100 manually counted spores were sucked up from a vial with deionized water and placed in each petri dish with a micro-pipette. The spores were cultured in axenic condition and maintained in the dark at 28 °C for five days before the image acquisition.

Since, after deposition, the water unevenly distributed and evaporated over the medium, the spores dispersed unevenly over the surface. Because of this, we could acquire more than one sample image from each petri dish, one for each spot.

To manually count the spores, we placed the sample under a vertical microscope (Nikon Eclipse Ni, Nikon Instruments Inc.) and used the Annotations and Measurements tool available with the NIS-Elements D software (Nikon Instruments Inc.) to visualize and mark elements in the sample. Each sample was counted three times with consistent results. The Root Mean Square (RMS) error was estimated to compare automated vs. manual count.

2.2 Image Acquisition

Images were acquired with a Nikon AZ100M microscope equipped with an Andor Zyla sCMOS camera (VSC-10642), AZ Plan Fluor 5 × objective, and a white backlight. The microscope has a motorized stage to move the sample over a large area (up to 25 cm × 25 cm) and Z-stack motion. The microscope can be controlled through the NIS-Elements software (Nikon Instruments Inc.), which allows the acquisition of a single frame, a large image through stitching, and Z-stack automatized acquisitions.

As the samples are intrinsically 3D, we ran the Z-stack acquisition with a plane interval of 2 μm to capture the third-dimension information. The starting plane was set closest to the camera, and the end plane farthest from the camera. In one case, where an area larger than $25\mu m^2$ (max field of view of the optic) was imaged, the interval was increased to 5 μm.

2.3 Image Processing

The image analysis program was coded in MATLAB 2022 [21]. As input, it takes a set of Z-stacked grayscale images of *R. Irregularis* spores and mycelium. The process follows the steps in Algorithm 1.

The spores were typically circular and within a known size range (between 30 and 140 μm), so the CHT proposed in [22] was utilized for spore detection. This technique also allows estimating the radius of each identified object, and it is robust against overlapping objects. We used the implementation provided with the function *imfindcircles* in MATLAB [23].

The scale bar assigned by the microscope software was segmented through global thresholding and used to convert pixels to millimeters. This information was used to set the circle size limits. The scale bar was removed from the image by setting the scale bar pixels to correspond to the mean grayscale intensity to not interfere with the circle detection. To speed up computation, the images were resized using the function *imresize* so that the lower radius limit in millimeters corresponded to six pixels, which is the lowest limit for the circle detection algorithm to remain stable [23].

Algorithm 1: Sporify

Input : Images, L = 30μm, U= 140μm, ϵ = 3.5 μm, pts = 5, sensitivity = 0.8, margin = 5 pixels.

Output : Centers, Radii and Z-planes of Spores.

1 allcenters = $\emptyset$, allradii = $\emptyset$, allFMs = $\emptyset$ Centers = $\emptyset$ Radii = $\emptyset$ Z-planes = $\emptyset$

2 **for** *i in images* **do**

3      $\frac{\mu m}{pixel} \leftarrow$ scalebar

4   L $\leftarrow \frac{L}{\frac{\mu m}{pixel}}$

5   U $\leftarrow \frac{U}{\frac{\mu m}{pixel}}$

6   s $\leftarrow \frac{L}{6}$

7   I $\leftarrow$ resize(I, s)

8   [centers, radii] = imfindcircles(I, [L U], sensitivity)

9   centers $\leftarrow$ s·centers

10   radii $\leftarrow$ s·radii

11   FMs $\leftarrow \emptyset$

12   **for** *j in centers* **do**

13   patchCoordinates $\leftarrow$ center(j) ± radii(j) ± margin

14   patch $\leftarrow$ image(patchCoordinates)

15   FM $\leftarrow$ focusmeasure(patch)

16   FMs $\leftarrow$ FMs ∪ FM

17   allcenters $\leftarrow$ allcenters ∪ centers

18   allradii $\leftarrow$ allradii ∪ radii

19   allFMs $\leftarrow$ allFMs ∪ FMs

20 $\epsilon \leftarrow \frac{\epsilon}{\frac{\mu m}{pixel}}$

21 clusters $\leftarrow$ dbscan(centers, pts, ϵ)

22 **for** *c in clusters* **do**

23   clusterCenters $\leftarrow$ allcenters(c)

24   clusterRadii $\leftarrow$ allradii(c)

25   clusterFMs $\leftarrow$ allFMs(c)

26     $FM_{argmax} \leftarrow$ argmax(clusterFMs)

27   Centers $\leftarrow$ Centers ∪ clusterCenters(FM_{argmax})

28   Radii $\leftarrow$ Radii ∪ clusterRadii(FM_{argmax})

29   Z-planes $\leftarrow$ Z-planes ∪ clusterFM(FM_{argmax})

30 **Function** *focusmeasure(patch)*

31   edges $\leftarrow$ edge(patch, 'Canny')

32   gradients $\leftarrow$ imgradient(patch)

33   FM $\leftarrow$ median(gradients(edges))

34   return FM

As each sample was acquired in Z-stack, the same spore was often detected at different Z-planes. Because of camera distortions, each spore associates with more than one coordinate (one for each plane) (Fig. 1). For this reason, we applied the clustering algorithm Density Based Spatial Clustering of Applications with Noise (DBSCAN) [24] to group centers belonging to the same spore. We utilized the implementation in the function *dbscan* in [25]. The DBSCAN algorithm takes two parameters: the minimum number of points in a cluster and a maximum distance threshold (ε) to search neighboring elements. We set the minimum number of elements to five and ε to the number of pixels corresponding to 3.5 μm as the maximum Euclidean distance between centers to fall into the same cluster.

Because multiple spores can be present in the same image, and that they can distribute at any depth, it was necessary to estimate the plane where the spore was more focused and extract its Z-position. To this purpose, we propose an FM adapted to fungal spores, merging gradient-based and Laplacian features. To assess the FM of each spore, we looped over each candidate in a cluster. The candidate element has associated a center, a radius, and a Z-plane. For each candidate, a squared region of interest (ROI) was

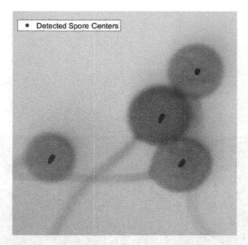

Fig. 1. The same spores are detected in several Z-planes. All the centers detected are shown with a blue dot. The small misalignment is the effect of camera distortion.

extracted around the center with a side length corresponding to the spore diameter plus a margin of five pixels. An ad-hoc FM was calculated for each ROI. Figure 2 shows visualizations of a single spore in three different set planes.

Specifically, Fig. 2A–C shows the considered spore in three different planes, where the most defined edge is the one that separates the spore from the background. We applied the Canny edge detector [26] with the *edge* function [23] (Fig. 2D–F). Besides computing the image gradients, the Canny edge detector applies local-maximum suppression, double thresholding, and hysteresis to obtain the edge in the image [26]. The median gradient magnitude (Fig. 2G–I) of the detected edge pixels represents the sharpness of the edge around the spore and is adopted in this study as FM. In Fig. 2G-I we see that, when the spore is in focus (Fig. 2H), the gradient magnitudes have higher values than the gradient magnitudes shown in Fig. 2G and in Fig 2I in the thin circle corresponding to the spore's edge. The Canny operator may identify some lines deriving from the spore's internal structure (Fig. 2D–E). However, since the median is considered, this does not represent an issue as long as these pixels are in minority.

Thus, we identified the in-focus plane and, consequently, the depth of each spore by selecting the plane associated with the maximum FM. Finally, a new image comprising all in-focus spores is obtained by stitching the in-focus ROI. Figure 3 illustrates an example of depth estimation within an all-in-focus image (Fig. 3A) and compares a zoom-in of the same sample with a single plane acquisition, where only a few spores are in focus (Fig. 3B), and a montage of all spores in focus (Fig. 3C). This resultant image offers a 2D view with an optimal definition of each spore border and texture, features essential for evaluating the state and vitality of the spores, which can be done manually or automatically.

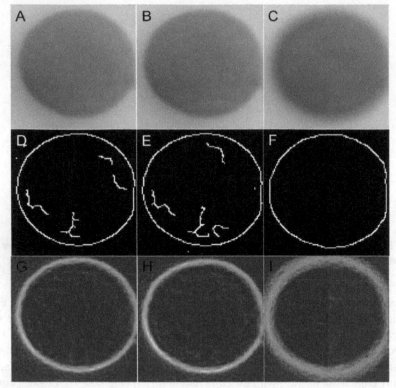

Fig. 2. Images of the same spore: (A) before entering focus, (B) in focus, (C) after moving past focus. (D-F) Edges identified by Canny operator. (G-I) Patch image gradient magnitudes.

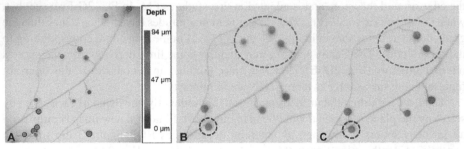

Fig. 3. (A) Detected spores with encircling color depending on estimated relative depth. (B) Single Z-plane with one spore (in blue) in focus and other spores (in red) out of focus. (C) Montage with all spores in focus.

3 Results

3.1 Spore Detection

We collected 16 samples with different numbers of spores, totaling 1338 spores according to our manual count, and 1277 spores with our tool. The mean diameter of the spores evaluated with the automatic analysis was 66.1μm (σ = 16.2 μm), with a median of 65μm (see Fig. 4A).

To assess the validity of our tool, we compared a manual count with the automatic count gained from our analysis (Fig. 4B). The tool can detect and count the spores with a maximum relative error of 7.15%, and the RMS value of the relative error was 3.25%.

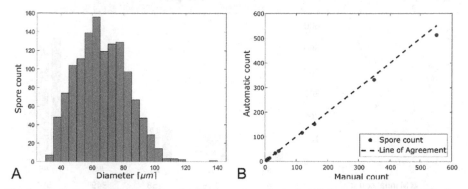

Fig. 4. Summary of results achieved with the automatic tool. (A) Spores diameter distribution. (B) Spores count yielded with the automatic analysis compared with a manual count.

Among the samples, two were particularly dense, with a spore density of over 30 spores per mm^2, where many spores were partially overlapped (Fig. 5A-B). These samples are particularly challenging to analyze either manually or with the automatic tool. From a manual count, they contained 349 and 551 spores. The automatic count yielded 332 (4.9% error) and 513 (6.9% error).

For the five samples with the highest spore count in our set, we compared the manual count, the automatic spore count derived from the all-in-focus image, and the result obtained from analyzing a single plane in the middle of the Z-stack. Figure 5C reports the results and highlights that, for samples with a high quantity of spores, using Z-stacked images improves the detection substantially with respect to a single plane analysis, reducing the distance with a manual count. Indeed, for the Z-stack method, the relative error for the five largest samples was between 2.5%–6.9%, with a median of 4.5%, while for the single plane method, it was between 6.8%–33.4%, with a median of 13.4%. The two errors result significantly different from a 1-factor ANOVA test (p-value = 0.043 with significance level 0.05).

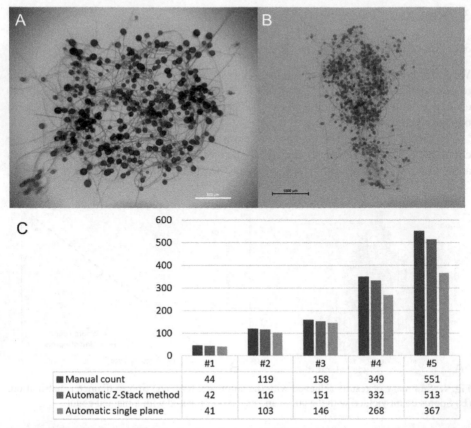

Fig. 5. Difference between the single plane image and full Z-stacked image. (A) Spore cloud #4. (B) Spore could #5. (C) Comparison of manual count, automatic count including all Z-planes, and Automatic Count with a single Z-plane.

3.2 Focus Plane Selection

Figure 6 shows the optimal focus planes attributed to some example spores. We observe that CONT and GDER tend to select more in-depth planes than the others; they appear less focused in the first row than the other FMs, and the WAVS performs worse in the third row than the others.

Generally, our FM tends to identify a plane closer (or the same, last raw Fig. 6) to the ones obtained with LAPM, WAVS, and LAPV methods, then to GDER, CONT. This suggests that our FM selects the plane where the border sharpness is maximized while at the same time neglecting artifacts like the partially overlapping spore in the first row of Fig. 6.

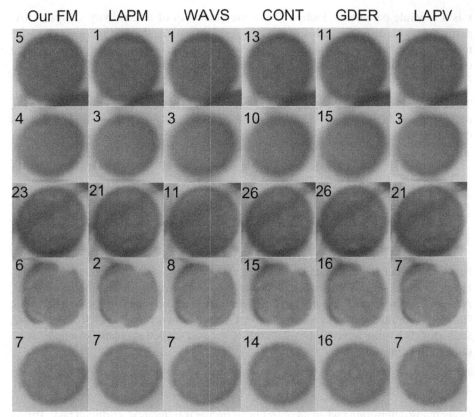

Fig. 6. Optimal focus of diverse spores, according to (from left to right): our FM, LAPM, WAVS, CONT, GDER, and LAPV. The resulting optimal Z-plane obtained from each FM is reported in the upper left corner of each image patch.

4 Discussions

4.1 Spore Detection

Our results demonstrate that the automatic detection produces an RMS error of 3.25% that increases with spores number (Fig. 4B), in our case, up to a maximum relative error of 7.15%. The main factor increasing the error is that large spore samples tend to become denser, with more overlapping spores. The Z-stack solution overcomes the problem of overlapping spores to some extent. However, if samples are extremely dense, having a single observation point imposes a limitation. A linear regression applied to the relative error estimated a coefficient of 0.00012, implying that the relative error can be expected to grow by 1.2 percentage points per 100 spores. However, for samples with $\gg$ 500 spores, the error likely would grow much faster due to the lack of visibility. Spores stacked on each other led to detect spore coordinates belonging to different spores close to each other, causing the clustering algorithm to merge them falsely. Further reducing the distance threshold (ε) could generate more clusters than actually present. Consequently,

ε is a sensible parameter. Table 1 shows the outcomes of a sensitivity analysis (SA) performed with different values of ε. The SA demonstrates that the spore count varies in very dense samples. A future perspective of this work may consist of embedding robustness against such faulty mergers or divisions of clusters.

Table 1: Sensitivity of the clustering distance threshold in high spore density samples. The spore count is provided for different ε values. The accuracy significantly reduces with the crowdedness of the sample.

	$\varepsilon = 2.5\,\mu m$	$\varepsilon = 3.5\,\mu m$	$\varepsilon = 4.5\,\mu m$
Cloud 1	334	332	330
Cloud 2	529	513	505

Spores surrounded by other spores represent another factor affecting the discrepancy between manual and automatic spore count. They may have insufficient edge contrast. Hence, a more sensitive detection algorithm may improve the detection performance. A detector with higher sensitivity and specificity may be obtained through machine learning techniques, such as a convolutional neural network, as in [14, 16]. However, such models require large training data sets (e.g., over 40,000 annotated examples were utilized in both studies).

4.2 Focus Measures

Objectively determining when an object in an image is in focus is a difficult task. Pertuz et al. (2013) aimed to estimate an object's depth and compare this measurement to a ground truth of known distances [19]. The method proposed by Pertuz et al. (2013) does not apply to our analysis because the spores' positions are unknown *a priori*. The evaluations of the FMs were conducted on five example spores, one with very weak texture, one partially overlapped, one with hyphae growing behind it, one with broken cell wall, and one more typical. Thus, even though the evaluated set of spores was small, a diverse range of cases is considered. While other FM techniques used in [19] generally analyze the entire region of interest to estimate the depth for all the objects, our approach considers only a small subset of the pixels in the examined patch. For this reason, we could assume that most detected edge pixels correspond to the edge of interest; thus, it is not a general-purpose focus measure. However, it may be suitable for some applications where the object is detected before evaluating the FM value. In Fig. 6, we can observe that the resulting optimal spore images all seem to be close to each other. Indeed, the largest observed difference in identified Z-plane for a given spore is only 15 planes, corresponding to 30 μm, which is less than the radius of an average spore.

4.3 Vitality Assessment

This study offers a first step toward automatizing several labor tasks. Among these, assessing spores' vitality is a critical analysis to be performed prior to experimentation.

Figure 7 shows spores displaying different features because of their different vital state. From left to right, we can see one vital spore (A), perfectly round, with a clear contrast with the background, an intact and sharp wall, and a peculiar internal texture induced by the presence of lipids. One spore with a broken cell wall (B), with fragmented edges and irregular color. Another spore is empty (C), characterized by transparency induced by the loss of lipids. And the last spore (D) was subjected to excessive thermal stress due to being autoclaved. Its shape is less circular than the vital one, and the internal texture seems equalized.

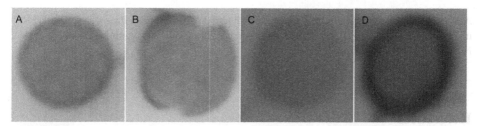

Fig. 7. (A) Healthy spore. (B) Spore with a broken cell wall. (C) Empty spore. (D) Spore exposed to excessive thermal stress.

In Vidal et al. (2019), the geometry of spores is assessed by first segmenting them through manual hysteresis thresholding and then computing the diverse geometric properties of each connected component in the image [8]. The spore detection algorithm presented in this paper detects and estimates the radius for all the spores shown in Fig. 7. However, the non-circular aspects are not accounted for yet, and it needs further elaboration for determining spore vitality.

5   Conclusions

This paper presents a methodology for automatically detecting, quantifying and obtaining an in-focus image of fungal spores, which considers Z-stack acquisitions of the biological sample. By incorporating depth information into the analysis, the proposed approach intends to improve the performance of spore detection and enhance the accuracy of the results.

We developed a fully automated program to count spores in the sample through the detection and clustering of the spores over multiple planes. It also estimates the Z-plane where the spore is more in focus with a custom FM, which is preliminary investigated to preserve relevant features of the spore, e.g., border and texture, useful for further sample analysis.

Here, we assessed the validity of our process by comparing automatic spores count with a manual count performed by an operator. We demonstrated that our method detects the spores with a relatively small error (RMS of 3.25%) and that the Z-stacked image acquisition can yield a significantly (p-value = 0.043) more accurate result than a classic 2D image analysis (median relative error of about a) 13.4% for manual vs. single plane and b) 4.5% for manual vs. Z-stack). Additionally, we propose a specialized focus measure to determine the Z-position of spores and qualitatively compare its performance with other general-purpose focus measures primarily used in the literature. Whereas the proposed FM is able to localize a plane where relevant features (borders and texture) are preserved, further improvements and analyses are required to better assess the performance.

Possible future works include developing a more sensitive segmentation technique for crowded samples to automate additional operations that are labor-intensive for an operator, including assessing the spore vitality.

Acknowledgments. This work has received funding from the European Research Council (ERC) under the European Union's Horizon 2020 Research and Innovation Programme Grant Agreement No. 101003304 (I-Wood).

References

1. Gorzelak, M.A., Asay, A.K., Pickles, B.J., Simard, S.W.: Inter-plant communication through mycorrhizal networks mediates complex adaptive behaviour in plant communities. In: AoB PLANTS, vol. 7, p. plv050 (2015). https://doi.org/10.1093/aobpla/plv050
2. Beiler, K.J., Durall, D.M., Simard, S.W., Maxwell, S.A., Kretzer, A.M.: Architecture of the wood-wide web: Rhizopogon spp. genets link multiple Douglas-fir cohorts. New Phytol. **185**(2), 543–553 (2010). https://doi.org/10.1111/j.1469-8137.2009.03069.x
3. Simard, S.W., Beiler, K.J., Bingham, M.A., Deslippe, J.R., Philip, L.J., Teste, F.P.: Mycorrhizal networks: mechanisms, ecology and modelling. Fungal Biol. Rev. **26**(1), 39–60 (2012). https://doi.org/10.1016/j.fbr.2012.01.001
4. Alaux, P., Zhang, Y., Gilbert, L., Johnson, D.: Can common mycorrhizal fungal networks be managed to enhance ecosystem functionality? Plants People Planet **3**(5), 433–444 (2021). https://doi.org/10.1002/ppp3.10178
5. Bonfante, P., Genre, A.: Mechanisms underlying beneficial plant–fungus interactions in mycorrhizal symbiosis. Nat. Commun. **1**(1), 48 (2010). https://doi.org/10.1038/ncomms1046
6. Paul, G.C., Kent, C.A., Thomas, C.R.: Viability testing and characterization of germination of fungal spores by automatic image analysis. Biotechnol. Bioeng. **42**(1), 11–23 (1993). https://doi.org/10.1002/bit.260420103
7. Melo, C.A.O.D., Lopes, J.G., Andrade, A.O., Trindade, R.M.P., Magalhães, R.S.: Semi-automated counting model for arbuscular mycorrhizal fungi spores using the circle hough transform and an artificial neural network. An. Acad. Bras. Ciênc. **91**(4), e20180165 (2019). https://doi.org/10.1590/0001-3765201920180165
8. Vidal-Diez de Ulzurrun, G., Huang, T.-Y., Chang, C.-W., Lin, H.-C., Hsueh, Y.-P.: Fungal feature tracker (FFT): a tool for quantitatively characterizing the morphology and growth of filamentous fungi. PLoS Comput. Biol. **15**(10), e1007428 (2019). https://doi.org/10.1371/journal.pcbi.1007428
9. Xu, P., Li, J.: Computer assistance image processing spores counting. In: 2009 International Asia Conference on Informatics in Control, Automation and Robotics, Bangkok, Thailand, pp. 203–206. IEEE (2009). https://doi.org/10.1109/CAR.2009.10
10. Zhang, Y., Li, J., Tang, F., Zhang, H., Cui, Z., Zhou, H.: An automatic detector for fungal spores in microscopic images based on deep learning. Appl. Eng. Agric. **37**(1), 85–94 (2021). https://doi.org/10.13031/aea.13818

11. Tahir, M.W., Zaidi, N.A., Blank, R., Vinayaka, P.P., Vellekoop, M.J., Lang, W.: Fungus detection through optical sensor system using two different kinds of feature vectors for the classification. IEEE Sensors J. **17**(16), 5341–5349 (2017). https://doi.org/10.1109/JSEN.2017.272 3052

12. Wang, Y., Mao, H., Xu, G., Zhang, X., Zhang, Y.: A rapid detection method for fungal spores from greenhouse crops based on CMOS image sensors and diffraction fingerprint feature processing. JoF **8**(4), 374 (2022). https://doi.org/10.3390/jof8040374

13. Tahir, M.W., Zaidi, N.A., Blank, R. , Vinayaka, P.P., Vellekoop, M.J., Lang, W.: An efficient and simple embedded system of fungus detection system. In: 2017 International Multi-topic Conference (INMIC), Lahore, pp. 1–4. IEEE (2017). https://doi.org/10.1109/INMIC.2017. 8289477

14. Tahir, M.W., Zaidi, N.A., Rao, A.A., Blank, R., Vellekoop, M.J., Lang, W.: A fungus spores dataset and a convolutional neural network based approach for fungus detection. IEEE Trans. Nanobiosci. **17**(3), 281–290 (2018). https://doi.org/10.1109/TNB.2018.2839585

15. Perner, P., Perner, H., Janichen, S., Buhring, A.: Recognition of airborne fungi spores in digital microscopic images. In: Proceedings of the 17th International Conference on Pattern Recognition, 2004. ICPR 2004, vol. 3, pp. 566–569. IEEE Cambridge, UK (2004). https:// doi.org/10.1109/ICPR.2004.1334592

16. Zhao, Y., Lin, F., Liu, S., Hu, Z., Li, H., Bai, Y.: Constrained-focal-loss based deep learning for segmentation of spores. IEEE Access **7**, 165029–165038 (2019). https://doi.org/10.1109/ ACCESS.2019.2953085

17. Sugiura, Y., et al.: Myristate can be used as a carbon and energy source for the asymbiotic growth of arbuscular mycorrhizal fungi. Proc. Natl. Acad. Sci. U.S.A. **117**(41), 25779–25788 (2020). https://doi.org/10.1073/pnas.2006948117

18. Forster, B., Van De Ville, D., Berent, J., Sage, D., Unser, M.: Complex wavelets for extended depth-of-field: a new method for the fusion of multichannel microscopy images. Microsc. Res. Tech. **65**(1–2), 33–42 (2004). https://doi.org/10.1002/jemt.20092

19. Pertuz, S., Puig, D., Garcia, M.A.: Analysis of focus measure operators for shape-from-focus. Pattern Recogn. **46**(5), 1415–1432 (2013). https://doi.org/10.1016/j.patcog.2012.11.011

20. Bécard, G., Fortin, J.A.: Early events of vesicular–arbuscular mycorrhiza formation on Ri T-DNA transformed roots. New Phytol. **108**(2), 211–218 (1988). https://doi.org/10.1111/j. 1469-8137.1988.tb03698.x

21. The MathWorks Inc., "MATLAB (R2022a)." The MathWorks Inc, Natick, Massachusetts, United States (2022). https://www.mathworks.com

22. Atherton, T.J., Kerbyson, D.J.: Size invariant circle detection. Image Vis. Comput. **17**(11), 795–803 (1999). https://doi.org/10.1016/S0262-8856(98)00160-7

23. The MathWorks Inc., "Image Processing Toolbox." The MathWorks Inc., Natick, Massachusetts, United States (2022). https://se.mathworks.com/products/image.html?s_tid=src htitle_image_1

24. M. Ester, H.-P. Kriegel, J. Sander, and X. Xu, "A Density-Based Algorithm for Discovering Clusters in Large Spatial Databases with Noise," *Knowledge Discovery and Data Mining*, 1996

25. The MathWorks Inc., "Statistics and machine learning toolbox." The MathWorks Inc., Natick, Massachusetts, United States (2022). https://www.mathworks.com/help/stats/index.html

26. Canny, J.: A computational approach to edge detection. IEEE Trans. Pattern Anal. Mach. Intell. PAMI-8(6), 679–698 (1986)

192   O. Sten et al.

A Comparison of Absolute and Relative Neural Encoding Schemes in Addition and Subtraction Functional Subnetworks

Cody Scharzenberger$^{(\boxtimes)}$ and Alexander Hunt

Portland State University, Portland, OR 97201, USA
`cscharz2@pdx.edu`

Abstract. As neural networks have become increasingly prolific solutions to modern problems in science and engineering, there has been a congruent rise in the popularity of the numerical machine learning techniques used to design them. While numerical methods are highly generalizable, they also tend to produce unintuitive networks with inscrutable behavior. One solution to the problem of network interpretability is to use analytical design techniques, but these methods are relatively underdeveloped compared to their numerical alternatives. To increase the utilization of analytical techniques and eventually facilitate the symbiotic integration of both design strategies, it is necessary to improve the efficacy of analytical methods on fundamental function approximation tasks that can be used to perform more complex operations. Toward this end, this manuscript extends the design constraints of the addition and subtraction subnetworks of the functional subnetwork approach (FSA) to arbitrarily many inputs, and then derives new constraints for an alternative neural encoding/decoding scheme. This encoding/decoding scheme involves storing information in the activation ratio of a subnetwork's neurons, rather than directly in their membrane voltages. We show that our new "relative" encoding/decoding scheme has both qualitative and quantitative advantages compared to the existing "absolute" encoding/decoding scheme, including helping to mitigate saturation and improving approximation accuracy. Our relative encoding scheme will be extended to other functional subnetworks in future work to assess its advantages on more complex operations.

Keywords: Neural Encoding Schemes · Functional Subnetwork Approach · Analytical Network Design Methods

1 Introduction

Over the past decade, there has been an explosion of academic interest in neural networks, both in their capacity as biological computational units and as

---

Supported by NSF DBI 2015317 as part of the NSF/CIHR/DFG/FRQ/UKRI-MRC Next Generation Networks for Neuroscience Program.

F. Meder et al. (Eds.): Living Machines 2023, LNAI 14158, pp. 193–205, 2023.
https://doi.org/10.1007/978-3-031-39504-8_13

potential solutions to a plethora of problems across disparate fields of scientific inquiry. Accompanying the precipitous ascendance of neural network research, there has been an escalation in the quantity and quality of techniques used in their design and training. Since the advent of backpropagation [2] made it possible to train networks comprised of multiple layers of neurons, techniques such as stochastic gradient descent (SGD) [1] and its many variations (e.g., Adagrad [5], Adam [4], etc.) have cemented numerical methods as the dominant approach to tuning network parameters. While numerical methods are excellent in terms of their ease of application and scalability, especially given modern advances in graphical processing units (GPU) [3], their key limitation is that they tend to produce networks whose decision making and computational processes are inscrutable. This makes them inappropriate for designing networks for applications where transparency is essential, such as when building high fidelity biological models. Fortunately, some analytical techniques for designing interpretable neural networks do exist (e.g., the functional subnetwork approach (FSA) [6,7]), but these methodologies remain relatively underdeveloped and need additional investigation to facilitate their broader utilization. Among the many open questions concerning analytical techniques, one of particular interest is how best to encode information in these networks to facilitate their design and enhance their approximation accuracy. After all, different encoding schemes require different network design constraints and may be more or less appropriate depending on the application. Since the existing work of the FSA is currently limited to a single encoding scheme that represents information directly in the membrane voltages of the neurons, this work extends these techniques to a new encoding scheme: one that stores information in neural activation ratios. While potentially less intuitive, such an encoding scheme is prudent since it allows for the simple integration of multiple subnetworks that might other operate over significantly different representational domains.

1.1   Our Contribution

In this manuscript we derive simple, yet novel analytical design rules for creating functional subnetworks that encode information in neural activation ratios rather than directly in membrane voltages. Our analysis indicates that this "relative" information encoding scheme has a variety of qualitative advantages (e.g., saturation prevention, biological plausibility, etc.), while also improving the approximation accuracy of the resulting subnetworks. For the purpose of generating quantitative results, we use our unique design rules to build small functional subnetworks that perform addition and subtraction operations. We then compare the design rules and performance of our custom "relative" addition and subtraction subnetworks to the "absolute" variations of the FSA [6] to emphasize the advantages of our approach. In this way, the work discussed here serves as an alternative to the non-spiking FSA formulation, with advantages that make it easier to use for some problems while offering improved accuracy.

2 Background

The two fields of information that are required to understand our work on encoding schemes in functional subnetworks are those pertaining to neuron modeling and the existing non-spiking FSA design rules.

2.1 Neuron Model

We use the same rate-based LIF model as [6] to facilitate direct comparisons with their results. Suppose that we want to analyze the behavior of a system of $n \in \mathbb{N}$ neurons over some time domain $\mathcal{T} = [0, T_f]$ where $T_f \in \mathbb{R}_{>0}$ is the final time of interest. Then the membrane voltages of these neurons form a first order dynamical system comprised of $n \in \mathbb{N}$ state variables $U_i \in \mathbb{R}$ that satisfy

$$C_{m,i}\dot{U}_i = I_{leak,i} + I_{syn,i} + I_{app,i}, \tag{1}$$

$\forall i \in \mathbb{N}_{\leq n}$, where the leak and synaptic currents are defined as

$$I_{leak,i} = -G_{m,i}U_i, \tag{2}$$

$$I_{syn,i} = \sum_{j=1}^{n} g_{s,ij} \min\left(\max\left(\frac{U_j}{R_j}, 0\right), 1\right)(\Delta E_{s,ij} - U_i), \tag{3}$$

respectively, and the applied currents $I_{app,i} : \mathcal{T} \to \mathbb{R}$ are known functions of time. Throughout this work, the following definitions hold: $U_i \in \mathbb{R}$ is the membrane voltage of the ith neuron with respect to its resting potential, $C_{m,i} \in \mathbb{R}_{>0}$ is the membrane capacitance of the ith neuron, $G_{m,i} \in \mathbb{R}_{>0}$ is the membrane conductance of the ith neuron, $R_j \in \mathbb{R}_{>0}$ is the activation domain of the jth neuron with respect to its resting potential, $g_{s,ij} \in \mathbb{R}_{>0}$ is the maximum synaptic conductance from neuron j to neuron i, and $\Delta E_{s,ij} \in \mathbb{R}$ is the synaptic reversal potential from neuron j to neuron i with respect to neuron i's resting potential. Substituting the leak current Eq. (2) and synaptic current Eq. (3) into the dynamical system Eq. (1) we have the governing equation

$$C_{m,i}\dot{U}_i = -G_{m,i}U_i + \sum_{j=1}^{n} g_{s,ij} \min\left(\max\left(\frac{U_j}{R_j}, 0\right), 1\right)(\Delta E_{s,ij} - U_i) + I_{app,i}. \tag{4}$$

2.2 Functional Subnetwork Approach (FSA)

The functional subnetwork approach (FSA) refers to the analytical methods developed in [6] for designing subnetworks of non-spiking neurons to perform basic tasks, including: (1) signal transfer such as transmission and modulation; (2) arithmetic operations such as addition, subtraction, multiplication, and division; and (3) calculus operations such as differentiation and integration. One of the main attractions of this work lies in the fact that it combines *simple* neural architectures with *analytical* design rules constrained by biological limitations, a combination of features that ensures that the resulting subnetworks are both meaningful and interpretable. For a thorough explanation of the existing FSA design rules refer to [6].

3   Methodology

To begin our analysis of information encoding schemes in addition and subtraction functional subnetworks, we derive the analytical design rules that are necessary to create these subnetworks in the first place. In order to compare the absolute encoding scheme, which stores information in the membrane voltages of a network's neurons, and the relative encoding scheme, which stores information in the percent activation of a network's neurons, we derive the design rules of both approaches using arbitrarily many inputs. Since the absolute encoding scheme is the same as that used in [6], the design rules for our absolute addition and subtraction subnetworks simplify to those of [6] when each subnetwork is assumed to have only two inputs. Similarly, since addition is just a special case of subtraction, we exclusively derive analytical design rules for subtraction subnetworks, because these rules can be simplified to apply to addition subnetworks by removing the inhibitory synapses.

3.1   Subtraction Subnetwork Architecture and Equilibrium

Consider a system of $n \in \mathbb{N}$ neurons, with each of the first $n - 1$ neurons connected to the final nth neuron via some combination of excitatory and inhibitory synapses as shown in Fig. 1a. Let $U_i^\star \in \mathbb{R}$ be the steady state membrane voltage of the ith neuron with respect to its resting potential $\forall i \in \mathbb{N}_{\leq n}$. Given this architecture, the steady state membrane voltage of the output neuron $U_n^\star$ can be written in terms of the steady state membrane voltages of the first $n - 1$ input neurons by

$$U_n^\star = \frac{\sum_{i=1}^{n-1} g_{s,ni} \min\left(\max\left(\frac{U_i^\star}{R_i}, 0\right), 1\right) \Delta E_{s,ni} + I_{app,n}}{G_{m,n} + \sum_{i=1}^{n-1} g_{s,ni} \min\left(\max\left(\frac{U_i^\star}{R_i}, 0\right), 1\right)}. \tag{5}$$

Equation (5) describes the natural steady state behavior of our subtraction subnetwork given our chosen neuron model and architecture.

3.2   Absolute and Relative Notions of Subtraction

Given the baseline steady state behavior of our subtraction subnetwork in Eq. (5), we now consider how we want our subnetwork to behave for each of our two encoding schemes. For the absolute encoding scheme we want the membrane voltage of the output neuron to be the sum of the membrane voltages of the excitatory input neurons less that of the inhibitory input neurons, scaled by

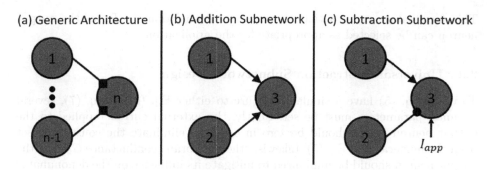

Fig. 1. (a) Generic subtraction subnetwork architecture. (b) Addition subnetwork example. (c) Subtraction subnetwork example. Triangular synapses are excitatory, circular synapses are inhibitory, and square synapses may be either.

some gain $c \in \mathbb{R}_{>0}$. Let $s_i \in \mathcal{S} = \{-1, 1\}$ be the sign associated with each input neuron $\forall i \in \mathbb{N}_{\leq n-1}$, where -1 is assigned to each inhibitory synapse and 1 is assigned to each excitatory synapse. In this case, the steady state membrane voltage of the output neuron should satisfy

$$U_n^\star = c \sum_{i=1}^{n-1} s_i U_i^\star. \tag{6}$$

While the absolute formulation in Eq. (6) is convenient for directly representing differences, it requires a potentially biologically unfeasible representational domain R_n at the output neuron. Consider an example where there are many more positive inputs than negative inputs in our subtraction subnetwork, such as when approximating an addition operation. When this happens, Eq. (6) requires that the representation domain R_n of the output neuron be the sum of the representational domains of the input neurons in order to prevent the output from saturating prematurely. Yet, as the number of input pathways grows, so too does the required output representational domain R_n, allowing for potentially impractically large values.

To address this problem, we can instead create a relative formulation for desired subtraction subnetwork behavior wherein the steady state activation ratio of the output neuron $\frac{U_n^\star}{R_n}$ is the average steady state activation ratio of the excitatory input neurons less that of the inhibitory input neurons, scaled by some gain $c \in \mathbb{R}_{>0}$. Let $n^+, n^- \in \mathbb{N}$ be the number of excitatory and inhibitory subtraction subnetwork inputs, respectively. Similarly, let $i_k^+ \in \mathcal{I}^+ = \{i \in \mathbb{N}_{\leq n-1} : s_i = 1\}$ and $i_k^- \in \mathcal{I}^- = \{i \in \mathbb{N}_{\leq n-1} : s_i = -1\}$ be the sets of indexes associated with excitatory and inhibitory input neurons, respectively. In this case, the steady state membrane voltage of the output neuron should satisfy

$$U_n^\star = cR_n \left(\frac{1}{n^+} \sum_{k=1}^{n^+} \frac{U_{i_k^+}^\star}{R_{i_k^+}} - \frac{1}{n^-} \sum_{k=1}^{n^-} \frac{U_{i_k^-}^\star}{R_{i_k^-}} \right). \tag{7}$$

This formulation ensures that the representational domain R_n of the output neuron can be selected as appropriate for the application.

3.3   Universal Subtraction Subnetwork Design

To make Eq. (5) have a similar structure to either Eq. (6) or Eq. (7), several common parameters must be set. Firstly, the external current applied to the output neuron $I_{app,n}$ should be zero in order to eliminate the constant offset from the numerator of Eq. (5). Likewise, the membrane conductance $G_{m,n}$ of the output neuron should be minimized to mitigate its influence on the denominator of Eq. (5), though it can not be completely eliminated and still allow the neuron to behave as a leaky integrator. Finally, in order to emphasize the impact of the membrane voltage terms $U_i^\star$ in the numerator of Eq. (5) compared to those in the denominator, we must maximize the synaptic reversal potentials $\Delta E_{s,ni}$ of the excitatory synapses and minimize those of the inhibitory synapses. While the synaptic reversal potentials $\Delta E_{s,ni}$ are in theory unbounded, they are in practice limited by biological constraints. As such, we use $\Delta E_{s,ni} = 194\,\text{mV}$, which describes calcium ion channels, for excitatory synapses, and $\Delta E_{s,ni} = -40\,\text{mV}$, which describes chloride channels, for inhibitory synapses.

3.4   Absolute Subtraction Subnetwork

For an absolute subtraction subnetwork, the membrane voltage of the nth neuron should satisfy Eq. (6). To achieve this, we start by substituting Eq. (5) into Eq. (6) and solving for the gain c to find

$$c = \frac{\sum_{i=1}^{n-1} g_{s,ni} \min\left(\max\left(\frac{U_i^\star}{R_i},0\right),1\right)\Delta E_{s,ni} + I_{app,n}}{\left(\sum_{i=1}^{n-1} s_i U_i^\star\right)\left(G_{m,n} + \sum_{i=1}^{n-1} g_{s,ni} \min\left(\max\left(\frac{U_i^\star}{R_i},0\right),1\right)\right)}. \tag{8}$$

There are numerous parameters in Eq. (8) that need to be set in order to achieve the desired gain c, most of which are already constrained by the principles discussed in Sect. 3.3. Among the remaining parameters, the most appropriate to adjust to achieve the desired gain c are the $n-1$ maximum synaptic conductances $g_{s,ni}$. However, since there are $n-1$ maximum synaptic conductances $g_{s,ni}$ and only one constraining equation (e.g., Eq. (8)), there are infinitely many sets of maximum synaptic conductances $g_{s,ni}$ that produce the desired gain c for a single steady state input membrane voltage point $\vec{U}^\star = \begin{bmatrix} U_1^\star \cdots U_{n-1}^\star \end{bmatrix}^T \in \mathbb{R}^{n-1}$. To constrain the number of solutions, we choose $n-1$ steady state input membrane voltage points $\vec{U}_j^\star \in \mathbb{R}^{n-1}$ at which to enforce the gain relationship in Eq. (8), $\forall j \in \mathbb{N}_{\leq n-1}$. For notational convenience, let $\mathbf{U}^\star \in \mathbb{R}^{(n-1)\times(n-1)}$ be such that $\mathbf{U}^\star = \begin{bmatrix} \vec{U}_1^\star \cdots \vec{U}_{n-1}^\star \end{bmatrix}$. Enforcing Eq. (8) at each of the $n-1$ steady state membrane voltage points $\vec{U}_j^\star$ that comprise the columns of $\mathbf{U}^\star$ yields the system of equations

$$c = \frac{\sum_{i=1}^{n-1} g_{s,ni} \min\left(\max\left(\frac{\mathbf{U}_{ij}^\star}{R_i},0\right),1\right) \Delta E_{s,ni} + I_{app,n}}{\left(\sum_{i=1}^{n-1} s_i \mathbf{U}_{ij}^\star\right)\left(G_{m,n} + \sum_{i=1}^{n-1} g_{s,ni} \min\left(\max\left(\frac{\mathbf{U}_{ij}^\star}{R_i},0\right),1\right)\right)}, \tag{9}$$

$\forall j \in \mathbb{N}_{\leq n-1}$. Rearranging Eq. (9) into matrix-vector form and isolating the maximum synaptic conductances $g_{s,ni}$ yields a linear system of equations

$$\mathbf{A}\vec{g}_{s,n} = \vec{b} \tag{10}$$

where $\mathbf{A} \in \mathbb{R}^{(n-1)\times(n-1)}$ such that $\forall i,j \in \mathbb{N}_{\leq n-1}$

$$\mathbf{A}_{ij} = \left(c \sum_{k=1}^{n-1} s_k \mathbf{U}_{ki}^\star - \Delta E_{s,nj}\right) \min\left(\max\left(\frac{\mathbf{U}_{ji}^\star}{R_j},0\right),1\right), \tag{11}$$

$\vec{g}_{s,n} \in \mathbb{R}^{n-1}$ such that $\vec{g}_{s,n} = \left[g_{s,n1} \cdots g_{s,n(n-1)}\right]^T$, and $\vec{b} \in \mathbb{R}^{n-1}$ such that $\forall i \in \mathbb{N}_{\leq n-1}$

$$\vec{b}_i = I_{app,n} - cG_{m,n}\sum_{k=1}^{n-1} s_k \mathbf{U}_{ki}^\star. \tag{12}$$

While any linearly independent choice of $n-1$ steady state input membrane voltage points $\vec{U}_j^\star$ would be sufficient for computing a unique set of maximum synaptic conductances $g_{s,ni}$, certain choices are more insightful than others. For example, if we choose $\vec{U}_j^\star$ such that $\forall i,j \in \mathbb{N}_{\leq n-1}$

$$\mathbf{U}_{ij}^\star = \begin{cases} R_i, & i = j \\ 0, & i \neq j \end{cases} \tag{13}$$

then the system matrix in Eq. (10) becomes diagonal and the associated design requirement for each $g_{s,ni}$ simplifies substantially. To see this, substitute Eq. (13) into Eq. (10) such that the system becomes

$$\begin{bmatrix} cs_1 R_1 - \Delta E_{s,n1} & \cdots & 0 \\ \vdots & \ddots & \vdots \\ 0 & \cdots & cs_{n-1}R_{n-1} - \Delta E_{s,n(n-1)} \end{bmatrix} \begin{bmatrix} g_{s,n1} \\ \vdots \\ g_{s,n(n-1)} \end{bmatrix} = \begin{bmatrix} I_{app,n} - cG_{m,n}s_1 R_1 \\ \vdots \\ I_{app,n} - cG_{m,n}s_{n-1}R_{n-1} \end{bmatrix}. \tag{14}$$

Solving the system of equations described by Eq. (14) for each $g_{s,nk}$ yields

$$g_{s,nk} = \frac{I_{app,n} - cs_k G_{m,n} R_k}{cs_k R_k - \Delta E_{s,nk}}, \tag{15}$$

$\forall k \in \mathbb{N}_{\leq n-1}$. The design requirement from Eq. (15) allows for absolute subtraction subnetworks to be designed with arbitrarily many input neurons. Note that choosing a different linearly independent set of steady state membrane voltage points $\vec{U}_j^\star$ at which to enforce the gain relationship Eq. 9 will yield a modified variation of the design requirement in Eq. 15 that prioritizes error minimization at those specific points.

3.5   Relative Subtraction Subnetwork

For a relative subtraction subnetwork, the membrane voltage of the nth neuron should satisfy Eq. (7). If we substitute Eq. (5) into Eq. (7) and solve for the gain c we find

$$c = \frac{\sum_{i=1}^{n-1} g_{s,ni} \min\left(\max\left(\frac{U_i^\star}{R_i}, 0\right), 1\right) \Delta E_{s,ni} + I_{app,n}}{R_n \left(\frac{1}{n^+} \sum_{k=1}^{n^+} \frac{U_{i_k^+}^\star}{R_{i_k^+}} - \frac{1}{n^-} \sum_{k=1}^{n^-} \frac{U_{i_k^-}^\star}{R_{i_k^-}}\right) \left(G_{m,n} + \sum_{i=1}^{n-1} g_{s,ni} \min\left(\max\left(\frac{U_i^\star}{R_i}, 0\right), 1\right)\right)}. \tag{16}$$

Following the same procedure as in Sect. 3.4, let $\vec{U}_j^\star = \left[U_{1,j}^\star \cdots U_{n-1,j}^\star\right]^T \in \mathbb{R}^{n-1}$, $\forall j \in \mathbb{N}_{\leq n-1}$ be the $n-1$ steady state membrane voltage points at which we want to achieve Eq. (16). Similarly, let $\mathbf{U}^\star \in \mathbb{R}^{(n-1)\times(n-1)}$ be such that $\mathbf{U}^\star = \left[\vec{U}_1^\star \cdots \vec{U}_{n-1}^\star\right]$. Enforcing Eq. (16) at each of the $n-1$ steady state membrane voltage points $\vec{U}_j^\star$ that comprise the columns of $\mathbf{U}^\star$ yields the system of equations

$$c = \frac{\sum_{i=1}^{n-1} g_{s,ni} \min\left(\max\left(\frac{\mathbf{U}_{ij}^\star}{R_i}, 0\right), 1\right) \Delta E_{s,ni} + I_{app,n}}{\left(R_n \left(\frac{1}{n^+} \sum_{k=1}^{n^+} \frac{\mathbf{U}_{i_k^+ j}^\star}{R_{i_k^+}} - \frac{1}{n^-} \sum_{k=1}^{n^-} \frac{\mathbf{U}_{i_k^- j}^\star}{R_{i_k^-}}\right)\right) \left(G_{m,n} + \sum_{i=1}^{n-1} g_{s,ni} \min\left(\max\left(\frac{\mathbf{U}_{ij}^\star}{R_i}, 0\right), 1\right)\right)},$$

$$\tag{17}$$

$\forall j \in \mathbb{N}_{\leq n-1}$. To compress the following notation, let

$$C_j = R_n \left(\frac{1}{n^+} \sum_{k=1}^{n^+} \frac{\mathbf{U}_{i_k^+ j}^\star}{R_{i_k^+}} - \frac{1}{n^-} \sum_{k=1}^{n^-} \frac{\mathbf{U}_{i_k^- j}^\star}{R_{i_k^-}}\right), \tag{18}$$

$\forall j \in \mathbb{N}_{\leq n-1}$. Rearranging Eq. (17) into matrix-vector form and isolating the maximum synaptic conductances $g_{s,ni}$ yields a linear system of equations

$$\mathbf{A}\vec{g}_{s,n} = \vec{b} \tag{19}$$

where $\mathbf{A} \in \mathbb{R}^{(n-1)\times(n-1)}$ such that $\forall i, j \in \mathbb{N}_{\leq n-1}$

$$\mathbf{A}_{ij} = (cC_i - \Delta E_{s,nj}) \min\left(\max\left(\frac{\mathbf{U}_{ji}^\star}{R_j}, 0\right), 1\right), \tag{20}$$

$\vec{g}_{s,n} \in \mathbb{R}^{n-1}$ such that $\vec{g}_{s,n} = \left[g_{s,n1} \cdots g_{s,n(n-1)}\right]^T$, and $\vec{b} \in \mathbb{R}^{n-1}$ such that $\forall i \in \mathbb{N}_{\leq n-1}$

$$\vec{b}_i = I_{app,n} - cG_{m,n}C_i \tag{21}$$

Choosing the same $n-1$ steady state input membrane voltage points $\vec{U}_j^\star$ as in Eq. (13), the system matrix in Eq. (19) becomes diagonal. Such a choice for the $\vec{U}_j^\star$ simplifies the parameters C_j from Eq. (18) to

$$C_j = \frac{s_j R_n}{n_j^\pm}, \tag{22}$$

where $s_j \in \mathcal{S} = \{-1, 1\}$ is defined as

$$s_j = \begin{cases} -1, & j \in \mathcal{I}^- \\ 1, & j \in \mathcal{I}^+ \end{cases}, \tag{23}$$

and $n_j^{\pm} \in \mathcal{N} = \{n^-, n^+\}$ is defined as

$$n_j^{\pm} = \begin{cases} n^-, & j \in \mathcal{I}^- \\ n^+, & j \in \mathcal{I}^+ \end{cases}, \tag{24}$$

$\forall j \in \mathbb{N}_{\leq n-1}$. The associated system of equations in Eq. (10) then becomes

$$\begin{bmatrix} \frac{cs_1 R_n}{n_1^{\pm}} - \Delta E_{s,n1} & \cdots & 0 \\ \vdots & \ddots & \vdots \\ 0 & \cdots & \frac{cs_{n-1} R_n}{n_{n-1}^{\pm}} - \Delta E_{s,n(n-1)} \end{bmatrix} \begin{bmatrix} g_{s,n1} \\ \vdots \\ g_{s,n(n-1)} \end{bmatrix} = \begin{bmatrix} I_{app,n} - \frac{cG_{m,n}s_1 R_n}{n_1^{\pm}} \\ \vdots \\ I_{app,n} - \frac{cG_{m,n}s_{n-1} R_n}{n_{n-1}^{\pm}} \end{bmatrix}. \tag{25}$$

Solving Eq. (25) for each $g_{s,nk}$ yields

$$g_{s,nk} = \frac{n_k^{\pm} I_{app,n} - cs_k G_{m,n} R_n}{cs_k R_n - n_k^{\pm} \Delta E_{s,nk}}, \tag{26}$$

$\forall k \in \mathbb{N}_{\leq n-1}$. The design requirement from Eq. (26) allows for relative subtraction subnetworks to be designed with arbitrarily many input neurons. As before, choosing a different linearly independent set of steady state membrane voltage points $\vec{U}_j^*$ at which to enforce the gain relationship Eq. 17 will yield a modified variation of the design requirement in Eq. 26 that prioritizes error minimization at those specific points.

4   Results

After deriving the analytical design rules necessary to build addition and subtraction subnetworks for each information encoding scheme, it is possible to determine how these different approaches impact subnetwork approximation accuracy by applying these techniques to example subnetworks. Toward this end, we employ the design constraints from Sect. 3.3, as well as from Eq. (15) and Eq. (26), to build simple addition and subtraction subnetworks for each encoding scheme. The example addition and subtraction subnetworks that we consider here have the architectures shown in Figs. 1b, 1c, respectively. To ensure that the output neurons of our subtraction subnetworks stay positive throughout the entire input domain, we apply a constant current to the output neuron so that it is tonically excited to half of its maximum value in the absence of inputs.

The steady state results obtained from simulating the two addition subnetworks are represented graphically in Fig. 2, while those associated with the two subtraction subnetworks are displayed in Fig. 3. Both figures are divided into

four sections, where plots (a) and (b) show the steady state response of the subnetworks when using the absolute and relative information encoding schemes,
respectively; plot (c) shows the steady state approximation error associated with
each encoding scheme; and plot (d) shows the difference in steady state approximation error between the two encoding schemes. Comparing plots (a) and (b)
from Fig. 2, it is clear that the maximum approximation error for each encoding
scheme occurs when the input neurons are maximally active. Plots (a) and (b)
from Fig. 2 also indicate that the relative encoding scheme tends to have less
error across the input domain than the absolute encoding scheme. This fact is
confirmed by plot (c) from Fig. 2 where both the maximum and average approximation error associated with the relative encoding scheme are less than that of
the absolute encoding scheme. Finally, plot (d) from Fig. 2 makes the difference
in approximation accuracy explicit by showing that the approximation error for
relative addition subnetwork never exceeds that of the absolute addition subnetwork.

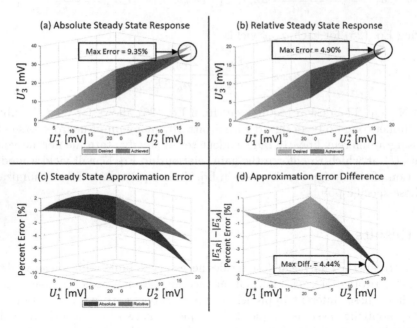

Fig. 2. Addition subnetwork information encoding scheme comparison. (a) Absolute
steady state response. (b) Relative steady state response. (c) Steady state approximation error. (d) Difference in approximation error.

Figure 3 tells a similar story concerning the approximation accuracy of the
subtraction subnetwork. In this case, plots (a) and (b) from Fig. 3 show that
the maximum approximation error occurs for both encoding schemes when the
first input neuron value is minimized and the second input neuron value is maximized. Similarly, plot (c) of Fig. 3 indicates that the approximation error of the

relative subtraction subnetwork is typically less than that of the absolute subtraction subnetwork, except for when the first input neuron value is small. This relationship is confirmed in plot (d) of Fig. 3, wherein the relative subtraction subnetwork typically outperforms the absolute subtraction subnetwork, but not for the entire input domain.

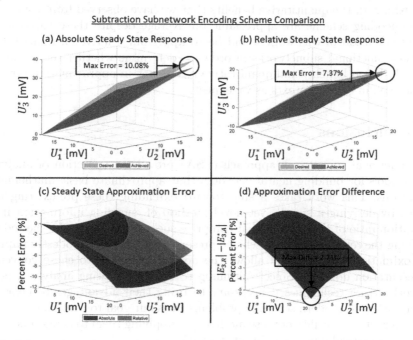

Fig. 3. Subtraction subnetwork information encoding scheme comparison. (a) Absolute steady state response. (b) Relative steady state response. (c) Steady state approximation error. (d) Difference in approximation error.

5 Discussion

Our results indicate that there are both qualitative and quantitative advantages to using a relative information encoding scheme compared to an absolute one. The design constraints derived in Sect. 3 allow the representation domain of the output neuron to be unconstrained when using a relative encoding scheme, meaning that a biologically realistic value may be selected by the designer without risking saturation for expected inputs. Although only addition and subtraction subnetworks are considered here, this feature may be even more salient in the context of certain mathematical operations, such as division, that tend toward infinity under certain input conditions. When this happens, an absolute subnetwork would be unable to represent the infinite output value, but a relative subnetwork would simply encode the result as a maximally active output. In addition to these qualitative benefits, the results shown in Figs. 2 and 3 demonstrate that the relative subnetworks tend to experience less approximation error, though the extent to which this is true is somewhat modest at about 4.44% for addition subnetworks and 2.71% for subtraction subnetworks. While differences in approximation error do vary across the input domain and the operation being approximated, the quantitative benefits that we have observed from using a relative encoding scheme are appreciable on average despite these variations. A logical extension of this work would be to apply our relative encoding scheme to other functional subnetworks in order to determine whether the qualitative network design benefits and quantitative reductions in approximation error are maintained in other contexts as we expect.

6   Conclusions

The functional subnetwork approach (FSA) provides a collection of analytical design tools for building neural networks that approximate basic mathematical operations. This work takes a step toward extending these pre-existing techniques by deriving a simple, yet novel method of encoding information in the activation ratio of the neurons that comprise such subnetworks. We showed that applying the relative encoding scheme presented in this work modestly improves approximation accuracy and allows the designer freedom to chose convenient representation domains. Since continuing to improve existing analytical neural network design techniques is necessary to bring their advantages to bear on a wider variety of modern scientific problems, it is our goal to continue to expand the generality and utility of these methods by applying them to new subnetworks and mathematical operations in future work.

Acknowledgements. The authors acknowledge support by NSF DBI 2015317 as part of the NSF/CIHR/DFG/FRQ/UKRI-MRC Next Generation Networks for Neuroscience Program.

References

1. Bottou, L.: Stochastic gradient descent tricks. In: Montavon, G., Orr, G.B., Müller, K.-R. (eds.) Neural Networks: Tricks of the Trade. LNCS, vol. 7700, pp. 421–436. Springer, Heidelberg (2012). https://doi.org/10.1007/978-3-642-35289-8_25
2. Hecht-Nielsen, R.: Theory of the backpropagation neural network. In: Neural Networks for Perception, pp. 65–93. Elsevier (1992). https://linkinghub.elsevier.com/retrieve/pii/B9780127412528500108
3. Keckler, S.W., Dally, W.J., Khailany, B., Garland, M., Glasco, D.: GPUs and the future of parallel computing. IEEE Micro **31**(5), 7–17 (2011). http://ieeexplore.ieee.org/document/6045685/
4. Kingma, D.P., Ba, J.: Adam: a method for stochastic optimization. arXiv:1412.6980 [cs] (2017)

5. Mukkamala, M.C., Hein, M.: Variants of RMSProp and Adagrad with Logarithmic Regret Bounds (2017)
6. Szczecinski, N.S., Hunt, A.J., Quinn, R.D.: A functional subnetwork approach to designing synthetic nervous systems that control legged robot locomotion. Front. Neurorobot. **11** (2017). http://journal.frontiersin.org/article/10.3389/fnbot.2017.00037/full
7. Szczecinski, N.S., Quinn, R.D., Hunt, A.J.: Extending the functional subnetwork approach to a generalized linear integrate-and-fire neuron model. Front. Neurorobot. **14**, 577804 (2020). https://www.frontiersin.org/articles/10.3389/fnbot.2020.577804/full

GANGLIA: A Tool for Designing Customized Neuron Circuit Patterns

Ashlee S. Liao[1]([✉]) [iD], Yongjie Jessica Zhang[1] [iD],
and Victoria A. Webster-Wood[1,2] [iD]

[1] Carnegie Mellon University, Pittsburgh, PA 15217, USA
{ashleel,jessicaz,vwebster}@andrew.cmu.edu
[2] McGowan Institute for Regenerative Medicine, University of Pittsburgh, 4200 Fifth
Ave, Pittsburgh, PA 15260, USA
http://engineering.cmu.edu/borg,
https://www.meche.engineering.cmu.edu/faculty/
zhang-computational-bio-modeling-lab.html

Abstract. Current biological neural controllers in biohybrid robotics
rely on networks of self-assembled neurons. However, to be able to repro-
ducibly create neuron circuits optimized for specific functions, the connections that the neurons form need to be controlled. Towards addressing this need, we have developed a tool for the Generation of Automatic
Neuron Graph-Like Interconnected Arrangements (GANGLIA), which
automatically generates micro-patterns using graph drawing algorithms
to place the cells based on an input array of neuron connections and
generate micro-patterns in a variety of common file formats. Four network connectivities, ranging in levels of complexity, were used to assess
GANGLIA's performance. As the complexity increased, the number of
intersections of neurite paths and the amount of time GANGLIA took
to generate the pattern increased. However, for the most complex circuit
tested here, GANGLIA took less than 8 s to generate a micro-pattern,
which is faster than manually generating an equivalent model. The fast,
automatic generation of micro-patterns has the potential to support the
design and fabrication process of complex neuron circuits *in vitro* for
biohybrid control.

Keywords: neuron · graph drawing · biohybrid controllers · circuit

1 Introduction

Biohybrid controllers incorporate live biological neurons to process information
and generate signals to control a periphery. Biological neural controllers for
biohybrid robots have been fabricated using a variety of methods, including
directly using intact networks, such as intact brains in live animals [6], spinal
explants [17], and intact neuromuscular tissues [40]. Alternatively, cultured neurons can be used for biohybrid control, either on a multi-electrode array to control a simulated animal [9] or a robot [18,29,39] or as neurospheres co-cultured

F. Meder et al. (Eds.): Living Machines 2023, LNAI 14158, pp. 206–216, 2023.
https://doi.org/10.1007/978-3-031-39504-8_14

with muscle actuators [2,3]. Although these studies made several advances to implement neural controls *in vitro* for biohybrid systems, the neurons stochastically self-assembled into circuit configurations. Not only does this make the resulting controller difficult to replicate, but this does not enable researchers to prescribe specific circuit configurations or control dynamics. Techniques and tools are needed to design and optimize a controller for specific functionalities and fabricate controllers with custom and repeatable circuit connectivity.

To control the network connectivity of neurons *in vitro*, microfabrication techniques can be used to control the placement and growth directions of neurites. One common technique is to use microcontact printing to constrain cell growth. Microcontact printing takes advantage of the neurons' natural chemical and mechanical sensitivity to control neuron polarization and guide network formation, by either using a gradient pattern of proteins [28] or patterning areas with cytophilic proteins on a cytophobic surface [24,37,42]. Another technique uses microstructures and microfluidics to limit where neurons can grow physically. This can allow for the isolation and placement of individual cells using optimized channel geometries [15,38], microsieves [25], or microwells [27,36]. Specialized designs of the channel geometry also enabled the control of regions that selectively allow for only neurite outgrowth using channels with bottlenecks [21] or narrow, straight microgrooves [26,30,35]. Using similar microfabrication techniques could enable researchers to produce biohybrid controllers with reproducible biological neuronal networks. Although these techniques already demonstrate the capability to guide the formation of simple neuronal circuits between cells [24,42] or specific populations of cells [21,30,35], manually designing and generating pattern layouts to represent more complex circuits, becomes increasingly difficult and time-consuming as network complexity increases, particularly if circuits must be designed manually.

Current existing neuron network modeling tools, such as NEURON [5], Brian 2 [33], and NEST [14], focus on the network and cellular dynamics, rather than producing network layouts for *in vitro* fabrication. Other visualization tools, such as BlenderNEURON [4], are suited for creating reconstructions of biological neurons and circuits akin to those in the brain, which would be challenging to reproduce using current *in vitro* constrained neuron circuit microfabrication techniques. Furthermore, the manual editing of each neuron's morphology to create specific circuits will also suffer from challenges similar to those encountered in the manual design of microfabrication pattern layouts for complex circuits. Therefore, to bridge the gap between *in vitro* constrained neuron culture techniques and producing specific complex circuits, a tool for automatically generating circuit layouts using existing experimental techniques is needed.

To supplement the existing microfabrication techniques towards reproducible, customized biohybrid controllers, we present a new 2D neuron circuit layout tool for the Generation of Automatic Neuron Graph-Like Interconnected Arrangements (GANGLIA) to create micro-patterns from a list of neuron connections automatically. The automatic generation of patterns can greatly reduce the difficulty and time required to design viable stamps and scaffolds, especially for complex circuits. For neuron circuits to be achievable *in vitro*, the placement of each soma must be distinct, and paths for each neurite cannot overlap to control the network connectivity. Similar challenges are addressed when generating visualizations for complex graphs in discrete mathematics, particularly in the problem of crossing minimization and uniform distribution of vertices [11,34]. Thus, GANGLIA uses graph drawing algorithms to determine candidate locations for neuron somas and neurites to rapidly produce patterns in seconds based on the desired circuit connectivity. The entire micro-pattern can be exported to common model files, including STEP, DXF, and SVG. These files can be used either to fabricate a 3D-printed scaffold for microfluidic chips or for microcontact printing stamps created using soft lithography.

2   Methods

2.1   Micro-Pattern Generation Algorithm

To automatically design micro-patterns for custom biological neuron network circuitry, a pipeline for GANGLIA was developed in Python 3.9.7 (https://www.python.org/). GANGLIA takes an input of neuron connections, paired in an array format, and determines candidate soma and branching node locations for the micro-pattern using either the Fruchterman-Reingold [7,13] or Kamada-Kawai [7,16] graph drawing algorithms from the iGraph (0.9.11) Python library (https://python.igraph.org/) [7] (Refer to Algorithm 1). Then, GANGLIA parametrically generates a micro-pattern for the circuit using CadQuery (2.2.0) (https://cadquery.readthedocs.io/). CadQuery enables the micro-pattern to be exported to several formats (STEP, DXF, SVG, PNG), which can then be used in external software to physically create the micro-pattern using other methods, such as 3D printing (STEP file) or microcontact printing (DXF, SVG).

By implementing Algorithm 1, GANGLIA generates two potential layouts for the placement of the somas using the Kamada-Kawai [7,16] and Fruchterman-Reingold [7,13] graph drawing algorithms (Fig. 1). After the user selects the

---

Algorithm 1. Determine candidate soma and branching node locations

---

Input: Neuron Connectivity: $C = (N_{pre,1}, N_{post,1}) \ldots (N_{pre,i}, N_{post,i})$
Output: Soma Locations: $(x_{N_1}, y_{N_1}) \ldots (x_{N_j}, y_{N_j})$

    for Each Neuron j **do**
        if N_j has > 1 post-synaptic connections **then**
            Append C to insert a branching node.
        end if
    end for
Input connection list into the graph drawing algorithms
Display intermediate visual output from graph algorithm
User input on which graph drawing result to use $\rightarrow (x_{N_1}, y_{N_1}) \ldots (x_{N_j}, y_{N_j})$

Algorithm 2. Generate neural circuit micro-patterns

Inputs: Neuron Connectivity: $C = (N_{pre,1}, N_{post,1}) \ldots (N_{pre,i}, N_{post,i})$
Soma Locations: $(x_{N_1}, y_{N_1}) \ldots (x_{N_j}, y_{N_j})$
Outputs: Neural Circuit Micro-Patterns (STEP, DXF, SVG, PNG)

    Adjust soma and branching nodes positions based on scaling factor
    for Each connection pair i **do**
        if Cells are mutually connected without connections to other cells **then**
            Add a curved path connecting the two cells
            Add a gap to separate the axonal path from the dendritic path
        else if The pre-synaptic cell connects to a branching node **then**
            Add a long, straight path between branching node and pre-synaptic cell
        else
            Add a short path from post-synaptic cell towards the pre-synaptic cell
            Add a long path from pre-synaptic cell toward post-synaptic cell
            Leave a short gap between axonal path and dendritic path
        end if
    end for
    for Each Neuron j **do**
        $a_j \leftarrow$ Number of Connections for N_j
        if $a_j < 4$ **then**
            if N_j does not have an axon **then**
                Add one long path for the axon
                Add $(4 - a_j - 1)$ short paths for dendrites
            else
                Add $(4 - a_j)$ short paths for dendrites
            end if
        end if
        Add circle for soma at (x_{N_j}, y_{N_j})
    end for
    Output neural circuit micro-patterns as desired file type

---

desired layout, Algorithm 2 generates a micro-pattern. Representations of the micro-pattern can be exported into several file types for 3D-printable CAD models (STEP file) and 2D representations (DXF, SVG, PNG) (Fig. 1).

2.2 Performance Assessment of GANGLIA

To test the functionality of GANGLIA, micro-patterns were generated for four different connectivity networks: (1) a half-center oscillator inspired by central pattern generators [22], (2) a human-generated network composed of 9 cells, (3) a network for the control of a single limb joint for rat locomotion [10], and (4) a Boolean network for the control of *Aplysia* feeding [41]. These networks varied in their level of complexity, as determined by their number of cells and cell-to-cell connections. For each circuit, after determining the soma and branching node locations using the graph drawing algorithm, the circuit pattern is generated and scaled based on the desired lengths for the dendritic and axonal paths. To scale the pattern, the average distance of each connection was calculated based on the initial soma and branching node locations. The average distance was used to scale the final pattern size relative to a target length between the center of two somas. The target length is the sum of the following: target axon length, dendrite length, gap distance between the axon and the dendrite ("synaptic cleft"), and the soma diameter. This ratio between the target length and the average distance was used to scale the initial soma and branching node positions. After scaling the positions, the neurite pathways for each connection were generated (Algorithm 2). The dendrite length and gap distance were kept constant, but the axon length was variable for each cell, depending on the final distance between the two connected cells (See Algorithm 2). Each neurite connection must have distinct pathways between the pre- and post-synaptic cell that do not intersect with other pathways to pattern these networks *in vitro* using microcontact printed stamps or microfluidic chips. Thus, to assess GANGLIA's performance in generating micro-patterns for these networks, the number of intersections between neurite pathways and the computational run time were measured for each pattern generated.

To measure the computational run time, the tool was used on a Windows 10 machine with an AMD Ryzen 7 3700X 8-core processor, 16 GB RAM, and an NVIDIA GeForce RTX 2080 SUPER graphics card. The tool was run in the Anaconda 3 distribution of Spyder 5.4.2. The run-time calculated included the time the tool took to complete the two procedures in Algorithms 1 and 2 but excluded the time in which the tool waited for any user inputs and the time the tool took to export the files.

3   Results and Discussion

GANGLIA automatically generated micro-patterns for all four connectivity networks used as test cases (Fig. 2). Since the automatic pattern generation is parametrically driven, different elements of the network, such as the area for the soma and the lengths of the axons and dendrites, can be used to scale the pattern to a larger or smaller size. The area designed for the soma can easily be scaled to either support smaller single-cell bodies or larger neurospheres. Furthermore, the lengths of the neurites can be either user-defined or potentially driven by realistic sizes based on experimental studies of neuron development [12,19,20]. However, with thicker neurite widths, there is an increased risk of overlaps between distinct neurite paths.

The number of intersections also increased with network complexity, as characterized by the number of cells, branching nodes, and connections (Table 1). Overlapping neurite paths is not desirable since these would not allow for the control of the connectivity between cells. Thus, these points of intersection could indicate locations where the layout of the somas and branching nodes may need to be modified to make distinct neurite paths. One potential option could be including additional graph drawing algorithms, such as the Davidson-Harel layout [7,8], the distributed recursive graph layout (DrL) [7,23], or the large graph layout (LGL) [1,7], to provide more options for soma placements that might

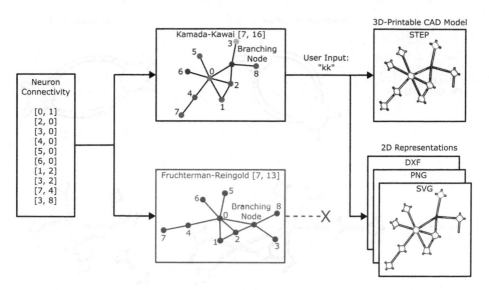

Fig. 1. Using only a list of paired values, indicating which two neurons are connected, GANGLIA can generate a micro-pattern for visually representing the network. Currently, GANGLIA provides the user with two possible layout options; each determined using a different graph drawing algorithm (Fruchterman-Reingold [7,13] or Kamada-Kawai [7,16]). Once the user inputs the desired layout (in this figure, Kamada-Kawai or "kk" was selected, as indicated by the continuing solid black arrows), GANGLIA can finalize the micro-pattern design and export the design in four file types: STEP, DXF, SVG, and PNG. The dashed line from the Fruchterman-Reingold result indicates that the user did not select that layout.

not include these intersections. Another alternative could be scaling GANGLIA to use a three-dimensional space, rather than only creating planar patterns, to accommodate increasingly complex patterns. Several graph drawing algorithms have already been implemented as part of the iGraph library, such as the 3D Fruchterman-Reingold [7,13], 3D Kamada-Kawai [7,16], and 3D DrL [7,23]. Furthermore, complex circuits could potentially be split into smaller, simpler subcircuits with 2D layouts, which could be combined to form a 3D network. However, when translating these designs to physical stamps or scaffolds, creating a 3D, user-defined circuit *in vitro* may require more complex cell manipulation techniques. Furthermore, experimental validation for fabricating these networks *in vitro* by verifying expected synaptic connections and circuit activity is needed.

In addition to the number of intersections, the time to generate a micro-pattern also increased with complexity (Table 1). The difference between the time to generate a pattern using either graph drawing algorithm was small since most of the computational time was spent to generate the CAD model (Algorithm 2, Table 1). Despite the increase in run time, GANGLIA still only takes seconds to generate a full 3D-printable CAD model for the micro-pattern, which could take a human designer several minutes to hours to generate manually.

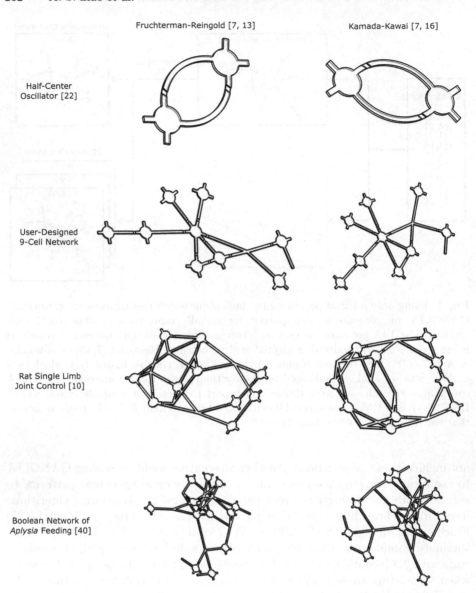

Fig. 2. Four different networks (half-center oscillator [22], user-generated 9-cell network, rat single limb joint control [10], and Boolean network of *Aplysia* feeding [41]) were used to test GANGLIA's micro-pattern generation capabilities. For each network, GANGLIA generated distinct layouts using different graph drawing algorithms (Fruchterman-Reingold [7,13] or Kamada-Kawai [7,16]).

Table 1. The run time for each procedure described in Algorithms 1 and 2 automatically create a 3D-printable CAD model for a neuron network micro-pattern and the number of resulting neurite path intersections correspond to the complexity of the network, as characterized by the number of cells, branching nodes, and synapses (cell-to-cell connections). The first procedure (Algorithm 1) determine candidate positions and the second procedure (Algorithm 2) generate the micro-pattern are indicated by $p1$ and $p2$, respectively.

Network	Cells	Nodes	Synapses	Algorithm	Intersections	Run Time (s)	
						$p1$	$p2$
Half-Center Oscillator [22]	2	0	2	FR	0	0.178	0.278
				KK	0	0.178	0.275
User-Designed 9-Cell Network	9	1	10	FR	0	0.207	2.304
				KK	0	0.205	2.322
Rat Single Limb Joint Control [10]	10	6	20	FR	4	0.241	4.831
				KK	9	0.238	5.200
Boolean Network of *Aplysia* Feeding [41]	12	6	22	FR	9	0.241	7.252
				KK	9	0.242	7.148

4 Conclusion

Biohybrid controllers using biological neurons have demonstrated the ability to control different peripheries but need to employ fabrication methods that are repeatable and enable a user to implement a designed circuit scheme. Current microfabrication and micromanipulation techniques enable researchers to control neuron cell placement and circuit formation when fabricating biohybrid controllers. However, existing techniques require the user to manually design the circuit schematic, which becomes increasingly difficult and time-consuming with increasingly more complex network requirements. To supplement existing microfabrication tools for creating user-designed circuits of biological neurons *in vitro*, GANGLIA was developed to automatically generate a micro-pattern using an input of paired neuron connections and graph drawing algorithms. To assess the performance of GANGLIA's pattern generation, four network connectivities, with varying complexity, were used: a half-center oscillator [22], a human-designed 9-cell network, a control network for a single rat limb joint [10], and a control network for *Aplysia* feeding [41]. With the increase in complexity, the number of intersections and the computational run time increased. However, the run time for the most complex network (*Aplysia* feeding) was far less than the time required to generate an equivalent model manually. In the future, GANGLIA could be further extended into 3D design space, which may reduce or eliminate the number of intersections. Additionally, patterns generated by GANGLIA could be coupled with neuron growth simulations [31,32] to predict how networks will form and function when grown on resulting patterns. Overall, the automatic generation of micro-patterns for more complex neuron circuits provided by GANGLIA will greatly reduce circuit prototyping design cycle time and supports the future creation *in vitro* biohybrid controllers.

Acknowledgments. This material is based upon work supported by the National Science Foundation (NSF). ASL was supported by the Graduate Research Fellowship Program under Grant No. DGE1745016. ASL and VAW were supported by the NSF Faculty Early Career Development Program under Grant No. ECCS-2044785. Any opinions, findings, and conclusions or recommendations expressed in this material are those of the author(s) and do not necessarily reflect the views of the NSF. ASL was also supported by the Carnegie Mellon University Jean-Francois and Catherine Heitz Scholarship. ASL, YJZ, and VAW were also supported by a Pennsylvania Infrastructure Technology Alliance grant. The authors would like to thank Ravesh Sukhnandan and Medinat Akindele for their insightful feedback during manuscript editing.

Code Availability. The designs and the pattern-generation tool GANGLIA presented in this paper are available at https://doi.org/10.5281/zenodo.7790394.

References

1. Adai, A.T., Date, S.V., Wieland, S., Marcotte, E.M.: LGL: creating a map of protein function with an algorithm for visualizing very large biological networks. J. Mol. Biol. **340**(1), 179–190 (2004). https://doi.org/10.1016/j.jmb.2004.04.047
2. Aydin, O., et al.: Development of 3D neuromuscular bioactuators. APL Bioeng. **4**(1), 016107 (2020). https://doi.org/10.1063/1.5134477
3. Aydin, O., et al.: Neuromuscular actuation of biohybrid motile bots. Proc. Natl. Acad. Sci. **116**(40), 19841–19847 (2019). https://doi.org/10.1073/pnas.1907051116
4. Birgiolas, J., Haynes, V., Gleeson, P., Gerkin, R.C., Dietrich, S.W., Crook, S.: NeuroML-DB: sharing and characterizing data-driven neuroscience models described in NeuroML. PLoS Comput. Biol. **19**(3), e1010941 (2023). https://doi.org/10.1371/journal.pcbi.1010941
5. Carnevale, N.T., Hines, M.L.: The NEURON Book. Cambridge University Press, Cambridge (2006). https://doi.org/10.1017/CBO9780511541612
6. Chapin, J.K., Moxon, K.A., Markowitz, R.S., Nicolelis, M.A.L.: Real-time control of a robot arm using simultaneously recorded neurons in the motor cortex. Nat. Neurosci. **2**(7), 664–670 (1999). https://doi.org/10.1038/10223
7. Csardi, G., Nepusz, T.: The igraph software package for complex network research. InterJ. Complex Syst **1695**, 1–9 (2006). https://igraph.org/
8. Davidson, R., Harel, D.: Drawing graphs nicely using simulated annealing. ACM Trans. Graph. **15**(4), 301–331 (1996). https://doi.org/10.1145/234535.234538
9. DeMarse, T.B., Wagenaar, D.A., Blau, A.W., Potter, S.M.: The neurally controlled animat: biological brains acting with dimulated bodies. Auton. Rob. **11**(3), 305–310 (2001). https://doi.org/10.1023/A:1012407611130
10. Deng, K., et al.: Neuromechanical model of rat hindlimb walking with two-layer CPGs. Biomimetics **4**(1), 21 (2019). https://doi.org/10.3390/biomimetics4010021
11. Di Battista, G., Eades, P., Tamassia, R., Tollis, I.G.: Graph Drawing: Algorithms for the Visualization of Graphs. Prentice Hall PTR, Upper Saddle River (1998)
12. Dotti, C.G., Sullivan, C.A., Banker, G.A.: The establishment of polarity by hippocampal neurons in culture. J. Neurosci. **8**(4), 1454–1468 (1988). https://doi.org/10.1523/jneurosci.08-04-01454.1988

13. Fruchterman, T.M.J., Reingold, E.M.: Graph drawing by force-directed placement. Softw.: Pract. Exp. **21**(11), 1129–1164 (1991). https://doi.org/10.1002/spe.4380211102
14. Gewaltig, M.O., Diesmann, M.: Nest (neural simulation tool). Scholarpedia **2**(4), 1430 (2007)
15. Göbbels, K., Thiebes, A.L., van Ooyen, A., Schnakenberg, U., Bräunig, P.: Low density cell culture of locust neurons in closed-channel microfluidic devices. J. Insect Physiol. **56**(8), 1003–1009 (2010). https://doi.org/10.1016/j.jinsphys.2010.05.017
16. Kamada, T., Kawai, S.: An algorithm for drawing general undirected graphs. Inf. Process. Lett. **31**(1), 7–15 (1989). https://doi.org/10.1016/0020-0190(89)90102-6
17. Kaufman, C.D., et al.: Emergence of functional neuromuscular junctions in an engineered, multicellular spinal cord-muscle bioactuator. APL Bioeng. **4**(2), 026104 (2020). https://doi.org/10.1063/1.5121440
18. Li, Y., Sun, R., Wang, Y., Li, H., Zheng, X.: A novel robot system integrating biological and mechanical intelligence based on dissociated neural network-controlled closed-loop environment. PLoS ONE **11**(11), e0165600 (2016). https://doi.org/10.1371/journal.pone.0165600
19. Liao, A.S., Cui, W., Zhang, Y.J., Webster-Wood, V.A.: Semi-automated quantitative evaluation of neuron developmental morphology in vitro using the change-point test. Neuroinformatics **21**(1), 163–176 (2023). https://doi.org/10.1007/s12021-022-09600-8
20. Liao, A.S., Webster-Wood, V.A., Zhang, Y.J.: Quantification of neuron morphological development using the change-point test. In: 2021 Summer Biomechanics, Bioengineering and Biotransport Conference. Virtual (2021)
21. Malishev, E., et al.: Microfluidic device for unidirectional axon growth. J. Phys: Conf. Ser. **643**, 012025 (2015). https://doi.org/10.1088/1742-6596/643/1/012025
22. Marder, E., Bucher, D.: Central pattern generators and the control of rhythmic movements. Curr. Biol. **11**(23), R986–R996 (2001). https://doi.org/10.1016/S0960-9822(01)00581-4
23. Martin, S., Brown, W., Wylie, B.: Dr.L: Distributed recursive (graph) layout (2007). https://doi.org/10.11578/dc.20210416.20
24. Matsumura, R., Yamamoto, H., Hayakawa, T., Katsurabayashi, S., Niwano, M., Hirano-Iwata, A.: Dependence and homeostasis of membrane impedance on cell morphology in cultured hippocampal neurons. Sci. Rep. **8**(1), 9905 (2018). https://doi.org/10.1038/s41598-018-28232-0
25. Moonen, E., Luttge, R., Frimat, J.P.: Single cell trapping by capillary pumping using NOA81 replica moulded stencils. Microelectron. Eng. **197**, 1–7 (2018). https://doi.org/10.1016/j.mee.2018.04.010
26. Park, J., Kim, S., Park, S.I., Choe, Y., Li, J., Han, A.: A microchip for quantitative analysis of CNS axon growth under localized biomolecular treatments. J. Neurosci. Methods **221**, 166–174 (2014). https://doi.org/10.1016/j.jneumeth.2013.09.018
27. Park, J.Y., et al.: Single cell trapping in larger microwells capable of supporting cell spreading and proliferation. Microfluid. Nanofluid. **8**(2), 263–268 (2010). https://doi.org/10.1007/s10404-009-0503-9
28. von Philipsborn, A.C., et al.: Microcontact printing of axon guidance molecules for generation of graded patterns. Nat. Protoc. **1**(3), 1322–1328 (2006). https://doi.org/10.1038/nprot.2006.251
29. Pizzi, R., Rossetti, D., Cino, G., Marino, D., Vescovi, A.L., Baer, W.: A cultured human neural network operates a robotic actuator. Biosystems **95**(2), 137–144 (2009). https://doi.org/10.1016/j.biosystems.2008.09.006

30. Poddar, S., et al.: Low density culture of mammalian primary neurons in compartmentalized microfluidic devices. Biomed. Microdevices **21**(3), 67 (2019). https://doi.org/10.1007/s10544-019-0400-2

31. Qian, K., et al.: Modeling neuron growth using isogeometric collocation based phase field method. Sci. Rep. **12**(1), 8120 (2022). https://doi.org/10.1038/s41598-022-12073-z

32. Qian, K., Liao, A., Gu, S. Webster-Wood, V., Zhang, Y.J.: Biomimetic IGA Neuron Growth Modeling with Neurite Morphometric Features and CNN-Based Prediction. Comput. Methods Appl. Mech. Eng. (2023). https://doi.org/10.1016/j.cma.2023.116213

33. Stimberg, M., Brette, R., Goodman, D.F.: Brian 2, an intuitive and efficient neural simulator. eLife **8**, e47314 (2019). https://doi.org/10.7554/eLife.47314

34. Tamassia, R., Rosen, K.H.: Handbook of Graph Drawing and Visualization, 1 edn. Chapman and Hall/CRC (2016)

35. Taylor, A.M., Blurton-Jones, M., Rhee, S.W., Cribbs, D.H., Cotman, C.W., Jeon, N.L.: A microfluidic culture platform for CNS axonal injury, regeneration and transport. Nat. Methods **2**(8), 599–605 (2005). https://doi.org/10.1038/nmeth777

36. Tu, C., et al.: A microfluidic chip for cell patterning utilizing paired microwells and protein patterns. Micromachines **8**(1), 1 (2016). https://doi.org/10.3390/mi8010001

37. Vogt, A., Lauer, L., Knoll, W., Offenhausser, A.: Micropatterned substrates for the growth of functional neuronal networks of defined geometry. Biotechnol. Prog. **19**(5), 1562–1568 (2003). https://doi.org/10.1021/bp034016f

38. Walczuch, K., et al.: A new microfluidic device design for a defined positioning of neurons in vitro. Biomicrofluidics **11**(4), 044103 (2017). https://doi.org/10.1063/1.4993556

39. Warwick, K., et al.: Controlling a mobile robot with a biological brain. Defence Sci. J. **60**(1), 5–14 (2010). https://doi.org/10.14429/dsj.60.11

40. Webster, V.A., et al.: 3D-printed biohybrid robots powered by neuromuscular tissue circuits from *Aplysia Californica*. In: Mangan, M., Cutkosky, M., Mura, A., Verschure, P.F.M.J., Prescott, T., Lepora, N. (eds.) Living Machines 2017. LNCS (LNAI), vol. 10384, pp. 475–486. Springer, Cham (2017). https://doi.org/10.1007/978-3-319-63537-8_40

41. Webster-Wood, V.A., Gill, J.P., Thomas, P.J., Chiel, H.J.: Control for multifunctionality: bioinspired control based on feeding in Aplysia Californica. Biol. Cybern. **114**(6), 557–588 (2020). https://doi.org/10.1007/s00422-020-00851-9

42. Yamamoto, H., Matsumura, R., Takaoki, H., Katsurabayashi, S., Hirano-Iwata, A., Niwano, M.: Unidirectional signal propagation in primary neurons micropatterned at a single-cell resolution. Appl. Phys. Lett. **109**(4), 043703 (2016). https://doi.org/10.1063/1.4959836

The Tall, the Squat, & the Bendy: Parametric Modeling and Simulation Towards Multi-functional Biohybrid Robots

Saul Schaffer[iD] and Victoria A. Webster-Wood[(✉)][iD]

Carnegie Mellon University, Pittsburgh, PA 15213, USA
vwebster@andrew.cmu.edu
http://engineering.cmu.edu/borg

Abstract. Efficient computational mechanical models are needed to develop complex, multifunctional soft robotics systems. The field of bio-hybrid robotics is no exception and is currently limited to low degree-of-freedom lab-chained research devices due in part to limitations in existing design tools and limitations in the morphological sophistication of existing biohybrid structures. Here, we present an expanded use of an existing soft body modeling tool PyElastica, along with a parametric design pipeline for generating and simulating a lattice-based distributed actuation biohybrid robot. Our key contribution in this work is the parameterization of the geometry defining the lattice robot architecture both in terms of the bulk structure and the patterning of the muscles on that structure. By encoding multifunctionality in the robot's architecture, we demonstrate extension, compression, and bending motion primitives exhibited by the same base lattice structure. We achieve structure-wide strains of 49.73% for extension, 30.59% for compression, and a 48.60° bend angle for the bent configuration, with all simulations completing in less than 45 s. From this pilot study, the computational model will be expanded to capture more complex and functional behaviors, such as esophageal-inspired peristalsis for internal transport, as well as earthworm-inspired locomotion. The computational modeling of these behaviors is a critical step toward the eventual design, fabrication, and deployment of complex biohybrid robots.

Keywords: Biohybrid · Distributed actuation · Soft-body modeling · Lattice · PyElastica

1 Introduction

Biohybrid robots show substantial promise for applications ranging from medicine to agriculture and environmental monitoring. Living muscle-based

Supplementary Information The online version contains supplementary material available at https://doi.org/10.1007/978-3-031-39504-8_15.

actuators can endow mechanical systems with desirable capabilities such as high compliance [9,21], self-healing [13], and biocompatibility [14]. To date, most bio-hybrid robots consist of low-degree-of-freedom systems that can achieve basic motions such as crawling [2,7,11,19], swimming [1,6,8,12], and flexion [9]. While promising, these modes of motion are limited. To achieve higher levels of functionality, biohybrid robots with more complex behavioral capabilities are needed.

A major challenge in designing and realizing complex biohybrid robots capable of multifunctional behavior is the limited number of modeling tools well-suited for biohybrid simulation [21]. Due to the time and expense required to fabricate and assess biohybrid robots, experimentally iterating to refine designs for complex, multifunctional robots is impractical. Unfortunately, many existing robot modeling tools focus on rigid body systems and traditional modes of actuation [10]. Few tools can capture the mechanics of multi-actuator biohybrid systems [15,18]. One could use approaches from solid mechanics modeling. However, traditional finite element tools are not well-suited for handling complex morphologies with large deformations in a reasonable (sub-hour) amount of time, resulting in long design-iteration cycle times. To enable the design of complex, multifunctional biohybrid robots, modeling tools need to be computationally efficient, amenable to large deformations, modular enough to allow the implementation of biologically relevant muscle contraction profiles, and accessible enough that they do not pose major barriers to entry to new researchers in the field [20].

To address the need for an accessible modeling pipeline for biohybrid robotics researchers, this work presents a novel framework for parametrically defining model morphology in the open-source soft modeling tool PyElastica [4,22]. Our pipeline is developed specifically for biohybrid robots with distributed muscle-actuators and lattice-based architectures, inspired by the "Meshworms" from MIT [16] and Case Western Reserve University [3]. These lattice-based architectures provide the physical complexity needed to achieve multifunctional behaviors while remaining amenable to both parameterization for design exploration and future physical fabrication via 3D bioprinting methods [5]. Our lattice robot features tens of muscle actuators that are patterned across their bulk structure (Fig. 3), which would be challenging to implement in PyElastica manually. As a test case for our parametric model definition approach, we use our tool to automatically create the biohybrid lattice robot model and position muscles based on user input. For this pilot study, we then demonstrate the simulated lattice robot achieving three basic motion primitives: extension (*i.e.* making the robot tall), compression (squat), and bending. By strategically combining these motion primitives, future research will build off the work presented here to demonstrate functional behaviors using this lattice architecture, such as esophageal-inspired peristalsis and locomotion. Furthermore, this work has the potential to broaden participation in biohybrid robotics by making biohybrid robot modeling and design more accessible through parametric model definition.

2   Methods

Simulation of the lattice worm (Fig. 1) was conducted using PyElastica (version 0.3.0) [4,22]. PyElastica is a software package for simulating assemblies of soft slender bodies using Cosserat Rod theory. A Cosserat rod is a mathematical description that captures the 3D dynamics of 1D slender bodies while accounting for all modes of deformation (*i.e.* bending, twisting, stretching, and shearing as well as mechanical instabilities such as buckling) [22]. For a detailed explanation of Cosserat Rod Theory, readers are encouraged to visit www.cosseratrods.org, a site managed by the creators of PyElastica.

For curved rods, PyElastica requires that every node be defined by an (x, y, z) position. Thus, generating architectures within PyElastica comprised of multiple curved rods can be challenging. To generate the helices that comprise our lattice structure, we created a pipeline for parametrically generating the discrete elements that comprise each helix, as well as all necessary connections and boundary conditions. This pipeline is a suite of custom Python functions that enable the facile instantiation and simulation of lattice-based biohybrid structures.

2.1   Parametric Model Generation for a 3D Biohybrid Lattice Robot

The pipeline for generating the structural rods and connections of the lattice as well as the muscle rods and their connections, is detailed in Fig. 2. In the proof-of-concept work described here, we have focused on lattice structures composed of 12 rods. However, this framework can be extended to other rod quantities by implementing the appropriate intersection geometry calculations. At a high level, the geometric parameters that define the rods (*i.e.* height h, width w, phase angle ϕ, and chirality χ) are input by the user into a Parametric Structure Rod Generator. From these parameters, all 12 rods that compose the bulk structure of the lattice (Fig. 1, purple rods) are generated. The intersections R between structure rods are automatically calculated based on the geometry and discretization of the structure. These intersections are used to

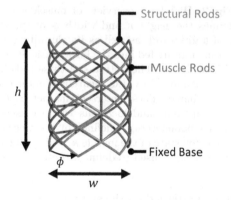

Fig. 1. The geometry of the lattice worm is defined and generated parametrically based on user-specified height, width, phase, chirality, and muscle locations. The structural rods (purple) are generated first, and all intersections are connected. The user then specifies which muscle rods (red) to include, and they are automatically connected at the appropriate nodes. For this work, the structure's base was grounded with a fixed boundary constraint on the first node of each structural rod. (Color figure online)

define connections between structure rods, as well as locations for muscle rods

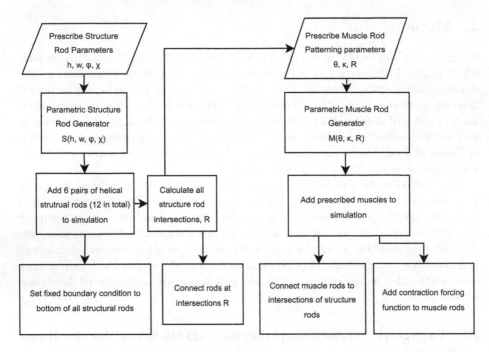

Fig. 2. High-level overview of muscle-actuated lattice generation pipeline. The user defines the height h and width w of the bulk lattice structure and the phase offset ϕ of a given rod, as well as its chirality χ (*e.g.* clockwise or counterclockwise). These parameters are fed into the Parametric Structure Rod Generator, which outputs 6 pairs of helical rods. The bottoms of these rods have a fixed boundary condition applied to them. Additionally, the location of intersections between interlaced structure rods R is calculated. These intersections act as both the location for connections between structure rods and locations where muscle rods can connect to the bulk structure. Muscle parameters are defined by the muscles orientation θ (*e.g.* vertical or horizontal), the on/off state of the muscle κ, and the locations R of the muscles on the lattice, which is the same R used to define structure rod connections.

to be patterned on the structure. Muscle rod (Fig. 1, red rods) orientation θ and on/off state κ are also prescribed by the user. These three muscle patterning parameters are then input into the Parametric Muscle Rod Generator, which outputs all prescribed muscles onto the correct location and with correct orientation on the lattice. Then, the muscles are programmatically connected to the structural rod elements at the appropriate intersections.

The geometry of the structural rods is defined by the parametric functions,

$$x(t) = \frac{d}{2}\cos(\frac{2\pi t}{T} + \phi)$$

$$y(t) = \frac{d}{2}\sin(\frac{2\pi t}{T} + \phi)$$

$$z(t) = t$$

for $0 < t < h$, where $x(t)$, $y(t)$, and $z(t)$ correspond to the x, y, and z positions for each node of a structural rod. h refers to the total height of the structure, and t is the parameterized variable. Variables d and T correspond to the diameter of the lattice and the period of the sinusoid defining individual structure rods, respectively. To achieve the desired closed lattice morphology, an additional geometrical constraint $T = \frac{3}{2}h$ was enforced. The numerical values of all the parameters that govern the simulation are detailed in Table 1.

Table 1. Parameters that define the lattice worm morphology, material model, and simulation variables.

Simulation Parameters	Value & Units
Structural rod elements	40 elements
Muscle rod elements	2 elements
Lattice height (h)	100 mm
Lattice diameter (d)	75 mm
Damping coefficient	30 mNs/m
Contraction magnitude	500 mN
Muscle Young's modulus	25 kPa
Structure Young's modulus	70 kPa
Muscle Poission's ratio	0.5
Structure Poission's ratio	0.5
Structure density	1070 kg/m^3
Muscle density	1060 kg/m^3
Structure rod radius	5 mm
Muscle rod radius	5 mm
Connection stiffness (k)	100 mN/mm

The parameters that define the lattice worm morphology were selected to create a tubular, closed lattice worm with element nodes located at structure rod intersections. The density and Young's modulus for the structure rods are an approximation taken from the Smooth-On website for their Ecoflex 00-30 product [17]. The muscle material model is the same as that in work detailed by Pagan-Diaz and colleagues [11]. Simulation variables (e.g., damping coefficient, connection stiffness) were hand-tuned to ensure simulation stability.

2.2 Quantifying Lattice Deformations

To assess our pipeline, we used it to generate three lattice models with *i)* circumferential, *ii)* symmetric longitudinal, and *iii)* asymmetric longitudinal and circumferential muscles. These muscle patterns give rise to the three motion primitives (*i.e.* extension, compression, and bending) that, when properly coordinated, can facilitate multifunctional behaviors such as locomotion and peristalsis. We evaluated the ability of the pipeline to successfully generate these lattice-based biohybrid robots in which all structural elements and muscles successfully attach and interact. During simulation, the muscles applied force to the lattice, and lattice extension and compression deformations were quantified by calculating how much the bulk structure of the lattice had deformed along its longitudinal axis. This deformation was calculated by finding the average change in the z position of the top of the lattice using the formula:

$$\frac{1}{n}\sum_{r=1}^{n}(z_{r,f} - z_{r,i})$$

where n is 12 for the number of structural rods, $z_{r,f}$ and $z_{r,i}$ are the initial and final z positions, respectively, of the top-most node of a given rod r. From this calculation, we get the average displacement of the top of the structure, which serves as a metric for the deformation of the structure as a whole. This displacement is divided by the height h of the structure to calculate the strain.

To quantify bending due to asymmetric longitudinal and circumferential actuation, we first created a plane that spanned the top of the lattice defined by three structure rod end nodes. The normal vector **n** of this plane, which initially pointed vertically, bends away from vertical due to the lattice's bulk deformation due to asymmetric actuation. To calculate the final angle change of that normal vector (*i.e.* the angle that the lattice bent), we used the following formula:

$$\theta = \cos^{-1}\left[\frac{\mathbf{n_i} \cdot \mathbf{n_f}}{|\mathbf{n_i}||\mathbf{n_f}|}\right]$$

where θ is the angle between the planes, $\mathbf{n_i}$ and $\mathbf{n_f}$ are the normal vectors that define where the lattice is pointing before and after deformation, respectively, and $|\mathbf{n_i}|$ and $|\mathbf{n_f}|$ are the magnitudes of those normal vectors. The nature of the lattice worm's deflection leads to the surface formed by the distal nodes of the lattice being non-planar due to its asymmetric deformation. The authors have incorporated this non-planar deformation into our calculations, and have selected coplanar nodes that are representative of the distal end of the robot.

For all actuation modalities, if any of the structural rod intersections or muscle rod connections have not been successfully defined by the parametric pipeline, the lattice would become unstable and disintegrate. In addition to assessing the deformation of each lattice quantitatively, each lattice simulation result was visually inspected to ensure that no rods were buckled or detached after muscle actuation.

2.3   Simulation Hardware

All simulations in this study were executed on a local computer workstation running Ubuntu 22.04, equipped with an Nvidia GeForce RTX 2080 SUPER graphics card and an AMD Ryzen 7 3700 8-core Processor, offering 2 threads per core. It is important to note that the version of PyElastica used in this work is not easily parallelizable, as it runs on a single CPU thread. Consequently, CPU clock speed becomes the most relevant hardware metric for enhancing simulation performance.

Despite this limitation, it is still possible to run multiple PyElastica simulations simultaneously on the same machine. In our case, we were able to successfully run up to 15 concurrent simulations, reserving one thread for maintaining operating system stability. This approach effectively increases the overall throughput of simulation runs, allowing for faster evaluation of different design parameters and system configurations. "These simulation's wall time for a given actuation condition was very consistent, always under one minute on the hardware used in this work.

3   Results and Discussion

Using our parametric lattice-robot design pipeline, we were successfully able to generate biohybrid structure models with user-specified geometry and muscle placements. All structure-structure intersection connections and muscle-structure connections translated successfully into PyElastica. Additionally, we were able to successfully demonstrate all three desired motion primitives of extension, contraction, and bending (Fig. 3). A quantitative assessment of these deformational modes is detailed in Table 2. Each mode deforms as expected, with no unexpected actuation asymmetries indicating muscle rods have not been properly connected to the structure.

Table 2. Quantified performance of three deformational modes demonstrated. Videos of each deformation can be found in supplementary materials.

Motion	Value & Unit	Wall Time (s)	Final Sim. Time (s)	Timestep (ms)
Extension	49.73 % strain	25.90	0.5	0.2
Compression	−30.59 % strain	29.27	0.3	0.1
Bending	48.60 °	44.31	0.5	0.1

These preliminary results support the prospect of a lattice-based biohybrid architecture being capable of multifunctional behavior and successfully demonstrate our parametric model definition pipeline. While these deformational modes (*i.e.* extension, compression, bending) do not accomplish any functional task when executed alone, we believe that being able to extend, compress, and bend are the motion primitives necessary for more complex behaviors in lattice-based biohybrid robots, such as locomotion and esophageal-inspired peristalsis. The speed of these simulations, all under 45 s, provides the computational efficiency needed for a biohybrid design robot tool. The strains the bulk structure

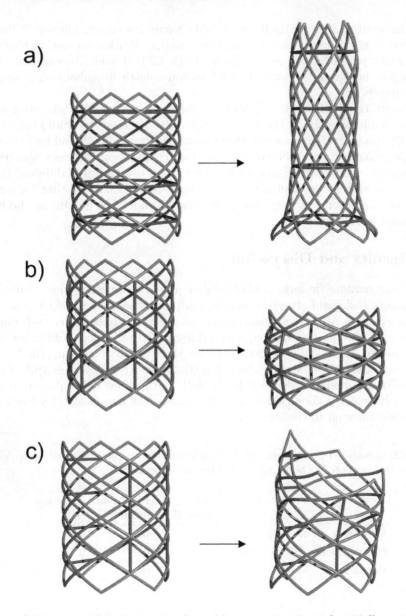

Fig. 3. a) Extension of the lattice is achieved by actuating circumferentially patterned muscles. **b)** Compression is achieved by actuating longitudinally patterned muscles. **c)** Bending is achieved by actuating circumferentially patterned muscles on the posterior of the lattice and actuating longitudinally on the anterior of the lattice. Videos of extension, compression, and bending can be found in the supplementary materials.

was able to undergo demonstrate that the simulation could generate large deformations required for future functional behavior.

4   Conclusions

This work presents a pilot study towards the design and simulation of multi-degree-of-freedom, functional lattice-based biohybrid robots. We present a parametric tool for computer-aided modeling of lattice-based structures using PyElastica and demonstrate the success of this pipeline by simulating three motion primitives *i.e.* extension, compression, and bending. These preliminary results indicate that careful coordination of actuators on this lattice architecture may enable more functional behaviors such as locomotion and peristalsis. Simulations for biohybrid robots, perhaps even more so than other mechanical systems, are crucial to the continued advancement of the field, as they allow researchers to perform countless iterations *in silico* before committing to the costly, time-intensive experiments needed to fabricate a functional living machine. Future work on this project will include verification of our computational predictions for biohybrid lattice robot behavior through physical, *in vitro* experimentation. Furthermore, the parametric model generation approach presented here makes simulating these lattice-based biohybrid robots more accessible, thereby reducing barriers to entry to biohybrid robot modeling.

Acknowledgements. This material is based on work supported by a Carnegie Mellon University (CMU) Dean's Fellowship and the National Science Foundation Graduate Research Fellowship Program under grant No. DGE1745016 and by the National Science Foundation CAREER award program (grant No. ECCS-2044785). The authors would also like to acknowledge OpenAI's ChatGPT for answering innumerable inane coding questions.

References

1. Aydin, O., et al.: Neuromuscular actuation of biohybrid motile bots. Proc. Natl. Acad. Sci. **116**(40), 19841–19847 (2019). https://doi.org/10.1073/pnas.1907051116
2. Cvetkovic, C., et al.: Three-dimensionally printed biological machines powered by skeletal muscle. Proc. Natl. Acad. Sci. U.S.A. **111**(28), 10125–10130 (2014). https://doi.org/10.1073/pnas.1401577111
3. Daltorio, K.A., Boxerbaum, A.S., Horchler, A.D., Shaw, K.M., Chiel, H.J., Quinn, R.D.: Efficient worm-like locomotion: slip and control of soft-bodied peristaltic robots. Bioinspiration Biomimetics **8**(3), 035003 (2013). https://doi.org/10.1088/1748-3182/8/3/035003
4. Gazzola, M., Dudte, L.H., McCormick, A.G., Mahadevan, L.: Forward and inverse problems in the mechanics of soft filaments. R. Soc. Open Sci. **5**(6), 171628 (2018). https://doi.org/10.1098/rsos.171628
5. Guix, M., et al.: Biohybrid soft robots with self-stimulating skeletons. Sci. Robot. **6**(53), eabe7577 (2021). https://doi.org/10.1126/scirobotics.abe7577
6. Herr, H., Dennis, R.G.: A swimming robot actuated by living muscle tissue. J. NeuroEng. Rehabil. **1**, 1–9 (2004). https://doi.org/10.1186/1743-0003-1-6
7. Kim, Y., et al.: Remote control of muscle-driven miniature robots with battery-free wireless optoelectronics. Sci. Robot. **8**, eadd1053 (2023). https://doi.org/10.1126/scirobotics.add1053

8. Lee, K.Y., et al.: An autonomously swimming biohybrid fish designed with human cardiac biophysics. Science **375**(6581), 639–647 (2022). https://doi.org/10.1126/science.abh0474

9. Morimoto, Y., Onoe, H., Takeuchi, S.: Biohybrid robot powered by an antagonistic pair of skeletal muscle tissues. Sci. Robot. **3**, 4440 (2018). https://doi.org/10.1126/scirobotics.aat4440

10. Naughton, N., Sun, J., Tekinalp, A., Parthasarathy, T., Chowdhary, G., Gazzola, M.: Elastica: a compliant mechanics environment for soft robotic control. IEEE Robot. Autom. Lett. **6**(2), 3389–3396 (2021). https://doi.org/10.1109/LRA.2021.3063698

11. Pagan-Diaz, G.J., et al.: Simulation and fabrication of stronger, larger, and faster walking biohybrid machines. Adv. Funct. Mater. **28**(23), 1801145 (2018). https://doi.org/10.1002/adfm.201801145

12. Park, S.J., et al.: Phototactic guidance of a tissue-engineered soft-robotic ray. Science **353**(6295), 158–162 (2016). https://doi.org/10.1126/science.aaf4292

13. Raman, R., et al.: Optogenetic skeletal muscle-powered adaptive biological machines. Proc. Natl. Acad. Sci. **113**(13), 3497–3502 (2016). https://doi.org/10.1073/pnas.1516139113

14. Ricotti, L., et al.: Biohybrid actuators for robotics: a review of devices actuated by living cells. Sci. Robot. **2**(12), eaaq0495 (2017). https://doi.org/10.1126/scirobotics.aaq0495

15. Schaffer, S., Lee, J.S., Beni, L., Webster-Wood, V.A.: A computational approach for contactless muscle force and strain estimations in distributed actuation biohybrid mesh constructs. Biomimetic Biohybrid Syst. **13548**, 140–151 (2022). https://doi.org/10.1007/978-3-031-20470-8_15

16. Seok, S., Onal, C.D., Cho, K.J., Wood, R.J., Rus, D., Kim, S.: Meshworm: a peristaltic soft robot with antagonistic nickel titanium coil actuators. IEEE/ASME Trans. Mechatron. **18**(5), 1485–1497 (2013). https://doi.org/10.1109/TMECH.2012.2204070

17. Smooth-On: Ecoflex 00–30 (2023). https://www.smooth-on.com/products/ecoflex-00-30/, Accessed 15 Jan 2023

18. Wang, J., et al.: Computationally assisted design and selection of maneuverable biological walking machines. Adv. Intell. Syst. **3**, 2000237 (2021). https://doi.org/10.1002/aisy.202000237

19. Webster, V.A., et al.: Aplysia Californica as a novel source of material for biohybrid robots and organic machines. Biomimetic Biohybrid Syst. (2016). https://doi.org/10.1007/978-3-319-42417-0

20. Webster, V.A., Nieto, S.G., Grosberg, A., Akkus, O., Chiel, H.J., Quinn, R.D.: Simulating muscular thin films using thermal contraction capabilities in finite element analysis tools. J. Mech. Behav. Biomed. Mater. **63**, 326–336 (2016). https://doi.org/10.1016/j.jmbbm.2016.06.027

21. Webster-Wood, V.A., Akkus, O., Gurkan, U.A., Chiel, H.J., Quinn, R.D.: Organismal engineering: toward a robotic taxonomic key for devices using organic materials. Sci. Robot. **2**(12), 1–19 (2017). https://doi.org/10.1126/scirobotics.aap9281

22. Zhang, X., Chan, F.K., Parthasarathy, T., Gazzola, M.: Modeling and simulation of complex dynamic musculoskeletal architectures. Nat. Commun. **10**(1), 4825 (2019). https://doi.org/10.1038/s41467-019-12759-5

A Simple Dynamic Controller for Emulating Human Balance Control

J. Stu McNeal[✉] and Alexander Hunt

Department of Mechanical and Materials Engineering, Maseeh College of Engineering and
Computer Science, Portland State University, Portland, OR 97201, USA
mcneal@pdx.edu

Abstract. This paper presents a biologically inspired control system developed
for maintaining balance in a simulated human atop an oscillating platform. This
work advances our previous research by adapting a human balance controller to
an inverted pendulum and controlled by linear-Hill muscle models. To expedite
neuron/synapse parameter value selection, we employ a novel two-stage process
that pairs a previously developed analytic method with particle swarm optimization. Using the parameter values found analytically as inputs for particle swarm
optimization (PSO), we take advantage of the benefits of each method while
avoiding their pitfalls. Our results show that PSO optimization allowed improved
balance control from modest (<10%) changes to the synaptic parameters. The
improved performance was accompanied by muscle coactivations, however, and
further refinement is needed to better align overall behavior of the neural controller
with biological systems.

Keywords: Neural Controller · Balance Control · Functional Subnetwork
Approach · Particle Swarm Optimization

1 Introduction

Robots and neural networks are gaining in popularity, but studies that make use of
synthetic nervous systems (SNSs) as robotic controllers, especially in motor control
applications, have thus far not found much traction in the research community. Most
studies are preoccupied with image processing, pattern recognition, or decision-making
(e.g. [1–3]). Here we pause to draw a distinction between SNS models such as the
one used in this study, and artificial- or recurrent neural networks (ANNs or RNNs),
namely that the former features neurons and synapses governed by differential equations
(see §2.1 below) that make them behave similarly to the structures they mimic. Of the
works interested in the motor control of SNS-driven robots, most explore the utility
of CPGs (e.g. [4–6]), with few concerned with balance control. This work presents a
novel approach in developing a muscle-actuated adaptive balance controller driven by a
synthetic nervous system.

This work was supported by NSF DBI 2015317 as part of the NSF/CIHR/DFG/FRQ/UKRI-MRC
next Generation Networks for Neuroscience Program

It is our hypothesis that the addition of numerical optimization to our previously developed analytic methods [7], will enable a synthetic nervous system (SNS) to dynamically balance a muscle-actuated inverted pendulum. We test our hypothesis by adapting our previously developed SNS-driven balance controller [8] to be more biorealistic by replacing the torque-controlled motor with simulated muscles and refining the values of the parameters with particle swarm optimization. Our results show the viability of the method and allow us to more quickly and accurately find parameter values that produce desirable model behaviors.

2 Background

One of the primary inspirations for this work is the balance studies of Peterka (2002, 2003) [23]. During the experiments, the balance of patients with severe vestibular conditions was measured by situating them atop an oscillating platform and securing their trunk and legs to a vertical plank that restricted bulk motion to bending at the ankle (Fig. 1, left). The patients were subjected to a pseudorandom stimulus that tilted their feet back and forth along the sagittal plane. Angle and velocity data were collected from sensors situated at the ankle. Their results introduced the common "Independent Channel" bipedal balance control model that connects weighted sensory inputs to muscle activations, and was later validated by [24] using PostuRob II. Peterka's subsequent 2003 study [25] repeated the analysis on a subset of the original study focusing on patients whose inputs were limited to proprioception and found that the best control equation that described the human balance data was a PD controller with force feedback and passive muscle dynamics (see Fig. 2,[25]). This control equation was used as the basis for the Hilts et al., (2018) SNS model [8], which was adapted for use here. The Hilts SNS incorporated force feedback but not passive muscle dynamics since it drove a torque motor rather than muscles.

The present study extends our previous work, in which an SNS emulated proprioception-based human balance control on an inverted pendulum controlled by a torque motor [8, 9]. Here, we employ a novel two-stage approach to parameter value selection. To understand the theoretical framework used in this study, an understanding of two subjects is required: the functional subnetwork approach (FSA) constraint equations that begin in §2.1 with a description of the neurons and synapses used, and particle swarm optimization (PSO).

2.1 Neurons and Synapses

The neuron model used in this study is a conductance-based non-spiking variant [10, 11], chosen because it captures neuronal subthreshold behavior while keeping computational costs low. Another benefit of this model is that it allows a single neuron to represent the aggregate behavior of a population of neurons [12]. The mathematical framework starts with calculating the membrane voltage V as the sum of various currents I:

$$C_m \frac{dV}{dt} = I_{leak} + I_{syn} + I_{app}, \tag{1}$$

where the leak and synaptic currents can be modeled as:

$$I_{leak} = G_m \cdot (E_r - V) \tag{2}$$

$$I_{syn} = \sum_{i=1}^{n} G_{s,i} \cdot (E_{s,i} - V) \tag{3}$$

and I_{app} is an optional applied current. Here C_m is the membrane capacitance, G_m and G_s are the neuronal and synaptic conductance, respectively. The reversal potentials, E, are in units of mV and the subscripts indicate whether they apply to the membrane (i.e. E_r) or the synapse (E_s). The synaptic conductance, $G_{s,i}$, is envisioned as a piecewise-linear function for simplicity:

$$G_{s,i} = \begin{cases} 0, & if\ V_{pre} \leq E_{lo}, \\ g_{s,i} \cdot \frac{V_{pre} - E_{lo}}{E_{hi} - E_{lo}}, & if\ E_{lo} \leq V_{pre} \leq E_{hi}, \\ g_{s,i}, & if\ V_{pre} \geq E_{hi}. \end{cases} \tag{4}$$

where $g_{s,i}$ represents the synapse's maximum conductance, E_{lo} and E_{hi} represent the lower threshold and saturation, respectively. Here we introduce the variable $R = E_{hi} - E_{lo}$ that describes the operating range of the network, in mV. For this study, we assign a value of $R = 20$ mV. Also, we introduce $\Delta E_s = E_{s,i} - E_{r,post}$, where $E_{r,post}$ is the resting potential of the post-synaptic neuron. Based on the design rules set forth in [7], parameter value selection is primarily a matter of estimating the values of $g_{s,i}$ and ΔE_s.

2.2 Functional Subnetwork Approach

The functional subnetwork approach (FSA) refers to a set of constraint equations analytically derived by [7], that provide design rules that can be used to build subnetworks for specific mathematical functions (i.e. addition, subtraction, etc.). The constraints are based on the observation that small clusters of neurons can be envisioned as mathematical operators, leading to their classification of synapses as being either for signal transmission or signal modulation. FSA allows designers to analytically develop networks that perform mathematical operations and to quickly find parameter values for the model. We refer the reader to [7] for the full derivation.

While the FSA provides a vehicle with which to find parameter values, the output constraint equations rely on simplifications that can introduce error [7]. As a result, some additional tuning of parameters is often required for optimal model behavior.

2.3 Particle Swarm Optimization

To further tune the SNS, we implement particle swarm optimization (PSO), a metaheuristic genetic algorithm created in 1995 by Kennedy and Eberhart [13]. It was originally envisioned for deployment in describing natural systems [14], as a simplified social milieu of collision-proof birds and fish [13]. PSO was quickly applied to optimization problems with success and has since been the subject of much interest and study. PSO makes use of parameter sets (swarms) called particles (X_t) that move through the solution space at some velocity (V) determined by some error measurement (X_i). This study makes use of the PSO framework where

$$V_{t+1} = w * V_t + c_1 r_1 (P_{best,i} - X_i) + c_2 r_2 (g_{best,i} - X_i) \qquad (5)$$

$$X_{t+1} = X_t + V_{t+1} \qquad (6)$$

with Eq. (4) having three terms that we call the inertia term, personal term, and group term, from left to right, respectively. The inertia term, which describes the particle's previous velocity, is weighted by w, and the personal and group terms contain a random number $0 \leq r_{1,2} \leq 1$ and a weighting variable $c_{1,2}$ that scale the calculated error in the solution space. The new velocity V_{t+1} is the sum of the weighted inertial term plus weighted inputs based on comparisons of the current error X_i with the particle's *personal* best configuration, $P_{best,i}$, and the best *group* configuration, $g_{best,i}$.

Rapid convergence is a hallmark characteristic of PSO but can lead to swarm stagnation if the early solution is sub-optimal [15]. Some modified methods have attempted to address this, with varying degrees of success. Some efforts, for example, have found means of guaranteeing convergence (GCPSO) (see [16]), but these algorithms require a priori solution knowledge and have shown to perform similarly to PSO in multimodal problems [15]. Riget and Vesterstrom (2002) implemented a scheme that alternated attraction and repulsion phases, resulting in better algorithm performance that scaled with model dimensionality [17]. Silva et al., 2002 utilized a predator particle that forces other particles to disperse [18]. While these latter strategies proved effective, they introduce further complexity and computational cost to the effort. Veeramachaneni et al. (2003) sought to avoid stagnation by slowing convergence using at fitness-distance-ratio-PSO [19]. This study addresses stagnation by setting the weights such that increment is slowed by small parameter values. Here w was set to 0.8 and both c values in Eq. (5) were set to 0.1 so that the overall influence of the personal and group terms was 10% per epoch.

Although PSO converges quickly, the algorithm's continuous reliance on g_{best} means that particles naturally move toward convergence. This behavior makes PSO ill-suited to deployment in vast solution spaces, which is a significant barrier for SNSs and ANNs alike. To combat this and access PSO's rapid convergence, several studies have shown the utility of pre-seeding the particles so that they are proximal to solution troughs. Parsopolous and Vrhatis (2002) [20] initialized particles using Nelder-Mead (1965)'s Nonlinear Simplex Method NSM [21]. While the NSM overhead added to the overall cost, the benefits could be significant. Trelea (2003) added to this effort by adding evidence-based guidance on this while investigating the exploration-exploitation tradeoff inherent to optimization algorithms [22]. This study bypasses this limitation by using FSA output parameter values as a seed for PSO.

3 Experimental Methods

Physical Model. A physical model was developed that approximates the humans tested during the balance trials (Fig. 1, right) [23]. Wherever possible, physical model parameters represent the average physical characteristics of the patients who participated in the original study. Average height (165 cm), mass (60 kg), and center of mass (80 cm) were used. The model, henceforth called the block person, consists of a single body and a foot situated atop an oscillating platform. A simple hinge joint between the body and the foot represented the ankle joint and was controlled by two muscles, situated contralaterally on the posterior and anterior sides of the lower portion of the body. Thus, balance is maintained by actuating either the anterior or posterior muscle, controlled by the SNS. Note that no effort was made to consider human physiology when creating or placing the linear-Hill muscle models (see [26]) between the lower section of the body and the feet. However, the model does capture the basic mechanics of actuation that connect an input signal to muscle activation. Angle data from the ankle joint is transformed to an applied current and sent to the SNS and used as an input for balance control.

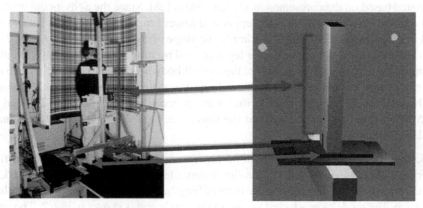

Fig. 1. (Left) Human on platform during balance experiments. (Right) Human balance control model generated in AnimatLab [27]. Lines indicate analogous elements. Red: body, blue: ankle joint, green: foot. Image on left courtesy of [23]

Hill Muscles. AnimatLab makes use of a linear-Hill muscle model. While the modeled muscles do not precisely mimic the detailed properties of the muscles they emulate, they readily capture the essential relationships between force, length, and velocity that underlie their biological counterparts. The muscles consist of a serial spring with coefficient k_{se} with a parallel combination of a force actuator A, dashpot with damping coefficient b, and a parallel spring with coefficient k_{pe}. Contractile tension T is generated by the model when one or more motor neurons depolarize the muscle membrane, according to

$$\frac{dT}{dt} = \frac{k_{se}}{b}\left(k_{pe}x + b\dot{x} - \left(1 + \frac{k_{pe}}{k_{se}}\right)\cdot T + A\right) \tag{7}$$

where x is the displacement of the resting muscle length, $x = l - l_{rest}$. Actuation A is the product of a sigmoid adapter, A_m, and a length-tension component, A_l, such that $A = A_m * A_l$. The sigmoid adapter equation,

$$A_m = \frac{F_{max}}{1 + e^{C(V_o-V)} + B}, \tag{8}$$

relates the maximum muscle force F_{max} to the motor neuron membrane voltage V by a slope coefficient C. V_o and B control the V and F offsets, respectively. The length-tension relation scales A according to

$$A_l = 1 - \frac{x^2}{l_{width}^2} = 1 - \frac{(l - l_{rest})^2}{l_{width}^2} \tag{9}$$

where l_{width} is the length at which the muscle can no longer produce force.

Implementation of the linear-Hill muscle model in AnimatLab was accomplished by setting the necessary coefficient values. Wherever possible, reference values were chosen as the average from values representing people in the 45–69-year range, the demographic containing the patients in the balance experiments. For this study, F_{max} (2300 N) was estimated based on data presented in Thelen (2003) [28]. Since the SNS model operates between -40 mV and -60 mV, the upper and lower limits, respectively, V_o was set to -50 mV. Steepness (530 N/mV) is simply the slope of the sigmoid at V_o. l_{rest} (40 cm) is estimated as the length of the lower leg, deduced by subtracting the average length of the upper leg (~41.4 cm)[1] from half of the overall body height (82.5 cm). l_{width} (2.6 cm) was calculated by manipulating Eq. (9) and represents the length at which <1% tension can be attained. Finally, k_{se} (575 KN/m) was set according to data from [29], and k_{pe} (9.75 KN/m) was set based such that the muscle deflects 4% of its upper limit under maximum loading conditions [30].

SNS. The Hilts SNS model is a faithful representation of the transfer function from Peterka (2003) describing a PD controller + force feedback [25]. A passive time delay was incorporated into the model in the form of lengthened time constants in the feedback gain loop. The model was adapted for use in this study and is shown in Fig. 2. The ankle joint angle θ serves as the input and is mapped such that $-R/2 \le \theta \le R/2$, and is transformed to an applied current that bounds the receiving neuron, θ_{now}, between -40 mV and -60 mV. Since the calculations made by the SNS model must be "positive" and align with the relative value of the input and output neurons, error calculations are made in parallel such that the reference voltage (-50 mV) is subtracted from the incoming θ voltage, and vice versa. The difference is conveyed along excitatory synapses, and out-of-bounds (i.e. inhibitory) values are ignored. To account for this limitation, the model is symmetrical about the horizontal midline (Fig. 2) with most structures featured twice. The SNS model is configured such that the neurons in the top half are active when the body is rotated counterclockwise relative to the foot and the neurons in the bottom half are active when the body is rotated clockwise relative to the foot. Structures appearing equivalently in the CW and CCW halves were grouped during the optimizations. The network outputs muscle activation to the CW and CCW muscles from the Sum neurons that represent the sum of the Kp and Kd pathways. The Kt force feedback circuit functions to minimize steady state errors (see Eq. 6, [31]). Parameter values were initially set to those reported in [8] and according to the FSA constraints.

Optimization. Gain in the Hilts SNS is the product of a tonic input current and the parameter it attenuates, manifested as multiplication subnetworks as described by [7].

---

[1] See Table 29, https://www.cdc.gov/nchs/data/series/sr_03/sr03-046-508.pdf.

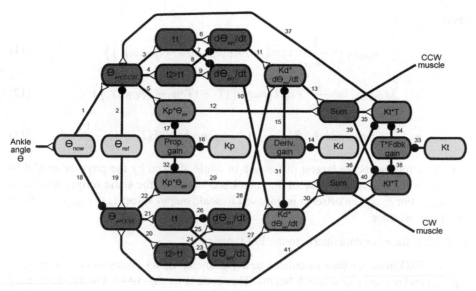

Fig. 2. The synthetic nervous system (SNS) developed by Hilts (2018) and modified for use in this study. For this study, a new system identification was performed using PSO.

For example, the *Kp* neuron (Fig. 2) receives a tonic stimulus and is multiplied times θ_{err} at $Kp \cdot \theta_{err}$. The multiplications subnetworks are comprised of a single excitatory neuron and two inhibitory neurons with synapse E_s-g_s values set identically (e.g., synapses $16 = 17 = 32$). Consequently, each SNS gain circuit is comprised of two sets of E_s-g_s values and a tonic stimulus. To avoid mathematically ambiguous solutions, optimization of the gain circuits was done in two steps, beginning with finding optimized tonic stimulus values. In total, two optimizations were performed. The parameters optimized during the experiment are shown with their start/end values in §4 in Tables 1 and 2.

To perform the PSO, python code was written that implements PSO and iterates AnimatLab simulation files in a standalone capacity, saving time and computational cost. Optimizations are divided into epochs that begin by assigning new parameter values to each particle, using Eqs. (5) and (6). For each particle during an epoch, the code.

- Writes a standalone AnimatLab file using the newly calculated parameter values.
- Runs an AnimatLab iteration using the file generated in the previous step.
- Reads from the AnimatLab text file and fetches the output orientation data for the platform and the block person.
- Calculates the particle error. Error estimations are comprised of three calculations that measure $\theta_{platform}$-θ_{person} variance, muscle tensions $T_{\{CW,CCW\}}$ (a proxy for preventing muscle coactivation), and a muscle activation roughness metric that addresses SNS instabilities. Each error element is scaled such that muscle activation is the most heavily penalized component, and curve roughness is the least. The error for each particle is calculated after each iteration according to:

$$Error = e_{angles} + e_{tensions} + e_{rough} \tag{10}$$

where

$$e_{angles} = \frac{1}{\theta_{max}} \cdot sqrt\left(mean\left((\theta_{platform} - \theta_{person})^2\right)\right) \qquad (11)$$

$$e_{tensions} = \frac{1}{T_{max}} \cdot sqrt\left(mean\left((T - (T_{CW} + T_{CCW}))^2\right)\right) \qquad (12)$$

$$e_{rough} = (mean(abs(diff(T_{CW}))) + mean(abs(diff(T_{CW})))) \cdot \frac{1}{2} - \phi \qquad (13)$$

Here θ_{max} represents the largest difference in angle allowed by the physical model (8 °), T_{max} is the maximum value of T, calculated based on the static torque needed at $\theta = \theta_{max}$. For e_{rough}, an offset ϕ is imposed to scale output values (i.e. $e_{rough} \to 0$) for target performance.

- Returns the error data matrix to the PSO manager.

The PSO manager then calculates new parameter values (velocities) according to Eqs. (5) and (6) and a new epoch begins. This code is on the AARL GitHub repository and available to the public.

Test Conditions. During the experiments, the oscillating platform, which mapped to oscillations described by a cosine wave $\theta = sin(t)$, where θ is in degrees and t is in seconds, from $\pi \leq t < 60$. This configuration differs from the original experiments in that it only captures a single frequency, although it represents the maximum point-to-point variance of 4 degrees used for the patients with vestibular issues. Error was calculated on values during the interval from $\pi \leq t < 60$ seconds according to Eq. (10). Since PSO convergence conditions are difficult to establish analytically [32], tests were performed to establish convergence based on parameter variance across the particles optimized. Bench tests showed the lowest variance occurred at about 60 epochs and 20 particles. Trials performed during the experiments incorporated 20 particles and 200 epochs, and the output solution was the particle configuration with the lowest overall error, g_{best} from Eq. (5).

4   Results

Figure 3 shows a comparison the block body orientation in various solution stages plotted with the platform orientation. During the simulations, the overall goal of the model was to actuate the muscles such that the body and platform maintained alignment. For reference, line (2) shows the output orientation of the block body when the muscles failed to actuate: the body slumped to one side and remained stationary for the duration of the run. Line (3) shows orientation after FSA-guided parameter value selection. The muscles actuated, but the behavior is erratic and the muscles are overcompensating. Line (4) shows orientation after FSA and PSO optimization. The body tracks well with the platform as it oscillates and the phase lag appears to show a delay similar to that seen in human balance control.

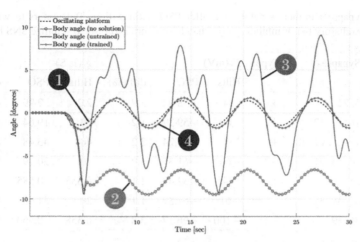

Fig. 3. Orientation of the oscillating platform (1) plotted with block person orientation for various solutions. (2) shows the results where the muscles failed to support the body and slumped to one side, (3) shows orientation after setting synapse parameters according to FSA constraints, indicating a partial solution, and (4) shows body orientation after FSA and PSO solution.

Tables 1 and 2 show the optimized parameter values before and after PSO. Since the mass and overall dimensions of the block body are much larger than that of Hilts' inverted pendulum, gain values are expected to be lower in this study. The tonic stimulus' shown in Table 1 decreased overall, with a 2/3 reduction to Kd and about an order of magnitude for the Kd and Kt inputs. Parameter value change during PSO was modest overall (<10%), with the largest shift to g_s in the inhibitive side of the Kt circuit. The modesty of the changes by PSO lend further validate the analytic methods performed ahead of this work.

Table 1. Neuronal parameters from Hilts SNS optimized by during the first PSO of this study.

Neuron	Parameter	Hilts	PSO
Kd	Stim Current, I_{App} (nA)	12.5	4.2
Kp	Stim Current, I_{App} (nA)	13.5	1.42
Kt	Stim Current, I_{App} (nA)	0.8	0.08

Table 2. Synapse parameters before and after PSO optimization. Type refers to whether the synapse is excitatory (+) or inhibitory (-). * hand-tuned prior to PSO to stabilize SNS behavior.

Circuit	Synapses	Type	E_s(mV)			$g_s(\mu\,S)$		
			Hilts	PSO	diff (%)	Hilts	PSO	diff (%)
Kp	5, 22	+	134	138.92	3.7	2.2	2.29	4.3
	16–17, 32	−	−60	−59.29	1.2	20	19.64	1.8
Kd	10–11, 27–28	+	134	138.24	3.2	40*	43.48	4.3
	14–15, 31	−	−60	−61.37	3.2	20	20.19	0.9
Kt	35, 40	+	134	132.49	1.1	0.558	0.585	4.8
	33–34, 38	−	−61	−61.37	1.1	20	21.68	8.4
	36, 39	−	−100	−96.17	3.8	0.558	0.560	0.3

5 Discussion

We hypothesized that the methods presented here would produce dynamic balance control using muscle activations. We demonstrated that by adopting the FSA-PSO method to a modified SNS, the model successfully found a solution that resulted in good body-platform alignment. This proof-of-concept exercise shows that balance can be maintained by actuating muscles in a fashion that approximates the basic mechanics of proprioception-based human balance control.

Although the method found a viable solution that produces the target behavior, the solution it found relies on high muscle coactivation (Fig. 4), which is not very efficient. The expectation is that only one muscle should be activated during peak output, and during the simulation minimum muscle activation only fell to about 20% of the peak rather than to zero. This is the result of an underconstrained cost function that permitted unrealistic neural activity that caused the muscles to remain activated during most of the simulation. To better approximate the energy minimizing nature of the biology, our next steps will refine the PSO cost calculations to further penalize muscle activation and produce behavior that better mimics that found in humans.

The methods used in this study can be generalized to encompass a broad range of balance and control applications where muscle actuation is required. Increasingly realistic SNSs that incorporate features like type Ib feedback can now be tuned with minimal increases to optimization time and computational cost. Additionally, increases in tuning efficiency allow modelers to devote more time to other aspects of biomimetic modeling, like hardware implementation.

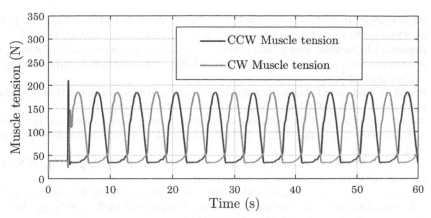

Fig. 4. Muscle activation data output from AnimatLab simulation of the FSA-PSO solution. While the controller maintained good alignment with the platform, it did so by keeping both muscles actuated throughout the simulation.

References

1. Franco, J.A.G., Padilla, J.L. del V., Cisneros, S.O.: Event-based image processing using a neuromorphic vision sensor. In: 2013 IEEE International Autumn Meeting on Power Electronics and Computing (ROPEC), pp. 1–6 (2013). https://doi.org/10.1109/ROPEC.2013.670 2715

2. Chu, M., et al.: Neuromorphic hardware system for visual pattern recognition with memristor array and CMOS NEURON. IEEE Trans. Ind. Electron. **62**, 2410–2419 (2015). https://doi. org/10.1109/TIE.2014.2356439

3. Corradi, F., You, H., Giulioni, M., Indiveri, G.: Decision making and perceptual bistability in spike-based neuromorphic VLSI systems. In: 2015 IEEE International Symposium on Circuits and Systems (ISCAS), pp. 2708–2711 (2015). https://doi.org/10.1109/ISCAS.2015. 7169245

4. Chen, W., Ren, G., Wang, J., Liu, D.: An adaptive locomotion controller for a hexapod robot: CPG, kinematics and force feedback. Sci. Chin. Inf. Sci. **57**(11), 1–18 (2014). https://doi.org/ 10.1007/s11432-014-5148-y

5. Deng, K., et al.: Neuromechanical model of rat hind limb walking with two layer CPGs and muscle synergies. In: Vouloutsi, V., et al. (eds.) Living Machines 2018. LNCS (LNAI), vol. 10928, pp. 134–144. Springer, Cham (2018). https://doi.org/10.1007/978-3-319-95972-6_15

6. Endo, G., Morimoto, J., Matsubara, T., Nakanishi, J., Cheng, G.: Learning CPG-based biped locomotion with a policy gradient method: application to a humanoid robot. Int. J. Robot. Res. **27**, 213–228 (2008). https://doi.org/10.1177/0278364907084980

7. Szczecinski, N.S., Hunt, A.J., Quinn, R.D.: A Functional subnetwork approach to designing synthetic nervous systems that control legged robot locomotion. Front. Neurorobotics. **11**, (2017). https://doi.org/10.3389/fnbot.2017.00037

8. Hilts, W.W., Szczecinski, N.S., Quinn, R.D., Hunt, A.J.: Emulating balance control observed in human test subjects with a neural network. In: Vouloutsi, V., et al. (eds.) Living Machines 2018. LNCS (LNAI), vol. 10928, pp. 200–212. Springer, Cham (2018). https://doi.org/10. 1007/978-3-319-95972-6_21

9. Hilts, W.W., Szczecinski, N.S., Quinn, R.D., Hunt, A.J.: Simulation of human balance control using an inverted pendulum model. In: Mangan, M., Cutkosky, M., Mura, A., Verschure,

P.F.M.J., Prescott, T., Lepora, N. (eds.) Living Machines 2017. LNCS (LNAI), vol. 10384, pp. 170–180. Springer, Cham (2017). https://doi.org/10.1007/978-3-319-63537-8_15

10. Hopfield, J.J.: Neurons with graded response have collective computational properties like those of two-state neurons. Proc. Natl. Acad. Sci. **81**, 3088–3092 (1984). https://doi.org/10.1073/pnas.81.10.3088

11. Beer, R.D., Gallagher, J.C.: Evolving dynamical neural networks for adaptive behavior. Adapt. Behav. **1**, 91–122 (1992). https://doi.org/10.1177/105971239200100105

12. Wilson, H.R., Cowan, J.D.: Excitatory and inhibitory interactions in localized populations of model neurons. Biophys. J. **12**, 1–24 (1972). https://doi.org/10.1016/S0006-3495(72)86068-5

13. Kennedy, J., Eberhart, R.: Particle swarm optimization. In: Proceedings of the ICNN95 - International Conference Neural Network (1995)

14. Kennedy, J.: The particle swarm: social adaptation of knowledge. In: Proceedings of 1997 IEEE International Conference on Evolutionary Computation (ICEC 1997), pp. 303–308 (1997). https://doi.org/10.1109/ICEC.1997.592326

15. Banks, A., Vincent, J., Anyakoha, C.: A review of particle swarm optimization. Part I: background and development. Nat. Comput. **6**, 467–484 (2007). https://doi.org/10.1007/s11047-007-9049-5

16. van den Bergh, F., Engelbrecht, A.P.: A new locally convergent particle swarm optimiser. In: IEEE International Conference on Systems, Man and Cybernetics, vol. 3, p. 6 (2002). https://doi.org/10.1109/ICSMC.2002.1176018

17. Riget, J., Vesterstrøm, J.S.: A diversity-guided particle swarm optimizer-the ARPSO. Dept. Comput. Sci Univ Aarhus Aarhus Den. Technical report. 2, 2002 (2002)

18. Silva, A., Neves, A., Costa, E.: An empirical comparison of particle swarm and predator prey optimisation. In: O'Neill, M., Sutcliffe, R.F.E., Ryan, C., Eaton, M., Griffith, N.J.L. (eds.) Artificial Intelligence and Cognitive Science. AICS 2002. Lecture Notes in Computer Science, vol. 2464, pp. 103–110. Springer, Heidelberg (2002). https://doi.org/10.1007/3-540-45750-X_13

19. Veeramachaneni, K., Peram, T., Mohan, C., Osadciw, L.A.: Optimization using particle swarms with near neighbor interactions. In: Cantú-Paz, E., et al. (eds.) GECCO 2003. LNCS, vol. 2723, pp. 110–121. Springer, Heidelberg (2003). https://doi.org/10.1007/3-540-45105-6_10

20. Parsopoulos, K.E., Vrahatis, M.N.: Initializing the particle swarm optimizer using the nonlinear simplex method. Adv. Intell. Syst. Fuzzy Syst. Evol. Comput. **216**, 1–6 (2002)

21. Nelder, J.A., Mead, R.: A simplex method for function minimization. Comput. J. **7**, 308–313 (1965). https://doi.org/10.1093/comjnl/7.4.308

22. Trelea, I.C.: The particle swarm optimization algorithm: convergence analysis and parameter selection. Inf. Process. Lett. **85**, 317–325 (2003). https://doi.org/10.1016/S0020-0190(02)00447-7

23. Peterka, R.J.: Sensorimotor integration in human postural control. J. Neurophysiol. **88**, 1097–1118 (2002)

24. Pasma, J.H., Assländer, L., van Kordelaar, J., de Kam, D., Mergner, T., Schouten, A.C.: Evidence in support of the independent channel model describing the sensorimotor control of human stance using a humanoid robot. Front. Comput. Neurosci. **12**, 13 (2018)

25. Peterka, R.J.: Simplifying the complexities of maintaining balance. IEEE Eng. Med. Biol. Mag. **22**, 63–68 (2003). https://doi.org/10.1109/MEMB.2003.1195698

26. Hill, A.V.: The heat of shortening and the dynamic constants of muscle. Proc. R. Soc. Lond. B Biol. Sci. **126**, 136–195 (1938). https://doi.org/10.1098/rspb.1938.0050

27. Cofer, D., Cymbalyuk, G., Reid, J., Zhu, Y., Heitler, W., Edwards, D.: AnimatLab: a 3D graphics environment for neuromechanical simulations. J. Neurosci. Meth. **187**, 280–288 (2010). https://doi.org/10.1016/j.jneumeth.2010.01.005

28. Thelen, D.G.: Adjustment of muscle mechanics model parameters to simulate dynamic contractions in older adults. J. Biomech. Eng. **125**, 70–77 (2003). https://doi.org/10.1115/1.153 1112

29. Pearson, K.G., Ekeberg, Ö., Büschges, A.: Assessing sensory function in locomotor systems using neuro-mechanical simulations. Trends Neurosci. **29**, 625–631 (2006). https://doi.org/ 10.1016/j.tins.2006.08.007

30. Meijer, K., Grootenboer, H.J., Koopman, H.F.J.M., van der Linden, B.J.J.J., Huijing, P.A.: A Hill type model of rat medial gastrocnemius muscle that accounts for shortening history effects. J. Biomech. **31**, 555–563 (1998). https://doi.org/10.1016/S0021-9290(98)00048-7

31. Hilts, W.W., Szczecinski, N.S., Quinn, R.D., Hunt, A.J.: A Dynamic neural network designed using analytical methods produces dynamic control properties similar to an analogous classical controller. IEEE Control Syst. Lett. **3**, 320–325 (2019). https://doi.org/10.1109/LCSYS. 2018.2871126

32. Clerc, M., Kennedy, J.: The particle swarm - explosion, stability, and convergence in a multidimensional complex space. IEEE Trans. Evol. Comput. **6**, 58–73 (2002). https://doi.org/10. 1109/4235.985692

Motivational Modulation of Consummatory Behaviour and Learning in a Robot Model of Spatial Navigation

Alejandro Jimenez-Rodriguez[1,3]([✉]) [iD] and Tony J. Prescott[2,3] [iD]

[1] Sheffield Hallam University, Sheffield, UK
a.jimenez-rodriguez@sheffield.ac.uk
[2] University of Sheffield, Sheffield, UK
t.j.prescott@sheffield.ac.uk
[3] Sheffield Robotics, Sheffield, UK

Abstract. We present a biomimetic model of motivated behaviour based on the network architecture of the mammalian hypothalamus and its interaction with brain systems involved in reward, memory and decision-making. Specifically, a novel model of the hypothalamus, viewed as a layered structure, is integrated with a previously-developed model of the hippocampal-striatal network controlling a simulated robot in a navigation task. Hypothalamic modulation of model dopamine signals allows the robot to learn the location of reward while regulating simulated food intake. When 'satiated' the robot explores, when 'hungry' it moves towards the learned food source. We discuss the potential uses and future challenges of such models in the development of autonomous robots.

Keywords: Hypothalamus · Motivation · Reinforcement learning · Navigation

1 Introduction

Behaviour in animals is orchestrated to satisfy different needs arising from the homeostatic constraints that make life possible [23]. A hungry animal, for example, needs to forage for food while remembering the location of reliable food sources that can be exploited in the future. On the other hand, a satiated animal is free to explore and engage in other behaviours, typically in order to the satisfy other needs (e.g. mating, nesting, etc.). Robots lack natural needs and therefore have no intrinsic motivational grounding for their behaviour [14]. The absence of any genuine needs has been argued to be a fundamental and immutable difference between robots and animals [4]. On the other hand, one could argue that robots can have needs in the sense that they require certain resources and inputs (power and maintenance, for example) to function properly. The instantiation of goals, provided by humans, in robot control systems can also play a similar role to natural needs in co-ordinating behaviour.

Supported by Horizon 2020, Horizon Europe, and UK Research and Innovation.

F. Meder et al. (Eds.): Living Machines 2023, LNAI 14158, pp. 240–253, 2023.
https://doi.org/10.1007/978-3-031-39504-8_17

Many animal physiological needs, for instance, to maintain blood oxygen and sugar levels, hydration, body temperature and so on, are regulated by the central and autonomic nervous systems. A layered architecture of brain systems is involved in this regulation [8,25,26,29], where the hypothalamus, a forebrain structure situated near the midline of the brain, plays a critical role. In this work, we propose a biomimetic model of the hypothalamus and its interaction with brain systems involved in decision-making (basal ganglia) and navigation (hippocampus). We show that this model can simulate alternation between consummatory behaviour and learning through the regulation of simulated physiological variables. Our long-term goal is to better understand the neural basis of motivated behaviour in animals, including humans. We consider that such an understanding could help illuminate these critical differences between evolved organisms and intelligent artefacts such as robots.

2   The Role of the Hypothalamus in Motivated Behaviour

As noted, in mammalian brains, the hypothalamus plays a critical role in the orchestration of motivated behaviour. In particular, it acts as an integrator for bodily signals that provide an up-to-date picture of homeostatic needs, and delivers outputs based on these signals to a wide network of brain regions that drive different aspects of behaviour [5,25]. The hypothalamus is a heteregeneous structure composed of multiple subregions, of particular importance, to the current work, are the dorsal and lateral areas. The dorsal hypothalamus (DH) is in contact with physiological milieu and generates signals that correlate with lower and higher levels of a variety of substances within the body. Those signals are used to drive a motivational state representation in the lateral hypothalamus (LH) that also integrates signals from other cortical and subcortical structures [3,10,24].

Approach and avoid signals generated by the LH are used to modulate the downstream dopaminergic neurons in the ventral tegmental area (VTA) [17,24] which project to major areas of the brain, and prominently to the nucleus accumbens (NAcc), which is an input structure for action selection systems in the basal ganglia [9,21]. VTA dopamine acts as both a motivational proxy and as a saliency signal that drives learning [13,16,21]. Motivational functions of dopamine include stimulation of behavioural activation, effort and appetite [1] and modulation of action selection in the basal ganglia [19], Phasic increases and decreases in dopamine, locked to environmental stimuli, allow for the modulation of reinforcement learning in regions including the striatum and the hippocampus [22]. Hence, in the current model simulated dopamine signals act as both a learning signal and to activate different motivational systems. GABAergic signals from the VTA have been found to act along with dopamine to allow associative learning in the NAcc [7]. In this work we use a similar chollinergic signal to modulate the plasticity of the hippocampal-striatal network.

In previous work, we presented a robotic model of the hippocampal-striatal network that allows the robot to learn the location of a reward [28]; we have also separately introduced a layered dynamical model of motivation [11]. The current model combines simulation of some of the neuronal networks involved in motivation, representing the different regions discussed in the previous paragraphs. This model is integrated with the hippocampal network in a layered architecture [18,29] and tested using a simulation of the animal-like robot platform, MiRo-e [15].

In the following sections we introduce the main components of the architecture: the motivational model, the cholinergic network and the navigational model. Then we present some simulation results.

3 The Motivational Model

As described in the introduction, our motivational model is composed of three layers as shown in Fig. 1. In each layer we have abstracted a network motif that performs specific computations relevant for the encoding motivational state of the agent and the corresponding modulation of learning and behaviour. Each of the neurons in the model is a rate neuron:

$$\tau \frac{dx_k}{dt} = -x_k + f(\sum w_{jk}x_j + \theta_k), \tag{1}$$

where, x_k is the firing rate of the k_{th} neuron, w_{jk} the synaptic weights and θ_i a bias term. The activation function is sigmoidal $f(x) = 1/(1+\exp(-\beta x))$. Table 1 shows the different neuron populations in the model.

Table 1. Abbreviations used for the different neuron populations in the model.

Variable	Description
x_s	Sensitive neurons in the Hammel network
x_i	Insensitive neurons in the Hammel network
x_h	Hunger neurons
x_s	Satiety neurons
x_{app}	Approach pathway neurons
x_{av}	Avoid pathway neurons
x_{acc}	Nucleus accumbens neurons
x_{vta_gaba}	VTA GABA neurons
x_{da}	Dopaminergic neurons
x_{msn}	Medium Spiny Neurons in the striatum
x_{cin}	Collinergic interneurons

In the upper layer or ventricular part, representing the dorsal hypothalamus, we propose a version of the network motif known as the *Hammel model* [6] in order to encode "hunger" and "satiety" states. This mechanism effectively defines a set-point based upon physiological signals, which are modeled as first order ODEs:

$$\tau \frac{du}{dt} = \alpha(1 - u) - ur(t), \tag{2}$$

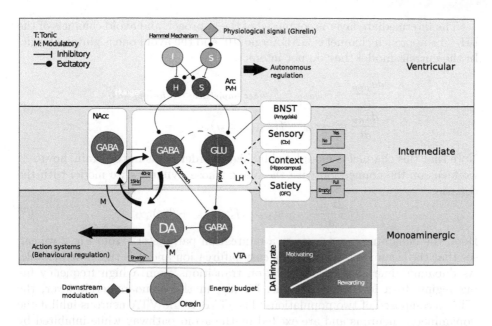

Fig. 1. Motivational circuit inspired by the hypothalamus architecture. The ventricular part, modelled on the dorsal hypothalamus, is in contact with the physiological millieu, and drives hunger (H) and satiety (S) signals that activate approach and avoid channels in the Lateral Hypothalamus (LH). These signals are reinforced by the nucleus accumbens. The approach pathway drives behavioural activation by disinhibiting VTA dopamine neurons (DA), shown here in the monoaminergic layer, by removing tonic inhibition from GABA cells. Inset: From the accumbens perspective, different dopamine regimes drive exploration/explotation trade-offs. See text for further explanation.

where $r(t)$ is the reward obtained from the environment, α, an accumulation rate, and τ a time constant that determines the timescale. Physiological signals accumulate indicating increasing levels of thirst, hunger, etc. The four neurons in the mechanism evolve according to the dynamics:

$$
\begin{aligned}
\tau_s \frac{dx_s}{dt} &= -x_s + f(w_u u), \\
\frac{dx_i}{dt} &= 0, \\
\tau \frac{dx_h}{dt} &= -x_h + f(w_{s \to h} x_s + w_{i \to h} x_i), \\
\tau \frac{dx_{st}}{dt} &= -x_{st} + f(w_{s \to st} x_s + w_{i \to st} x_i).
\end{aligned}
\tag{3}
$$

Here, the sensitive neurons x_s need to overcome the constant firing rate of the insensitive ones x_i to elicit hunger x_h state; otherwise the output x_{st} indicate a satiety state. We assume $\tau = 1$ for the rest of the model, except for τ_s which is adjusted to the particular choice of physiological signal.

The intermediate layer is composed of the approach and avoid channels of the LH. The approach channel is GABAergic [10] and the avoid one is glutamatergic. In the current model they do not interact.

$$\frac{dx_{app}}{dt} = -x_{app} + f(w_{acc \to app}x_{acc} + w_{h \to app}x_h),$$
$$\frac{dx_{av}}{dt} = -x_{av} + f(w_{st \to av}x_{st}),$$
(4)

Note that this channel is modulated by higher order areas in the brain, however, we focus on the connection with the NAcc whose dynamics we model with the equation:

$$\frac{dx_{Acc}}{dt} = -x_{Acc} + f(wx_{Acc} + \theta_{da}).$$
(5)

Here, the dopamine input, acts as a bifurcation parameter. From Fig. 2 we can see that the accumbens undergoes a cusp bifurcation and it is therefore bistable. As dopamine increases, the population transitions from a high frequency firing regime to a low frequency one. Finally, in the monoaminergic layer, the VTA is composed of two populations. The GABAergic VTA neurons inhibit the dopaminergic neurons and are excited by the avoid pathway while inhibited by the approach pathway. Thus, behavioural activation works by disinhibition of dopamine neurons. The full model of the VTA is:

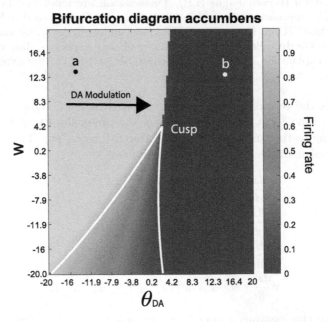

Fig. 2. Bifurcation diagram of the nucleus accumbens showing a cusp catastrophe. The dopamine signal drives the firing rate to a low frequency firing in an abrupt change. This allows for sharp transition between motivated behaviour and exploration.

$$\frac{dx_{vta\_gaba}}{dt} = -x_{vta\_gaba} + f(w_{app \to vta\_gaba}x_{app} + w_{av \to vta\_gaba}x_{av})$$

$$\frac{dx_{da}}{dt} = -x_{da} + f(w_{vta\_gaba \to da}x_{vta\_gaba} + \theta_{orexin}). \tag{6}$$

Note that we have added an *orexin* related modulation term to modulate the excitability of the dopaminergic neurons and therefore the timescales used by acetylcholine in the next section. As shown in Fig. 1, the approach and avoid pathways in the intermediate part are subject to modulation from different brain areas [5].

4   Cholinergic Signal

To modulate learning, we generate a transient signal λ_{ach} by combining the GABAergic and dopaminergic outputs from the VTA in two steps circuit similar to [7]:

$$\frac{dx_{msn}}{dt} = -x_{msn} + f(w_{vta\_gaba \to msn}x_{vta\_gaba} + \theta_{msn})$$

$$\frac{dx_{cin}}{dt} = -x_{cin} + f(w_{da \to cin}x_{da} + w_{msn \to cin}x_{msn} + \theta_{cin}) \tag{7}$$

with $\lambda_{ach} = \Theta(x_{cin} - b)$. Note that the GABA input disinhibits the cholinergic output which is being excited by dopamine; the parameters are chosen in such a way that the CIN output tracks the start and end of the consummatory behaviour (see Fig. 3). On the other hand, the teaching signal is a binary value that determines when learning should occur (see next section).

5   The Navigation Model

The hippocampal-striatal model has been previously published in [28], here we show only an overview of the important parts of its integration with the motivational model. The main parts of the model are shown in Fig. 4. For the model we assume the MiRo-e is located in a simulated open arena and its coordinates are known at each step.

5.1   Hippocampal Network

The hippocampal network is composed of 100 place cells connected in a grid to their immediate neighbours (Fig. 4). Their firing rate is given by:

$$x_j = \begin{cases} 0 & \text{if } x_j^{'} < 0 \\ 100 & \text{if } x_j^{'} > 100 \\ x_j^{'} & \text{otherwise.} \end{cases} \tag{8}$$

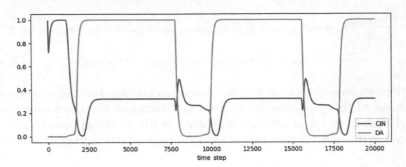

Fig. 3. The activity of the Cholinergic interneurons tracks the start and end of behavioural activation. Shown is a fraction of the simulation DA and CIN time series to illustrate this behaviour.

with the rate defined as rectified function of its current:

$$x'_j = \alpha \left(I_j - \epsilon \right)$$

The dynamics of this current are given by:

$$\tau_I \frac{d}{dt} I_j = -I_j + \psi_j I_j^{syn} + I_j^{place}, \tag{9}$$

where, I_j^{syn} is the synaptic current from neighboring place cells, ψ_j is the intrinsic plasticity (see paper [28] for details) and I_j^{place} is the input due to a place field given by:

$$I_j^{place} = I_{max}^p \exp \left[-\frac{(x_{MiRo}^c - x_j^c)^2 + (y_{MiRo}^c - y_j^c)^2}{2d^2} \right], \tag{10}$$

where the position of the robot is assumed to be known. The synaptic input is modulated by the cholinergic output of the motivational model (see previous section). Additionally it possesses depression and facilitation terms D_k and F_k to ensure the correct dynamics during learning:

$$I_j^{syn} = \lambda_{ach} \sum_{k=1}^{8} w_{jk}^{place} x_k D_k F_k, \tag{11}$$

see [28] for details on the depression and facilitation dynamics.

5.2   Action Cells

There are 72 action cells, each coding for $1/360$ degrees of orientation. Firing rates are drawn from a normal distribution

$$y_i \sim \mathcal{N} \left(\tilde{y}_i, \sigma^2 \right), \tag{12}$$

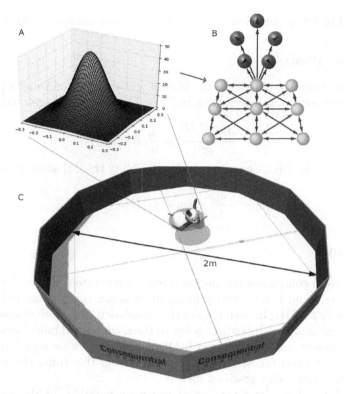

Fig. 4. Hippocampal striatal network. A. Each place field is a Gaussian centered at a given preferred position. B. The network is composed of the hippocampal network that has a feed-forward projection to action cells. C. The simulations are performed in a circular arena with the robotic platform MiRo-e.

where the mean is computed according to

$$\tilde{y}_i = \frac{x_{da}}{1 + \exp\left[-c_1 \sum_{j=1}^{100} w_{ij}^{PC\text{-}AC} x_j - c_2\right]}, \tag{13}$$

and where x_{da} is the output of the dopaminergic cells in the VTA. Note that firing rate is modulated by the place cells. The target direction of the robot is computed by tallying the preferred directions of all cells weighted by their firing rates:

$$\theta_{target} = \arctan\left(\frac{\sum_i y_i \sin\theta_i}{\sum_i y_i \cos\theta_i}\right). \tag{14}$$

The magnitude of the activation in that direction is computed as the magnitude of the population vector.

$$m_{target} = \sqrt{\left(\sum_i y_i \sin\theta_i\right)^2 + \left(\sum_i y_i \cos\theta_i\right)^2}, \tag{15}$$

this is used in action selection (exploration vs. consummatory behaviour).

5.3   PC → Plasticity

The synapses from the place cells are plastic and are updated using a policy gradient RL methods (see full derivation in [28]). The weights are updated according to:

$$\frac{dw_{ij}^{PC\text{-}AC}}{dt} = \frac{\eta}{\sigma^2} R e_{ij}, \tag{16}$$

where $R = \lambda_{ach}$ in this case and e_{ij} is the eligibility trace that evolves according to

$$\frac{de_{ij}}{dt} = -\frac{e_{ij}}{\tau_e} + (y_i - \tilde{y}_i)(1 - \tilde{y}_i)\tilde{y}_i x_j. \tag{17}$$

6   Results

We performed a continuous simulation during 300000 steps where the simulated MiRo-e robot could behave freely in an open arena using Gazebo 11 and the MiRo MDK (v201904). In each step of the simulation, the motivational model is integrated first and then its output is fed to the navigational model whose output is the presence or absence of reward. Once a Acetylcholine signal is detected, behaviour is stopped for as long as it lasts; during this time, the weights are updated using the policy gradient method.

In Fig. 5 we show the dynamics of the main variables of the motivational model during the whole session. We chose the hormone *Ghrelin* to act as the physiological proxy of hunger. The robot manages to keep the hormone levels from saturating and therefore is able to survive. Note that the location of the reward is not known before hand. If learning is turned off (Fig. 6), the robot only randomly satisfies its needs when passing by the location of the rewards.

It is useful to investigate the trajectories from the start to the end of behavioural activation, as indicated by the cholinergic signal (Fig. 3). When learning is activated, the trajectories clearly converge to the reward position during the consummatory behaviour and away from it when the robot is satiated (Fig. 7). The transparency of the trajectories has been made proportional to the index of the consummatory event. On the other hand, when learning is deactivated, trajectories remain random (Fig. 8).

7   Conclusions and Future Work

We have proposed a model of motivated consummatory behaviour that integrates hypothalamic and hippocampal-striatal networks showing that this model is able to modulate learning whilst satisfying certain homeostatic constraints. The simulated MiRo-e robot, with this control architecture, is able to find and remember the reward location, satisfying its needs continuously, while performing exploratory behaviour whenever the energy budget allows.

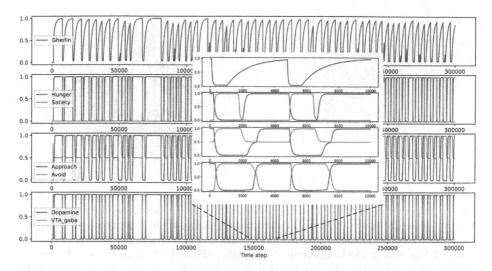

Fig. 5. Time series of the main variables of the motivational model during the whole recording session. Note that the needs are better satisfied over time. From top to bottom. The hormone representing hunger increases over time and decreases once the reward has been consumed. The hunger and satiety signals alternate depending upon the hormone levels. The approach and avoid pathways drive behavioural activation. Dopaminergic and GABAergic signals in the VTA alternate to modulate behaviour and learning.

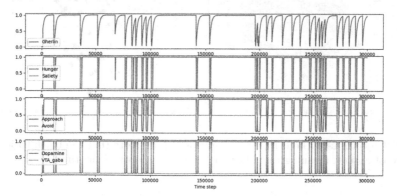

Fig. 6. Time series without learning. The robot satisfies its needs only when it finds the reward by accident.

Although our motivational model simplifies the dynamics of each of the regions involved we consider that it captures important roles of key circuits involving the hypothalamus and VTA in the control of behavioural activation. In particular, it demonstrates that a push-pull motivational system that operates through parallel approach and avoid channels can allow the orchestration of motivational systems in order to satisfy needs and to generate useful reward pre-

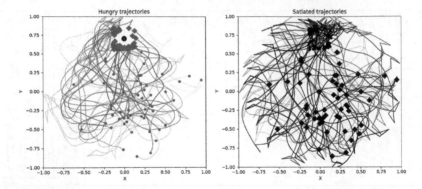

Fig. 7. Trajectories of MiRo during consummatory and exploratory behaviours. The starting point of the trajectory is marked with a circle, while the ending point with a diamond. The place of the reward is marked with a cross. The alpha channel represents time, with opaque trajectories representing later trials. Left. Trajectories of consummatory behaviours when the robot gets hungry, it can be seen that the location of the rewards has been learn and performance improves over time. Right. Once the robot is satiated, it is free to engage of exploration away from the reward until its energy reserves are depleted.

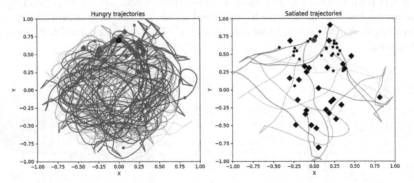

Fig. 8. Trajectories without learning. Same as before. Note that the black trajectories are almost absent, meaning that the robot is hungry most of the time.

diction errors. We intend to explore potential uses for this model in biomimetic control of autonomous robots for continual learning, and as a platform to investigate motivation-related disorders such as addiction and compulsive eating.

Future work will also include developing a more detailed model of the avoid pathway that involves serotonin and different regions of the nucleus accumbens [27]. This will allow extinction and punishment to be explored alongside reward. The role of acetylcholine in the model should also be refined and, importantly, the roles of nucleus accumbens and amygdala in motivational phenomena such as "wanting" and "liking" [2], the current model can be considered to represent only wanting.

Even though the model comprises just one explicit motivation vs. an explicit drive to explore, we think that the layered architecture presented could harbor multiple motivations as a result of the separation between physiological state (in the ventricular layer) and motivational state (in the intermediate layer). Indeed, this excitatory-inhibitory balanced networks have been shown to support the creation of multiple assemblies and are a good target for modulation of higher areas as shown in Fig. 1.

Overall, this work is a contribution to the ongoing effort to integrate motivational aspects in robotic cognitive architecture and in machine learning in general [12,20,29]. Looking further ahead, in animals, needs and motivation are closely related to emotions and feelings, and are processed in similar areas of the brain. This relationship between the motivational and experiential aspects of being is poorly understood, however, as noted by Craig:

"...our affective feelings derive from the brain networks that generate flexible and adaptable emotional behaviors, which evolution built by expanding upon the ancient homeostatic neural systems that automatically take care of the body. In other words, the affective feelings that you experience are interoceptive reflections of emotional motivations, which are expressed by activity throughout the peripheral and central autonomic systems of your body and your brain and which produce behavior that you "feel" as it happens." [8](p. 12).

We therefore consider that robot modelling that illuminates the neural basis for motivation could ultimately provide a better understanding of the role of the brain in generating affective experience.

Acknowledgements. This work was supported by the EU H2020 Programme as part of the FET Flagship Human Brain Project (HBP-SGA3, grant no. 945539), and specifically, through the CATRA (Cognitive Architecture for Therapy Robots and Avatars) project which was supported by the EBRAINS Research Infrastructure Voucher Programme. It was also supported by the UK Research and Innovation (UKRI) under the UK government's Horizon Europe funding guarantee for the EIC Pathfinder CAVAA project. We are grateful to Matthew Whelan and Eleni Vasilaki with whom the hippocampal model was developed.

Declaration of Interest. TJP is a director and shareholder of Consequential Robotics Ltd which develops the MiRo robot, and Bettering Our Worlds (BOW) ltd which develops robot software. AJR has no competing interests.

Code Availability. The code is available at https://github.com/aljiro/motivation_lm.

References

1. Beeler, J.A., Frazier, C.R., Zhuang, X.: Putting desire on a budget: dopamine and energy expenditure, reconciling reward and resources. Front. Integr. Neurosci. **6**, 49 (2012)

2. Berridge, K.C.: Food reward: brain substrates of wanting and liking. Neurosci. Biobehav. Rev. **20**(1), 1–25 (1996)
3. Berthoud, H.R., Münzberg, H.: The lateral hypothalamus as integrator of metabolic and environmental needs: from electrical self-stimulation to optogenetics. Physiol. Behav. **104**(1), 29–39 (2011)
4. Boden, M.: Robot says: Whatever (2018). https://aeon.co/essays/the-robots-wont-take-over-because-they-couldnt-care-less
5. Bonnavion, P., Mickelsen, L.E., Fujita, A., De Lecea, L., Jackson, A.C.: Hubs and spokes of the lateral hypothalamus: cell types, circuits and behaviour. J. Physiol. **594**(22), 6443–6462 (2016)
6. Boulant, J.A.: Neuronal basis of Hammel's model for set-point thermoregulation. J. Appl. Physiol. **100**(4), 1347–1354 (2006)
7. Brown, M.T., Tan, K.R., O'Connor, E.C., Nikonenko, I., Muller, D., Lüscher, C.: Ventral tegmental area GABA projections pause accumbal cholinergic interneurons to enhance associative learning. Nature **492**(7429), 452–456 (2012)
8. Craig, A.D.: How Do You Feel? Princeton University Press, Princeton (2015)
9. Humphries, M.D., Prescott, T.J.: The ventral basal ganglia, a selection mechanism at the crossroads of space, strategy, and reward. Prog. Neurobiol. **90**, 385–417 (2010). https://doi.org/10.1016/j.pneurobio.2009.11.003
10. Jennings, J.H., Rizzi, G., Stamatakis, A.M., Ung, R.L., Stuber, G.D.: The inhibitory circuit architecture of the lateral hypothalamus orchestrates feeding. Science **341**(6153), 1517–1521 (2013)
11. Jimenez-Rodriguez, A., Prescott, T.J., Schmidt, R., Wilson, S.: A framework for resolving motivational conflict via attractor dynamics. In: Living Machines 2020. LNCS (LNAI), vol. 12413, pp. 192–203. Springer, Cham (2020). https://doi.org/10.1007/978-3-030-64313-3_19
12. Keramati, M., Gutkin, B.: A reinforcement learning theory for homeostatic regulation. Adv. Neural Inf. Process. Syst. **24** (2011)
13. Kremer, Y., Flakowski, J., Rohner, C., Lüscher, C.: Context-dependent multiplexing by individual VTA dopamine neurons. J. Neurosci. **40**, 7489–7509 (2020). https://doi.org/10.1523/JNEUROSCI.0502-20.2020
14. McFarland, D., Bösser, T., Bosser, T.: Intelligent Behavior in Animals and Robots. MIT Press, Cambridge (1993)
15. Mitchinson, B., Prescott, T.J.: MIRO: a robot mammal with a biomimetic brain-based control system. In: Lepora, N.F.F., Mura, A., Mangan, M., Verschure, P.F.M.J.F.M.J., Desmulliez, M., Prescott, T.J.J. (eds.) Living Machines 2016. LNCS (LNAI), vol. 9793, pp. 179–191. Springer, Cham (2016). https://doi.org/10.1007/978-3-319-42417-0_17
16. Mohebi, A., et al.: Dissociable dopamine dynamics for learning and motivation. Nature **570**(7759), 65–70 (2019)
17. Nieh, E.H., et al.: Inhibitory input from the lateral hypothalamus to the ventral tegmental area disinhibits dopamine neurons and promotes behavioral activation. Neuron **90**(6), 1286–1298 (2016)
18. Prescott, T.J., Redgrave, P., Gurney, K.: Layered control architectures in robots and vertebrates. Adapt. Behav. **7**(1), 99–127 (1999)
19. Redgrave, P., Prescott, T.J., Gurney, K.: The basal ganglia: a vertebrate solution to the selection problem? Neuroscience **89**, 1009–1023 (1999). https://doi.org/10.1016/S0306-4522(98)00319-4
20. Rosado, O.G., Amil, A.F., Freire, I.T., Verschure, P.F.: Drive competition underlies effective allostatic orchestration. Front. Robot. AI **9** (2022)

21. Salamone, J.D., Correa, M.: The mysterious motivational functions of mesolimbic dopamine. Neuron **76**(3), 470–485 (2012)
22. Sjulson, L., Peyrache, A., Cumpelik, A., Cassataro, D., Buzsáki, G.: Cocaine place conditioning strengthens location-specific hippocampal coupling to the nucleus accumbens. Neuron **98**(5), 926–934 (2018)
23. Sterling, P.: Allostasis: a model of predictive regulation. Physiol. Behav. **106**(1), 5–15 (2012)
24. Stuber, G.D., Wise, R.A.: Lateral hypothalamic circuits for feeding and reward, January 2016. https://doi.org/10.1038/nn.4220
25. Swanson, L.W.: Cerebral hemisphere regulation of motivated behavior. Brain Res. **886**(1–2), 113–164 (2000)
26. Swanson, L.W.: Brain Architecture: Understanding the Basic Plan. Oxford University Press, Oxford (2003)
27. Wert-Carvajal, C., Reneaux, M., Tchumatchenko, T., Clopath, C.: Dopamine and serotonin interplay for valence-based spatial learning. Cell Rep. **39**(2), 110645 (2022)
28. Whelan, M.T., Jimenez-Rodriguez, A., Prescott, T.J., Vasilaki, E.: A robotic model of hippocampal reverse replay for reinforcement learning. Bioinspiration Biomi. **18**(1), 015007 (2022)
29. Wilson, S.P., Prescott, T.J.: Scaffolding layered control architectures through constraint closure: insights into brain evolution and development. Philos. Trans. R. Soc. B **377**(1844), 20200519 (2022)

Biomimetic Research Analyzed

Topical Grouping of Thousands of Biomimetics Articles According to Their Goals, Results and Methods

Théophile Carniel[1,2(✉)], Leo Cazenille[1], Jean-Michel Dalle[2,3], and José Halloy[1]

[1] Université Paris Cité, CNRS, LIED UMR 8236, 75006 Paris, France
[2] Agoranov, Paris, France
tc@agoranov.com
[3] Sorbonne Université, Paris, France

Abstract. Here we discuss the limitations of current topic modeling methods for scientific documents, which are often too coarse-grained to identify the specific themes of an article accurately. This is particularly challenging in interdisciplinary research, such as in the field of Living Machines, where scientific methods from different fields may be used to achieve a scientific goal. To address this problem, we extend previous methods and propose a new targeted topic modeling method that goes beyond a simple thematic classification. Our data processing relies on ChatGPT to extract information from abstracts of the corpus, which are then classified into thematic clusters using topic modeling algorithms. This approach adds clustering of the articles according to the scientific goal, the type of method used, and the type of results obtained. By using this technique, each document is associated with three targeted themes and one general theme, allowing for more fine-grained clustering. We demonstrate the effectiveness of this method in biomimetics with a representative corpus of 2099 documents. Our framework provides a detailed scientometric analysis of different topics in the field.

Keywords: Bioinspiration · Text Mining · Bibliography · Natural Language Processing · BERT · Scientometrics · ChatGPT

1 Introduction

The Living Machines conference began a decade ago with a focus on developing real-world technologies by understanding principles underlying living systems and communication signals between living and artificial systems. This led to the emergence of an interdisciplinary scientific field, drawing from robotics, computer science, biology, and natural sciences [11,17] However, due to the field's interdisciplinary nature and rapid development, it is challenging for any one person to have a comprehensive understanding of the current state-of-the-art in Living Machines.

F. Meder et al. (Eds.): Living Machines 2023, LNAI 14158, pp. 257–272, 2023.
https://doi.org/10.1007/978-3-031-39504-8_18

More generally, as the number of scientific publications continues to grow exponentially, it becomes increasingly difficult to get an overview of the state of the art in a scientific or technical field. Researchers are no longer able to process and keep up with all of the information contained in the ever-increasing number of articles in order to keep up with their research community. This is particularly difficult for interdisciplinary research that requires tracking the state of the art in different areas of science and technology.

Recent progress in the field of Natural Language Processing (NLP) made possible the automatic identification of the themes of a scientific document. Namely, topic modeling methods can be used to regroup the documents of a corpus into thematic clusters.

Our previous works proposed a topic modeling approach able to automatically regroup Biomimetics articles according to their overarching topics [4,5]. While these approaches were a significant progress towards the thematic characterization of Biomimetics articles, they had difficulty classifying documents linking several scientific sub-fields together.

Indeed, current topic modeling methods for scientific documents are currently too coarse-grained. For instance, it is currently difficult to disentangle the sub-field of the scientific goal of an article (e.g. solve a robotic task) from the sub-fields used to accomplish this goal (e.g. bioinspired optimization) and to the type of obtained results (e.g. increased energy efficiency). This is especially relevant in interdisciplinary research where the scientific methods of an article may be from a different field than the scientific goal.

Objectives

Here, we describe a new targeted topic modeling method for scientific documents that rely only on specific parts of the document ("aspects") to perform clustering: scientific goal, type of method, type of results. As such, each document is associated with four clusters (three targeted aspects and one general theme), which allows a more fine-grained clustering. We show that this approach provides a fine-grained scientometric analysis of different topics in the field of Biomimetics. We apply this method to analyze a corpus of 2099 articles defined in [5] and comprised of all *Living Machines* conference proceedings (from March 2006 up to May 2022), all *Bioinspiration & Biomimetics* articles and all *Soft Robotics* articles. This allow us to extract and characterize current and emerging topics in this sub-field of Biomimetics.

Our contribution to the existing literature is three-fold: first, we add a knowledge extraction step where we create several versions of each article (*aspects*) with specific information extracted (thus reducing the noise introduced by text not directly relevant to the targeted information) and we study how the clusters retrieved in the different aspects compare to each other. Second, we introduce a new methodology to generate word embedding-based keywords on relatively large corpora, allowing us to quickly generate keywords that are conceptually relevant to each cluster rather than purely statistically relevant keywords. Third,

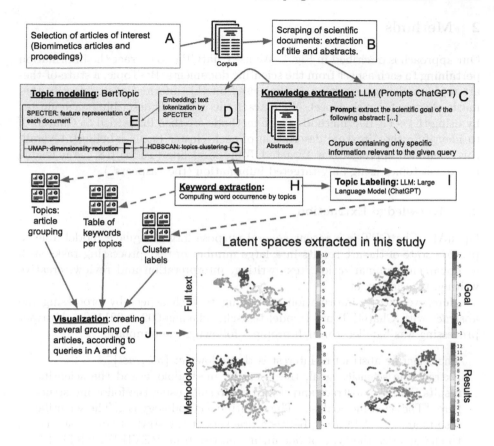

Fig. 1. Workflow of our methodology to group articles by thematic clusters according to user-defined queries. The corpus is comprised of Biomimetics articles (**A**). We extract the title and abstract from each document (**B**), which are then filtered (**C**) using knowledge extraction techniques based on ChatGPT [2] to only keep information related to one contextual part of the article ("aspects" of the article, e.g. the scientific goal, or the method, of the type of results uncovered). This knowledge is then further processed by Topic Modeling tools (**D**–**G** inspired by BERTopic [10]) to automatically extract the scientific topics of the corpus and generate keywords (based on word occurrence) related to each topical cluster (**H**). These keywords are analyzed by ChatGPT to generate descriptive labels for each cluster (**I**). This results into several thematic groupings of articles, either based on the full text of the abstracts, or on the three extracted aspects (**J**). For each aspect, we show a 2-D visualization of the embedding space and the cluster allocation of documents in our corpus. Each dot represents a single scientific article and its color the cluster to which it has been allocated. The gray color represents unlabeled articles.

we propose a new methodology using the extracted keywords and a Large Language Model (LLM) to perform topic labeling (*i.e.* give a label to the topics retrieved using topic modeling), an unsupervised machine learning task.

2   Methods

Our approach is described in Fig. 1. We use ChatGPT to extract the information pertaining to each aspect from the scientific documents. BerTopic, a state-of-the-art topic modeling algorithm, is then used on this information to identify thematic clusters for each aspect. We extract the keywords describing each cluster by using the c-TF-IDF method. These methods are then forwarded to ChatGPT to identify a short textual description of each cluster (topic labeling). Overall, this combined approach is a Targeted Topic Modeling (TTM) [18], as it is able to extract topics using only targeted information (the "aspects").

2.1   Knowledge Extraction

OpenAI's ChatGPT is a recent general-purpose large language model able to provide state-of-the-art results in a large number of text processing tasks such as document summarization, text writing, interpretation and review, creative writing, translation, etc.

Here, we extract information pertaining to each aspect by processing the abstract with ChatGPT pro (model text-chat-davinci-002-20221122). Abstract processing was handled through prompts following the template:

> The scientific abstract of interest is the following: {*abstract*}
> Extract the scientific goal, the scientific methodology and the scientific results from the abstract and return the results using the following structure: "The scientific goal is ... The scientific methodology is ... The scientific results are ...". Add a tag between brackets at the start of your response to characterize the type of document (choose from REVIEW, ARTICLE and OTHER).

This allowed us to extract the three targeted aspects in only one prompt. Having all aspects listed into one prompt signaled to ChatGPT that overlaps of content between aspects should be avoided. The tags were then used to filter out documents that were not scientific articles or reviews, such as author commentaries or editorial letters. We used ChatGPT instead of other models, such as GPT-3, Bloomz, or LLaMA, because we observed more accurate results with the former in term of information extraction.

Note that it is currently impossible to use ChatGPT alone to perform topic modeling, as it only allows context windows of 4096 tokens (i.e. around 3000 words), which would render impossible the comparison and grouping of a large corpus of documents. Furthermore, ChatGPT would be prone to hallucination and bias for this task, as there could be a multitude of possible grouping of articles. A direct topic modeling prompt would also be particularly complex, resulting in ChatGPT answers containing fabricated facts. In our approach, ChatGPT is only used to extract aspect information from the abstracts – associated results do not exhibit strong bias or fabricated facts, as it is a task akin to abstractive summarization of explicitly provided information.

2.2   Topic Modeling

We present a methodology based on [10] that automatically analyzes scientific corpora. Specifically, this methodology involves the creation of a vectoral representation, referred to as an "embedding", for each article in the corpus. These embeddings are subsequently used to cluster similar articles together based on their topic, thereby enabling further analysis.

The algorithm used in this study involves the analysis of the title and abstract of each article to generate a latent representation of the topics examined in the article. The resulting embedding of the articles enables the identification of articles that discuss similar topics, as they are positioned more closely in the latent space. This embedding process employs the use of Transformers [16], which is a type of neural network that has gained widespread acceptance in natural language processing in recent years. Transformers excel in learning the context and meaning of language by identifying statistical relationships between sequential data, such as the words within sentences. One of the most significant advantages of Transformers is the self-attention mechanism, which allows the model to better comprehend language by learning the general context of words and the interdependence of terms within the context of a sentence. Here, we used SPECTER [8], a pre-trained sentence-BERT architecture specifically designed for analyzing scientific literature based on the SciBERT Transformer model [1].

Each token is subjected to a 768-dimensional embedding process using the proposed model. Since this space is not latent, we use the UMAP [13] algorithm to project this space into a low-dimensional projected latent space. The chosen dimension for this projection varies based on the dataset and is manually selected to optimize the interpretability of the results by humans while minimizing the number of unlabeled articles by the clustering algorithm presented below. This dimensionality reduction step condenses the information and improves the performance of the HDBSCAN [12] clustering algorithm. Additionally, this reduction in dimensionality significantly reduces memory requirements and computational time, which is especially crucial when dealing with more extensive sets of data, such as complete corpora of scientific articles. It is worth noting that the qualitative validity of the results obtained is not compromised when higher-dimensional UMAP projections are used.

The projected latent representations of all articles are utilized to filter out outliers in the corpus, which may include articles that do not contain valuable information, such as those with empty abstracts or titles, errata, and corrigenda. To achieve this, we use two different methods to compute the radius of the complete corpus in latent space, depending on the dimensionality of the projected latent space. For dimensions 5 and lower, we compute the convex hull of all points and measure the pairwise euclidean distance of all points on the hull to determine the radius of the corpus. However, since convex hull algorithms operate in $\mathcal{O}(n^{d/2})$ time [6], where d represents the dimension of the latent space, this method is not suitable for higher dimensions. Instead, for dimensions greater than 5, we simply compute the pairwise euclidean distance of all points in the corpus and select the maximum pairwise distance. Although this method may not be suitable for larger corpora, it works for relatively small ones.

Using the radius obtained, we compute the mean distance of each article to the 5% closest articles in the corpus using a K-nearest neighbors (KNN) model. If this mean distance exceeds one-third of the radius, we consider the article to be an outlier and remove it from the corpus. It is worth noting that some groups of legitimate articles may be located relatively far from the centroid of the corpus in the latent space. This methodology, however, allows us to differentiate between such articles, which are specific but relevant to our analysis, and true outliers.

The HDBSCAN algorithm is employed to perform unsupervised clustering in the latent space projection generated using our low-dimensional vectorial representations. This clustering algorithm automatically groups items based on their main themes. HDBSCAN is capable of identifying points in the dataset that do not belong to any cluster and therefore considers them as *noise*. Such points are referred to as *unlabeled*.

2.3 Keyword Extraction

The keyword extraction algorithm has two phases combining methods from [9, 10].

In the first phase, we extract the vocabulary most relevant to each cluster. To do so, we use a model called class-based TF-IDF (c-TF-IDF) [10]. This consists in applying the standard TF-IDF method [15] where each cluster is treated as a single document in order to retrieve the top n-grams with the highest values computed following Eq. 1, where n-grams here are defined as sequences of n adjacent words from a given cluster. Since the TF-IDF score reflects how important an n-gram is to a document in a corpus, the c-TF-IDF score reflects how important an n-gram is to a cluster in a collection of clusters. The c-TF-IDF score is computed using the following equation:

$$x_{w,c} = \frac{w_c}{A_c} \times \log \frac{m}{\sum_{j=0}^{n} t_j} \qquad (1)$$

where $x_{w,c}$ is the c-TF-IDF score (importance) of n-gram w within cluster c, w_c is the number of occurrences of n-gram w in cluster c, A_c is the total number of n-grams in cluster c, m is the number of documents in the sample, n is the number of different clusters and t_j is the frequency of n-gram t across all clusters.

We then add an additional processing step to remove similar keywords (e.g. *attention* and *attentions*) by sequentially going through the keywords in descending order of c-TF-IDF score and only keeping those that have Levenshtein similarity with all keywords of higher score **lower** than a threshold (we set the threshold at 0.8) until we have the desired top k keywords.

We retrieve the top k 1-grams, 2-grams and 3-grams using the aforementioned method, and amalgamate them before beginning the second phase of our keyword extraction algorithm. All these n-grams combined together are henceforth referred to as *candidate keywords* for a given cluster (note that a given n-gram can be a candidate keyword for several clusters).

In the second phase, we endeavor to select a small number of most relevant and diverse keywords from all the n-grams previously extracted. In order to do so, we compare for each cluster c the individual embeddings $e(w)$ of the selected n-grams with the global embedding $\mathbf{p_c}$ (Eq. 2) of the cluster. We refer to all n-grams selected by the following method as *selected keywords*. At the beginning of this algorithm, all n-grams are thus candidate keywords and the list of selected keywords is empty. For each candidate keyword w, we compute the similarity of its embedding with the cluster's embedding $sim_{candidate}(w)$ and the similarity of its embedding with the maximally similar selected keyword $sim_{selected}(w)$ (Eq. 5). We then compute the mmr (Maximal Marginal Relevance [3]) value over all candidate keywords following Eq. 6 and pick the keyword with the maximum mmr value, which we add to our list of selected keywords and remove from the list of candidate keywords. We repeat this process until we have the desired number n of selected keywords for each cluster. This combination of the two methods presents several advantages:

- by first performing a selection of relevant n-grams with c-TF-IDF, we greatly reduce the number of candidate keywords (and thus the time and hardware requirements) of the mmr phase.
- by using n-gram embeddings instead of statistical methods such as c-TF-IDF for our keyword selection, we can explicitly add a diversity parameter and select n-grams based on their *semantic meaning* rather than pure mathematical frequency.
- using embeddings gives a more diverse mixture of 1-, 2- and 3-grams compared to just using c-TF-IDF which tends to over-represent higher order n-grams. This bias still exists as higher order n-grams are more numerous and are structurally able to be more descriptive than 1-grams, but it exists to a weaker extent.

$$\mathbf{p}_{c_i} = \frac{\sum\limits_{k=1}^{n_{c_i}} \mathbf{e}(c_i^k)}{n_{c_i}} \tag{2}$$

where n_{c_i} is the number of documents in cluster i and $\mathbf{e}(c_i^k)$ is the embedding of the k-th document in cluster i with $k \in [1, n_{c_i}]$.

$$\cos(\mathbf{a}, \mathbf{b}) = \frac{\mathbf{a} \cdot \mathbf{b}}{||\mathbf{a}|| \, ||\mathbf{b}||} \tag{3}$$

$$sim_{candidate}(w) = \cos(\mathbf{p}_{c_i}, \mathbf{e}^\mathsf{T}(w)) \tag{4}$$

$$sim_{selected}(w) = \max(\cos(\mathbf{e}(w), \widehat{\mathbf{K}}^\mathsf{T})) \tag{5}$$

where $\cos(..., ...)$ is the cosine similarity as defined in Eq. 3, $\mathbf{e}(w)$ is the embedding vector of candidate keyword w, $\widehat{\mathbf{K}}$ is the matrix containing the embeddings of all selected keywords and max(...) corresponds to the maximum of the resulting similarity vector (we find the selected keyword most similar to candidate keyword w).

$$mmr(w) = (1 - d) \times sim_{candidate}(w) - d \times sim_{selected}(w) \qquad (6)$$

with $d \in [0, 1]$ a diversity parameter to control the diversity when sequentially selecting keywords ($d = 0$ corresponds to no diversity parameter, $d = 1$ corresponds to maximally diverse keywords).

2.4 Topic Labeling

Topics were labeled using the ChatGPT Plus API (model text-chat-davinci-002-20221122). In order to label each topic, the top 20 keywords were extracted following Sect. 2.3, which were then used to query the ChatGPT API in order to label the topic. The query used was: "The keywords of interest are the following: {$processed\_keywords$}. Provide in 5 words or less the name of a thematic cluster related to these keywords.".

2.5 Adjusted Rand Index

We use the scikit-learn [14] implementation of the Adjusted Rand Index. From the documentation, "the Rand Index computes a similarity measure between two clusterings by considering all pairs of samples and counting pairs that are assigned in the same or different clusters in the predicted and true clusterings". The index has lower bound -0.5 for maximally discordant clusterings, value 0 for random (independent) clusterings and value 1 for identical clusterings.

2.6 Intercluster Similarity

The intercluster similarity is computed following Eqs. 7 and 8:

$$s(c_i^k, c_i^l) = 1 - \frac{||\mathbf{e}(c_i^k) - \mathbf{e}(c_i^l)||_2}{\max\limits_{k,l}(||\mathbf{e}(c_i^k) - \mathbf{e}(c_i^l)||_2)} \qquad (7)$$

$$S(c_i, c_j) = \frac{\sum\limits_{k=1}^{n_{c_i}} \sum\limits_{l=1}^{n_{c_j}} s(c_i^k, c_j^l)}{n_{c_i} n_{c_j}} \qquad (8)$$

$$\hat{S}(c_i, c_j) = \frac{S(c_i, c_j)}{\max\limits_{j}(S(c_i, c_j))} \qquad (9)$$

where $\hat{S}(c_i, c_j)$ is the intercluster similarity between clusters i and j and $s(c_i^k, c_i^l)$ is the euclidean similarity between articles c_i^k and c_i^l. As a final step, we divide each row of the matrix by its maximum, making this similarity measure i.e. $\hat{S}(c_1, c_2) \neq \hat{S}(c_2, c_1)$. The euclidean distance was chosen to measure similarity between two embeddings as we are working in a low-dimensional version of the latent space.

Table 1. Hyperparameters used for the UMAP and HDBSCAN algorithms.

UMAP parameters		HDBSCAN parameters		
n_components	n_neighbors	min_samples	cluster_epsilon	min_cluster_size
10	3	1	0.45	40

3   Results

We apply our complete methodology and retrieve a clustering for each of the four selected aspects (*Full, Goal, Methodology, Results*). Clusterings were retrieved for all aspects using hyperparameters shown in Table 1. Figure 2 shows for each aspect the proportion of articles in each cluster and their temporal evolutions. Tables 3 and 2 show, for each cluster in each aspect, the top 5 keywords retrieved following Sect. 2.3 and the topic labels retrieved following Sect. 2.4. The number of clusters retrieved ranges between 8 (for aspect *Goal*) and 13 (for aspect *Results*), and we can study their temporal evolution as shown on the figure. No massive evolution in terms of topic of study is observed, we however see that "Soft Robotics"-related clusters become increasingly represented in all aspects.

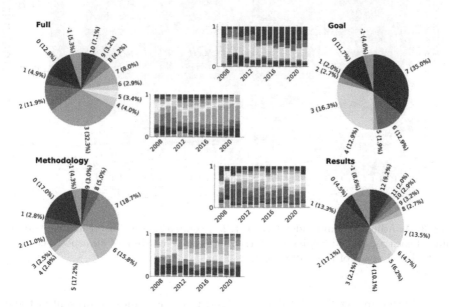

Fig. 2. Proportion of articles in each cluster for each aspect and their temporal evolution. Barplots are ordered starting from the bottom with cluster −1 and then follow the numbered order of the clusters.

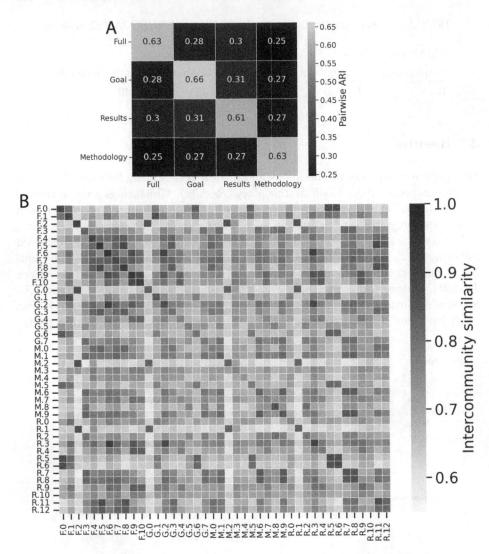

Fig. 3. A: Adjusted Rand Index (see Sect. 2.5) comparing the clustering results over 30 runs of each aspect. **B:** Similarity matrix between all clusters of all aspects computed on the latent space of the *Full* aspect.

As shown in Fig. 2 and Table 2, we find that the 3 most represented themes in the *Full* aspect are "Fish-Inspired Robotic Locomotion", "Biomimetic Flapping Wing Flight" and "Soft Robotics Actuation & Design". The most represented themes in the *Goal* aspect are "Biomimetic Materials & Structures Design", "Biomimetic Robotic Fish Propulsion" and "Soft Robotics and Bioinspired Actuation". The most represented themes in the *Methodology* aspect are "Biomimetic Materials and Design", "Fish-Inspired Robotic Locomotion

Table 2. Topic labels for all clusters of all aspects.

	Full	Goal	Methodology	Results
0	Fish-Inspired Robotic Locomotion	Flapping Wing Aerodynamics and Biomechanics	Biomimetic Materials and Design	Biomimetic Underwater Sensing & Acoustics
1	Underwater Biomimetic Robotics	Underwater Biomimetic Robotics & Sensing	Soft Robotics for Locomotion and Design	Flapping Wing Aerodynamics & Performance
2	Biomimetic Flapping Wing Flight	Biomimetic Touch Sensing for Robots	Biomimetic Flapping Wing Flight	Biomimetic Legged Robot Locomotion
3	Soft Robotics Actuation & Design	Biomimetic Materials & Structures Design	Bioinspired Unmanned Aerial Swarms	Biomimetic Tactile Sensors and Robotics
4	Bio-inspired Photonic & Robotic Systems	Biomimetic Robot Navigation & Performance	Biomimetic Underwater Sonar Systems	Bio-inspired Robotics Control Architecture
5	Bioinspired Materials and Structures	Snake-Inspired Robotic Locomotion	Fish-Inspired Robotic Locomotion Research	Aquatic Robotic Propulsion and Design
6	Biomimetic Touch Sensing Technology	Biomimetic Robotic Fish Propulsion	Soft Robotics Actuators and Design	Fish-inspired Swimming Dynamics & Propulsion
7	Bio-Inspired Robotics and Design	Soft Robotics and Bioinspired Actuation	Biomimetic Locomotion Robotics	Soft Robotics Actuators & Design
8	Biomimetic Composite Materials & Structures		Bipedal/Quadrupedal Locomotion Robotics	Soft Robotics and Bio-Inspiration
9	Human-Robot Symbiotic Interaction & Therapy		Soft Pneumatic Artificial Muscle Actuation	Bio-inspired Swarm Robotics
10	Insect-Inspired Aerial Robotics Navigation			Bioinspired Multi-modal Locomotion Dynamics
11				Biomimetic Adhesion & Lubrication Mechanics
12				Biomimetic Materials and Design

Research" and "Biomimetic Locomotion Robotics". The most represented themes in the *Results* aspect are "Flapping Wing Aerodynamics & Performance", "Biomimetic Legged Robot Locomotion" and "Soft Robotics Actuators & Design". The "Biomimetic Swimming", "Biomimetic Flying", "Soft Robotics Actuation" and "Biomimetic Locomotion" themes are among the most represented in 3 aspects. The "Biomimetic Materials" and "Biomimetic Locomotion" themes are among the most represented in 2 aspects.

Table 3. The 5 most significant n-grams (see Sect. 2.3) and the cluster labels (see Sect. 2.4) for each cluster of each aspect.

Full

F.0: Fish-Inspired Robotic Locomotion	F.1: Underwater Biomimetic Robotics & Sensing.	F.2: Biomimetic Flapping Wing Flight.	F.3: Soft Robotics Actuation & Design.	F.4: Bioinspired Photonic & Robotic Systems.
biomimetic robotic fish	underwater active electrolocation	flapping wings hovering	actuated soft robots	biomimetic photonic systems
fin based propulsion	biomimetic flow sensors	aerodynamics dynamic flight	flexible fluidic actuators	robots inspired plant
swimming kinematics	adjacent robotic fish	aerodynamic performance flapping	multi legged	actuated cellular structures
underwater propulsion	small underwater robots	wing design	field soft robotics	dynamic nanoindentation technique
underwater legged locomotion	upstream oscillating fin	model flapping wing	soft pneumatic actuators	analysis prismatic bioinspired

F.5: Bioinspired Materials and Structures	F.6: Biomimetic Touch Sensing Technology.	F.7: Bioinspired Robotics and Design.	F.8: Biomimetic Composite Materials & Structures	F.9: Human-Robot Symbiotic Interaction & Therapy.
biomimetic scale covered	biomimetic tactile sensor	bionic soft hexapod	biomimetic fibre reinforced	human robot symbiotic
biocomposite structures	hybrid tactile sensing	bio inspired robotics	shaped microstructures gecko	cognitive architecture
tissue engineering cell	fingered tactile robot	biomimetics seed dispersal	biomimetic adhesive pads	effectiveness biomimetic robots
shaping biohybrid components	biomimetic tactile	material biohybrid robots	biomimetic model	robot individuals
hydrogel based microcapsules	tactile sensor array	computer aided biomimetics	inspired composites functionally	robot expressive

F.10: Insect-Inspired Aerial Robotics Navigation
fly robot
neuronal dynamics simulation
optomotor response
insect inspired
vision sensor dvs

Goal

G.0: Flapping Wing Aerodynamics and Biomechanics	G.1: Underwater Biomimetic Robotics & Sensing	G.2: Biomimetic Touch Sensing for Robots.	G.3: Biomimetic Materials & Structures Design.	G.4: Biomimetic Robot Navigation & Performance
flapping wing kinematics	sensor inspired fish	biomimetic tactile sensor	biomimetic approach architectural	effectiveness biomimetic robots
investigate aerodynamic performance	analysis underwater navigational	skins soft robots	art biomimetics sep	cell fly brain
dynamic flight stability	aquatic locomotion research	highly compliant tactile	bioinspired engineering	navigation behavior desert
aerodynamic performance flapping	line fish hydrodynamic	biomimetic fingertip	biomimetic design processes	bio inspired motion
wing kinematics aerodynamic	underwater active electrolocation	soft tactile sensor	shaped microstructures gecko	flytrap inspired robot

G.5: Snake-Inspired Robotic Locomotion	G.6: Biomimetic Robotic Fish Propulsion	G.7: Soft Robotics and Bioinspired Actuation.
underwater snake robots	biomimetic robotic fish	actuated soft robot
gait transition snake	fin propulsion	bioinspired variable stiffness
robot serpentine locomotion	propelled swimming flexible	bioinspired legged robot
thrust assisted perching	fish like propulsion	field soft robotics
gliding flying snake	artificial micro swimmer	soft pneumatic actuators

(*continued*)

Table 3. (*continued*)

	M.0: Biomimetic Materials and Design	M.1: Soft Robotics for Locomotion and Design	M.2: Biomimetic Flapping Wing Flight	M.3: Bioinspired Unmanned Aerial Swarms	M.4: Biomimetic Underwater Sonar Systems.
Methodology	art biomimetics sep	softworms design control	flapping wing kinematics	swarms unmanned aerial	biomimetic sonar head
	coaxial electrospun biomimetic	locomotion modular mesh	aerodynamic performance model	design aerodynamics autonomy	multi frequency excitation
	biomimetic shark	insect exoskeletons	dynamic flight stability	flight dynamics	octopus inspired
	dynamic nanoindentation technique	inspired soft robot	wing air vehicle	flying high	acoustic near field
	biomimetic design	earthworm like locomotion	dimensional hovering wing	adaptive networks physarum	sonarhead inspired

	M.5: Fish-Inspired Robotic Locomotion Research	M.6: Soft Robotics Actuators and Design.	M.7: Biomimetic Locomotion Robotics	M.8: Bipedal/Quadruped Locomotion Robotics.	M.9: Soft Pneumatic Artificial Muscle Actuation.
	inspired robotic fish	soft robotic actuators	robots biomimetic solution	quadruped locomotion	pneumatic soft actuators
	locomotion flexible propulsors	dielectric elastomer actuators	multi modal locomotion	walking bipedal model	artificial muscle
	jet underwater vehicle	soft biomimetic finger	insects legged robots	leg stiffness	contraction stiffness models
	biomimetic fish sep	pneumatic bending actuator	biomimetic solution locomotion	multi legged robots	flexible fluidic actuators
	fin swimming	actuated soft micromold	inspired controller	bipedal spring	polymers artificial muscles

	R.0: Biomimetic Underwater Sensing & Acoustics	R.1: Flapping Wing Aerodynamics & Performance.	R.2: Biomimetic Legged Robot Locomotion.	R.3: Biomimetic Tactile Sensors and Robotics	R.4: Bioinspired Robotics Control Architecture.
Results	underwater autonomous	flapping wings hovering	multi legged robot	biomimetic tactile sensor	robot self organizes
	biomimetic flow	aerodynamic performance	biomimetic solution locomotion	biomimetic tactile arrays	inspired control architecture
	biomimetic smart ears	compared rigid wings	leg stiffness energy	soft tactile sensor	determination appropriate motor
	acoustic near field	aerodynamic performance flapping	legged locomotion	previously achieved tactile	architecture robot controller
	fish lateral line	wing stroke plane	robots biomimetic solution	biomimetic tactile	robot symbiotic interaction

	R.5: Aquatic Robotic Propulsion and Design.	R.6: Fish-inspired Swimming Dynamics & Propulsion	R.7: Soft Robotics Actuators & Design	R.8: Soft Robotics and Bioinspiration	R.9: Bioinspired Swarm Robotics.
	aquatic robotic propellers	biomechanics fish swimming	soft actuators based	soft robotics	robotic fish swarm
	fin based propulsion	self propelled swimmers	world congress biomimetics	dielectric elastomer actuators	bioinspired navigation
	swimming soft robotic	fin swimming	bending soft robot	healing soft robots	virtual fence swarm
	bionic robotic fish	pulsed jet underwater	soft cylindrical actuator	soft actuators	integration fish robots
	aquatic soft robots	swimming kinematics	dielectric elastomer actuators	like soft robots	swarms unmanned aerial

	R.10: Bioinspired Multi-modal Locomotion Dynamics.	R.11: Biomimetic Adhesion & Lubrication Mechanics	R.12: Biomimetic Materials and Design
	multi modal locomotion	adhesion lubrication biomacromolecules	biomimetic approach architectural
	flying	flexible porous superhydrophobic	biomimetic design
	bio inspired locomotion	inspired micro origami	biomimetics sep scientific
	thrust assisted perching	design elastomer	shaping biohybrid components
	biohybrid fly robot	microstructures	mechanical properties

Figure 3 presents a comparison of the different aspect-based clusterings. Panel **A** shows the average ARI (see Sect. 2.5) value between aspects computed over the article clusterings obtained for 30 random seeds of the algorithm. Each cell denotes the similarity between the row aspect and the column aspect. High ARI values correspond to similar clusterings, and values close to zero correspond to uncorrelated clusterings. Here, we see that all matrix values are positive, meaning that some structure of the clusterings is retained between the various aspects. The diagonal values are markedly higher than the rest, suggesting that there is a qualitative difference in the information retrieved by each of the aspects that is not only the consequence of the stochasticity of the algorithm used. This thus shows that, for a given corpus, taking into account the aspect adds a new level of information.

Panel **B** shows the intercluster similarity computed following Eq. 8. We computed the intercluster similarity for all cluster pairs from all aspects in the latent space of the *Full* aspect. Panel **A** shows that there are differences at the aspect-level, here we study these differences on a cluster-level. We see that a few clusters are very similar across all aspects (for instance *F.2*, *G.0*, *M.2* and *R.1* that deal with "Biomimetic Flying" or *R.5*, *R.6*, *G.1*, *G.6*, *M.5* and *F.0* that deal with "Biomimetic Swimming"), suggesting that the associated theme of these clusters can be found in all aspects. Some clusters such as *M.8* are also very well-identified in a given aspect and quite dissimilar to all clusters in other aspects, suggesting that these clusters deal with aspect-specific topics that are not as salient when clustering articles through their full abstracts.

Note however that comparing clusterings in Fig. 3B is an ill-defined process as the knowledge extraction step occurs for each document before the embedding step, and thus the position of the document in the latent space of the *Full* aspect would not necessarily correspond to its position in another aspect. Nevertheless, it remains a proxy for the similarity of the various clusterings.

The results from the topic modeling, keyword extraction and topic labeling stages were manually validated by human experts and were found to be both precise (*i.e.* the themes extracted were relatively fine-grained) and coherent (*i.e.* the collection of articles allocated to each of the clusters were accurate according to the extracted topic label and keywords).

4   Discussions and Conclusion

We proposed an extension of our previous topic modeling methods in [4,5], that is able to automatically regroup Biomimetic articles extracted from three different academic sources into several thematic clusters, according to several thematic aspects related either to the scientific goals of the documents, or the type of methods used, or the types of results uncovered, or related to the entire documents. Our method is also able to make use of ChatGPT to perform topic labeling, and provide a descriptive name to each uncovered cluster. We use this methodology on a corpus of scientific articles representative of the Biomimetics community, and analyze the similarity in content between clusters and their temporal evolution.

Our methodology could still be improved further. For instance, it should be noted that our current methodology solely examines the abstract and title of the articles, and does not consider their entire content. This is because abstracts are already abridged versions of the articles, and it is simpler for the algorithm to correctly identify the research topic from them than from the entire text. Besides, the authors' writing style or the type of article (research article versus review) may affect how the full text is written, making its analysis more complicated for the algorithm.

Comparing our results with other language processing methods such as ontologies or thesauri in order to build the topical clusters could also bring interesting insights complementary to those presented here, but would still need to be supplemented with embedding-based methods in order to quantitatively compare results. LLMs would still be required in order to perform the knowledge extraction and topic labeling steps.

Our approach could be applied to generate hierarchical thematic clusters (*i.e.* each cluster would contain several sub-clusters). Hierarchical clusterings over several aspects may be necessary to characterize larger corpus. This could be achieved through the hierarchical topic modeling capabilities of BERTopic, or by executing our method iteratively on each found clusters, as to find sub-clusters.

Finally, the use of ChatGPT as a tool for knowledge extraction and topic labeling back-end raises important technical and ethical issues. Preliminary tests have shown that lighter and freely distributed models such as [7] performed similarly to ChatGPT on our samples, providing more transparent alternatives to ChatGPT; as they are still under development, however, we decided to use ChatGPT as it provides API access. While the technology is indeed able to aptly process scientific information, there is a risk of bias and inaccuracy in the results produced by the algorithm. Moreover, there are concerns around the ownership and privacy of the data used to train the model. The training data should be made public and clarified as well as the training method. It is crucial to carefully consider and address these ethical considerations in the development and implementation of ChatGPT as a tool for knowledge extraction from scientific documents. More specialized versions of these tools, oriented towards scientific and technical fields, should be developed in an open science framework.

References

1. Beltagy, I., Lo, K., Cohan, A.: SciBERT: a pretrained language model for scientific text. In: Proceedings of the 2019 Conference on Empirical Methods in Natural Language Processing and the 9th International Joint Conference on Natural Language Processing (EMNLP-IJCNLP), pp. 3615–3620 (2019)
2. Brown, T., et al.: Language models are few-shot learners. In: Advances in Neural Information Processing Systems, vol. 33, pp. 1877–1901 (2020)
3. Carbonell, J., Goldstein, J.: The use of MMR, diversity-based reranking for reordering documents and producing summaries. In: Proceedings of the 21st Annual International ACM SIGIR Conference on Research and Development in Information Retrieval, pp. 335–336 (1998)

4. Carniel, T., Cazenille, L., Dalle, J.M., Halloy, J.: Ten years of living machines conferences: transformers-based automated topic grouping. In: Hunt, A., et al. (eds.) Biomimetic and Biohybrid Systems. Living Machines 2022. LNAI, vol. 13548, pp. 13–26. Springer, Cham (2022). https://doi.org/10.1007/978-3-031-20470-8_2

5. Carniel, T., Cazenille, L., Dalle, J.M., Halloy, J.: Using natural language processing to find research topics in living machines conferences and their intersections with bioinspiration & biomimetics publications. Bioinspiration Biomim. **17**(6), 065008 (2022)

6. Chazelle, B.: An optimal convex hull algorithm in any fixed dimension. Discrete Comput. Geom. **10**(4), 377–409 (1993). https://doi.org/10.1007/BF02573985

7. Chiang, W.L., et al.: Vicuna: an open-source chatbot impressing GPT-4 with 90%* ChatGPT quality (2023)

8. Cohan, A., Feldman, S., Beltagy, I., Downey, D., Weld, D.S.: SPECTER: document-level representation learning using citation-informed transformers. arXiv preprint arXiv:2004.07180 (2020)

9. Grootendorst, M.: KeyBERT: minimal keyword extraction with BERT (2020). https://doi.org/10.5281/zenodo.4461265

10. Grootendorst, M.: BERTopic: neural topic modeling with a class-based TF-IDF procedure. arXiv preprint arXiv:2203.05794 (2022)

11. Lepora, N.F., Verschure, P., Prescott, T.J.: The state of the art in biomimetics. Bioinspiration Biomim. **8**(1), 013001 (2013)

12. McInnes, L., Healy, J., Astels, S.: HDBSCAN: hierarchical density based clustering. J. Open Source Softw. **2**(11), 205 (2017)

13. McInnes, L., Healy, J., Melville, J.: UMAP: uniform manifold approximation and projection for dimension reduction. arXiv preprint arXiv:1802.03426 (2018)

14. Pedregosa, F., et al.: Scikit-learn: machine learning in Python. J. Mach. Learn. Res. **12**, 2825–2830 (2011)

15. Ramos, J., et al.: Using TF-IDF to determine word relevance in document queries. In: Proceedings of the First Instructional Conference on Machine Learning, vol. 242, pp. 29–48. Citeseer (2003)

16. Vaswani, A., et al.: Attention is all you need. In: Advances in Neural Information Processing Systems, vol. 30 (2017)

17. Vouloutsi, V., Cominelli, L., Dogar, M., Lepora, N., Zito, C., Martinez-Hernandez, U.: Towards Living Machines: current and future trends of tactile sensing, grasping, and social robotics. Bioinspiration Biomim. **18**, 025002 (2023)

18. Wang, S., Chen, Z., Fei, G., Liu, B., Emery, S.: Targeted topic modeling for focused analysis. In: Proceedings of the 22nd ACM SIGKDD International Conference on Knowledge Discovery and Data Mining, pp. 1235–1244 (2016)

Biomimetics Analyzed: Examples from an Epistemological and Ontological Perspective

Manfred Drack[1]([⊠]) [iD] and Ludger Jansen[2,3] [iD]

[1] University of Tübingen, Auf der Morgenstelle 28, 72076 Tübingen, Germany
`manfred.drack@uni-tuebingen.de`
[2] University of Rostock, Institute for Philosophy, 18051 Rostock, Germany
`ludger.jansen@uni-rostock.de`
[3] PTH Brixen, Piazza Seminario 4, 39042 Bressanone, Italy

Abstract. The theoretical foundations of biomimetics have not been extensively studied. Therefore we examine both epistemological and ontological aspects of biomimetics. Here, we describe the state of the art and show that an important requirement for future research is the development of a coherent conceptual framework to account for functions, working principles, and constructions. We demonstrate the connection of these concepts via the design space and show that important working principles can be modeled as complex dispositions. As a proof of concept, we investigate the epistemological and ontological profile of two famous examples from the history of biomimetics: bird wings for flying and (artificial) neural networks. The investigation of these examples indicates that biomimetics can be understood as a unique scientific discipline.

Keywords: Biomimetics · Epistemology · Ontology · Working principles

1 Introduction

During the last few decades, knowledge of biological systems has increased significantly because of innovative analysis and simulation methods, both at the molecular and the mesoscopic (organismal) level. Moreover, advances in production methods in engineering have considerably boosted biomimetic output. Biomimetics is a growing field of research (Lepora et al. 2013), with its own societies (such as Biokon, biokon.de, or the International Society of Bionic Engineering, isbe-online.org), handbooks (Bar-Cohen 2012; Jabbari et al. 2014; Prescott et al. 2018), and journals. Lenau et al. (2018) report that both publications and patents in the field of biomimetics have steadily increased since the 1990s. In addition, a wide field of work can be considered as being biomimetic without explicit use of that label, e.g., in robotics, swarm intelligence and artificial neural networks.

Despite their importance and successes, the new developments at the crossroads of biology and technology still lack a theoretical foundation as a basis for the systematization of the knowledge generated in these fields. This lack has previously been

F. Meder et al. (Eds.): Living Machines 2023, LNAI 14158, pp. 273–289, 2023.
https://doi.org/10.1007/978-3-031-39504-8_19

explicitly pointed out for biomimetics (Schmidt 2002; Nachtigall 2010:149), and the situation is no different today. The bibliographic database philpapers.org, for example, lists only few philosophical papers explicitly addressing biomimetics. For instance, Dicks (2023) deals with the general philosophical features of biomimicry, a field that focuses on sustainability and that partly overlaps with biomimetics, and Zoglauer (1994) has analyzed the transfer of models from nature to technology. Some authors suggest sub-classifications of biomimetics (von Gleich et al. 2010; Marzi et al. 2018). For example, Schmidt (2002) distinguishes various kinds of mimesis of which function-mimesis is a sub-area of biomimetics. This approach has been criticized by Nachtigall (2010) because all biomimetics is about function. Biomimetics has also been described as a technoscience (Nordmann 2005), which does not seem to be an adequate depiction as the term "technoscience" refers to research areas without a clear separation between representation and intervention ("Darstellung und Eingriff"). However, the description of biological systems and the intervention in the form of a technical application are clearly distinguishable in biomimetics. Related discussions can be found in the broader philosophical literature, ranging from Kapp's famous claim that all technical products have a biological precursor model (Kapp 1877) to Janich's skepticism with regard to the technical potential of biomimetics (Janich 1989).

A formal theoretical framework for biomimetic research should remove obstacles for biomimetic research projects as identified by von Gleich et al. (2010). Whereas some of these obstacles are merely of an organizational nature, e.g., bringing together necessary expertise and supporting infrastructure, others are more principled. Tension between the scientific wish to gain insight and the engineering need to build market-viable applications might be ameliorated if such a formal framework provides a way of thinking shared by all members of biomimetic research teams. Such a foundation requires that both the epistemology and the ontology of biomimetics are known. Epistemology and ontology are two disciplines within philosophy. Epistemology (from Greek *epistêmê* for knowledge, and *logos* for explanation) is the study of knowledge and its justification, including the ways how knowledge is acquired. Ontology (from Greek *ontos*, 'of being') in contrast, is the study of being. As a philosophical discipline, ontology is the study of the most general kinds of the most general kinds of being and the relations between them. Applied to biomimetics, these two perspectives boil down to the double question: *how* does biomimetics acquire knowledge (epistemology), and *about what* (ontology)?

2 Current State of the Art

2.1 The Epistemology of Biomimetics

Recently, Tamborini (2022) presented a socio-historical study of what he describes as the blurring of the disciplinary boundaries between engineering and the life sciences taken at large. However, with the exception of Zoglauer's (1994) study concerning model transfer from nature to technology, hardly any research has been carried out on the epistemological reconstruction of biomimetics. This is surprising, as the topic of artificial devices imitating and improving on nature was a standard topos already in ancient philosophy (Schiemann 2014). So far, methodological analyses of such transfer have been conducted from a pragmatic point of view in order to arrive more easily at technical applications. Only a few attempts have been made at posing more conceptual questions and at developing a theoretical basis (e.g., Vogel 2000; Vincent et al. 2006; Speck and Speck 2008; Nachtigall 2010; Fayemi et al. 2017). Commonly used labels such as "technology pull" and "biology push" (DIN-ISO-18458 2015) can, unfortunately, often be applied post hoc only; they are descriptive rather than explanatory and do not provide any insight into the rational structure of biomimetic research.

The lack of a theoretical foundation brings into doubt whether biomimetics should be seen as a unified discipline. This controversy is also fueled by the ambiguous use of terms such as "biomimetics", "bionics", or "biomimicry", on the one hand (Drack and Gebeshuber 2013), and by lumping together various fields under umbrella terms such as "bio-transformation", on the other hand. Situated at the crossroads between biology and engineering, biomimetics seems to have neither a clearly delineated object of research, nor a unified method or objective. One characteristic of biomimetics is that it combines knowledge from natural sciences with that from engineering. This implies that it can adhere neither to standard biological thinking, nor to standard engineering routines. For this reason, neither established theoretical considerations about biology (e.g., Mahner and Bunge 1997; Krohs and Toepfer 2005), nor theories of engineering (e.g., Kroes and Meijers 2000; Kornwachs 2012; Kroes 2012; Hansson 2017) are sufficient to elucidate the status of biomimetics. The question as to how these established aspects and other recent developments at the biology–engineering interface (which have also received little epistemological attention so far) can serve as starting points for investigations into biomimetics remains unanswered.

Based on observations of the interdisciplinary workflow within biomimetic projects of the DFG Collaborative Research Center SFB TRR 141 "Biological Design and Integrative Structures" (https://www.trr141.de last accessed 2023/03/10), Drack et al. (2018, 2020) have developed a conceptual framework that is applicable to any biomimetic development, including those of material products, material processes, and information processes. Their main finding is that the engineering design approach of Pahl et al. (2007) can be successfully used to describe biomimetic transfer processes involving five levels of engineering design, namely (1) the *overarching system* (biological or engineering system, e.g., organism, machine), (2) the *construction* level (specifying the concrete parameters of the interacting entities), (3) the *working principles* (i.e., constellations of abstract causal relations, covering also so-called mechanisms), (4) the *function* in question, enabling the construction (or the concrete design) for the performance of (5) the *task* for which a machine, device or process is built. Whereas the overarching system, the technical construction, and the task will differ from the biological role model, the function and working principles remain the same indicating that these are at the core of biomimetic knowledge transfer. Nachtigall (2010:83) has suggested to use the term "abstraction" for the research process that derives what Drack et al. (2018) have identified as the function and working principle from the biological system. Nachtigall has also introduced the term "concretization" which can best be understood as referring to the process of implementing function and working principle in the technical application (Drack et al. 2018). Combining these two ideas, the promising hypothesis emerges that the core of biomimetic knowledge generation involves the identification and implementation of functions and working principles that are transferred together from biology to engineering.

2.2 The Ontology of Biomimetics

Ontology development in biomimetics is still in its infancy. Several attempts have been made to structure and organize biomimetic knowledge in formal ontological structures from a computer-science perspective. Yim et al. (2008) have developed a bio-inspired design ontology based on functions, strategies, and design solutions. The approach of Kozaki and Mizoguchi (2014) aims at retrieving knowledge for technical applications, and Vincent (2014, 2017) discusses a systematization of biomimetic knowledge based on biological and technical trade-offs. Whereas all of these approaches include interesting components, they also exhibit shortcomings because they have been designed to serve as practical tools for technical innovation (McInerney et al. 2018) and not as adequate representation of the biomimetic domain of research. The latter remains an important requirement.

Our previous work suggests the centrality of functions, working principles, and constructions. Relevant functions can be characterized by verb phrases (Pahl et al. 2007 suggest verb+noun combinations). Their theoretical analysis, however, is still a desideratum, as the word "function" itself is ambiguous and there are various competing theories of functions in both biology and artifacts. A rich literature exists with regard to functions in the philosophy of biology and technology (e.g., Buller 1999; Krohs and Kroes 2009; Mossio et al. 2009; Houkes and Vermaas 2010). Usually, causal-dispositional approaches are distinguished from etiological approaches to functions, whereby the former considers the causal effects of functions, whereas the latter analyzes functions in terms of their origins, where these origins can be grounded in a better adaptation to a given environment, or selective advantages in the phylogenetic past (Bedau 1998), or, in case of technical artefacts, the intentions of designers or users. In addition, the notion of normalcy or typicality is often held to be relevant (Wachbroit 1994; Schurz 2001; Krohs 2004). For the formal-ontological analysis of functions, we can build on previous work on functions in formal ontologies (Röhl and Jansen 2014; Jansen 2018; cf. Spear et al. 2016).

Considerably less extensive literature is available concerning the analysis of working principles and constructions as the causal principles that help to fulfil a function but that are distinct from it. On the one hand, however, interest in mechanisms in the philosophy of biology is growing (e.g., Machamer et al. 2000; Krickel 2018; for a critique see Nicholson 2012). On the other hand, the modeling of working principles as complexes of dispositions, i.e., in terms of systems of causal properties that can be achieved by certain types of processes, seems to show promise. For the latter, we can again build on own work (Jansen 2007; Röhl and Jansen 2011; Barton et al. 2017) to develop an account of working principles appropriate for the domain of biomimetics.

3 Epistemological and Ontological Hypotheses

Our overall goal is to deepen our understanding of the developments at the crossroads of biology and technology by a thorough analysis and consolidation of the theoretical foundations of biomimetics, by focusing on two basic questions:

- Can biomimetics be conceived as a coherent field of research? What is the nature of biomimetic knowledge, and how is it derived?
- What is the specific object of biomimetic research and how can it be analyzed ontologically?

Our leading hypothesis is that biomimetics is unified by epistemological features including the transfer of working principles for functions from biological to technical constructions.

Our hypotheses regarding the epistemological profile of biomimetics are that: (1) the central unifying objects of biomimetics are the functions and working principles that can be transferred together from biology to engineering (cf. Fig. 2), and that (2) the biomimetic workflow always includes abstraction and concretization processes. We also hypothesize that (3) a unique set of methods (including technical biology and reverse biomimetics) cycles between conventional biological methods and engineering methods by using a model simultaneously as a model *of* a biological system and a model *for* an application (Masselter et al. 2012; Nachtigall 2010:86ff). We further hypothesize that whereas (4) the ultimate goal is always the technical application, an understanding of the underlying biology is indispensably instrumental for reaching this goal, and hence, is a sub-goal in all examples. We further expect evidence for (5) a pluralistic account with respect to the body of knowledge generated: Not only is knowledge of an application (*Anwendungswissen*) generated, but this also yields new scientific knowledge about the biological system, enriched by usage knowledge (*Gebrauchswissen*; Gaycken 2010) from developing biomimetic products. We expect that knowledge can be "double checked" by both biological evidence and engineering tests.

With respect to the ontological foundational categories, our hypothesis is that biomimetics has three basic categories: functions, working principles, and constructions. The first task will be to develop a theory of function able to cover all functional phenomena in biomimetics. We suggest that we need to develop a new (or to modify an existing) account of functions (that include causal-dispositional approaches and etiological approaches) in order to agree with the description of the working principle. With regard to working principles, our hypothesis is that they can be modeled as complexes of dispositions, i.e., causal properties that can be realized by certain types of processes (Jansen 2007; Röhl and Jansen 2011; Barton et al. 2017). The abstract working principles are embodied in a concrete construction in which all parameters (material properties, size, shape, etc.) must be set in such a way that the function is adequately fulfilled.

4 Distinguishing Functions from Working Principles

The term function is used with various meanings, and a vast literature exists concerning their exact ontological analysis. However, across the various ontological approaches, a broad agreement has been reached that a function can be described by a verb phrase.

As these constructions are ambiguous insofar as they can also be used to describe the respective processes, we prefix the phrase "the function to..." when necessary, in order to distinguish functions from the processes that are their realizations. For example, the function of the heart can be described as the *function to pump blood* or, more generically, the *function to pump liquid*. Functions (e.g., the function of the heart to pump blood) can be achieved in degrees of performance, down to outright malfunctioning or dysfunctioning (Jansen 2018). Furthermore, they can be described specifically and in greater or lesser detail (*function to pump blood* vs. *function to transport liquid*). They can also further be analyzed into sub-functions (e.g., the *sub-function to prevent reflux*, performed by the cardiac valves). Further examples for function descriptions are "to attach object reversibly", "to move a surface", "to conduct light", or "to keep mechanical stress on a surface constant" (Fig. 1).

Of similar importance is the capacity to distinguish functions from the working principles that make their realization possible. One and the same function can be achieved by different working principles, and one and the same working principle can contribute to achieve different functions. That functions can be fulfilled through different working principles (consider the way that pumps can work differently in biology and engineering) seems at the same time to rule out all causal-dispositional approaches for the analysis of functions.

The term "working principle" is often used in engineering literature to refer to the natural law or basic physical, chemical, or biological effect that is used to solve a certain construction problem. The exact definition of a working principle is generally left in the dark. As a first approximation, working principles can be considered as constellations of causal relations that can exist without any function but that can also be utilized for different functions. Such working principles often need to be combined to fulfill a function. Our hypothesis is that mechanisms, in general, and working principles, in particular, can be modeled as complex dispositions.

In both engineering and biomimetics, working principles are often not described verbally but are depicted by means of schematic images. Examples for such depictions are shown in Fig. 1. Our aim here is to show the way in which these working principles can be analyzed in terms of dispositions. For this, we need to identify (a) the bearer of the respective disposition, which might be a single material thing or a system composed of several such things, (b) the type of processes that the disposition allows to be achieved, and (c) the type of processes that trigger the realization of the disposition in question. In the case of a complex bearer for the disposition, we also need to identify (d) how the components of the complex bearer and their dispositions contribute to the resulting complex disposition.

The working principles in Fig. 1 can be analyzed as follows:

1. *Friction* due to normal force. In this image, the vertical force vector F_N depicts the trigger, whereas the horizontal force vector F_F suggests the realization. The bearer of the disposition is the complex out of work piece and surface. The disposition in question is the *disposition to resist to resist any movement if a potentially moving horizontal force (not shown) is below a certain threshold*, i.e., if it is smaller than the static friction force.

Functions

„to attach object reversibly"
„to pump liquid"
„to move surface"
„to conduct light"
„to keep mechanical stress on surface constant"

Working principles

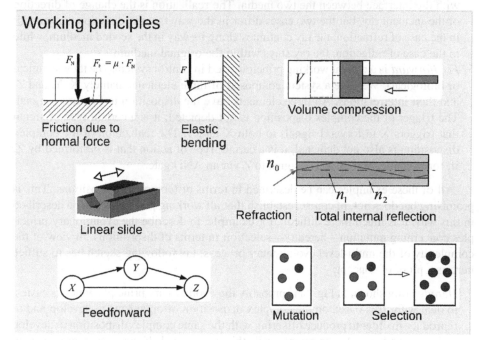

F_N $F_r = \mu \cdot F_N$

Friction due to normal force

F

Elastic bending

V

Volume compression

Linear slide

n_0

n_1 n_2

Refraction   Total internal reflection

X Y Z

Feedforward

Mutation   Selection

Fig. 1. Examples of function descriptions and basic working principles from different domains (mechanics, optics, control engineering, biology). Some of the functions listed can be connected to one of the depicted working principle: To attach an object reversibly can involve elastic bending (see Fig. 2). To pump liquid may use volume compression. To conduct light can be done by means of refraction and total internal reflection.

2. *Elastic bending.* In this case, the force vector depicts the trigger, and the deviation of the beam from the horizontal line depicts the realization. The bearer of this *disposition to deform in a reversible way when a force is applied* is the beam that is to be bent.
3. *Volume compression.* Here, the depicted unit consists of a container and a piston. The container has the disposition not to be permeable for the particles contained within it, and the piston is moved and thus changes the volume of the container. The trigger is the movement of the piston, the realization is the change in volume and pressure of the material contained in the compressor.
4. *Linear slide.* The point of this working principle is that the top sliding part has exactly one degree of freedom, namely to slide along the rail. In the construction depicted, the slider has the disposition to do so, but it lacks the disposition to move in any other

direction (translation or rotation), unless extraordinary force is applied, probably leading to the destruction of either the sliding part or the rail. The rail has, of course, the matching disposition to prevent any movement of the sliding part in any other direction, unless extraordinary force is applied.

5. *Refraction and total internal reflection* are cases in which the bearer of the disposition is the combination of two optical materials, e.g., the air and a glass fiber. The trigger is the contact between the incident light-ray (coming from the left in the diagram) with the interface between the two media. The realization is the change of direction of the incident ray, but the two cases differ in the way that the direction is changed: in the case of refraction, the ray continues along its way in the second medium, while in the case of reflection, the ray stays within the original medium.

6. *Feedforward* is a typical working principle used in control systems (be they technical or biological). We have a system composed of three elements, namely X, Y, and Z, and their interrelations. All three elements have the disposition to forward a signal. The trigger of the complex disposition is not depicted; it is a certain type of signal that triggers X to forward signals to both X and Y. The realization of the complex disposition is also not depicted; it is a certain type of action that is performed by Z, if, for example, both X and Y signal to Z via an AND gate.

All of these examples can be described in terms of (complex) dispositions. This is promising but does not, of course, establish that all working principles can be described in this way. It is much more difficult, for example, to describe the evolutionary principles concerning mutation—heredity—selection in terms of dispositions. In view of the complexity of the multi-level evolutionary process, the following sketch has to suffice here as a proof of concept:

7. *Heredity* (not shown in Fig. 1) is probably the evolutionary principle which is easiest to deal with. It is based on the complex disposition of organisms to develop and to reproduce in order to produce offspring with the same complex disposition to develop and to reproduce. On the micro-level, this organismal disposition is grounded in certain chemical dispositions of DNA and other biomolecules.

8. *Mutation* is a process that occurs within single organisms, more specifically, within the genetic material of single cells of single organisms. In order to be passed on to the next generation, the mutation has to occur within the germline. It happens because chromosomes can alter under certain conditions. The disposition in question here is surely a multi-track disposition, i.e., a disposition that is not adequately described by a single pair of triggers and ensuing realizations but that allows various triggers and realizations. The realizations of this multi-track disposition can be generically described as "to change the DNA". The causes of these changes, i.e., the potential triggers of this multi-track disposition, can be of quite different kinds. They can be exogenous factors, such as strong radiation hitting and eventually altering DNA, or endogenous factors, such as an intrinsic change of the DNA.

9. *Selection*, finally, considered on the population level, is a complex process that realizes the disposition of a whole population to favor organisms with a certain phenotype within a given environment (and, indirectly, with a certain genotype). Whereas it is difficult to account for this complex disposition fully in terms of the dispositions

of the components of the population, it is plausible that any population has such a disposition.

More work is required if we are to obtain more complete catalogs of working principles or even systematic routines to describe them in terms of dispositions.

5 Interconnections of Function, Working Principle, and Construction

Functions and working principles are central for biomimetic transfers, because they seem to be the same in the biological system and in the engineering system. At least, the same descriptions of functions (i.e., the same verb+noun combination) can be used for both domains. This can be seen in the example of Velcro® in Fig. 1 left (Drack et al. 2018, 2020). In the biological model, the overarching system comprises the interaction of a dog and a burdock plant, leading to seed dispersal. The construction level indicates details of the interacting parts and their properties. Observations suggest that the function in question is to attach an object reversibly. The working principles in this case are elastic bending (cf. Fig. 1) and positive interconnection as represented by the two drawings. The task is seed dispersal. In its technical application, Velcro® is used, for example, to buckle a shoe as the overarching system. Whereas the technical construction and task differ from the biological (role) model (termed "concept generator" by biomimeticists), the function and working principles remain the same and, hence, lie at the core of biomimetic knowledge transfer (Drack et al. 2018).

The conceptual levels that need to be considered in particular in biomimetics are function, working principle, and construction, all of which can easily be linked to the design space (Fig. 2 right). A function such as the *function to attach an object reversibly* provides the indication for an objective and a performance measure. A particular performance measure can be interpreted as a quantified specification of a function. For an engineering construction, one can, for instance, use a specified performance measure such as the attachment force after 1000 cycles of attaching and detaching for the *function to attach an object reversibly*.

At the level of the working principle, the connection to the design space is straightforward. Working principles directly indicate the parameters that can and need to be changed in the process of optimization. For instance, parameters that can be changed in the Velcro® example include the diameter of a single hook, the diameter of the loop, the aspect ratio of the hook, and material parameters such as Young's modulus or the overall hook density.

At the construction level, the parameters determined by the working principles are set to specific values represented by a particular point in the design space. In the final construction, the parameters are set in such a way that performance is high, i.e., the construction adequately fulfills the function. Hence, the concept of optimization via the design space can be seen as connecting the three levels of the scheme, namely function, working principle, and construction (Fig. 2).

A parallel to the categories used in this schema can be seen in computer science in the conceptual distinction of David Marr. Marr's "computational theory", "representation and algorithm" and "hardware implementation" (Marr 2010/1982:25) resemble function, working principle, and construction.

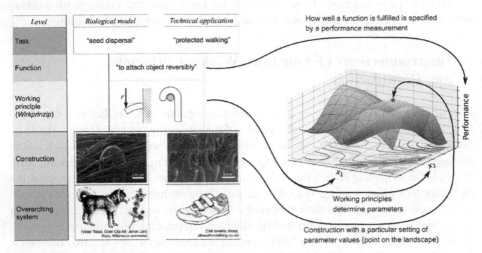

Fig. 2. Conceptual connection of the levels of biomimetic analysis using abstraction and concretization (left) with the design space (right). Further explanation in the text. Modified from Drack and Betz (2022).

6   Two Examples

Two paradigmatic cases of transfers from biological systems to engineered systems will now be described and analyzed in more detail, namely Lilienthal's flying machines and artificial neural networks. Philosophers of science standardly distinguish between the *context of discovery* and the *context of justification* (Seo and Chang 2015). We here focus only on the justification of biomimetic knowledge only along the abstraction and concretization steps from biological system to technical system. In contrast, the discovery of biomimetic knowledge is normally more complex and often iterative in overcoming difficulties, and also involves the transfer of technical knowledge to biology. This is, however, beyond the scope of this paper.

6.1   From Bird to Airplane Wings

The transfer from bird flight to the building of flying machines is in so far remarkable, as the whole research and development (abstraction and concretization) was performed and documented mainly by one person, namely by Otto Lilienthal. Lilienthal's breakthrough was based on a thorough investigation of birds (Lilienthal 1943/1889; Otto Lilienthal Museum n.d.). While anyone can see that birds fly, many observations and experiments were necessary to obtain an understanding and abstraction of the important features and to upscale them for human purposes, in the absence of a physical understanding of aerodynamics. One crucial point was to overcome the idealized conviction that plane foils should be used, whereas Lilienthal found that curved foils produce a much better lift-to-drag ratio.

With regard to our hypotheses about the epistemological profile of biomimetics detailed in Sect. 3, the following can be stated for airplane development:

1. The objects here are the function and working principle, even though a great amount of research into the construction level of the biological "concept generator" and development regarding the engineering construction level were necessary.
2. The abstraction and concretization processes are obvious in Lilienthal's work, with observations of birds, the measurement of lift and drag of various wing profiles, and the building of several gliders with which he flew. The muscles, joints, feathers, etc. are abstracted away in order to derive a parabolic wing profile used in the technical system.
3. Although having an interest mainly in engineering rather than in biology, Lilienthal observed the behavior and morphology of birds, an aspect that can be understood as using the method of technical biology. He also back-tracked from building technical devices to research into birds, i.e., in what we would call today 'reverse biomimetics'. The physical models of wings with parabolic shapes for measurements can be seen as simultaneously being the model of the biological system and model for the application.
4. The ultimate goal clearly was a technical application, a glider (and later an airplane) for humans. The investigations of Lilienthal, however, also clearly show the importance of the goal of understanding the underlying biology in the achievement of building a flying machine.
5. The knowledge for an application (*Anwendungswissen*) grew by investigating birds and performing measurements on wing models. This was accompanied by the introduction of new conceptual tools that formed the basis for scaling airplanes. Diagrams that are today known as drag polar or drag curve (a plot of drag coefficient versus lift coefficient) are rooted in Lilienthal's research. His conclusions concerning curved wing profiles were central, and they contradicted the state-of-the-art knowledge. Lilienthal grasped the working principle only empirically, as the theoretical basis of the emerging field of aerodynamics has only been described many years later. Usage knowledge (*Gebrauchswissen*) was gained throughout the development of several constructed, refined, and tested flying machines, whereby aspects such as steering also played an important role.

It is sometimes said that the development of working airplanes was only possible when birds were not imitated (e.g., Blumenberg 2020). This is partly true (wing flapping is not useful for large machines), but it misses the point that gliding birds (e.g., storks) use the same working principle and function as those early gliders. Creation of thrust with a propeller was the next step; despite the fact that the propeller rotates, the working principle of the bird wing is also applied here.

The ontological analysis shows that the key function for flying is "to generate lift" (even though Lilienthal did not use the terms "lift" or "Auftrieb"). The key working principle is that shapes of airfoils at the proper angle of attack, when in an airflow, create a force, namely the lift, perpendicular to the airflow. Schematically, this working principle is depicted in Fig. 3. Following the discussion in Sect. 4, this working principle can also be described in terms of dispositions. The vertical arrow in Fig. 3 depicts the realization of the disposition. The bearer of the disposition is the wing depicted in a cross-section. The trigger of the disposition is the air flow indicated by the parallel arrows coming from the left. Hence, the working principle consists of the disposition of the bearer experiencing lift force when exposed to an air flow in the perpendicular direction indicated.

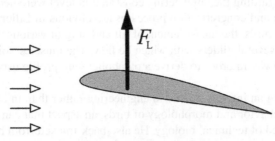

Fig. 3. Key working principle for wings, lift attributable to airflow. Trigger: airflow along a foil. Realization: generated lift.

6.2   From Biological to Artificial Neural Networks

Just as in their biological pre-figurations, artificial neural networks can be used for various goals, e.g., to classify images of dogs and cats. Although the paper of McCulloch and Pitts (1943) is seen as a milestone in the development of artificial neural networks, it does not propose a technical application. However, the abstracted neurons that are logically connected at the synapses form the basis for the development of artificial neural networks, as pursued by Rosenblatt (1958) and others.

With regard to our hypotheses concerning the epistemological profile of biomimetics detailed in Sect. 3, the following can be stated for the development of artificial neural networks:

1. The function of a whole (artificial) neural network may be to classify images of dogs and cats. Therefore, the function of a single neuron may be to process many input signals with learnable (changeable) weights for producing an output signal that can be fed to further neurons. Depending on the level that one considers, the working principle can be a feed-forward loop consisting of several to many neurons (Fig. 1) or the working principle of a single neuron (Fig. 4). The construction level also plays a role here, although the extent to which the pioneers of artificial neural networks (also after the above-mentioned researchers) back-tracked to the construction of nervous systems remains unclear. Other than a history of neuro- and brain science (Breidbach 2016), a detailed historical account of artificial neural networks is apparently still missing.

2. The biomimetic workflow clearly includes abstraction steps toward a logical or mathematical description concerning the way that neurons apparently work. Moreover, a

concretization processes toward applications can be found that importantly includes the training and learning of the various weighting parameters (not further investigated here).

3. Methods of biology and medicine were used to investigate brains from which abstractions were made followed by the utilization of engineering methods (computer science) for simulation and implementation. Historical in-depth analysis of early developments in artificial neural networks is scarce (Rojas 1996), in particular with respect to knowledge transfer from application to biology. Hence, a definitive answer regarding the hypothesis of the circulation of knowledge and the simultaneous use of model of a biological system and model for an application awaits detailed historical research.

4. The ultimate goal for artificial neural networks was the technical application. An understanding of the underlying biology seemed to have occurred independently before bio-inspiration in engineering took place. Hence, biological understanding was indispensable but probably not part of the agenda of the computer scientists.

5. Based on biological knowledge, knowledge for an application (*Anwendungswissen*) was generated for artificial neural networks and was enriched throughout many computer implementations with usage knowledge (*Gebrauchswissen*). Whether and to what extent this (implicitly) enriched the scientific knowledge about the biological system remains to be investigated in detail.

In a first approximation, a neural network can be described as a pair of mathematical functions (activating function and output function) that maps the values of a range of input variables p_1, p_2, ..., p_n to an output variable a via a matching set of weighting parameters w_1, w_2, ..., w_n (Fig. 4). Ontologically, this can easily be described as a multi-track disposition with the network as the bearer, any constellation for the input variables as a trigger, and the outputting of the respective value of a as the realization. However, the particular idea of a neural network is not to have a direct connection between input and output, but to have many cells combined in a directed, but possibly cyclical, structure consisting of many cells (e.g., in a feed-forward way indicated in Fig. 1) that can be described in a similar mathematical way. The single cell of the network is the bearer of the respective multi-track disposition, although any constellation for the input variables is the trigger, and the outputting of the respective value of a is the realization.

7   Conclusion

Our aim has been to analyze biomimetics both from an epistemological and an ontological perspective. For both, we have tested several hypotheses by using the historical examples of airplane wings based on bird wings and artificial neural networks based on biological neural networks.

All the tested hypotheses on the epistemological profile show unique features for Lilienthal's developments and go beyond pure biology and pure engineering. The analysis of the development of (artificial) neural networks hints in the same direction, although more detailed historical investigations are needed if we are to grasp the complete knowledge transfer that took place.

Our guiding ontological hypothesis is that biomimetics concerns three main categories: functions, working principles, and constructions. In this paper, we have especially

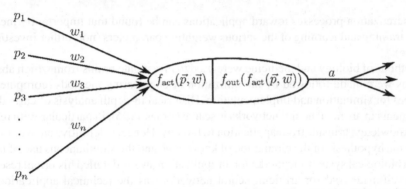

Fig. 4. Key working principle of a neuron cell as used in neural networks. Trigger: input p_1, ... p_n—which is then processed with weights w_1, ... w_n via activation function f_{act} and output function f_{out}. Realization: output a.

discussed our hypothesis that working principles can be modeled as complex dispositions. We have analyzed examples from classical mechanics, optics, cybernetics, and evolutionary biology in order to test this assumption. As a proof of concept, we discuss our two examples from an ontological point of view. In both cases, our ontological hypotheses support the analysis of the underlying working principles.

Acknowledgments. We thank Lena Hinderer for her input on the epistemic profile. This research is funded by the German Research Foundation (DFG) within the project 492191929, "Learning from Nature: Epistemological and Ontological Foundations of Biomimetics".

References

Bar-Cohen, Y. (ed.): Biomimetics: Nature-Based Innovation. CRC Press, Boca Raton (2012)

Barton, A., Jansen, L., Ethier, J.-F.: A taxonomy of disposition-parthood. In: Proceedings of the Joint Ontology Workshops, Bolzano (2017). http://ceur-ws.org/Vol-2050/FOUST_paper_10.pdf. Accessed 9 Mar 2020

Bedau, M.: Where's the good in teleology? In: Allen, C., Bekoff, M., Lauder, G. (eds.) Nature's Purposes, pp. 261–291. MIT Press, Cambridge (1998)

Blumenberg, H.: Nachahmung der Natur. Reclam, Stuttgart (2020)

Breidbach, O.: Die Materialisierung des Ichs, 2nd edn. Suhrkamp, Frankfurt (2016)

Buller, D.J. (ed.): Function, Selection, and Design. SUNY Press, Albany (1999)

Dicks, H.: The Biomimicry Revolution: Learning from Nature How to Inhabit the Earth. Columbia University Press, New York (2023)

DIN-ISO-18458. Biomimetics: Terminology, concepts and methodology. Beuth, Berlin (2015)

Drack, M., Betz, O., Nebelsick, J.H.: Konstruktionslehre, Bionik und phylogenetische Aspekte. In: Werneburg, I., Betz, O. (eds.) Phylogenie, Funktionsmorphologie und Bionik – 60. Phylogenetischen Symposium in Tübingen, pp. 27–38. Scidinge Hall, Tübingen (2020)

Drack, M., Betz, O.: A technomorphic conceptualisation of biological 'constructions' and their evolution. Vertebrate Zool. **72**, 839–855 (2022)

Drack, M., Gebeshuber, I.C.: Comment on "Innovation through imitation: biomimetic, bioinspired and biokleptic research" by A.E. Rawlings, J.P. Bramble and S.S. Staniland, Soft Matter, 2012, 8, 6675. Soft Matter **9**, 2338–2340 (2013)

Drack, M., Limpinsel, M., de Bruyn, G., Nebelsick, J.H., Betz, O.: Towards a theoretical clarification of biomimetics using conceptual tools from engineering design. Bioinspir. Biomim. **13**, 016007 (2018)

Fayemi, P.E., Wanieck, K., Zollfrank, C., Maranzana, N., Aoussat, A.: Biomimetics: process, tools and practice. Bioinspir. Biomim. **12**, 011002 (2017)

Hansson, S.O.: Philosophie der Ingenieurwissenschaften. In: Lohse, S., Reydon, T. (eds.) Grundriss der Wissenschaftsphilosopie: Die Philosophien der Einzelwissenschaften, pp. 357–380. Meiner, Hamburg (2017)

Houkes, W., Vermaas, P.E.: Technical Function. On the Use and Design of Artefacts. Springer, Dordrecht (2010)

Jabbari, E., Kim, D.-H., Lee, L.P., Ghaemmaghami, A., Khademhosseini, A.: Handbook of Biomimetics and Bioinspiration, 3 vols. World Scientific Publishing, Singapore (2014)

Janich, P.: Der Natur nach konstruieren. Erkenntnistheorie und Anwendung. In: Bendele, M., Reiner, R., Reiner, U., Rodeit, S.-H., Wirth, H. (eds.) Natürliche Konstruktionen: Beiträge zum I. Internationalen Symposium des SFB 230 Natürliche Konstruktionen. Leichtbau in Architektur und Natur, pp. 47–53. SFB 230, Stuttgart (1989)

Jansen, L.: Functions, malfunctioning, and negative causation. In: Christian, A., Hommen, D., Retzlaff, N., Schurz, G. (eds.) Philosophy of Science. ESPS, vol. 9, pp. 117–135. Springer, Cham (2018). https://doi.org/10.1007/978-3-319-72577-2_7

Jansen, L.: Tendencies and other realizables in medical information sciences. Monist **90**, 534–555 (2007)

Kapp, E.: Grundlinien einer Philosophie der Technik. Westermann, Braunschweig (1877)

Kornwachs, K.: Strukturen technologischen Wissens. Edition Sigma, Berlin (2012)

Kozaki, K., Mizoguchi, R.: An ontology explorer for biomimetics database. In: Horridge, M., Rospocher, M., van Ossenbruggen, J. (eds.) ISWC: Proceedings of the International Semantic Web Conference 2014 Posters & Demonstrations Track, 13th International Semantic Web Conference, Riva del Garda, pp. 469–472 (2014)

Krickel, B.: The Mechanical World. The Metaphysical Commitments of the New Mechanistic Approach. Springer, Cham (2018)

Kroes, P.: Technical Artefacts: Creations of Mind and Matter. Springer, Dordrecht (2012)

Kroes, P., Meijers, A. (eds.): The Empirical Turn in the Philosophy of Technology. JAI Elsevier, Amsterdam (2000)

Krohs, U.: Eine Theorie biologischer Theorien. Springer, Berlin (2004)

Krohs, U., Kroes, P. (eds.): Functions in Biological and Artificial Worlds. MIT Press, Cambridge (2009)

Krohs, U., Toepfer, G. (eds.): Philosophie der Biologie. Suhrkamp, Frankfurt am Main (2005)

Lenau, T.A., Metze, A.-L., Hesselberg, T.: Paradigms for biologically inspired design. In: Proceedings of SPIE 10593, Bioinspiration, Biomimetics, and Bioreplication VIII: 1059302 (2018)

Lepora, N.F., Verschure, P., Prescott, T.J.: The state of the art in biomimetics. Bioinspir. Biomim. **8**, 013001 (2013)

Lilienthal, O.: Der Vogelflug als Grundlage der Fliegekunst, 4th edn. Oldenburg Wissenschaftsverlag, Berlin (1943/1889)

Machamer, P., Darden, L., Craver, C.F.: Thinking about mechanisms. Philos. Sci. **67**, 1–25 (2000)

Mahner, M., Bunge, M.: Foundations of Biophilosophy. Springer, Berlin (1997)

Marr, D.: Vision. MIT Press, Cambridge (2010/1982)

Marzi, T., Knappertsbusch, V., Marzi, A., Naumann, S., Deerberg, G., Weidner, E.: Fragen zu einer biologischen Technik. UMSICHT-Diskurs Heft 2. Laufen, Oberhausen (2018)

Masselter, T., Bauer, G., Gallenmüller, F., et al.: Biomimetic products. In: Bar-Cohen, Y. (ed.) Biomimetics: Nature-Based Innovation, pp. 377–429. CRC Press, Boca Raton (2012)

McCulloch, W.S., Pitts, W.: A logical calculus of the ideas immanent in nervous activity. Bull. Math. Biophys. **5**, 115–133 (1943)

McInerney, S.J., et al.: E2BMO: facilitating user interaction with a biomimetic ontology via semantic translation and interface design. Designs **2**, 53 (2018)

Mossio, M., Saborido, C., Moreno, A.: An organizational account of biological functions. Br. J. Philos. Sci. **60**, 813–841 (2009)

Nachtigall, W.: Bionik als Wissenschaft: Erkennen, Abstrahieren Umsetzen. Springer, Berlin (2010)

Nicholson, D.J.: The concept of mechanism in biology. Stud. Hist. Philos. Biol. Biomed. Sci. **43**, 152–163 (2012)

Nordmann, A.: Was ist TechnoWissenschaft? – Zum Wandel der Wissenschaftskultur am Beispiel von Nanoforschung und Bionik. In: Rossmann, R., Tropea, C. (eds.) Bionik, pp. 209–218. Springer, Berlin (2005)

Otto Lilienthal Museum. http://www.lilienthal-museum.de/olma/ehome.htm. Accessed 18 Mar 2023

Pahl, G., Beitz, W., Feldhusen, J., Grote, K.H.: Engineering Design: A Systematic Approach. Springer, London (2007)

Prescott, T.J., Lepora, N.F., Verschure, P.F.M.J. (eds.): Living Machines: A Handbook of Research in Biomimetic and Biohybrid Systems. Oxford University Press, Oxford (2018)

Röhl, J., Jansen, L.: Representing dispositions. J. Biomed. Semant. **2**(Suppl. 4), S4 (2011)

Röhl, J., Jansen, L.: Why functions are not special dispositions: an improved classification of realizables for top-level ontologies. Journal of Biomedical Semantics **5**, 27 (2014)

Rojas, R.: Neural Networks. Springer, Berlin (1996)

Rosenblatt, F.: The perceptron: a probabilistic model for information storage and organization in the brain. Psychol. Rev. **65**, 386–408 (1958)

Schiemann, G.: Die Relevanz nichttechnischer Natur. Aristoteles' Natur-Technik-Differenz in der Moderne. In: Hartung, G., Kirchhoff, T. (eds.) Welche Natur brauchen wir?, pp. 67–96. Alber, Freiburg (2014)

Schmidt, J.C.: Vom Leben zur Technik? Kultur- und wissenschaftstheoretische Aspekte der Natur-Nachahmungsthese in der Bionik. Dialektik. Zeitschrift für Kulturphilosophie **2**, 129–142 (2002)

Schurz, G.: "What is normal?" An evolution-theoretic foundation of normic laws and their relation to statistical normality. Philos. Sci. **28**, 476–497 (2001)

Seo, M., Chang, H.: Context of discovery and context of justification. In: Gunstone, R. (ed.) Encyclopedia of Science Education, pp. 229–232. Springer, Dordrecht (2015). https://doi.org/10.1007/978-94-007-2150-0_239

Spear, A.D., Ceusters, W., Smith, B.: Functions in basic formal ontology. Appl. Ontol. **11**, 103–128 (2016)

Speck, T., Speck, O.: Process sequences in biomimetic research. WIT Trans. Ecol. Environ. **114**, 3–11 (2008)

Tamborini, M.: Entgrenzung: Die Biologisierung der Technik und die Technisierung der Biologie. Meiner, Hamburg (2022)

Vincent, J.F.V., Bogatyreva, O.A., Bogatyrev, N.R., Bowyer, A., Pahl, A.K.: Biomimetics: its practice and theory. J. R. Soc. Interface **3**, 471–482 (2006)

Vincent, J.F.V.: An ontology of biomimetics. In: Goel, A.K., McAdams, D.A., Stone, R.B. (eds.) Biologically Inspired Design: Computational Methods and Tools, pp. 269–285. Springer, London (2014)

Vincent, J.F.V.: The trade-off: a central concept for biomimetics. Bioinspired Biomimetic Nanobiomaterials **6**, 67–76 (2017)

Vogel, S.: Rhino horns and paper cups: deceptive similarities between natural and human designs. J. Biosci. **25**(2), 191–195 (2000). https://doi.org/10.1007/BF03404914

von Gleich, A., Pade, C., Petschow, U., Pissarskoi, E.: Potentials and Trends in Biomimetics. Springer, Berlin (2010)

Wachbroit, R.: Normality as a biological concept. Philos. Sci. **61**, 579–591 (1994)

Yim, S., Wilson, J.O., Rosen, D.W.: Development of an ontology for bio-inspired design using description logics. In: International Conference on Product Lifecycle Management, Seoul (2008)

Zoglauer, T.: Modellübertragungen als Mittel interdisziplinärer Forschung. In: Maier, W., Zoglauer, T. (eds.) Technomorphe Organismuskonzepte, pp. 12–24. Frommann-Holzboog, Stuttgart (1994)

Biohybrid Systems and Interactions

Feed Me: Robotic Infiltration of Poison Frog Families

Tony G. Chen[1](✉), Billie C. Goolsby[2], Guadalupe Bernal[1],
Lauren A. O'Connell[2], and Mark R. Cutkosky[1]

[1] Department of Mechanical Engineering, Stanford University, Stanford,
CA 94305, USA
agchen@stanford.edu
[2] Department of Biology, Stanford University, Stanford, CA 94305, USA
http://bdml.stanford.edu

Abstract. We present the design and operation of tadpole-mimetic robots prepared for a study of the parenting behaviors of poison frogs, which pair bond and raise their offspring. The mission of these robots is to convince poison frog parents that they are tadpoles, which need to be fed. Tadpoles indicate this need, at least in part, by wriggling with a characteristic frequency and amplitude. While the study is in progress, preliminary indications are that the TadBots have passed their test, at least for father frogs. We discuss the design and operational requirements for producing convincing TadBots and provide some details of the study design and plans for future work.

Keywords: Biomimetic · Robotic · Animal Studies

1 Introduction

Complex behavioral interactions govern animal social life, especially in relation to parental care and coordination critical for the survival of a species. The mimetic poison frog, *Ranitomeya imitator*, a monogamous poison frog native to the north-central region of eastern Peru, is biparental, meaning that both mothers and fathers must work together as a team for their offspring to have the greatest chances of survival [1–3]. *R. imitator* fathers transport their tadpoles piggy-back style into pools of water situated in bromeliad plant cavities, which they visit and guard at least daily [1–3]. The father deposits one tadpole per pool because the tadpoles are cannibalistic to their sibling conspecifics as a consequence of their low-resource environments [3]. At any time, *R. imitator* parents normally care for one to three tadpoles [22]. When the father observes that a tadpole needs to be fed, he calls for his partner to provision one

Supplementary Information The online version contains supplementary material available at https://doi.org/10.1007/978-3-031-39504-8_20.

F. Meder et al. (Eds.): Living Machines 2023, LNAI 14158, pp. 293–302, 2023.
https://doi.org/10.1007/978-3-031-39504-8_20

to two unfertilized egg meals [15,22]. The tadpoles signal that they are in need of nutritional resources by intensely wriggling, which both parents can observe [22]. When a frog makes contact with the pond, the tadpole also vibrates against the frog's abdomen to elicit care. Rather than using kin recognition, poison frogs use spatial memory of the pool sites to determine which tadpoles to provide with care [16,17,19]. We exploit this characteristic to add robotic tadpole infiltrators into poison frog families, to study parenting and explore which tadpole signals are relevant to care (Fig. 1).

In other work, model frogs, robotic frogs, and even electrodynamic shakers have been used across multiple species to test social decision-making, including treefrogs and tungara frogs [3–5,11,14,20]. In the present case, we are interested in producing tadpole-mimetic robots that can influence parental decision-making. In this context, the test for a robot is whether it can convince *R. imitator* parents that it is a tadpole that needs to be guarded and fed.

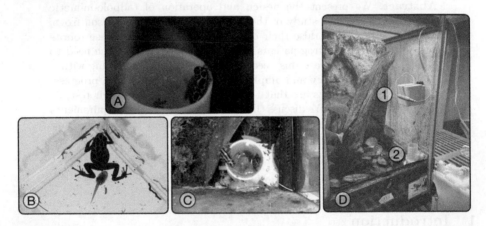

Fig. 1. Infiltration of Poison Frog Families with TadBots. (A) Frogs enter the pools of water with their heads facing away from the tadpole. (B) Young tadpoles, approximately 3/4 the length of a frog, approach the vent of the frog to beg. (C) Parents attempt to coordinate TadBot care. (D) Typical experiment chamber with camera ① positioned above a TadBot canister ②; the canister is identical to those used for biological offspring. Photos A-B courtesy of Daniel Shaykevich.

1.1   Characteristics of Begging in *Ranitomeya imitator*

Begging as a form of parent-offspring communication has independently evolved multiple times across the vertebrate lineages and also within the Amphibia class [6,11,12,21,22]. However, research on what begging actually signals in poison frogs has reached conflicting conclusions. In the strawberry poison frog, *Oophaga pumilio*, which is a female uniparental system, only tadpoles of greater fitness beg, meaning that begging is a signal of quality rather than need [6]. In *R. imitator*, which are biparental and spread the parental burden of care, smaller

and more nutritionally needy tadpoles beg more, suggesting, that begging in
R. imitator is a signal of need [22]. These conflicting signals of quality versus
need reflect a theoretical schism concerning the function of begging in parental
decision-making. In either case, what has not been demonstrated is whether
begging *intensity* acts as a signal that influences parental care.

To investigate whether begging intensity is a signal that influences parental
effort, we need a tractable method of modifying single or multiple features of the
begging signal. *R. imitator* poison frogs are an ideal model to investigate what
information begging signals contain, as poison frogs do not recognize individual
offspring but remember the spatial locations of their nurseries [19]. Therefore, we
hypothesized that it would be possible to cross-foster biological offspring with
robotic tadpole imposters.

In order to maximize our chances with a robotic infiltrator, we first considered the sensory modalities that poison frogs likely employ when interacting
with their offspring: olfactory, visual, and tactile. Nursery water for tadpoles is
often dirty, as it contains detritus, algae, and dirt – all of which are desirable
to poison frogs for hosting offspring in well-resourced environments with stagnant water. Studies suggest that poison frogs likely prioritize olfactory cues in
decision-making about which pools of water to populate [18]. Other studies across
Anurans have shown that touch, especially vibrational processing, is critical for
life-or-death decision-making [6,9]. In red-eyed treefrogs, vestibular mechanoreception dictates the escape-hatch response of embryos [10]. Mechanoreception
presents an evolutionary response to detecting predators like snakes, that may
eat embryos growing on rainforest canopy leaves [10]. Early experimental studies showed that vibration – not olfaction or vision – was the necessary cue to
stimulate egg feeding behavior [11]. In summary, these findings illustrate that
vibration and touch are an important language for frogs with the capacity to
have different meanings in different social contexts.

Begging in *R. imitator* is a dazzling visual and tactile display. During six
minutes of exposure to mothers, tadpoles can beg for 1–4 min intensely wriggling and vibrating their bodies against a parent entering the nursery [22]. For
comparison, studies have shown in other species of poison frog tadpoles that the
mean duration of a begging bout is 12–15 s [6].

1.2   Design Requirements

As noted above, olfactory, visual, and haptic (vibrational and tactile) cues evi-
dently play a role in *R. imitator* parenting. To match olfactory signals, the robot
should function in tadpole-conditioned water, achieved when a tadpole has lived
in the water for at least 24 h, supplemented with detritus such as waste from
frogs and dead flies, which are common to tadpole nurseries. For scale, the neu-
trally buoyant body should be roughly 75%–100% of the length of a parent
(adult size: 16.0–17.5 mm, [2]) to proportionally mimic a tadpole between the
Gosner stages 30–40 [8]. To encapsulate the body we require a soft material to
match the feel of a tadpole's skin which contains its viscera. It is also desirable
to match the tadpole's color, as poison frogs appear to rely on contrast for visual

detection. Finally, we want to mimic the stereotypical begging motion in which the tail undulates with respect to the head, which also vibrates side-to-side. We desire to match the frequencies, amplitudes, and durations recorded in previous observations of tadpoles [6] and our own observations [5]. These parameters are summarized in Table 1 and govern the mechanism design in Sect. 2.1.

Table 1. Required Parameters for TadBot Design.

Requirement	Range	Requirement	Range
overall length	≤20 mm	mass	0.15–0.3 g
head major diameter	≈8 mm	minor diameter	≈6 mm
oscillation freqs	5–25 Hz	amplitude	≈5 mm
skin	dark gray/brown	hardness	≈Shore A 00-20

2   Methods

2.1   Mechanism Design

To meet the design requirements, we have designed and built TadBots that mimic the appearance and begging dynamics of *R. imitator* tadpoles. The body of the TadBot has four major components (Fig. 2). To keep the body small, and isolate any noise and high-frequency motor vibrations from the nursery canister, the TadBot is driven remotely by a motor and crank mechanism that connects to the body using a 30 cm long tendon running through a soft plastic sleeve (Fig. 3C). The tendon acts upon a lever inside the TadBot body that rotates about a dowel pin as a pivot. An elastic band maintains tension and restores the lever position as the tendon relaxes.

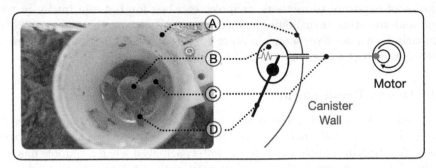

Fig. 2. Tadbot resides inside a plastic canister (A). The body (B) encloses a tail lever (D) that rotates about a pivot under the action of a motor-driven tendon (C) and restoring elastic band.

The TadBot body is suspended inside a water-filled plastic canister, the usual habitat of *R. imitator* tadpoles in the laboratory. This is achieved by having the

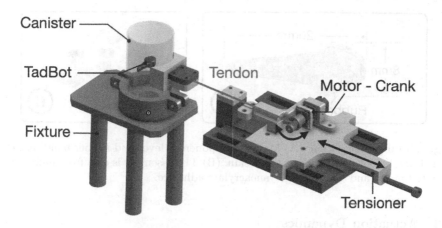

Fig. 3. CAD rendering of TadBot system. TadBot is suspended inside a canister, mounted on a platform in the terrarium where the parents live. The actuation assembly is mounted remotely and consists of a motor-crank mechanism and tensioner.

soft plastic sleeve glued to the TadBot body at one end and to the canister wall at the other end. The tendon terminates at the motor-crank and tensioner mechanism (Fig. 3). TadBots have a mass of 0.3 g and outer dimensions of 20 mm by 8 mm by 5 mm (L×W×D).

For adjustment, the motor-crank assembly is mounted on a platform that slides on a fixed stand, and the relative position of the two can be adjusted by turning a tensioning screw to ensure that (i) the motor-crank assembly is providing enough range of motion to the oscillating lever and (ii) the tendon tension does not exceed the buckling strength of the plastic sleeve.

2.2 Body and Skin

A soft silicone skin approximates the texture and feel of tadpole skin when it comes into contact with a parent. A black pigment is mixed into Ecoflex 00-20 to match the dark gray skin tone of a tadpole. The skin is 1 mm thick and is made in pieces, shown in Fig. 4B. The top and bottom pieces are identical. The side piece is molded to provide the desired profile and enclose the moving parts. The tail is made from a two-part mold so that it can slip onto the end of the oscillating lever. The silicone pieces are glued together with cyanoacrylate adhesive (it is not necessary to form a watertight seal).

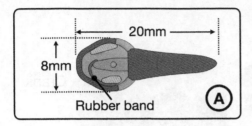

Fig. 4. TadBot fabrication: (A) Moving components (lever and rubber band) are contained in a SmoothOn Eco-Flex 00-20 skin. (B) The assembly is cast from multiple 3D prointed molds and glued using cyanoacrylate adhesive.

2.3 Actuation Dynamics

A frequency and amplitude characterization was conducted to ensure that Tad-Bot's tail achieves the desired wiggling displacement at the desired operating frequencies (Table 1). Two markers were drawn on the head of a TadBot spaced 4.2 mm apart, with a 15° offset from the transverse plane (Fig. 5). Then a line is drawn from the bisection point between these two points and the pivot point of the tail to establish the median line along the sagittal plane. An additional marker is placed at the tip of the tail, and the amplitude is measured between this marker and the median line. The results are plotted in Fig. 5.

At frequencies below 8 Hz, consistent with gentle, non-begging swimming, the tail appears relatively free of inertial effects and undergoes a low amplitude oscillation. As the frequency increases 10 Hz, there is some additional displacement due to the inertia of the silicone tail. The behavior, however, is not noticeably resonant, and the amplitude plateaus between 15–28 Hz, which covers the upper limit of observed begging frequencies in tadpoles (Table 1).

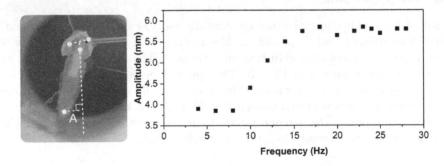

Fig. 5. Relationship between wiggling frequency and amplitude (A) of the tail displacement, measured with a camera at 240 fps tracking markers on the head and tail.

2.4   Experiment Setup and Procedure

Multiple aquarium tanks are set up for the pair-bonded frog parents (Fig. 1). Tadpoles inside the habitat are swapped out with TadBots after successful feeding behaviors from the parents are observed. To normalize care efforts across pairs, the number of tadpoles was controlled by limiting the number of nurseries available for parents to deposit. Any extra tadpoles deposited were subsequently removed from the tank. The experiment setup is shown in Fig. 1D.

All *R. imitator* used in the laboratory study were captive-bred in our poison frog colony or purchased from Ruffing's Ranitomeya (Tiffon, Ohio, USA). One adult male and female are housed together in a $45.72 \times 30.48 \times 30.48$ cm terrarium (Exoterra, Rolf C. Hagen USA, Mansfield, MA) containing sphagnum moss substrate, driftwood, live Pothos plants, horizontally mounted film canisters as egg deposition sites, and additional film canisters filled with water, treated with reverse osmosis (R/O Rx, Josh's Frogs, Owosso, MI) for tadpole deposition. Terraria were automatically misted ten times daily for 20 s each, and frogs were fed live *Drosophila melanogaster* flies dusted with vitamin powder, thrice weekly. The tanks were also supplemented with *Folsomia candida* and *Trichorhina tomentosa*. The observation housing was set on a 12:12 light cycle from 07:00 to 19:00 h. The average temperature and humidity were recorded for each day of observation, usually around 25° and 95% humidity within the tank. The experiment is approved under Stanford APLAC protocol 34242.

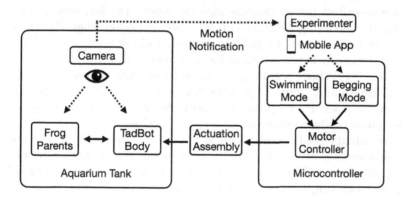

Fig. 6. System diagram of the experiment. A camera observes the interaction between the frog parents and the TadBot. Once a motion is detected, a notification is sent to the experimenter, who can control the operation of TadBot through a mobile app.

Wyze v3 cameras were adhered by velcro onto the side of the Exoterra tanks and suspended above the tadpole canisters, with the face of the camera approximately 17.5 cm above the bottom of the canister. Cameras were given 256 GB SD cards to store a month of recording. The camera observation methods are described in previous work [7].

A motion detection notification is sent to the experimenters when the Wyze camera detects any frog movements. Then, based on the reaction of the frogs, and at the experimenter's discretion, TadBot is activated using one of two modes through the use of a mobile app. The two modes are intended to make TadBot more analogous to living tadpoles, with different paradigms of movement to reflect affiliative and neutral behaviors. The *swimming* mode commands Tad-Bot to intermittently wiggle its tail in 8 Hz (15 s on, 10 s off, repeat 3 times). The *begging* mode issues a wiggling signal 16 Hz with the same pattern. Using swimming mode versus begging mode enables the experimenter to test which frequencies a frog uses to make care decisions. The microcontrollers used in this experiment, Particle Argons, are connected to the cloud through local WiFi (Fig. 6).

To determine the influence of begging on parental decision-making, poison frog families are placed into randomized trials after a biological tadpole has been deposited into a nursery and is confirmed to be fed at least once. Parents are exposed to, in randomized order: a cross-foster living tadpole (a positive control); a TadBot with no actuation assembly (negative control); and a TadBot with an actuation assembly (experimental group). Parents are provided with two weeks per experimental stimulus, the approximate time necessary to observe repeated bouts of paternal monitoring, and at least one bout of maternal provisioning.

3   Conclusions and Future Work

We have described how a tadpole-mimetic robot, TadBot, was developed for studying the parenting behaviors of *R. imitator* poison frogs. TadBots physically resemble *R. imitator* tadpoles, operate in tadpole nurseries, and mimic the tadpoles' begging behavior which includes vigorous tail wiggling at characteristic frequencies. To evaluate parenting response to begging intensity, an experiment involving multiple *R. imitator* parents has been constructed in which TadBots are substituted for live tadpoles and controlled remotely using cameras and a mobile app to produce swimming or begging motions.

A preliminary study is in progress with $n = 4$ parenting pairs. In all of these pairs we have observed on multiple occasions that fathers, after observing begging signals from TadBots, have begun to coordinate care, distinguished by calling and soliciting mothers to tadpole nurseries to provision them (Fig. 1C). The calls are consistent with those documented in [15]. Examples of the behaviors can be seen in videos posted at http://bdml.stanford.edu/TadBot to accompany this paper. Tadpoles beg to both their mothers and fathers [22]. Mothers decide to provision eggs based on signals that are not entirely clear but may include vibrational signals from the tadpoles (which may include physical contact) and acoustic signals from the fathers. Thus far we have observed the mothers visiting the begging tadbot, but no unfertilized eggs were deposited More longitudinal work is necessary to determine quantitatively the amount of care that robotic tadpoles receive versus biological offspring.

Ongoing work includes refinement of TadBots based on the preliminary study. In the next generation we will employ a softer and more flexible tubing for the tendon, to allow more movement inside of canister – in part so that TadBots can more convincingly vibrate their heads against the mothers. Another refinement will be to coat the skin with a hydrogel, as described in [13], to increase tactile realism.

Acknowledgements. The authors acknowledge that this research was conducted on the ancestral lands of the Muwekma Ohlone people at Stanford. We thank the Laboratory of Organismal Biology for support, assistance, and input. We thank Dave Ramirez and Madison Lacey for their continued care of our poison frog colony.

Funding. T.G.C was supported by a NSF Graduate Research Fellowship. B.C.G. was supported by an HHMI Gilliam Fellowship (GT15685) and a NIH Cellular Molecular Biology Training Grant (T32GM007276). This research was funded with grants from the NIH (DP2HD102042) and the New York Stem Cell Foundation. LAO is a New York Stem Cell Foundation-Robertson Investigator.

References

1. Brown, J.L., Morales, V., Summers, K.: A key ecological trait drove the evolution of biparental care and monogamy in an amphibian. Am. Nat. **175**(4), 436–446 (2010)
2. Brown, J.L., et al.: A taxonomic revision of the neotropical poison frog genus ranitomeya (amphibia: Dendrobatidae). Zootaxa **3083**(1), 1–120 (2011)
3. Brown, J., Morales, V., Summers, K.: Divergence in parental care, habitat selection and larval life history between two species of Peruvian poison frogs: an experimental analysis. J. Evol. Biol. **21**(6), 1534–1543 (2008)
4. Caldwell, M.S., Johnston, G.R., McDaniel, J.G., Warkentin, K.M.: Vibrational signaling in the agonistic interactions of red-eyed treefrogs. Curr. Biol. **20**(11), 1012–1017 (2010)
5. Coss, D.A., Ryan, M.J., Page, R.A., Hunter, K.L., Taylor, R.C.: Can you hear/see me? multisensory integration of signals does not always facilitate mate choice. Behav. Ecol. **33**(5), 903–911 (2022)
6. Dugas, M.B., Strickler, S., Stynoski, J.L.: Tadpole begging reveals high quality. J. Evol. Biol. **30**(5), 1024–1033 (2017)
7. Goolsby, B.C., Fischer, M.T., Pareja-Mejia, D., Lewis, A.R., Raboisson, G., O'Connell, L.A.: Home security cameras as a tool for behavior observations and science equity. bioRxiv, pp. 2023–04 (2023)
8. Gosner, K.L.: A simplified table for staging anuran embryos and larvae with notes on identification. Herpetologica **16**(3), 183–190 (1960)
9. Hill, P.S., Mazzoni, V., Stritih-Peljhan, N., Virant-Doberlet, M., Wessel, A.: Biotremology: Physiology, Ecology, and Evolution. Springer, Cham (2022). https://doi.org/10.1007/978-3-030-97419-0
10. Jung, J., Kim, S.J., Pérez Arias, S.M., McDaniel, J.G., Warkentin, K.M.: How do red-eyed treefrog embryos sense motion in predator attacks? assessing the role of vestibular mechanoreception. J. Exp. Biol. **222**(21), jeb206052 (2019)
11. Jungfer, K.H.: Reproduction and parental care of the coronated treefrog, Anotheca spinosa (Steindachner, 1864)(Anura: Hylidae). Herpetologica **52**, 25–32 (1996)

12. Kam, Y.C., Yang, H.W.: Female-offspring communication in a Taiwanese tree frog, Chirixalus eiffingeri (Anura: Rhacophoridae). Anim. Behav. **64**(6), 881–886 (2002)
13. Kight, A., et al.: Decoupling transmission and transduction for improved durability of highly stretchable, soft strain sensing: Applications in human health monitoring. Sensors **23**(4), 1955 (2023)
14. Klein, B.A., Stein, J., Taylor, R.C.: Robots in the service of animal behavior. Commun. Integr. Biol. **5**(5), 466–472 (2012)
15. Moss, J.B., Tumulty, J.P., Fischer, E.K.: Evolution of acoustic signals associated with cooperative parental behavior in a poison frog. Proc. Natl. Acad. Sci. **120**(17), e2218956120 (2023)
16. Ringler, E., Barbara Beck, K., Weinlein, S., Huber, L., Ringler, M.: Adopt, ignore, or kill? male poison frogs adjust parental decisions according to their territorial status. Sci. Rep. **7**(1), 1–6 (2017)
17. Ringler, E., Pašukonis, A., Ringler, M., Huber, L.: Sex-specific offspring discrimination reflects respective risks and costs of misdirected care in a poison frog. Anim. Behav. **114**, 173–179 (2016)
18. Serrano-Rojas, S.J., Pašukonis, A.: Tadpole-transporting frogs use stagnant water odor to find pools in the rainforest. J. Exp. Biol. **224**(21), jeb243122 (2021)
19. Stynoski, J.L.: Discrimination of offspring by indirect recognition in an egg-feeding dendrobatid frog, Oophaga pumilio. Anim. Behav. **78**(6), 1351–1356 (2009)
20. Taylor, R.C., Klein, B.A., Stein, J., Ryan, M.J.: Faux frogs: multimodal signalling and the value of robotics in animal behaviour. Animal Behaviour (2008)
21. Wright, J., Leonard, M.l.: The Evolution of Begging: Competition, Cooperation and Communication. Springer, Dordrecht (2007). https://doi.org/10.1007/0-306-47660-6
22. Yoshioka, M., Meeks, C., Summers, K.: Evidence for begging as an honest signal of offspring need in the biparental mimic poison frog. Anim. Behav. **113**, 1–11 (2016)

Triboelectric Charging During Insect Walking on Leaves: A Potential Tool for Sensing Plant-Insect Interactions

Serena Armiento⬤, Fabian Meder(✉) ⬤, and Barbara Mazzolai(✉) ⬤

Istituto Italiano di Tecnologia (IIT), 16163 Genova, GE, Italy
{fabian.meder,barbara.mazzolai}@iit.it

Abstract. Plant-insect interactions are crucial for most ecosystems, and they are still not fully understood. Detecting and monitoring interactions of insects with plants could enable tools to observe pollination and circumvent potential damage to crop plants by pests. Sensorized artificial traps have made significant advances in monitoring pests in crop fields. Nevertheless, a direct measurement from the leaf level could further improve the resolution of such technologies. Here, we explore the opportunity to use the plant leaf itself as a biohybrid sensor for plant-insect interactions. Instead of measuring electrophysiological signals, we investigate the spontaneous charging of a *Nerium oleander* leaf surface during walking of *Halyomorpha halys* (better known as Asian stink bug) by contact or triboelectrification using high-resolution current recordings and the ion-conductive leaf tissue as a measurement electrode. Our results suggest that the insect's walking and take-off from the leaf surface produce characteristic static surface charges potentially due to contact/triboelectrification that are electrostatically induced into the cellular tissue. Although further investigations are required to understand the phenomenon and its capabilities, it suggests that the leaf could be directly used as a sensor for insect-leaf interactions. This could be a tool to investigate insect-plant interactions under controlled laboratory conditions and may, in the future, benefit technologies like smart and precision agriculture and even measuring interactions of robotic insects with plants on the leaf level by tuning the triboelectric signals.

Keywords: Plant-insect interactions · biohybrid sensors · plant-hybrid energy conversion · contact electrification

1 Introduction

Plants and insects interact in various ways with each other, either both organisms can benefit from the interaction, or one or both partners are harmed. Developing methods and technologies to study and understand the interplay between the two organisms at a molecular level as well as at an ecological level is essential [1–4]. Especially crop and food security depend on plant-insect interactions: whereas insect-mediated pollination is essential and needs to be supported, destructive pests can be a risk to crops. An example of an invasive species and common agricultural pest is the stink bug *Halyomorpha*

© The Author(s), under exclusive license to Springer Nature Switzerland AG 2023
F. Meder et al. (Eds.): Living Machines 2023, LNAI 14158, pp. 303–317, 2023.
https://doi.org/10.1007/978-3-031-39504-8_21

halys (Heteroptera: Pentatomidae) which has become an agricultural and urban plague diffusing from Asia to the USA (mid 90s) to Europe (early 2000s) and more recently to Australia, New Zealand, and Chile [1] *H. halys* not only has few natural biological enemies in its new territories, it is also characterized by a varied diet, both crop and wild plants, and high mobility, making it a potentially destructive species difficult to contain. One effective means of control are broad spectrum pesticides, which, however, are environmentally questionable, cause damage, and even secondary pests [1, 2].

Knowledge of population dynamics and associated ecological factors is fundamental to efficient pest management design. However, monitoring insect pests in many cases is still performed by manually counting the specimens found in the fields or by costly, not widely accessible, techniques like radar technologies monitoring pest migration, high-resolution video equipment to observe flying insects, thermal imaging, satellite-based telemetry, ultrasound detections. Yet, additional methods are being developed like automatized sensor systems such as sensorized traps in which machine learning techniques are used to count and recognize insect species based on images. Furthermore, some systems use species-specific acoustic traces to detect their presence [3–7]. Especially the widely used trap-based techniques require the insect to interact with artificial devices. Interesting for further and better integration of insect monitoring technology in the ecosystem would be, if the plant itself could be used as sensor to detect the insects.

A possibility to monitor insects could be the contact between the insect's feet and the leaf surface. Plant leaves have recently been shown to act as energy converters producing electric currents from mechanical forces applied on their surface by solid contacts and raindrops hitting the leaf cuticle [8, 9]. This phenomenon is mainly based on the physical interaction of materials and known as tribo- or contact electrification; it has been used both for energy harvesting and sensing purposes [8–12] Dielectric materials exchange charges when coming in transient periodic contact with each other [13–16]. The charges on plant leaves are produced on the dielectric cuticle, the outermost leaf surface, and are then electrostatically induced into the inner tissues, an ionic conductor. The surface charges can be analyzed by inserting an electrode into the living plant tissue [17]. Measurements of triboelectric charges, especially when recorded on living organisms by a single electrode, are not akin to recording electrophysiological signals since they arise from the materials' interaction (here the leaf cuticle and the insect exoskeleton) and not from a physiological response.

Here we analyze the charges and resulting currents produced in an *N. oleander* leaf while a brown-marmorated stink bug (*H. halys*) is interacting with the leaf surface. We use a typical circuit that allows to detect triboelectrification of the leaf cuticle [17, 18]. By current measurements and video recordings, we identified three specific patterns in the electrical recordings that relate to the observed insect motion (walking, pausing, and take-off). To investigate the nature of the currents produced by the insect on the leaf in more detail, we reproduced the interactions using a single foot and artificially actuate it at a controlled frequency towards the leaf surface. The current signal shape and dynamics suggest a triboelectric mechanism producing the signals and the measurements, thus showing that this could be used for sensing different dynamics of insects on the leaves. Such a tool, in combination with others, could be useful in laboratory settings to study plant-insect interactions, and provide new sensing technologies for smart and precision agriculture or monitoring robotic insects in the future.

2 Materials and Methods

2.1 Plant Samples

Leaves were freshly picked before each experiment from an *N. oleander* growing outdoors in Genoa, Italy. The leaves were used for a maximum period of 1–2 h. A gold-coated pin electrode was inserted in the petiole where it was removed from the stem for electrical measurements.

2.2 Insect Specimen

Alive and dead Heteroptera, most likely *H. halys*, also known as brown-marmorated stink bugs, were collected close to the windows in our laboratories during autumn 2022. Alive stinkbugs were captured only for the period of the experiments. The bugs were gently handled and carefully placed on the *N. oleander* leaf. The leaf was kept at an angle of about 30°, which triggered the bug to walk upwards to reach the "highest point" and then take off from the leaf. After the period of the experiments (typically 1–2 h), the bugs were released outdoors. No harm was done to the insects. The collected dead insects have been used for microscopy and controlled triboelectric stimulation. For this, legs were removed from the dead specimen and installed on a mechanical actuator to perform the experiments detailed below.

2.3 Experiments

Electric Measurements with Live Insects. The free-standing *N. oleander* leaf was mounted in a holder that kept it inclined at an angle of ~30°, and it was then connected to a high input impedance electrometer (6517B, Keithley, USA) through a gold-plated pin electrode that was inserted into the petiole. Figure 1 illustrates the setup using a typical configuration to measure triboelectric surface charges on leaves [17]. The insect was then placed on the leaf tip and typically walked upwards along the leaf blade. The short circuit currents generated in the leaf upon walking of the insect take-off were measured in fA resolution and in high time resolution (20000 samples per second) by an oscilloscope (MSO7014A, Agilent Technologies, USA) connected to the electrometer. All measurements have been performed in a Faraday cage under ambient conditions (temperature typically 22 °C and 50% relative humidity, RH).

Controlled Mechanical Stimulation with Single Legs. The exoskeleton of a single *H. halys* leg was carefully removed from the main body of the dead specimen using tweezers and glued onto a sample holder with a drop of hot glue. The sample holder was mounted on a self-made actuator that allowed to apply a regular, vertical motion to the leg to precisely control its interaction with the leaf surface (the setup is described in detail elsewhere) [17]. In short, the setup consists of a linear actuator (4O HiFi full range driver, diameter 8 cm, model FRS, Visaton, Germany) driven by a monolithic power amplifier

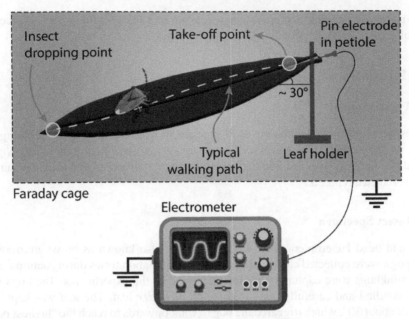

Fig. 1. Schematic of the experimental approach to record the triboelectric signals generated by contact electrification during leaf-insect interactions. The leaf is fixed in an inclined position, and the living bug is dropped onto the tip of the leaf (here *N. oleander*). The inclination triggers *H. halys* to walk upwards along the leaf blade, where it typically takes off from the leaf. The setup is placed in a Faraday cage to reduce noise. The current signals are measured at a pin electrode inserted into the petiole.

(OPA549T, Burr-Brown, USA) controlled by a function generator (GFG-8217A, GW Instek, Taiwan) used to create a vertical motion to stimulate the leaves selecting waveform, frequency, amplitude, and offset. A sinusoidal stimulus with a frequency of 5 Hz was applied. The electrical signals generated in the leaf were then measured as described above.

Microscopy. The exoskeleton of a dead *H. halys* was imaged by digital microscopy using a KH-8700 (Hirox, Japan) and by scanning electron microscopy (SEM) using an EVO MA10 (Zeiss, Germany).

3 Results

3.1 Characteristics of Electric Signals Generated by Leaf-Insect Interaction

Figures 2a and 2b show the time-resolved short circuit current signals that have been recorded at the electrode inserted in the inner leaf tissue after the *H. halys* specimen has been released on the leaf tip, as described in Fig. 1. A total of ten experiments have been conducted, and the graphs shown represent the behaviors that we have observed. The release of the insect on the leaf causes a negative peak at the beginning of each graph.

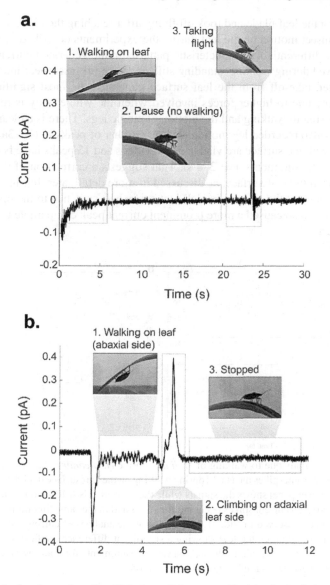

Fig. 2. Electric signals produced by *H. halys* walking on an *N. oleander* leaf. a) and b) show the currents measured at an electrode inserted in the leaf's petiole as a function of time and insect behavior. Characteristic patterns in the current measurements for walking, standing still, take-off, and switching leaf sides are highlighted. The inset images are frames from Video 1 showing the insect movement during the measurements. The first peak that has not been highlighted in the yellow boxes is an artefact due to the release of the insect on the leaf tip.

We excluded this peak from our analysis as it is not directly related to the leaf-insect interaction. It may be partially due to touching the leaf while releasing the arthropod or noise from opening the Faraday cage. Subsequently, the insects typically walked upwards along the leaf blade and took off flying after reaching the highest point. Video 1 shows the insect motion on the leaf during the experiments described in Figs. 2a and 2b. Distinctly differentiable, characteristic patterns in the generated current amplitude can be observed during walking, standing still, and take-off insect-leaf interactions. As discussed later, take-off from the leaf surface generated the most significant current peaks, possibly due to higher forces involved when the whole body is released from the leaf compared to walking and the motion of single legs. There is a clear correlation between the video recorded leg motion and the number of peaks in Fig. 3a (14 leg lifts and contacts with the surface are visible in the videos and 13 peaks have been observed in the current measurements, t = 2–4 s). That suggests a correlation of the contact of the leg/foot with the leaf surface, as discussed in more detail later. In Fig. 2b, the walk of *H. halys* started at the lower (abaxial) leaf surface. It switched to the upper (adaxial leaf side), which also caused a more prominent current peak comparable to the take-off peak in Fig. 2a.

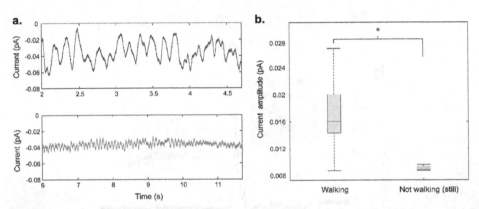

Fig. 3. Current signals due to walking of *H. halys* on the *N. oleander* leaf. a) The upper panel shows the in situ current spikes measured during walking on the leaf surface in high time resolution. In contrast, the lower panel shows the signals while the arthropod is still standing on the leaf blade as a reference. Sixteen current spikes occur within ~2.7 s and in the same timeframe and 16 visible footsteps have been observed in Video1. b) Boxplot of the analysis of current amplitudes during walking and still standing on the leaf showing a significant difference confirming the sensing of walking using a single electrode in the leaf (seven measurements for walking and three for still standing, respectively, two-sample t-test, p-value <0.05).

Further analysis of the current amplitudes during walking and resting on the leaf is given in Fig. 3b. Walking produces distinct signals with a median amplitude of 0.016 pA. When the insect remains still, the signals immediately reduce to noise level with a median amplitude of 0.009 pA. The boxplot in Fig. 3b shows the statistics of the current patterns registered during walking and still standing from seven measurements with about 10–20 steps each and three recordings with a standing insect, respectively. The average current amplitudes were tested with a two-sample t-test showing that the values are significantly different with a p-value of <0.05. The results confirm that the current amplitude is significantly increased during walking. Thus, they seem to be caused by the dynamic interaction of the foot and leg with the leaf surface. The movements that involve the expectedly largest forces between feet and the leaf surface are switching between leaf surfaces and the take-off for flying. These motions generated current spikes up to 0.4 pA. Typically, positive current spikes have been observed for this event, and the signal shape varied slightly, i.e., the take-off was usually associated with narrower peak widths compared to that for switching leaf sides.

The video also shows episodes where a standing bug lifts off one or two feet and touches down. This seems to lead to more subtle signals. The reasons could be a) the signals are of lower magnitude and hidden in noise, b) the camera recordings do not allow to justify if a real surface contact occurred, and c) the surface contact did not generate sufficient surface charges for example due to very low contact forces. Although this effect may help to distinguish a moving from a standing insect, further studies are required with detailed tracking of insect motion and leaf interaction, potentially coupled with force measurements.

3.2   Electric Signals Produced by an Artificially Actuated Arthropod Leg *ex vivo*

To further investigate the origin of the signals produced by *H. halys* on the *N. oleander* leaf in more detail, we mounted a leg from the exoskeleton of a dead specimen on a linear actuator to apply a controlled touch-release stimulus with the foot *ex vivo* on the leaf surface. The motion thus resembles a single step on the leaf surface with a single foot, and the setup is shown in Fig. 4a. The actuator was programmed to move the leg vertically at a frequency of 5 Hz with a vertical displacement of about 5 mm.

The experiment was designed to test if contact/triboelectric charging could be a potential source of the observed electrical signals. We used a previously described setup that we have developed to test charging events on the leaf cuticle upon interactions with solid and liquid materials [17, 18]. The leaf was then elevated to achieve repeated contact and separation between the leaf surface and the ablated foot. Figure 4b shows the multicycle current signals that the repeated motion caused in the inner leaf tissue showing a distinct current peak each time the leaf surface is touched. The reference measurement shows the signals during the motion of the actuated leg above the leaf surface but without contacting it, which shows that only contact and subsequent release from the surface create significant current spikes. The zoom-in in a single signal in Fig. 4c suggests a positive current peak during the approach of the foot towards the leaf surface and a negative current spike when the foot is released from the surface after contact. The alternating current signal is characteristic for a triboelectric mechanism coupled with electrostatic induction of the charges caused by contact electrification of the leaf and foot surfaces, as discussed in more detail below. Amplitudes of up to 1.7 nA are observed, which are about four times higher than those observed during the take-off of the freely moving insect. This is likely due to higher impact forces and repeated stimulation of the same position by the artificially actuated leg. It could be a further hint towards contact electrification as a mechanism for the current generation since the charge generation on the leaf surface is force dependent [17].

Figures 5a–d show digital microscopy and scanning electron microscopy (SEM) images of the structure of the exoskeleton of *H. halys* legs and feet. *H. halys* have six legs consisting of mostly chitin and proteins like resilin [19, 20]. The close-up micrographs

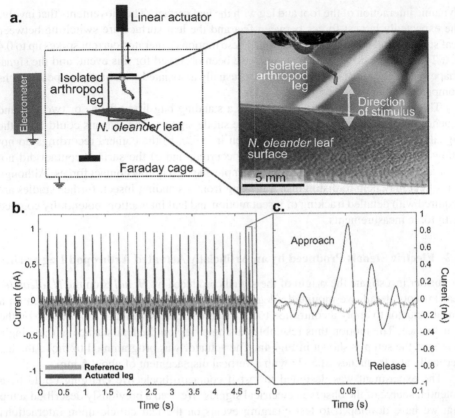

Fig. 4. Electric signals produced by an artificially actuated foot of *H. halys ex vivo* on a living *N. oleander* leaf. a) Overview of the measurement setup and photograph showing the isolated leg and leaf surface. b) Current signals generated by the foot-leaf contact during a 5 Hz sinusoidal multicycle stimulation of the leaf surface with the isolated foot *ex vivo* (blue line). The reference curve (yellow line) shows data obtained from actuating the same leg over the leaf surface but without contacting the surface. c) Zoom-in of a single current peak. It is assumed that the positive peak relates to the approach of the foot towards the surface, whereas the negative peak results from the release of the foot from the leaf surface after contact, as further detailed in the discussion. (Color figure online)

reveal the presence of the attachment hairs setae. The primary function of the setae is to improve adhesion with substrates by van der Waals forces [21]. A claw is visible at the end of the feet (Fig. 5d), which is believed to improve grasping on slippery surfaces. Although we did not observe pulvilli, the adhesive pads are expected to be present on the living *H. halys* feet, contributing to the surface contact [20]. Consequently, a series of different structures will be in contact with the leaf surface during walking and take-off. The resulting contact and separation motion each time a leg is lifted, and a foot separated from the leaf surface could lead to contact electrification of the leaf surface which is suggested to cause the current signals in our measurement configuration.

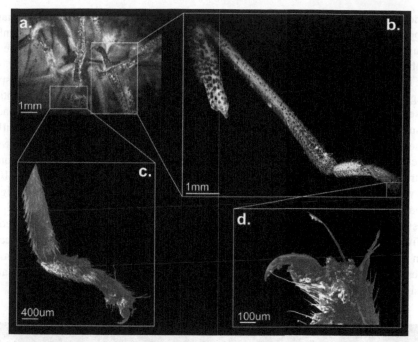

Fig. 5. Micrographs of *H. halys* feet and illustration of the current generation mechanism based on a triboelectric mechanism. a) and b) digital microscopy and c) and d) SEM images of the exoskeleton of the feet, respectively.

4 Discussion

4.1 Origin of the Current Signals

Our measurements suggest a contribution of contact-/triboelectrification and electrostatic induction as a possible explanation for the currents we measured in the leaf tissue during insect walking. First, the currents only occur when a contact is coupled with a release motion. Still standing of *H. halys* on the leaf does not cause current spikes. Hence, both contact and separation are necessary. It has been reported earlier that the leaf cuticle, surface lipids, and waxes tend to charge positively upon contact with other materials through contact electrification [17, 18, 22–24]. The polarity and mixture of charged species created on surfaces during contact electrification strongly depend on the material pair that comes in contact, which occurs on most materials [14, 15, 25–28]. When materials come in direct contact or so close that van der Waals forces occur, the subsequent separation often leads to surface charges. These charges affect ion motion in the cellular tissue acting as electrodes into which charges on the leaf surface are electrostatically induced.

Figure 6 illustrates the potential mechanism of current generation due to the triboelectric effect. The contact between the *H. halys* feet and the leaf surface creates charges on both objects by contact electrification. The figure shows the charge distribution at separation after the previous contact. In the separation stage, the static charges created on the dielectric leaf cuticle are electrostatically induced and compensated by charges of opposite polarity in the ion-conductive cellular tissue. This creates the electron inflow through the electrode connected to the tissue resulting in a negative current spike that we observed during stimuli with a single foot *ex vivo*.

The multicycle experiment of Fig. 4 can indeed explain the positive current spike. It suggests that the foot bears positive static surface charges due to previous contacts. These charges balance the negative charges on the leaf surface when it reapproaches the surface, causing an opposite current in the tissue characterized by a current outflow in the measurement instrument resulting in the positive current spike. This shows an AC current generation that is typical for a repeated contact and coupling of contact electrification and electrostatic induction. Also, the signal peak duration of about ~10 ms (full width at half maximum) is a time domain typically observed for triboelectric signals in leaves [17]. Although time domains and signal shapes of the current peaks during measurements with *H. halys in vivo* (Fig. 3a) differ from those with the actuated leg *ex vivo* (Fig. 4b), the results obtained by the isolated leg suggest that surface electrification upon contact may contribute to the signal generation. Then contact duration, impact forces, multiple contact-release patterns, pre-charging, and the environment will affect the signal amplitude and time domains.

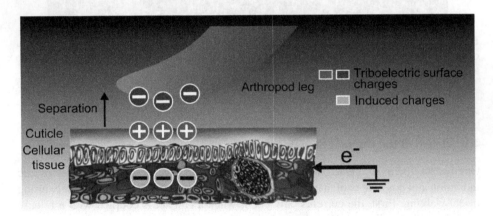

Fig. 6. Illustration of the suggested current generation mechanism due to the triboelectric effect between the *H. halys* feet and the leaf surface. The figure shows the moment of separation after a previous contact. The contact generates charges on the leaf and feet surface materials by contact electrification. After separation, the charges on the leaf's surface are electrostatically induced into the ion-conductive cellular tissue of the leaf, where it creates an electron inflow through the electrode connected to the tissue.

Here, it is interesting to mention that the signals for take-off and switching leaf sides have a significantly higher time duration and amplitude, which could indicate that other mechanisms play an additional role which would need to be investigated in more detail in the future. The higher forces exerted during take-off could also possibly play a role, potentially causing higher triboelectric signals. However, also a pre-charge of the main insect body, such as reported for bumble bees, would generate additional electric fields acting on the ions in the tissue which may be another factor influencing the signals' shape. Electric fields play a crucial role in insect-plant interactions, especially in bumblebees and honeybees [29–33]. Recent studies indicate that insects charge positively by walking on dielectric surfaces or by atmospheric electric fields during flight [34–36]. It would be interesting to include those species in the future together with measurements of the body charge.

Electrophysiological responses have also been recorded upon plant-insect interactions, especially upon mechanical damage caused by feeding [37–39]. However, our electrode configuration differs from typical electrophysiological measurements and would likely not pick up the related potential differences but focuses instead on materials-based contact charging. In summary, our analysis strongly suggests that insect feet-leaf interactions can cause contact electrification of the leaf surface and currents in the leaf tissue, yet further analysis is required to fully clarify the mechanism.

4.2 Using the Leaf as a Sensor for Insect Interactions

Our results show that characteristic signals for insect-leaf interactions can be measured using a single electrode in the cellular tissue. Contact electrification is likely causing the reported signals. Thus, the leaf acts as a mechanical-to-electrical energy converter that facilitates the registration of the current signals, even for traction forces as low as that of single arthropod footsteps which have been reported to be in the range of 2–25 mN [40]. The exerted forces show a strong dependency on the leaf morphology [19, 40–42] and we expect that traction forces and current signals may change in other plants and could be particularly interesting in those species which present specific adaptations that obstruct insect navigation on the leaf surface [43, 44].

Moreover, different behaviors like walking and take-off can be clearly distinguished. Detailed information on the leaf-insect interaction can be sensed straightforwardly. This could be especially interesting for research and laboratory settings in which, for example, the response of insects to leaf treatments which affect adhesion and other pest controls are developed and tested. Further tests are required for example using different species (both insects and plants) and performing measurements paired with high-speed camera tests from different angles. Moreover, setups that allow registering adhesion forces could give further information on the leg-leaf interaction forces [43, 44]. Yet, our results show that information in high resolution like interactions of single steps could be straightforwardly obtained by our method. A critical factor is adequate control of the electrical noise in the environment to allow measuring currents in the fA to nA range. Although this can be easily achieved in laboratory settings using a Faraday cage, outdoors and in the field, this will be more difficult, and noise elimination will play a more crucial role. We previously showed that plants pick-up also radiofrequency signals causing significant peaks in a similar measurement configuration that likely impedes registration of the insect-caused signals [45]. It needs to be tested if advanced signal processing using simultaneous measurements of background noise levels, amplitude and time-resolved analysis could be used to distinguish low currents caused by insects on the leaves in outdoor settings from other environmental factors that could produce triboelectric signals like raindrops and wind-driven leaf contacts. An approach could be integrating additional sensors that specifically track wind and rain as complementary measurements together with analysis of the frequency domains.

In addition, it needs to be investigated how insects that possess different locomotion patterns, morphologies and exoskeleton compositions would be distinguished ideally by automatic, in-depth analysis of the resulting leaf electrification. Although machine learning techniques may help, a better understanding of the signal generation is required at first. Overall, especially when noise shielding is possible as under controlled laboratory conditions, the straightforward measurements of leaf-insect interactions using the leaf itself as a sensor, as presented in this study, could provide an additional tool to gain information on how insects interact with leaves and the physical mechanisms occurring during the interaction.

Studying the electric patterns produced by insects upon interaction with crop plants in more detail may provide opportunities for smart and precision agriculture, especially for tracking pests where early detection is crucial or in the development phase of new pesticides. Moreover, it could also be a way to sense interactions of robotic insects with plants where tailored triboelectric materials could be applied on the feet that produce characteristic charging patterns on leaves.

5 Conclusions

Here we investigated the current signals in leaves produced by insect walking, climbing, and take-off on the leaf surface. The signals were typically in the fA-nA range. They allowed us to clearly distinguish the arthropod's motion patterns on the leaf surface. The origin of the current signals is likely charges formed by contact electrification during contact between the insect's feet and the leaf cuticle that are electrostatically induced into the ion-conductive inner cellular tissue. Even single footsteps can be observed. The specific sensing properties preliminarily shown here might lead to a new strategy to track and monitor plant-insect interactions in situ on leaves. Yet, the study strongly suggests that a larger multidisciplinary investigation is required including experts from insect locomotion, materials surface science, contact electrification, and plant science to better investigate the specific electrification patterns, the signal formation mechanism and the potential use of the reported results.

Acknowledgements. The authors acknowledge the support by the GrowBot project, the European Union's Horizon 2020 Research and Innovation Programme under Grant Agreement No. 824074.

References

1. McPherson, J.E.: Invasive Stink Bugs and Related Species (Pentatomoidea): Biology, Higher Systematics, Semiochemistry, and Management (2018). https://doi.org/10.1201/978131537 1221
2. Knight, K.M.M., Gurr, G.M.: Review of *Nezara viridula* (L.) management strategies and potential for IPM in field crops with emphasis on Australia. Crop Prot. **26**(1), 1–10 (2007). https://doi.org/10.1016/j.cropro.2006.03.007

3. Cardim Ferreira Lima, M., de Almeida Leandro, M.E.D., Valero, C., Pereira Coronel, L.C., Gonçalves Bazzo, C.O.: Automatic detection and monitoring of insect pests—a review. Agriculture 10, 161 (2020). https://doi.org/10.3390/agriculture10050161

4. Amarathunga, D.C., Grundy, J., Parry, H., Dorin, A.: Methods of insect image capture and classification: a systematic literature review. Smart Agric. Technol. 1, 100023 (2021). https://doi.org/10.1016/j.atech.2021.100023

5. Kasinathan, T., Singaraju, D., Uyyala, S.R.: Insect classification and detection in field crops using modern machine learning techniques. Inf. Process. Agric. 8, 446–457 (2021). https://doi.org/10.1016/j.inpa.2020.09.006

6. Li, W., Zheng, T., Yang, Z., Li, M., Sun, C., Yang, X.: Classification and detection of insects from field images using deep learning for smart pest management: a systematic review. Ecol. Inform. 66, 101460 (2021). https://doi.org/10.1016/j.ecoinf.2021.101460

7. Johnson, J.B.: An overview of near-infrared spectroscopy (NIRS) for the detection of insect pests in stored grains. J. Stored Prod. Res. 86, 101558 (2020). https://doi.org/10.1016/j.jspr.2019.101558

8. Armiento, S., Mondini, A., Meder, F., Mazzolai, B.: A plant-hybrid system for wind monitoring connected with social media. In: 2022 IEEE 5th International Conference on Soft Robotics (RoboSoft), pp. 287–292. IEEE (2022). https://doi.org/10.1109/RoboSoft54090.2022.9762083

9. Meder, F., Thielen, M., Mondini, A., Speck, T., Mazzolai, B.: Living plant-hybrid generators for multidirectional wind energy conversion. Energy Technol. 8, 2000236 (2020). https://doi.org/10.1002/ente.202000236

10. Meder, F., Armiento, S., Naselli, G.A., Thielen, M., Speck, T., Mazzolai, B.: Biohybrid generators based on living plants and artificial leaves: Influence of leaf motion and real wind outdoor energy harvesting. Bioinspir. Biomim. 16, 055009 (2021). https://doi.org/10.1088/1748-3190/ac1711

11. Wang, Z.L.: From contact electrification to triboelectric nanogenerators. Rep. Prog. Phys. 84, 096502 (2021). https://doi.org/10.1088/1361-6633/ac0a50

12. Dharmasena, R.D.I.G., et al.: Triboelectric nanogenerators: providing a fundamental framework. Energy Environ. Sci. 10, 1801–1811 (2017). https://doi.org/10.1039/C7EE01139C

13. Wang, Z.L., Wang, A.C.: On the origin of contact-electrification. Mater. Today 30, 34–51 (2019). https://doi.org/10.1016/j.mattod.2019.05.016

14. Lowell, J., Rose-Innes, A.C.: Contact electrification. Adv. Phys. 29, 947–1023 (1980). https://doi.org/10.1080/00018738000101466

15. Lacks, D.J., Mohan Sankaran, R.: Contact electrification of insulating materials. J. Phys. D Appl. Phys. 44(45), 453001 (2011). https://doi.org/10.1088/0022-3727/44/45/453001

16. Özel, M., Demir, F., Aikebaier, A., Kwiczak-Yiğitbaşl, J., Baytekin, H.T., Baytekin, B.: Why does wood not get contact charged? Lignin as an antistatic additive for common polymers. Chem. Mater. 32, 7438–7444 (2020). https://doi.org/10.1021/acs.chemmater.0c02421

17. Meder, F., et al.: Energy conversion at the cuticle of living plants. Adv. Funct. Mater. 28, 1806689 (2018). https://doi.org/10.1002/adfm.201806689

18. Armiento, S., Filippeschi, C., Meder, F., Mazzolai, B.: Liquid-solid contact electrification when water droplets hit living plant leaves. Commun. Mater. 3, 79 (2022). https://doi.org/10.1038/s43246-022-00302-x

19. Salerno, G., Rebora, M., Gorb, E., Gorb, S.: Attachment ability of the polyphagous bug *Nezara viridula* (Heteroptera: Pentatomidae) to different host plant surfaces. Sci. Rep. 8, 10975 (2018). https://doi.org/10.1038/s41598-018-29175-2

20. Voigt, D., Perez Goodwyn, P., Sudo, M., Fujisaki, K., Varenberg, M.: Gripping ease in southern green stink bugs *Nezara viridula* L. (Heteroptera: Pentatomidae): coping with geometry, orientation and surface wettability of substrate. Entomol. Sci. 22, 105–118 (2019). https://doi.org/10.1111/ens.12345

21. Feldmann, D., Das, R., Pinchasik, B.-E.: How can interfacial phenomena in nature inspire smaller robots. Adv. Mater. Interfaces **8**, 2001300 (2021). https://doi.org/10.1002/admi.202 001300
22. Kim, D.W., Kim, S.W., Jeong, U.: Lipids: source of static electricity of regenerative natural substances and nondestructive energy harvesting. Adv. Mater. **30**, 1804949 (2018). https://doi.org/10.1002/adma.201804949
23. Jie, Y., et al.: Natural leaf made triboelectric nanogenerator for harvesting environmental mechanical energy. Adv. Energy Mater. **8**, 1703133 (2018). https://doi.org/10.1002/aenm.201703133
24. Wu, H., Chen, Z., Xu, G., Xu, J., Wang, Z., Zi, Y.: Fully biodegradable water droplet energy harvester based on leaves of living plants. ACS Appl. Mater. Interfaces **12**, 56060–56067 (2020). https://doi.org/10.1021/acsami.0c17601
25. Baytekin, H.T., Patashinski, A.Z., Branicki, M., Baytekin, B., Soh, S., Grzybowski, B.A.: The mosaic of surface charge in contact electrification. Science **333**(6040), 308–312 (2011). https://doi.org/10.1126/science.1201512
26. Baytekin, H.T., Baytekin, B., Incorvati, J.T., Grzybowski, B.A.: Material transfer and polarity reversal in contact charging. Angew. Chem. **124**, 4927–4931 (2012). https://doi.org/10.1002/ange.201200057
27. Musa, U.G., Cezan, S.D., Baytekin, B., Baytekin, H.T.: The charging events in contact-separation electrification. Sci. Rep. **8**, 1–8 (2018). https://doi.org/10.1038/s41598-018-204 13-1
28. Xie, L., He, P.F., Zhou, J., Lacks, D.J.: Correlation of contact deformation with contact electrification of identical materials. J. Phys. D Appl. Phys. **47**, 215501 (2014). https://doi.org/10.1088/0022-3727/47/21/215501
29. Clarke, D., Whitney, H., Sutton, G., Robert, D.: Detection and learning of floral electric fields by bumblebees. Science **340**(6128), 66–69 (2013). https://doi.org/10.1126/science.1230883
30. Vaknin, Y., Gan-Mor, S., Bechar, A., Ronen, B., Eisikowitch, D.: The role of electrostatic forces in pollination. Plant Syst. Evol. **222**, 133–142 (2000). https://doi.org/10.1007/BF0098 4099
31. Sutton, G.P., Clarke, D., Morley, E.L., Robert, D.: Mechanosensory hairs in bumblebees (*Bombus terrestris*) detect weak electric fields. Proc. Natl. Acad. Sci. **113**, 7261–7265 (2016). https://doi.org/10.1073/pnas.1601624113
32. Morley, E.L., Robert, D.: Electric fields elicit ballooning in spiders. Curr. Biol. **28**, 2324–2330 (2018). https://doi.org/10.1016/j.cub.2018.05.057
33. Clarke, D., Morley, E., Robert, D.: The bee, the flower, and the electric field: electric ecology and aerial electroreception. J. Comp. Physiol. **203**, 737–748 (2017). https://doi.org/10.1007/s00359-017-1176-6
34. Lapidot, O., Bechar, A., Ronen, B., Ribak, G.: Can electrostatic fields limit the take-off of tiny whiteflies (*Bemisia tabaci*)? J. Comp. Physiol. A **206**(6), 809–817 (2020). https://doi.org/10.1007/s00359-020-01439-1
35. Jackson, C., McGonigle, D.: Direct monitoring of the electrostatic charge of house-flies (*Musca domestica* L.) as they walk on a dielectric surface. J. Electrostat. **63**, 803–808 (2005). https://doi.org/10.1016/j.elstat.2005.03.075
36. Edwards, D.K.: Electrostatic charges on insects due to contact with different substrates. Can. J. Zool. **40**, 579–584 (1962). https://doi.org/10.1139/z62-051
37. Toyota, M., et al.: Glutamate triggers long-distance, calcium-based plant defense signalling. Science **361**(6407), 1112–1115 (2018). https://doi.org/10.1126/science.aat7744
38. Johns, S., Hagihara, T., Toyota, M., Gilroy, S.: The fast and the furious: rapid long-range signaling in plants. Plant Physiol. **185**(3), 694–706 (2021). https://doi.org/10.1093/plphys/kiaa098

39. Hilker, M., Meiners, T.: How do plants "notice" attack by herbivorous arthropods? Biol. Rev. **85**, 267–280 (2010). https://doi.org/10.1111/j.1469-185X.2009.00100.x

40. Voigt, D., Goodwyn, P.P., Fujisaki, K.: Attachment ability of the southern green stink bug, *Nezara viridula* (L.), on plant surfaces. Arthropod-Plant Interact. **12**(3), 415–421 (2017). https://doi.org/10.1007/s11829-017-9591-8

41. Salerno, G., Rebora, M., Piersanti, S., Matsumura, Y., Gorb, E., Gorb, S.: Variation of attachment ability of *Nezara viridula* (Hemiptera: Pentatomidae) during nymphal development and adult aging. J. Insect Physiol. **127**, 104117 (2020). https://doi.org/10.1016/j.jinsphys.2020.104117

42. Salerno, G., Rebora, M., Kovalev, A., Gorb, E., Gorb, S.: Contribution of different tarsal attachment devices to the overall attachment ability of the stink bug *Nezara viridula*. J. Comp. Physiol. A **204**(7), 627–638 (2018). https://doi.org/10.1007/s00359-018-1266-0

43. Surapaneni, V.A., Bold, G., Speck, T., Thielen, M.: Spatio-temporal development of cuticular ridges on leaf surfaces of *Hevea brasiliensis* alters insect attachment: Leaf growth and insect walking forces. Roy. Soc. Open Sci. **7**, 201319 (2020). https://doi.org/10.1098/rsos.201319

44. Prüm, B., Florian Bohn, H., Seidel, R., Rubach, S., Speck, T.: Plant surfaces with cuticular folds and their replicas: influence of microstructuring and surface chemistry on the attachment of a leaf beetle. Acta Biomater. **9**, 6360–6368 (2013). https://doi.org/10.1016/j.actbio.2013.01.030

45. Meder, F., Mondini, A., Visentin, F., Zini, G., Crepaldi, M., Mazzolai, B.: Multisource energy conversion in plants with soft epicuticular coatings. Energy Environ. Sci. **15**, 2545–2556 (2022). https://doi.org/10.1039/D2EE00405D

Slug Battery: An Enzymatic Fuel Cell Tested *in vitro* in *Aplysia californica* Hemolymph

Theo Cockrell[1] ⓘ, Kevin Dai[2] ⓘ, Michael J. Bennington[2] ⓘ,
and Victoria A. Webster-Wood[2,3(✉)] ⓘ

[1] Department of Electrical and Computer Engineering, Carnegie Mellon University,
Pittsburgh, PA, USA
[2] Department of Mechanical Engineering, Carnegie Mellon University, Pittsburgh,
PA, USA
vwebster@andrew.cmu.edu
[3] McGowan Institute for Regenerative Medicine, Carnegie Mellon University,
Pittsburgh, PA, USA

Abstract. Supplying continuous power is a major challenge in the creation and deployment of sensors and small robots for marine applications. Glucose-based enzymatic fuel cells (EFCs) are a possible solution for sustainably powering such devices when mounted on or implanted in living organisms. The two main barriers to developing implantable EFCs for marine organisms are their power output and *in vivo* feasibility. Ideally, an *in vivo* EFC should be minimally invasive, remain mechanically secure, and output relatively consistent power over a predefined lifespan, ranging from weeks to months. The shape and chemistry of EFC electrodes can each contribute to or detract from the overall power production potential of the cells. This paper assesses the feasibility of EFCs using the marine sea slug, *Aplysia californica*'s, hemolymph as an analyte and presents methods to enhance the power produced by EFCs by altering their chemistry and form factor. We found that perfluorodecalin-soaked cathodes and spirally-rolled cells demonstrated increased power output compared to their respective control specimens. Cells tested in *Aplysia* saline mirrored the power output trends of cells tested in hemolymph but with higher power output. This work suggests the feasibility of creating implantable EFCs for marine sea slugs that could one day serve as sustainable biohybrid robotic platforms.

Keywords: Enzymatic Fuel Cell · *Aplysia* · Hemolymph

This work was supported by NSF DBI2015317 as part of the NSF/CIHR/DFG/FRQ/UKRI-MRC Next Generation Networks for Neuroscience Program, by the NSF Research Fellowship Program under Grant No. DGE1745016, and by internal funding through Carnegie Mellon University. Any opinions, findings, and conclusions or recommendations expressed in this material are those of the authors and do not necessarily reflect the views of the National Science Foundation. T. Cockrell and K. Dai—These authors contributed equally to the work.

F. Meder et al. (Eds.): Living Machines 2023, LNAI 14158, pp. 318–334, 2023.
https://doi.org/10.1007/978-3-031-39504-8_22

1   Introduction

As commercial electronic devices have become smaller and more energy efficient, it has become feasible to create small-scale electronic devices and sensors for wearable and implantable applications [14]. However, powering these devices for long-term usage typically requires long charging cycles or may otherwise result in limited lifetimes [1]. Powering electronic payloads for long-term environmental monitoring poses unique challenges. Devices may need to be deployed for long periods in various environmental conditions without human intervention [6] and with limited access to charging infrastructure.

In marine environments, powering these devices is further hindered by reduced access to sunlight and harsh salinity conditions. Despite these limitations, marine environments may be among the most compelling application spaces for low-power, sustainable power sources due to the need for persistent aquatic sensors that monitor ongoing changes in ocean ecosystems. For these same reasons, sustainably-powered sensors could be utilized in the rapidly growing field of aquaculture [6,13]. Su et al. detailed the many factors that affect water quality and aquaculture cultivations [13]; some of these factors, including pH, temperature, and salinity, are able to be measured by sensors with power requirements in the microwatt range [12].

One possible solution to sustainably power implantable sensors and microelectronics is an enzymatic fuel cell (EFC) that consumes glucose [6,14]. Glucose-based EFCs generate electricity through biocatalytic oxidation of glucose at the anode [5]. A number of implantable biofuel cells have been previously reported in the literature, including in the retroperitoneal space of rats [2], in rabbit blood vessels [3], in the caudal area of fish [6], in the hemocoel of lobsters [10], and in living land snails [5]. However, to our knowledge, no biocatalytic EFCs have been previously developed for use in sea slugs to target marine applications.

To begin addressing the need for implantable fuel cells in marine applications, we have developed enzymatic fuel cells for use with hemolymph from the marine sea slug, *Aplysia californica*. *Aplysia*'s body structure lends itself to the introduction of glucose-based EFCs due to its large body cavity and open circulatory system [9]. In this work, we build on the state-of-the-art in implantable EFCs and compare the performance of EFC designs in *Aplysia* hemolymph. Through a series of benchtop proof-of-concept studies, we have identified the baseline performance of these cells and demonstrated the effect of perfluorodecalin treatment on cell voltage in hemolymph. These preliminary studies suggest the feasibility of using enzymatic fuel cells to power future implantable aquatic sensors in *Aplysia* for applications including marine environmental monitoring.

2   Methodology

Two battery geometries, two electrode chemistries, and two testing solutions were evaluated in a fractional design of experiments to establish feasibility and identify process improvements for an *Aplysia* hemolymph-powered enzymatic fuel cell (EFC). The electrodes utilized a chemical reaction that converted glucose and oxygen to electricity and water, building on prior work demonstrated in land snails [5]. In addition to testing the electrode chemistry described by Halamkova et al., we compared the performance of cells with and without the addition of perfluorodecalin to the cathode [5]. Perfluorodecalin is a fluorocarbon that acts as a solvent for oxygen, allowing higher oxygen concentrations to be dissolved in the working fluid [7]. We hypothesized that perfluorodecalin's oxygen-transporting properties could increase local oxygen concentration at the cathode, and thus increase power output [8]. We also compared the performance of a rolled cell, with cathodic perfluorodecalin, in both extracted hemolymph and *Aplysia* saline. We decided to use *Aplysia* saline for our tests since previous works had proved it to be an appropriate analog for sea slug hemolymph [11]. Other works had also used an analog solution to mimic the properties of hemolymph in their earlier testing [5]. By using *Aplysia* saline in all experiments that did not depend on hemolymph itself as a variable, we only had to extract hemolymph from *Aplysia* one time. This minimized the harm done to the animal since hemolymph extraction could be detrimental to the slug, especially if multiple extractions are performed.

2.1   Electrode Fabrication

All electrodes used in this work were built using a multi-wall carbon nanotube (MWCNT) base material (20 gsm buckypaper, Nano Tech Labs), adapting procedures described by Halamkova et al. [5]. Briefly, to prepare the electrodes, MWCNT strips were manually cut from the stock material using a razor blade to a size of 52.6 mm × 14 mm (Figure 1). All electrode strips underwent a three-step wash preparation with gentle shaking at 60 RPM via an orbital shaker (VWR 3500I) at 21°C. First, electrodes were submerged in 10 mM 1-pyrenebutanoic acid succinimidyl ester (PBSE, VWR) in dimethyl sulfoxide (DMSO, Thermo Fisher Scientific) for 1 h. Electrodes were then transferred to DMSO and washed for 5 min. Finally, electrodes were transferred to a 10 mM potassium phosphate buffer for an additional 5 min.

Following the three-step wash process, the anode and cathode materials underwent separate preparation steps. All anodes were incubated in 1 mg/mL PQQ-dependent glucose dehydrogenase (PQQ-GDH, Toyobo) and 1 mM CaCl$_2$ in potassium phosphate buffer (10 mM, pH 7) for 1 h with gentle shaking. In contrast, cathodes were incubated in 1.5 mg/mL laccase from *Trametes versicolor* (Sigma-Aldrich) in 10 mM potassium phosphate buffer (pH 7) for 1 h with gentle shaking. For cells constructed with perfluorodecalin, the cathode was then shaken in 0.1 M perfluorodecalin in de-ionized water for an additional hour. EFCs constructed without the addition of perfluorodecalin were considered "control chemistry" cells for our data analysis. Anodes and non-perfluorodecalin cathodes were stored in separate containers containing 0.1 M potassium phosphate buffer until they were tested or used to create a cell. Cathodes that were soaked in 0.1 M perfluorodecalin were kept in the perfluorodecalin solution at 4°C until testing or construction.

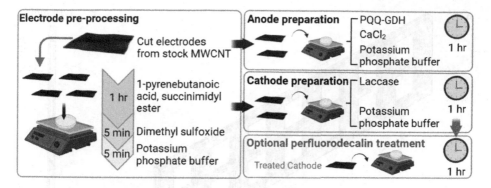

Fig. 1. Electrode fabrication process for glucose-based enzymatic fuel cells. The electrodes are fabricated from buckypaper with multi-wall carbon nanotubes and soaked in a series of solutions that will coat the electrodes in their respective enzymes. All electrodes follow the same series of pre-processing solutions. Then, the anodes are incubated with PQQ-dependent glucose dehydrogenase and the cathodes are incubated with laccase. Some cathodes are additionally coated with perfluorodecalin for improved oxygen transport.

2.2   Elastomer Separator Fabrication

The two EFC electrodes should be separated by a thin gap that prevents shorting and reduces the cell's internal resistance, while simultaneously providing sufficient fluid flow between the electrodes for fresh reagent to contact the electrodes' surfaces. To create this gap, a hollow-frame elastomeric separator was designed with 0.3 mm-thick walls on the upper and lower surfaces and a 0.5 mm-thick gap between walls (Fig. 2). 4.5 mm × 5 mm cutouts in the walls enable fluid to contact the electrodes and are supported by 2.4 mm × 12.2 mm pillars between the walls. The separator was constructed out of a flexible elastomer (Asiga DentaGUM, Shore 30A) on an Asiga Pico 2 HD printer (27 μm XY resolution, 0.1 mm layer height) to enable rolling the electrodes into cylindrical cell geometries. The length and width of the separator measured 50.8 mm × 14 mm. The length of the separator was undersized compared to the electrodes to provide potential capability for wrapping the electrodes around their respective wires for better electrical contact, although the wrapping was not implemented in the work presented here.

2.3   Enzymatic Fuel Cell Construction

Each cell was constructed using one anode and one cathode, three 3D-printed elastomer separators, and two wires (Fig. 3). Cyanoacrylate adhesive (CA 100, Mitreapel) was used to attach all layers at their centers and edges.

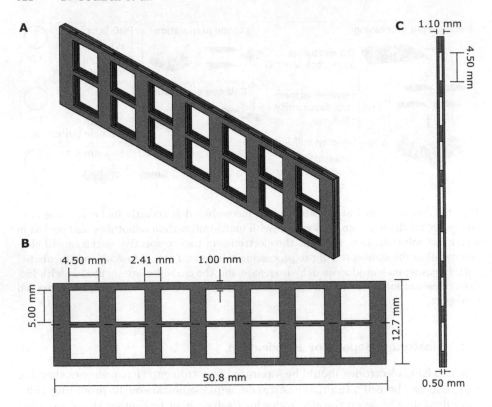

Fig. 2. a) Isometric view of a hollow elastomer separator, 3D printed from Asiga Den-taGUM, which separates the electrodes of the battery while enabling fluid flow between the electrodes. b) Front view of a separator. c) Top view of a separator. Due to the flexibility of the elastomer, both flat and rolled cell geometries can be constructed using the same separator design.

"Flat" Cell Construction. A flat enzymatic fuel cell design was created by sequentially layering the electrodes between elastomer separators, with conductive wire (24 AWG) sandwiched between each electrode and their respective outer elastomer separator. The electrodes were attached to the separators using cyanoacrylate adhesive at their centers and their edges. The wires were attached to the electrodes by applying cyanoacrylate adhesive to a 3 mm section of the 12 mm-long bare wire contacting the electrode, while leaving the remainder of the bare wire free of adhesive.

"Rolled" Cell Construction. A rolled cell geometry, inspired by the power-dense jelly-roll design of electrolytic capacitors, was also designed and tested. The spiral winding of the rolled cell was hypothesized to facilitate more chemical reactions and decrease electrical resistance between the two electrodes due to an increased active surface area; by rolling the cell, each side of the cathode

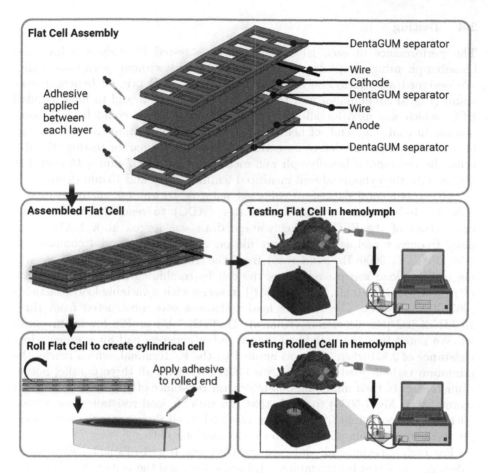

Fig. 3. The tested EFCs are assembled by layering electrodes between thin elastomer separators (DentaGUM). Each EFC uses two electrodes, three elastomer separators, and two conductive wires. Wires are stripped bare and placed adjacent to their respective electrode before sandwiching between elastomer separators. Cyanoacrylate adhesive secures the assembled cells together. Rolled cells are formed by rolling a completed flat cell along its length. Assembled cells are placed in a 3D-printed test stand (blue), which contains wells for either cell form factor. Extracted *Aplysia* (Color figure online) hemolymph or synthetic *Aplysia* saline is applied to the cell during testing. In each test, the load resistance across the cell is varied by a microcontroller and the cell voltage is continuously logged to a PC.

would face the anode, and vice versa. To create a rolled cell, we first created a complete flat cell and then rolled the cell length-wise. To ensure that the cylindrical structure was maintained, cyanoacrylate adhesive was applied to attach the loose end of the cell to the rest of the body.

2.4   Testing

The performance of each EFC geometry was tested in *Aplysia* saline and hemolymph using electrodes constructed with and without perfluorodecalin. We designed a polyethylene terephthalate (PETG) 3D printed benchtop test stand (Fig. 3) containing a well to hold a flat EFC and a well to hold a rolled EFC, which was used for all tests. Flat and rolled EFCs could be fully submerged in 6 mL and 4 mL of hemolymph, respectively, minimizing the amount of hemolymph that needed to be extracted from the animal for testing. For flat cells, the rectangular hemolymph well measured 55 mm × 7 mm × 15 mm. For round cells, the cylindrical well measured 9 mm radially and 15 mm deep.

All experimental data were collected using a Teensy 4.0 microcontroller's onboard 10-bit analog-to-digital converter (ADC) to read the analog voltage output of the EFC. Analog voltage data was logged at a 1 kHz sampling frequency and saved to a text file on a PC through serial communication (PuTTY, 9600 Hz baud rate) from the Teensy microcontroller. A varying resistive load was placed across the cell by combining fixed-value resistors ($R_f \in [0\Omega, 4.7 \text{ k}\Omega, 10 \text{ k}\Omega, 22 \text{ k}\Omega, 47 \text{ k}\Omega]$) in series with a variable load resistance (667–4000Ω range). The variable load resistance was constructed from three 10 kΩ digital potentiometers (Adafruit DS3502, 7-bit or 128 levels) in parallel. We noted that the individual digital potentiometers had an average wiper resistance of 2 kΩ when 15 V was applied to the V_+ terminal, which is why the minimum variable load resistance was 667Ω even with all three parallel potentiometers set to their minimum potentiometer resistance of 0Ω. We used an LCR meter (Atrix MCR-5030) to verify that the variable load resistance was within 10Ω of the expected 4000Ω resistance value when all three potentiometers were set to their maximum potentiometer resistance of 10 kΩ.

For each experimental configuration that was tested (Table 1), EFCs were submerged in either hemolymph or *Aplysia* saline, and the voltage was recorded during a sweep of resistance values, beginning at $(667 + R_f)\Omega$ and ending at $(4000 + R_f)\Omega$, where R_f is the resistance of the fixed-value resistor. To provide the varying load resistance, only one of the three potentiometers was actively changed at a time while the other two inactive potentiometers were held at either 0Ω or 10 kΩ, depending on whether or not they had been previously active. The actively changing potentiometer was monotonically swept from 0-10 kΩ in single level steps corresponding to a 78Ω step increase in potentiometer resistance. The EFC's analog voltage was sampled 50 times at the 1 kHz sampling frequency for each step change in resistance. With a 6 ms pause before transitioning to the subsequent resistance values, each resistance value was set for a total time of 56 ms. Since the variable load was swept through 384 resistance values, one full sweep of load resistances spanned 21.5 s. Once the actively changing potentiometer reached a resistance of 10 kΩ, it was held at a static resistance of 10 kΩ while the next potentiometer swept from 0-10 kΩ. When all three potentiometers had completed their sweeps and were each held at resistances of 10 kΩ (+2 kΩ of wiper resistance), the EFC's load resistance had reached its final value of $(4000 + R_f)\Omega$. Considering the 2 kΩ wiper resistances and

Table 1. Experimental conditions and parameters. *Italics* indicate the independent variable for a particular test type.

Test Type	EFC Specimen	Experimental Variables		
		Form Factor	Perfluoro. (Y/N)	Testing Fluid
Cell Form Factor	1	*Rolled*	N	Hemolymph
	2	*Flat*	N	Hemolymph
Perfluorodecalin v. Control Chemistry	1	Rolled	*N*	Hemolymph
	2	Flat	*N*	Hemolymph
	3	Rolled	*Y*	Hemolymph
	4	Flat	*Y*	Hemolymph
Testing Fluid	3	Rolled	Y	*Hemolymph*
	3	Rolled	Y	*Saline*

the parallel arrangement of the three potentiometers, each 78Ω step increase in potentiometer resistance corresponded to a change in EFC load resistance that varied between $0.5\text{-}43.9\Omega$, depending on the resistances of the static potentiometers.

2.5 Hemolymph Extraction

A wild-caught *Aplysia californica* specimen (421 g) was obtained from Marinus Scientific (Long Beach, CA) and maintained in a 40 L tank of artificial sea water (16°C, specific gravity 1.026). Hemolymph was extracted from this animal in a survival procedure using the anesthetization protocol described by Gill et al. (2020) [4]. Briefly, the animal was anesthetized with a 30% (volume [mL]: body mass [g]) injection of 333 mM magnesium chloride. The injected fluid was spread throughout the body with manual palpation. Then the animal was transferred to a bath of 2–5°C artificial seawater and allowed to chill for 10 min. Approximately 20 mL of hemolymph was then drawn from the animal with a syringe. For both the injection and extraction, 21 gauge needles were used, and all punctures were sealed with cyanoacrylate adhesive (Mitreapel). To avoid vital organs, the injection and extraction points were placed in the cheek of the animal, below the buccal mass. The extracted hemolymph was stored in a 100 mL specimen jar for testing immediately after the surgery. After testing, the extracted hemolymph container was stored at 4°C. *Aplysia* saline was created following the process outlined by McManus et al. [11] and also stored at 4°C.

3 Results

3.1 "Flat" Vs. "Rolled" Cells

Rolled cells demonstrated a much higher peak power compared to flat cells (Fig. 4). For flat cells, the mean and standard deviation of peak power was

0.83 ± 0.04 µW at 5390Ω. For the rolled cell, the power spiked to 6.94 ± 0.41 µW and 7.29 ± 0.16 µW at 667Ω and 5370Ω, respectively. Above resistances of 5370Ω, the power output of both cells decreased with increasing resistance.

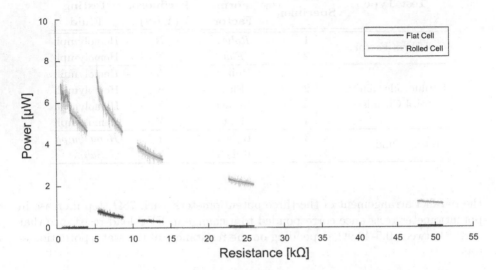

Fig. 4. Both flat and rolled cell geometries were tested in *Aplysia* hemolymph using 52.6 mm long electrodes that were not coated in perfluorodecalin. The rolled cell exhibits a much higher power output than the flat cell, especially at load resistances lower than 10.7 kΩ. The power from both cells decreases with increasing resistance after 5370Ω. The rolled cell shows two peaks in power, which is not expected because cells typically exhibit a single power peak. This double power peak could be due to charge that built up in the EFC prior to testing and dissipated once the cell was put under a load, or due to rapid consumption of reagents at low load resistances. Solid lines show the mean power value for a given resistance, with shaded regions showing the full range of measured power values.

3.2   Cells with Perfluorodecalin Vs. Without

The addition of perfluorodecalin to the electrode chemistry of a rolled cell led to an increase in power output (Fig. 5A). At their respective peaks, the control chemistry cell output 7.29 ± 0.16 µW while the cell with perfluorodecalin output 15.1 ± 0.34 µW, a 107% increase in power. For the cell without perfluorodecalin, we note two peaks at 667Ω and 5370Ω, whereas the peak power for the cell with perfluorodecalin is measured at 1500Ω. Both cells exhibit a visually similar trend in slope at resistances above 5370Ω.

In contrast to the rolled cell, a flat cell that utilized perfluorodecalin was not consistently more powerful than a flat cell utilizing the control chemistry (Fig. 5B). The cell with control chemistry produced a peak power of 0.83 ± 0.04 µW at 5390Ω, which was 207% greater than the peak of 0.27 ± 0.03 µW

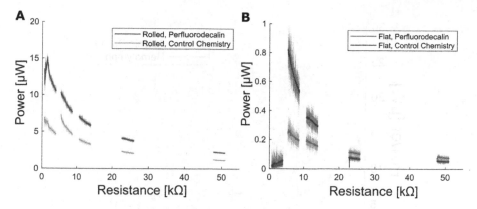

Fig. 5. Power comparisons of (A) rolled and (B) flat cells in hemolymph with different electrode preparations. (A) Using perfluorodecalin with rolled cells led to a 100% peak power increase compared to control chemistry. Both cells demonstrate visually similar slopes at resistances above 5370Ω. (B) For flat cells, the control chemistry cell demonstrated a peak power of 0.83 ± 0.04 µW, which was 207% higher than the peak power produced by the cell with perfluorodecalin, 0.27 ± 0.03 µW. This was substantially less than the power levels observed in the rolled cells. The power from both cells decreases with increasing resistance after 5370Ω. As before, solid lines show the mean power level for a given resistance, with shaded regions showing the full range of measured powers. In this preliminary study, it is unclear why the flat and rolled cells showed opposite effects of the perfluorodecalin treatment, but this should be further investigated in future work.

produced by the cell with perfluorodecalin at 5620Ω. It was only at resistances above 22.7 kΩ that the cell with perfluorodecalin began to produce more power than the control chemistry cell consistently.

3.3 Submerged in *Aplysia* saline vs. Submerged in Extracted Hemolymph

The rolled cell with perfluorodecalin demonstrated visually similar trends when submerged in either *Aplysia* saline or extracted *Aplysia* hemolymph, albeit with a higher power output in *Aplysia* saline (Fig. 6). Tests in *Aplysia* saline yielded a 70% peak power increase compared to the peak power from tests in hemolymph. In both tested fluids, the rolled cell exhibited visually similar slopes at resistances above 5370Ω. The *Aplysia* saline data set demonstrated a double power peak at 683Ω and 1470Ω, measuring 25.7 ± 0.74 µW and 25.1 ± 0.46 µW respectively. The hemolymph data set exhibited a single 15.1 ± 0.34 µW power peak at 1500Ω.

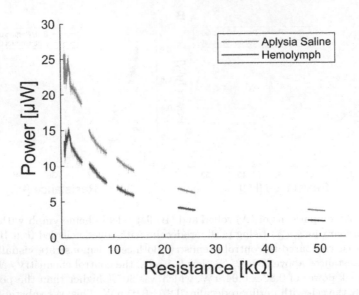

Fig. 6. The perfluorodecalin-treated rolled cell demonstrated visually similar trends in both *Aplysia* saline and hemolymph, but generated a 70% higher peak power output when submerged in *Aplysia* saline. As before, solid lines show the mean power level for a given resistance, with shaded regions showing the full range of measured powers.

4   Discussion

4.1   Analysis of Results

We observed that variables such as changing to a rolled cell geometry and adding perfluorodecalin each impacted the peak power output of our EFCs more percentage-wise than changing the testing fluid. Given the identical fabrication methods between flat cells and rolled cells prior to rolling, we expected a slight increase in power due to a more secure connection between the wires and electrodes in the rolled cell. Instead, even with the control chemistry, we saw an increase in peak power for rolled cells vs. flat when testing in hemolymph. Note that in the tests with rolled cells, the power output was in the 1.13 μW to 7.29 μW range, while the tests with flat cells were consistently lower in the 0.01 μW to 0.83 μW range. This could be due to the spiral winding of the rolled cell, which may create better contact between the wires and electrodes of the rolled cell when compared to the flat cell. We noticed that the cells' power outputs were sensitive to small perturbations in the wire, so we attempted to keep the wires stable during testing. However, the contact between the wire and the cells' electrodes could vary regardless of whether the wires were held manually or mounted on an external fixture. We also note that the choice of alligator clips and method of clamping to the EFC wires may have had an effect on the observed difference in power output of rolled and flat cells. Alligator clips were used to connect to the rolled cells, while mini probe hooks were used to

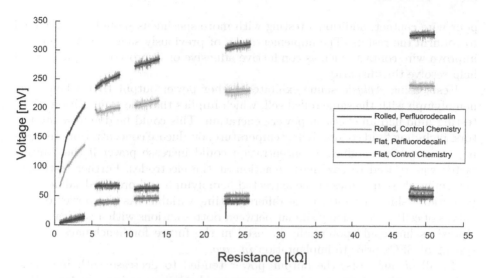

Fig. 7. Across multiple EFC specimens of different compositions, the cell voltage appears to plateau with increased load resistance. The inverse relationship between power and resistance, demonstrated by all tested cells, is due to the plateau in voltage at higher resistances. EFCs with higher peak power output also had higher voltage. Similar to earlier plots, lines show the mean voltage level for a given resistance, with the shaded region showing the full range of measured voltages.

connect to the wires on flat cells. This was due to varying amounts of exposed wire extending from the cells after fabrication. Mini probe hooks were used for shorter lengths of exposed wire extending from the flat cells compared to the rolled cells. Additional experiments with consistent wire connection methods should be conducted in the future to clarify the difference between rolled and flat cell power output. In the future, application of a conductive adhesive at the wire-electrode connection could improve the performance of any cells suffering from insufficient wire contact. Regardless, rolled cells demonstrated the ability to generate several microwatts across a range of resistances (Fig. 4).

Across all measured resistances, the rolled cell with perfluorodecalin exhibited a power output that was always at least 0.98 μW greater than the rolled cell without perfluorodecalin. The increased power output from cells with perfluorodecalin is expected from previous work [8] that demonstrated increased current density and power output after modifying a cathode with perfluorodecalin. Perfluorodecalin's oxygen-transporting properties can provide greater oxygen concentration at the cathode [8]. As the addition of perfluorodecalin increased our EFC's power output, this implies that oxygen could be the limiting factor in the enzymatic reaction taking place in the cell.

Interestingly, the flat control chemistry cell performed better than the flat cell with perfluorodecalin at resistances below 22.7 kΩ. The perfluorodecalin cell's peak power was only 32% of the peak power generated by the control chemistry cell. While the low power output of the perfluorodecalin cell could be due to poor wire contact, additional testing with more specimens should be conducted to confirm the results. The implementation of previously suggested methods to improve wire contact, such as conductive adhesive or improved clamping, could help resolve this disparity.

Tests using *Aplysia* saline exhibited higher power output than when using hemolymph with the same rolled cell, which implies that the composition of the testing fluid had an effect on power generation. This could be due to many factors, including fluid conductivity, temperature, or glucose concentration. Increasing temperature or glucose concentration could increase power if the limiting factor was related to enzymatic reaction at the electrodes. Further testing to determine these qualities of the extracted hemolymph and prepared saline could potentially shine a light on the differentiating variable. As the power output curves of cells were visually similar between both solutions with a vertical offset, *Aplysia* saline could potentially be used in the future for benchmark *in vitro* testing of EFCs prior to implantation *in vivo*.

In all of our tests, the output power tended to decrease with increasing resistance, although the trend was sometimes broken at resistances lower than 10.7 kΩ. The relationship between power and resistance can be described by $P = \frac{V^2}{R}$, where P is power, V is voltage, and R is resistance. In tested EFCs, the voltage plateaued at higher resistance values (Fig. 7). As the resistance increased while the EFC voltage stayed near constant, we expected to see decreased power output. However, we also note that our testing methodology could contribute to the inverse relationship between power and resistance. As the EFC's load resistances were sequentially swept from low to high values, reagent depletion could account for reduced power output at higher resistance values in later stages of testing. That being said, each sweep of load resistance between $(667 + R_f)\Omega$ to $(4000 + R_f)\Omega$ was conducted within a span of approximately 20 s for a given value of R_f.

For regions where the cell power increased with increasing resistance, it is implied that the voltage increases sufficiently rapidly to compensate for the inverse relationship with resistance. A special case in our test data occurred when a double power peak was exhibited at resistances below 10.7 kΩ. These double peaks are likely a consequence of previously mentioned issues, such as poor electrical wire contact or limited reagent, but additional testing is needed to confirm. Since these peaks occurred at low load resistances that were the first to be tested in each of our experiments, it is also possible that charge had accumulated on the EFC's electrodes prior to testing and dissipated during experimentation. This charge buildup could be due to the cell's exposure to reagents prior to testing, such as after placing the cell in test solution. Additional testing with alternative experimental methods, such as randomizing the sequence of tested load resistances, could determine if charge buildup is a significant variable.

We note that the method for sweeping the potentiometers' resistance values was not ideal for collecting data at evenly-spaced load resistance values. As mentioned previously, only one potentiometer at a time was actively swept from 0-10 kΩ while the remaining two potentiometers were fixed at values of either 0Ω or 10 kΩ. This resulted in step changes in load resistance that varied between 0.5-43.9Ω. The smallest, 0.5Ω, step changes in load resistance occurred when the first active potentiometer was sweeping to high potentiometer resistances near 10 kΩ and the remaining inactive potentiometers were held at 0Ω. The largest, 43.9Ω, step changes in load resistance occurred when the third active potentiometer was sweeping from low potentiometer resistances near 0Ω and the remaining inactive potentiometers were held at 10 kΩ. We intend to implement an improved potentiometer resistance sweeping method in future work for more evenly-spaced load resistance values. The improved method would alternate between active potentiometers after each 78Ω step change in potentiometer resistance, such that the difference between any two given potentiometers' resistances is never greater than $2 \times 78\Omega = 156\Omega$. With the improved method for sweep potentiometer resistances, the step change in EFC load resistance will vary between 8.5-9.0Ω, which is a much smaller range than the 0.5-43.9Ω variation exhibited by the current method.

It is also possible that glucose levels in a cell's test solution decreased significantly throughout multiple tests. In future experiments, either a glucose monitor or colorimetric glucose assays will be used to measure the glucose levels in the test solution before and after a test. This should help determine how much glucose levels are decreasing during testing. The test solution will also be replaced after every sweep of load resistances, rather than after testing each cell. This should reduce the temporal impact of glucose consumption on subsequent tests' results.

An interesting point of comparison between our EFC and previous works is the power density of said EFCs. In particular, Halamkova et al. generated a maximum power density of 30 μW cm^{-2} with their implanted biofuel cell [5]. Our rolled cell, when implanted in hemolymph, generated a maximum power density of 0.99 μW cm^{-2}. Further testing and characterization of our EFC should help us understand the difference in power density given the similar electrode fabrication methods.

4.2   Experimental Process Improvements

Through the pilot studies presented here, we have identified several process improvements for reliable EFC fabrication. First, the MWCNT electrodes were prone to tearing during handling in the washing and incubation steps. We found that carefully handling the electrodes away from their edges using curved tweezers was effective at reducing tearing occurrences. Furthermore, large sample containers in which the electrodes are less likely to contact the wall should be used during the incubation steps, as electrodes were more likely to tear after sticking to the container wall. We also found that gently shaking the cathode in 0.1 M perfluorodecalin was sufficient to observe noticeably improved power output, as opposed to using a perfluorodecalin slurry spray [8]. We observed that three 52.6 mm electrodes could be gently shaken in the same container with no loss in efficacy.

Our current cell design uses flexible elastomer separators that maintain a thin gap between the electrodes, which prevents shorting while also allowing fluid flow to carry fresh reagents to the electrode surfaces. As an additional benefit, the flexibility of the elastomer allows any flat cell to be rolled into a rolled cell with minor changes in fabrication methods. The rolled geometry could provide increased active electrode surface area for increased power output. Rolled cell geometry could also be a better option for spaces that are length-constrained or where fluid flow is predominantly in an axial direction rather than through a thin-walled duct. Further development of similar structures that enable high flow rate and high roll density could be beneficial for improving the performance of high power density EFCs.

4.3 Future Work

We identified several routes for future improvements related to experimental design to improve our understanding of the power output provided by EFCs for use in *Aplysia* hemolymph. Among these are reducing variability in electrical contact resistance, improving the sequence of applied load resistances, and evaluating the reagent-limited and time-dependent responses of fabricated cells. As only one specimen was evaluated during each test, additional experimentation is needed to collect data and confirm the trends presented in this paper. In addition, we would consider exploring new electrode materials with higher power output and improved structural integrity [3]. As glucose-based EFCs are developed further, we will consider *in vivo* implantation into aquatic invertebrates such as *Aplysia*, which could enable remote monitoring in harsh marine environments using non-invasive microelectronics. EFC-powered sensors mounted on *Aplysia* could record environmental data and autonomously transfer the data to researchers through nearby relay stations without requiring personnel stationed on site. Since the EFCs are self-sustaining as long as the *Aplysia* continues feeding and producing glucose, we would expect the lifespan of the implanted sensor and integrated circuitry to surpass the lifespan of the animal. The suggested remote sensing capability would ideally enable the monitoring of marine habitats with low environmental impact and minor upkeep.

The power output of the presented EFCs could enable the operation of small sensor payloads by utilizing capacitive charge pump circuitry, as demonstrated by Huang et al. [6]. The available supply voltage could also be increased by connecting multiple EFCs in series. In future experiments, the efficacy of EFC's could be benchmarked by long-term, stable power generation for powering energy-efficient sensors [12].

5 Conclusion

The glucose-based enzymatic fuel cells (EFCs) explored in this paper are a step towards tractable implanted electronics within *Aplysia* for operation in aquatic environments. We found visually similar electrical performance between cells extracted in *Aplysia* hemolymph and synthetic *Aplysia* saline, which could be used in future benchtop experiments for estimating the performance of *in vitro* electrodes before *in vivo* usage. We also demonstrated the effects of several key factors on EFC power output, including electrode chemistry and cell form factor. Improved power output from electrodes using perfluorodecalin and rolled cell geometry suggests that these design elements should be considered in the further development of EFCs. Additional experimentation with more specimens should be conducted to confirm the trends presented in this paper. Future improvements to EFC designs could investigate alternative electrical connection methods for consistently low contact resistance and utilize alternative base materials for electrodes. As EFCs become more powerful, they could support a realm of applications, including robotic operation in locations without existing infrastructure and self-sustaining aquatic sensors in harsh marine environments.

Acknowledgements. Figures 1 and 3 were created with graphical assets from Biorender.com.

References

1. Chen, X., et al.: Stretchable and flexible buckypaper-based lactate biofuel cell for wearable electronics. Adv. Func. Mater. **29**(46), 1905785 (2019)
2. Cinquin, P., et al.: A glucose biofuel cell implanted in rats. PLoS ONE **5**, e10476 (2010)
3. El Ichi-Ribault, S., et al.: Remote wireless control of an enzymatic biofuel cell implanted in a rabbit for 2 months. Electrochim. Acta **269**, 360–366 (2018)
4. Gill, J.P., Chiel, H.J.: Rapid adaptation to changing mechanical load by ordered recruitment of identified motor neurons. Eneuro **7**(3) (2020)
5. Halámková, L., Halámek, J., Bocharova, V., Szczupak, A., Alfonta, L., Katz, E.: Implanted biofuel cell operating in a living snail. J. Am. Chem. Soc. **134**(11), 5040–5043 (2012)
6. Huang, S.H., Chen, W.H., Lin, Y.C.: A self-powered glucose biosensor operated underwater to monitor physiological status of free-swimming fish. Energies **12**(10), 1827 (2019)
7. Jägers, J., Wrobeln, A., Ferenz, K.B.: Perfluorocarbon-based oxygen carriers: from physics to physiology. Pflügers Arch.-Eur. J. Physiol. **473**, 139–150 (2021)
8. Karaskiewicz, M., Biernat, J.F., Rogalski, J., Roberts, K.P., Bilewicz, R.: Fluoroaromatic substituents attached to carbon nanotubes help to increase oxygen concentration on biocathode in biosensors and biofuel cells. Electrochim. Acta **112**, 403–413 (2013)
9. Koester, J., Koch, U.: Neural control of the circulatory system of Aplysia. Experientia **43**, 972–980 (1987)
10. MacVittie, K., et al.: From "cyborg" lobsters to a pacemaker powered by implantable biofuel cells. Energy Environ. Sci. **6**(1), 81–86 (2013)
11. McManus, J.M., Lu, H., Chiel, H.J.: An in vitro preparation for eliciting and recording feeding motor programs with physiological movements in Aplysia Californica. JoVE (J. Visualized Exp.) (70), e4320 (2012)
12. Olatinwo, S.O., Joubert, T.H.: Energy efficient solutions in wireless sensor systems for water quality monitoring: a review. IEEE Sens. J. **19**(5), 1596–1625 (2018)

13. Su, X., Sutarlie, L., Loh, X.J.: Sensors, biosensors, and analytical technologies for aquaculture water quality. Research **2020**, 1–15 (2020)
14. Wang, L., Wu, X., Su, B.Q.W., Song, R., Zhang, J.R., Zhu, J.J.: Enzymatic biofuel cell: opportunities and intrinsic challenges in futuristic applications. Adv. Energy Sustain. Res. **2**(8), 2100031 (2021)

Mycelium Bridge as a Living Electrical Conductor: Access Point to Soil Infosphere

Hana Geara, Kadri-Ann Valdur, and Indrek Must$^{(\boxtimes)}$

Institute of Technology, Intelligent Materials and Systems Lab, University of Tartu, Nooruse 1, 50411 Tartu, Estonia
indrek.must@ut.ee

Abstract. Fungal mycelium, a sensor and commutation highway for information in the form of electrical signals and biomarkers, covers a large section of the Earth's biosphere, giving access to the "wood-wide web". A bio-hybrid robot with fungal mycelium as a living agent for information collection and commutation is the missing link for data-driven precision agriculture – one of the ways to sustainability. Currently, we do not have effective access points due to the high localization of existing sensing approaches deriving us from holistic data on the mycelium level. Here we show a method for isolating the electrical signals within a living mycelium and characterize the ion movements with impedance and open circuit potential (OCP) study. The colonizing nature of the fungus was used to form a mycelium bridge between the grounded and floating nodes to isolate the electrical signals within the living organism. The average real part of the impedance (80 kΩ) demonstrates the effectiveness of the mycelium as a distributed salt bridge and the fluctuations in impedance ($\sim$10 kΩ) and OCP ($\sim$20 mV) at a predictable period (28–30 h) evidence the life processes of the fungus, e.g. the opening of Ca^{2+} channels. The use of living fungus as a biological sensor and connector shows important insight into truly biohybrid robotics. Access to fungal networks enables cooperation between ecosystems and data-driven decisions, leading to sustainability.

Keywords: biohybrid · fungal mycelium · precision agriculture · mycelium bridge · bioimpedance · biopotential · decentralized sensor network · soil infosphere

1 Introduction

Biohybrid robotics incorporating living agents native to soil can revolutionize precision agriculture. Sustainability in agriculture is driven by real-time data collection and decision-making, needing intricate access to biologically relevant information over a large area. Agricultural land covers 39% of the total land of the EU [1]. Most of the agricultural fields are in the range of 5 hectares [1], which is a challengingly large area to supervise with current solutions.

A single fungal mycelium – a complex 3D network assembled through radial growth and anastomosis of relatively independent 2D hypha [9] - can cover an area up to 3

© The Author(s), under exclusive license to Springer Nature Switzerland AG 2023
F. Meder et al. (Eds.): Living Machines 2023, LNAI 14158, pp. 335–347, 2023.
https://doi.org/10.1007/978-3-031-39504-8_23

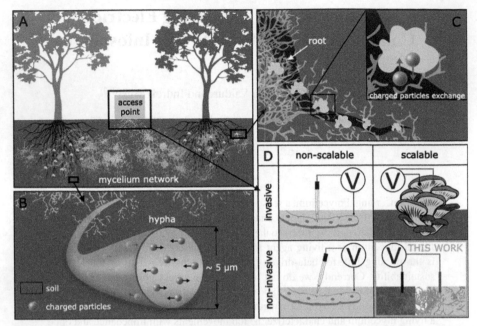

Fig. 1. Mycelium as a sensing electrical entity. A) Fungi form underground networks that connect plants and mediate nutrient exchange [2]. A feasible access point to these networks is currently missing. B) For convenience we can think of hypha as a microwire filled with electrolyte along which charged particles move. In this simplified model the resistance of the hyphal microwire is determined by the diameter of the hypha. C) We show a hypothetical arbuscular mycorrhiza connection through which the fungus provides the plant with vital nutrients such as nitrogen and phosphates while the plant is the main carbon source for the fungus [3, 4]. D) The state of art methods for measuring fungal electricity are either invasive, non-scalable, or both [5]–[8]. Our work proposes a non-invasive scalable method for measuring mycelial electrical activity.

times (15 ha) the range of most agricultural fields [10]. While symbiotic fungi form networks directly connecting plants (Fig. 1A) [2, 11] through mycorrhizal formations, which enable plant-fungus nutrient exchange as well as mediate plant-plant nutrient exchange[2, 11], non-symbiotic fungal networks can also act as water and nutrient distributers and stocks in soil.

Mycorrhizal networks can be seen as biological market networks where goods are exchanged between individuals similarly to human economic market [12]. Moreover, the direction of the trade depends on environmental conditions and the resource value can be influenced by individuals [12]. Therefore, despite it is commonly stated that fungi are dependent on carbon originating from plants [13] while plants receive up to 90% of their nutritional needs from fungi [14], reversed trade can also be observed. A substantial example are myco-heterotrophic plants that get all their carbon from mycorrhizal networks [15]. Altogether, mycorrhizal networks, also referred to as the "wood-wide web" [16], is an information-sharing platform for entire ecosystems and indicator of a healthy natural community [17].

One of the mechanisms for coordinating the hyphal network growth and functioning is, similar to neuronal networks and convenient for robotics, electricity [18]. Endogenous electrical currents shown to be critical for the fungus for the location of plant roots and formation of mycorrhiza [18, 19] (Fig. 1C). Additionally, electrical currents in fungi can be measured in response to many stimuli: light, humidity, temperature, pH, electromagnetic fields, mechanical pressure, chemical compounds, and other organisms [5, 18, 20].

Bioelectrical measurements are an appealing opportunity for recording the changes in physiology as a simple setup of electrodes enables to record responses of varying origins. [7]. Cable theory [21], primarily developed for computational neuroscience applications, is especially relevant for describing electrical activity in fungal hypha [7], where aligned cells are connected through a continuum of cytoplasm via special connections – septal pores. Similarly to neural cells, fungal hypha exhibit action-potential-like activity. The cable approximation allows to consider the hypha as a microwire in which longitudinal electrical currents depend on capacitive and conductive components of transmembrane ion movement as well as endogenous longitudinal conductivity [7, 21]. Simultaneous measurements of ionic flow along the hypha and ionic flux across the hyphal membrane have shown that K^+ and Cl^- ions contribute the most to the change in membrane potential in *Neurospora crassa* while for example Ca^{2+}, Na^+ ions, and organic acids are likely to contribute to the endogenous ionic flow. Although consisting of transmembrane and along membrane components, the electrical signals propagate along the conductive hyphal tube, in which the presence of septas exhibits a minimal effect on ion movement [7] and can therefore be neglected, this is illustrated in the simplified wire model in Fig. 1B. In that the mycelium can be considered as a distributed conductive bridge across signal input and output, bearing resemblance to a salt bridge – a method often used in electrochemistry to acquire conductive pathways without altering the measurement itself [22, 23].

First attempts of implementing fungi into electronics have already been made [24] but the methods for measuring fungal electricity are localized, often invasive, and need delicate handling (Fig. 1D). Olsson and Hansson [6] inserted invasive glass microelectrodes filled with KCl solution into hyphae to show both spontaneous and stimulated neuron-like activity in mycelial strands. Adamatzky [5, 8] pinned invasive stainless steel needle electrodes in the dense mycelium and fruiting bodies to detect exogenous changes in potential. As an example of a non-invasive method, the vibrating probe method for measuring extracellular currents was introduced by Jaffe and Nuccitelli [25] and was successfully applied by Lew [26] for measuring Ca^{2+} and H^+ fluxes along hyphal tips of *Neurospora crassa* and *Saprolegnia ferax*. However, present research does not enable us to study the mycelium as an access point to widely distributed underground communication network.

In this work we show a scalable and non-invasive method to isolate the electrical signals within a living mycelium and treat the mycelium as an information pathway for external signals for prospective use in biohybrid robotics. The real part of the impedance and open circuit potential (OCP) are used to characterize the ion movements. *Pleurotus ostreatus*, a decomposer fungus is used as a model because of cultivability, rapid growth and previous use in electrical measurements [5].

2 Living Fungus as an Electrical System

Herein we present the idea of the mycelium bridge for connecting a living fungus into an electrical system in a way that incorporates the whole mycelium and is non-invasive.

2.1 Colonizing Behavior as the Key to Non-invasiveness

Living mycelium is a conductive network of tubular hyphae filled with electrolyte. As the natural growing environment for soil fungi is conductive [normal soil conductivity (EC) is 4 dS/m [27]] it is critical to isolate the electrical signals from the mycelium and surrounding environment. An electrochemical cell filled with conductive growing medium and divided into two nodes separated by a common isolation medium – air. One of the cell nodes is grounded and can be referred to as the natural soil habitat (Fig. 2B, node 1) while the other node is electrically isolated (Fig. 2B, node 2). The connection between the two nodes is completed by the mycelium itself via colonization from one node to the other (hereinafter the mycelium bridge, Fig. 2A).

Mycelial growth is investigative and colonizing by its nature. Leading hyphae at the edge of the mycelium form the foraging front colonizing new territories in search of nutrients and food [14]. Meanwhile, the hyphae behind the foraging front develop and reinforce the 3D network through anastomosis to fuel the leading hyphae [14]. This suggests that in sufficient humidity mycelium can bridge nutrient-deprived environments to colonize new nearby nutrient-rich environments.

Most of the present methods for measuring fungal electricity place the electrodes in the pre-grown mycelium invasively. In the setup depicted in Fig. 2, the foraging behavior of the fungus is used to achieve a noninvasive contact by letting the mycelium form the mycelium bridge and thereby grow into gel/soil mediated contact with fixed electrodes.

While the mycelium bridge is in contact with moist air only, the mycelium within the nodes is exposed to the growing medium – an electrolytic environment, where trans-membrane currents that act as signals of fungal life processes are evoked as a result of the activity of ion channels. Consequently, the signals of fungal life processes are mainly localized inside the nodes. However, the contact area between hypha and electrolytical medium is much larger compared to the cross-section area of the bridge. Therefore, when measuring electrical signals between the two nodes, the electrical connection is likely dominated by the bridge characteristics, while the electrical parameters are the result of fungal life processes in the nodes.

2.2 Mycelium Bridge as 'Living Wires'

The mycelium bridge can be approximated as an arrangement of elongated electrolyte-filled chambers. Thus, once formed, the mycelium bridge bears resemblance to salt bridges, a classical method in electrochemistry for establishing the galvanic connection between dissimilar cells. Indeed, the salt bridge separates solutions while allowing for ion mobility and closing the electric circuit for cell potential measurement. The electrolyte-filled structures appear to be optimal for longitudinal signal transfer while the environment connection is of large cross-section area and spatially highly distributed -features hardly available with human-made salt bridges.

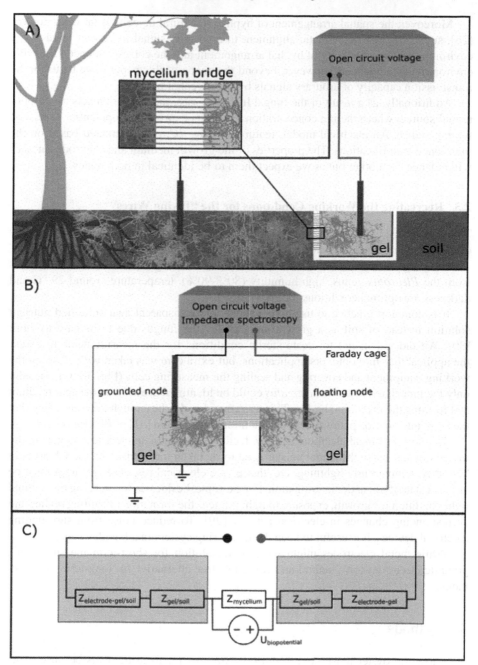

Fig. 2. Concept of the mycelium bridge measurements. A) Theoretical concept in natural environment. B) Laboratory setup. C) Simplified electrical scheme of the measuring system.

Moreover, the spatial arrangement of hyphae in natural mycelia is far from random [26], suggesting also systematic alignment to a specific signal to be registered in the environment. The specificity of hyphal arrangement and the correspondence to specific environmental signals are, however, beyond the scope of this paper – we focus on the transmission capacity of arbitrary signals by the mycelial bridge.

Additionally, as a result of the fungal life processes, the mycelium acts as a biopotential source, where the ion concentration gradients express as biopotential as well as bioimpedance. An electrical model, featured in Fig. 2C, can be created based on the mentioned simplifications. The properties of the growth medium and electrode surfaces will balance each other out as we expect them to be identical in both nodes.

2.3 Recreating the Working Conditions for the "Living Wires"

To incorporate a living fungus into an electrical circuit the basic needs and life processes of the mycelium need to be taken into consideration.

Fungal growth relies on intra cell water pressure - turgor [14, 22]. For the species from the *Pleurotus* genus, high humidity (80%-90%), temperature around 29 °C and darkness are optimal conditions for growth [29].

It is common practice to use homogenous and transparent agar-solidified nutrient solution instead of soil as a growth medium for the fungus due to its ease to work [30]. We did not intend to create sterile conditions for the measurements to assess the applicability into outdoors applications, but extra care was taken with cleaning the working equipment and covering and sealing the measuring cells (Fig. 3B, C). Visually only the inoculated *Pleurotus ostreatus* could be identified growing on the agar medium and forming the mycelium bridge. This was considered to be enough for concluding that the main information pathway was the intentional mycelium [31] of *Pleurotus ostreatus*.

To interpret fungal electrical activity, factors that stimulate electrical signals in the mycelium and make the signal noisier need to be taken into consideration. Changes in humidity, temperature, lightning, etc. that evoke electrical responses in fungi must be kept constant if not under investigation. For example, besides darkness being the optimal light condition for growth, exposure to light induces the formation of fruiting bodies and corresponding changes in electrical activity [29]. To reduce noise from surrounding electrical devices, it is useful to keep the measuring system in a Faraday cage.

While metal electrodes might be a good solution for short-term measurements, graphite electrodes are a neutral and corrosion-free alternative for long-term measurements.

3   Methods

We chose the oyster mushroom *Pleurotus ostreatus* for measurements because of its rapid growth, undemanding growing environment, and reliability as fungal bioelectrical measurements with this genus have previously been performed [5, 8]. The oyster mushroom *Pleurotus ostreatus*, strain TFC202336 was gained from Tartu Fungal Culture Collection (TFC). *Pleurotus ostreatus* mycelium was inoculated on malt extract agar (MEA, 2% malt extract + 2% agar + deionized water) Petri dishes. Following the incubation of *Pleurotus ostreatus* isolates at 23 °C the mycelium covered the entire surface of Petri dishes within 7 days after which they were kept at 5 °C. The measuring cell (see dimensions in Fig. 3A) was designed with the Fusion 360 software and 3D printed from polylactic acid (PLA) with Original Prusa i3 MK3S printer.

Malt Extract Agar (MEA) medium (2% malt extract + 1,5% agar + deionized water) was used as the substrate, and 2 mm diameter graphite electrodes were used for measuring potential differences between two nodes. The fast-growing mycelium of *Pleurotus ostreatus* was inoculated at the vicinity of the electrode, approximately in the center of the grounded node (Fig. 3B). The floating and grounded nodes, covered with a transparent lid and sealed with Parafilm (Fig. 3C) was placed into a sealed chamber together with a small container filled with deionized water to keep the mycelium from drying. The whole setup was placed into a Faraday cage and was kept in darkness during measurements. Measurements were conducted at room conditions, at a temperature of 22 °C $\pm$ 2 °C. Bio Logic BP-300 potentiostat was used to measure open circuit potential (OCP) and impedance. OCP was recorded at one sample per second with 10 μV resolution. 10 mV AC voltage in the frequency range of 1–100 kHz was applied to measure the impedance.

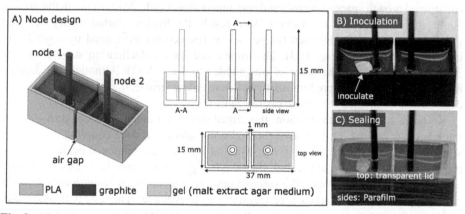

Fig. 3. Measuring set-up. A) Design and arrangement of the two mirror-symmetric growth cells as floating and grounded node. B) Photograph immediately after inoculation of the mycelium into the grounded node. C) Sealing of the inoculated two-node system.

4   Results and Discussion

4.1   Formation and Longevity of the Mycelium Bridge

For consideration of the mycelium as a communication channel, the living mycelium bridge needs to be formed *in situ* and the life processes limit the longevity of the connection. The first step is to determine the stability and quality of the formed mycelial bridge.

Although herein we represent one set of measurements, our results clearly characterize the main functioning phases of the mycelium bridge (Fig. 4; 0–3). *Pleurotus ostreatus* was inoculated to the centre of the grounded node, starting rapid growth towards the borders of the node. We recorded changes in OCP during 18 days from inoculation, shown in Fig. 4 A. Phase 0–1 in Fig. 4 marks the time when the mycelium bridge had not formed yet, implying effectively an open-circuit condition. Before the mycelium reached the borders to start forming a bridge, the OCP between nodes fluctuated at about 400 mV peak-to-peak (Fig. 4A; 0–1), attributed to the coupling of the high-input-impedance and low-capacitance electrometer channel to the node cap. The impedance between the nodes was primarily determined by charging characteristics of the parallel-plate capacitor formed of the surfaces of two growth substrates facing each other (capacitance: estimated 1.0 pF). In about three days from inoculation, the fast-growing mycelia occupied most of the 2.2-cm^2 node surface area, reached the border of the node, and the first hyphae crossing the gap between nodes was visually confirmed. Phase 2 in Fig. 4 corresponds to the formed viable mycelial bridge. A well-formed mycelium bridge was evidenced by OCP switching from white to pink (low-frequency-dominated) noise characteristic (Fig. 4A). The impedance was drastically decreased to around 100 kΩ, almost frequency-invariable (Fig. 4B; 2). By day 14, the mycelium had occupied most of the constricted growth space (1.8 cm^3) and consumed most available nutrients in the growth media in both nodes (2 x 1.8 cm^3). As a result, the hyphae started to dry out, and the mycelial bridge degenerated (as per visual inspection), evidenced by a gradually increased noise figure (Fig. 4; 3). The impedance for the declination stage (Fig. 4B; 3) increased by about one order of magnitude (to a few MΩ). Although the degrading mycelium retained a predominantly resistive characteristic, the rapid progression of degradation terminated the usable operation time.

In terms of signal transmission, the impedance is a fundamental concern – lower impedance is desired for decreased thermal noise and can reduce coupling to adjacent signal sources. In our experiment, the mycelial bridge was composed of thousands of individual hyphae acting in parallel, thus the bridge conductance increases proportionally to the number of hyphae. The suitable optimal scale of the measurements depends on the application. Some applications require single hypha level access, such as ion flux and current measurements across the cell membrane [6, 25], where the microelectrode is suitable. Others need access to the collective entity of the mycelium, well represented in [8] where needle electrodes are pinned into a composite material with living fungus to test for its sensing ability to external stimuli. In all cases the methodological choice is a compromise between averaging and resolution of information. Although our measurements suggest that the extrapolated real impedance to a single hypha bridging the gap would be at an appropriate level, we emphasize the lower impedance benefit of multiple parallel hyphae that is hardly achievable by invasive approaches. While it still comprises the idea of conveying environment driven changes in electrical potential within the hyphae (embodied by the grounded node) to the measurement electronics (connection made within the other floating node) this approach is more convenient in a larger scale. The signal pathway was large enough to average the behaviors of individual hypha, yet small enough to render interfacial impedance between the gel and the electrode negligible ($Z_{electrode-gel} = 60$–80 kΩ, much smaller than the $Z_{mycelium}$).

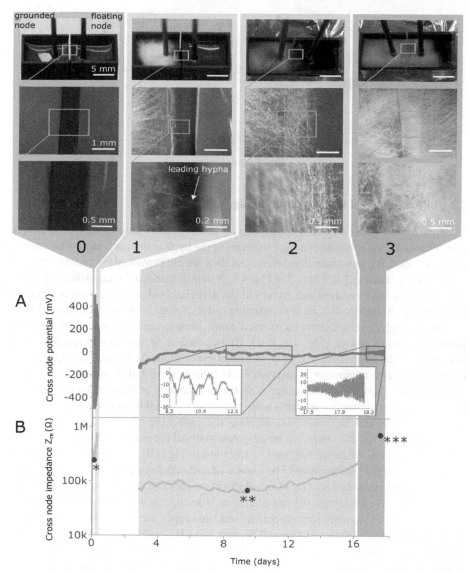

Fig. 4. Electrical activity of the mycelium bridge. 0) Mycelium is inoculated, 1) Mycelium bridge is not formed, 2) Mycelium bridge is formed and functions normally, 3) Mycelium bridge starts to dry out. A) Open circuit potential evidences mycelial life artifacts and shows cycling behavior throughout phase 2. B) Impedance Zre monitors the impedance of the mycelium bridge and shows distinct behavior during the phases 0-3. C) PSD analysis for potential fluctuations indicates a period of 30 h D) PSD analysis for the Zre indicates a period of 28 h. E) Impedance measured at day 1 (*), 9 (**) and 18 (***). Impedance at 10 kHz was chosen for monitoring, as it is high enough to represent purely resistive compo-nents of the impedance but low enough to neglect noise from surrounding electronics.

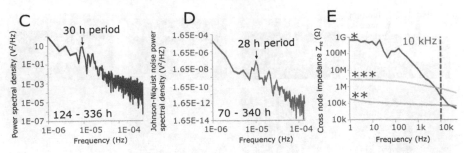

Fig. 4. (*continued*)

4.2 Life Artifacts of the Mycelium Bridge

Consideration of the body of a living mycelium as a conductor could not be done without contribution by the spontaneous life processes of the hyphae themselves on transmission characteristics. By spontaneous we mean that they are not provoked by intentional external stimuli as stated in [5]. Phase 2 in Fig. 4A, B demonstrates a distinguishable periodic pattern during the formation and growth of the mycelial bridge. The period is estimated to be around 30 h (Fig. 4C), in the consistent order of magnitude with literature [5].

Interestingly, cyclic behaviour is even more pronounced in connection establishment and growth phases (Fig. 4B; 0–2). Bioimpedance, Z was monitored during the life cycle of the mycelium, taking a spectrum every hour. At broad, bioimpedance is composed of two components: resistance (R) which is attributed to total body water, and reactance (Xc) which associates with the capacitance of the cell membrane [25]. Resistive and capacitive components both contribute to signal transmission: higher resistive components can increase noise whereas the capacitive effect can induce shifts in OCV magnitude. In this study, we investigated in detail the resistive component, allowing for the approximation of hyphae to a microwire (Fig. 1B). The resistive component dominates at higher frequencies. The choice of methodology is always a compromise between signal, noise and artefacts from electrode wiring and depend on particular setup. We chose 10 kHz frequency for impedance monitoring, as it is high enough to expect the dominance of the resistive component and thus apply the microwire model and the analogy to predominately resistive salt bridges. 10 kHz was found to be the best compromise as it is also low enough to neglect the noise from wires and measuring apparatus which increases at higher frequencies. Figure 4D reveals a clear oscillating behaviour in transient impedance (bioimpedance) with an average period of 28 h, pronounced in growth phase (Fig. 4B; 2), monitored at 10 kHz (Fig. 4E).

Considering, in first approximation, hyphae as electrolyte-filled tubes, the measurement suggests fluctuations in ion concentrations within the tubes as a result of ion channel's activities across the mycelium, and changes in effective tube diameter, which affects the impediment to longitudinal movement. In the case of the mycelium bridge, both sources can provide valuable signals. Establishing a stable bridge connection with low enough impedance is essential for evidencing the life artifacts of the fungus. Meanwhile we could investigate ′the wire′ – mycelium bridge itself. Hyphal surface in the growing medium is much larger compared to mycelium bridge cross-section area. Therefore, we expect the latter to be the dominant impeding feature. Change in the tube effective diameter (compare phases 0–1, 2, and 3 in Fig. 4B) represents the quality of the established connection, and phase 2 is clearly the best state for evidencing the life processes of the fungus.

5 Conclusion

Mycelium is, among other functions, an important messenger in soil, facilitated by its highly distributed structure and large area giving an excellent access to any information, including those represented by electric potential fluctuations. We considered mycelial bridge as a living messenger between the robotic domain and the environment. This suggests vast potential for 'tapping' the information carried by self-forming mycelia for data-driven decisions in precision agriculture.

This work focused on practical aspects in non-invasive interfacing measurement electronics to a living mycelium. We constructed a system of two nodes equipped with electrodes and separated by a common isolation medium – air. The electrical circuit was completed by the mycelium growing from the grounded inoculation node to the floating node. Formation of the connection - mycelium bridge occurred relatively fast – in three days from inoculation, hinting to even faster formation with a pre-inoculated node. This suggests to a rapid deployment procedure of non-invasive measurement point, avoiding the complexity, laboriousness of the currently popular method of invasive tapping of a single hypha, yet still delivering information on mycelium interior environment. The self-forming and self-replenishing bridge suggest potential for distributed deployment of a large number of nodes in nature, whereas each node delivers information from a network existing in soil. A conceptual parallel to internet access points is subtly noted.

Although this work represents one set of measurements, the life processes of the mycelium bridge were clearly isolated and the experiments conducted in [31] support our results. Our measurements showed best performance for the communication channel in rapid growth phase of the mycelium, restricted by nutrient source and free space. This suggests a practical lifetime of the mycelial bridge as a sensing node of approximately 15 days. In addition to the expected potential fluctuation (30 h), the impedance across the bridge also demonstrated cyclic behaviour, with a period of approximately 28 h. As the experiment focused on longitudinal signal transmission via an aligned arrangement of a limited number of hyphae, minimizing interfacial effects, the measurements suggest fluctuations in intra-hyphae electrolytic conductivity. This gives inspiration for development of self-oscillatory ionic machines.

At predictable and periodic characteristic, the life artefacts could be compensated for in restoring the original signal – or applied as a confirmation sign of an active bridge. Indeed, consideration of hyphae as wires with spontaneous quality monitoring brings new thought to sensing electronics development.

Further studies should concentrate on detecting and interpreting electrical responses to specific stimuli on species level as well as on inter-species variations as noted in [32].

The hyphal wires carry not only electrical signals but also chemical signals. The mycelium bridge concept can therefore act also as an access point for sending and receiving other types of messages than electrical. In the consideration of precision agriculture, pinging individual plants on their actual nutrition level would greatly reduce the fertilizer oversupply issue in today's agriculture.

At broad, our experiments were aimed on better understanding the practical implications of deployment of a living organism (*Pleurotus ostreatus*) as a pathway for electrical signal – knowledge widely appreciated in biohybrid robotics, and gateway to precision agriculture.

Acknowledgements. This research was supported by the Estonian Research Council grants PRG1498 and Kristjan Jaak Scholarship for short study visits (provided by Estonian Ministry of Education and Research and the Education and Youth Board).

The authors thank colleagues from the University of Tartu Leho Tedersoo, Professor in Mycorrhizal Studies for support and providing the oyster mushroom (Pleurotus ostreatus) strains and Hanna Hõrak, Associate Professor of Molecular Plant Physiology for allowing to use her laboratories for experimenting with fungi.

References

1. 'Farms and farmland in the European Union-statistics', eurostat- Statistics Explained (2018). https://ec.europa.eu/eurostat/statistics-explained/index.php?title=Farms_and_farmland_in_the_European_Union_-_statistics. Accessed 27 Oct 2022
2. Simard, S.W., Jones, M.D., Durall, D.M.: Carbon and nutrient fluxes within and between mycorrhizal plants. In: van der Heijden, M.G.A., Sanders, I.R. (eds.) Mycorrhizal Ecology, Ecological Studies, vol. 157, pp. 33–74. Springer, Berlin (2003). https://doi.org/10.1007/978-3-540-38364-2_2
3. Drigo, B., et al.: Shifting carbon flow from roots into associated microbial communities in response to elevated atmospheric CO_2. Proc. Natl. Acad. Sci. **107**(24), 10938–10942 (2010). https://doi.org/10.1073/pnas.0912421107
4. Heijden, M.G.A., Martin, F.M., Selosse, M., Sanders, I.R.: Mycorrhizal ecology and evolution: the past, the present, and the future. New Phytol. **205**(4), 1406–1423 (2015). https://doi.org/10.1111/nph.13288
5. Adamatzky, A.: On spiking behaviour of oyster fungi Pleurotus djamor. Sci. Rep. **8**(1), 7873 (2018). https://doi.org/10.1038/s41598-018-26007-1
6. Olsson, S., Hansson, B.S.: Action potential-like activity found in fungal mycelia is sensitive to stimulation. Naturwissenschaften **82**(1), 30–31 (1995). https://doi.org/10.1007/BF01167867
7. Lew, R.R.: Ionic currents and ion fluxes in Neurospora crassa hyphae. J. Exp. Bot. **58**(12), 3475–3481 (2007). https://doi.org/10.1093/jxb/erm204
8. Adamatzky, A., Gandia, A., Chiolerio, A.: Towards fungal sensing skin. Fungal Biol. Biotechnol. **8**(1), 6 (2021). https://doi.org/10.1186/s40694-021-00113-8
9. Rayner, A.D.M.: The challenge of the individualistic mycelium. Mycologia **83**(1), 48–71 (1991). https://doi.org/10.1080/00275514.1991.12025978
10. Smith, M.L., Bruhn, J.N., Anderson, J.B.: The fungus Armillaria bulbosa is among the largest and oldest living organisms. Nature **356**(6368), 428–431 (1992). https://doi.org/10.1038/356428a0
11. Simard, S.W., Beiler, K.J., Bingham, M.A., Deslippe, J.R., Philip, L.J., Teste, F.P.: Mycorrhizal networks: mechanisms, ecology and modelling. Fungal Biol. Rev. **26**(1), 39–60 (2012). https://doi.org/10.1016/j.fbr.2012.01.001

12. Van't Padje, A., Werner, G.D., Kiers, E.T.: Mycorrhizal fungi control phosphorus value in trade symbiosis with host roots when exposed to abrupt 'crashes' and 'booms' of resource availability. New Phytol. **229**(5), 2933–2944 (2021). https://doi.org/10.1111/nph.17055

13. Jiang, Y., et al.: Plants transfer lipids to sustain colonization by mutualistic mycorrhizal and parasitic fungi. Science **356**(6343), 1172–1175 (2017). https://doi.org/10.1126/science.aam 9970

14. Lew, R.R.: How does a hypha grow? The biophysics of pressurized growth in fungi. Nat. Rev. Microbiol. **9**(7), 509–518 (2011). https://doi.org/10.1038/nrmicro2591

15. Merckx, V., Bidartondo, M.I., Hynson, N.A.: Myco-heterotrophy: when fungi host plants. Ann. Bot. **104**(7), 1255–1261 (2009). https://doi.org/10.1093/aob/mcp235

16. Nature **388**(6642) (1997).https://www.nature.com/nature/volumes/388/issues/6642#Article

17. Angrish, R.: The wood wide web: tree talk in the forest. Resonance **27**(8), 1429–1441 (2022). https://doi.org/10.1007/s12045-022-1435-x

18. Berbara, R.L.L., Morris, B.M., Fonseca, H.M.A.C., Reid, B., Gow, N.A.R., Daft, M.J.: Electrical currents associated with arbuscular mycorrhizal interactions. New Phytol. **129**(3), 433–438 (1995). https://doi.org/10.1111/j.1469-8137.1995.tb04314.x

19. Wang, W., Shi, J., Xie, Q., Jiang, Y., Yu, N., Wang, E.: Nutrient exchange and regulation in arbuscular mycorrhizal symbiosis. Mol. Plant **10**(9), 1147–1158 (2017). https://doi.org/10.1016/j.molp.2017.07.012

20. Adamatzky, A.: Towards fungal computer. Interface Focus **8**(6), 20180029 (2018). https://doi.org/10.1098/rsfs.2018.0029

21. Rall, W.: Core conductor theory and cable properties of neurons. Compr. Physiol., 39–97 (2011). https://doi.org/10.1002/cphy.cp010103

22. Herman, K.C., Bleichrodt, R.: Go with the flow: mechanisms driving water transport during vegetative growth and fruiting. Fungal Biol. Rev. **41**, 10–23 (2022). https://doi.org/10.1016/j.fbr.2021.10.002

23. Kakiuchi, T.: Salt bridge in electroanalytical chemistry: past, present, and future. J. Solid State Electrochem. **15**(7–8), 1661–1671 (2011). https://doi.org/10.1007/s10008-011-1373-0

24. Adamatzky, A., et al.: Fungal electronics. Biosystems **212**, 104588 (2022). https://doi.org/10.1016/j.biosystems.2021.104588

25. Jaffe, L.F., Nuccitelli, R.: An ultrasensitive vibrating probe for measuring steady extracellular currents. J. Cell Biol. **63**(2), 614–628 (1974). https://doi.org/10.1083/jcb.63.2.614

26. Lew, R.R.: Comparative analysis of Ca2+ and H+ flux magnitude and location along growing hyphae of saprolegnia ferax and neurospora crassa. Eur. J. Cell Biol. **78**(12), 892–902 (1999). https://doi.org/10.1016/S0171-9335(99)80091-0

27. Abegunrin, A.: Effect of kitchen wastewater irrigation on soil properties and growth of cucumber (Cucumis sativus). J. Soil Sci. Environ. Manag. **4**(7), 139–145 (2013). https://doi.org/10.5897/JSSEM2013.0412

28. Toju, H., Guimarães, P.R., Olesen, J.M., Thompson, J.N.: Assembly of complex plant–fungus networks. Nat. Commun. **5**(1), 5273 (2014). https://doi.org/10.1038/ncomms6273

29. Aghajani, H., et al.: Influence of relative humidity and temperature on cultivation of pleurotus species. Maderas. Ciencia y tecnología **20**(4), 571–578 (2018). https://doi.org/10.4067/S0718-221X2018005004501

30. Indian Institute of Science Education and Research Kolkata (IISER-K), Mohanpur, West Bengal – 741246, India et al.: Evolution of bacterial and fungal growth media. Bioinformation **11**(4), 182–184 (2015). https://doi.org/10.6026/97320630011182

31. Thomas, M.A., Cooper, R.L.: Building bridges: mycelium–mediated plant–plant electrophysiological communication. Plant Biol. (2022). https://doi.org/10.1101/2022.07.20.500447

32. Adamatzky, A.: Language of fungi derived from their electrical spiking activity. R. Soc. Open Sci. **9**(4), 211926 (2022). https://doi.org/10.1098/rsos.211926

Living Organisms as Sensors
for Biohybrid Monitoring Systems

Wiktoria Rajewicz$^{(\boxtimes)}$ ⓘ, Nikolaus Helmer ⓘ, Thomas Schmickl ⓘ,
and Ronald Thenius ⓘ

University of Graz, Graz, Austria
wiktoria.rajewicz@uni-graz.at

Abstract. Many aquatic habitats have become vulnerable to rapid and long-term changes induced by industrialism, air pollution, tourism, fishing activities etc. These factors created an urgent need for extensive water monitoring and conservation. By observing the behaviour of lifeforms, we can monitor the state of the environment. Here, we present the methodology, calibration approaches and preliminary results of designing a biohybrid entity for aquatic monitoring. Biohybrid robots combine mechanical and electronic elements with living organisms or tissues. This biohybrid consists of several modules, each hosting or attracting different species and communities. We focus on animals such as *Daphnia* sp., zebra mussel *Dreissena polymorpha* and various representatives of the plankton community. The first results showed that 1) both *Daphnia* and *D. polymorpha* show no clear signs of confinement-induced stress, 2) the designed structures are examples of suitable tools for hosting the organisms, observing their behaviour and collecting and storing data and 3) their behaviour can be calibrated under laboratory conditions to be able to extrapolate the field data into environmental data.

Keywords: Biohybrid · Animal-Robot Interaction · Environmental Monitoring

1 Introduction

1.1 Organisms as Sensors

The term "biosensor" began and was popularised in the late'80s by Clark Jr. (1988) [5] and has been gaining interest since. Currently, many methods of using living sensors are being implemented for various purposes ranging from ecological studies, and detection of substances to developing functional robots actuated by living cells [12,29,33]. An example is the use of trained dogs for the detection of chemicals at airport security [30]. We take advantage of the dog's superior sense of smell to detect the olfactory cues emitted by toxic substances. An analogous

Supported by EU-H2020 Project Robocoenosis, grant agreement No 899520.

F. Meder et al. (Eds.): Living Machines 2023, LNAI 14158, pp. 348–362, 2023.
https://doi.org/10.1007/978-3-031-39504-8_24

scenario is the use of canaries in mines for the detection of high carbon monoxide concentration [32].

The need for aquatic monitoring arose with the increasing water and air pollution that came with intense industrialism [7]. This has caused an urgent need to gather extensive data on the limited freshwater supplies. In order to protect these habitats, large-scale monitoring needs to be established and perfected. One of the projects researching this, is project Robocoenosis [25], which aims at developing a biohybrid system that will serve as a complementary element to traditional water monitoring.

In contrast to living organisms, classical sensors, such as oxygen probes or conductivity sensors are a more precise source of information on the environment, due to their narrow specificity. The aforementioned examples of using organisms as sensors (such as dogs and canaries) are performed with the naked eye thanks to the relatively simple observation methods. However, the monitoring of the aquatic environment is more complex due to its inaccessibility. Continuous observation of the lifeforms inhabiting is much more logistically complex with human observers.

To overcome this limitation, the development of so-called biohybrids gained interest. A biohybrid entity (also called "biohybrid") is a device connecting living organisms or tissues with mechanical and electrical parts [20,37]. Biohybrids have many functions, for example as actuators in the functioning of muscles or as actuators for motile cells and can operate on a variety of levels [15,27,28]. Here, we present a methodology for using this approach to extract data on the surrounding environment through the observation of living organisms by electronic components.

Several companies have used this methodology to create robust water quality monitoring tools. Devices such as Daphtox II ® and MosselMonitor ® [2] have incorporated animals like *Daphnia* and *Dreissena polymorpha* for in-house monitoring. *Daphnia* is used as a living detection tool for ecological, toxicological and pharmaceutical studies [16,18,31]. The findings show altered swimming behaviour and physiology depending on the presence/absence and the intensity of toxic substances, such as paracetamol, antidepressants, microcystin, etc. The majority of these studies focus on visual observation or post-experimental video analysis with the use of various object-tracking software. Here, we translate this approach into the field aiming at an autonomous, long-term monitoring device.

Observing the behaviour of living organisms in a biohybrid module developed by Project Robocoenosis provides a different type of data compared to classical sensors. It is a broad-range sensor which focuses on the detection of a wide variety of changes (see Table 1) resulting in a lower precision for individual stressors (for example, the behavioural reaction to a change in temperature is a less precise reading than a temperature probe). The sensitivity of this biohybrid depends on the animal's tolerance of the stimuli and our ability to interpret its behaviour. To be able to extract data from the organisms we need to: 1) have the background knowledge on the organism's tolerance to changes and 2) have performed calibration experiments on the changing behaviour to establish the magnitude and possible sources of stress.

1.2   Project Robocoenosis

In this work, we present the most recent results of selected modules of a biohybrid entity, that incorporates multiple living organisms. The biohybrid modules (here, also called "modules") attract or host different species and communities and observe them in a non-invasive way. This biohybrid includes several features:

Automated Observation of the Organisms: The biohybrid incorporates several species and communities in order to extrapolate more precise data on the environment, due to different lifeforms having different sensitivity to certain pollutants (for details, see Table 1).

Long-Term Data Collection: The biohybrid operates over long runtimes (relative to other autonomous biohybrid approaches such as [21,23]: 6 days and 7 days respectively), aiming for several months/years, with little to no maintenance required.

Self-sustainable Energy Source: The biohybrid uses Microbial Fuel Cells (MFCs) as an energy harvesting mechanism allowing the entity to forgo external batteries and be entirely self-sustainable, The MFCs also serve as an additional sensor, giving an insight into the bacterial activity in the sediments. For more details, please see [24,25,36].

The biohybrid modules designed and investigated by the project are listed in Table 1. In this work, we present the working principles and preliminary results of selected modules in Robocoenosis.

Table 1. Biohybrid modules developed by the project Robocoenosis and their functions.

Organism	Method	Raw data obtained	Aimed information on the ecosystem
Daphnia sp	Video analysis	Swimming speed, swarming, spinning, sinking, inhibition	Oxygen, temperature, salinity, microplastics, pesticides
Dreissena polymorpha	Hall sensor, heartbeat sensor	Valve movements, heartbeat	Oxygen, temperature, salinity, heavy metals, pesticides
Microbial activity	MFC power output	Energy produced by the MFC	Oxygen, temperature
Planktonic community	Video analysis	Community structure, species present/absent, structure fluctuations, mass mortality	Oxygen, temperature, toxins, heavy metals, pesticides

For more information on the project's first concepts and goals, the reasoning behind the choice of organisms and the preliminary results of the biohybrid modules, please see publications [24,25,36] respectively. Here, we present a further development of several biohybrid modules and the results of various calibration experiments. This work focuses on the presentation of a Hall sensor approach (Sect. 2.5, furthering the "Daphnia module" development (Sect. 2.4) and the first advances in creating a "Plankton community module" (Sect. 2.6).

2 Module Development

2.1 Test Sites

Field tests and calibration experiments take place in two Austrian lakes: Lake Millstatt and Lake Neusiedl. They represent vastly different habitats which allow for more extensive testing of the biohybrid. Lake Millstatt (46°47′N 13°34′E) located in Carinthia (Austria) is an oligotrophic lake, characterized by small amounts of nutrients and clear waters [38]. Its depth reaches 150 m which allows for testing the biohybrid on different depths and provides optimal conditions for video-based approaches [26].

Lake Neusiedl (47°50′N 16°45′E), in Burgenland (Austria), provides vastly different conditions, being a highly eutrophic water body [8]. It is characterized by a high nutrient and algae content. It is extremely shallow (<1.8 m) while being the largest body of freshwater in Central Europe, surface-wise. During multiple workshops per year, both of these lakes are being used for field experiments.

2.2 Proper Setup Design and Its Calibration

The constructed experimental setups and the final modules must meet the following guidelines:

Enable Normal Behaviour: The animals observed by the biohybrid must have the ability to show their natural behaviours, such as feeding and breeding. For this, the modules cannot be overly restricting, must allow for access to food, etc. To test this, long-term tests are compared to laboratory observations and literature.

Observation Unit: The module hosting the organisms must be able to record their movements, store the data and potentially analyze it on board. The setup for collecting the visual data needs to be adjusted taking external factors into account, such as the water turbidity, light conditions and water movement. This is continuously adjusted and improved depending on the changing conditions.

Calibration of the Biohybrid Entity: In the approach of observing organisms in their natural habitat, classical calibration is challenging due to a wide variety of factors influencing their behaviour in the field. We carry out the calibration in two ways:

- Traditional calibration: a series of experiments are carried out under laboratory conditions in order to be able to distinguish normal behaviour from a disrupted one.
- Long-term observation within the setup: it is essential to test whether the confinement brings an additional stress factor for the animals. This is then compared against environmental data taken from classical probes.
- Data extrapolation: finally, two previous methods can be combined to be able to interpret data from the field and compare it against the laboratory- and literature-based studies. This will enable us to classify different behaviours of lifeforms under different conditions.

2.3 "Daphnia Module"

"Daphnia Module" Description

One of the organisms used in the Robocoenosis biohybrid entity is *Daphnia* sp. It is a small, planktonic crustacean in the suborder Diplostraca, ranging in size from 0.5 to 6 mm [10]. *Daphnia* is one of the most intensely studied freshwater organisms [22]. Thanks to its high abundance and broad distribution, it is an important part of the aquatic food chain. In recent years, it also gained popularity in toxicological and pharmaceutical studies because of its high sensitivity to even minor changes in the water chemistry or to the presence of pollutants [4, 19, 34].

One of the modules incorporated into the biohybrid entity is the "Daphnia module" (Fig. 1). This module consists of a flow-through chamber, a camera, a Raspberry Pi (a single-board computer), and a power source. The flow-through chamber hosts *Daphnia* in a layer of water which can be monitored by the camera. The camera used is a wide-angle camera with an OV5647 sensor with an adjustable focus and focal length of 6mm. Recordings were taken at 30 fps. This camera was chosen because it allowed the closest proximity of the camera to the *Daphnia* cage without having any areas out of view. The design of this module is comparable to the one described in [25]. This setup allows for continuous observation of the behaviour and detects any changes in the swimming pattern or other behavioural characteristics (for example, attraction to light).

2.4 *Daphnia* Calibration Experiments

The calibration of the "Daphnia module" follows the steps described in Sect. 2.2. An observation unit presented in Fig. 1 was tested in the field for 5 days to check its ability to host the lifeforms and offer them conditions suitable for presenting normal behaviour in semi-long-term conditions. *Daphnia* calibration experiments took place both in the field and in the laboratory. In the field, the "Daphnia

Fig. 1. "Daphnia module" before a mission in Lake Neusiedl. A: *Daphnia* swimming in a flow-through chamber, B: Camera module recording the swimming animals and C: Raspberry Pi plugged into the energy source.

module" setup was placed in water for several days, with the animals placed manually in the chamber. The recordings were then extracted when the mission was terminated.

Laboratory experiments focused on classifying the animal's swimming behaviour in response to a stressor, where increasing salinity (2.5, 3, and 4 ppt, parts per thousand) was chosen for the first tests. Five *Daphnia* individuals were placed in Petri dishes filled with aquarium water (total number of individuals tested was $n = 65$, 100 and 100 for salinity levels 2.5, 3 and 4.5 ppt respectively). After a one-hour acclimation period, an adequate salt solution was added to each Petri dish. The animals were then recorded for 24 h and their swimming trajectories were extracted post-experiment.

2.5 "Mussel Module"

Bivalves are another group of organisms that are used in the Robocoenosis biohybrid entity. Bivalves are recognised as suitable indicator organisms for aquatic environmental monitoring since they can be easily handled and respond with different patterns of behaviour to toxicants and pollutants [3]. Currently, zebra mussels (*Dreissena polymorpha*) are used in a biohybrid entity due to their wide distribution in natural water bodies in Austria and Europe [17]. However, since *Dreissena polymorpha* is also a highly invasive species the experimental fieldwork is restricted to Lake Millstatt where the species has been previously confirmed in the project.

The "Mussel module" is currently based on an Arduino UNO R3 microcontroller and is able to get data from up to five zebra mussels simultaneously. This setup collects valve movement data from the zebra mussels by attaching a Hall effect sensor (Honeywell SS495A) to one valve and neodymium magnets

(HKCM Z04x04Au-N35) to the other valve of the mussel. This Hall effect sensor was chosen since it provides a linear output with high precision. This enables accurate readings of the mussel valve movement.

In previous works [25,36], camera-based approaches were used. Taking a step away from visual analysis, where possible, allows for quicker data collection from multiple individuals with reduced power consumption, as cameras and software required for image analysis tend to reduce the run-time of the module. The collected raw sensor data is combined with a timestamp obtained from a real-time clock and saved to an SD Card every 200 ms (Fig. 2).

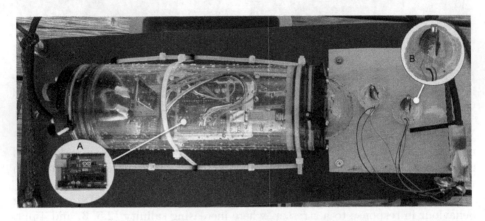

Fig. 2. Field setup of the Mussel organ tested at Lake Millstatt. A: Arduino UNO R3 with a real-time clock and an SD card board. B: Zebra mussel (*Dreissena polymorpha*) situated on a Hall sensor with a neodymium magnet on the opposite valve.

The "Mussel module" has been tested in the field at Lake Millstatt with locally-collected zebra mussels as well as in the laboratory with specimens of a colony of zebra mussels to compare their behaviour in different settings (data not shown). We also tested the reaction of the mussels to artificial stimulation.

In the preliminary experiment at Lake Millstatt, two zebra mussels collected in the field were used and data was obtained over 25 h. The reaction of the zebra mussels to artificial stimuli was tested by dropping stones next to the "Mussel module".

2.6   "Plankton Community Module"

The composition of the plankton community in limnic water bodies is a very important indicator to estimate the water quality and the ecological status [14]. To include information on the plankton community in the respective lakes, we are currently developing an optical system based on the work by Cowen & Guigand [6]. With this optical system, called "Shadowgraph", it is possible to observe plankton organisms in a larger volume of water without having to account for focus planes which limit normal camera systems. A "Shadowgraph" projects 3D objects in a volume (in this case plankton organisms) to a 2D plane by having two plano-convex lenses which parallelize the light through the volume. By using a combination of lenses and cameras, the light is collimated and then refocused. This allows for a sharp image of plankton organisms throughout the volume of water. By developing a laboratory setup with off-the-shelve parts, custom 3D-printed parts, and an aluminium frame, it is possible to calibrate the current "Plankton community module" using *Daphnia* specimens (Fig. 3).

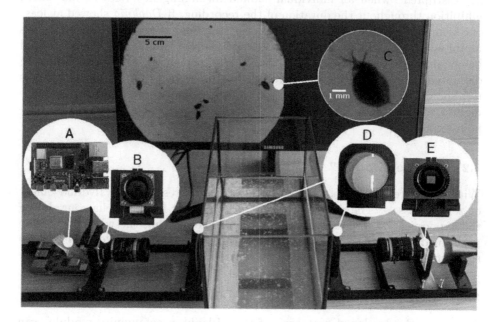

Fig. 3. Laboratory prototype of the "Plankton community module" (PCO). A: Raspberry Pi 4 B: Raspberry Pi HD Camera. C: Image of *Daphnia* sp. made with the PCO. D: Plano-convex lenses. E: Modified C-Mount with acrylic glass as a light diffuser. Both the Raspberry Pi HD Camera and the light source are combined with a camera lens with a 16 mm focal length. The black scale bar refers to the overall image and the white scale bar refers to the magnified *Daphnia* image.

3   Results

3.1   "Daphnia Module" Results

Field results of the "Daphnia module" addressed two calibration questions: 1) How do the animals react to prolonged confinement and 2) Can the module successfully film and identify *Daphnia* in the field?

Firstly, long-term experiments performed in both Lake Millstatt and Lake Neusiedl showed that *Daphnia* not only survives the confinement but also breeds inside it. This shows that the animals are able to preserve their normal behaviours of which extent will be compared against laboratory experiments.

Secondly, the "Daphnia module" allowed us to successfully take underwater recordings of the swimming animals. With post-mission video analysis, it is possible to identify *Daphnia* and draw their swimming trajectories. Further analysis will be performed.

Further, laboratory-based calibration experiments aimed for investigating in more detail *Daphnia*'s stress responses to rising salinity. Behaviour was classified as "disrupted" when an individual showed swimming in circles or movement inhibition throughout the duration of the recording. If *Daphnia* showed at least one spinning movement, it was classified as "spinning", while if its movement was inhibited for 15 s consecutively, it was classified as "inhibited". The combined behaviours were classified as "disrupted". The percentage of *Daphnia* showing disrupted behaviour is presented for each salinity in Fig. 4. A Kruskal-Wallis test showed that *Daphnia* present significantly more disrupted behaviour in the highest salinity range compared to the two lower ranges ($p < 0.05$) after a 22-hour exposure.

3.2   "Mussel Module" Results

With the current "Mussel module", we can clearly resolve the valve movement of zebra mussels. The mussels showed no abnormal feeding behaviour during the experiment. The preliminary experiment showed that the water disruption performed during the experiment caused both zebra mussels to close their valves simultaneously (Fig. 5).

3.3   "Plankton Community Module" Results

The currently developed prototype of the "Plankton community module" can observe plankton organisms, in this case, *Daphnia* specimens, in the size between 500 μm (size of newborn *Daphnia*) and 5 mm (large adult female *Daphnia*). Various random water samples from the lakes were also added to the preliminary experiments. The combination of off-the-shelve parts with custom 3D printed parts works excellent to test different combinations and qualities of plano-convex lenses, camera sensors and objective lenses and provides insight into future improvements.

4   Discussion

In this work, we present the most recent results obtained from testing selected modules of the biohybrid entity for environmental monitoring developed by the project Robocoenosis. The biohybrid modules host or attract various species and communities in order to monitor their well-being in the environment (Table 1). From this data, we can draw conclusions about the state of the lake. Project Robocoenosis is developing a biohybrid incorporating a combination of those

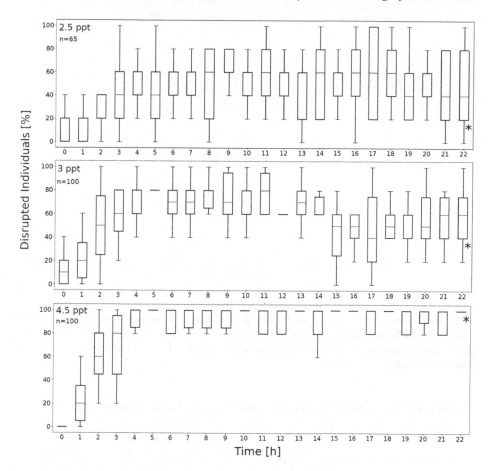

Fig. 4. The percentage of disrupted *Daphnia*'s individuals (compiled from "spinning" and "inhibited" behaviours) plotted against rising salinity (2.5, 3 and 4.5 ppt). There was a statistically significant (Kruskal-Wallis test, p < 0.05*) difference in *Daphnia*'s reactions at a 22 h mark between the three salinity levels. The whiskers of the box plots represent Q1 (lower whiskers), Q2 (box with the median line) and Q3 (upper whiskers) reaching maximum).

modules to gain insight into both rapid and long-term changes in limnic systems. The most crucial findings of this work are:

1. *Daphnia* can be incorporated into automated biohybrid systems to be used as a living sensor. The flow-through cage allows them to feed and breed inside it. Laboratory behavioural experiments gave preliminary calibration results that indicate *Daphnia*'s varying behaviour depending on the presence and the intensity of the stressor.
2. Zebra mussel *D. polymorpha* can be incorporated into automated biohybrid systems to be used as a living sensor. The attachment to the underwater

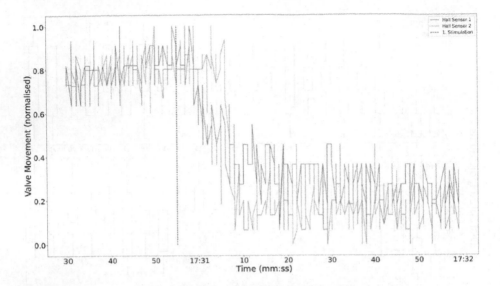

Fig. 5. Normalised Hall sensor data obtained from two zebra mussels. Top means open shell, and bottom means closed shell. The dotted line represents a stimulus (a dropped stone) to which the mussels reacted by closing their shell. Data are normalized against the minimum and maximum values of the whole data (where 1 is maximally open and 0 is a maximally closed shell).

setup did not inhibit the mussels' ability to feed and breathe. Both field and laboratory experiments show results enabling the detection of change in its behaviour. Preliminary results of the calibration experiments show the change in behaviour in case of a disruption in the environment. The data also shows, that the noise of the Hall effect sensors (e.g. due to temperature change) is insignificant in comparison to the behaviour readings.

3. Shadowgraph is a working setup that allows for the identification of plank-tonic organisms. Its openness to the water column (lack of confinement for the lifeforms) creates a community-based sensor that could be able to detect large-scale changes in the water chemistry. It is expected that through the Shadowgraph, it will be possible to observe the behaviours that indicate changes in the environment, such as the appearance or absence of certain groups. Then, literature data will be used to compare the observations to life cycles, seasonality and other natural periodicity.

4.1   Similar Initiatives

The use of organisms as sensors has been developed for decades in a multitude of fields. An example of a continuous real-time observation of the *Daphnia*'s swimming behaviour is a piece of laboratory equipment called DaphTox II ® [11,13]. It hosts several *Daphnia* individuals and using image analysis tracks the swimming behaviour of the animals and sounds an alarm in case of an abnormality.

A similar approach was used for mussel observation in a MosselMonitor ® [2]. The system evaluates the behaviour of several mussels in a continuous manner and measures the degree of valve opening, activity levels and mortality. It can be used with both freshwater and marine mussels. Here, we present an adaptation of this approach, moved directly into the field which allows the mussels to remain in their natural habitat. By combining their reactions with several other species we are also able to narrow down the possible cause of stress.

In contrast to the mentioned approaches, project Robocoenosis aims to move the monitoring process into the field and provide an autonomous power source. Although other approaches provide high-resolution data, they are limited in terms of power requirements and cost. Reading of the behaviour is done in real-time in the natural environment of the organisms which bypasses the need for laboratory facilities and staff making the process less costly and time-consuming. This work differs from other approaches as it incorporates multiple organisms and interprets their cumulative reactions. Here, we aim for low-price, long-term observations in off-grid locations.

4.2   Challenges

As mentioned previously, organisms provide a wide spectrum sensor. The interpretation of the behavioural data provides insight into the overall state of the environment. The specifications of the changes occurring can only be as good as our knowledge of their reactions and sensitivity to certain compounds. For this reason, we offer the usage of biohybrids as an additional monitoring tool, rather than a substitute. Should the monitoring mission be focused on a specific parameter, such as oxygen, we suggest using an adequate classical probe. However, especially in protected areas exposed to a multitude of anthropogenic pollution, it is of merit to broaden the spectrum of the detection.

These prototypes of biohybrid modules function continuously over the period of 5 days for the "Mussel module" and 2 days for the "Daphnia module" on various power sources. This period will be extended substantially with the use of energy harvesting and low-power electronics.

5   Outlook

This approach to environmental monitoring is novel in the way it hosts multiple lifeforms in their natural habitat and draws conclusions from a non-invasive observation of their natural reactions to the environment. In order to provide optimal readings, several experiments and improvements need to be carried out.

To further the calibration of the "Daphnia module", long-term confinement tests will be performed both in the field and under laboratory conditions. The calibration of *Daphnia*'s normal breeding behaviour must be carried out for various animal densities in the flow-through chamber and for changing water quality. The preliminary results showing no mortality or reproduction inhibition are promising as they show that *Daphnia* is able to continue its natural processes within the setup. Additionally, more tests will be carried out to optimise the robustness of the module.

The mussels showed feeding behaviour during the experiment and reacted to environmental stimuli such as waves, noise and changes in light. Those changes in valve opening are minor and can be clearly distinguished from a strong stress response (see Fig. 5). Valve movements are a normal occurrence, as shown in literature [1, 9, 35], caused by natural behaviours, like feeding and respiration. The responses to toxic substances and other stressors can be clearly identified and what is more, it is possible to distinguish different stressors from the movement patterns [9]. For example, alarm cues (sent by an injured mussel) cause it to close its valves for a significantly longer period than when being exposed to only predator presence. These and other calibration experiments will be carried out and accounted for in further experiments.

Acknowledgements. This work was supported by EU-H2020 Project Robocoenosis, grant agreement No 899520. Furthermore, this work was supported by The Field of Excellence COLIBRI (COmplexity of LIfe in Basic Research and Innovation) at the University of Graz. We further thank the "Österreichische Bundesforste AG", the "Burgenländische Landesregierung, Abt. 4 (Natur- und Klimaschutz)" and the "Biologische Station Illmitz" for their support.

References

1. Alexander, J.E., Jr., McMahon, R.F.: Respiratory response to temperature and hypoxia in the zebra mussel *Dreissena polymorpha*. Comp. Biochem. Physiol. Part A: Mol. Integr. Physiol. **137**(2), 425–434 (2004)

2. AquaDect: Mosselmonitor®. https://aquadect.nl/en/. Accessed 28 Mar 2023

3. Bae, M.J., Park, Y.S.: Biological early warning system based on the responses of aquatic organisms to disturbances: a review. Sci. Total Environ. **466–467**, 635–649 (2014). https://doi.org/10.1016/j.scitotenv.2013.07.075

4. Bownik, A.: *Daphnia* swimming behaviour as a biomarker in toxicity assessment: a review. Sci. Total Environ. **601**, 194–205 (2017)

5. Clark, L.C., Jr., Spokane, R.B., Homan, M.M., Sudan, R., Miller, M.: Long-term stability of electroenzymatic glucose sensors implanted in mice. An update. ASAIO Trans. **34**(3), 259–265 (1988)

6. Cowen, R.K., Guigand, C.M.: In *situ* ichthyoplankton imaging system (ISIIS): system design and preliminary results. Limnol. Oceanogr. Methods **6**(2), 126–132 (2008). https://doi.org/10.4319/lom.2008.6.126

7. Damania, R., Desbureaux, S., Rodella, A.S., Russ, J., Zaveri, E.: Quality Unknown: the Invisible Water Crisis. World Bank Publications (2019). https://doi.org/10.1596/978-1-4648-1459-4

8. Dokulil, M.T., Herzig, A.: An analysis of long-term winter data on phytoplankton and zooplankton in Neusiedler See, a shallow temperate lake, Austria. Aquat. Ecol. **43**, 715–725 (2009)

9. Dzierżyńska-Białończyk, A., Jermacz, Ł, Zielska, J., Kobak, J.: What scares a mussel? Changes in valve movement pattern as an immediate response of a byssate bivalve to biotic factors. Hydrobiologia **841**, 65–77 (2019)

10. Ebert, D.: Ecology, epidemiology, and evolution of parasitism in *Daphnia*. National Library of Medicine (2005)
11. Enviro-Analytical: Daphnia Toximeter II. A powerful instrument for water toxicity assessment- continuous visual analysis of Daphnia behaviour (2021). http://www. enviro-analytical.com/preview/enviroproducts/daphnia_toximeter.html. Accessed 25 Feb 2021
12. Gao, L., et al.: Recent progress in engineering functional biohybrid robots actuated by living cells. Acta Biomater. **121**, 29–40 (2021)
13. Green, U., Kremer, J.H., Zillmer, M., Moldaenke, C.: Detection of chemical threat agents in drinking water by an early warning real-time biomonitor. Environ. Toxicol. **18**(6), 368–374 (2003). https://doi.org/10.1002/tox.10138
14. Jeppesen, E., Nõges, P., Davidson, T.A., Haberman, J., Nõges, T., Blank, K., et al.: Zooplankton as indicators in lakes: a scientific-based plea for including zooplankton in the ecological quality assessment of lakes according to the European Water Framework Directive (WFD). Hydrobiologia **676**(1), 279–297 (2011). https://doi. org/10.1007/s10750-011-0831-0
15. Lee, K.Y., et al.: An autonomously swimming biohybrid fish designed with human cardiac biophysics. Science **375**(6581), 639–647 (2022)
16. Lomba, L., et al.: Ecotoxicological study of six drugs in *Aliivibrio fischeri, Daphnia magna* and *Raphidocelis subcapitata*. Environ. Sci. Pollut. Res. **27**, 9891–9900 (2020). https://doi.org/10.1007/s11356-019-07592-8
17. Lopes-Lima, M., Sousa, R., Geist, J., Aldridge, D.C., Araujo, R., Jakob, B., et al.: Conservation status of freshwater mussels in Europe: state of the art and future challenges. Biol. Rev. **92**, 572–607 (2017). https://doi.org/10.1111/brv.12244
18. Ma, Y., et al.: Combined toxicity and toxicity persistence of antidepressants citalopram and mirtazapine to zooplankton *Daphnia magna*. Environ. Sci. Pollut. Res. **29**(44), 66100–66108 (2022)
19. Martins, J., Soares, M., Saker, M.L., Oliva-Teles, L., Vasconcelos, V.: Phototactic behavior in *Daphnia magna* Straus as an indicator of toxicants in the aquatic environment. Ecotoxicol. Environ. Saf. **67**(3), 417–422 (2007)
20. Mestre, R., Patiño, T., Sánchez, S.: Biohybrid robotics: from the nanoscale to the macroscale. Wiley Interdisc. Rev.: Nanomed. Nanobiotechnol. **13**(5), e1703 (2021)
21. Morimoto, Y., Onoe, H., Takeuchi, S.: Biohybrid robot powered by an antagonistic pair of skeletal muscle tissues. Sci. Robot. **3**(18), eaat4440 (2018). https://doi.org/ 10.1126/scirobotics.aat4440
22. Nikitin, O.: Aqueous medium toxicity assessment by *Daphnia magna* swimming activity change. Adv. Environ. Biol. **8**(13), 74–78 (2014)
23. Park, S.J., et al.: Phototactic guidance of a tissue-engineered soft-robotic ray. Science **353**(6295), 158–162 (2016)
24. Rajewicz, W., et al.: Freshwater organisms potentially useful as biosensors and power-generation mediators in biohybrid robotics. Biol. Cybern. **115**, 615–628 (2021)
25. Rajewicz, W., Schmickl, T., Thenius, R.: The use of robots in aquatic biomonitoring with special focus on biohybrid entities. In: Müller, A., Brandstötter, M. (eds.) RAAD 2022. Mechanisms and Machine Science, vol. 120, pp. 521–527. Springer, Cham (2022). https://doi.org/10.1007/978-3-031-04870-8_61
26. Reynolds, C.S., O'Sullivan, P.E.: The Lakes Handbook: Lake Restoration and Rehabilitation. Blackwell Publishing (2003)
27. Ricotti, L., et al.: Biohybrid actuators for robotics: a review of devices actuated by living cells. Sci. Robot. **2**(12), eaaq0495 (2017). https://doi.org/10.1126/ scirobotics.aaq0495

28. Romano, D., Donati, E., Benelli, G., Stefanini, C.: A review on animal-robot inter-action: from bio-hybrid organisms to mixed societies. Biol. Cybern. **113**, 201–225 (2019)
29. Schmidt, P.L.: Companion animals as sentinels for public health. Vet. Clin. North America: Small Animal Pract. **39**(2), 241–250 (2009)
30. Schoon, G.: The effect of the ageing of crime scene objects on the results of scent identification line-ups using trained dogs. Forensic Sci. Int. **147**(1), 43–47 (2005)
31. Sousa, A.P., Nunes, B.: Dangerous connections: biochemical and behavioral traits in *Daphnia magna* and *Daphnia longispina* exposed to ecologically relevant amounts of paracetamol. Environ. Sci. Pollut. Res. **28**, 38792–38808 (2021)
32. Spencer, T.: Effects of carbon monoxide on man and canaries. Ann. Occup. Hyg. **5**, 231–234 (1962)
33. Suckling, D.M., Sagar, R.L.: Honeybees Apis mellifera can detect the scent of Mycobacterium tuberculosis. Tuberculosis **91**(4), 327–328 (2011)
34. Szabelak, A., Bownik, A.: Behavioral and physiological responses of *Daphnia magna* to salicylic acid. Chemosphere **270**, 128660 (2021)
35. Tang, B., Riisgård, H.U., et al.: Physiological regulation of valve-opening degree enables mussels *Mytilus edulis* to overcome starvation periods by reducing the oxygen uptake. Open J. Mar. Sci. **6**(03), 341 (2016)
36. Thenius, R., et al.: Biohybrid entities for environmental monitoring. In: ALIFE 2022: The 2022 Conference on Artificial Life. MIT Press (2021)
37. Webster-Wood, V.A., et al.: Biohybrid robots: recent progress, challenges, and perspectives. Bioinspiration Biomimetics (2022)
38. Wieser, G., Schulz, L.: Alpine Lakes Network SILMAS Beitrag Kärnten-Endbericht. Publikationen des Kärntner Instituts für Seenforschung **79**, 1–44 (2013)

Autonomous Versus Manual Control of a Pasture Sanitation Robot

Ian Adams[1]($\boxtimes$), Roger Quinn[1], Greg Lee[2], Alexandra Kroeger[3], and Erica N. Feuerbacher[3]

[1] Department of Mechanical and Aerospace Engineering, Case Western Reserve University, Cleveland, OH 44106-7222, USA
ija2@case.edu
[2] Department of Electrical Engineering and Computer Science, Case Western Reserve University, Cleveland, OH 44106-7222, USA
[3] Department of Animal and Poultry Science, Virginia Tech, Blacksburg, VA 24061, USA

Abstract. This work presents the collection and analysis of data from animal-robot interactions in two different control schemes. Cows (*B. taurus*) and horses (*E. caballus*) were introduced in pasture to a robot controlled either manually via teleoperation and autonomously via a costmap-based navigation algorithm. The robot maneuver at random, simulating a manure collection task, until all animals in the pasture lost vigilant attention to the robot. The time of initial loss of interest, interest over time, and time of ultimate loss of interest (10 consecutive seconds of non-vigilance) were recorded. The pasture sanitation robot was successful in manual and autonomous navigation of pastures. The robot was able to operate autonomously in pasture safely without changing qualitative response from the animals, as compared to manual methods. The deployment of autonomous control did not increase stress as a function of vigilance as compared to manual teleoperation. Both methods contribute to the development and evaluation of future pasture sanitation robots.

Keywords: Autonomous Robotics · Unmanned Ground Vehicle · Livestock Management · Sanitation

1 Introduction

Greener Pastures is a project which aims to automate pasture management and sanitation using autonomous robots. Findings of animal-robot interactions and the performance of an established autonomous robot in an occupied pasture are presented here.

Crop farming is usually performed in a highly controlled and cultivated pasture, which is free from animal agents. Consequently, cattle and horse farming which both require large tracts of land, are relegated to terrain which is otherwise unsuitable for crop farming. This heterogeneous terrain is frequently higher in

© The Author(s), under exclusive license to Springer Nature Switzerland AG 2023
F. Meder et al. (Eds.): Living Machines 2023, LNAI 14158, pp. 363–377, 2023.
https://doi.org/10.1007/978-3-031-39504-8_25

biodiversity and hydrological sensitivity. This presents challenges to maintaining minimal ecological impact. The difficulty in manual or automated cultivation of these pastures combined with their sensitivity to waste runoff means manure removal is difficult to do at scale, and infrequently done [1]. Consequently, cattle are disproportionately responsible for and waste runoff into water systems [2,3]. As a global increase in population drives up the demand for food, crop-unsuitable land can cultivate human inedible protein into human edible food [4,5].

Autonomous robotic waste control presents a solution to many negatives of livestock cultivation on these pastures. Autonomous robots in such pastures present an opportunity to gather data from embedded sensor technologies. In-situ monitoring from sensors both on and off a mobile robot would allow for a greater depth of pasture management. However, animal-occupied and highly difficult terrain are challenges which have historically hampered robotic development [1]. Both cattle ($B.taurus$) and horses($E.\ caballus$) are large and unpredictable animals. Animals can act in unexpected ways which can damage or hinder the robot, and the robot can stress or harm animals if not controlled safely [6,7]. Additionally, animals can be stressed by the robot's presence and behavior, which should be mitigated as much as possible.

In order to assess the viability of a future autonomous system for pasture management, we explore capacity of operation and animal response for manual and autonomous operation of a mobile robot. Successful autonomous operation in pasture demonstrates that the robot is capable of operating in the difficult terrain without human feedback. Comparing animal stress as a function of time to initial non-vigilance, and time to ultimate non-vigilance, we can assess if the autonomous control scheme produces similar stress responses as compared to manual control. Both safety and minimization of induced stress are critical to further development of a pasture sanitation robot.

1.1 Robot Platform

Pasture sanitation robot 1 (PSR1) is a lightweight unmanned ground vehicle (UGV) serving as the sensor testbed for the wider greener pastures project. PSR1 is a skid-steer differential drive robot with a footprint of approximately $1\,\mathrm{m}^2$ and with a mass of approximately 90 Kg. Its payload of sensors and motion control hardware is enclosed in an onboard Pelican hardcase. The robot is constructed with a welded steel chassis and is actuated by a pair of wheelchair motors which drive a chain-linked, all-wheel drive wheelbase.

PSR1, shown in Fig. 1 has sensing and processing electronics which enable it to be driven manually, as well as autonomously. It utilizes an Intel NUC running Ubuntu 18.04 and ROS Melodic. The Robot Operating System (ROS) is a software framework used for real-time communication between sensors and actuators, which enables data collection and motion control. Existing ROS infrastructure and software libraries allow for rapid sensor integration and software sharing to other platforms such as future pasture management robots or systems.

PSR1 utilizes an Ouster OS-1-32 360° field of view 3D LIDAR to perform ranging measurements, obstacle detection, and mapping. The LIDAR is well-

Fig. 1. Pasture Sanitation Robot 1. PSR1's control electronics and GPS sensor are protected by the Pelican hardcase on the rear of the vehicle. The Ouster 3D LIDAR is mounted on a section of construction rail at the front.

suited to detecting and visualizing animals within that range. For absolute geospatial localization, PSR1 is equipped with a Ublox ZED-F9P RTK GPS module. As PSR1 is used autonomously during these trials, it is equipped with a long range remote E-stop which can be triggered by an operator in the event of imminent hazard to animal or property.

1.2   Localization

Robust localization is a prerequisite to safe autonomous motion. To ensure this, PSR1 uses a combination of position estimates from different sensors through an Unscented Kalman Filter (UKF) to create robust localization. The two major contributing odometry sensors were GPS projection odometry from the UBlox, and Simultaneous Localization and Mapping (SLAM) from the LIDAR. Steep hills, combined with a lack of reference infrastructure challenge the use of either sensor individually. Fusing the high latency absolute positioning from GPS with the low-latency relative positioning from SLAM made PSR1 localization more robust in less than ideal circumstances.

SLAM gives high data rate, low latency, and recoverable odometry. The Velodyne HDL graph SLAM package leverages LIDAR readings over time to build a more and more detailed map of the environment [8]. The longer that PSR1 maneuvers in a pasture, the more detailed the map generated from SLAM and the more robust the position estimate.

Lastly, the UKF incorporates input from the issued motor commanded velocity. Listening to the motor commands can be useful to counteract drift while the robot is stationary. However, the input produces diminishing returns if the motor commands are not moving the robot, for instance while the robot is stuck.

1.3   Navigation

The robot used the well-developed ROS Nav-stack to maneuver autonomously. The ROS Nav-stack is a set of packages for environment mapping and trajectory planning. Nav-stack uses sensors such as LIDAR to populate a local occupancy grid map, marking spaces which are occupied by obstacles or empty and traversable. Obstacles in the map are inflated by a variable radius to generate a costmap. Using the costmap, one of several optimization algorithms solves for a path of least cost between robot position and a goal position.

In order to minimize turf destruction and to have greater synergy with future platforms, PSR1 uses the Dynamic Window Approach (DWA) algorithm for motion planning. The DWA planner is compatible with Ackermann or skid-steered vehicles making it an ideal method to test for both. The DWA planner creates trajectories by simulating constrained forward motion. Given a range of maximum and minimum linear and angular velocities, DWA simulates a series of trajectories, and selects the simulated trajectory with the least cost to traverse.

To ensure safety for animals, we selected an inflation radius of 1.5 m, and disabled recovery behaviors. Therefore, if the robot was unable to complete a path to goal, or was in close proximity to animals, it would default to a stop rather than continue motion, potentially stressing or harming the animals.

1.4   Animal Testing

A pasture management robot must be able to maneuver safely around animals, and navigate adverse terrain while performing tasks. Animals can act unpredictably to new stressors [6,12,20]. Accurately replicating the kinds of behaviors a robot will exhibit while performing its tasks may not be possible with remote operation. Here we collect animal behavior data from two livestock species: Cows (*B.taurus*) and horses(*E. caballus*) as they become acclimated to PSR1 in pastures.

The principal metric for this work explores the time to acceptance of the robot. Even after deliberate provocation of stress by the robot, horses and cattle recovered and returned to sharing space with the robot. However in future applications a pasture sanitation robot will spend longer time around animals, ideally without deliberately provoking a response. To gauge the stress of animals, we categorize animal response to robot presence as vigilant or non-vigilant.

Vigilance refers to a set of characteristic behaviors, different between both species, which indicate stress [9]. Non-vigilance conversely represents apathy or lack of stress imposed by the robot. Introducing the robot to animals starts a period of vigilance which ultimately gives way to ignoring the robot while it performs its tasks.

For the purposes of this work, signs of vigilance in horses include: focused eyes or ears towards the robot, flared nostrils, yawning, defecation while looking

Fig. 2. Two scenes from animal trials. Above: Cattle pastures have steep hills which can block line of sight between the animals and robot. Below: PSR1 interacts with a different group of cattle in a pasture.

at the robot, pinned ears while looking at the robot, general rigid posture, head held high and attentive [10,11]. For the purposes of this work, we also consider all motion towards or away from the robot to be classified as vigilance. This is to not under-represent these behaviors which can be vigilant or non-vigilant depending on context. Signs of non-vigilance for horses, are considered to be the opposite behaviors of vigilance, including: relaxed posture, head lowered, grazing, especiallyz grazing facing away from the robot, and no motion towards or away from the robot.

We consider signs of vigilance for cattle to include: head down as if to charge the robot, ears attentive towards the robot, body posture or head facing the robot, as well as motion towards or away from the robot [12]. Cattle tend to be obscured by grouping together, and their posture is less apparent than horses. Therefore, a greater emphasis is placed on the facing and ears of cattle. Signs for non-vigilance in cattle include opposite behaviors from vigilance: orientation facing away from the robot, head looking elsewhere from the robot, grazing and relaxed posture.

Fig. 3. The PSR1 platform navigating around horses during a trial at Virginia Tech.

2   Methods

2.1   Animal Testing

Between June 2022 and March 2023, cattle and horses were tested in Blacksburg and Middleburg VA, using pastures at the Virginia-Maryland College of Veterinary Medicine Center for One Health Research, Smithfield Horse Center, and MARE Center. The data were collected on three trips, each taking place over three to four days. During each trip, pastures for both species were tested no more than once per day, in order to prevent animals from becoming familiar with the robot, and to minimize potential stress animals experienced during trials. Each trip was several months apart and used unexposed animals whenever possible to avoid animals building longer-term familiarity with the robot.

Populations of horses and cattle were separated into roughly equal populations in each pasture. Horses ranged from 5–7 individuals of various breeds and ages, a mix of mares (various breeds), and geldings (all Thoroughbred). The groups were tested in their home pastures and were allowed to acclimate for more than 3 weeks prior to testing.

The cattle were heifers, Angus and Charolais breed mix. One large herd of cattle was split into two smaller herds for a pair of pastures with approximately 15 members in each. The cattle were allowed to acclimate for multiple days prior to each round of testing.

The pastures ranged from 0.5 acre to 30 acres in horse pastures and 3–6 acres for the cow pastures. Pastures for both species had significant topography, with the cattle pastures especially having steep hills (shown in Fig. 2) which were challenging for robot localization and animal sight lines. Steep hills allowed animals and PSR1 to enter and leave line of sight during trials more easily. The cattle pastures had minimal landmarks, challenging SLAM, while the horses had shelters and fences which were readily visible, contributing to SLAM accuracy. Lastly, cattle pastures tended to feature rougher terrain which caused the robot to pitch and rock while traveling.

Building on previous animal acceptance work, this test aims to emulate a sanitation robot at work in pastures. During each trial the robot maneuvers (either by autonomy or teleoperation) to random points. This serves to increase and decrease the distance to animals in the way a future sanitation robot would be expected to behave. During manual operation, the pilot was focused on driving the robot, and not on scanning and coding herd behavior. The pilot altered or ceased motion only in the case of imminent collision with an animal. The autonomous portions also explore the ability to safely and successfully maneuver around animals in the pasture such as in Fig. 3. Each round of testing follows these steps:

1. Introduce the robot into a pasture within line of sight of the animals.
2. Begin random motion, either by manual control or autonomous waypoint navigation.
3. Either after a set number of random turns or when autonomously achieving a goal, halt the robot for approximately 10 s.
4. Resume a random motion scheme.

This random motion sequence was repeated for at least 20 min, or 1 min past the time where the herd is non-vigilant for 10 continuous seconds, as observed by the supervising researcher.

Using LIDAR and external video cameras, animal behavior around the robot is recorded. Off-robot cameras were crucial, as the robot is jostled and broke line of sight with the animals. Additionally, as the distance between robot and animal increased, LIDAR data density decreased, making real-time animal detection and behavior classification impractical for artificial intelligence at this time.

After each completed trial, the LIDAR and video recordings were segmented into 5 s intervals. Individual animals visible in each scan were manually coded according to their behavior to be either vigilant or non-vigilant. Behavior coding was done independently by two people, and then compared to confirm results. If any member of the herd was considered vigilant, the herd was considered to be vigilant. Once the herd was coded for behavior we recorded the time to initial non-vigilance, time to ultimate non-vigilance, and vigilance as a function of time. Time to initial non-vigilance represents the time from trial start until all members of the herd are non-vigilant for at least 5 s. Time to ultimate non-vigilance represents the time when the trial is considered complete, as two scan periods have passed without vigilant behavior from any animal in the herd. For each species, vigilance as a function of time is reported as a cumulative graph. The cumulative number of 5 s observations windows with vigilant animals is plotted versus time to show how stress changes over time. A linear trend indicates a continuous period of vigilance, and any deviations from linear indicate when in the trial animals drop vigilance. Trends which are highly linear and end abruptly are examples of animals which abruptly lose interest in the robot. Trends which often deviate from linear indicate animals which frequently drop vigilance for short intervals.

3   Results

During manual teleoperation the robot was able to be maneuvered successfully without risk of damage to animals or itself. During autonomous control, the robot was able to successfully autonomously navigate environments in both the cattle and horse pastures. In both cases, the robot encountered and then successfully maneuvered around animals and static obstacles such as fences and buildings. The robot was able to retain localization through most of the runs. The robot localization and path planning are dependent on Kalman-filtered sensor data, which can quickly diverge given noisy data or absent data. In these cases, the robot's filtered position estimate becomes erratic, which leads to undesired operation. In order to combat this, in the event of a divergent position estimate, the localization and navigation stack would be reset to be reset to preserve functionality. The vigilance metrics observed for each species are as follows.

3.1   Results: Cows

In manual teleoperation, cattle had an average time to initial non-vigilance of 56.4 s, with a standard deviation of 27.3 s. Cattle time to ultimate non-vigilance was an average of 426.7 s, with a standard deviation of 241.1 s. Comparing the ratio of initial non-vigilance to ultimate non-vigilance, cattle had an average ratio of 0.15 with standard deviation 0.049. This suggests that in manual operation, the time to initial non-vigilance may be correlated to time to ultimate non-vigilance.

While these metrics show consistent behavior during manual operation, the autonomous control regime was much less consistent. Autonomous control had average time to initial and ultimate non-vigilance as 69.0 s, and 838.0 s with standard deviations of 47.9 and 202.1 s, respectively. These were consistently higher than the corresponding manual teleoperation trials. The ratio of initial to ultimate time of non-vigilance for autonomous operation was lesser at 0.087 with standard deviation 0.070, which suggests time to initial non-vigilance was not a clear indicator for time to ultimate non-vigilance. Cattle time to initial non-vigilance and time to ultimate non-vigilance show at least overlapping ranges, if not overlapping interquartile ranges (IQR) for both metrics as shown in Fig. 4. The changes in vigilance over time, shown in Fig. 5 show similar trends for both control schemes, with animals having strong vigilance at first, followed by greater vacillation in vigilance/non-vigilance as the trials reached around the halfway time. The combination of time to initial and ultimate non-vigilance overlap,

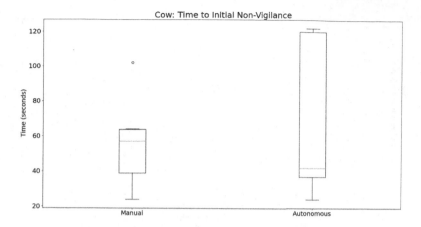

(a) Cattle time to initial non-vigilance.

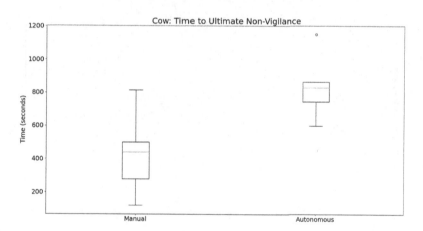

(b) Cattle time to ultimate non-vigilance.

Fig. 4. The cattle time to initial and ultimate non-vigilance show lower averages than the manually controlled regime. Autonomous control showed high variance in the time to initial non-vigilance but much less variance in time to ultimate non-vigilance as compared to manual.

and trends of vigilance versus time show behavioral similarity. Further animal trials can resolve numerical details about the differences, if any, between the two control methods.

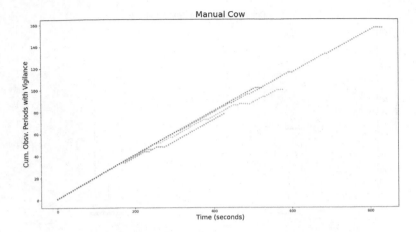

(a) Cattle manual control vigilance vs time.

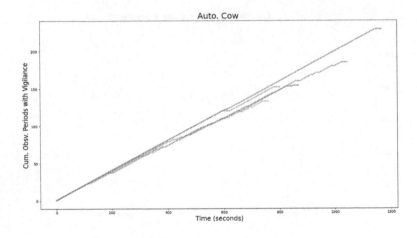

(b) Cattle autonomous control vigilance vs time.

Fig. 5. Manual and autonomous cattle trials, showing cumulative number of observation windows with vigilant animals. Both modes of control had comparable levels of vigilance over time. Manual teleoperation was slightly less consistent, but had a shorter time to ultimate non-vigilance. Autonomous control had slightly longer average times to ultimate non-vigilance, but with fewer changes in vigilance.

3.2 Results: Horses

During teleoperation, horses had an average time to initial non-vigilance of 84.4 s, with a standard deviation of 78.8 s. The time to ultimate non-vigilance had an average of 755.0 s, with a standard deviation of 621.9 s. Comparing the ratio of initial non-vigilance to ultimate non-vigilance, the horses had an average ratio

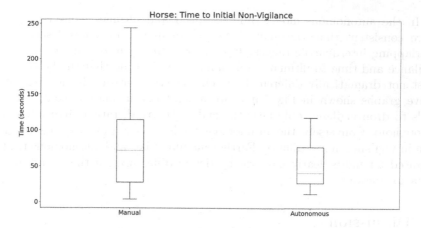

(a) Horse time to initial non-vigilance.

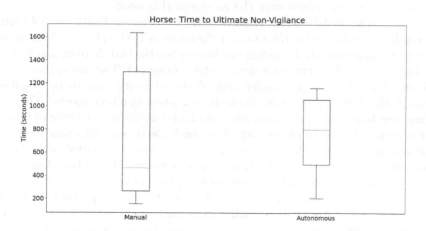

(b) Horse time to ultimate non-vigilance.

Fig. 6. Both regimes had similar averages for time to initial non-vigilance (84.4 s manual, 50.8 s autonomous) and identical averages for time to ultimate non-vigilance (755.0 s for manual and autonomous). In both time to initial non-vigilance, and time to ultimate non-vigilance, the autonomous control regime was more consistent.

of 0.11 with standard deviation 0.060. All metrics in the manual operation mode show horses as behaving less consistently. Autonomous control had average time to initial and ultimate non-vigilance as 50.8 s, and 755.0 s with standard deviations of 33.8 and 334.3 s respectively. The ratio of initial to ultimate time of non-vigilance for autonomous operation was lesser at 0.084 with standard deviation 0.068, which may suggest again that time to initial non-vigilance may be a poor indicator for time to ultimate non-vigilance in horses as well.

In the autonomous mode, time to initial and ultimate non-vigilance were more consistent than the manual control regime. Both control schemes had overlapping interquartile ranges (IQR) shown in Fig. 6 for time to initial non-vigilance and time to ultimate non-vigilance, indicating that the behavior is at least not dramatically different between the two control schemes. The cumulative graphs shown in Fig. 7 indicate a tendency in manual control for animals to drop vigilance only near the end of the trial, rather than infrequently throughout. Conversely, the autonomous trials show a greater degree of vacillation in vigilance/non-vigilance. Further manual trials and autonomous trials are required for more clearly numerically define differences, if they exist, in these behavior metrics.

4   Discussion

Despite the high variability and limited available number of trials involved, we can draw a few conclusions from the results of this work.

Both manual PSR1 control regimes, and autonomous PSR1 control regimes showed large variances for time to non-vigilance in both species, which make it difficult to draw statistical conclusions. In general, the two share similar features, and have overlapping ranges for most metrics observed. The initial time to non-vigilance tended to be just under 10% of the ultimate time to non-vigilance, although this metric was not particularly consistent in either species. Therefore, initial time to non-vigilance does not seem to be a reliable predictor of ultimate time to non-vigilance for either control method. Cattle showed a mild increase in time to ultimate non-vigilance when using the autonomous control, and relatively consistent vigilance over time for both control schemes. Horses had similar times to ultimate non-vigilance for both control schemes, but with a very wide variance.

Results from animal interactions with novel stressors in pasture are not well represented in literature. Other similar work such as the introduction of robotic scrapers to penned sows [6] or the introduction of a drone to horses in pasture [21] are related, but not directly comparable.

In our previous work, we demonstrated that both cattle and horses would interact with a mobile robot before and after the approaching robot caused animals to flee. Animals re-approached and increased in interaction after fleeing, showing a lack of serious induced stress [22].

Here we demonstrate that PSR1 is capable of successfully maneuvering in the adverse pasture terrain, and performing a simplified version of the expected manure removal procedure. During this autonomous operation, the robot successfully navigated to coordinates, avoiding animals and other obstacles. The qualitative similarities between the autonomous and manual control suggest that PSR1's autonomous behavior are at least comparably stressful to the animals as compared to manual control, and that the autonomy did not incur noteworthy added stress.

Manual control and autonomous control yielded similar stress on animals, we can therefore expect that work done using manual control is not dissimilar to an autonomous method. This suggests that in such cases where animal-robot

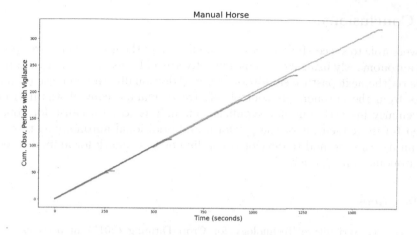

(a) Horse manual control, vigilance vs time.

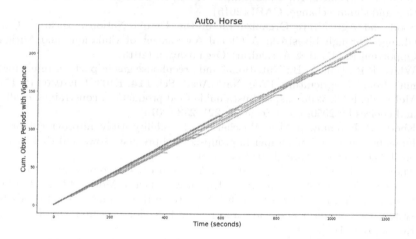

(b) Horse autonomous control vigilance vs time.

Fig. 7. Manual and autonomous horse trials, with cumulative number of observation windows with vigilant animals versus time. Manual control had higher constant vigilance, shown by a strong linear trend over time. Autonomous control had more fickle vigilance, shown by a greater dispersion away from pure a linear trend.

interaction situations via autonomous control would be unlikely or impractical, it is possible manual methods may be a comparable stand-in.

Data collected during these trials may eventually contribute to AI for behavior coding, which could be used to track animal behaviors in other animal husbandry projects. Future work can also explore using the platform to explore methods for reducing animal stress, such as through the use of audio or visual stimuli, novel approach or avoidance behaviors, and/or silhouette alterations to the robot.

5   Conclusions

We were able to successfully operate a simulation of the greener pastures project goal autonomously using a combination software and sensors which are similar to those on the next pasture sanitation robot. Additionally, the increase of animal stress from the autonomous control relative to manual control was noticeable particularly in cattle but not significant enough as to be a cause for concern. Given future refinement of the platform and additional autonomous test runs, we can use this method to develop a baseline or benchmark for animal response to autonomous navigation.

References

1. Precision Agriculture Technology for Crop Farming (2015) https://doi.org/10.1201/b19336
2. Malik, P.K., Bhatta, R., Takahashi, J., Kohn, R., Prasad, C.S.: Livestock production and climate change. CABI (2015)
3. Food and Agriculture Organization of the United Nations. Tackling Climate Change Through Livestock: A Global Assessment of Emissions and Mitigation Opportunities. Food & Agriculture Organization (2013)
4. White, R.R., Hall, M.B.: Nutritional and greenhouse gas impacts of removing animals from US agriculture. Proc. Natl. Acad. Sci. **114**, E10301–E10308 (2017)
5. McKenzie, F.C., Williams, J.: Sustainable food production: constraints, challenges and choices by 2050. Food Secur. **7**, 221–233 (2015)
6. Ebertz, P., Krommweh, M.S., Büscher, W.: Feasibility study: improving floor cleanliness by using a robot scraper in group-housed pregnant sows and their reactions on the new device. Animals **9**, 185 (2019)
7. Thomas, B.L., Cutler, M., Novak, C.: A modified counterconditioning procedure prevents the renewal of conditioned fear in rats. Learn. Motiv. **43**, 24–34 (2012)
8. Koide, K., Miura, J., Menegatti, E.: A portable three-dimensional LIDAR-based system for long-term and wide-area people behavior measurement. Int. J. Adv. Robot. Syst. **16** (2019)
9. McFarland, D.: A Dictionary of Animal Behaviour. Oxford University Press, Oxford (2014)
10. Waring, G.H.: Horse Behavior: The Behavioral Traits and Adaptations of Domestic and Wild Horses, Including Ponies. Noyes Series in Animal Behavior (1983)
11. Austin, N.P., Rogers, L.J.: Limb preferences and lateralization of aggression, reactivity and vigilance in feral horses, Equus caballus. Anim. Behav. **83**, 239–247 (2012). https://doi.org/10.1016/j.anbehav.2011.10.033
12. Welp, T., Rushen, J., Kramer, D.L., Festa-Bianchet, M., de Passillé, A.M.B.: Vigilance as a measure of fear in dairy cattle. Appl. Anim. Behav. Sci. **87**, 1–13 (2004). https://doi.org/10.1016/j.applanim.2003.12.013
13. Doerfler, R.L., Lehermeier, C., Kliem, H., Möstl, E., Bernhardt, H.: Physiological and behavioral responses of dairy cattle to the introduction of robot scrapers. Front. Veterinary Sci. **3**, 106 (2016)
14. Kleinman, P.J.A., et al.: Managing agricultural phosphorus for water quality protection: principles for progress. Plant Soil **349**, 169–182 (2011)
15. Encyclopedia of Energy, Natural Resource, and Environmental Economics. Newnes (2013)

16. Schacht, W.H., Reece, P.E.: Impact of livestock grazing on extensively managed grazing lands. In: Environmental Impacts of Pasture-Based Farming, pp. 122–143 (2008). https://doi.org/10.1079/9781845934118.0122
17. Soupir, M.L., Mostaghimi, S., Yagow, E.R., Hagedorn, C., Vaughan, D.H.: Transport of fecal bacteria from poultry litter and cattle manures applied to pastureland (2006)
18. Wang, H., Aguirre-Villegas, H.A., Larson, R.A., Alkan-Ozkaynak, A.: Physical properties of dairy manure pre- and post-anaerobic digestion. Appl. Sci. **9**, 2703 (2019)
19. Walter, M., Walter, M., Brooks, E., Steenhuis, T., Boll, J., Weiler, K.: Hydrologically sensitive areas: variable source area hydrology implications for water quality risk assessment. J. Soil Water Conserv. **55**, 277–284 (2000)
20. Boissy, A.: Fear and fearfulness in animals. Q. Rev. Biol. **70**, 165–191 (1995). https://doi.org/10.1086/418981
21. Howell, R.G., et al.: Evaluating changes in horse behavior as a response to small unmanned aerial vehicles. Rala **44**, 121–128 (2022). https://doi.org/10.1016/j.rala.2021.12.004
22. Adams, I., Quinn, R.D., Lee, G., Kroeger, A., Thompson, R., Feuerbacher, E.: Animal acceptance of an autonomous pasture sanitation robot. In: Hunt, A., et al. (eds.) Biomimetic and Biohybrid Systems. LNCS, vol. 13548, pp. 366–377. Springer, Cham (2022). https://doi.org/10.1007/978-3-031-20470-8_36

A Novel Steerable Catheter Controlled with a Biohybrid Actuator: A Feasibility Study

Carlotta Salvatori[1,2], Diego Trucco[1,2], Ignazio Niosi[1,2], Leonardo Ricotti[1,2], and Lorenzo Vannozzi[1,2(✉)]

[1] The BioRobotics Institute, Scuola Superiore Sant'Anna, 56127 Pisa, Italy
Lorenzo.vannozzi@santannapisa.it

[2] Department of Excellence in Robotics & AI, Scuola Superiore Sant'Anna, 56127 Pisa, Italy

Abstract. Targeted therapies allow increasing the efficacy of treatments for several diseases, including cancer. The release of drugs or chemicals directly in the site of interest will be beneficial for maximizing the therapy and minimize side effects.

Here, we report the concept and a preliminary analysis of an innovative intravascular steerable catheter guided by an on-board biohybrid actuator, aiming to release drugs into deep and tortuous regions within the cardiovascular systems. The catheter performance has been estimated through analytical and numerical analyses, varying catheter diameter, wall thickness, and actuator force. Results show how larger catheter deflections can be obtained with a smaller outer diameter and decreasing wall thickness. Besides, improved outcomes can be achieved by applying the biohybrid actuator distant from the catheter tip extremity and maximizing the magnitude of the applied forces. Despite the need to further improve the performance of this concept (e.g., by decreasing material stiffness), these preliminary results show great promise in view of future experimentation of such kind of actuation to drive microcatheters through the cardiovascular network.

Keywords: catheter · biohybrid actuator · drug release · living machine

1 Introduction

Cancer is a worldwide disease consisting of uncontrolled growth of cells, which can even go beyond their usual boundaries to invade nearby parts of the body. The American Cancer Society reports that, for solid cancers, more than 1.8 million cases are expected in 2023 [1].

The current gold standards for cancer therapy depend on the cancer location. They include surgical removal, radiation therapy, and chemotherapy [2]. In particular, chemotherapy aims to stop the growth of cancer cells, either by killing the cells or preventing their division. Chemotherapy is typically given through injection or infusion by central venous catheters or orally taken as pills. The drugs used in chemotherapy, such as cisplatin, are meant to attack cells that proliferate quickly, including cancer cells, and those found in the blood and hair bulbs. Thus, systemic administration may result in many undesirable effects on the patient, such as hair loss, nausea, and vomit.

F. Meder et al. (Eds.): Living Machines 2023, LNAI 14158, pp. 378–393, 2023.
https://doi.org/10.1007/978-3-031-39504-8_26

To mitigate such side effects, a desirable approach would be to target the tumor directly navigating the arteries through a catheterization, allowing for the delivery of the medication in the target area. A recent example of a therapy developed to treat a specific organ, such as the liver, is the hepatic arterial infusion therapy (*HAI*) [3]. Hepatocellular carcinoma is one of the most common cancers worldwide and, nowadays, the only curative treatment is surgery, liver transplantation, and percutaneous ablation. HAI therapy consists of a surgical procedure to implant a wireless pump at the level of the abdomen, connected to a catheter that supplies a drug directly to the hepatic artery. Thus, the therapy is administered only to the liver over a period of time and cycles. The main limitations of HAI are the need for surgery (some patients cannot undergo surgery because of their impaired health status) and the risks associated with surgery complications [4, 5].

Understanding the anatomy of the arteries supplying the cancer is crucial for improving the treatment by catheterization. However, conventional catheters may not effectively reach the target due to the high degree of tortuosity in the artery network, which becomes increasingly complex toward the target organ and organ region. Therefore, there are ongoing studies to develop steerable catheters with an orientable tip, which can enhance their ability to access deeper and tortuous regions. Steerable catheters can be categorized based on their actuation method, which either generates force at the tip or transmits force to the tip. The former can be further classified into electric, thermal, and magnetic actuation, while the latter can be subdivided into hydraulic actuation and mechanical cable actuation [6]. Each category has its own set of limitations. In the case of electrical actuation, an electrical current is supplied to the actuator to generate a bending force and movement at the distal tip. Such an approach has inherent restrictions on the degree of bending movement that can be obtained. Additionally, there are concerns about the safety of the materials used in an aqueous environment, such as the bloodstream in which the catheter is immersed, due to the intensity of the current needed to actuate the catheter. Instead, thermal actuation exploits shape memory alloys, thus encountering problems in fabrication procedures, overheating hazards, and temperature dependence.

The principle behind magnetic actuation is typically the manipulation of a magnetic field, applied to the distal end of the catheter containing magnetic-responsive elements. Kim et al. recently conducted an interesting study in which they developed a 500 μm diameter steerable catheter, magnetically controlled thanks to the presence of NdFeB nanoparticles dispersed in the soft polymer matrix of the body, composed of silicone (polydimethylsiloxane, PDMS) or thermoplastic polyurethane [7]. However, the limitations associated with magnetic actuation are mainly due to the cost and complexity of the external field-generating system to be used in a surgical scenario.

Regarding the approaches developed to transmit force to the tip, the hydraulic actuation takes advantage of channels running through the entire length of the catheter, through which a fluid or air is injected to generate pressure capable of steering the catheter. Recently, Goseph *et al.* developed a tip with hydraulic actuation, characterized by an outer diameter of 900 um and four channels of 50 um diameter filled with saline solution [8]. However, drawbacks include limitations inherent in the catheter design, the need for manual manipulation of the proximal tip movements, the extended length of the catheter, and the requirement for pressures as high as 4 Bar. Catheters are usually steered by cable-driven systems controlled by mechanical wires that are driven from their base, and require the passage through the entire length of the catheter [9]. Many commercial solutions have been developed with this technology. For example, a steerable microcatheter with cable actuation and remote control via a steering dial placed proximally on the grip was developed in 2014. The catheter, characterized by a diameter of 900 μm, was connected to the steering dial by two wires inserted through lumens in the wall, and the tip could be manipulated by applying tension to the cables [10]. Therefore, they also have limitations in design due to the cables themselves, difficulties in control by the physician, and they can be impeded by twisting and instability that can lead to undesired tip movements.

However, remotely controlling miniaturized catheters intravascularly to deliver drugs to difficult-to-access regions remains a challenge. In this paper, we propose a novel approach to drive a steerable catheter, based on a biohybrid actuator integrated on-board, in the catheter tip (Fig. 1).

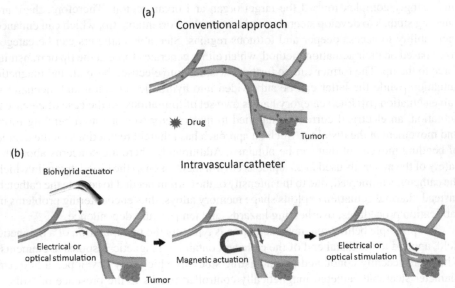

Fig. 1. Comparison between a conventional catheter-assisted drug release and the proposed biohybrid catheter concept, in which the scalability of the biohybrid motors may assist the achievement of a narrower district to deliver a chemotherapeutic drug. (a) Traditional catheters allow to deliver chemotherapeutic drugs relatively far from the cancer location; consequently, a considerable amount of drug is delivered to healthy tissues, with side effects. (b) The newly proposed biohybrid catheter combines magnetic steering and bending of the tip exploiting the force produced by a biohybrid actuator integrated on-board (that can be triggered on-demand by the user through electrical stimuli or optical ones, in the case of optogenetically-modified cells. This allows the release of chemotherapeutic drugs in a highly targeted way, minimizing the side effects.

Biohybrid actuators integrate living organisms, such as contractile muscle cells, with artificially engineered structures, to develop machines with unconventional functionalities. Natural muscle is a soft biological actuator derived from millions of years of evolution, featured by performance invariance with scalability, outstanding driving capability, compliance, and additional functions such as self-healing. Biohybrid actuators offer the advantage of maintaining contractile performance and high actuation efficiency, particularly when scaled down from centimeter to micrometer sizes [11–13]. Moreover, muscle cell-based actuators can generate a significant force on the milli and micrometer-scale, higher than $100\,\mu N$ up to mN [14, 15]. Also, they exploit their ability to convert chemical energy from their environment into mechanical energy, eliminating the need for external power sources, which can be hardly scaled down in size.

In this work, we propose the innovative concept of a steerable catheter tip actuated by a muscle cell-based actuator. We explored the design of such a concept by envisioning the fabrication of a soft catheter tip made of silicone, which incorporates a biohybrid actuator based on skeletal muscle cells that can deflect the tip. A preliminary analysis of the physical and geometrical parameters of the catheter tip is reported, putting them in relationship with the estimated catheter deflection generated by the force produced with the biohybrid actuator. A numerical analysis has been performed to investigate the bending dynamic of the tip by varying the biohybrid actuator configuration, with the aim to maximize the tip deflection.

2 Materials and Methods

2.1 Material Selection, Preparation and Mechanical Evaluation

For the design of the catheter tip, we considered different types of soft silicones, such as PDMS (Sylgard 184 silicon elastomer kit, Dow), Ecoflex 00-10 (Smooth-On), and different ratios to tune their mechanical properties. Silicones were chosen because they are tunable and soft materials that can be modified to host cell cultures on their surface. Indeed, cell cultures on silicones can be promoted by activating their surface with a plasma treatment, which can favor protein coatings, thus an excellent cell adhesion and growth [16]. PDMS is biocompatible and can be functionalized through plasma [17]. On the other hand, Ecoflex 00–10 cannot be tailored easily through plasma-assisted modifications, but they have a smaller elastic modulus and larger viscosity [18, 19].

PDMS was tested at the monomer/curing agent ratio of 10:1 and 20:1, while Ecoflex 00-10 was prepared according to the manufacturer's instructions. PDMS was mixed with Ecoflex 00–10 by preparing each silicone separately to the desired ratio. After mixing for 2 min, the solution was degassed using a centrifuge, set at 1300 RCF for 5 min.

Tensile tests were performed using an INSTRON machine (model 2444, load cell: 1 kN, Instron, Norwood, MA, USA), with specimens obtained through a mold designed following ASTM-D638, applying a tensile speed of 10 mm/min. The Young's modulus was derived from the slope of the first 10% of the stress-strain graph.

2.2 Estimation of the Catheter Flexural Rigidity

The catheter's geometrical and physical properties influence the deflection of the catheter [20]. These parameters can be summarized in the flexural rigidity (F_l), which can be calculated as follow:

$$F_l = E * I_0 \tag{1}$$

where E is the Young's modulus and I_0 denotes the moment of inertia of a hollow structure:

$$I_0 = \frac{\pi \left(D^4 - d^4\right)}{64} \tag{2}$$

where D is the external diameter and d is the internal diameter.

Another encountered phenomenon when placing a catheter is kinking, which refers to the potential obstruction that may occur when the radius of curvature becomes smaller than a critical value ($R_{critical}$). This $R_{critical}$ can be defined as:

$$R_{critical} = \frac{\left(1 - v^2\right) * R^2}{K * t} \tag{3}$$

where R is the external radius of the catheter, t is the wall thickness, v is the Poisson's ratio (set to 0.48 [21]) and K is a constant (theoretically $= 0.99$; experimentally 0.72–1.14) [22].

2.3   Expected Deflection by Euler-Bernoulli Beam's Theory

Euler-Bernoulli's beam theory has been used to calculate catheter deflection, assuming a linear mechanical behaviour of the material at small deformations [23, 24]. Considering the force (F) exerted by the biohybrid actuator, the catheter will be subject to a moment M equal to:

$$M = F * \frac{D}{2} \tag{4}$$

Then, for the Euler-Bernoulli's beam theory, the deflection induced by the biohybrid actuator can be calculated as follows:

$$\delta = \frac{M * x1^2}{2 * E * I_0} \tag{5}$$

where $x1$ is the length of the biohybrid actuator (Fig. 2).

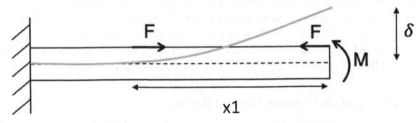

Fig. 2. Representation of applied forces, torque, and deflection generated on a beam, used as a model of the catheter tip.

2.4 Numerical Analysis of the Catheter Bending

Structural finite element model (FEM) simulations were performed using COMSOL Multiphysics v5.6 (COMSOL Inc., Sweden) to support the analytical modelling of catheter deflection. The module "solid mechanical" was used, and the mesh was set to normal (physics-controlled mesh, number of elements: 6065, minimum elements quality: 0.2046) after the evaluation of the mesh convergence. We defined a model consisting of a hollow cylinder with an outer radius of 1 mm ($D = 2$ mm), an inner radius of 0.75 mm ($d = 1.5$ mm) and a catheter tip length (lc) of 15 mm. Two axial load points were applied to the outer wall of the catheter ($p1$ and $p2$), with the same magnitude and opposite direction, simulating the biohybrid actuator contraction behavior as a strip of muscle tissue, with a length defined as $x1$ (Fig. 3).

The geometrical parameters of the biohybrid actuator, such as its positioning over the catheter wall, length, and the force magnitude applied, were varied in the analyses.

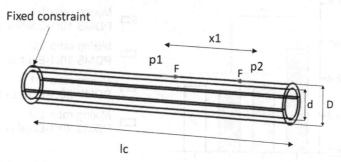

Fig. 3. Depiction of the model implemented in COMSOL, and of the variables considered in the analysis.

3   Results and Discussion

3.1 Mechanical Characterization

Figure 4 and Fig. 5 show the mechanical analysis results for PDMS 1:10, PDMS 1:20 Ecoflex 00–10 and mixes between PDMS and Ecoflex 00–10.

Among the materials examined, PDMS 10:1 was the stiffest one, Ecoflex 00–10 kept the lowest elastic modulus, whereas PDMS 20:1 displayed a medium elastic modulus. Then, we tried to mix PDMS 20:1 and Ecoflex to decrease the material Young's modulus to maintain the PDMS chemistry as a highly tailorable one for cell cultures. As can be seen in the Fig. 5, we noticed a saturation in Young's modulus variation, down to an average value close to 0.34 MPa for the mix between PDMS 1:10 and Ecoflex 00–10 in a ratio 1:2, and PDMS 1:20 and Ecoflex for both ratios (1:1 and 1:2). We kept this value as a reference for the following analyses.

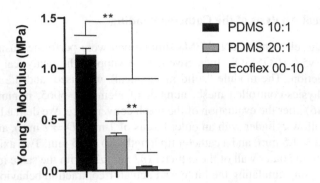

Fig. 4. Young's moduli of the silicones considered in this study. Data underwent ANOVA test and Tukey's post-hoc comparison, * = p < 0.05, ** = p < 0.01. N = 5.

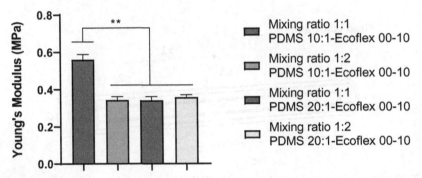

Fig. 5. Young's moduli of different combinations of PDMS and Ecoflex 00–10. Data underwent ANOVA test and Tukey's post-hoc comparison, * = p < 0.05, ** = p < 0.01. N = 5.

3.2 Flexural Rigidity, and the Influence of the Physical and Geometrical Parameters

In Fig. 6a and Fig. 6b, it is noticeable that as the outer diameter (from 0.5 to 6 mm) and the wall thickness (from 100 to 500 μm) increase, the catheter flexural rigidity also considerably increases, based on the analytical model described in Sect. 2.3. Flexural rigidity represents the tendency for the catheter to mechanically oppose when a moment is applied, and it is proportional to the stress that is applied on the vessel wall by the catheter itself. Therefore, a low value of flexural rigidity is desirable to maximize the catheter deflection. These results also suggested that catheters with smaller diameters will tend to oppose a lower resistance to the torque applied by the biohybrid actuator.

(a)

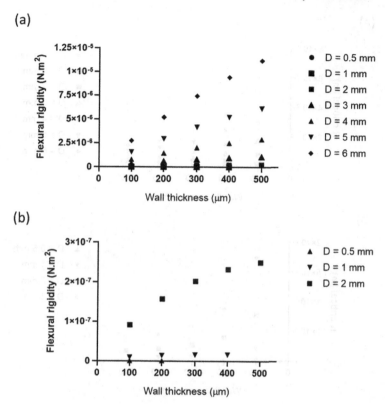

(b)

Fig. 6. (a) Flexural rigidity over the outer diameter and wall thickness variation. (b) Magnification for the cases D = 0.5 mm, D = 1 mm, and D = 2 mm.

Figure 7a and Fig. 7b show the critical radius to not incur in kinking phenomena. Here, it is noticeable how the wall thickness influences the $R_{critical}$, and how this value increases while decreasing the catheter size. Typical values of flexural rigidity of catheters range from 1 to 50 * 10^{-4} N * m^2, mainly due to the stiffness of the material used to fabricate the catheter (higher than silicones) [25]. The possible occurrence of kinking phenomena is an important parameter of catheters to take into account because of the need to avoid occlusions during steering. The final dimensioning of the catheter should be also driven by avoiding the achievement of such curvatures.

(a)

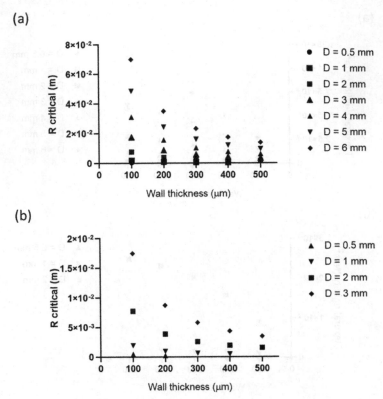

(b)

Fig. 7. (a) $R_{critical}$ over the outer diameter and wall thickness variation. (b) Magnification for the cases D = 0.5 mm, D = 1 mm, D = 2 mm, and D = 3 mm.

3.3 Estimation of the Catheter Deflection/Curvature

The catheter deflection has been analytically estimated by varying specific geometrical and physical parameters, such as the diameter, wall thickness and force applied by the actuator. It is possible to observe from Fig. 8a and Fig. 8b a drastic decrease in deflection as the outer diameter increases from 0.5 to 6 mm. When a catheter has a small diameter (e.g., D = 0.5 mm), it has a lower inertia, and can achieve greater deflection values than larger-diameter systems.

(a)

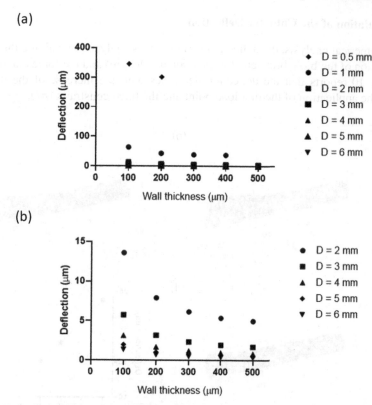

(b)

Fig. 8. (a) Analysis of the catheter deflection over the outer diameter and wall thickness variation. (b) Magnification for the cases D = 2 mm, D = 3 mm, D = 4 mm, D = 5 mm, and D = 6 mm.

We also analyzed the influence of the force for a specific case ($D = 2$ mm). That is a suitable diameter to move forward to the left or right branches of the hepatic artery [26]. As shown in Fig. 9, increasing the biohybrid actuator force from 100 μN to 500 μN [12], the expected deflection increased proportionally up to about 70 μm from 15 μm.

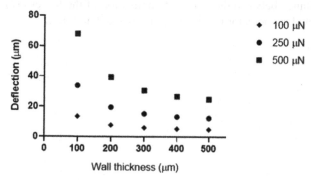

Fig. 9. Analysis of the catheter deflection over the wall thickness variation for the case D = 2 mm.

3.4   Simulation of the Catheter Deflection

For the numerical analysis, the deflection variation was analyzed by varying the spatial configuration of the biohybrid actuator (position and length) and the force magnitude.

Figure 10 reports that the deflection decreases with the increase of the distance between the application of the first load point and the fixed constraint (*p1*).

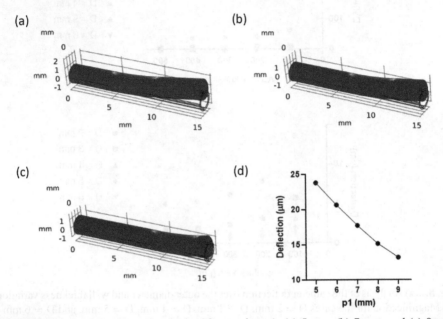

Fig. 10. Representation of results obtained by varying p1: (a) 5 mm, (b) 7 mm, and (c) 9 mm. Other parameters set are: D = 2 mm, t = 200 μm, lc = 15 mm, E = 0.34 MPa, x1 = 5 mm, F = 100 μN. Scale factor 50. (d) Deflection estimated by varying the distance p1.

The deflection was higher at the lowest value of *p1* (23.8 μm), and decreased up to 13.2 μm (*p1* = 9 mm). On the other hand, Fig. 11 shows the variation obtained by varying the distance between the points of application of the forces (*x1*), so essentially varying the biohybrid actuator length, keeping *p1* fixed at 8 mm.

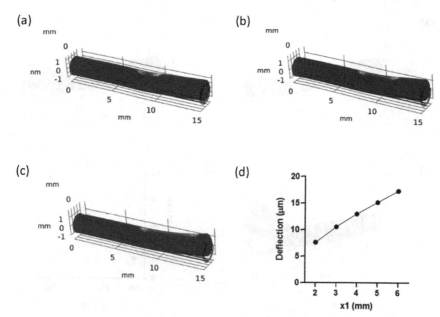

Fig. 11. Representation of results obtained by varying the length of the biohybrid actuator (x1): (a) 2 mm, (b) 4 mm, and (c) 6 mm. Other parameters set are: $D = 2$ mm, $t = 200$ μm, $lc = 15$ mm, $E = 0.34$ MPa, $p1 = 8$ mm, $F = 100$ μN. Scale factor 50. (d) Deflection estimated by varying the biohybrid actuator length (x1).

In this case, the deflection increases from 7.6 μm ($x1 = 2$ mm) up to 17.3 μm ($x1 = 5$ mm). As the distance between the points at which the forces are applied increases, there is a higher deflection of the catheter. This means that the length of the biohybrid actuator is relevant in improving the catheter deflection. Then, another important parameter that can help in maximizing the catheter deflection is the force applied by the biohybrid actuator. In Fig. 12, a variation of the force applied was investigated.

Here, the deflection increases proportionally to the applied force, from 15.7 μm (F $= 100$ μN) up to 75.7 μm (F $= 500$ μN). These simulations foresee the analysis of the forces applied on the outer surface of the catheter tip. In the case of forces applied in the inner wall of the catheter (e.g., biohybrid actuator placed internally), the expected deflection will be lower because of the generation of a torque with a lower magnitude due to the lower arm.

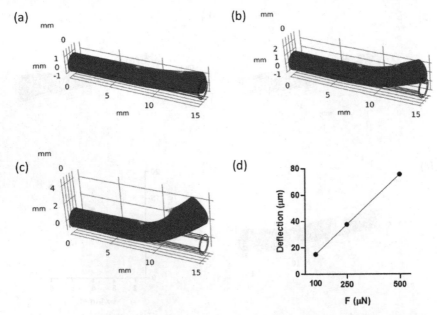

Fig. 12. Representation of results obtained by varying F: (a) 100 μN, (b) 250 μN, and (c) 500 μN. Other parameters set are: D = 2 mm, t = 200 μm, lc = 15 mm, E = 0.34 MPa, p1 = 8 mm and x1 = 5 mm. Scale factor 50. (d) Deflection estimated by varying the distance F.

Finally, an investigation of the parameters providing the highest deflection for each case (*p1* = 5 mm, *x1* = 6 mm, *F* = 500 μN) was performed to analyze the performance of the optimized configuration among the cases analyzed (Fig. 13). It can be observed that the deflection achieved a considerably higher value (133.4 μm) than the previous simulations, almost doubling the outcome of the most performing parameter (*F*).

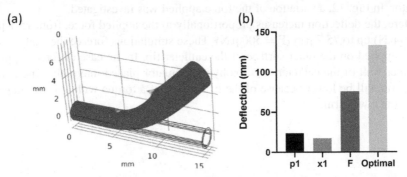

Fig. 13. Representation of the catheter bending by setting: D = 2 mm, t = 200 μm, lc = 15 mm, E = 0.34 MPa, p1 = 8 mm, x1 = 5 mm and F = 500 μN. Scale factor 50. (d) Comparison of the deflections estimated with the previous simulations.

This result demonstrates the need of playing with multiple parameters to improve the catheter deflection, and maximize the performance in view of a steerable catheter controlled with a biohybrid actuator.

4 Conclusions

This work reports the concept and preliminary considerations for the design of a steerable catheter actuated by a biohybrid actuator integrated on its tip. Analytical and numerical models were used to estimate the degree of catheter deflection by varying the catheter size, the force exerted by the biohybrid actuator, and its spatial configuration, considering some soft silicones that have been characterized for this application. Future efforts will be also directed to optimize the material properties to manufacture a softer catheter, more compliant to the torque generated by the actuator. Different microfabrication technologies will be explored, including molding, additive manufacturing, self-assembly techniques, and dip coating, by carefully assessing the strengths and limitations of each technology. Then, future work will regard the integration of a flexible electronic platform to facilitate the electrical stimulation required for the muscle cells [27]. Future evolutions may also include light-responsive cells (e.g., subjected to optogenetic modifications [28], or treated with azobenzenes [29]) to make the catheter tip bendable through light pulses transmitted through the catheter structure (that should act as an optical fiber).

Acknowledgments. This project has received funding from the European Union's Horizon Europe research and innovation program under grant agreement No. 101070328 (BioMeld project).

References

1. American Cancer Society. https://www.cancer.org/research/cancer-facts-statistics/all-cancer-facts-figures/2023-cancer-facts-figures.html. Accessed 03 Apr 2023
2. Zugazagoitia, J., Guedes, C., Ponce, S., Ferrer, I., Molina-Pinelo, S., Paz-Ares, L.: Current challenges in cancer treatment. Clin. Ther. **38**(7), 1551–1566 (2016)
3. Obi, S., Sato, S., Kawai, T.: Current status of hepatic arterial infusion chemotherapy. Liver Cancer **4**(3), 188–199 (2015)
4. OHSU Knight Cancer Institute. https://www.ohsu.edu/knight-cancer-institute/hepatic-arterial-infusion-hai. Accessed 29 May 2023
5. Song, M.J.: Hepatic artery infusion chemotherapy for advanced hepatocel-lular carcinoma. World J. Gastroenterol. **21**(13), 3843–3849 (2015)
6. Ali, A., Plettenburg, D.H., Breedveld, P.: Steerable catheters in cardiology: classifying steerability and assessing future challenges. IEEE Trans. Biomed. Eng. **63**(4), 679–693 (2016)
7. Kim, Y., Parada, G.A., Liu, S., Zhao, X.: Ferromagnetic soft continuum ro-bots. Sci. Robot. **4**(33), eaax7329 (2019)
8. Gopesh, T., et al.: Soft robotic steerable microcatheter for the endo-vascular treatment of cerebral disorders. Sci. Robot. **6**(57), eabf0601 (2021)
9. Hu, X., Chen, A., Luo, Y., Zhang, C., Zhang, E.: Steerable catheters for minimally invasive surgery: a review and future directions. Comput. Assist. Surg. **23**(1), 21–41 (2018)

10. Soyama, T., Yoshida, D., Sakuhara, Y., Morita, R., Abo, D., Kudo, K.: The steerable micro-catheter: a new device for selective catheterisation. Cardiovasc. Intervent. Radiol. **40**(6), 947–952 (2017). https://doi.org/10.1007/s00270-017-1579-3

11. Sun, L., et al.: Biohybrid robotics with living cell actuation. Chem. Soc. Rev. **49**(12), 4043–4069 (2020)

12. Ricotti, L., et al.: Biohybrid actuators for robotics: a review of devices actuated by living cells. Science Robotics **2**(12), eaaq0495 (2017)

13. Hasebe, A., et al.: Biohybrid actuators based on skeletal muscle-powered microgrooved ultra-thin films consisting of poly (styrene-block-butadiene-block-styrene). ACS Biomater. Sci. Eng. **5**(11), 5734–5743 (2019)

14. Guix, M., et al.: Biohybrid soft robots with self-stimulating skeletons. Sci. Robot. **6**(53), eabe7577 (2021)

15. Pagan-Diaz, G.J., et al.: Simulation and fabrication of stronger, larger, and faster walking biohybrid machines. Adv. Funct. Mater. **28**(23), 1801145 (2018)

16. Regehr, K.J., et al.: Biological implications of polydimethylsiloxane-based microfluidic cell culture. Lab Chip **9**(15), 2132–2139 (2009)

17. Genchi, G.G., et al.: Bio/non-bio interfaces: a straightforward method for obtaining long term PDMS/muscle cell biohybrid constructs. Colloids Surf. B **105**, 144–151 (2013)

18. Park, S., et al.: Silicones for stretchable and durable soft devices: beyond sylgard-184. ACS Appl. Mater. Interfaces **10**(13), 11261–11268 (2018)

19. Sollier, E., Murray, C., Maoddi, P., Di Carlo, D.: Rapid prototyping polymers for microfluidic devices and high pressure injections. Lab Chip **11**(22), 3752–3765 (2011)

20. I. Mechanical Properties of Catheters. Acta Radiol. Diagnosis **4**, 11–22 (1966)

21. Huang, C., Bian, Z., Fang, C., Zhou, X., Song, J.: Experimental and theoretical study on mechanical properties of porous PDMS. J. Appl. Mech. Trans. ASME **85**(4), 041009 (2018)

22. Evans, R.L., Bernstein, E.F., Johnson, E., Reller, C., Mechancia, C.R.: Mechanical properties of the living dog aorta. Am. J. Physiol.-Legacy Content **202**(4), 619–621 (1962)

23. Bauchau, O.A., Craig, J.I.: Euler-Bernoulli beam theory. In: Bauchau, O.A., Craig, J.I. (eds.) Structural analysis. Solid Mechanics and Its Applications, vol. 163, pp. 173–221. Springer, Dordrecht (2009). https://doi.org/10.1007/978-90-481-2516-6_5

24. Mestre, R., Patiño, T., Barceló, X., Anand, S., Pérez-Jiménez, A., Sánchez, S.: Force modu-lation and adaptability of 3D-bioprinted biological actuators based on skeletal muscle tissue. Adv. Mater. Technol. **4**(2), 1800631 (2019)

25. Hartquist, C.M., et al.: Quantification of the flexural rigidity of peripheral arterial endovascular catheters and sheaths. J. Mech. Behav. Biomed. Mater. **119**, 104459 (2021)

26. Basciano, C.A., Kleinstreuer, C., Kennedy, A.S., Dezarn, W.A., Childress, E.: Computer modeling of controlled microsphere release and targeting in a representative hepatic artery system. Ann. Biomed. Eng. **38**, 1862–1879 (2010)

27. Lai, S., Zucca, A., Cosseddu, P., Greco, F., Mattoli, V., Bonfiglio, A.: Ultra-conformable organic field-effect transistors and circuits for epidermal electronic applications. Org. Electron. **46**, 60–67 (2017)

28. Sakar, M.S., et al.: Formation and optogenetic control of engineered 3D skeletal muscle bioactuators. Lab Chip **12**(23), 4976–4985 (2012)

29. Vurro, V., et al.: Molecular design of amphiphilic plasma membrane-targeted azobenzenes for nongenetic optical stimulation. Front. Mater. **7**, 631567 (2021)

A Novel Aromatic Carbene Complex with a Bisphenol A ...   418

Open Access This chapter is licensed under the terms of the Creative Commons Attribution 4.0 International License (http://creativecommons.org/licenses/by/4.0/), which permits use, sharing, adaptation, distribution and reproduction in any medium or format, as long as you give appropriate credit to the original author(s) and the source, provide a link to the Creative Commons license and indicate if changes were made.

The images or other third party material in this chapter are included in the chapter's Creative Commons license, unless indicated otherwise in a credit line to the material. If material is not included in the chapter's Creative Commons license and your intended use is not permitted by statutory regulation or exceeds the permitted use, you will need to obtain permission directly from the copyright holder.

Author Index

F. Meder et al. (Eds.): Living Machines 2023, LNAI 14158, pp. 395–397, 2023.
https://doi.org/10.1007/978-3-031-39504-8

Printed in the United States
by Baker & Taylor Publisher Services